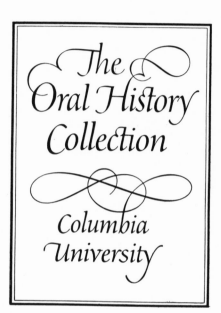

The
Oral History
Collection

Columbia
University

THE

Oral History Collection

of COLUMBIA UNIVERSITY

Edited by Elizabeth B. Mason
and Louis M. Starr

New York

ORAL HISTORY RESEARCH OFFICE

1979

Library of Congress Cataloging in Publication Data

Columbia University. Oral History Research Office.
The Oral History Collection of Columbia University.

1. United States—Civilization—Bibliography—Catalogs.
2. Oral history—Bibliography—Catalogs.
3. Columbia University. Oral History Research Office—Catalogs.
I. Mason, Elizabeth B.
II. Starr, Louis Morris, 1917–
III. Title.
Z1361.C6C64 1979   [E169.1]   016.973   79-11527
ISBN 0-9602492-0-6

Address inquiries regarding Oral History to
Box 20, Butler Library, Columbia University, New York 10027.

For Mary Nevins

Contents

UNIVERSITY ADVISORY COMMITTEE

Appointed by the President to serve to June 30, 1981

PATRICIA BATTIN, *Chairman*
Vice President for Information Services

ROBERT G. BARNES
President, Columbia University Press

ANNETTE K. BAXTER
Adolph S. and Effie Ochs Professor of History

CHARLES FRANKEL
Old Dominion Professor of Philosophy and Public Affairs

CHARLES V. HAMILTON
Wallace S. Sayre Professor of Government

NORMAN E. ISAACS
Editor in Residence, Journalism

WILLIAM E. LEUCHTENBURG
De Witt Clinton Professor of American History

HERBERT WECHSLER
Harlan Fiske Stone Professor of Constitutional Law

Introduction

WHEN THE FIRST edition of *The Oral History Collection of Columbia University,* a 120-page booklet that sold for two dollars, appeared in 1960, a copy landed in the hands of Supreme Court Justice Felix Frankfurter. His response contained this bit of word-weighing, in a wondrously elaborate, two-tense aside:

> I have gone through every item of it, and found it—at this point in my dictation I was pausing whether the word that came to my lips was an exaggeration, but it isn't—fascinating.

Oral history catalogues need readers like Justice Frankfurter. What would he say of this fourth edition, one that quadruples what the first had to offer? The Justice, noting we now term it a *dictionary* catalogue, might be put in mind of a celebrated dictum by an old favorite of his, Dr. Samuel Johnson: "Dictionaries are like watches; the worst is better than none, and the best cannot be expected to go quite true."

We borrow of these eminent scholars to give this edition the send-off it deserves, one tempering the Justice's enthusiasm with a pinch of Johnsonian skepticism.

There is ground for enthusiasm. The book carries word of hundreds of new memoirs, describes new projects, interrelates material through topical cross references for the first time, and takes note of over a thousand changes of access since the 1973 edition. Its format is new. So is its appearance. Warren Chappell, dean of American book designers, has given it fresh typography that cuts its girth and increases its stature. The aim has been to put in the hands of researchers the most inviting and straightforward guide we could devise: a dictionary catalogue marshalling all of its information in one alphabet.

The simplicity imposed by the new format is in order. This is a guide to the testimony of 3,638 persons interviewed over the last thirty years. The Collection now mirrors, however imperfectly, its University's interests in the arts, business, education, history, international affairs, journalism, labor, law, library science, literature, medicine, the social sciences, and the physical sciences. The largest of oral history collections, not surprisingly, is the most diversified.

If there is ground for skepticism, it is because researchers tend to expect more of a tool of this kind than it can deliver. Does a given memoir hold new answers to questions of moment? Is it related with candor and wit? What hypotheses are hiding here for a dissertation, what characterizations for a biography, what quotes, what anecdotes for next year's bestseller? Like the worst of Dr. Johnson's watches, the typical entry may be better than none; but it offers tantalizingly few clues. It lists, in a telegraphic style we have used from the first, the topics discussed. If one prints a glowing description of *this* memoir, what of *that* one? We have contained ourselves accordingly; but pity the scholar who cannot find what fascinated Felix Frankfurter!

ACKNOWLEDGEMENTS

Small foundations and individuals with an understanding of this work have been indispensable allies of Oral History from its earliest days —a dependence that helps assure our independence—and we are pleased to cite fresh instances. The funding of this catalogue resulted from their interest. From Chicago came a challenge grant from the Harris Foundation. Its chairman, Irving Harris, had come to know of our work through a graduate of our course, Richard Polsky. Another graduate, Irene Silverman of New York, responded at once with her own check, and matching it was one from her husband, Samuel Silverman. The Bydale Foundation of New York, thanks to Mrs. James P. Warburg, then put us over the top by meeting the Harris challenge.

An overhaul this extensive requires both money and resolve. The latter has come once again, as in all three editions before it, from the Associate Director, Elizabeth B. Mason. Her knowledge of the Collection, her judgment and unfailing attention to detail, saw us through. For the better part of nearly three years of compilation we had the competent aid of Kathryn Back and Katherine Rutkowski. More recently, three graduates of our course, Jeri Nunn, Russell Merritt and Theresa Bowers, assisted us. We are particularly indebted to graduate student Elma Barnes, for long hours of intelligent help.

We thank President William McGill and his associates for doing, generously and consistently, all that we have asked of them.

Lastly, we pay tribute to all the interviewers and transcribers who have served this cause across the years. They are credited on the front page of every memoir; their devotion to the work will merit the thanks of those who make use of it in the years to come.

Oral History Research Office
February, 1979   Louis M. Starr, Director

Coming to Terms: Oral History

W E SKETCH here, for those coming upon oral history for the first time, some background.

Allan Nevins once remarked it was well no one had showered millions on Oral History at Columbia, because the pinch of necessity had made us more active than we would otherwise have been. The same resolute optimism is needed in contemplating the name he applied to it, a misnomer that cloaked a brilliant idea in obscurity. Oral history has ratified his choice long since, slipping into more or less common usage for want of anything better; but the need to explain it lingers. The term impels oral historians to become propagandists, or at least partisans, for a cause that should need no urging. Its end product, they must explain all their lives, is not oral but written, not history but testimony from which history may be written.

The Merriam-Webster *New Collegiate Dictionary* has carried this entry since 1973:

> **oral history** *n:* historical information that is obtained in
> interviews with persons who have led significant lives and
> that is us. tape-recorded—**oral historian** *n*

Oral historians accept that as a capsule definition, but most would point out that one vital ingredient is missing. Oral history interviews are private. The best of them are told with what Sir Norman Angell (*q.v.*) refers to as "smoking room candor." The interviewee, once he feels secure in the knowledge that his wishes will be honored, that any part of what he says may be closed for as long as he likes, enjoys that rarest of privileges, the chance to speak for the record without let or hindrance. Not all avail themselves. Nor is anyone likely to deprive oral history of its many hazards for those on both sides of the recorder. The best one can say is that its triumphs amply redeem its disasters. The latter tend to be short and soon forgotten; the successes survive, not only in collections but—eventually—in ten thousand quotes and footnotes, fresh insights and new interpretations.

Name and hazards notwithstanding, oral history developed the momentum of a movement. From Columbia and a few other institutions in the middle years of the century it spread to every state. It has reached every continent. Oral history societies flourish in Canada, Great Britain and Australia in addition to the U.S., where the first was conceived at U.C.L.A. in 1966 and emerged at Columbia's Arden House in 1967. Courses on the creation and evaluation of oral history multiply on campuses. Oral history has its own literature and its own code of ethics. Beloit College, a few years ago, granted what was hailed as the first B.A. awarded an oral history major. Harvard, at about the same time, accepted an oral history memoir as a doctoral dissertation, albeit only after it had won Theodore Rosengarten a National Book Award for his rendering of the life story of a black Alabama tenant farmer, *All God's Dangers*. There were other signs, by the close of the 1970's, that oral history was emerging as a discipline. Not least were identity crises among oral historians whenever they got together, reminiscent of those suffered by folklorists, archaeologists, sociologists, and others in similar circumstances before them.

The Columbia office, recording this growth in its annual reports since its early years, has made the dissemination of information about oral history a second calling. In 1977 it developed kits for libraries and others in need, designed to fit in a vertical file. Components include a how-to-do-it manual, a 24-page encyclopedia article and reprints of other articles of interest, the current list of oral histories available on microfiche from Columbia's collection and others, samples of representative interviews, and Oral History Association information, including OHA's publications list.

The entire file of Columbia Oral History reports, beginning with typed carbons of the late 1940's, has been published for libraries on microfiche by Microfilming Corporation of America. An index is in the making. Since first attaining print in 1961, the report has been the most widely distributed serial in the field. In addition to dealing with matters of general interest, it describes recent accessions to the Collection, which continues to add from 15,000 to 25,000 pages of new material yearly.

Newcomers to oral history often inquire how it is put to use. The answer, for anyone curious enough to find out while in the vicinity of a reasonably well stocked library, is to have in hand an annotated list of books that illustrate use of one kind or another. From this one may choose titles of interest and see for himself. In making selections from among hundreds of books that have drawn upon COHC (Columbia's Oral History Collection as it is commonly abbreviated), we have limited ourselves to works of broad interest likely to be available in most any library:

Anderson, Jervis. A. PHILIP RANDOLPH: *A Biographical Portrait.* Harcourt Brace Jovanovich, 1973.
Although written before our Randolph memoir became available, six COHC memoirs are used.

Barnouw, Erik. A TOWER IN BABEL: *A History of Broadcasting in the United States to 1933.* Oxford University Press, 1966.

———. THE GOLDEN WEB: *A History of Broadcasting in the United States, Volume II, 1933–1953.* Oxford University Press, 1968.

———. THE IMAGE EMPIRE: *A History of Broadcasting in the United States from 1953.* Oxford University Press, 1971.
The first two volumes of this trilogy, the definitive history of the industry, make use of scores of memoirs in our Radio Pioneers series. The concluding one includes interviews conducted by the author and donated to COHC.

Buell, Thomas B. THE QUIET WARRIOR: *A Biography of Raymond A. Spruance.* Little, Brown, 1974.
The author, noting that Spruance resisted interviewing, says that Admiral Charles J. Moore, through his own massive COHC memoir, served as Spruance's Boswell. The Naval Institute's oral histories are also used.

Burner, David. HERBERT HOOVER: *A Public Life.* Alfred A. Knopf, 1979.

The first study of Hoover to make extensive use of oral history, this volume utilizes eight COHC memoirs in addition to many in the Hoover Presidential Library.

Caro, Robert A. THE POWER BROKER: *Robert Moses and the Fall of New York.* Alfred A. Knopf, 1974.
Twenty-four COHC memoirs, including the very first one ever done (George McAneny's), are drawn upon.

Cerf, Bennett. AT RANDOM. Random House, 1977.
This jaunty autobiography of a major figure in American publishing, edited by Phyllis Cerf Wagner and Albert Erskine from the Oral History that Cerf completed shortly before his death, is representative of a genre. Autobiographies of similar origin include Cass Canfield's *Up and Down and Around* (1971) and Arthur M. Schlesinger's *In Retrospect: The History of a Historian* (1963).

Dubofsky, Melvin and Warren Van Tine. JOHN L. LEWIS: *A Biography.* Quadrangle, 1977.
Despite their reservations about oral history, the authors list 12 "major" and 21 "minor" memoirs from COHC in their bibliography, along with others they utilized from the Penn State and Sangamon State oral history collections.

Hamby, Alonzo L. BEYOND THE NEW DEAL: *Harry S. Truman and American Liberalism.* Columbia University Press, 1973.
In this highly regarded study, COHC memoirs are used along with others in the Truman Library, University of California, Berkeley, and Wayne State University collections.

Harbaugh, William H. LAWYER'S LAWYER: *The Life of John W. Davis.* Oxford University Press, 1973.
COHC's memoir by Davis, obtained twenty years earlier, is pivotal in this biography.

Heckscher, August. WHEN LAGUARDIA WAS MAYOR. W. W. Norton, 1978.

Like Arthur Mann before him, the author turned to COHC for testimony unobtainable elsewhere, but he notes mixed results, which he ascribes to varying degrees of competence on the part of interviewers.

Hofstadter, Richard. THE PROGRESSIVE HISTORIANS: *Turner, Beard, Parrington.* Alfred A. Knopf, 1968.
The author's use of Arthur M. Schlesinger's Oral History, including a number of Charles A. Beard's letters embedded therein, and of Oral History interviews with Beard's daughter help offset the fact Beard destroyed his papers before his death.

Josephson, Matthew and Hannah. AL SMITH: *Hero of the Cities.* Houghton Mifflin, 1969.
Still the best biography of Smith, this volume draws extensively on Oral History's Frances Perkins memoir and others.

Josephy, Alvin M., Jr. THE AMERICAN HERITAGE HISTORY OF FLIGHT. American Heritage Publishing Company, Inc., 1962.
Some seventy persons prominent in the history of aviation testify about various phases of its development in excerpts taken from our Aviation project.

Kennan, George F. SOVIET-AMERICAN RELATIONS, 1917–1920: Volume II, *The Decision to Intervene.* Princeton University Press, 1958.
The Oral History memoir by DeWitt Clinton Poole, the last American diplomatist to leave the USSR when relations were severed, furnishes much for the final chapter, "The End at Moscow."

Kluger, Richard. SIMPLE JUSTICE: *The History of Brown v. Board of Education and Black America's Struggle for Equality.* Alfred A. Knopf, 1976.
The Oral History memoir of Federal Judge J. Waties Waring is put to good use here.

Lash, Joseph P. ELEANOR AND FRANKLIN. W. W. Norton, 1971.
COHC memoirs by Will Alexander, M. L. Wilson and half a dozen others are cited in the notes.

Leuchtenburg, William E. FRANKLIN D. ROOSEVELT AND THE
NEW DEAL, *1932–1940.* Harper & Row, 1963.
Thirty-two COHC memoirs are referred to in various sections of
the notes of this work, long a landmark in the historiography of the
period.

Martin, George. MADAM SECRETARY: *A Biography of Frances Per-
kins.* Houghton Mifflin, 1976.
The basic document for this is Columbia's 5,500-page Frances Perkins
Oral History.

Nevins, Allan. HERBERT H. LEHMAN AND HIS ERA. Charles
Scribner's Sons, 1963.
An extensive Oral History memoir by Governor Lehman forms one
of the principal sources for this biography.

Parmet, Herbert S. EISENHOWER AND THE AMERICAN CRU-
SADES. Macmillan, 1972.
Extensive use is made of COHC's Eisenhower Administration series
and of Princeton's oral history project on John Foster Dulles, in a
volume generally considered the first noteworthy one on its period.

Patterson, James T. MR. REPUBLICAN: *A Biography of Robert A.
Taft.* Houghton Mifflin, 1972.
Columbia's Robert A. Taft project is acknowledged as central to this
study.

Penkower, Monty Noam. THE FEDERAL WRITERS' PROJECT: *A
Study of Government Patronage of the Arts.* University of Illinois Press,
1978.
This title, drawing upon Holger Cahill and William Terry Couch
memoirs, is included here as representative of a host of well written
monographs utilizing COHC on subjects as wide-ranging as the Collection itself. See Oral History's annual reports for listings.

Thompson, Lawrance. ROBERT FROST: *The Years of Triumph.* Holt,
Rinehart & Winston, 1970.
A volume memorable for its use of a single anecdote about Frost and

Stark Young at Amherst, as related in Gardner Jackson's Oral History.

Williams, T. Harry. HUEY LONG. Alfred A. Knopf, 1969.
The author explains on the first page of his preface that the book was inspired by "the project in Oral History being conducted at Columbia University." He applied Columbia methodology to obtain much of his material, drawing as well on COHC memoirs about Long.

Butler Library, since its completion in 1934 the central facility of the Columbia libraries, is home for Oral History. The work began in a basement room in the back of this building in 1948.

...an Nevins in Oral
...tory's basement office,
...8. Below, with Thomas
...t Benton at the Truman
...rary, 1961. Opposite:
...l History memoirs line
... galleries of the
...nuscript Reading Room
...Butler's 8th floor.

Dean Albertson, pad in hand to catch spellings for the
transcriber, elicits a memoir from James P. Warburg, 1953.
Below, Mrs. Walter Gellhorn, similarly armed but markedly
less encumbered by machinery, tapes Anna Lord Strauss, 1973.

Opposite: Ed Reno, Microfilming Corporation of America (left)
presents a fresh batch of microfiche to Oral History's directors,
1977. In this form the best of the Collection, once restrictions
expire, may be shared with other libraries and scholars.

Three generations of the Henry A. Wallace family came to Columbia on November 18, 1975 to witness President McGill's opening of one of Oral History's longest, and longest sealed, memoirs. Wallace had closed his 5,500 pages until 10 years after his death. Left to right are Professor Starr, Mrs. Robert Wallace, David Wallace Douglas, a grandson, Ilo (Mrs. Henry A.) Wallace, President McGill, Mrs. Leslie Douglas, Wallace's daughter, and Madame Charles Bruggmann, his sister. At right: Moments later, Mrs. Wallace hears a voice coming from the tape recorder in the background: her husband, recorded a quarter of a century before.

A 30th anniversary luncheon fills the Columbia College auditorium with "an extraordinary gathering of scholars—and people . . . of interest to scholars," as the *New York Times* put it May 26, 1978. Among them, from the top of the page at left: Alfred A. Knopf with President McGill; Louise Nevelson and Marie (Mrs. Fiorello), La Guardia; R.M. Lumiansky, president of the American Council of Learned Societies, and Barbara Tuchman.

How to Use This Catalogue

Q: How do I go about using the Oral History Collection?

A: Begin here. Then scan the catalogue to find persons, topics and projects of interest. Each entry carries a notation in italic at the end regarding access: *Open; Permission required to cite or quote; Permission required;* or *Closed* until some specified time. Those in the first two categories are available to *bona fide* researchers.

Q: And establishing that one is bona fide?

A: Write, phone, or visit us, explaining your interest. No appointment is necessary, but writing or calling in advance can be helpful—Area Code 212 280-2273. Oral History is open weekdays, 9 to 5, the year round. Come to the southeast corner of Butler Library from the main entrance. Our offices are on the east mezzanine, one flight up via a doorway to the left just before you reach the Columbia College Library.

Q: Is it always necessary to come to Columbia?

A: No. That depends on your quest. Some 800 of the memoirs described here—the ones that carry the word *Micro* followed by *I, II, III,* or *IV* at the end of an entry or in a cross reference—are available in microform. These are to be found in major research libraries (and in some instances in smaller ones), or they may be ordered individually on 105 × 148mm microfiches directly from the publishers, Microfilming Corporation of America, Box 10, Sanford, N. C. 27330. Even if the memoirs you need are not obtainable in microform, you might be able to save a trip by employing our research service.

Q: How does the research service function?

A: We arrange for research in the Collection in response to precise instructions and a statement of purpose. There is a nominal charge per hour. We suggest you set a dollar limit, and in making your estimate, allow time for the writing of a report as well as for the research itself.

A graduate course in Oral History, offered since 1973 in Columbia's Herbert Lehman suite, plunges students into interviewing, critiquing, and research in the Oral History Collection.

Q: What about interlibrary loan?

A: We are prevented from participating by the terms of our agreements with memoirists.

Q: How can I examine memoirs that are Permission required?

A: You need the written permission of the oral author or his designee. We furnish addresses; you write for permissions. Often as not, they are readily granted. Be sure to bring them when you come.

Q: And Closed *means literally that?*

A: Precisely. Restrictions change, so there is no harm in asking us. No inference is to be drawn from the fact that a memoir is closed. In a few cases we imposed the restriction ourselves, in the absence of word from the memoirist.

*Q: Many individual entries in this catalogue carry labels in caps and small caps—*EISENHOWER ADMINISTRATION *and* SOCIAL SECURITY *and so forth. What does this signify?*

A: The label not only identifies a special project that you will find described elsewhere in the catalogue, it also tells you this particular memoir is of sufficiently broad interest to merit separate notice. More commonly, contributors are simply cross-referenced to the project entry, where the nature and scope of the project is described and related memoirs are listed.

Q: Several thousand entries tell us someone is "discussed in" a memoir or in several memoirs and projects. Are these comprehensive listings, or merely suggestive?

A: They are merely suggestive, calling attention to memoirs or special projects in which there are substantive references about that person.

Q: Then the absence of such an entry for an individual . . .

A: Tells nothing about whether the Collection has material concerning that person. By way of illustration, the *Dictionary of American Biography*'s Supplement V refers to the Columbia Oral History Collection as holding substantial material about biographees in 32 instances. As it happens, 27 of these rate entries herein; five do not, simply because compilers of our catalogue entries, from which "discussed ins" derive, did not mention them: Brien McMahon, Adam Clayton Powell, Sr., John Sloan, Oliver Sprague and Fred Vinson. For that matter, you won't find "discussed ins" for Carrie Chapman Catt or John D. Rockefeller, although the Collection has numerous references to each. The whole we are talking about now runs to 472,936 pages, so being comprehensive in this respect is quite beyond us.

Q: Then how is one to know if the Collection has material about a given person?

A: By consulting our master biographical card index, either in person or by mail or phone. We search it and respond without charge to inquiries made in good faith.

Q: What other finding aids are available?

A: Every memoir has its own biographical index. A few special projects have detailed indexes of their own, as noted in the project descriptions. A massive multiple-access index to *Micro I,* the first 55,000 pages in the micro series, may be consulted in our office. Indexing for parts II, III, and IV is to follow, and all will be available in book form. Inquire for these in the 1980s.

Q: Are tapes as well as transcripts available?

A: Yes. Restrictions permitting, you can listen to the tapes of most memoirs done since 1964. (Segments of a few pre-1964 tapes also are available.) Look for the year given at the end of each entry: this is the year of the concluding interview. Tapes are audited on our premises. Copying tape requires special permission.

Q: What about copying specified pages of transcript for research purposes, in lieu of note-taking?

A: Copyright law obtains. We can copy specified pages if they are among the 155,000 currently available in the *Micro* series, which is growing rapidly. Others still require the written permission of the oral author or his executor for copying. The office charges a copying fee.

Q: How does one cite and quote from the Collection for use in a book or an article or script?

A: Send us pertinent pages of your final draft; we assist in obtaining the necessary permissions. The form of citation normally used is, *"The Reminiscences of Norman Thomas,* Part II (1965), p. 149, in the Oral History Collection of Columbia University, hereafter Thomas, COHC."

Q: Are fees charged for published use?

A: Ordinarily, no. We follow trade practice in negotiating a fee for quotation that exceeds the "fair use" rule, generally more than 500 words taken from any single memoir. Scholarly monographs may be excepted. Every user is asked to furnish the Oral History Office with a copy of the published work.

Q: Does the Oral History Office still offer a free copy of the catalogue to anyone who discovers published use of which you were unaware?

A: Yes, and authors win mention in our annual reports, now widely distributed.

Q: The catalogue presents no problem if you know the names of persons to look up in it, but what if your approach is topical?

A: This edition introduces subject headings designed to help you find individual memoirs and special projects that are pertinent. For convenience, a checklist of these entries is appended, along with a list of all the special projects described in this edition.

SUBJECT HEADINGS

Abortion
Advertising/Public Relations
Agriculture
American Federation of Labor— Congress of Industrial Organizations (AFL-CIO)
American Indians
American Labor Party
Archaeology/Anthropology
Architecture
Art
Art Criticism
Athletics
Atomic Energy
Authors
Aviation
Black Communities
Black Issues
Blacks—Civil Rights

Books and Book Publishing
Business and Industry
Children
China
Civil Rights
Civil War
Columbia University
Communications
Communist Party
Conservation of Natural Resources
Dance
Democratic Party
Department of Defense
Depression of the 1930's
Diplomacy/International Affairs
Economics
Education
Engineering

Film

Finance/Banks and Banking

History

Hoboes

Immigration/Emigration

Industrial Workers of the World

Insurance

Integration/Segregation

Internal Security Investigations

Japan

Jewish Issues

Journalism

Judiciary

Korean War

Ku Klux Klan

Labor Relations

Latin America

Law

Law—Education

League of Nations

League of Women Voters

Liberal Party of New York State

Libraries

Lumber Industry

Medicine

Medicine—Education

Medicine—Research

Mining

Missions and Missionaries

Museums

Music

National Association for the Advancement of Colored People

New Deal

New Deal Agricultural Policies

New York City Politics

New York State Politics

North Atlantic Treaty Organization

Nursing

Oil

Oral History

Pacifism

Philanthropy

Philosophy

Physics

Police

Politics and Government—National

Politics and Government—State and Local

Prisons

Progressive Party (1912)

Progressive Party (1948)

Prohibition

Psychology/Psychiatry

Public Health

Race Relations

Religion

Republican Party

Sacco-Vanzetti Case

Science and Scientists

Social Work/Reform

Socialist Party

Sociology

South, U.S.

Spanish-American War

Spanish Civil War

Strikes

Student Activism

Suez Crisis

Theater

Trade—Retail/Import-Export

Transportation

Union of Soviet Socialist Republics	Urban Development/Housing
Unions	Vietnam War
United Nations	War Crimes Trials
U.S. Air Force	Women
U.S. Army	World War I
U.S. Navy	World War II

SPECIAL PROJECTS

Air Force Academy	Thomas Alva Edison Project
Alaskan Pioneers	Eisenhower Administration
American Association of Physics Teachers	Ethnic Groups and American Foreign Policy
American Cultural Leaders	Farm Holiday Association
American Historians	Federal Communications Commission
Architecture Project	
Argentina	Federated Department Stores
Henry H. Arnold Project	Robert J. Flaherty Project
Association for the Aid of Crippled Children	James Lawrence Fly Project
	Flying Tigers
Austrian Project	Forest History Society
Aviation Project	Friends of the Columbia Libraries
Benedum and the Oil Industry	John Robert Gregg Project
Book-of-the-Month Club	Dag Hammarskjold Project
Nicholas Murray Butler Project	Health Sciences
Carnegie Corporation	Richard Hofstadter Project
Children's Television Workshop	Hungarian Project
China Missionaries	Independence National Historical Park
Chinese Oral History	
Civil Rights in Alabama	International Negotiations
Civil War Centennial	Jackson Hole Preserve
Columbia Crisis of 1968	Benjamin A. Javits Project
Continental Group, Inc.	Jazz Project
Hart Crane Project	Journalism Lectures
James B. Duke Project	John F. Kennedy Project

Kirkland College
Alexandra Kollontai Project
La Follette Civil Liberties Committee
League of Nations Project
Herbert H. Lehman Project
Longwood Gardens
McGraw-Hill
Marine Corps
Marshall Plan
Mining Engineers
Mt. Sinai Hospital
Naval History
Allan Nevins Project
New York Bar
New York Botanical Garden
New York Political Studies
New York University
New York's Art World
Nobel Laureates on Scientific Research
Occupation of Japan
Robert P. Patterson Project
Poets on their Poetry
Popular Arts
Joseph M. Proskauer Project
Psychoanalytic Movement
Radio Liberty
Radio Pioneers
Rare Books
Rockefeller Foundation
Theodore Roosevelt Association
Social Security
Socialist Movement
Southern Intellectual Leaders
Adlai E. Stevenson Project
Robert A. Taft Project
Teachers Insurance and Annuity Association of America—College Retirement Equities Fund
United Nations Conference, San Francisco, 1945
Vietnam Veterans
Weyerhaeuser Timber Company
Women Journalists
Women's History and Population Issues
World Bank

ABBREVIATIONS

AAA	Agricultural Adjustment Administration	AEC	Atomic Energy Commission
ACLS	American Council of Learned Societies	AFL	American Federation of Labor
ACLU	American Civil Liberties Union	AHA	American Historical Association
ADA	Americans for Democratic Action	*AHR*	*The American Historical Review*

AID	Agency for International Development	EFC	Emergency Fleet Corporation
AMA	American Medical Association	EPIC	End Poverty in California
AP	Associated Press	ERA	Equal Rights Amendment
BAE	Bureau of Agricultural Economics	FAO	Food and Agriculture Organization
BEW	Board of Economic Warfare	FCC	Federal Communications Commission
CARE	Cooperative for American Remittances to Europe	FEAF	Far Eastern Air Force
CBI	China, Burma, India Theater of War	FEPC	Fair Employment Practices Committee
CCC	Civilian Conservation Corps	FERA	Federal Emergency Relief Administration
CCNY	College of the City of New York	FHA	Federal Housing Administration
CG	Commanding General	FSA	Farm Security Administration
CIA	Central Intelligence Agency	FTC	Federal Trade Commission
CIAA	Co-ordinator of Inter-American Affairs	HEW	Department of Health, Education, and Welfare
CIO	Congress of Industrial Organizations	HIP	Health Insurance Plan
CO	Commanding Officer	HQMC	Marine Corps Headquarters
CORE	Congress on Racial Equality	ICA	International Cooperation Administration
CPA	certified public accountant		
CREF	College Retirement Equities Fund	ICFTU	International Confederation of Free Trade Unions
DAB	*Dictionary of American Biography*		
EDC	European Defense Community	IFC	International Finance Corporation

IGY	International Geophysical Year	NLRA	National Labor Relations Act
IHB	International Health Board	NLRB	National Labor Relations Board
ILO	International Labor Office	NRA	National Recovery Administration
IPR	Institute of Pacific Relations	NSC	National Security Council
IRO	International Relief Organization	NYA	National Youth Administration
IWW	Industrial Workers of the World	NYU	New York University
MGH	Massachusetts General Hospital	OAS	Organization of American States
Micro	microform available	OCD	Office of Civilian Defense
MIT	Massachusetts Institute of Technology	ODT	Office of Defense Transportation
MSA	Mutual Security Administration	OES	Office of Economic Stabilization
NAACP	National Association for the Advancement of Colored People	OFRRO	Office of Foreign Relief and Rehabilitation Operations
NAM	National Association of Manufacturers	ONI	Office of Naval Intelligence
NATO	North Atlantic Treaty Organization	OPA	Office of Price Administration
NDRC	National Defense Research Committee	OPM	Office of Production Management
NEA	National Education Association	OSRD	Office of Scientific Research and Development
NIH	National Institutes of Health	OSS	Office of Strategic Services
NIMH	National Institute of Mental Health	OTC	Officers Training Corps
NIRA	National Industrial Recovery Act	OWI	Office of War Information

PAC	Political Action Committee	TIAA	Teachers Insurance and Annuity Association of America
P&S	College of Physicians and Surgeons		
PUMC	Peking Union Medical College	TNEC	Temporary National Economic Committee
PWA	Public Works Administration	TVA	Tennessee Valley Authority
RA	Resettlement Administration	UAW	United Automobile Workers
RAF	Royal Air Force	UJA	United Jewish Appeal
REA	Rural Electrification Administration	UMW	United Mine Workers
		UNESCO	United Nations Educational, Scientific and Cultural Organization
RFC	Reconstruction Finance Corporation		
ROTC	Reserve Officers Training Corps	UNICEF	United Nations International Children's Emergency Fund
SCAP	Supreme Commander Allied Powers		
SEATO	South East Asia Treaty Organization	UNRRA	United Nations Relief and Rehabilitation Administration
SEC	Securities and Exchange Commission		
SHAEF	Supreme Headquarters, Allied Expeditionary Force	USAF	United States Air Force
		USHA	United States Housing Authority
SHAPE	Supreme Headquarters Allied Powers Europe	USIA	United States Information Agency
SNCC	Student Non-violent Coordinating Committee	USIS	United States Information Service
SPAB	Supply Priorities and Allocations Board	USMC	United States Marine Corps
SSRC	Social Science Research Council	USO	United Service Organizations
TC	Teachers College, Columbia University	USPHS	United States Public Health Service

USSB	United States Shipping Board	WHO	World Health Organization
WCTU	Woman's Christian Temperance Union	WIB	War Industries Board
WFA	War Food Administration	WLB	National War Labor Board
WFC	War Finance Corporation	WPA	Works Progress Administration
WFTU	World Federation of Trade Unions	WPB	War Production Board
		WWI	World War I
		WWII	World War II

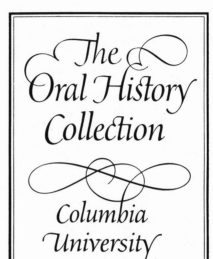

The
Oral History
Collection

Columbia
University

A

ABAD DE SANTILLAN, Diego. *See* Argentina.

ABBOTT, George. *Discussed in* Sol Jacobson; Richard Rodgers.

ABBOTT, Paul (1898–1971) *See* McGraw-Hill.

ABDUL, Raoul (1929–   ).
Musical background; journalistic work in Cleveland; work as Langston Hughes' private secretary, Harlem, 1957–67; Hughes' working methods, his attitudes toward black culture and artistic projects; work in the theater; Hughes' death.
  65 pp. *Permission required to cite or quote.* 1975.

ABEL, Elie (1920–   ) Journalist.
EISENHOWER ADMINISTRATION
Recollections of the Eisenhower administration, 1953–59; Washington correspondent, *NY Times,* 1949–59; press conferences, information leaks; Vietnam War. Impressions of John Foster Dulles, Richard M. Nixon, and Charles Wilson.
  45 pp. *Permission required to cite or quote.* 1970. *Micro III.*

ABEL, Walter Charles (1898–   ) *See* Popular Arts.

ABERBACH, Jean and Julius. *See* Popular Arts.

ABORTION *See* Albert Blumenthal; Women's History and Population Issues.

ABPLANALP, Alfred J. (1895–   ) *See* Continental Group.

ABRAHAM, Karl. *Discussed in* Edward Glover; Sandor Rado; Theodor Reik.

ABRAM, Morris Berthold (1918–   ) *See* Ethnic Groups and American Foreign Policy.

ABRAMS, Charles (1901–1970) Housing expert.
Urban renewal, social reform; National Committee Against Discrimination; First Houses, NYC; Morris Strunsky, Langdon W. Post.
  78 pp. *Permission required to cite or quote.* 1964. *Micro II.*

ABRAMS, Frank Whittemore (1889–1976) Executive.
Early life and education; career with Standard Oil of New Jersey; responsibilities of management; Council on Financial Aid to Education.
  48 pp. *Permission required to cite or quote.* 1954. *Micro IV.*

ABT, John J. (1904–   ) *See* La Follette Civil Liberties Committee.

ABZUG, Bella. *Discussed in* Edward I. Koch.

ACEIRO, Jorge. *See* Argentina.

ACHESON, Dean (1893–1971) *See* Journalism Lectures *and* Marshall Plan.
Discussed in Raymond Baldwin; William Benton; Spruille Braden; Sir Robert Jackson; Philip Jessup; Nelson Rockefeller; Henry Wallace; James P. Warburg.

ACHILLES, Theodore C. (1905–   ) *See* International Negotiations.

ACKENHAUSEN, Helen. *See* Eisenhower Administration.

ACKERMAN, Lauren V. *See* Occupation of Japan. *Micro II.*

(1)

ACOSTA, Bert. *Discussed in* Harry Bruno.

ACTING *See* Film; Theater.

ADAMS, Claude M. (1914–   ) *See* Continental Group.

ADAMS, John Charles (–1952) *See* Benedum and the Oil Industry.

ADAMS, Maude. *Discussed in* Richard Gordon; James W. Wood.

ADAMS, Sherman (1899–   ) Presidential aide.
EISENHOWER ADMINISTRATION
Eisenhower's decision to run for the Presidency; 1952 convention and campaign; Richard Nixon fund; Korea speech; Cabinet and White House staff; NSC; Council of Economic Advisors; foreign policy; congressional-executive relations; economic controls. Recollections of John Foster Dulles, Herbert Brownell, Thomas E. Dewey, Earl Warren, Emmett Hughes, Gabriel Hauge, Arthur F. Burns.
268 pp. *Permission required to cite or quote.* 1970.

EISENHOWER ADMINISTRATION
Duties as Chief of Staff, issues faced: desegregation, oil depletion allowance, vice-presidential nomination of 1956.
50 pp. *Permission required.* 1969.

Discussed in H. Meade Alcorn, Jr.; Edward L. Beach; Ralph H. Cake; Edgar Eisenhower; Barry Goldwater; Robert K. Gray; James C. Hagerty; William H. Lawrence; Edward A. McCabe; Kevin McCann; E. Frederic Morrow; Ilene Slater; John Steelman.

ADKINS, Bertha (1906–   ).
EISENHOWER ADMINISTRATION
Republican National Committee; 1952 convention; women in government; impressions of President and Mrs. Eisenhower.
72 pp. *Permission required to cite or quote.* 1967. *Micro III.*

ADLER, Alexandra (1901–   ) *See* Austrian Project.

ADLER, Felix. *Discussed in* James Gutmann; Joseph Jablonower; Henry Neumann; John Spargo.

ADLER, Kurt A. (1905–   ) *See* Austrian Project.

ADVERTISING/PUBLIC RELATIONS
See Frank Arnold; William Benton; Edward L. Bernays; Chester Bowles; Roy Durstine; George H. Gallup; Mary Bass Gibson; Dan Golenpaul; Alvin Grauer; L. Richard Guylay; Albert Hauptli; William Hutton; Albert Lasker; Paul F. Lazarsfeld; William Paley; Murray Snyder.

ADY, Merrill Steele. *See* China Missionaries.

AERONAUTICS *See* Aviation.

AFRO-AMERICANS *See* Black Issues.

AGEE, James (1909–1955) Author.
Recollections of Agee by John Huston, Fr. James Fly, Walker Evans, Ralph Ellison, Wilder Hobson, Nan Taylor, David McDowell and Alfred Kazin. Radio program written and produced by WBAI, NY.
33 pp. *Open.*

AGHNIDES, Thanassis (1889–   ) Greek diplomat.
LEAGUE OF NATIONS PROJECT
Education, University of Constantinople; League of Nations, 1919–41; Sir Eric Drummond, Joseph Avenol as Secretaries General; preparatory commission and disarmament conference, 1932; Under Secretary General, 1938; discussion of League Secretariat and degree of national influence on Secretariat members; political pressures in Europe with rise of Nazis; effects of Munich, Albania, Danzig, outbreak of WWII; Greek government-in-exile, 1942; UN organization meeting in San Francisco, drafting charter; chairman of advisory committee on administration and finance; review of 21 years of UN: description of major crises, recollections of Trygve Lie, Dag Hammarskjold, U Thant, many other League and UN staff members. The memoir is in French.
506 pp. *Permission required.* 1966.

AGRICULTURE *See* George Aiken; Will Alexander; Ezra Taft Benson; Karl Brandt; Earl Butz; Clarence Francis; J. George Harrar; Charles Holman; Chester Morrill; True D. Morse; Don Paarlberg; Daniel Powers; Arthur F. Raper; E.C. Stakman; Lewis L. Strauss; Louis Taber; Jesse W. Tapp; Charles E. Taylor; Henry C. Taylor; Howard R. Tolley; Leslie A. Wheeler; M.L. Wilson; Milton R. Young.
See also New Deal Agricultural Policies.

AIKEN, George David (1892–   ) Senator.
EISENHOWER ADMINISTRATION
Agricultural policies from late 1940's through 1950's; impressions of President Eisenhower.
31 pp. *Permission required to cite or quote.* 1967. *Micro III.*

AIR FORCE ACADEMY
In 1968 the faculty of the USAF Academy initiated a series of oral history interviews with significant figures in military aviation. The major topics discussed include strategy and tactics in WWI, WWII and Korea, the establishment of the Air Force Academy, and inter-service relationships. Two series of particular interest deal with blacks in the Air Force and the introduction of women cadets to the Academy.

Participants and pages: John R. Alison, 54 *(closed during lifetime);* James R. Allen, 30 *(permission required to cite or quote);* William Bower, 84; James E. Briggs, 61; Charles P. Cabell and Haywood S. Hansell, 133 *(closed during lifetime);* Charles C. Canfield, 53 *(closed during lifetime);* George Caron, 64 *(permission required to cite or quote);* Charles I. Carpenter, 72 *(closed during lifetime);* Benjamin W. Chidlaw, 23 *(closed during lifetime);* Prosper E. Cholet, 84; Anthony R. Cillo, 44 *(permission required);* A.P. Clark, 96 *(permission required);* Mrs. Albert B. Clark, 17 *(closed during lifetime);* Jacqueline Cochran, 165 *(permission required to cite or quote);* Robert L. Copsey, 48; Jarred V. Crabb, 150; Laurence C. Craigie, 81; Perry J. Dahl, 63 *(permission required);* Howard C. Davidson, 35; Benjamin O. Davis, 38 *(closed except to USAF historians);* Gen. and Mrs. Benjamin O. Davis, 56 *(closed during life-*

time); Charles Dolan, 25 *(permission required to cite or quote);* Charles D'Olive, 58; James H. Doolittle, 56; William R. Dunn, 74;

Ira C. Eaker, 56; Idwal Edwards, 35; James C. Evans, 47; Wendell H. Fertig, 18 *(permission required);* Judith Galloway, 79 *(permission required);* Paul Garber, 236 *(permission required);* Harold L. George and Haywood S. Hansell, 60 *(closed during lifetime);* James P. Goode, 26; Irene Graf and Terry Walter, 124 *(permission required);* Anthony Grossetta, 53; Haywood S. Hansell, 52; Mrs. H.R. Harmon, 40 *(closed during lifetime);* Jeanne Holm, 80; Daniel James, Jr., 24 *(permission required to cite or quote);* Ben H. Johnson, 58 *(permission required to cite or quote);* Edward G. Lansdale, 83; Oliver C. LeBoutillier, 43; Robert M. Lee, 35 *(closed during lifetime);* Curtis LeMay, 107 *(permission required);* Grover Loening, 9;

James P. McCarthy, 59; Gail McComas, 84 *(permission required);* John P. McConnell, 24; Robert McDermott, 207 *(permission required);* Jack Marr, 33 *(permission required to cite or quote);* S.L.A. Marshall, 70; Ben S. Martin, 62; Hughie E. Mathews, 37; Joseph O. Mauborgne, 79 *(permission required);* Francis E. Merritt, 116 *(permission required to cite or quote);* Francis E. Merritt, 80 *(permission required);* Danforth P. Miller, Jr., 101; Theodore R. Milton, 125; Atha Grace Moorman, 41 *(closed during lifetime);* Thomas Moorman, 134; Oliver K. Niess, 43; Emmett O'Donnell, Jr., 48 *(permission required);* Charles W. Oliver, 39 *(permission required to cite or quote);* Noel F. Parrish, 45; Earle E. Partridge, 85; Forrest Pogue, 39 *(permission required);*

Joseph Reich, 29 *(closed during lifetime);* Edward V. Rickenbacker, 19 *(permission required to cite or quote);* Reginald Sinclaire, 58; Jesse Smith, 37; Robert J. Smith, 72; Carl Spaatz, 26 *(permission required);* Delmar T. Spivey, 100; Donald R. Spoon, 66; Myra M. Stone, 43 *(permission required);* Keith A. Stowers, 29 *(closed during lifetime);* Dean C. Strother, 76 *(closed during lifetime);* Herbert B. Thatcher, 122 *(closed during lifetime);* Lucius Theus, 34; James C. Thomas and Robert E. Lushbaugh, 44; Thayer Tutt, 35; Nathan F. Twining, 47 *(permission required);* John F. Victory, 114 *(closed during lifetime);* Leigh Wade, 28 *(permission required);* Lewis Walt, 114 *(closed during lifetime);* Spann Watson, 61; Albert C. Wedemeyer, 90 *(closed during lifetime);* Sir Frank Whittle, 30.

5,754 pp. *Open except as noted.* 1968– *Contributed by the USAF Academy, Colorado.*

AITCHISON, A. E. *See* Weyerhaeuser Timber Company.

AKINS, Zoe. *Discussed in* John Hall Wheelock.

ALASKAN PIONEERS
This project gathers the reminiscences of pioneer settlers in Alaska, providing accounts of gold prospecting, mining, cattle driving, homesteading, and travel by trail and river. Included are descriptions of the social life of the pioneers, as well as accounts of the depression of 1893 and the Klondike strike.
Participants and pages: Jack Brooks, 7; Nat Browne, 33; Edward Crawford, 57; George Gasser, 23; Bobby Sheldon, 36; William R. Sherwin, 40; Sam White, 39; Oscar Winchell, 159.

394 pp. *Open.* 1959–62. *Contributed by Mrs. Sandy Jensen of Fairbanks, Alaska.*

ALBEE, Edward (1928–   ) and Alan Schneider. *See* Popular Arts.

ALBERTSON, Ralph (1866–1951) Clergyman.
Christian Commonwealth Movement, coworkers; Walter Lippmann; Russia, 1918–19.

46 pp. *Permission required to cite or quote.* 1950. *Micro II.* Papers (microfilm).

ALBIZU CAMPOS, Pedro. *Discussed in* Roger N. Baldwin.

ALBRIEU, Oscar. *See* Argentina.

ALBRIGHT, Horace Marden (1890–   ) Conservationist.
Department of the Interior, 1913; National Park Service, 1916–33; Superintendent of

Yellowstone, 1919–33; conservation problems; maintenance of park facilities, establishment of new parks, acquisition of lands; historical areas and national monuments; organization of CCC; Capital Parks and Planning Commission; borax mining and potash producing, US Potash Company; chemical code under NRA; labor problems; international cartel and price war; impressions of Franklin K. Lane, Woodrow Wilson, Albert B. Fall, Warren G. Harding, Owen Brewster, Gifford Pinchot, Calvin Coolidge, Herbert Hoover, John D. Rockefeller, Jr., Hiram Johnson, Franklin D. Roosevelt, Harold Ickes.

851 pp. *Permission required to cite or quote.* 1960. *Micro I.* Papers.
See also Jackson Hole Preserve.
Discussed in Harold P. Fabian.

ALBRIGHT, Horace M. and Newton Drury.
Comments on conservation, 1900–60.

49 pp. *Permission required to cite or quote.* 1961. *Contributed by the Regional Oral History Office, University of California, Berkeley.*

ALCORN, Hugh Meade, Jr. (1907–   ) Lawyer.
EISENHOWER ADMINISTRATION
Account of Republican Conventions, 1952 and 1964; Republican National Committee; Senatorial Campaign Committee and Congressional Campaign Committee; Operation Dixie. Recollections of Sherman Adams, John Foster Dulles, Richard Nixon, Harold Stassen, Leonard Hall, and Barry Goldwater.

159 pp. *Permission required to cite or quote.* 1967.

ALDERMAN, Sidney Sherrill (1892–1973) Lawyer.
Early life; Trinity College (now Duke University); law school and teaching; military training and WWI; law practice in North Carolina; General Solicitor, General Counsel and Vice President of the Southern Railway System; Nuremberg War Crimes trials.

1,817 pp. *Permission required to cite or quote.* 1953. Papers.

ALDERSON, Harold B. *See* Robert A. Taft Project.

ALDEWERELD, Siem (1909–) *See* World Bank.

ALDRICH, Winthrop Williams (1885–1974) *See* Eisenhower Administration. *Micro IV.*

ALEMANN, Roberto T. *See* Argentina.

ALEXANDER, Bill. *See* Robert J. Flaherty Project.

ALEXANDER, Franz. *Discussed in* Abram Kardiner; Mary Lasker; Sandor Rado.

ALEXANDER, Lonnie. *See* Vietnam Veterans.

ALEXANDER, Will Winton (1884–1956) Authority on race relations.
Childhood and education; Vanderbilt University; ministry, Methodist Church South, 1901–17; WWI; race riots; beginning work in race relations, Commission in Interracial Cooperation, 1919–30; lynching; Ku Klux Klan; Atlanta University merger; Dillard University, Acting President, 1931–35; RA, 1935–36; Greenbelt towns; Great Plains; subsistence homesteads; Bankhead-Jones Farm Tenant Act, FSA, 1937; Julius Rosenwald Fund; FEPC; organizing the American Council on Race Relations; impressions of C.B. Baldwin, John Fischer, Sidney Hillman, President and Mrs. Franklin D. Roosevelt, Julius Rosenwald, Frank Tannenbaum, Mr. and Mrs. Rexford G. Tugwell, Henry Wallace, and others.
756 pp. *Permission required to cite or quote.* 1952. *Micro I.*
Discussed in Arthur F. Raper.

ALEXANDER, Willard W. *See* Popular Arts.

ALEXANDERSON, Ernst F. W. (1878–1975) *See* Radio Pioneers. *Micro III.*

ALFORD, T. Dale (1916–) *See* Eisenhower Administration.
Discussed in Orval E. Faubus.

ALGER, George William (1872–1967) Lawyer.
Law practice in NYC at the turn of the century; Moreland commission; NY pris-

ons; Moreland commissioner to investigate NY superintendent of insurance in the guaranteed mortgage companies debacle on nearly two billion issues of bonds, 1933; NYC garment industry; Vermont boyhood. Observations on social reformers, including Lillian Wald and Florence Kelley; Theodore Roosevelt.
538 pp. *Permission required to cite or quote.* 1952. *Micro I.*

ALGREN, Nelson. *Discussed in* Roger W. Straus.

ALISON, John Richardson (1912–).
AVIATION PROJECT
Pre-WWII training and experience in Army Air Corps; demonstrating P-40's in England; London during the Blitz; duty in Russia, Lend-Lease program with Russian Air Force; combat assignments in CBI; kamikaze attacks on Pacific Fleet; Assistant Secretary of Commerce for Air; Northrop Corporation. Recollections of Harry Hopkins, Gens. Henry H. Arnold, Claire Chennault, and Orde Wingate.
132 pp. *Permission required to cite or quote.* 1960.
See also Air Force Academy.

ALLEN, Agnes. Author.
Family background; education, Vassar, 1916–17; Stuart Walker Portmanteau Theatre tour, 1916–17; *Harper's* magazine, 1919–35; marriage to Frederick Lewis Allen, 1932; development of photograph and picture book form; co-authorship with husband of *The American Procession,* 1933; *Metropolis,* 1934; *Women are Here to Stay,* 1949; OWI, Outposts Service, WWII; Reader's Digest Condensed Books, 1947.
231 pp. *Permission required to cite or quote.* 1977.

ALLEN, Chester Robinson (1905–1972) *See* Marine Corps.

ALLEN, Ed. *See* Radio Pioneers.

ALLEN, Ernest Mason (1904–) *See* Health Sciences.

ALLEN, Frederick Lewis. *Discussed in* Agnes Allen.

ALLEN, George Venable (1903–1970) Diplomat.
US Foreign Service, 1930; consular service, Shanghai, Greece; Middle East Division, State Department, 1938–46; Potsdam, 1945.
77 pp. *Permission required to cite or quote.* 1962. *Micro IV.*

EISENHOWER ADMINISTRATION
Ambassador to India; Director of USIA; recollections of John Foster Dulles and other Secretaries of State; Korea; Greece; US exhibition in Moscow and "Kitchen Debate"; Brussels Fair, 1958.
213 pp. *Permission required to cite or quote.* 1967. *Micro III.*

ALLEN, James E., Jr. (1911–1971) Educator.
Early work in West Virginia and at Princeton, Harvard, and Syracuse Universities; executive assistant to NY Commissioner of Education, later Commissioner; Presidential Commission on Higher Education.
55 pp. *Permission required to cite or quote.* 1966. *Micro II.*

ALLEN, James R. (1925–   ) *See* Air Force Academy.

ALLEN, Joseph H. (1916–   ) *See* McGraw-Hill.

ALLEN, Netta Powell (1890–   ) *See* China Missionaries.

ALLEN, William Harvey (1874–1963) Civic worker.
Youth and education; Universities of Chicago and Pennsylvania; Association for Improving the Condition of the Poor, 1903–07; Bureau of Municipal Research, 1907–14; Rockefeller Foundation and Carnegie Foundation; Training School for Public Service, 1911–14; University of Wisconsin Survey; Dr. Charles Van Hise; Institute for Public Service; NYC Municipal Civil Service Commission, 1934–37; NY politics; Mayors Fiorello La Guardia and James Walker, Thomas E. Dewey.
532 pp. *Permission required to cite or quote.* 1950. *Micro I.* Papers.

ALLIN, William M. (1910–   ) *See* Continental Group.

ALLISON, John M. *See* International Negotiations.

ALMARZA, Camilo (1904–   ) *See* Argentina.

ALMOND, Edward. *Discussed in* Oliver P. Smith.

ALOE, Carlos. *See* Argentina.

ALSBERG, Henry G. *Discussed in* William Couch.

ALSOP, Joseph Wright (1910–   ) *See* Eisenhower Administration.

ALTER, Gerald (1919–   ), John de Wilde and Harold Larsen. *See* World Bank.

ALTIER, Charles (1918–   ) *See* Continental Group.

ALTMEYER, Arthur Joseph (1891–1972) Administrator.
SOCIAL SECURITY
Education, background in health insurance movement, John R. Commons; Committee on Economic Security, 1934–35; Assistant Secretary of Labor, 1934; Advisory Council, National Conference on Health, 1938; administrative problems and policies in Social Security: training, relations with Congress, Treasury Department, Internal Revenue Service; influence of organized labor and professional associations. Impressions of Frances Perkins, Edwin Witte, Wilbur Cohen, Isidore Falk, and others.
231 pp. *Permission required to cite or quote.* 1967.
Discussed in Barbara Armstrong; A. Henry Aronson; Frank Bane; Bernice Bernstein; Eveline Burns; Ewan Clague; Wilbur Cohen; Isidore Falk; Maurine Mulliner; Paul and Elizabeth Raushenbush; Herman Somers; Jack B. Tate; Russell G. Wagenet.

ALTSCHUL, Helen (Mrs. Frank) (1887–   ) *See* Herbert H. Lehman Project.

AMBROSE, George M. (1905–   ) *See* Continental Group.

AMEN, John Harlan (1898–1960) Lawyer. Harvard Law School; Departments of Justice and of War; Nuremberg War Crimes trials.

36 pp. *Permission required to cite or quote. 1951. Micro I.*

AMERICAN ASSOCIATION OF PHYSICS TEACHERS
Founding members discuss the formation of the American Association of Physics Teachers in 1930 and describe its relations with the American Physical Society and the American Institute of Physics. Efforts to improve teaching methods and to achieve a balance between teaching and research; anecdotes and appraisals of leading American physicists, including Karl Compton, Arthur Compton, and F. K. Richtmyer.
Participants and pages: Homer L. Dodge, 47; Paul Klopsteg, 42; Frederic Palmer, 36; M. N. States, 31; D. L. Webster, 37.

193 pp. *Permission required to cite or quote. 1963. Underwritten by the American Association of Physics Teachers and the American Institute of Physics of New York City.*

AMERICAN CULTURAL LEADERS
This series of interviews was conducted by Joan Simpson Burns to provide material for a study of patterns in American cultural life. Mrs. Burns's interest centered on her subjects' family backgrounds and early exposure to the arts as well as on their later contributions to American culture. Her interviewing method, frankly experimental, encouraged free association and frequent digressions. The principals' memoirs are supplemented by conversations with their professional associates.
Participants and pages: William Arrowsmith and Roger Shattuck, 16; Mody Boatwright, 12; Robert Brustein, 17; Turner Catledge, 35; Hedley Donovan, 184; Ronnie Dugger, 33; Lloyd Goodrich, 86; John Hawkes, 51; Barnaby Keeney, 23; Goddard Lieberson, 95; W. McNeil Lowry, 296; Robert McCord, 50; Harry Ransom, 89; Gordon Ray, 18; Frank Stanton, 330; Frank Thompson, 138; Mrs. Marshall Thompson, 37.

1,510 pp. *Permission required. 1968. Contributed by Joan Simpson Burns, Williamstown, Massachusetts.*

AMERICAN FEDERATION OF LABOR —CONGRESS OF INDUSTRIAL ORGANIZATIONS (AFL-CIO) *See* Solomon Barkin; Joseph A. Beirne; John Brophy; Earl Browder; James B. Carey; Cyrus Ching; Nelson Cruikshank; Joseph Curran; John W. Edelman; Katherine Ellickson; John P. Frey; Albert J. Hayes; Benjamin McLaurin; H.L. Mitchell; Lee Pressman; Morris S. Rosenthal; Lisbeth B. Schorr; Boris B. Shishkin; M. Hedley Stone; Philip Taft; Florence Thorne; Eva M. Valesh.

AMERICAN HISTORIANS
A series of interviews with leading historians, conducted by Professor John Garraty, dealing with such topics as westward expansion and economic change to 1860; slavery in the US; American nationalism, social and cultural changes in the US between the Civil War and WWI; Reconstruction period; the US in world affairs from 1918 to 1945; and problems of interpretation of history.
Participants and pages: Bernard Bailyn, 83; Ray Allen Billington, 103; Stuart Bruchey, 92; Henry Steele Commager, 81; Robert D. Cross, 122; George Dangerfield, 82; Sigmund Diamond, 109; David Donald, 88; Clement Eaton, 89; Stanley Elkins, 87; Robert Ferrell, 111; Jack P. Greene, 161; Robert Heilbroner, 86; Richard Hofstadter, 58; Alfred Kazin, 82; Edward C. Kirkland, 67; Richard W. Leopold, 87; William E. Leuchtenburg, 99; Arthur S. Link, 96; Ernest R. May, 104; Richard B. Morris, 133; George Mowry, 92; Robert K. Murray, 114; Roy F. Nichols, 81; Russel B. Nye, 101; David M. Potter, 82; Arthur M. Schlesinger, Jr., 73; T. Harry Williams, 103; C. Vann Woodward, 86.

2,752 pp. *Permission required to cite or quote. 1968–69. Contributed by John A. Garraty, New York.*

AMERICAN INDIANS *See* Wesley D'Ewart; Charles Fahy; Arthur V. Watkins.

AMERICAN LABOR PARTY *See* Ben Davidson; Benjamin McLaurin; Paul O'Dwyer; Victor Rabinowitz; Paul Ross; Socialist Movement.

AMITAY, Morris. *See* Ethnic Groups and American Foreign Policy.

ANDERSON, Carl D. (1905–) *See* Nobel Laureates.

ANDERSON, Clinton (1895–) *Discussed in* Howard Bray, Nelson Cruikshank; Irwin Wolkstein; Henry Wallace.

ANDERSON, Dillon (1906–1974) Lawyer.
EISENHOWER ADMINISTRATION
Pre-convention and election campaigns, 1952; Tidelands issue; NSC; Draper Committee; Vietnam; Laos; Quemoy and Matsu; Open Skies proposal; Geneva Summit Conference; impressions of President Eisenhower and John Foster Dulles.
130 pp. *Permission required to cite or quote.* 1969. *Micro III.*

ANDERSON, Florence (1910–) Foundation officer.
CARNEGIE CORPORATION
Detailed account of her experiences with the Carnegie Corporation from 1934; relationships, functions and organizations of the various Carnegie enterprises; description of major programs undertaken by Carnegie Corporation with particular emphasis on philosophy, policy, restrictions, procedures, follow-up, and impact; trustees and staff members; relationship with federal government, Congressional investigations; impressions of Andrew Carnegie, Frederick Keppel, Charles Dollard, John Gardner, Nicholas Murray Butler, Alan Pifer, and many other educators and public figures.
656 pp. *Permission required.* 1967.
Discussed in Charles Dollard; Frederick Jackson; John M. Russell.

ANDERSON, Frank Maloy (1871–1961) Historian.
AHA politics and policies; *AHR;* Mississippi Valley Historical Association and its *Review.*
24 pp. *Open.* 1955.

ANDERSON, Gilbert M. (Bronco Billy) (1882–1971) *See* Popular Arts.

ANDERSON, Harold S. (1895–) *See* Thomas A. Edison Project.

ANDERSON, Harry G. *Discussed in* Solomon A. Klein.

ANDERSON, Hilda (1903–) Government official.
Childhood in Brooklyn; education, Columbia and Cornell; China 1931–37: arrival, evacuation, Japanese occupation; return to China, 1945; embassy work in Nanking; "China-Hand Purge"; McCarthyism; State Department reorganization, 1950; Foreign Service work in Taiwan 1953–56, Washington, D.C., Beirut 1959–63; retirement.
150 pp. *Permission required to cite or quote.* 1977.

ANDERSON, Jack Z. (1904–) *See* Eisenhower Administration.

ANDERSON, Maxwell (1888–1959) Author, playwright.
Experiences with the NY *World;* writing *Winterset* and other plays.
34 pp. *Permission required to cite or quote.* 1956. *Micro I.*

ANDERSON, Medford O. *See* Independence Park.

ANDERSON, Orvil A. (1895–1965) Air Force Officer.
HENRY H. ARNOLD PROJECT
Recollections of Gen. Arnold from 1938; War Department policy on planes; fighters vs. bombers; Lend-Lease; expansion of forces, 1941–42; problems of allocation and division of appropriations; organization of USAF; Joint Chiefs and Joint Planning Staff; Pearl Harbor attack; Ploesti raid, 1942. Impressions of President Franklin D. Roosevelt, Gen. George C. Marshall, Adm. Ernest J. King, and others.
113 pp. *Permission required.* 1959.
See also Aviation Project. *Micro II.*

ANDERSON, Robert B. (1910–1965) *See* Eisenhower Administration.
Discussed in C. Douglas Dillon; Thomas Gates; Clifford Roberts.

ANDERSON, Russell. *See* McGraw-Hill.

ANDERSON, Sherwood. *Discussed in* Mildred Gilman; Ben W. Huebsch.

ANDERSON, Walter Stratton (1881–) Naval officer.

Childhood and education; Naval Academy; Naval War College; teaching at Naval Academy and St. John's; NY Harbor Supervisor; sea commands; Naval attaché, London, 1934–37; Director of Naval Intelligence, 1939–41; Pearl Harbor attack; Board of Inspections; Commander, Gulf Sea Frontier; Automatic Electric Company, 1946–56. Impressions of Adms. Ernest King, Chester Nimitz, and Hugo Osterhaus and of Josephus Daniels and Frank Knox.

290 pp. *Permission required to cite or quote.* 1962. *Micro I.*

ANDERSON, Mr. and Mrs. Warwick. *See* Adlai E. Stevenson Project. *Micro III.*

ANDERSON, William Hamilton (1874–1959) Prohibitionist.
Organization, personnel and activities of Anti-Saloon League; Prohibition and NY politics, 1915–24; trial of Mr. Anderson.

148 pp. *Permission required to cite or quote.* 1950. *Micro IV.* Papers.

ANDERVONT, Howard B. (1898–) Biologist.
HEALTH SCIENCES
Family, educational background; chicken virus work, Johns Hopkins; teaching career, Harvard School of Public Health; virus and cancer research; Cancer Act and establishment of Cancer Institute.

108 pp. *Permission required to cite or quote.* 1964.

ANDREW, Geoffrey C. *See* Carnegie Corporation.

ANDREWS, Dana (1909–) *See* Popular Arts.

ANDREWS, Frank. *Discussed in* James Doolittle; Ira C. Eaker.

ANDREWS, John B. *Discussed in* Social Security.

ANDREWS, John Nevins. *See* China Missionaries.

ANGELL, James R. *Discussed in* Carnegie Corporation.

ANGELL, Sir Norman (1872–1967) Author.
Peace movements, British and American politics, and personal reflections, 1900–50; Lord Northcliffe and his newspaper empire. An informal memoir accompanied by an annotated bibliography of his work.

278 pp. *Permission required to cite or quote.* 1951. *Micro I.* Papers.

ANNAN, Robert. *See* Mining Engineers.

ANNETT, Fred A. (1879–1959) *See* McGraw-Hill.

ANNIS, Edward Roland (1913–) Physician.
SOCIAL SECURITY
The President of the AMA (1963–64) discusses debates with Hubert Humphrey, Walter Reuther, John Kennedy, Lyndon Johnson and George Smathers; King-Anderson and Kerr-Mills bills.

84 pp. *Closed during lifetime.* 1967.

ANSORGE, Martin Charles (1882–1967) Lawyer, congressman.
Columbia University, 1903; NYC politics, 1914–32; WWI; national politics during Warren Harding administration.

74 pp. *Permission required to cite or quote.* 1949. *Micro I.* Papers.

ANSTEY, Edgar and Daphne. *See* Robert J. Flaherty Project.

ANTHROPOLOGY *See* Archaeology/Anthropology.

APOLLINAIRE, Guillaume. *Discussed in* Jacques Barzun.

APPLEBY, Paul Henson (1891–1963) Political scientist.
Family background; Grinnell College; newspaper experiences; assistant to Secretary of Agriculture Henry A. Wallace, including detailed description of important New Deal leaders, agencies, politics and policies; trip to London and experiences with Lend-Lease; Department of State.

360 pp. *Permission required to cite or quote.* 1952. *Micro I.*
Discussed in Carl Hamilton.

APPLEMAN, Roy E. *See* Independence Park.

ARAM, John Lorenzo (1912–   ) *See* Weyerhaeuser Timber Company.

ARCHAEOLOGY/ANTHROPOLOGY
See Franziska Boas; Paul Fejos; Albert Giesecke; Theresa Goell; Athanasius Samuel.

ARCHBOLD, John. *Discussed in* Michael L. Benedum.

ARCHITECTURE *See* Architecture Project; Gilmore Clarke; William A. Delano; Constantinos Doxiadis; Douglas Elliman; Robert Greenstein; Wallace K. Harrison; Philip C. Johnson; I.M. Pei; Lawrence White; Frank Lloyd Wright.

ARCHITECTURE PROJECT
This material is drawn primarily from a 1961 program at Columbia University's School of Architecture in celebration of the four great founders of contemporary architecture: Charles-Edouard Le Corbusier, Walter Gropius, Ludwig Mies van der Rohe and Frank Lloyd Wright. It includes addresses by Le Corbusier and Gropius as well as an interview with Mies van der Rohe. Discussion focuses upon philosophies of design, aspects of their various architectural projects, and the juncture of architecture and city planning. Also included are earlier taped conversations with Walter Gropius and Frank Lloyd Wright.
Participants and pages: Walter Gropius, 32; Charles-Edouard Le Corbusier, 8; Ludwig Mies van der Rohe, 78; Frank Lloyd Wright, 15.
    133 pp. *Open.* 1961. *Contributed by Columbia University School of Architecture.*

ARECHAGA, Guillermo. *See* Argentina.

ARENDS, Leslie Cornelius (1895–   ) *See* Robert A. Taft Project.

ARES, Roberto (1912–   ) *See* Argentina.

ARGENTINA
This series of interviews provides a broad general view of Argentina at a critical period in that country's development. A joint effort of the Instituto Torcuato Di Tella in Buenos Aires and the Oral History Research Office of Columbia University, the project began in 1970 with a grant from the Tinker Foundation.
    While the memoirs focus primarily on the 1930's, there is much background information from prior years, and a number of the memoirists deal with events in the succeeding two decades. The institute plans to continue the project, concentrating next on the 1940's and the rise to power of Juan D. Peron.
    Taken together, the memoirs offer a richly detailed panorama of political, sociological, and economic developments unobtainable elsewhere. A group of labor leaders highlight the transition from craft to industrial unions, the factional and partisan conflicts within the labor movement, and attitudes toward ethnic and regional concentrations. Argentine industrial and manufacturing figures describe technological changes, relationships with foreign enterprises, and attitudes toward organized labor. Political leaders discuss internal organization and practices of political groups, with examples from municipal and national campaigns.
    The interviews, conducted by staff members of the institute, are in Spanish. The project is a continuing one.

Participants and pages: Diego Abad de Santillan, 20; Jorge Aceiro, 60; Oscar Albrieu, 156 *(closed during lifetime);* Roberto T. Alemann, 49; Camilo Almarza, 160; Carlos Aloe, 252; Guillermo Arechaga, 21; Roberto Ares, 34; Cecilio Benitez de Castro, 13; Lucio Bonilla, 103; Carlos Browne, 50; Andres Cabona, 116; Enrique Canepa, 232; Andres Caradonti, 38; Celestino Carbajal, 86; Ramon A. Cereijo, 26; Guido Clutterbuck, 61; Eduardo Colom, 138; Alfredo Concepcion, 22; Luis Danussi, 87; Jorge del Rio, 41; Virginio Demarchi, 54; Joaquin Diaz de Vivar, 197; Emilio Dickmann, 174; Jose Domenech, 192 *(certain pages closed);* Hector Duarte, 40;

Carlos Emery, 33; Jesus Fernandez, 31; Alfredo Fidanza, 21; Manuel Fossa, 61; Mateo Fossa, 77; Javier Gamboa, 20; Luis F. Gay, 107; Americo Ghioldi, 50; Ovidio Gimenez, 53; Rafael Ginocchio, 67; Roberto Giusti, 59; Alfredo Gomez

Morales, 88; Ricardo Guardo, 62; Jorge F. Haagen, 26; Esteban Habiague, 147; Hector Hidalgo Sola, 17; Carlos Ibarguren, 48; Julio Irazusta, 51; Alberto Iturbe, 57; Ernesto Janin, 57; Arturo Jauretche, 221; Emilio Jofre, 40; Julio A. Lagos, 31; Roberto Marcelo Levingston, 28; Roberto Lobos, 55;

Juan Maggi, 123; Ernesto Malaccorto, 64 *(closed until 1980);* Raul Margueirat, 103; Jose Heriberto Martinez, 71; Celina de Martinez Paiva, 15; Arturo Mathov, 58; Santiago Menendez, 152; Luciano F. Molinas, 25; Alberto Morello, 30; Adolfo Mugica, 483 *(certain pages closed);* Francisco Muro de Nadal, 59; Felipe Noe, 18; Juan Pablo Oliver, 87 *(closed during lifetime);* Maria Rosa Oliver, 57; Manuel Ordonez, 106; Cornelio Oswald, 22; Pedro Otero, 236;

Delia Parodi, 64; Leon Patlis, 40; Hipolito J. Paz, 42; Jose Luis Pena, 74; Francisco Perez Leiros, 180 *(permission required to cite or quote);* Osvaldo Perez Pardo, 71; Jorge Walter Perkins, 3; Federico Pinedo, 84 *(permission required to cite or quote);* Pedro Pistarini, 46; Jose Luis Portos, 47; Luis Ramicone, 43; Juan Jose Real, 55; Miguel Revestido, 28; Cipriano Reyes, 80; Juan Rodriguez, 70; Luis Maria Rodriguez, 21; Jose Luis Romero, 60; Eduardo Rumbo, 244; Vicente Saadi, 70; Julian Sancerni Gimenez, 7; Hilario Sanchez, 30; Silvano Santander, 81; Dario Sarachaga, 21; Fernando Sola, 50; Pablo Ove Sorensen, 23; Rene Stordeur, 581; Diogenes Taboada, 25; Mariano Tedesco, 78; Adolfo Vicchi, 173; Juan Fernandez Villegas, 34; Salvador Zucotti, 47.

8,110 pp. *Open except as noted.* 1971–73. *Underwritten by the Tinker Foundation, NYC.*

ARKHURST, Frederik. *See* International Negotiations.

ARMSEY, James W. (1917–   ) *See* New York University.

ARMSTRONG, Barbara (1890–1976) Lawyer.
SOCIAL SECURITY
Social Insurance Commission, California, 1915–19; attempts to get social and health insurance; *Insuring the Essentials,* 1932; consultant on unemployment insurance and old age insurance, Committee on Economic Security, 1934; detailed account of preparatory work for Social Security legislation: effect of Depression, Wisconsin plan, separation of taxing and spending provisions, constitutionality, relationship with insurance industry and Treasury, Edwin Witte, J. Douglas Brown, Arthur Altmeyer, Senator Robert La Follette, and others.

317 pp. *Permission required to cite or quote.* 1965.
Discussed in J. Douglas Brown.

ARMSTRONG, James Sinclair (1915–   ) Government official.
EISENHOWER ADMINISTRATION
Illinois Republican party; Commissioner SEC, 1952–57; Dixon-Yates case, Adams-Goldfine affair; Assistant Secretary for Financial Management of the Navy, 1957; military spending, closing down of naval installations; aircraft carriers, destroyer escorts; phasing out redundant weapons systems; Polaris.
125 pp. *Permission required.* 1972.

ARMSTRONG, Louis. *Discussed in* Max Gissen; Milton Hinton.

ARMSTRONG, Thomas N. III (1932–   ) *See* New York's Art World.

ARNER, Frederick B. *See* Social Security.

ARNOLD, Eleanor Pool (Mrs. Henry H.) (–1978).
HENRY H. ARNOLD PROJECT
Family background of Henry H. Arnold; early meetings; engagement and marriage, 1913; Gen. Arnold's experiences in Army Air Corps: Washington in WWI, planning and production problems, forest patrols, air mail; Mitchell trial, reprimand and exile; Morrow Board; Command and General Staff School; effects of Depression. Impressions of Gens. Douglas MacArthur, George C. Marshall, William L. Mitchell, Wendell Westover, and others.
108 pp. *Permission required.* 1959.

ARNOLD, Elizabeth. *See* Women's History and Population Issues.

ARNOLD, Frank Atkinson (1867–1958).
RADIO PIONEERS
Early advertising experiences; first contacts with radio; broadcasting and advertising; Director of Development for NBC; pre-recorded programs; early radio advertisers; *Broadcast Advertising: the Fourth Dimension;* advertising agencies, independent radio counsel; technical advances in radio; television and its problems.
 101 pp. *Open.* 1951.

ARNOLD, Henry H. *Discussed in* John R. Alison; Lawrence D. Bell; Henry H. Arnold Project; Robert J. Smith.

HENRY H. ARNOLD PROJECT
The life of the late Gen. Henry H. Arnold (1886–1950), first Commander of the Army Air Forces, as related by his associates. Included are interviews with veteran Air Force officers throughout the country and with retired RAF officers in Great Britain who worked with Gen. Arnold during WWII. Primary emphasis is upon Arnold's role in the Air Forces, his relations with his associates, the types of problems he met, and his contributions to the development of military aviation, including a wealth of material of value to Air Force historians. The material deals with Arnold as a student at West Point, as infantry officer in the Philippines, as student pilot under Orville Wright, as close associate of Gen. William Mitchell, as Chief of the Army Air Corps, and as Commanding General of the Air Forces and member of the Combined Chiefs of Staff during WWII.
Participants and pages: Orvil A. Anderson, 113; Eleanor Pool (Mrs. Henry H.) Arnold, 108; John Leland Atwood, 26; Eugene Beebe, 80; James Henry Burns, 26; Charles P. Cabell, 59; Benjamin Castle, 77; Frederick Warren Conant, 28; Donald Wills Douglas, 137; Ira C. Eaker, 184; Grandison Gardner, 54; Robert Ellsworth Gross, 29; W. Averell Harriman, 60; Sir Arthur Harris, 85;
James Howard Kindelberger, 57; Frank P. Lahm, 33; Robert Abercrombie Lovett, 69; Leroy Lutes, 32; Thomas D. Milling, 100; A. C. Peterson, 31; Elwood Quesada, 18; Arthur Emmons Raymond, 24; Sir Henry Self, 56; Sir John Slessor, 38; Carl Spaatz, 80; Henry Wyman Strangman, 38; Hayden

Wagner, 35; Kenneth B. Wolfe, 49.
 1,726 pp. *Permission required.* 1959–60.
Underwritten by friends of General Arnold.

ARNOLD, Leslie Philip (1894–) *See* Aviation Project. *Micro IV.*

ARNOLD, Thurman Wesley (1891–1970) Lawyer.
New Deal economic theories; NRA, TNEC; Assistant Attorney General, 1938–43; antitrust cases.
 46 pp. *Permission required to cite or quote.* 1962. *Micro IV.*
See also James Lawrence Fly Project.
Discussed in Horace Albright; Gordon Dean; Thomas Emerson; Henry Wallace.

ARNOLD, William W. (1878–1957) *See* Benedum and the Oil Industry.

ARONSON, A. Henry (1904–) Government official.
SOCIAL SECURITY
Director of personnel, Social Security Board; selection of administrators; field assistants; personnel problems in public assistance and unemployment insurance; merit system; recruitment; Bureau of Research and Statistics; authority of Civil Service Commission over Social Security Administration; Bureau of Old Age and Survivors Insurance; patronage problems; federal-state relationships in personnel administration. Recollections of Arthur Altmeyer, Vincent Miles, and John Winant.
 173 pp. *Closed during lifetime.* 1965.

ARRIGO, Joseph P. (1903–) *See* Continental Group.

ARROWSMITH, William (1924–) and Roger W. Shattuck. *See* American Cultural Leaders.

ART *See* American Cultural Leaders; Will Barnet; Jacques Barzun; Thomas Hart Benton; Isabel Bishop; Elizabeth Blake; Holger Cahill; Carnegie Corporation; Warren Chappell; Allan Crite; Edwin Dickinson; Joseph Domjan; Edward S. Edwin; Georg Eisler; Elton C. Fax; J. Paul Getty; Jill Kre-mentz; Leon Kroll; Mary Lasker; Jack Levine; Paul Manship; Duane Michals; Katherine P. Murphy; Roy Neuberger; New

York's Art World; John D. Rockefeller 3rd; Paul J. Sachs; Ben Shahn; Aaron Shikler; Max Weber; Mahonri M. Young; William Zorach.
See also Museums.

ART CRITICISM *See* Jacques Barzun; Thomas Hart Benton; Lloyd Goodrich; New York's Art World; Paul J. Sachs; Carl Van Vechten.

ARTHUR, George K. (1899–   ) *See* Popular Arts.

ARVEY, Jacob M. (1895–1977) *See* Adlai E. Stevenson Project. *Micro III.*

ASCHER, Charles (1899–   ) Urban planner.
Family history; boyhood, West Side NYC; Ethical Culture Society School; Columbia College and Law School; Legislative Drafting Fund; Kuhn, Loeb; Brooklyn Heights society, 1921–25; ACLU; Sunnyside and Radburn developments; Croton-on-Hudson; zoning law; Public Administration Clearing House, 1932–36; Martha's Vineyard, 1921–71; Regional Planning Association of America; SSRC, 1935–42; UNESCO; US and European regional and city planning; New Deal housing programs: PWA and WPA; Chicago World's Fair, 1933; management associations; National Association of Housing Officials; National Resources Planning Board; Urban studies; Maxwell School, Syracuse University; Greenbelt towns; Spelman Fund; FHA; TVA; National Housing Agency, 1942–47; city government; National Municipal League; impressions of Roger Baldwin, Dr. Mary Calderone, Louis Brownlow, Henry Beetle Hough, Julian Huxley, Harold Ickes, Lewis Mumford, Eleanor and Franklin D. Roosevelt, Clarence Stein, Harlan F. Stone, Rexford Guy Tugwell, Henry L. Wright.
In process.

ASHBERY, John (1927–   ) Poet.
POETS ON THEIR POETRY
Harvard days; early publishing; NYC art and film associates; Parisian life; production of *Art and Literature,* 1963–66.
30 pp. *Permission required.* 1974.

ASHE, Nathan. *See* Hart Crane Project.

ASKEW, Ed (1902–   ) *See* Continental Group.

ASPER, Levy J. *See* Eisenhower Administration.

ASSOCIATION FOR THE AID OF CRIPPLED CHILDREN
Until its reorganization in 1948, the Association had provided a variety of services to handicapped children in metropolitan New York for fifty years. Interviews with members of the Association's board and staff focus on the transition from service agency to foundation made possible by the bequests of Milo Belding. In the last quarter century, the Association's grants have supported research in prenatal and perinatal problems, genetics, and embryology, as well as conferences on prematurity, the placenta, limb morphology, and teratology. Studies of learning disabilities, mental retardation, and accident prevention are detailed. The Association's international collaborative studies with the University of Aberdeen, the Karolinska Institute, and the University of Kyoto are described. Staff cooperation with the NIH and the background of President Kennedy's Panel on Mental Retardation are recalled.
Memoirs include personal recollections of Drs. Howard Rusk, John Lind, Dugald Baird, and Clement Reid; and of William McPeak and Laurance Rockefeller.

Participants and pages: Herbert Birch and Stephen Richardson, 97; Lewis Cuyler, 58; Charles Dollard, 30; Mrs. Richard Emmet, 45; Alice FitzGerald, 78; Mrs. Ross McFarland, 31; Leonard Mayo, 71; Milton Senn, 46; Robert Slater, 67; Chester Swinyard, 52.
575 pp. *Permission required.* 1972. *Underwritten by the Association for the Aid of Crippled Children, New York City.*

ASTIN, Allen Varley (1904–   ) Physicist.
EISENHOWER ADMINISTRATION
National Bureau of Standards, 1932–67; recollections of Secretary of Commerce Sinclair Weeks; Kelly Committee; moving of

Bureau to Gaithersburg, Maryland; change to metric system.
57 pp. *Permission required.* 1967.

ASWELL, Edward C. (1900–1958) *See* McGraw-Hill.

ATCHLEY, Dana Winslow (1892–   ) Physician.
Early education at University of Chicago; Johns Hopkins Medical School; internship at P & S; impact of WWI; academic medicine at Johns Hopkins, 1921–23; P & S, 1924–56; developments in physiological medicine in association with Robert Loeb.
174 pp. *Permission required to cite or quote.* 1956. *Micro II.* Papers.
Discussed in Flora Rhind; Jules Stahl.

ATHLETICS *See* Willis Cummings; Miguel de Capriles; Ken Dryden; Harry L. Kingman; Albert Lasker; Ben Martin; John K. Norton; Charles Oliver; Glenn Resch; James Thomas and Robert Lushbaugh; Rudolph Von Bernuth.

ATKINSON, Joseph Hampton (1900–   ) *See* Aviation Project. *Micro II.*

ATKINSON, Justin Brooks (1894–   ) *See* Journalism Lectures.

ATOMIC ENERGY *See* Kenneth Bainbridge; Edward L. Beach; Albert S. Bigelow; Charles D. Coryell; J.R. Dunning; Thomas I. Emerson; Paul F. Foster; Leslie Groves; Menelaos Hassialis and John Palfrey; James R. Killian, Jr.; William F. Knowland; William L. Laurence; Kenneth D. Nichols; Adelaide Oppenheim; Norman Ramsey; Henry L. Stimson; Lewis L. Strauss; James J. Wadsworth; Henry Wallace.

ATTLEE, Clement. *Discussed in* Henry Wallace; Sir Robert Watson-Watt; Sir Muhammad Zafrulla Khan.

ATTWOOD, William (1919–   ) *See* Adlai E. Stevenson Project. *Micro III.*

ATWOOD, John Leland (1904–   ) *See* Henry H. Arnold Project.

AUB, Joseph Charles (1890–1973) Physician.
Education, Harvard College and Medical

School; internship, MGH; metabolic research, Russell Sage laboratories; WWI service; lead poisoning; calcium metabolism; cancer research, Huntington Memorial Hospital, 1929–43; impact of WWII on research; work at MGH, 1943–57; early use of radioisotopes; 1911 trip to Wilfred Grenfell Mission, Labrador; magnesium metabolism; radium poisoning; hormones and cell growth; liver regeneration; work in traumatic shock, WWII; growth studies of deer; American Cancer Society; Physiological Congress, 1929; Unitarian Service Committee mission, Czechoslovakia, 1946; WHO mission, India, 1953. Impressions of David Edsall, Walter Cannon, George Wislocki, Eugene DuBois, Ira Nathanson, Robley Evans.
566 pp. *Permission required to cite or quote.* 1957. *Micro II.* Papers.

AUDEMARS, Edmond. *See* Aviation Project.

AUNG, U H'tin (1909–   ) Burmese educator.
Early life; education, Burma and Europe; teaching experiences, University of Rangoon; Council of National Education; Thankin Movement; WWII experiences, 1942–45.
128 pp. *Permission required.* 1965.

AURAND, Evan Peter (1917–   ) Naval officer.
EISENHOWER ADMINISTRATION
Appointment as Naval aide to President Eisenhower, 1957; role as aide; use of helicopters; Nikita Khrushchev's visit and "Spirit of Camp David"; arrangements for Presidential travels to Bermuda, Europe, India, Latin America.
138 pp. *Permission required to cite or quote.* 1967. *Micro III.*

AURAND, Henry S. (1894–   ) Army officer.
EISENHOWER ADMINISTRATION
Impressions of President and Mrs. Eisenhower.
34 pp. *Permission required to cite or quote.* 1968.

AURELIO, Richard (1929–   ) Politician.
Childhood interest in politics; Boston University; *Newsday* reporter, 1950–60; press

secretary, administrative assistant to Senator Jacob Javits, 1960–68; campaign manager for Nelson Rockefeller, 1966, and John Lindsay, 1965, 1969, 1972; deputy mayor, NYC, 1969–71; impressions of NYC press.
In process.

AUSTIN, Warren. *Discussed in* James Barco; Ernest Gross; Philip Jessup.

AUSTRIAN PROJECT
Austrian immigrants to the US discuss their careers in music, painting, and writing, and the influence of colleagues and teachers such as Oskar Kokoschka.
Participants and pages: Alexandra Adler, 41 *(permission required);* Kurt A. Adler, 23 *(permission required);* Georg Eisler, 20 *(permission required);* Felix Popper, 28; Friedrich Torberg, 34 *(permission required);* Gertrude Urzidil, 61; Frederic Waldman, 40; Eric Werner, 55 *(permission required).*
261 pp. *Open except as noted.* 1976—.
Contributed by Rose Stein, NYC.

AUTHORS *See* Raoul Abdul; James Agee; Agnes Allen; Sir Norman Angell; Dorothy Baker; Erik Barnouw; William S. Braithwaite; Melville H. Cane; Joseph Collins; Hart Crane Project; Caroline K. Duer; Leon Edel; Helen W. Fall; Ford Maddox Ford; Mildred Gilman; Frank Ernest Hill; Eric Hodgins; John Clellon Holmes; Madeleine L'Engle; Walter Lippmann; Ellen C. Masters; Milton Meltzer; Richard B. Morris; Gunnar Myrdal; Allan Nevins; Poets on their Poetry; Theodore Rosengarten; Arthur M. Schlesinger; Upton Sinclair; Sharon Spencer; Frank Sullivan; Gertrude Urzidil; Carl Van Vechten; Robert Penn Warren; John Hall Wheelock; Margaret B. Young.
See also Books and Book Publishing; Journalism.

AVENOL, Joseph. *Discussed in* Thanassis Aghnides; Pablo de Azcarate; Branko Lukac.

AVERY, Oswald T. *Discussed in* Rene J. Dubos.

AVIATION *See* Air Force Academy; Henry H. Arnold Project; Aviation Project; John

J. Ballentine; William A.M. Burden; Emily Chapin; F. Trubee Davison; Clarence E. de la Chapelle; Joseph J. Clark; Walter S. Diehl; James H. Doolittle; Donald Duncan; Edward C. Dyer; Walter G. Farrell; Flying Tigers; Paul Frillman; Emory S. Land; Grover Loening; Vivian Nemhauser; William A. Read; Margaret Slaymaker; Felix B. Stump; George A. Vaughan; Eugene E. Wilson; Oscar Winchell.
See also Marine Corps; U.S. Air Force; U.S. Navy.

AVIATION PROJECT
A broad survey of the development of aviation, beginning with accounts by associates of the Wright brothers and other pioneers in the US and abroad. Those interviewed include designers, engineers, pilots and executives, stunt flyers, and barnstormers; their recitations are informal and seasoned with anecdote. Veterans of WWI describe the development of aerial warfare in that conflict. Scores of recollections trace the rapid progress of aviation between the two World Wars: commercial aviation, air mail development, record flights, technological improvements, air races and polar flights, gliders, and lighter-than-air craft. Gen. William Mitchell's campaign for strengthening military aviation and Charles Lindbergh's solo flight to Paris provide focal points for many accounts of this period.
Eyewitness stories of episodes in WWII deal with exploits of the RAF, the Luftwaffe, and the US air forces, and range from the Battle of Britain to Hiroshima. Research and production problems and achievements are detailed from the outset to the jet era and the beginnings of rockets and missiles.
The material includes descriptions of the breaking of the sound barrier, stories of test pilots for supersonic planes, and accounts of aerial warfare in Korea.

Participants and pages: John Alison, 132; Orvil A. Anderson, 51; Leslie P. Arnold, 25; Joseph H. Atkinson, 71; Edmond Audemars, 8; Leon Bathiat and Raymond Saladin, 8; Hillery Beachey, 25; Lawrence D. Bell, 288; Otis Benson, 38; Harold M. Bixby, 50; Adrienne Bolland, 16; Albert Boyd, 53; Lord Brabazon of Tara, 39; Gregory J. Brandewiede, 66; Carl A. Brandt, 34; William B. Bridgeman, 57;

James E. Briggs, 39; Sir Harry Brittain, 36; Georgia T. Brown, 27; Ross Browne, 115; Harry A. Bruno, 118 *(closed until May 1, 1985);*

Cyril C. Caldwell, 39; Felix Camerman, 7; Douglas Campbell, 30; Clarence Chamberlain, 11; Reed Chambers, 84; Ellen Church, 22; Jerrie Cobb, 8; Alan Cobham, 39; Jacqueline Cochran, 105; Frank T. Coffyn, 43; Franklin Rudolf Collbohm, 21; Sir Harold Roxbee Cox, 28; Laurence C. Craigie, 53; Albert Scott Crossfield, 30; Didier Daurat, 18; Luis de Florez, 39; James Dodson, 34; Charles Dollfus, 31; James H. Doolittle, 28; Lord Douglas of Kirtleside, 28; Hugh L. Dryden, 40; Delos C. Emmons, 21; Francis Evans, 37; Maurice Farman, 17; Benjamin D. Foulois, 81; Henry J. Friendly, 24;

Esther C. Goddard (Mrs. Robert H.), 85 *(closed until 5 years after death);* Dennis Handover, 42; Beckwith Havens, 75; A. Heurtaux, 13; H. Mansfield Horner, 28; Ben Odell Howard, 67; Jerome Clarke Hunsaker, 112; Leslie Irvin, 37; James Jabara, 21; Jack Jefford, 37; Robert S. Johnson, 35; Charles Sherman Jones, 45; Alexander Kartveli, 43; Aron Krantz, 60; Emory Scott Land, 42; William Powell Lear, 49; Kenneth Littauer, 30; William R. Lovelace, II, 30;

John A. Macready, 69; Willy Messerschmitt, 14; Richard M. Mock, 54; Mathilde Moisant, 52; Muriel E. Morrissey, 20; James P. Murray, 36; Ruth Rowland Nichols, 45; Umberto Nobile, 64; Blanche Noyes, 68; Ruth Law Oliver, 33; Alan Campbell Orde, 50; Ray Petersen, 80; Leroy Ponton de Arce, 23; Ramsay Potts, 39; Thomas S. Power, 35; Leroy Prinz, 60; Max Pruss, 20; Elwood Quesada, 76; Robert Reeve, 63; Hanna Reitsch, 44; Holden C. Richardson, 29; Edward Vernon Rickenbacker, 19; James Sargent Russell, 51; Ryan roundtable discussion, 57;

Christian Franklin Schilt, 23; H. Shaw, 57; Cyrus Rowlett Smith, 48; Dean Smith, 77; Merle Smith, 33; Sir Thomas Octave Murdoch Sopwith, 31; John Paul Stapp, 28; Katherine Stinson, 47; Paul Tibbets, Jr., 38; Roscoe Turner, 38; George A. Vaughan, 39; Alfred Verville, 85; Gabriel Voisin, 8; Theodore Von Karman, 15; Charles Wald, 32; Otto P. Weyland, 71; Robert M. White, 27; Thomas D. White, 47; Noel Wien, 68; A.S. Wilcockson, 24; Harold B. Willis, 75; Gill Robb Wilson, 89; Charles Yeager, 34.

5,200 pp. *Permission required to cite or quote except as noted.* 1961. *Some memoirs are available in microform; consult individual entries. Underwritten by American Heritage Publishing Company, Inc.*

AYLESWORTH, Merlin H. *Discussed in* Radio Pioneers.

AYMAN, Sven. *See* Dag Hammarskjold Project.

AZCARATE Y FLOREZ, Pablo de (1890–1971) Diplomat.
LEAGUE OF NATIONS PROJECT.
Discussion of recruiting international civil servants, illustrated by his own experience from 1922 in League of Nations; problems of conflict between national and international loyalties; morale; building of Palace of Nations in Geneva; role of Secretary General as illustrated by Sir Eric Drummond and Joseph Avenol. This memoir is in French.
80 pp. *Permission required to cite or quote.* 1966.

AZCARATE Y FLOREZ, Pablo de, Edouard de Haller and W. Van Asch Van Wijck.
LEAGUE OF NATIONS PROJECT
The three leaders of the Section on Minorities of the League of Nations during the 1920's and 30's recall how each came to the League and describe the Section: what it covered, how it operated, procedure, personnel, area of responsibility; committee of 3; relationship with other sections and with World Court; analysis of examples: Rumania, Czechoslovakia, Upper Silesia. This memoir is in French.
156 pp. *Permission required to cite or quote.* 1965.

B

BABBEL, Frederick W. *See* Eisenhower Administration.

BABBITT, Samuel. *See* Kirkland College.

BABCOCK, James. *Discussed in* Connie M. Guion.

BABCOCK, Margaret. *See* Hart Crane Project.

BACALL, Lauren (1924–   ) *See* Adlai E. Stevenson Project.

BACON, Edmund Norwood (1910–   ) *See* Independence Park.

BADEAU, John (1903–   ) Educator, diplomat.
Family background; education, Union College, 1923, New Brunswick Seminary Dutch Reformed Church, 1928; missionary work, life in Iraq, 1928–35: Arabic language training, political turmoil, ethnic and linguistic groups; professor of religion, philosophy, American University of Cairo, 1936–42, president, 1945–53; OWI, 1943–45; cultural and political developments in Egypt, Iraq, Iran, 1930s–'60s; effects of WWII, British and later US presence in Middle East; president, Near East Foundation, NYC, 1953–61, providing technical assistance to Greece, Syria, Iran, Afghanistan, others; Egypt after abdication of King Faruq, 1952: labor unrest, land redistribution, centrality of irrigation, roles of Naguib and Nasser; US Ambassador to Egypt, 1961–64: break-up of United Arab Republic, AID and counterpart funds, Yemen Revolution, crisis in Egyptian-Saudi relations; Middle East Institute, Columbia University, 1964–71. Impressions of King Faruq, Shah of Iran, Nasser, Anwar al-Sadat, many others.
In process. Underwritten by friends of Ambassador Badeau.

BADILLO, Herman (1929–   ) Politician.
Childhood in Puerto Rico and NYC; education, City College, Brooklyn Law School; NYC Commissioner, Department of Housing and Relocation, 1961; Bronx borough president; US Congressman, 1971–77; observations of NYC politics in 1960's, '70's.
In process.

BADINELLI, John L. (1910–   ) *See* Continental Group.

BAEHR, George (1887–1978) Physician.
Columbia Medical School, early 1900's; internship; European studies; Mt. Sinai Hospital: Division of General Pathology, typhoid fever research, Clinical Pathological Conferences 1919–50, professionalizing lab services, consultation service for people of moderate means, home care for housing development residents, Director of Clinical Research; WWII: Chief Medical Officer OCD, Red Cross; Mayor La Guardia; HIP; evaluation of 1965 Medicare, Medicaid amendments; state standards for nursing homes; medical provisions of Workmen's Compensation Act; NY Public Health Council; national health insurance proposals; Milbank Memorial Fund.
237 pp. *Permission required to cite or quote. 1976. Underwritten by Milbank Memorial Fund, NYC.*
See also Mt. Sinai Hospital. *Micro II.*

BAER, Abel (1893–1976) *See* Popular Arts.

BAER, Robert W. (1916–　) *See* Continental Group.

BAILEY, John. *Discussed in* Chester Bowles; Dorothy Bowles.

BAILYN, Bernard (1922–　) *See* American Historians.

BAINBRIDGE, Kenneth Tompkins (1904–　) Physicist.
Education and early research at MIT, Princeton, and the Cavendish Laboratory at Cambridge, England; teaching and research at Harvard, 1934; creation of NDRC Radiation Laboratory at MIT, 1940; technical mission to England on radar development, 1941; Los Alamos, 1943; security problems, testing first atom bomb, 1945; use of the bomb; May-Johnson and MacMahon bills; Federation of Atomic Scientists; Joseph McCarthy investigations. Impressions of Karl Compton, Henry D. Smyth, Leo Szilard, Robert Oppenheimer.
　150 pp. *Permission required.* 1960. Papers.

BAIRD, Dugald. *Discussed in* Association for the Aid of Crippled Children.

BAIRD, Peggy. *See* Hart Crane Project.

BAKER, Carl. Research scientist.
Health Sciences
Amino acids research; Director of Laboratories and Clinics, NIH; voluntary vs. federal research support; Cancer Act; development of Division of Research Grants; university program support; grants vs. contracts; debate over chemotherapy and viral research; drug patent problems; effects of Fountain Committee hearings; congressional pressures on cancer research programming; evolution of the Cancer Institute; institutional organization and research activities patterns. National Cancer Chemotherapy Program.
　191 pp. *Permission required to cite or quote.* 1964.

BAKER, Dorothy (1907–1968) Author.
Early life; beginnings as writer; reactions to writing and criticism; *Young Man With a Horn, Trio, Cassandra at the Wedding;* Robert Frost, Robert Penn Warren, Carson

McCullers, F.O. Matthiessen, May Sarton.
146 pp. *Open.* 1962.

BAKER, James Chamberlain (1879–　) *See* China Missionaries.

BAKER, Moses Nelson (1864–1955) *See* McGraw-Hill.

BAKER, Newton D. *Discussed in* Goldthwaite Dorr; Eugene Meyer; James W. Wadsworth.

BAKER, Walter Ransom Gail (1892–1960) *See* Radio Pioneers.

BAKHMETEFF, Boris Alexander (1880–1951) Diplomat.
Early life in Russia; engineering studies in Switzerland and US, 1903–05; political life in Russia, 1903–14; European politics, 1914; Russia in WWI; War Supply Mission to US, 1915–16; Russian Revolution; Kerensky government; Ambassador to US, 1917–22; impressions of Woodrow Wilson administration, J.P. Morgan, Edward Stettinius, Sr., Dwight Morrow, John Spargo, Frederic Coudert, Nicholas Murray Butler; US citizenship and career.
　568 pp. *Permission required.* 1950.
Discussed in Frederic R. Coudert.

BALANCHINE, George. *Discussed in* Richard Rodgers.

BALCON, Sir Michael (1896–1977) *See* Robert J. Flaherty Project.

BALDWIN, Calvin Benham (1902–1975) Executive.
Henry A. Wallace and the Progressive Party.
　37 pp. *Open.* 1951.
Discussed in Will Alexander.

BALDWIN, Hanson W. (1903–　) *See* Journalism Lectures.

BALDWIN, Joseph Clark (1897–1957) Congressman.
NY politics; national politics during WWII; Free French during WWII; Gen. Charles de Gaulle; Argentina and Palestine, 1947–48.
　73 pp. *Permission required to cite or*

quote. 1950. *Micro I.* Papers: 271 items (microfilm).

BALDWIN, Mildred. *See* James B. Duke Project.

BALDWIN, Raymond Earl (1893–   )
Public official.
Boyhood and education; naval service, WWI; early career in law and politics; Governor of Connecticut, 1939–41, 1943–46; Willkie campaign, 1940; US Senator, 1946–49; Armed Services, Post Office, Civil Service Committees, unification of armed services, investigation of Malmedy massacre, Joseph McCarthy; 1948 senatorial campaign, resignation, 1949; experiences as Connecticut Supreme Court Judge (1949–64), State referee, co-chairman of 1965 Constitutional Convention; impressions of Wilbur Cross, J. Henry Roraback, Franklin D. Roosevelt, Thomas E. Dewey, Herbert Hoover, Senators Robert A. Taft, Arthur Vandenburg, Leverett Saltonstall.
2,272 pp. *Permission required to cite or quote.* 1969–72. *Acquired from the University of Connecticut, Storrs.*

BALDWIN, Roger Nash (1884–   ) Political reformer.
Teacher of sociology, Washington University, 1906–09; pioneering work in probation, social and political reform movements, St. Louis, 1906–17; pacifist organizations in NYC, conscientious objectors; Free Speech League, Theodore Schroeder; ACLU: formation and development, 1920–50, cooperation with other organizations, defense policies, publicity tactics, relations with New Deal; celebrated cases: Mooney-Billings, Scottsboro, Sacco-Vanzetti; contact with anarchists; IWW, 1910–20; William D. Haywood; Negro rights; Indian independence movement, India League; travel abroad and work for international agencies, 1924–54; visits to Russia, postwar Japan, Korea, and Germany.
666 pp. *Permission required to cite or quote.* 1954. *Micro I.*

International League for the Rights of Man; UN, world tour, 1959; Margaret Sanger, Krishna Menon, Madame Pandit,

Jawaharlal Nehru, Mrs. Franklin D. Roosevelt.
183 pp. *Permission required to cite or quote.* 1963. *Micro I.* Papers.

Pedro Albizu Campos; visits in prison hospitals; defense by ACLU.
30 pp. *Permission required to cite or quote.* 1965. Papers.

OCCUPATION OF JAPAN
In Japan and Korea for ACLU during the occupation; impressions of MacArthur; differences between headquarters and the prefectures; the forming of a Japanese civil liberties organization; new Japanese constitution; the general strike; interview with the Emperor; women in public life; impressions from visit in 1960.
116 pp. *Permission required to cite or quote.* 1961. *Micro II.*

Reminiscences of ACLU; observations on 1960's: civil rights, anti-war and women's movements; obscenity question; privacy rights; labor relations; democratic government; international civil rights; impressions of Supreme Court judges, Ralph Nader, Kennedy family.
106 pp. *Permission required to cite or quote.* 1975. *Contributed by Alan F. Westin, NYC.*

Impressions of Eduardo Lindeman and his social philosophy.
74 pp. *Permission required to cite or quote.* 1975. *Contributed by Betty Lindeman Leonard, Portland, Ore.*

Discussed in Charles Ascher; Algernon D. Black; Philip Taft.

BALFOUR, Arthur. *Discussed in* Sir Robert Watson-Watt.

BALINT, Michael (1896–1970)
PSYCHOANALYTIC MOVEMENT
Early life; development of interest in psychoanalysis; predictions of future of psychoanalysis.
78 pp. *Permission required to cite or quote.* 1965.

BALL, George Wildman (1909–   ) *See* Adlai E. Stevenson Project, Ethnic Groups

and American Foreign Policy *and* International Negotiations.
Discussed in John Sharon; Marietta Tree.

BALL, Robert M. (1914–   ) *See* Social Security.

BALLANTINE, Arthur. *Discussed in* James P. Warburg; Walter Wyatt.

BALLANTINE, Joseph (1888–1973) Consular officer.
OCCUPATION OF JAPAN
Childhood in India; US consular service beginning at Tokyo, 1909; Dairen and Yokohama earthquakes; Japan Desk, State Department; London Naval Conference; Consul General, Canton and Mukden; Japanese government in Manchuria; adviser to Cordell Hull during Japanese conversations, 1941; Pearl Harbor investigations; Head, Far Eastern Division; Director, Office of Far Eastern Affairs; post-war program for Far East; occupation policies; Owen Lattimore, Joseph Grew, Eugene Dooman, Douglas MacArthur.
271 pp. *Permission required to cite or quote.* 1961. *Micro I.* Papers.

BALLENTINE, John Jennings (1896–1970) Naval officer.
Childhood and education; interest in naval air during WWI; flight training, Pensacola, Kelly Field; testing and development work, Dahlgren Naval Proving Grounds; Norden bombsight; Japanese naval aviation; air support, Operation Torch; command of *Bunker Hill;* Pacific operations: Rabaul, Tarawa, Kwajalein, Eniwetok; fleet liaison with Gen. MacArthur for Japanese surrender; Military Staff Committee, UN, 1947; Mediterranean, 1947–48; Commander, 6th Fleet. Impressions of Adms. Ernest King, H.K. Hewitt, Chester Nimitz, Richmond Turner and Gens. George Patton and Douglas MacArthur.
758 pp. *Permission required to cite or quote.* 1964. *Micro I.*

BAMPTON, Rose (1909–   ) Opera singer.
Childhood, early music studies in Buffalo; Curtis Institute; Metropolitan Opera, 1932–50; building a repertoire; preparation for roles and performances; teaching.

69 pp. *Permission required to cite or quote.* 1976.

BANE, Frank (1893–   ) Government official.
SOCIAL SECURITY
Executive director, American Public Welfare Association, 1931–35; consultant to FERA, 1932; Advisory Committee on Public Employment and Public Assistance; executive director, Social Security Board, 1935–38; Advisory Council to the Senate Finance Committee. Impressions of Harry Hopkins, Frances Perkins, John Winant, Arthur Altmeyer.
121 pp. *Permission required to cite or quote.* 1965. *Micro III.*

Experiences in public welfare administration; Brookings Institution, 1931–35; Social Security Board, Council of National Defense; Office of Civilian Defense, 1941; director of field operations, OPA, 1941–42; National Housing Authority, 1942; executive director, Council of State Governments.
281 pp. *Permission required to cite or quote.* 1965. *Acquired from University of California, Berkeley.*

Discussed in Ewan Clague; Lavinia Engle; Maurine Mulliner.

BANKHEAD, Tallulah. *Discussed in* S. Michael Bessie.

BANKS, Charles Louis (1914–   ) *See* Marine Corps.

BANKS AND BANKING *See* Finance/ Banks and Banking.

BANNISTER, Harry Ray (1894–1967) *See* Radio Pioneers.

BARA, Walter (1919–1966) *See* McGraw-Hill.

BARAGWANATH, John Gordon (1888–1965) *See* Mining Engineers.

BARBIERI, Matthew V. (1921–   ) *See* Continental Group.

BARCELO, Alberto. *Discussed in* Esteban Habiague.

BARCO, James William (1916–   ) Lawyer, ambassador.
EISENHOWER ADMINISTRATION
Family background, education in Michigan; Harvard Law School; Home Owners Loan Corporation, 1941–42; US Navy, WWII; wartime London, preparations for D-Day; US State Department posts, 1946 on; UN Good Offices, Commission for Indonesia, 1948; UN Conciliation Commission for Palestine, 1948–49; US mission to UN, 1949–61; various international problems and crises: Indonesian question, 1947–51; Middle East, Arab nationalism; Suez and Hungary, 1956; India; Congo; Cuba; US foreign relations; UN diplomacy; UN policies. Impressions of many international figures, including John Foster Dulles, Warren Austin, Philip Jessup, Jawaharlal Nehru, Achmed Sukarno, Nikita Khrushchev, Patrice Lumumba, Fidel Castro, Dag Hammarskjold.
1,061 pp. *Closed until January 1, 1984.* 1963.

BARDEEN, John (1908–   ) *See* Nobel Laureates.

BARE, Robert Osborne (1901–   ) *See* Marine Corps.

BARKAN, Alexander Elias (1909–   ) *See* Social Security. *Micro III.*

BARKER, George H. (1910–   ) *See* Continental Group.

BARKER, James Madison (1886–1974) Businessman.
Family background and childhood; education at MIT, first experiences in engineering; teaching at MIT, 1914–18; Manager, First National Bank, Buenos Aires, 1920–28; administrative experiences with Sears, Roebuck and Co., 1928–40, and with various business and educational institutions; Chairman of Board, Allstate Insurance, 1943–52; Overseas Consultants mission to Iran, 1948–49; Chief of World Bank mission to Turkey, 1949–50; philosophy of life and views on travel, modern education, government, foreign affairs; impressions of

George F. Swain, Daniel G. Wing, Julius Rosenwald, Charles G. Dawes, Gen. Robert E. Wood.
380 pp. *Permission required to cite or quote. 1952. Micro IV.*

BARKER, Ray W. (–1974) *See* Eisenhower Administration.

BARKIN, Solomon (1907–   ) Economist.
Economic and political studies at CCNY, 1920's; economist in various New Deal agencies; International Ladies' Garment Workers' Union; origins of the Textile Workers' Union of America and its role in the CIO.
141 pp. *Permission required to cite or quote. 1960. Micro IV.*

BARLOW, Howard (1892–1972) Orchestra conductor.
RADIO PIONEERS
Early life, education; NYC choral groups; early orchestral experiences; Neighborhood Playhouse; CBS: William S. Paley, public service programs, advertising; "Voice of Firestone"; planning and production problems in television. Recollections of Arthur Judson, Jerome Louckheim, Julius Sieback.
213 pp. *Open.* 1951.

BARNARD, Rollin D. (1922–   ) Post Office Official.
EISENHOWER ADMINISTRATION
Director of Real Estate, US Post Office Department, 1953–55; Deputy Assistant Postmaster General, 1955; Assistant Postmaster General, 1959–61.
60 pp. *Permission required to cite or quote. 1967. Micro IV.*

BARNES, Joseph Fels (1907–1970) Newspaperman.
Youth and family background; education, Harvard, 1927, London School of Slavonic Studies; IPR staff, 1932–34, in Russia and China; 1934–48, NY *Herald Tribune* foreign correspondent, editor in Moscow, Berlin and NY; deputy director, OWI overseas branch, 1941–44, Voice of America radio show; editor NY *Star,* 1948–49; impressions of Russia in the 1920's and '30's; effect of mass media on American life.
300 pp. *Permission required to cite or quote.* 1953.

BARNES, Patrick Henry (–1969) *See* Radio Pioneers.

BARNES, William. *Discussed in* John L. O'Brian; William Prendergast; Frederick Tanner.

BARNET, Will (1911–) Artist.
Family background, childhood interest in art; Boston Museum Art School; relationship of fine and commercial art; official printer, instructor, Art Students League; Depression; Artist-in-Residence, Virginia; opinions on: gallery vs. museum shows, critics, dealers, graphic arts, tradition, art education, composition materials, spiritual qualities, trends; teaching experiences, Famous Artists Schools; portrait painting.
523 pp. *Permission required to cite or quote.* 1976. *Micro IV.*

BARNETT, Joseph M. (–1978) *See* Radio Pioneers. *Micro II.*

BARNETT, Ross. *See* Journalism Lectures.

BARNOUW, Erik (1908–) Writer, educator.
Childhood, The Hague and NYC; Princeton, 1929; career in radio, 1930's and 40's: advertising, directing, writing for networks, government, and independent producers; establishment of Columbia University's Department of Radio and Television, 1946; editor, Center for Mass Communication, Columbia University Press, 1948; film and television production; writing a history of film industry, India, 1963; blacklisting in the 1950's; censorship; writers unions: Author's League, Radio Writers Guild, Authors Guild, Writers Guild of America.
280 pp. *Permission required to cite or quote.* 1975.

Preparation of history of US broadcasting and of volume on documentary films; Bancroft Prize; President, International Film Seminar; Fellow, Woodrow Wilson Center; television advisor to Library of Congress.
61 pp. *Permission required to cite or quote.* 1977.

BARR, David Preswick (1889–1977) Physician.
Early education at Cornell Medical School;

internship at Bellevue; physiological medicine.
130 pp. *Permission required to cite or quote.* 1957. *Micro IV.*

BARRETT, Edward W. (1910–) *See* International Negotiations.

BARRY, Gregory J. (1897–) *See* Continental Group.

BARSHOP, Irving. *See* Socialist Movement.

BARTHELMESS, Richard (1897–1963) *See* Popular Arts.

BARTLETT, David H. *See* Weyerhaeuser Timber Company.

BARTOK, Bela. *Discussed in* Hungarian Project.

BARTON, Bruce. *Discussed in* Roy S. Durstine.

BARUCH, Bernard Mannes (1870–1965) *See* James B. Duke Project *and* Robert P. Patterson Project. *Discussed in* Emory S. Land; Eugene Meyer; James P. Warburg.

BARZUN, Jacques (1907–) Author, educator.
Childhood in Passy, 1910–20; *salons* and *soirees;* observations on French artists and artistic movements of the decade; poetry and painting; effect of WWI on artists; Guillaume Apollinaire, Jean Cocteau.
In process.
See also Columbia Crisis of 1968.

BATE, Franklin L. (1921–) Lawyer, politician.
Democratic and Republican parties in New Jersey, 1954–75; Clean Government Group, 1960; Constitutional Convention, 1966.
19 pp. *Permission required to cite or quote.* 1975.

BATEMAN, Alan Mara (1889–1971) *See* Mining Engineers.

BATESON, William. *Discussed in* Leslie C. Dunn.

BATHIAT, Leon and Raymond Saladin. *See* Aviation Project.

BATTELL, William F. (1906–   ) *See* Marine Corps.

BATTLE, Lucius D. (1918–   ) *See* International Negotiations.

BATTLE, Samuel J. (1883–1966) Police officer.
Childhood and education; first Negro policeman in Manhattan; lieutenant and first Negro Parole Commissioner; race riots in Harlem; impressions of Eleanor Roosevelt, Mayors James Walker, Fiorello La Guardia, and William O'Dwyer; other NYC political figures.
60 pp. *Permission required to cite or quote.* 1960. *Micro I.*
Contributed by John K. Kelly of Newark, Delaware.

BAYNE-JONES, Stanhope (1888–1971) *See* Robert A. Taft Project.

BEACH, Edward Latimer (1918–   ) Naval officer.
EISENHOWER ADMINISTRATION
Early Navy days; WWII submarine service; Atomic Defense Section, Naval Operations; atomic submarine development; Adm. Hyman Rickover; Peace Ship; Naval Aide to Gens. Omar Bradley and Dwight D. Eisenhower; White House social aides; arrangement of presidential trips; ship launchings; NSC; the *Williamsburg;* Camp David; Secret Service; press conferences; Atoms for Peace; President Eisenhower at ease: family relaxation, hobbies; Eisenhower's relations with staff. Recollections of Sherman Adams, Robert Schulz, Lewis Strauss.
470 pp. *Permission required.* 1967.

BEACHEY, Hillery. *See* Aviation Project. *Micro IV.*

BEACHEY, Lincoln. *Discussed in* Hillery Beachey; Lawrence Bell.

BEADLE, George Wells (1903–   ) *See* Nobel Laureates.
Discussed in Warren Weaver.

BEALE, Elizabeth. *See* Adlai E. Stevenson Project.

BEAME, Abraham. *Discussed in* Robert F. Wagner.

BEAN, Lillian (–1974) *See* Allan Nevins Project.

BEAN, Louis H. (1896–   ) Economist.
Early life as immigrant; statistics, Department of Agriculture; price and economic analysis, BAE; economic adviser, AAA Agricultural-Industrial Relations Section; fiscal analyst, Bureau of the Budget; economic adviser, Office of the Secretary of Agriculture; change of administration, 1953; long-range weather forecasting.
303 pp. *Permission required to cite or quote.* 1953. *Micro I.* Papers.

BEANS, Fred D. (1906–   ) *See* Marine Corps.

BEARD, Charles A. *Discussed in* Guy Ford; Alfred A. Knopf.

BEARD, Robert L. (1896–1965) *See* McGraw-Hill.

BEARD, William Kelly, Jr. (1898–   ) *See* McGraw-Hill.

BEAUX, Cecilia. *Discussed in* Elizabeth Blake.

BECK, David D. (1894–   ) Labor executive.
Childhood occupations in Seattle, early 1900's; efforts building Teamsters International Union, 1919–57, organizer, executive vice president, 1947–52, general president, 1952–57; chairman, Teamsters' Western Conference; organizing tactics, administrative structures, philosophy of trade unionism; relationship of labor and national economy; relationship of Teamsters and other unions. Impressions of Jimmy Hoffa, John L. Lewis, Dan Tobin.
187 pp. *Permission required.* 1978.

BECKER, Carl. *Discussed in* Allan Nevins.

BECKER, Harry J. (1909–   ) *See* Social Security.

BECKER, J. Bill. *See* Eisenhower Administration. *Micro III.*

BEDONI, Sidney. *See* Marine Corps.

BEEBE, Eugene. *See* Henry H. Arnold Project.

BEEBY, Clarence Edward (1902–   )
CARNEGIE CORPORATION
Carnegie Commonwealth Program in New Zealand; New Zealand Council for Educational Research, 1934–63; effect on New Zealand educational policy; travel grants, museum development, public libraries, rural education, National Library Association, publications, adult education.
89 pp. *Permission required.* 1968.

BEECHER, Henry. *Discussed in* Edward D. Churchill.

BEHR, Karl Howell (1885–   ) *See* Theodore Roosevelt Association. *Micro IV.*

BEHRENS, Earl C. (1892–   ) Newspaperman.
EISENHOWER ADMINISTRATION
Political editor, San Francisco *Chronicle;* William F. Knowland Senate campaign; 1948 Presidential campaign. Recollections of Earl Warren, Richard M. Nixon.
44 pp. *Permission required to cite or quote.* 1967. *Micro IV.*

BEINECKE, Walter. *See* Kirkland College.

BEIRNE, Joseph Anthony (1911–1974) Labor leader.
Early experiences in Western Electric maintenance shop; communications workers in the Depression; origins of Communications Workers of America, role in CIO; unification of AFL and CIO.
66 pp. *Permission required to cite or quote.* 1957.

BELKNAP, Chauncey (1891–   ) Lawyer.
NEW YORK BAR
Harvard Law School; law clerk for Oliver Wendell Holmes, 1915–16; WWI, relationship with George C. Marshall; counsel for Rockefeller Foundation; selection of judges; lawyers' respect for law, Watergate;

impressions of Louis D. Brandeis, Charles Evans Hughes, John D. Rockefeller, Jr.
58 pp. *Permission required to cite or quote.* 1975. Papers.
See also Robert P. Patterson Project.

BELL, Daniel (1919–   ) *See* Richard Hofstadter Project *and* Socialist Movement.

BELL, Daniel Wafena (1891–1971) Banker.
Department of the Treasury, 1911–46: foreign loans, 1919–20; Commissioner of Accounts and Deposits, 1931–35; acting director of the Bureau of the Budget, 1934–39; Under Secretary of the Treasury, 1940–46; President of the American Security & Trust Company; observations of Congress, the Depression, Federal Reserve System, NRA, New Deal, RFC, public works, WWI and WWII.
526 pp. *Closed until October 3, 1996.* 1954.

BELL, Jack L. (1904–1975) Newspaperman.
ROBERT A. TAFT PROJECT
Association with Senator Taft as AP representative.
22 pp. *Permission required.* 1969.
See also Eisenhower Administration. *Micro IV.*

BELL, Lawrence Dale (1894–1956) Corporation executive.
AVIATION PROJECT
Speeches from management dinners, Bell Aerospace Co.; broadcast from world-record helicopter flight, Texas to Niagara Falls, 1952; Larry Bell Library dedication, Mentone, Indiana, 1955; first contact with airplane; exhibition flying; developing various types of planes; barnstorming; Bell Aircraft from 1935: developing the company, new techniques, new planes, work for military; world records; developing the helicopter; first supersonic flight. Impressions of Glenn Martin, Lincoln Beachey, Gens. Henry H. Arnold and William S. Knudsen and others.
288 pp. *Permission required to cite or quote.* 1955.

BELLAMY, Ralph (1904–   ) *See* Popular Arts.

BELMONT, August. *Discussed in* John T. Hettrick; Morris L. Strauss.

BELMONT, Eva. *Discussed in* Alice Paul.

BELSER, Jess L. (1924–) *See* Continental Group.

BENALLY, John. *See* Marine Corps.

BENCHLEY, Robert. *Discussed in* Mildred Gilman.

BENDER, Morris P. *See* Mt. Sinai Hospital.

BENDER, Thomas Harry (1944–) Urban historian.
San Francisco childhood; education in California; teaching at University of Wisconsin, Green Bay; specialization in urban cultural history; teaching at NYU.
36 pp. *Open.* 1976.

BENEDICT, Stephen (1927–) Consultant.
EISENHOWER ADMINISTRATION
1952 pre-convention campaign for Eisenhower; campaign train; speech writing; transition between administrations, 1952; White House staff and activities. Recollections of Gabriel Hauge, C. D. Jackson, Richard M. Nixon, George Marshall, Joseph McCarthy, Harry Dexter White.
137 pp. *Permission required.* 1968.

EISENHOWER ADMINISTRATION
1952 pre-convention research, Citizens for Eisenhower; White House staff assistant positions, 1953–55, USIA 1955–59.
33 pp. *Permission required.* 1969.

BENEDUM, Darwin (1902–) *See* Benedum and the Oil Industry.

BENEDUM, James Claxton (1909–) *See* Benedum and the Oil Industry.

BENEDUM, Michael Late (1869–1959) Oil executive.
BENEDUM AND THE OIL INDUSTRY
Firsthand account of early days of oil development: wildcatting, buying leases and royalty rights, experiences drilling and opening fields in Pennsylvania, West Virginia, Illinois; later larger operations in Texas and Louisiana; expansion, financial arrangements; building gas pipelines and marketing natural gas; transportation and storage problems; geology and geophysics; Mexican undertakings with E. L. Doheny; impressions of John Archbold, Joseph Trees.
144 pp. *Open.* 1951.

BENEDUM, Paul (1902–1977) Oil executive.
BENEDUM AND THE OIL INDUSTRY
Ohio State University; early interest in petroleum industry; experiences as geologist in Texas and Louisiana oilfields for M. L. Benedum during 1920's and '30's: oilbearing formations, leasing, financing, drilling, pipelines; Air Corps during WWII, development of aviation gasoline facilities worldwide; history and description of Benedum holdings; role and influence of M. L. Benedum.
87 pp. *Open.* 1951.

BENEDUM, Sophie and Pearl. *See* Benedum and the Oil Industry.

BENEDUM AND THE OIL INDUSTRY
A record of the oil industry from 1890 to 1950 as shown in the development of the Benedum oil interests and the experiences of Michael Late Benedum (1869–1959) and his associates, notably Joseph Clifton Trees (1869–1943). The material consists of interviews with people having special knowledge of leasing, financing, geology, oil and gas production, legal and tax problems. The memoirs contain several accounts of Benedum and Trees as wildcatters, going into virgin territory and finding new sources of oil and gas in the US (Illinois, 1905, Caddo, Louisiana, 1908, Central Texas, 1918, Big Lake and Yates fields in West Texas, 1923–26); problems of oil exploration outside the US (Mexico, 1911–16, Colombia, 1915, Rumania, 1918–19, the Philippines, 1920, and China, 1936); development of companies and corporate holdings including Transcontinental Oil Co. (1919), Plymouth Oil Co. (1923), Hiawatha Oil and Gas Co. (1926), and Bentex Oil Corp. (1936); storage, transportation, marketing, and refining; conservation and proration practices leading to Interstate Oil Compact Commission, 1933; US income tax claim against M. L. Benedum and Foster B. Parriott for $79,000,000,

1925, Supreme Court decision in their favor, 1937; extensive biographical material on M. L. Benedum, including early life and political activities.

Incidental material of interest includes: impressions of Woodrow Wilson at Princeton (McClintock memoir), E. L. Doheny, Senator Joseph Guffey, John Archbold (M. L. Benedum memoir), John W. Davis (Johnson memoir); Texas General Land Office (Giles memoir) and Slick Research Foundation (Slick memoir).

Participants and pages: John Charles Adams, 32; William W. Arnold, 15; Darwin Benedum, 6; James Claxton Benedum, 16; Michael Late Benedum, 144; Paul Benedum, 87; Sophie and Pearl Benedum, 30; Charles E. Beyer, 38; Al A. Buchanan, 14; Clem S. Clarke, 17; A. B. Dally, Jr., 36; Margaret E. Davis, 71; John W. Dieringer, 13;

Bascom Giles, 18; William Morris Griffith, 22; Walter Simms Hallanan, 63; Houston Harte, 37; Harry B. Hickman, 26; David Dean Johnson, 42; Caswell S. Jones, Thomas J. Newlin and Alex U. McCandless, 18; William J. Jones, 22; Winchester Kelso, 13; W. B. Lane and Roy Gardner, 44; Charles A. McClintock, 11;

Will E. Odom, 16; Alexander P. Olivey, 43; Foster B. Parriott, 30; Andrew Donaldson Robb, 13; Ovid Daniel Robinson, 71; Frank B. Shepard, 17; Tom Slick, 38; Ernest A. Stiller, 14; Milton E. Witherspoon, 8.

1,085 pp. *Open.* 1951.
Underwritten by a gift of Michael Late Benedum.

BENES, Edward. *Discussed in* Jan Papanek.

BENITEZ DE CASTRO, Cecilio. *See* Argentina.

BENJAMIN, Curtis G. (1901–   ) Publisher.
MCGRAW-HILL
College representative of McGraw-Hill, 1928; book publishing policies of the company; growth of college and technical book and visual education departments; development of export markets; evolution of corporate organization and operation.
78 pp. *Permission required.* 1953.

MCGRAW-HILL
Delegate to Russian publishers cultural exchange meeting, 1962; development of *Encyclopedia of World Art, Encyclopedia of Science and Technology, Catholic Encyclopedia;* computer information systems; company goals; developments in text films.
51 pp. *Permission required.* 1964.

BENJAMIN, Herbert. Political activist.
Jewish family life, boyhood reading, job-hunting in Chicago, 1912; early interest in Communist Party; growth of political convictions, leadership in IWW, Socialist and Communist Parties, 1910–35; factionalism in US Left—issues, reasons, leaders; organizing Communist Party districts and Unemployed Councils in Philadelphia, Washington, NYC; black participation in Communist Party; history, policies, organization of US Unemployed Movement, 1920–35; major strikes, demonstrations, marches; renditions of Jewish, Yiddish, protest and Wobbly songs.
545 pp. *Permission required.* 1977.

BENJAMIN, Robert S. (1909–   ) *See* Adlai E. Stevenson Project. *Micro III.*

BENNET, William Stiles (1870–1962) Lawyer, congressman.
NYC politics, 1898–1945; NY politics, 1901–18; national politics, Grover Cleveland to Franklin D. Roosevelt; NY election, 1910.
216 pp. *Permission required to cite or quote.* 1951. *Micro I.*

BENNETT, Charles Edward (1910–   ) *See* Eisenhower Administration. *Micro III.*

BENNETT, John (1902–   ) *See* Socialist Movement.

BENSON, Ezra Taft (1899–   ) *See* Eisenhower Administration.
Discussed in Earl Butz; Don Paarlberg; Edward Thye; Milton R. Young.

BENSON, Frank. *See* Vietnam Veterans.

BENSON, Otis (1902–   ) *See* Aviation Project. *Micro II.*

BENTLEY, Richard (1894–1970) *See* Adlai E. Stevenson Project. *Micro III.*

BENTON, Thomas Hart (1889–1975) Artist.
Family background; Washington; Paris art circles; populism; film work; Armory Show, 1913; WWI naval experiences; Missouri murals; art criticism: walking tours; Jose Clemente Orozco; WPA lecture tour; social function of art; regionalist movement.
185 pp. *Permission required to cite or quote. 1972. Micro III. Contributed by Robert S. Gallagher, La Crosse, Wisconsin.*

BENTON, William (1900–1973) Senator, publisher.
Family background, schooling in Minnesota, Montana; Carleton College, Yale University; National Cash Register Co.; advertising agencies, Lord & Thomas, Batten Company, Benton & Bowles, 1929–36; new techniques of consumer research, General Foods accounts; vice president, University of Chicago, 1937–45; America First; government research at University of Chicago, WWII; Assistant Secretary of State, 1945–47; Senator from Connecticut, 1949–53: resolution to expel Senator Joseph McCarthy, 1951; Smith-Mundt Bill; creation of Commission for Economic Development; vignettes of Chester Bowles, Robert E. Wood, Charles Lindbergh, Nelson Rockefeller, Anna Rosenberg, James Byrnes, Will Clayton, Arthur Vandenburg, Robert A. Taft, and many others.
213 pp. *Permission required to cite or quote. 1968. Micro II.* Papers.
See also Adlai E. Stevenson Project. *Micro IV.*
Discussed in Chester Bowles; Dorothy Bowles; Robert M. Hutchins.

BERDING, Andrew H. (1902–   ) Government official.
EISENHOWER ADMINISTRATION
Deputy Director USIA, 1953–57; Assistant Secretary of State for Public Affairs, 1957–61.
38 pp. *Permission required to cite or quote. 1967. Micro III.*

BERELSON, Bernard R. (1912–   ) Educator.
CARNEGIE CORPORATION
Carnegie grants for library studies, graduate education, behavioral science; Educa-

tional Testing Service; Ford Foundation and Carnegie Corporation.
119 pp. *Permission required. 1967.*

BERENSON, Bernard. *Discussed in* Thomas C. Kinkaid; Paul J. Sachs.

BERGER, Lawrence. *See* Columbia Crisis of 1968.

BERGER, Victor. *Discussed in* John Spargo.

BERGSON, Henri. *Discussed in* Frederic R. Coudert.

BERGSTROM, Harold A. (1905–   ) *See* Continental Group.

BERKELEY, James Phillips (1907–   ) Marine Corps officer.
China duty, Peking, 1932–34; formation of Fleet Marine Force, prewar communications training, procedures, and equipment; WWII communications personnel procurement; Iwo Jima, occupation of Japan; duty in office of Secretary of the Navy, Joint Army-Navy Secretariat; Adviser, Argentina: Naval War College and Marine Corps; Student and Instructor, Armed Forces Staff College, Naval War College; Chief of Staff, 1st Marine Division, Korea, 1954–55; Assistant Chief of Staff, G-1, HQMC, 1955–58, personnel; subsequent commands. Major USMC events, decisions, personalities.
481 pp. *Open.* 1969.

BERKNER, Lloyd Viel (1905–1967) Physicist.
Organization and results of IGY, 1957–58.
60 pp. *Permission required to cite or quote. 1959. Micro I.*

BERKSON, Bill (1939–   ) *See* Poets on their Poetry.

BERLE, Adolf Augustus, Jr. (1895–1971) Lawyer.
Education; early law career; Justice Louis Brandeis' law office; Versailles Peace Conference; land rights 1920–24 in the Dominican Republic; Pueblo Indian land act, 1924; early teaching career; *The Modern Corporation and Private Property,* 1931; impressions of Harlan Stone, Nicholas Murray

Butler, Lillian Wald, Huges Jervey, Samuel E. Morison, William Z. Ripley; Henry Street Settlement; Raymond Moley, Rexford Tugwell, Franklin D. Roosevelt and the New Deal Brain Trust.
190 pp. *Permission required to cite or quote.* 1970. *Micro II.* Papers.

Depression; First Hundred Days after Roosevelt's inauguration, Bank Holiday; Charles W. Taussig.
36 pp. *Permission required.* 1969.
Contributed by James E. Sargent, Roanoke, Virginia.

See also Journalism Lectures (A).
Discussed in Nelson Rockefeller; Henry Wallace; James P. Warburg.

BERNAYS, Edward L. (1891–   ) Public relations counselor.
Psychological and legal ramifications of public relations; societal techniques; symbolism and propaganda; "engineering of consent"; social consciousness-raising and consumerism; Gallup polls; corporations and research; segmental approach; industrial and labor relations; politicans and pollsters; reminiscences of the Sigmund Freud family; the Franklin D. Roosevelt family; Senator Joseph McCarthy; opera and ballet personalities; impressions of many public figures.
403 pp. *Closed during lifetime.* 1971.

BERNHARDT, Sarah. *Discussed in* Eddie Dowling.

BERNSTEIN, Bernice (1908–   ) Lawyer.
SOCIAL SECURITY
Wisconsin unemployment legislation, influence of Senator Robert La Follette; NIRA, Social Security Board, Social Security Administration: legal problems and procedures, preparation of Draft Act; federal-state relationships; 1939 amendments to Social Security Act; effect of WWII; War Manpower Commission; 1947, regional attorney for Federal Security Agency; impressions of Thomas H. Eliot, Jack B. Tate, John Winant, Arthur Altmeyer.
125 pp. *Permission required to cite or quote.* 1965.

BERNSTEIN, Leonard. *See* Andre Watts. *Discussed in* Schuyler Chapin; Aaron Copland; Otto Luening.

BERNSTEIN, Louis (1878–1962) *See* Popular Arts.

BERNSTIEN, Oscar (1885–1974) *See* New York Political Studies (A).

BERRY, Frank Brown (1892–1976) Physician.
Family background; boyhood; Harvard College and Medical School, 1910–17; respiratory experiments under Walter Boothby, WWI: US Army Medical Corps, France, 1918–19; training in surgery and internal medicine; thoracic surgery; WWII: 9th Evacuation Hospital, North Africa and Italy; treatment of chest wounds, blood supplies, penicillin; consultant surgeon, 7th Army, France and Germany, 1943–45; postwar German medical facilities; Bellevue Hospital, 1946–54.
193 pp. *Permission required to cite or quote.* 1972. *Micro II. Contributed by Dr. William Ward Heroy, Huntington, N.Y.*

BERRY, Watson (1870–1963) *See* Journalism Lectures.

BERSON, Solomon (1918–   ) *See* Mt. Sinai Hospital.

BERTRAM, James. *Discussed in* Carnegie Corporation.

BESSIE, Simon Michael (1916–   ) Publisher.
NY childhood, Harvard; *Newark Star-Eagle;* research at RKO-Radio pictures; *Look* magazine; Director, news division, OWI, Algiers and London, 1943–45; USIS, Paris, 1945–46; Harper & Brothers, 1946–59: editorial and personal experiences with authors John Cheever, Tallulah Bankhead, Alfred Kinsey, Alice B. Toklas, Grandma Moses, Kenneth Tynan, others; teaching publishing courses, Columbia, 1950's, and New School; founding, operating Atheneum Books, 1959–75: books and authors, finances, policy; return to Harper & Row, 1975; impressions of New York publishing; visit to Egyptian President Anwar al-Sadat, 1976.

307 pp. *Permission required to cite or quote.* 1976.
Discussed in Evan Thomas II.

BEST, Marshall A. (1901–   ) Publisher.
Family background, education; founding of Viking Press, 1925; *Ulysses* incident; impressions of Viking authors; Literary Guild, Book-of-the-Month Club; Viking *Portable Library;* juvenile book publishing; wartime publishing; Armed Services Editions; American vs. English editing; work with Ben W. Huebsch, Thomas Guinzburg.
239 pp. *Permission required to cite or quote.* 1976.

BETHEL, Ion Maywood (1900–   ) *See* Marine Corps.

BETHUNE, Mary McLeod. *Discussed in* John Warren Davis, Dorothy Height.

BEYER, Charles E. *See* Benedum and the Oil Industry.

BIDDLE, Francis. *Discussed in* Thomas I. Emerson; Robert H. Jackson; Henry Wallace.

BIEMILLER, Andrew John (1906–   ) *See* Social Security.
Discussed in Nelson Cruikshank; Kenneth Williamson.

BIGELOW, Albert Smith (1906–   ) Author, artist.
Family background; US Navy, WW II; work with Hiroshima maidens; Quakerism; participation in freedom rides, Golden Rule voyage 1958, Seabrook demonstration 1977; problems of AEC, power plants, military technology; impressions of Linus Pauling and other scientists.
77 pp. *Permission required to cite or quote.* 1978.

BIGELOW, Karl Worth (1898–   ) Educator.
CARNEGIE CORPORATION
Carnegie grants for African educational programs; TC; Afro-Anglo-American Program in teacher education; ICA; Teachers for East Africa; AID; Peace Corps; Overseas Liaison Committee.
138 pp. *Permission required.* 1967.

BILLEY, Wilfred. *See* Marine Corps.

BILLINGTON, Ray Allen (1903–   ) *See* American Historians *and* Allan Nevins Project.

BING, Rudolph. *Discussed in* Schuyler Chapin.

BINGHAM, Barry (1906–   ) Editor.
ADLAI E. STEVENSON PROJECT.
Campaigns of 1952 and 1956; Far East trip; impressions of Jawaharlal Nehru, Dwight Eisenhower, John F. Kennedy, Estes Kefauver.
117 pp. *Permission required to cite or quote.* 1969. *Micro III.*

BINGHAM, Hiram. *Discussed in* Albert Giesecke.

BINGHAM, Jonathan B. (1914–   ) *See* Ethnic Groups and American Foreign Policy.

BINKERD, Robert Studebaker (1882–n.d.) Businessman, civic worker.
Municipal Voters League of Buffalo; Citizens Union of NYC; NY State politics, 1904–18; NYC politics, 1910–32; national politics during Wilson administration; WWI, railroads; WWII, OPA.
107 pp. *Permission required to cite or quote.* 1949. *Micro IV.*

BIRCH, Herbert (1918–1973) and Stephen A. Richardson. *See* Association for the Aid of Crippled Children.

BIRD, Hobart Stanley (1873–1960) Journalist, lawyer.
William McKinley administration; Puerto Rico, 1898–1904; election of 1924; railroad finance, 1925; NY State finances, 1932.
55 pp. *Permission required to cite or quote.* 1949. *Micro I.*

BIRD, John A. (1910–   ) *See* Eisenhower Administration.

BISHOP, Isabel (Mrs. Harold G. Wolff) (1902–   ) Artist.
Early life and training; the life of an artist; philosophy of art; painting techniques; the creative process; commentary on some of

her own work (illustrated); process of producing an effective painting through etchings, drawings; abstract art.

107 pp. *Permission required to cite or quote.* 1956. *Micro II.*

BISHOP, J.W. *See* Eisenhower Administration.

BISHOP, Jack. *See* Weyerhaeuser Timber Company.

BISHOP, Walter. *See* Popular Arts.

BISSELL, Richard Mervin, Jr. (1909–) Economist.
EISENHOWER ADMINISTRATION
Guatemala, Bay of Pigs; U-2 project; Harold Stassen.

48 pp. *Permission required to cite or quote.* 1967. *Micro IV.*

BIXBY, Harold McMillan (1890–1965) *See* Aviation Project. *Micro II.*

BLACK, Algernon David (1900–) Educator, civil libertarian.
Immigrant background, Ethical Culture School, Harvard; early interest in civil liberties; Roger N. Baldwin; settlement house work, 1926–33; work with West Virginia mining families, 1933; teacher and leader at Ethical Culture from 1933; co-chairman, city-wide Committee on Harlem, 1941–47; job opportunities for blacks; state committee on fair housing, 1949; chairman of board of National Committee on Discrimination in Housing, 1950–67; black militancy in late '60's; chairman of Civilian Complaint Review Board of Police Department, NYC, 1966; encampments for citizenship from 1939; writing and broadcasting on ethical issues; internal security investigations.

210 pp. *Permission required to cite or quote.* 1978.

BLACK, Douglas M. (1895–1977) Publisher.
EISENHOWER ADMINISTRATION
The publication of *Crusade in Europe;* Eisenhower as president of Columbia University.

53 pp. *Permission required to cite or quote.* 1967.

BLACK, Eugene Robert (1898–) Banker.
WORLD BANK
Experiences as American Executive Director, later President, of World Bank: decisions on foreign loan defaults, bond issues and corollary legislation, domestic and foreign bond marketing, National Advisory Council, technical assistance services, mediation of disputes on Indus River development and Suez Canal seizure.

62 pp. *Permission required to cite or quote.* 1961.
Discussed in Davidson Sommers; James P. Warburg; Walter Wyatt.

BLACK, Hugo. *Discussed in* Clifford J. Durr; Virginia Durr; Robert H. Jackson; Henry Wallace.

BLACK, Richard Blackburn (1902–) Naval officer, explorer.
Education in North Dakota and on NYU's floating university, 1926–27; mining, rescue, and recovery work; Adm. Richard Byrd and second Antarctic expedition, 1933–34; Hawaii, 1936; Antarctic Service Expedition, 1939; Hawaii and Pearl Harbor, 1941; Antarctic Support Forces, 1954–56; Adm. Byrd's staff, 1956–57; Office of Naval Research.

89 pp. *Permission required to cite or quote.* 1962. *Micro I.*

BLACK, Mrs. Robert L. *See* Robert A. Taft Project.

BLACK COMMUNITIES *See* Raoul Abdul; James E. Booker; Mamie Clark; Allan Crite; Ed Edwin; Elton C. Fax; Dorothy Height; Jean B. Hutson; A. Philip Randolph; George Schuyler.

BLACK ISSUES *See* Algernon D. Black; James E. Booker; Kenneth Clark; Louis Cowan; John Warren Davis; J. Curtis Dixon; W.E.B. Du Bois; Ed Edwin; John Hammond; Jazz Project; Malcolm X; Ernest R. McKinney; Esther Raushenbush; William J. Schieffelin; George S. Schuyler; Felice N. Schwartz; Charles Smith; Wesley J. Streater; Carl Van Vechten.
See also Black Communities; Blacks—Civil Rights; Integration/Segregation; Ku Klux Klan; NAACP; Race Relations.

BLACKBURN, James Edward, Jr. (1902–) *See* McGraw-Hill.

BLACKIE, Hood River (Ralph Gooding) (1926–) Hobo.
Western American hobo legends, biographical sketches from 1900's–'60's; definitions of slang; life-style differences among road kids, hippies, tramps, winos and hobos; plans to build a ranch for retired "old-timers"; hobo code of ethics, personalities, motivations for travel, habits.
477 pp. *Permission required.* 1973. *Contributed by Dan Carlinsky, NYC.*

BLACKMER, Sidney (1898–1973) *See* Popular Arts.

BLACKS—CIVIL RIGHTS *See* Civil Rights in Alabama; Clifford J. Durr; Lester B. Granger; Dorothy Height; Edward I. Koch; John Lewis; Benjamin McLaurin; E. Frederic Morrow; Constance B. Motley; Theodore Rosengarten; Hobart Taylor, Jr.; William L. Taylor; Roy Wilkins; Margaret B. Young.
See also NAACP; Integration/Segregation.

BLAIR, Beatrice (1929–)
WOMEN'S HISTORY AND POPULATION ISSUES
Rochester Planned Parenthood clinic work, 1950's; outreach clinics, counseling, contraception issues; Director, New York State Abortion Education Program; 1973, Supreme Court decision on abortion; Women's Lobby work; executive director, National Abortion Reform, 1974– ; seminary training.
94 pp. *Permission required to cite or quote.* 1976.

BLAIR, Paxton (1892–1974) Lawyer.
Assistant Corporation Counsel in Fiorello La Guardia administration; NYC politics, Welfare Department and education.
25 pp. *Open.* 1949.

BLAIR, William McCormick, Jr. (1916–) Ambassador.
ADLAI E. STEVENSON PROJECT
Governor Stevenson's administration in Illinois; the Presidential campaigns of 1952, 1956, 1960.
94 pp. *Permission required.* 1969.

Discussed in Elizabeth S. Ives; Newton Minow.

BLAKE, Elizabeth (Mrs. William H.) Artist.
National Association of Women Artists; life in Paris; art classes in New York, 1920's; impressions of Cecilia Beaux, F. Luis Mora, Louis Tiffany, others; Tiffany Foundation; Riverside Church; Armory Show 1913; Women's Archives; faculty functions, Columbia University.
211 pp. *Permission required to cite or quote.* 1975. *Micro IV.*

BLAKE, Robert (1894–) *See* Marine Corps.

BLANCHFIELD, Richard D. *See* Vietnam Veterans.

BLANKENHORN, Heber (1884–1956) Labor researcher.
Ohio childhood; Worcester College, Columbia University; NY *Sun,* early labor reporting; war research, leaflet warfare, WWI; Commission to Negotiate Peace, 1918; Bureau of Industrial Research, 1919–21; Steel Strike Report; Cabot Fund report; coal strike, 1922; Sidney Hillman, Amalgamated Clothing Workers, 1920; NY *Call, Leader;* London correspondent, *Labor,* 1926–31; Italian anti-fascism; Dillon Reed Corporation analyst; Spanish Civil War, 1931–33; NIRA; National Labor Board, assistant to Senator Robert Wagner; passage of Wagner Act; investigation of industrial espionage; La Follette Committee.
564 pp. *Permission required to cite or quote.* 1955. *Micro IV.*

BLATCHFORD, Paul. *See* Marine Corps.

BLEDSOE, Samuel B. (1898–) Agriculturist.
Childhood and education; newspaper work in Memphis, 1921–23, and Washington, D.C., 1928–35; AAA Information Section, 1935–40; assistant to Vice President Henry Wallace, 1941; assistant to Secretary of Agriculture Wickard: preparing for war; commodity production and price ceilings; Farm Bureau Federation and the Farmers' Union; political influence of the Department of Agriculture; Pearl Harbor, reorganization and prices; control of food pro-

duction and agricultural manpower; WPB; congressional relations; relations of the FSA with labor and the political left; production and supply of farm machinery; control of the WFA; departmental reorganization, November, 1942; Herbert W. Parisius and the Food Production Administration; Gardner Jackson; Claude Wickard as War Food Administrator, 1941–43; work with NY *Times, US News,* National Cotton Council, NAM, 1943–53.

689 pp. *Permission required to cite or quote.* 1954. *Micro I.* Papers.

BLERIOT, Louis. *Discussed in* Ross Browne.

BLIGHTON, Frank. *Discussed in* James T. Williams, Jr.

BLISS, Anthony. *Discussed in* Schuyler Chapin.

BLISS, C. Presby (1900–) *See* McGraw-Hill.

BLIVEN, Bruce Ormsby (1889–1977) Editor.
Youth and education; early experiences in journalism with NY *Globe;* editor, *New Republic;* Henry A. Wallace and the Progressive Party; Twentieth Century Fund.

60 pp. *Permission required to cite or quote.* 1964. *Micro II.*

BLOCH, Ernest. *Discussed in* Roger Sessions.

BLOCH, Felix (1905–) *See* Nobel Laureates.

BLOCK, Herbert (1909–) *See* Journalism Lectures.

BLOOM, Andrew. *Discussed in* William Maxwell.

BLOOM, Samuel. *See* Mt. Sinai Hospital.

BLOSER, Bernard D. (1908–) *See* Continental Group.

BLOSSOM, Virgil. *Discussed in* Orval Faubus; A.F. House.

BLOUGH, Roger M. (1904–) Chairman, US Steel.
Family background and education; Yale Law School; corporate and labor cases, White & Case, 1931–41; Depression, New Deal legislation; US Steel, 1942–69: wartime production, steel prices and wages, WLB; subsidiaries, raw materials procurement, Korean War, seizure of steel industry, 1952; military vs. civilian production needs; 1962 confrontation of President Kennedy and steel industry; worker safety and environmental protection measures; business liaisons with government.

316 pp. *Permission required to cite or quote.* 1975.

BLUITT, Tim. *See* Vietnam Veterans.

BLUMENTHAL, Albert H. (1928–) Lawyer, public official.
Childhood; education, William and Mary, NYU Law School; law career, involvement in NYC clubhouse politics; New York Civil Liberties Union Board member; elected Assemblyman 1962, Health Committee Chairman, 1966; divorce and abortion legislation reform efforts; penal legislation; impressions of politics and NY politicians.
In process.

BLYER, Bob and Doc Richardson. *See* Flying Tigers.

BOAS, Franz. *Discussed in* Franziska Boas.

BOAS, Franziska.
Reminiscences of her father, Franz Boas (1858–1942).
76 pp. *Permission required to cite or quote.* 1972. *Contributed by John R. Cole, New York.*

BOATWRIGHT, Mody. *See* American Cultural Leaders.

BOBROW, Davis. *See* International Negotiations.

BOEING, William. *Discussed in* Eugene E. Wilson.

BOESCHENSTEIN, Harold (1896–1972) *See* Eisenhower Administration. *Micro III.*

BOGAN, Louise (1897–1970) *See* Ford Maddox Ford.

BOGER, Robert Forrester (1900–1968) *See* McGraw-Hill.

BOHEMAN, Erik. *See* Alexandra Kollontai Project.

BOHLEN, Charles Eustis (1904–1974) *See* Eisenhower Administration. *Micro IV.*

BOHR, Niels. *Discussed in* I.I. Rabi; Warren Weaver.

BOHRER, Joseph. *See* Adlai E. Stevenson Project.

BOHS, Louis G. (1895–   ) *See* Continental Group.

BOITANO, Ernie. *See* Vietnam Veterans.

BOK, Edward. *Discussed in* James M. Wood.

BOLENIUS, William. *See* Kirkland College.

BOLLAND, Adrienne. *See* Aviation Project.

BONAPARTE, Marie. *Discussed in* Rudolph M. Loewenstein.

BOND, Nelson L. (1903–1974) *See* McGraw-Hill.

BOND, Walter Elder (1912–   ) *See* Continental Group.

BONILLA, Lucio. Labor leader.
ARGENTINA
Textile industry in Argentina, 1920–46: formation of Workers' Textile Union, 1930, new products, wages, unemployment, benefits achieved by union pressure, political influences, factional divisions; General Confederation of Workers (CGT) during 1940's; rise of Juan Peron and role of unions in 1943 revolution; relations with Department of Labor.
103 pp. *Open.* 1971.

BONN, Louis A. *See* Popular Arts.

BOOHER, Edward E. (1911–   ) *See* McGraw-Hill.

BOOK-OF-THE-MONTH CLUB
The founding and development of the Book-of-the-Month Club from 1926 to 1955. The material consists of interviews with the founders, members of the Selection Committee, executive and technical personnel. In the most detailed of these memoirs, Harry Scherman, founder and board chairman, describes his own background, gives the origins of the idea of selling current books by mail to subscribers, tells of the first judges and later additions to the Selection Committee, discusses problems of editorial policy and the preferences of various judges, and recalls many of the selections and their reception. Mr. Scherman and other participants also deal with: the reader system for culling books submitted by publishers, attempts of outsiders to influence selection, relationships with publishers, membership and sales through the years, characteristics of subscribers, the book dividend system, the use of premiums, the preparation and testing of advertisements, distribution of art reproductions and musical recordings, book design and calligraphy, the Literary Guild and other book clubs, opposition of the book sellers, book manufacture, corporate structure of the company, problems of servicing subscribers, personnel and employee relations. Students of the literary scene in these years will find the Canby, Fadiman, Fisher, Highet, Loveman, Marquand, Scherman and Wood memoirs of particular interest.
Participants and pages: Henry Seidel Canby, 28; Harry Dale, 22; Clifton Fadiman, 45; Helen R. Feil, 16; Dorothy Canfield Fisher, 129; George Gallup, 32; Robert K. Haas, 31; Gilbert Highet, 18; Gordon Hyle, 24; Edwina Kohlman, 18; Amy Loveman, 17; Warren Lynch, 28; John Marquand, 30; Oscar Ogg, 35; Axel Rosin, 45; Maxwell Sackheim, 17; Harry Scherman, 367; Ralph Thompson, 28; Lester Troob, 26; Edith Walker, 40; Meredith Wood, 103.
1,099 pp. *Permission required to cite or quote. 1955. Some memoirs are available in microform; consult individual entries. Underwritten by a gift of the Book-of-the-Month Club, Inc.*

(33)

BOOKBINDER, Hyman (1916–) *See* Ethnic Groups and American Foreign Policy.

BOOKER, James E. Journalist.
Long Island childhood; Hampton Institute and Howard University; *Amsterdam News,* 1947–50 and 1954–66; information director, White House Conference on Civil Rights; consultant, White House Conference on Education; relationship with Adam Clayton Powell; organization of Congressional Black Caucus; changes in Harlem and other black communities since 1960's; impressions of J. Raymond Jones, Robert Wagner, Earl Brown.
In process.

BOOKS AND BOOK PUBLISHING *See* Agnes Allen; William Benton; S. Michael Bessie; Marshall A. Best; Douglas Black; Book-of-the-Month Club; William S. Braithwaite; D. Angus Cameron; Melville H. Cane; Cass Canfield; Bennett Cerf; Warren Chappell; Dorothy Commins; Daniel Cosio Villegas; William Couch; Elton C. Fax; Beulah Hagen; Ralph E. Henderson; Frank Ernest Hill; Eric Hodgins; Ben W. Huebsch; Oliver Jensen; Donald Klopfer; Alfred A. Knopf; Jill Krementz; Freeman Lewis and Leon Shimkin; Kenneth D. McCormick; McGraw-Hill; Frank MacGregor; Helen Macy; Joseph A. Margolies; May Massee; Arthur W. Page; S. Phelps Platt; Poets on their Poetry; Rare Books; M. Lincoln Schuster; Edwin Seaver; Roger W. Straus; Evan Thomas II; Phyllis Cerf Wagner; John Hall Wheelock.

BOOLE, Ella Alexander (Mrs. William H.) (1858–1952) Church and temperance worker.
Development, political activities and personnel of WCTU; Prohibition.
28 pp. *Permission required to cite or quote. 1950. Micro IV.*

BOONE, Richard Allen (1917–) *See* Popular Arts.

BOOTHBY, Walter. *Discussed in* Frank B. Berry.

BORAH, William E. *Discussed in* James A. Farley; Burton K. Wheeler.

BORIE, Lysbeth Boyd. *See* Independence Park.

BORLENGHI, Angel. *Discussed in* Ernesto Janin.

BORROWMAN, Steve. *See* Vietnam Veterans.

BORTON, Hugh (1903–) State Department official.
Training in Japanese studies; US State Department, 1942–48; US-Japan relations during WWII and Occupation; Gen. Douglas MacArthur.
52 pp. *Permission required to cite or quote. 1956. Micro II.*

BOSCH, John. *See* Farm Holiday Association.

BOSCH, Richard. *See* Farm Holiday Association.

BOSLER, Gustave A. *See* Radio Pioneers.

BOTSFORD, Gardner (1917–) Editor.
New Yorker reporter, editor, 1941– ; impressions of William Shawn, Harold Ross, Raoul Fleischman.
61 pp. *Permission required to cite or quote. 1976. Micro IV.*

BOULANGER, Nadia. *Discussed in* Aaron Copland; Elie Siegmeister; Virgil Thomson.

BOULEZ, Pierre. *Discussed in* William Schuman.

BOURKE, Thomas Eugene (1896–1978) *See* Marine Corps.

BOW, Clara. *Discussed in* Popular Arts.

BOWER, William (1917–) *See* Air Force Academy.

BOWERS, Claude Gernade (1878–1958) Ambassador, historian.
Boyhood in Indiana; Senate in the Progressive era; NY *Evening World;* William Randolph Hearst; *The Tragic Era* and other books; Democratic Conventions, 1924 and 1928; Ambassador to Spain during Civil War, and to Chile during WWII.

149 pp. *Permission required to cite or quote.* 1956. *Micro I.*
Discussed in Theodore F. Kuper; Allan Nevins.

BOWERS, Faubion (1917–) *See* Occupation of Japan. *Micro II.*

BOWIE, Robert Richardson (1909–) Lawyer, educator.
EISENHOWER ADMINISTRATION
Policy Planning Board; NSC; foreign policy; Project Solarium; impressions of Dwight D. Eisenhower, John Foster Dulles.
51 pp. *Permission required to cite or quote.* 1967. *Micro III.*
See also Robert P. Patterson Project.

BOWLES, Chester (1901–) Diplomat, government official.
Education at Choate and Yale; advertising, 1925; Benton & Bowles; radio advertising, product research and pricing; Defense Council; America First movement; Connecticut rationing administrator; Price Administrator; relations with Congress, Cabinet, and government officials; OPA; stabilization, postwar period; campaign for Democratic gubernatorial nomination, Connecticut, 1946; ADA; UNESCO, UNICEF, UNRRA, 1946–47; Governor, Connecticut, 1948–50; appointment of William Benton as Senator from Connecticut; 1950 campaign; Ambassador to India, 1951–53; Senate campaign, 1958; posts and relationships, Kennedy administration; Ambassador to India, 1963. Observations on national and international political figures, especially Franklin D. Roosevelt, Eleanor Roosevelt, Harry Truman, John F. Kennedy, James Byrnes, Donald Nelson, Jawaharlal Nehru, Adlai E. Stevenson.
866 pp. *Permission required to cite or quote.* 1963. *Micro III.*
Discussed in Raymond Baldwin; William Benton; Dorothy Bowles; Thomas I. Emerson; Henry Wallace.

BOWLES, Dorothy Stebbins (Mrs. Chester)
Description of the political events in the life of Chester Bowles, especially in Connecticut; John Bailey, William Benton.
89 pp. *Permission required to cite or quote.* 1963. *Micro III.*

BOWMAN, Karl M. (1888–1973) Psychiatrist.
Medical education and early practice; psychiatric treatment for soldiers, 1917–19; Jungian and Freudian influences; Boston Psychopathic Hospital, Harvard Medical School, Bellevue Hospital; American Psychiatric Association: president, 1944–45, internal politics, use of shock treatment; chemical and organic aspects of mental disease; relation of law to mental disorders: *Research on Alcoholism, Sexual Deviation, Narcotics;* Leopold-Loeb trial; Langley Porter Clinic, 1941–56. Recollections of teachers, students, and colleagues.
102 pp. *Open.* 1968. *Contributed by Alden B. Mills, Sacramento.*

BOWMAN, Waldo G. (1900–) *See* McGraw-Hill.

BOWSER, Alpha Lyons (1910–) *See* Marine Corps.

BOYD, Albert (1906–) *See* Aviation Project. *Micro IV.*

BOYD, Ralph. *See* Weyerhaeuser Timber Company.

BOZELL, Harold Veatch (1886–) *See* McGraw-Hill.

BOZELL, Lewis (1892–) *See* Continental Group.

BRABAZON OF TARA, Lord (1884–1964) *See* Aviation Project.

BRACKETT, Charles (1892–) *See* Popular Arts.

BRADEMAS, John (1927–) *See* Adlai E. Stevenson Project. *Micro IV.*

BRADEN, Anne (Mrs. Carl) (1924–) Journalist, civil rights activist.
Girlhood, education, Alabama; reporter, Birmingham, Louisville; postwar race relations in the South, especially in Louisville; the Bradens' arrest for sedition, 1954; Southern Educational Conference Fund, 1957–66.
In process.

BRADEN, Spruille (1894–1978) Diplomat, mining engineer.
Childhood and education; development of copper mining in Chile; business enterprises in NY and Latin America; experiences as chairman of the NY State Crime Commission; detailed description of career with the government, with special emphasis on the Chaco Peace Conference, 1935–39; embassies to Colombia, 1939–42, Cuba, 1942, and Argentina, 1945, and role as Assistant Secretary of State for Latin American Affairs, 1945–47; impressions of Cordell Hull, Sumner Welles, and Carlos Saavedra Lamas.
3,188 pp. *Permission required to cite or quote.* 1956. *Micro IV.* Papers.

BRADLEY, Carter. *See* Social Security.

BRADLEY, Michael Joseph (1897–   ) *See* Independence Park.

BRADLEY, Omar Nelson (1893–   ) Army officer.
EISENHOWER ADMINISTRATION
Recollections of Dwight D. Eisenhower: West Point, Africa, Normandy.
23 pp. *Permission required to cite or quote.* 1965.
Discussed in Edward L. Beach; John L. Hall, Jr.; Alan Kirk.

BRADSHAW, Homer V. *See* China Missionaries.

BRADY, Thomas F. (1914–   ) *See* Continental Group.

BRAGDON, Everett L. *See* Radio Pioneers.

BRAINARD, C.L. (1903–   ) *See* Eisenhower Administration.

BRAINERD, Bertha. *Discussed in* Radio Pioneers.

BRAITHWAITE, William Stanley Beaumont (1878–1962) Author.
Work on the Boston *Transcript;* reminiscences of literary friends, including E. A. Robinson, Amy Lowell, Robert Frost, and Sara Teasdale; experiences in publishing and teaching.
233 pp. *Open.* 1956.

BRANCH, Hilarion Noel (1880–1966) Lawyer.
Boyhood, British West Indies; teaching in Mexico, 1900–10; Mexican Embassy, Washington; oil industry in Mexico, 1920's and 30's. Impressions of William Gibbs McAdoo, Edward L. Doheny, Dwight Morrow.
182 pp. *Permission required to cite or quote.* 1966. *Micro I.*

BRANDEIS, Louis D. *Discussed in* Chauncey Belknap; Adolf A. Berle; Virginia Durr; Learned Hand; Gardner Jackson; James M. Landis; John L. O'Brian; Paul and Elizabeth Raushenbush; Bernard G. Richards.

BRANDEWIEDE, Gregory J. (1899–   ) *See* Aviation Project.

BRANDT, Carl Amandus (1906–   ) *See* Aviation Project.

BRANDT, Harry (1897–   ) *See* Popular Arts.

BRANDT, Karl (1899–1975) *See* Eisenhower Administration.

BRANHAM, Danny. *See* Vietnam Veterans.

BRANNAN, Charles Franklin (1903–   ) Government official.
Education; early law practice; first experiences in politics; work with the government during the New Deal and WWII, with emphasis on his association with the RA and FSA; Secretary of Agriculture, 1948–53.
183 pp. *Closed during lifetime.* 1953.

BRANTING, Hjalmar. *Discussed in* Hokan B. Steffanson.

BRANTON, Wiley Austin (1923–   ) *See* Eisenhower Administration.

BRATTAIN, Walter Houser (1902–   ). *See* Nobel Laureates.

BRAY, Howard.
SOCIAL SECURITY
Work for Senator Clinton Anderson in late 1950's and '60's; Medicare legislation; health insurance role of private insurance

companies, Blue Cross, and federal government.
112 pp. *Closed during lifetime.* 1966.

BRECHER, Edward. *See* James Lawrence Fly Project.

BRECKINRIDGE, Henry (1886–1960) Lawyer.
Family background; Princeton; Harvard Law School; law clerk in Baltimore; practice in Lexington, Ky.; election of 1912; appointment as Assistant Secretary of War; the Army (generals, red tape, Board of Review); Woodrow Wilson and the New Freedom; Mexico; WWI in Europe; mission to Europe; *Lusitania;* preparedness and the administration; congressional relations; Supreme Court justices; Army justice and discipline; soldiers in alien lands; growth of aviation; the New Deal.
327 pp. *Permission required to cite or quote.* 1953. *Micro I.* Papers.

BRECKINRIDGE, James. *Discussed in* Robert B. Luckey.

BREITENBACH, Harry P. *See* Radio Pioneers.

BREWER, Joseph. *See* Ford Maddox Ford.

BREWER, Vivion (Mrs. Joe) *See* Eisenhower Administration.

BREWSTER, Owen. *Discussed in* Horace M. Albright.

BRICE, William O. (1898–1972) *See* Marine Corps.

BRICKER, John W. (1893–   ) Senator.
EISENHOWER ADMINISTRATION
Republican Conventions of 1944 and 1952; Eisenhower administration; Bricker amendment.
40 pp. *Permission required.* 1968.

BRIDGEMAN, William B. (1916–   ) *See* Aviation Project. *Micro IV.*

BRIDGES, C.B. *Discussed in* Theodosius Dobzhansky.

BRIDGES, Hal (1918–   ) (with John Niven) *See* Allan Nevins Project.

BRIDGES, Harry. *Discussed in* John P. Frey; M. Hedley Stone; Frances Perkins.

BRIGGS, Ellis O. (1899–1976) Writer, ambassador.
EISENHOWER ADMINISTRATION
Duties of an ambassador; relations with State Department and John Foster Dulles; ambassador to Czechoslovakia, 1949; Oatis spy trial; ambassador to Korea (1952), Peru (1955), Brazil (1956); American business interests in Latin America; ambassador to Greece, 1959–61; Eisenhower's visit to Greece.
139 pp. *Permission required to cite or quote.* 1972. *Micro IV.*

BRIGGS, James Elbert (1906–   ) *See* Aviation Project, *Micro IV, and* Air Force Academy.

BRILL, A.A. *Discussed in* Abram Kardiner.

BRINDLE, James and Martin Cohen. *See* Social Security. *Micro IV.*

BRISCOE, Robert. *See* Journalism Lectures.

BRISTOL, Arthur. *Discussed in* Robert B. Carney.

BRITTAIN, Sir Harry E. (1873–1974) *See* Aviation Project. *Micro IV.*

BRITTON, Mason (1890–   ) *See* McGraw-Hill.

BROADWELL, Edward H. (1917–   ) *See* Continental Group.

BROCKWAY, George. *Discussed in* Evan Thomas II.

BRODE, Wallace Reed (1900–1974) *See* Eisenhower Administration.

BROOKE, Bryan. *See* Mount Sinai Hospital.

BROOKLYN POLITICS, 1930–50. *See* New York Political Studies (A).

BROOKS, Jack. *See* Alaskan Pioneers.

BROOKS, Van Wyck. *Discussed in* John Hall Wheelock.

BROPHY, John (1883–1963) Labor union official.
Family background and childhood; miners' organizations in England and US before 1900; life of a typical miner; organizational work with UMW, Western Pennsylvania and Michigan, 1899–1917; struggles of UMW, 1899–1940; John L. Lewis; visits to England and Russia, 1927; UMW and AFL, 1918–35; emergence of new CIO, 1935–41; posts and activities with CIO, 1935–41; relations of CIO and AFL, 1935–55; national director, Industrial Union Councils, 1940–47; wartime labor relations boards, 1941–45; Philip Murray's Industrial Council Plan; opening conference, WFTU and ILO, 1945; ICFTU, 1949; comments on labor's view of socialism, the New Deal, Communists and the labor movement, the Department of Labor, future of the labor movement. Impressions of labor figures: William B. Wilson, Samuel Gompers, William Z. Foster, Philip Murray, Sidney Hillman, William Green, Walter Reuther, Lee Pressman, Frances Perkins, Maurice Tobin.
1,036 pp. *Permission required to cite or quote.* 1955. *Micro I.*

BROSIO, Manlio (1897–   ) *See* International Negotiations.

BROUN, Heywood. *Discussed in* Mildred Gilman; Dan Golenpaul.

BROWDER, Earl (1891–1973) Communist leader.
Childhood in Kansas; Populist Party; social and economic characteristics of Kansas; socialism; Office Workers Union, AFL, union activities, 1914; WWI; anti-war group; Tom Mooney; Russian Revolution, 1917; Communist Party, 1919; IWW vs. AFL; International Trade Union Congress, Russia, 1921; 3rd Congress Communist International; La Follette movement; Chinese Revolution, 1927; Pan-Pacific Trade Union Secretariat, 1928; Communist magazines; development of CIO, 1930's; Scottsboro case; Negro rights; 1936 presidential campaign; leftist organizations, 1930's; United Front and 7th Congress Communist International, 1935; Spanish Civil War and International Brigade; Stalin-Hitler Pact, 1939; WWII; postwar changes in Communist Party; discussion of ideology; impressions of Communist leaders.
525 pp. *Permission required to cite or quote.* 1964. *Micro II.* Papers.

BROWER, David. *Discussed in* Stewart Ogilvy.

BROWN, Earl. *Discussed in* James E. Booker.

BROWN, Emerson Lee (1901–   ) *See* McGraw-Hill.

BROWN, Georgia T. *See* Aviation Project.

BROWN, Harry. *Discussed in* Carl Hamilton.

BROWN, James Douglas (1898–   ) Economist.
SOCIAL SECURITY
Chairman of Advisory Council, Subcommittee of Senate Finance Committee; Social Security Board, 1937–38; advisory councils, 1947–48, 1957–58, 1963–64; efforts toward old age insurance legislation; impressions of Edwin Witte, Barbara Armstrong, Murray Latimer.
148 pp. *Permission required to cite or quote.* 1965. *Micro III.*
Discussed in Barbara Armstrong.

BROWN, John Mason. *Discussed in* Alan Kirk.

BROWN, John Paulding. *See* Adlai E. Stevenson Project.

BROWN, John R. (1913–   ) *See* Continental Group.

BROWN, Katharine Kennedy. *See* Robert A. Taft Project.

BROWN, Ralph E. *See* Jazz Project.

BROWN, Sevellon Ledyard (1886–1956) Editor, publisher.
Early years on Washington newspapers and

with the UP; President William H. Taft and the press; NY *Herald* Washington bureau during WWI; career with the Providence *Journal* and *Evening Bulletin;* origins of the AP Managing Editors' Association and the American Press Institute; comments on American journalism.

99 pp. *Permission required to cite or quote.* 1956. *Micro I.*

BROWN, Stephen L. (1916–   ) *See* Continental Group.

BROWN, Wilburt Scott (1900–1968) *See* Marine Corps.

BROWN, William Wilbur (1889–   ) *See* Radio Pioneers.

BROWNE, Carlos Eduardo. *See* Argentina.

BROWNE, George Chalmers. *See* China Missionaries.

BROWNE, Nat. *See* Alaskan Pioneers.

BROWNE, Ross (–1963) Flyer.
AVIATION PROJECT
With Louis Bleriot in France, 1908; Wilbur Wright and the first circular flight; first flight across the English Channel; aviation meet in Belmont Park; touring with "International Aviators"; aviation pictures.

115 pp. *Permission required to cite or quote.* 1960. *Micro II.*

BROWNE, Scoville (1915–   ) *See* Jazz Project.

BROWNELL, Herbert (1904–   ) Lawyer, politician.
EISENHOWER ADMINISTRATION
1952 pre-convention and election campaigns; Republican Party; selection of the Cabinet; other appointments; Justice Department and Attorney General's Office; immigration; integration; Emmett Till case; Brown case; Tidelands case; Bricker amendment; Julius and Ethel Rosenberg; Joseph R. McCarthy; Adam Clayton Powell; Civil Rights Act of 1957; Little Rock crisis; presidential incapacity legislation; national security; labor racketeering prosecution; anti-trust law enforcement; impressions of Dwight Eisenhower.

347 pp. *Permission required to cite or quote.* 1967.

EISENHOWER ADMINISTRATION
Pre-convention campaigning with General Lucius D. Clay for Dwight Eisenhower; 1951 Republican Convention; vice-presidential and cabinet nominee consideration.

16 pp. *Permission required to cite or quote.* 1971.

NEW YORK BAR
Childhood, education; corporate law practice, Lord & Day, 1929–53, 1957–   ; work with SEC law, New Deal administration while in New York State Assembly, 1934–37; counsel for 1940 World's Fair, NY; responsibilities as Dewey's presidential campaign manager, 1944–48; corporate law in 1940's–50's; US Attorney General, 1953–57; 1973 Mexican-American Water Treaty dispute; impressions of Richard Nixon and Justice Warren Burger.

141 pp. *Permission required to cite or quote.* 1977.

See also additional interview in Eisenhower Administration. *Discussed in* Sherman Adams; Lucius D. Clay; M. Hedley Stone.

BROWNELL, Samuel Miller (1900–   ) Educator.
EISENHOWER ADMINISTRATION
Service on US delegation to UNESCO, 1954; Conference of Ministers of Education of the Americas, 1956; International Conference on Education, 1960.

83 pp. *Permission required to cite or quote.* 1967. *Micro III.*

BROWNING, Gordon (1889–1976) Governor.
Early years and family background in Tennessee; education, law training; early experience in law and politics; WWI; Congressman, description of Washington political scene in the 1920's and 30's; Senate campaign, 1934; Governor of Tennessee, 1937–39, TVA, state finances; WWII; Governor, 1949–53. Anecdotes of many political figures: Huey Long, Edward H. Crump, Kenneth McKellar, Estes Kefauver.

144 pp. *Open.* 1965. *Contributed by Joseph H. Riggs and the Memphis Public Library.*

(39)

BROWNLOW, Louis. *Discussed in* Charles Ascher; Frances Perkins; Henry Wallace.

BRUCHEY, Stuart (1917–   ) *See* American Historians.

BRUERE, Henry (1882–1958) Civic worker, financier.
NYC politics, 1904–17; Bureau of Municipal Research from its founding; US-Mexico relations, 1916; banking, 1926–1933; national politics under Franklin D. Roosevelt.
170 pp. *Permission required to cite or quote.* 1949. *Micro I.*

BRUNDAGE, Percival Flack (1892–   ) Consultant.
EISENHOWER ADMINISTRATION
The Budget Bureau during the Eisenhower Administration; consultations with departments and with President Eisenhower.
52 pp. *Permission required to cite or quote.* 1967.

BRUNO, Harry A. (1893–1978) Public relations counsel.
AVIATION PROJECT
First experiences in glider aviation, 1910; School of Military Aeronautics, University of Toronto; Aeromarine Airways, 1919–23; aviation public relations, 1923; flight safety; Airplane Owners and Pilots Association; women's contribution to world aviation; impressions of Bert Acosta, Wiley Post.
118 pp. *Closed until May 1, 1985.* 1960.

BRUNSWICK, Ruth Mack. *Discussed in* Muriel Gardiner.

BRUSTEIN, Robert (1927–   ) *See* American Cultural Leaders.

BRYAN, Julien (1899–   ) *See* Robert J. Flaherty Project.

BRYAN, William Ray (1905–   ) *See* Health Sciences.

BRYANT, William Cullen II. *See* Allan Nevins Project.

BRYSON, Lyman Lloyd (1888–1959) Educator.
RADIO PIONEERS
Family background and education; journal-

ism instructor, University of Michigan; Army, 1917; American Red Cross; lecturer, University of California, 1925; director, San Diego Museum; TC; radio commentator from 1927; educational broadcasts for CBS; networks and local stations; radio and fiscal matters; views on broadcasting; impressions of academic and broadcasting personalities.
254 pp. *Permission required to cite or quote.* 1951. *Micro IV.*

BUCHANAN, Al A. *See* Benedum and the Oil Industry.

BUCHANAN, Clarence E. *See* James B. Duke Project.

BUCHANAN, Wiley Thomas, Jr. (1914–   ) *See* Eisenhower Administration.

BUCHANAN, William Walter (1914–   ) *See* Marine Corps.

BUCHER, E. R. *See* James B. Duke Project.

BUCK, Paul Herman (1899–1978) Author, university dean.
CARNEGIE CORPORATION
Discussion of grants received from Carnegie Corporation and programs carried out in educational fields at Harvard University.
87 pp. *Permission required.* 1967.

BUCK, Solon Justus (1884–1962) Historian, archivist.
AHA: policies, financial problems, administration, members and officers; AHR and Annual Reports.
44 pp. *Permission required to cite or quote.* 1955. *Micro I.*

BUCKNER, Elmer LaMar (1922–   ) *See* Eisenhower Administration. *Micro III.*

BUCKNER, Emory. *Discussed in* David W. Peck.

BUGBEE, Emma (1888–   ) *See* Women Journalists.

BUHROW, Herbert (1914–   ) *See* McGraw-Hill.

BULLITT, William. *Discussed in* James P. Warburg.

BULLOCK, Earl R. (1912–   ) *See* Weyerhaeuser Timber Company.

BUNCHE, Ralph. *Discussed in* John Warren Davis; Gunnar Myrdal.

BUNDY, Harvey Hollister (1888–1963) Lawyer.
Childhood and education; legal experience in Boston; government service in the Departments of State and War. Impressions of Henry L. Stimson, Herbert Hoover, Gen. George Marshall, and many other national figures.
    313 pp. *Permission required to cite or quote.* 1960. *Micro I.* Papers.

BUNDY, McGeorge. *Discussed in* Carnegie Corporation; F. Peterson Jessup.

BUNKER, Arthur Hugh (1895–1964) *See* Mining Engineers.

BUNKER, Ellsworth (1894–   ) *See* Robert J. Flaherty Project.

BUNZL, Mrs. Walter (1907–1968) Research assistant to Mayor La Guardia.
NYC politics and the Citizens Union; Fiorello La Guardia.
    24 pp. *Permission required to cite or quote.* 1949. *Micro I.* Papers.

BURCKHARDT, Frederick H. (1912–   ) Educator.
CARNEGIE CORPORATION
Carnegie grants to Bennington College; ACLS, SSRC, and Council on Higher Education in the American Republics; Carnegie personnel and administration.
    84 pp. *Permission required.* 1968.

BURDEN, William Armistead Moale (1906–   ) Diplomat.
EISENHOWER ADMINISTRATION
National Aeronautics and Space Council; State Department; Department of Defense; Belgium; Congo crisis.
    81 pp. *Closed during lifetime.* 1968.

BURGER, Joseph Charles (1902–   ) Marine Corps officer.

Early training and assignments; China duty, 1927, 1935–37; development of amphibious warfare doctrine in early 1930's; operations planning in South Pacific, 1st Marine Amphibious Corps, 1942–43; Military Secretary to Gen. Alexander Vandegrift, 1944–46; CO, Basic School, 1949–50; Chief of Staff, Fleet Marine Force, Pacific, 1950–51, Korean War; Director of Information, Director of Reserve, HQMC, 1954–56; CG, Recruit Depot, Parris Island, 1956, Ribbon Creek affair; CG, Camp Lejeune and 2d Marine Division, 1956–59; Marine operations in Lebanon; CG, Fleet Marine Force, Atlantic, 1959–61. USMC operational planning, developments, personalities.
    377 pp. *Open.* 1969.

BURGESS, Carter L. (1916–   ) Corporation executive.
EISENHOWER ADMINISTRATION
Gen. Walter B. Smith, WWII; Wriston Report; studies on White House organization; Assistant Secretary of Defense for Manpower, 1954–57; impressions of the Eisenhower administration.
    40 pp. *Permission required to cite or quote.* 1967. *Micro III.*

BURGESS, Gelett. *Discussed in* Ben W. Huebsch.

BURGESS, Warren Randolph (1889–1978) Government official.
CARNEGIE CORPORATION
Trustee of the Carnegie Corporation; vignettes of fellow trustees and discussions of policies.
    50 pp. *Permission required.* 1967.
See also International Negotiations.

BURKE, Agnes (–1974) Educator.
Childhood and Normal School, Winona, Minnesota; Miss Wheelock Kindergarten Training School, Boston; TC; experiences as tutor, reading consultant, teacher.
    50 pp. *Permission required to cite or quote.* 1969. *Micro II.*
Discussed in Charlotte Garrison.

BURKE, Arleigh Andrew (1901–   ) *See* Eisenhower Administration.

BURKE, James Vincent, Jr. (1911–   ) *See* Eisenhower Administration. *Micro III.*

BURKE, John P. (1902–   ) *See* McGraw-Hill.

BURLINGHAM, Charles Culp (1858–1959) Lawyer.
Legal and political recollections of NYC; impressions of prominent jurists.
45 pp. *Permission required to cite or quote.* 1949. *Micro I.* Papers.

BURNEY, Leroy E. (1906–   ) *See* Health Sciences.

BURNS, Arthur Edward (1908–   ) Economist.
EISENHOWER ADMINISTRATION
Technical Cooperation Administration; Foreign Operations Administration, 1953–57; Consultant, Joint Federal State Action Committee, White House staff, 1957–60; economic policies of the Eisenhower Administration.
45 pp. *Permission required to cite or quote.* 1967. *Micro III.*
Discussed in Gabriel Hauge; Neil H. Jacoby.

BURNS, Arthur F. *Discussed in* Sherman Adams.

BURNS, Eveline Mabel (1900–   ) Economist.
SOCIAL SECURITY
Board of the Consumer's League of New York; grant to study unemployment security in England and Germany; staff member, Committee on Economic Security, 1934; committee on social security, National Resources Planning Board, 1939; studies of social security programs; impressions of Mary W. Dewson, Edwin Witte, Wilbur Cohen, Arthur Altmeyer, John Winant.
180 pp. *Permission required to cite or quote.* 1965. *Micro III.*

BURNS, Frank W. (1898–   ) *See* Continental Group.

BURNS, James Henry (1885–   ) *See* Henry H. Arnold Project.

BURNS, Lucy. *Discussed in* Alice Paul.

BURROUGHS, Edgar Rice. *Discussed in* Sol Lesser.

BURT, Katharine Newlin (Mrs. Struthers) *See* Jackson Hole Preserve.

BURWELL, Sidney. *Discussed in* Edward D. Churchill.

BUSE, Henry W., Jr. (1912–   ) *See* Marine Corps.

BUSH, Prescott (1895–1972) Banker, Senator.
EISENHOWER ADMINISTRATION
Yale; WWI; early business experience; investment banking; W. A. Harriman & Co., 1926–31, Brown Brothers Harriman, from 1931, role of private banking; early political activities, Republican Party in Connecticut; Senator, 1952–62: committees, legislation, Randall Commission on tariff and trade; campaign of 1956, development of Republican platform; impressions of President Eisenhower, John Foster Dulles, Senators Robert A. Taft and Joseph McCarthy; Averell Harriman, Robert Roosa.
454 pp. *Permission required to cite or quote.* 1966.

BUSH, Vannevar (1890–1974) Administrator, engineer.
CARNEGIE CORPORATION
Discussion of Carnegie Institution of Washington and Carnegie Corporation of New York, 1939–55.
58 pp. *Permission required.* 1967.

BUSINESS AND INDUSTRY *See* Frank W. Abrams; James M. Barker; Benedum and the Oil Industry; Roger Blough; John Carmody; Guido Clutterbuck; Continental Group; Lewis B. Cullman; Donald W. Douglas; James B. Duke Project; Charles Edison; Federated Department Stores; Forest History Society; J. Paul Getty; Edwin T. Gibson; Carl Henrikson, Jr.; Paul G. Hoffman; John K. Jenney; Nicholas Kelley; Goddard Lieberson; William Lusk; Anthony C. McAuliffe; Dennis O'Rourke; Marjorie Merriweather Post; Louis Rabinowitz; Morris S. Rosenthal; Felice Schwartz; Bernard (Toots) Shor; Hokan B. Steffanson; Weyerhaeuser Timber Company; Eugene E. Wilson; Robert E. Wood.

BUTLER, Nicholas Murray. *Discussed in* Boris Bakhmeteff; Adolf A. Berle; Nicholas

Murray Butler Project; Carnegie Corporation; Frederic R. Coudert; Malcolm W. Davis; Frank D. Fackenthal; James Gutmann; Alvin Johnson; William H. Kilpatrick; Marjorie Nicolson; Lindsay Rogers; William J. Schieffelin; Constance M. Winchell.

NICHOLAS MURRAY BUTLER PROJECT
This series of interviews provides a general view of Columbia University during the Butler administration, 1902–45, and specific recollections of Nicholas Murray Butler as President.
    Participants and pages: Virginia Gildersleeve, 8; Philip M. Hayden, 11; Carlton J.H.Hayes, 23; Isadore Mudge, 50; E. Berthol Sayre, 16; Eugene Sheffer, 55; James T. Shotwell, 23.
    186 pp. *Open.* 1955–71.

BUTLER, Richard Austen (1902–   ) Statesman.
Recollections of Sir Winston Churchill, his speeches.
    9 pp. *Open.* 1971. *Contributed by Benjamin D. Wood, New York.*

BUTLER, Richard C. (1910–   ) *See* Eisenhower Administration. *Micro IV.*

BUTLER, Smedley. *Discussed in* Merwin H. Silverthorn.

BUTZ, Earl Lauer (1909–   ) Government official.
Eisenhower Administration
Assistant Secretary of Agriculture, 1954–57; programs of the Department of Agriculture, and relations with Congress and other departments; impressions of Ezra Taft Benson and President Eisenhower.
    51 pp. *Permission required to cite or quote.* 1968. *Micro III.*

BUXMAN, William (1884–1954) *See* McGraw-Hill.

BYRD, Harry, Sr. *Discussed in* Virginius Dabney.

BYRD, Richard. *Discussed in* Richard B. Black.

BYRNES, James F. *Discussed in* William Benton; Chester Bowles; Lucius D. Clay; Will Clayton; William H. Davis; Marvin Jones; Eugene Meyer; James P. Warburg.

BYRNES, John W. (1913–   ) *See* Social Security. *Micro III.*

C

CABELL, Charles Pearre (1903–1971) *See* Henry H. Arnold Project.

CABELL, Charles Pearre and Haywood S. Hansell. *See* Air Force Academy.

CABONA, Andres(1899–   )Labor leader.
Argentina
Joined union of wicker workers, 1917; official in various labor organizations, 1922– 55; development of unions, 1930's: percentage of workers organized, political tendencies and influences, personalities; relations of labor movement with different administrations; formation and internal organization of General Confederation of Workers; effects of unemployment and Depression, 1930's and '40's; workers in petroleum industry; factionalism.
    116 pp. *Open.* 1970.

CAESAR, Irving (1895–) *See* Popular Arts.

CAGE, John. *Discussed in* Otto Luening.

CAGNEY, James (1904–) *See* Popular Arts.

CAHILL, Holger (1893–1960) Writer, art director.
Early life in North Dakota, wanderings and odd jobs; arrival in NYC, newspaper work, Greenwich Village; NY art world in the 1920's; folk art; Americana; collecting; Mrs. John D. Rockefeller, Jr.; politics in art; the Depression; relief of artists; Federal Arts Project; NY World's Fair, art, especially abstract expressionism, since 1943. Memoir includes brief interviews with Dorothy Canning Miller (Mrs. Cahill) and Clair Laning.
622 pp. *Permission required to cite or quote.* 1957. *Micro II.*

CAHILL, Kevin. *Discussed in* Lawrence C. Kolb.

CAHOON, Herbert (1918–) *See* Rare Books (A).

CAKE, Ralph Harlan (1891–1973) Executive.
EISENHOWER ADMINISTRATION
Experience in law and finance in Oregon; Republican National Committee, 1940; conventions of 1940, 1944, 1948; detailed description of National Committee meeting and convention of 1952; campaign; citizens' groups; impressions of Gen. Eisenhower, Sherman Adams, Robert Taft, and other political figures; Panama Canal Company.
78 pp. *Permission required to cite or quote.* 1969. *Micro III.*

CALDERONE, Mary Steichen (1904–)
See Women's History and Population Issues.
Discussed in Charles Ascher; Emily Hartshorne Mudd.

CALDWELL, Cyril C. *See* Aviation Project.

CALDWELL, Orestes Hampton (1888–1967) *See* Radio Pioneers.

CALLAHAM, John (1911–) *See* McGraw-Hill.

CALVIN, Melvin (1911–) *See* Nobel Laureates.

CAMERMAN, Felix. *See* Aviation Project

CAMERON, Allan (1903–) *See* Continental Group.

CAMERON, D. Angus (1908–) Editor, publisher.
Childhood and education, rural Indiana; DePauw University, 1930; editor: Bobbs-Merrill Co., 1935–38, Little, Brown & Co., 1938–51; Massachusetts Progressive Party, Henry Wallace campaign, 1948; break with Little, Brown; appearances before Senate committees, House Un-American Activities Committee; establishment of private publishing house in Adirondacks, 1953; Cameron and Kahn, later Cameron Associates, Liberty Book Club; Alfred A. Knopf, Inc., senior editor, 1959, trip to Russia; anecdotes on publishing history, publishing and literary figures including Alfred McIntyre, Alfred and Blanche Knopf, Thomas Mann, C.S. Forester, Ogden Nash, Norman Mailer.
640 pp. *Permission required.* 1977.

CAMERON, Peter. *See* Vietnam Veterans.

CAMERON, William M. (1908–) *See* Continental Group.

CAMIL, Scott. *See* Vietnam Veterans.

CAMP, W.B. *Discussed in* Cully A. Cobb.

CAMPBELL, Douglas (1896–) *See* Aviation Project. *Micro II.*

CAMPBELL, Hugh B. *See* Weyerhaeuser Timber Company.

CAMPBELL, James Winchester (1903–) Foundation executive.
CARNEGIE CORPORATION
Associations with the Carnegie Corporation in 1925 and 1928–29; sale of US Steel

bonds; accountant for Corporation, 1933; impressions of the Treasurer's office and other parts of the Corporation, fiscal matters; Assistant Treasurer, 1953; Treasurer, 1961; the role of the treasurer in a foundation. Impressions of various foundation personalities.
151 pp. *Permission required.* 1967.

CAMPBELL, Loraine Leeson (1905–) *See* Women's History and Population Issues.

CAMPBELL, Russell. *See* Vietnam Veterans.

CANBY, Henry Seidel (1878–1961) *See* Book-of-the-Month Club.

CANE, Melville Henry (1879–) Lawyer, poet.
Columbia University, 1900; legal practice specializing in copyright and publishing matters; recollections of Sinclair Lewis, John Erskine, Thomas Wolfe, Harry Houdini; commentary on writing poetry.
83 pp. *Permission required to cite or quote.* 1956. *Micro I.*

CANEPA, Enrique. *See* Argentina.

CANFIELD, Cass (1897–) Publisher.
Early youth, education, NY and abroad; Harvard; graduate study at Oxford, 1920; walked Burma Road, 1920; Harper & Bros. president from 1932; crossing on *Hindenburg,* 1936; interview with Leon Trotsky, 1940; BEW; OWI, 1944; International Planned Parenthood Federation; history of Harper's and comprehensive discussion of publishing; anecdotes about many notable literary and political figures including Edith Wharton, Julian and Aldous Huxley, Edna St. Vincent Millay, Franklin and Eleanor Roosevelt, Adlai Stevenson, Sumner Welles, and Jacqueline Kennedy.
417 pp. *Permission required to cite or quote.* 1966. *Micro II.*
Discussed in Beulah Hagen; Evan Thomas II.

CANFIELD, Charles C. *See* Air Force Academy.

CANNELLA, Leonard G. (1907–) *See* Continental Group.

CANNON, Charles A. (1892–1971) *See* James B. Duke Project.

CANNON, John D. *See* Columbia Crisis of 1968.

CANNON, Walter. *Discussed in* Joseph C. Aub.

CANTRIL, Hadley. *Discussed in* Paul F. Lazarsfeld.

CAPERS, Roberta. Fine arts consultant.
CARNEGIE CORPORATION
Arts adviser for Carnegie Corporation, 1926–34: studies in Europe, 1925–26, College arts sets, arts fellowships; Metropolitan Museum; American Federation of Arts; museum programs; chairman of Arts Department, Tulane College. Impressions of Frederick Keppel, Morse Cartwright, Robert Lester, and other Corporation officials.
124 pp. *Permission required.* 1967.

CAPONE, Al. *Discussed in* Edwin A. Lahey.

CAPOTE, Truman. *Discussed in* Phyllis Cerf Wagner.

CAPPA, Joseph D. *See* Radio Pioneers.

CAPRA, Frank (1897–) *See* Popular Arts. *Micro II.*
Discussed in Samson Raphaelson; Albert E. Sutherland.

CARADONTI, Andres. *See* Argentina.

CARALEY, Demetrios (1932–) *See* New York Political Studies (B).

CARBAJAL, Celestino. *See* Argentina.

CARDON, Philip Vincent (1889–1965) Agriculturist.
Childhood and education; Nephi, Utah, Agricultural Station, 1909–14; cotton investigations and dry-land agriculture, 1914–18; Montana State Agricultural College and Experiment Stations, 1918–21; Utah State Agricultural College, *Utah Farmer,* Utah

Agricultural Experiment Station, 1921–34; subsistence homesteads, land-use planning, 1934–35; Bureau of Plant Industry, 1935–42; Agricultural Research Administration, 1942–44; FAO; Department of Agriculture Graduate School, 1946–52.

806 pp. *Permission required to cite or quote. 1952. Micro I.*

CARDOZO, Benjamin. *Discussed in* Frederic R. Coudert; James M. Landis; John L. O'Brian.

CARELLI, Gabor (1915–   ) Opera singer.
HUNGARIAN PROJECT
Voice studies, Budapest and with Beniamino Gigli in Italy, 1936–39; reminiscences of Gigli; 1939 immigration to US; touring with American Civic Opera Company; house tenor with Dallas Symphony; Metropolitan Opera, 1951; precision and expression in opera; feasibility of television and radio broadcast opera; original language vs. translation.

119 pp. *Permission required to cite or quote. 1975.*

CAREY, James Barron (1911–1973) Labor executive.
Early experiences in the Philco plant in Philadelphia; formative years of the United Electrical, Radio and Machine Workers; CIO; labor and New Deal; Communist Party and the labor movement; Secretary of the CIO; formation of WFTU; London and San Francisco labor conferences, 1945; merger of AFL and CIO.

352 pp. *Permission required to cite or quote. 1958. Micro II.*
Discussed in Edwin A. Lahey; Lee Pressman.

CAREY, Lee A. (1917–   ) *See* Continental Group.

CARLE, Albert H. (1892–   ) *See* Continental Group.

CARLIN, Phillips (1894–1971) *See* Radio Pioneers.

CARLISLE, Henry (–1964) *See* Mining Engineers.

CARLSON, James V. (1916–   ) *See* Continental Group.

CARLTON, Richard L. (1903–   ) *See* Continental Group.

CARLTON, Winslow. *See* Social Security. *Micro III.*

CARMAN, Harry James (1884–1964) Educator.
Board of Higher Education, NYC, 1938–61: practices and policy, budgets, relationships with city and state administrations, problems of tenure, day and evening sessions; Russell case; Rapp-Coudert Committee and Strayer committee; impressions of Mayors Fiorello La Guardia, William O'Dwyer, and Robert F. Wagner.

221 pp. *Permission required to cite or quote. 1961. Micro IV.*

CARMEN, Arlene (1936–   ) *See* Women's History and Population Issues.

CARMICHAEL, Oliver C. *Discussed in* Carnegie Corporation.

CARMODY, John Michael (1881–1963) Administrator.
Family background and description of life in northern Pennsylvania and upstate NY at the turn of the century; education and early work experiences as a steel inspector; later as an executive in the garment industry and coal mining industry; editor-in-chief successively of *Coal Age* and *Factory & Industrial Management* for the McGraw-Hill Publishing Company; detailed account of service in government: Civil Works Administration, FERA, National Defense Mediation Board, NLRB, REA, President's Power Policy Committee, the Cabinet-rank position as head of the Federal Works Agency (encompassing PWA, WPA, USHA, Bureau of Public Roads, Bureau of Public Buildings, Fine Arts Commission, and Lanham Act Defense Housing Program), US Maritime Commission, Maritime War Emergency Board, and Federal Interdepartmental Safety Council.

763 pp. *Permission required to cite or quote. 1954. Microfiche copies available.*

CARNEGIE, Andrew. *Discussed in* Carnegie Corporation; Burton J. Hendrick.

CARNEGIE, Mrs. Andrew. *Discussed in* Carnegie Corporation.

CARNEGIE CORPORATION

This project traces the first 58 years of Andrew Carnegie's central philanthropic organization. Officers, staff members, and grant recipients discuss its work in adult education, area studies, art education, cognitive research, education testing, library science, music education, national security, social science research, teacher education, and other areas. The Corporation's relations with other Carnegie institutions over the years are delineated in many memoirs. Others detail its own administrative history, as well as its relations with other major foundations and with the federal government. Still others trace the work of independent agencies which originally received all or part of their funds from the foundation. In general, the design was to provide comprehensive and candid information about the foundation, its work, and those who have served its end, "to promote the advancement and diffusion of knowledge and understanding."

The material is rich in personal recollections of grantees and members of the Corporation's board and staff. Prominent among them are James R. Angell, James Bertram, Nicholas Murray Butler, Oliver C. Carmichael, Robert Franks, Walter Jessup, Nicholas Kelley, Frederick Paul Keppel, Clyde Kluckhohn, Thomas W. Lamont, William S. Learned, Russell C. Leffingwell, Arthur Page, Henry Pritchett, Elihu Root and Elihu Root, Jr., Beardsley Ruml, James E. Russell, William F. Russell, Whitney H. Shepardson, Irvin Stewart, and Samuel A. Stouffer.

There is a comprehensive index.

Participants and pages: Florence Anderson, 656; Geoffrey Andrew, 64; Clarence Beeby, 89; Bernard Berelson, 119; Karl Bigelow, 138; Paul Buck, 87; Frederick H. Burckhardt, 84; W. Randolph Burgess, 50; Vannevar Bush, 58; James W. Campbell, 151; Roberta Capers, 124; Morse Cartwright, 242; Henry Chauncey, 88; Eric Clarke, 76; James B. Conant, 88; Lawrence

Cremin, 107; Cornelis de Kiewiet, 117; Rene d'Harnoncourt, 65; Harold W. Dodds, 70; Charles Dollard, 329; Katherine Ford, 61; William T. R. Fox, 97; John W. Gardner, 221;

Morris Hadley, 84; Samuel S. Hall, Jr., 115; Caryl P. Haskins, 251; Edward Pendleton Herring, 129; Alger Hiss, 67; Alice Hoctor, 48; Kenneth Holland, 35; John C. Honey, 82; Robert Hoppock, 49; Everett C. Hughes, 43; Frederick Jackson, 305; Guion G. Johnson, 67; Guy B. Johnson, 64; Joseph Johnson, 50; Devereux C. Josephs, 150; Francis Keppel, 61; Eric Larrabee, 89; Robert M. Lester, 872; R. McAllister Lloyd, 67; Trevor Lloyd, 45; Dorothy R. Loemker, 73;

Thomas R. McConnell, 86; Constance McCue, 60; Earl McGrath, 107; Margaret Mahoney, 86; Ernst G. Malherbe, 68; William Marvel, 278; Lloyd Morrisett, 214; Lois Murkland, 24; Gunnar Myrdal, 122; Isabelle C. Neilson, 42; Frederick Osborn, 140; G. Raleigh Parkin, 152; Talcott Parsons, 41; James Perkins, 64; Alan Pifer, 273; Alan Pifer and Eli Evans, 149; David Riesman, 84; John Russell, 290; Frederick Sheffield, 61; Arthur Singer, 138; Harold Spivacke, 76; Stephen Stackpole, 398; Ralph Tyler, 139; Robert E. Ward, 81; Robertson D. Ward, 49; Bethuel Webster, 25; Robert J. Wert, 200; Benjamin D. Wood, 123; John E. F. Wood, 52; Henry Wriston, 219; Donald Young, 180.

9,948 pp. *Permission required.* 1966–70. *Underwritten by the Carnegie Corporation.*

CARNEY, Robert Bostwick (1895–   ) Naval officer.
Family background, Naval Academy, 1916; first cruises, assignments; WWI convoying; navigation instructor, Naval Academy, 1923–24; Interior Control Board manual, 1928; Orange Plan and naval preparedness, 1940; Adm. Arthur Bristol, organization of Support Force Operation; North Atlantic convoy duty; Chief of Staff, Adm. William Halsey, South Pacific theater: strategy, operations, logistics, personalities, problems; theater of war approach, Adm. Chester Nimitz, Gen. Douglas MacArthur; 3d Fleet operations, Central Pacific; Leyte Gulf and China Sea,

1945; British participation; Japan's defeat and surrender; Deputy Chief of Naval Operations for Logistics, 1946–50; computers; War College, problems of command and staff training, postwar Navy; unification of services, 1947; impressions of many military figures.

768 pp. *Closed until July 1, 1989.* 1964.

CARNOVSKY, Morris (1897–   ) *See* Popular Arts.

CARON, George (1919–   ) *See* Air Force Academy.

CARPENDER, Arthur. *Discussed in* James Fife.

CARPENTER, Charles I. (1906–   ) *See* Air Force Academy.

CARPENTER, Edmund. *See* Robert J. Flaherty Project.

CARPENTER, Mrs. John. *See* Adlai E. Stevenson Project.

CARR, William George (1901–   ) Educator.
UN Conference, San Francisco; UNESCO; various international teachers' associations; NEA.

31 pp. *Permission required to cite or quote.* 1961. *Micro II.*
Discussed in John K. Norton.

CARREL, Alexis. *Discussed in* Frederic R. Coudert.

CARREL, Clarence E. (1901–   ) *See* Continental Group.

CARSON, Clarence. *Discussed in* William T. Couch.

CARSON, John. *Discussed in* Maurine Mulliner.

CARSON, Mrs. Joseph. *See* Independence Park.

CARSTENSON, Blue.
SOCIAL SECURITY
Technical director for education for aging at HEW, 1959; chairman of the technical directors for the White House Conference on Aging; staff member of the Democratic National Committee; Executive Director, National Council of Senior Citizens, 1961–65; Legislative Representative, National Farmers Union, 1965–72; organizing senior citizens; efforts toward medical legislation; impressions of Ivan Nestingen, Abraham Ribicoff.

227 pp. *Permission required to cite or quote.* 1966. *Micro IV.* Papers.
Discussed in Ray Henry; James C. O'Brien; Charles Odell.

CARTER, Hodding (1907–1972) *See* Journalism Lectures (C).

CARTWRIGHT, Morse Adams (1890–1974) Educational administrator.
CARNEGIE CORPORATION
Assistant to Frederick Keppel at the Carnegie Corporation, 1924–26; developing a program; policies; trustees and staff; studies at the Rockefeller Foundation; adult education; American Association for Adult Education; executive director, Des Moines Experiment; leisure programs; the Association's relationship with the Carnegie Corporation; TC; comments on grants through the years. Impressions of Frederick Keppel, Walter Jessup, Devereux Josephs, and other Corporation officials.

242 pp. *Permission required.* 1967.
Discussed in Roberta Capers; Trevor Lloyd; John M. Russell.

CARY, Edward K. *See* Thomas A. Edison Project.

CASHMORE, John. *Discussed in* New York Political Studies (A).

CASSAVETES, John (1929–   ) *See* Popular Arts.

CASTELLI, Leo (1907–   ) *See* New York's Art World.

CASTELLI, Leo and Roy Lichtenstein. *See* New York's Art World.

CASTELLI, Leo and James Rosenquist. *See* New York's Art World.

CASTLE, Benjamin. *See* Henry H. Arnold Project.

CASTLE, William. *Discussed in* Leslie C. Dunn.

CASTRO, Fidel (1927–   ) Revolutionary leader.
Recordings of several speeches in Spanish, followed by a series of tape-recorded interviews in English (with the aid of an interpreter). The interviews cover a range of subjects on Cuba: agricultural policy, especially the sugar industry, land use, and people's farms; economy in general and foreign trade, future potentialities; revolutionary philosophy, how the Communist revolution worked in different regions, political prisoners and indemnification; local government organizations; questions of leadership, nature and use of power; education, creative arts, voluntary exiles and counter-revolutionaries; relations with the US: Vietnam, Dominican Republic; missile crisis; US press; relations with Russia.
381 pp. *Permission required.* 1965. *Contributed by Lee Lockwood, Boston, Massachusetts.*
Discussed in James Barco; Charles Cook; Leo Cherne; Milton Eisenhower; Thomas C. Mann; Ray Rubottom, Jr.

CASWELL, Hollis (1901–   ) Educator.
Family, education; experiences as graduate student at TC; consultant to southern state departments of education, General Education Board; school surveys, curricula, national associations; return to TC, 1937–62: head of department of curriculum and teaching, 1937–47, director, division of instruction, 1938–50, President, 1954–62; relations with Fund for Advancement of Education and Carnegie Corporation; teaching as a profession, teachers' unions, trustees, administration; travel; consultant to *World Book Encyclopedia;* retirement. Vignettes of James Russell and William Russell, Professor George Strayer, James B. Conant and many others in education.
262 pp. *Permission required to cite or quote.* 1969. *Micro II.*

CATES, Clifton Bledsoe (1893–1970) Marine Corps officer.
Education; WWI; aide to Commandant

Marine Corps and CG, Department of the Pacific, 1920–23; China, 1929–32; War Plans Division, 1935–37; Shanghai, 1937–39, Sino-Japanese War; Army War College: wartime training program; President, USMC Equipment Board and Commandant, USMC Schools, 1947; USMC Commandant, 1948–51, unification fight; Korea; USO.
254 pp. *Open.* 1967.
Discussed in John H. Masters.

CATES, Louis Shattuck (1881–1959) *See* Mining Engineers.

CATHER, Willa. *Discussed in* Alfred A. Knopf.

CATLEDGE, Turner (1901–   ) *See* American Cultural Leaders.

CAVANAUGH, Robert William (1914–   ) *See* World Bank.

CELLER, Emmanuel (1888–   ) *See* Herbert H. Lehman Project.

CEREIJO, Ramon A. *See* Argentina.

CERF, Bennett Alfred (1898–1971) Publisher.
Childhood and education in NYC; Columbia College: *Spectator, Jester;* journalism; Wall Street; Boni & Liveright; purchase of Modern Library; partnership with Donald Klopfer; travels and meetings with European authors; marriage to Sylvia Sidney; trip to Russia; building up Random House: contacts with authors, editors, other publishers; marriage to Phyllis Fraser; WWII publishing; *Try and Stop Me* and later books; magazine columns, radio programs, lecture tours; paperbacks, reprints, Bantam books; "What's My Line?"; role of an editor in a publishing house; dictionary and its promotion; purchase of other publishing houses: Singer, Knopf; stock issue, going public, 1959; purchase by RCA, 1965; educational developments, teaching machines; juvenile lists; spurt of growth in all publishing after WWII; purchase of Pantheon; foreign contacts; Peabody Awards Committee; director of MGM; Miss America pageant; Famous Writers School; many anecdotes about well

known personalities in literary and entertainment fields.
  1,029 pp. *Permission required.* 1968.
Discussed in Donald Klopfer; Phyllis Cerf Wagner.

CERF, Christopher and Jonathan. *Discussed in* Phyllis Cerf Wagner.

CHADBOURNE, William Merriam (1879–1964) *See* Theodore Roosevelt Association.

CHADWICK, Howard B. and Anthony J. Civitello. *See* Continental Group.

CHAMBERLAIN, Clarence (1893–1976) *See* Aviation Project.

CHAMBERLAIN, Owen (1920–   ) *See* Nobel Laureates.

CHAMBERLAIN, Thomas Gassner (1892–1978) Lawyer.
Law career; experiences with William H. Taft, 1919–20; Herbert Hoover campaign in California, 1920; Pro-League Republicans' campaign for James M. Cox; Finance Committee of the Republican Party.
  181 pp. *Closed until May 9, 1983.* 1951.

CHAMBERLIN, Waldo (1905–   ) Historian.
UN Conference, San Francisco, 1945; Preparatory Commission, London, 1945; Secretariat, NY, 1945–48.
  112 pp. *Permission required to cite or quote.* 1952. *Micro II.*

CHAMBERS, Reed. *See* Aviation Project. *Micro II.*

CHAMBERS, Whittaker. *Discussed in* Max Gissen; Alger Hiss.

CHANDLER, George Fletcher (1872–1964) Surgeon, penologist.
Early life, medical research; organization of NY State Police Force, 1919–1926; Governors Charles S. Whitman and Alfred E. Smith; Lackawanna steel strike; NY State Police School; Auburn prison riots.
  113 pp. *Open.* 1950.

CHANDLER, Harry. *Discussed in* Donald W. Douglas.

CHANG Fa-k'uei. *See* Chinese Oral History.

CHAPIN, Emerson. *See* International Negotiations.

CHAPIN, Emily (1916–   ) Pilot.
Early pilot training in New York; British Air Transport Auxiliary, 1942–44; freelance ferrying in New York, 1944; impressions of Women's Air Service Pilots training; experiences as woman pilot.
  52 pp. *Open.* 1977.

CHAPIN, Schuyler Garrison (1923–   ) Music administrator.
Family background; aviation cadet, China-Burma theater, 1943–45; NBC radio, TV, 1947–51; general manager, Tex and Jinx McCrary, 1950–52; booking director, Columbia Artists' Management; tour manager for Jascha Heifetz, 1952–56; Community Concert Subscription system, NBC Opera Co., 1959–63; Vice-President, programming at Lincoln Center, 1964–69; executive producer, Amberson Enterprises, 1969–71; Goeran Gentele's death; acting general manager Metropolitan Opera, 1972–73; general manager, 1973–75; impressions of past and present Metropolitan directors, performers' temperaments, structures and conflicts of artistic administration; productions, daily schedule, fund-raising, labor negotiations. Impressions of performers, impresarios, particularly Leonard Bernstein, Herbert Von Karajan, Rudolph Bing, Franco Corelli, Anthony Bliss.
  783 pp. *Permission required to cite or quote.* 1977.

CHAPLIN, Charlie. *Discussed in* Albert E. Sutherland.

CHAPMAN, Alger Baldwin (1904–   ) Lawyer.
NY Republican politics, 1930–49.
  76 pp. *Closed during lifetime.* 1949.
See also New York Political Studies (C).

CHAPPELL, Warren (1904–   ) Artist, book designer.
Family background; childhood in Virginia; study and teaching at Art Students League, NYC, 1926–35; promotional art director, *Liberty* magazine, 1928–31; study with Ru-

dolf Koch, 1931; assistant to Boardman Robinson, Colorado Springs, 1935–36; juvenile book illustration; design of Trajanus and Lydian typefaces; book design for Alfred Knopf, George Macy, Book-of-the-Month Club, 1940 on; *A Short History of the Printed Word,* 1970; Oscar Ogg.
403 pp. *Permission required to cite or quote.* 1978.

CHARLTON, Lillian. *See* McGraw-Hill.

CHARTERS, W. W. *Discussed in* W. H. Cowley.

CHASE, Mary Ellen. *Discussed in* Marjorie Nicolson.

CHASE, Harry W. *Discussed in* William T. Couch.

CHASE, William. *Discussed in* Edwin Dickinson.

CHASINS, Abram (1903–   ) *See* Radio Pioneers. *Micro II.*

CHATELAIN, Nicolas (1913–1976) Journalist.
Experiences as US correspondent for *Le Figaro;* comments upon coverage of the US by the press of Europe; Presidential press conferences; trip to Russia; comparison of US and European journalism.
55 pp. *Open.* 1961.

CHAUNCEY, Henry (1905–   ) *See* Carnegie Corporation.

CHEEVER, John. *Discussed in* S. Michael Bessie.

CHEN, Theodore. *See* International Negotiations.

CH'EN Kuang-fu (K.P. Chen) *See* Chinese Oral History.

CH'EN Li-fu. *See* Chinese Oral History.

CHENNAULT, Anna and Thomas Corcoran. *See* Flying Tigers.

CHENNAULT, Claire. *Discussed in* John R. Alison; Flying Tigers; Paul W. Frillman.

CHERNE, Leo (1912–   ) Economist, political analyst.
Childhood and education, NYC; New York Law School; Depression and rise of leftist movements; Research Institute of America; figures and policies of Dwight D. Eisenhower Administration; 1960 presidential campaign; International Rescue Committee in Germany, Hungary, Vietnam; US policy toward Vietnam; Cuba under Fidel Castro. Impressions of Senator Joseph McCarthy, President Ngo Dinh Diem, Gen. Douglas MacArthur, Dr. Tom Dooley.
590 pp. *Closed during lifetime.* 1961.

CHEVALIER, Willard Townshend (1886–1961) Editor, publisher.
MCGRAW-HILL
Early training and occupations; joined *Engineering News-Record* as associate editor, 1922; formation of McGraw-Hill Publishing Company; evolution of various trade magazines; administration and policies of McGraw-Hill; impressions of James H. McGraw.
129 pp. *Permission required.* 1953.

CHIANG Kai-Shek. *Discussed in* Walter H. Judd, Thomas C. Kinkaid; George Sokolsky; William A. Worton.

CHIAPPE, Wayne T. (1924–   ) *See* Continental Group.

CHIDLAW, Benjamin W. (1900–   ) *See* Air Force Academy.

CHILDREN *See* Association for the Aid of Crippled Children; Agnes Burke; Children's Television Workshop; Kenneth Clark; Mamie Clark; Martha May Eliot; Charlotte Garrison; Dorothy Gordon; Willi Hoffer; Katharine Lenroot; Margaret Mahler; May Massee; Edith Miller; Lucy Sprague Mitchell; Henry Mulhearn; Helenka Pantaleoni; Vincent Riccio; Joseph Sandler; Charles I. Schottland.

CHILDREN'S TELEVISION WORKSHOP
This series of interviews traces the development of the Children's Television Workshop and the creation of "Sesame Street" in the words of some of those principally re-

sponsible. They recall 1966 discussions of how television might be made to serve preschool children, preliminary studies, the roles of the Carnegie Corporation, of Harold Howe II as US Commissioner of Education, and of the Ford Foundation in advancing the concept and helping to finance it, the founding of the Workshop and its staffing, and the emergence of the Sesame Street format, as well as the changing relationship of the Workshop with National Educational Television, from which it became independent.

Participants and pages: David Connell, 33; Joan Cooney, 24; Robert Davidson, 36; Barbara Finberg, 11; Louis Hausman, 21; Edward Meade, 14; Lloyd Morrisett, 12; John White, 13.

164 pp. *Permission required to cite or quote.* 1972. *Most of the memoirs are available in microform; consult individual entries.*

Contributed by Richard M. Polsky, New York.

CHILDS, John. *Discussed in* William H. Kilpatrick.

CHILDS, Marquis William (1903–   ) Journalist.
Education and early work on the St. Louis *Post-Dispatch;* impressions of Chicago and St. Louis journalists; coverage of the 1936 presidential campaign; impressions of members of the Supreme Court: Robert H. Jackson, Harlan Stone, and Felix Frankfurter.

132 pp. *Permission required to cite or quote.* 1958. *Micro I.*
See also Adlai E. Stevenson Project. *Micro IV.*

CHILDS, Richard Spencer (1882–1978) Businessman, civic worker.
Growth of the city manager plan of government; short ballot movement; Citizens Union.

48 pp. *Permission required to cite or quote.* 1950. *Micro II.*

Experiences with National Municipal League, City Club; NYC politics since 1902.

78 pp. *Permission required to cite or quote.* 1975.

CHILSON, O. Hatfield. (1903–   ) *See* Eisenhower Administration.

CHINA *See* Hilda Anderson; China Missionaries; Chinese Oral History; Paul W. Frillman; L. Carrington Goodrich; John B. Grant; Nelson T. Johnson; Walter H. Judd; Harry L. Kingman; Brij Mohan Kaul; Marine Corps; Walter S. Robertson; Frank W. Rounds, Jr.; Helen F. Snow; George E. Sokolsky.

CHINA MISSIONARIES
The Oral History Program at Claremont Graduate School, Claremont, California launched a project to assess the influence of the China missionary movement, 1900–50. Christian workers of various denominations give their recollections of conditions and experiences in China; they include educators, medical administrators, teachers, ministers, authors, and translators. The accounts deal with local conditions in urban and rural China and interaction between American residents and Chinese communities. A few interviews with China missionaries, conducted by the Columbia Oral History Office, are included also.

Participants and pages: Merrill S. Ady, 97; Netta P. Allen, 83; John N. Andrews, 31; James C. Baker, 26; Homer V. Bradshaw, 54; George Chalmers Browne, 83; Earl Cranston, 127; Mildred W. Cranston, 78; Rowland McLean Cross, 200; Helen Dizney, 23; Leslie and Mary Fairfield, 75; Cyril Faulkner, 52; Glen V. Fuller, 24; Oswald J. Goulter, 44; Edward P. Hayes, 23; Egbert M. Hayes, 39; Alfred D. Heininger, 62; Clarence H. Holleman, 95; Lyda S. Houston, 79; Ethel L. Hylbert, 31; Ernest L. Ikenberry, 32;
Lydia Johnson, 36; Francis P. Jones, 65; Lucille W. Jones, 46; Claude R. Kellogg, 27; Mary L. Latimer, 44; John J. Loftus, 49; James H. McCallum, 26; Sr. Mary Colmcille McCormick, 28; William S. Morton, 41; Jay C. Oliver, 27; Alice C. Reed, 122; Grace M. Rowley, 52; Agnes Scott, 53; Roderick Scott, 113; Margaret T. Simkin, 62; Lewis S. C. Smythe, 114; Margaret G. Smythe 82; Louise H. Stanley, 83; Marjorie R. Steurt, 127; F. Olin Stockwell, 46; George T. Tootell, 31; William H. Topping, 23; Katherine Ward, 90; Martha Wiley,

106; Eleutherius Winance, 125; Pearl F. Winans, 47;

2,941 pp. *Open.* 1969–76.

Underwritten by the Henry Luce Foundation of New York.

CHINESE ORAL HISTORY

In 1958 Professors Franklin L. Ho and C. Martin Wilbur formulated a project within the East Asian Institute of Columbia University to record the oral recollections of prominent Chinese leaders of the Republican era, 1911–49. In the ensuing two decades seventeen outstanding figures have devoted hundreds of hours to compiling oral records of their careers. These have been transcribed, translated, researched, and edited to produce memoirs for use by scholars interested in this half-century of Chinese history. Many are accompanied by private papers. The memoirs represent the lives of men who played major roles in Republican China in such capacities as Acting President, Vice President, Ambassador to the UN, Ambassador to the US and other countries, Minister of Foreign Affairs, Commanders in the National Revolutionary Army, mayors of the capitals in WWII, governors of provinces divided by the Sino-Japanese War and by civil war, philosopher and spokesman for the Literary Revolution, financier, industrialist, educator, founders of a new political party opposed to and outlawed by both the Chinese Communist Party and the Kuomintang, and activists in the Third Force.

Many attended American universities and returned to China bringing modern attitudes to the still traditional society. Their detailed reminiscences help clarify hitherto confused areas of scholarly inquiry: the historian, sociologist, literary historian, economist, and political scientist will find a wealth of material for research. Most of the private papers are in Chinese.

Participants and pages: Chang Fa-k'uei, ca. 1,000 *(closed);* Ch'en Kuang-fu (K.P. Chen), 167; Ch'en Li-fu *(in process);* Jun-ke Choy, 341; Franklin L. Ho, 450; Hu Shih, 295; Shen I-yun Huang, 489; V.K. Wellington Koo, ca. 11,000; H.H. Kung, 147; Li Han-hun, 239 *(certain pages closed);* Li Huang, 1,013; Li Shu-hua, 243 *(certain pages closed);* Li Tsung-jen, ca. 1,000, 4 vols., 54 chapters; J. Heng Liu, 8 *(closed);* Ting-fu F. Tsiang, 239; Tso Shun-sheng, 489; K.C. Wu, 391.

17,511 pp. *Open except as noted. Descriptions of individual memoirs available on request.* 1958–76. *Some memoirs are available in microform; consult individual entries. Underwritten by the Ford Foundation, NYC, and the National Endowment for the Humanities.*

CHING, Cyrus Stuart (1876–1967) Industrial relations expert.

Labor relations in US, 1914–65; supervisor of industrial relations, US Rubber Co., 1919–47: centralizing personnel policies, factory councils, arbitration, industrial and craft unions; boyhood and education, Prince Edward Island; career with Boston Elevated Railway, 1901–19: air brakes, rapid transit unions, Storrow arbitration board, state receivership; a mediator's qualifications; American Management Association; NAM; US Chamber of Commerce; NLRB; NIRA industrial codes; organization of rubber industry by International Rubber Workers; Bethlehem Steel strike, 1939; 1941 National Defense Mediation Board cases: Allis-Chalmers, North American Aviation, Federal Shipbuilding, Air Associates, mineworkers; closed shop; WLB, 1942–43: Little Steel formula, auto industry; Federal Mediation and Conciliation Service, 1947–52: steel and auto industries, longshoremen, Taft-Hartley Act, General Electric; AEC Labor Relations Panel, 1953–67; Commerce Department Business Advisory Council; 1966 elections; AFL-CIO merger; Wage Stabilization Board, 1950; UMW; effectiveness of wage-price controls. Anecdotes of leaders in industry, labor, and government. Memoir includes a joint interview with Ralph T. Seward, executive secretary of National Defense Mediation Board.

805 pp. *Permission required to cite or quote.* 1967. *Micro II.*

Acquired from Cornell Program in Oral History, Cornell University.

CHISHOLM, Shirley. *Discussed in* Wesley McD. Holder.

CHOATE, Joseph. *Discussed in* Allen Wardwell.

CHOLET, Prosper E. *See* Air Force Academy.

CHORLEY, Kenneth (1893–1974) Conservationist.
JACKSON HOLE PRESERVE
Conservationist activities of John D. Rockefeller, Jr.; the beginning of Jackson Hole Preserve; Robert E. Miller and the buying of land; cattlemen; the Forest Service versus the Park Service; political opposition; the Monument; the hotels; famous guests at Jackson Hole; notes for official reports; impressions of John D. Rockefeller, Jr. and his family.
160 pp. *Permission required.* 1966.

CHOU En-lai. *Discussed in* Walter S. Robertson; William A. Worton

CHOY, Jun-ke. *See* Chinese Oral History.

CHRISTAKIS, George. *See* Mt. Sinai Hospital.

CHRISTIE, Agatha. *Discussed in* S. Phelps Platt.

CHRISTO (1935–   ) and Jean-Claude Christo. *See* New York's Art World.

CHURCH, Ellen. *See* Aviation Project.

CHURCHES *See* Religion.

CHURCHILL, Edward Delos (1895–1972) Surgeon.
Family history and boyhood; education, Northwestern University and Harvard Medical School; clinical training, Faulkner and MGH, 1919–24; techniques of surgery, anesthesiology, and blood transfusion, 1920's; anecdotes of Boston medical profession, 1920–40; observations in European clinics and laboratories, 1926–27; Boston City Hospital, 1929–52; relationship of Harvard teaching hospitals and University; cancer research; Huntington and Vincent Hospitals; medical planning, WWII; Surgical Consultant, North African and Mediterranean Theaters, 1943–46; battle wound management; shock research; debate on plasma use; postwar Veterans Administration; chairman, advisory committee to Secretary of War Robert P. Patterson, 1946;

impressions of colleagues in medicine, education, and government, especially Cecil Drinker, David Edsall, Harvey Cushing, Elliott Cutler, James B. Conant, Henry Beecher, Edwin Cohn, Sidney Burwell, Evarts Graham, Howard Snyder, Michael De Bakey, and Henry L. Stimson.
691 pp. *Permission required to cite or quote.* 1957. Notes, correspondence, supplementary documents interfiled with pages of memoir.
Discussed in Joseph C. Aub.

CHURCHILL, Sir Winston. *Discussed in* Raymond Baldwin; Richard A. Butler; Ira Eaker; William Fechteler; James Hagerty; Livingston T. Merchant; S. Phelps Platt; Sir Robert Watson-Watt; Sir Muhammad Zafrulla Khan.

CIANO, Galeazzo. *Discussed in* Thomas C. Kinkaid.

CILLO, Anthony R. *See* Air Force Academy.

CITIZENS BUDGET COMMISSION. *See* New York Political Studies (B).

CITY PLANNING *See* Urban Development/Housing.

CIVIL RIGHTS *See* Charles Ascher; Roger Baldwin; Albert Blumenthal; Clifford J. Durr; Virginia Durr; Thomas I. Emerson; Osmond K. Fraenkel; Walter Gellhorn; Harry L. Kingman; Edward I. Koch; La Follette Civil Liberties Committee; Corliss Lamont; Alice Paul; Terry Sanford; Edwin Seaver; John Seigenthaler; Socialist Movement; Norman Thomas; Elbert P. Tuttle; Emily Smith Warner; Margaret B. Young. *See also* Blacks—Civil Rights; NAACP.

CIVIL RIGHTS IN ALABAMA
Leaders and participants in the movement at Tuscaloosa, Alabama in 1964 describe clashes with local law enforcement personnel, culminating in the tear gassing of the First Baptist Church. Included are the transcripts of two mass meetings and interviews with residents expressing widely varying attitudes towards the movement.
Participants and pages: Rev. Willie Herzfeld, 39; James Jacquith, 50; George Le

Maistre, 31; Jay Murphy, 20; T. Y. Rogers, 60; Robert Shelton, 59.
259 pp. *Open.* 1964.
Contributed by Harvey Burg, New York.

CIVIL WAR *See* American Historians; Civil War Centennial; Lester A. Dessez; Frederick H. Meserve.

CIVIL WAR CENTENNIAL
Civil War scholars at the final Centennial meeting in Springfield, Illinois discuss sources, problems in historiography, and research experiences in the field.
Participants and pages: Harold M. Hyman, 15; E. B. Long, 53; Bell I. Wiley, 44; T. Harry Williams, 31.
143 pp. *Permission required to cite or quote.* 1965.

CIVITELLO, Anthony J. and Howard B. Chadwick. *See* Continental Group.

CLAGUE, Ewan (1896–   ) Economist.
Education; work at Brookings Institution; New Deal legislation; social security; relationship of Bureau of Labor Statistics to other Federal agencies; Department of Labor under Franklin D. Roosevelt, Harry S. Truman, and Dwight D. Eisenhower; Frances Perkins and subsequent Secretaries of Labor; John Winant, Arthur Altmeyer, Isador Lubin, John Steelman, and others.
468 pp. *Permission required.* 1958.

SOCIAL SECURITY
Student days at University of Wisconsin and relations with John R. Commons; work with Bureau of Employment Security, Social Security Board and development of unemployment insurance; impressions of Frank Bane, John Winant; appointment as Commissioner of Labor Statistics.
152 pp. *Permission required to cite or quote.* 1966. *Micro III.*

CLAIR, Mary F. (1890–   ) *See* Continental Group.

CLAPP, Norton (1906–   ) *See* Weyerhaeuser Timber Company.

CLARK, A.P. *See* Air Force Academy.

CLARK, Mrs. Albert B. *See* Air Force Academy.

CLARK, Grenville (1882–1967) *See* Robert P. Patterson Project.

CLARK, Harold Florian (1899–   ) Educator.
Early education; London School of Economics, 1926–27; teaching, Indiana University, 1923–25, TC, 1928 on; Sloan project in applied economics; work abroad: India, Southeast Asia, South America; consultant to Special Assistant for USAF Academy; political activities; impressions of educators, especially John Dewey and William H. Kilpatrick.
306 pp. *Permission required to cite or quote.* 1963. *Micro II.*

CLARK, J. Reuben. *Discussed in* James T. Williams, Jr.

CLARK, Joseph James (1893–1971) Naval officer.
Early life in Indian Territory; Oklahoma A&M; Naval Academy; WWI convoys and patrols; Turkey; destroyer duty; teaching at Naval Academy; naval aviation; Adm. William Moffett and Gen. William Mitchell; Naval Air Stations; stunt and test flying; relationships with members of Congress; Inspector of Naval Aircraft; early Pacific operations; North African landings; "Fighting Lady," 1943; detailed descriptions of Pacific operations; Task Group Commander, Assistant Chief of Naval Operations for Air; the "Revolt of the Admirals," Korea; Command of 7th Fleet, 1952. Impressions of many military, naval, and political figures, especially Adms. John H. Towers, Ernest King, Chester Nimitz, Arthur Radford, Marc Mitscher, and Raymond Spruance, and Secretaries of the Navy John L. Sullivan and James V. Forrestal.
840 pp. *Permission required.* 1962. Papers.

CLARK, Kenneth Bancroft (1914–   ) Psychologist, educator.
Family background, childhood and education, Howard University, 1936, PhD, Columbia University, 1940; teaching career at City College; with wife Mamie, NAACP

witness on psychological damage of racial segregation; founding of Northside Center for Child Development, 1946; political clashes involving Harlem Youth Opportunities; impressions of Adam Clayton Powell, Malcolm X; *Dark Ghetto,* 1965; establishment of Metropolitan Applied Research Center, 1967; federal and local education commissions; American Psychological Association, 1972, presidential address and aftermath.
In process.

CLARK, Mamie (1917–   ) Child psychologist.
Arkansas childhood; BS, MS, Howard University; PhD., Columbia University, 1946; Riverdale Children's Association; founding of Northside Center, 1946; child psychology with underprivileged urban children; relationship of community and Center; impressions of Adam Clayton Powell.
In process.

CLARK, Mark Wayne (1896–   ) Army officer.
EISENHOWER ADMINISTRATION
Association with Dwight D. Eisenhower at West Point and during WWII; US involvement in Korea; military tactics, negotiations to end Korean War; Eisenhower as President-elect.
91 pp. *Permission required to cite or quote.* 1970.

CLARK, Maud. *See* McGraw-Hill.

CLARK, Thomas Edward (1869–1962).
RADIO PIONEERS
Chicago World's Fair, 1893; Edison General Electric in Schenectady; experiments with wireless; automatic radio train control; police car radios.
38 pp. *Open.* 1951. *Micro IV.*

CLARK, Tom. *See* Poets on their Poetry.

CLARKE, Clem S. (1897–   ) *See* Benedum and the Oil Industry.

CLARKE, Eric. *See* Carnegie Corporation.

CLARKE, Gilmore David (1892–   ) Landscape architect.
Training at Cornell; early work on Bronx

River Parkway; WWI; Westchester County park system; planning parks, parkways, and expressways, 1930's through 1950's; housing projects, including Metropolitan Life Insurance Company; city planning in Portland, Oregon, and Nashville, Tennessee; National Commission of Fine Arts, 1932–50; NYC traffic control report; NY World's Fair, 1939; College of Architecture, Cornell, 1935–50; planning for NY State Power Authority, Naval Academy, Military Academy; UN headquarters; consulting services to universities and colleges.
372 pp. *Permission required to cite or quote.* 1959. Papers and pamphlets.

CLAY, Alexander Stephen. *Discussed in* Lucius D. Clay.

CLAY, Lucius DuBignon (1897–1978) Army officer.
EISENHOWER ADMINISTRATION
Alexander Stephen Clay: political career, US Senate, 1897–1915; Europe, 1919; Marietta, Georgia politics, the Negro vote during early 1900's; West Point, 1914–21, 1924–28; military training, instructorship; beginning of ROTC; assignment to Panama, mapping the terrain; Rivers and Harbors Division; Depression in Pittsburgh; effect of New Deal, WPA policies on Rivers and Harbors; Franklin D. Roosevelt, Harry Hopkins; Los Angeles Flood Control project; Europe during early 1930's; TVA controversy; Harold Ickes; flood control bill in early 1930's; Douglas MacArthur; duty in the Philippines; building Denison Dam, Texas; Sam Rayburn.
1,101 pp. *Permission required to cite or quote.* 1971. *Micro III.*

EISENHOWER ADMINISTRATION
Career relations with Gen. and President Eisenhower; drafting Eisenhower for President in 1952; selection and evaluation of the Cabinet members.
113 pp. *Permission required to cite or quote.* 1967. *Micro III.*

EISENHOWER ADMINISTRATION
Impressions of President Eisenhower; 1952 presidential drafting and campaign; issues faced: Korea, military-industrial complex lobbying.
39 pp. *Permission required.* 1969.

See also Continental Group.
Discussed in Herbert Brownell; Lucius D. Clay, Jr; Maxwell Rabb.

CLAY, Lucius DuBignon, Jr. (1919–   ) Air Force officer.
EISENHOWER ADMINISTRATION
Reminiscences of his father, Gen. Lucius D. Clay, particularly Panama experiences, 1928–29, and interest in community projects; own career in aerospace programs, Deputy Chief of Staff, Programs and Resources, 1967–68.
25 pp. *Permission required to cite or quote.* 1969. *Contributed by Jean E. Smith, Toronto, Canada.*

CLAYTON, William Lockhart (1880–1966) Cotton executive, government official.
Childhood and education in Mississippi; Jerome Hill and the cotton business; Anderson, Clayton and Co.; Congressional investigations; New Deal agricultural policy; Liberty League; John W. Davis, Jesse Jones, Nelson Rockefeller, Henry Wallace, Edward Stettinius, James Byrnes, George Marshall, the Marshall Plan.
235 pp. *Permission required to cite or quote.* 1962. *Micro II.*
See also Marshall Plan.
Discussed in William Benton; Sir Robert Jackson.

CLEMENT, Travers. *See* Socialist Movement.

CLEMENTS, Barbara Evans. Historian.
ALEXANDRA KOLLONTAI PROJECT
Mme. Kollontai's significance in Russian politics; activities for Women's Bureau; relationships with men; interpretations of writings at different times in Mme. Kollontai's life; contemporary relevance of ideas.
110 pp. *Permission required.* 1976.

CLEVELAND, Grover. *Discussed in* William S. Bennet; Charles Warren.

CLIFFORD, Cornelius. *Discussed in* Frederic R. Coudert.

CLOSE, Chuck (1940–   ) *See* New York's Art World.

CLOTHIER, Florence (1903–   ) *See* Women's History and Population Issues.

CLOUD, George Harlon (1904–   ) *See* Marine Corps.

CLUTE, R. V. *See* Weyerhaeuser Timber Company.

CLUTTERBUCK, Haroldo Rodolfo Guido (1907–   ) *See* Argentina.

COAKLEY, John C.F. *See* Thomas A. Edison Project.

COAKLEY, John C.F. and Thelda. *See* Thomas A. Edison Project.

COASH, Carl (1905–   ) *See* McGraw-Hill.

COATNEY, George Robert (1902–   ) *See* Health Sciences.

COBB, Candler (1887–1955) Lawyer.
Childhood and education at Harvard and Oxford; assistant in office of US District Attorney; commercial attaché to London Embassy, repayment of WWI debts, techniques of diplomatic service; Andrew Mellon, George Harvey, William H. Taft; law practice in London, 1932–40.
175 pp. *Permission required to cite or quote.* 1951. *Micro I.*

COBB, Cully Alton (1884–   ) Agriculturist.
Detailed account of the AAA Cotton Section, 1933–37; establishment of program and work with state extension directors, sources of support and opposition, public and press relations, dispute over landlord-tenant relations; Meyers Report. Recollections of W. B. Camp, Jerome Frank, Chester C. Davis, Gen. Stephen D. Lee, Walter F. George, Henry A. Wallace.
130 pp. *Permission required to cite or quote.* 1966. Papers. *Acquired from Regional Oral History Office, University of California, Berkeley.*

COBB, Jerrie (1931–   ) *See* Aviation Project.

COBB, Ned (Nate Shaw). *Discussed in* Theodore Rosengarten.

COBHAM, Sir Alan (1894–1973) *See* Aviation Project.

COCHRAN, Jacqueline (Mrs. Floyd B. Odlum).
AVIATION PROJECT
Pilot's license, 1932; the Australian race; instrument flying; aviation medicine; ferry flights during WWII; women pilots in the Air Force; use of jet planes; world records; FAI; visits to Russia; Northeast Airlines. Recollections of Howard Hughes, Amelia Earhart.
105 pp. *Permission required to cite or quote.* 1960. *Micro II.*
See also Air Force Academy *and* Eisenhower Administration.

COCKCROFT, John. *Discussed in* Warren Weaver.

COCKE, Norman Atwater (1884–1974) Lawyer.
JAMES B. DUKE PROJECT
Educational background; founding of Duke Power Co., 1912; anti-trust case, American Tobacco Co., 1911–12; impressions of James B. Duke as a businessman; planning the Duke Endowment; building and operating Duke University; trustee of the Duke Endowment, 1924; President, Duke Power Co., 1953; description of the Duke home in Charlottesville. Grady Rankin participates in one interview.
204 pp. *Permission required.* 1964.

COCTEAU, Jean. *Discussed in* Jacques Barzun.

COFFIN, Henry Sloane. *Discussed in* Willard E. Givens.

COFFYN, Frank T. (–1960) *See* Aviation Project. *Micro IV.*

COGGESHALL, Lowell T. (1901–   ) *See* Health Sciences.

COHEN, Henry (1933–   ) *See* New York Political Studies (B).

COHEN, Martin and James Brindle. *See* Social Security. *Micro IV.*

COHEN, Morris R. *Discussed in* Joseph J. Klein.

COHEN, Wilbur J. (1913–   ) Government official.
Work with Edwin Witte and President's Committee on Economic Security, 1934; drafting Truman health message, 1945; Hill-Burton Act, 1946; studies undertaken as Research Director, Universal Military Training Commission; roles with Commission on Social Security; Professor, School of Social Work, University of Michigan, 1956–61; passage of 1965 Medicare bill; Assistant Secretary, HEW, 1961–68; Secretary, HEW, 1968–69; observations of US politics, 1930's–70's; impressions of Samuel Rosenman, Theodore Sorensen, Arthur Altmeyer, Lyndon B. Johnson.
191 pp. *Permission required.* 1974.
See also Social Security *and* Eisenhower Administration.
Discussed in Arthur Altmeyer; Eveline Burns; Nelson Cruikshank; Charles Odell; Roswell B. Perkins; William Reidy; Sidney Saperstein; Charles I. Schottland; Harold Sheppard; Herman M. Somers; Elizabeth Wickenden; Alanson W. Willcox; Kenneth Williamson; Irwin Wolkstein.

COHN, Edwin. *Discussed in* Edward D. Churchill.

COHN, Harry. *Discussed in* Samson Raphaelson.

COHN, Marcus (1913–   ) *See* James Lawrence Fly Project.

COHN, Roy Marcus (1927–   ) *See* Eisenhower Administration.

COKER, Walter J., Jr. (1927–   ) *See* Continental Group.

COLAHAN, Thomas S. *See* Columbia Crisis of 1968.

COLBY, Bainbridge. *Discussed in* William A. Prendergast.

COLBY, Ursula J. *See* Kirkland College.

COLEAN, Miles (1898–   ) Consulting economist.
Education, University of Wisconsin and

Columbia, 1916–24; FHA, Director, Technical and Rental Housing Divisions; 1940, housing research, 20th Century Fund; 1945–   , consultant, Mortgage Bankers Association; organization and functions of FHA; lending reforms; multiplication of housing agencies; private market vs. social welfare orientation; housing and lending industries in Depression, WWII, postwar, Eisenhower and Nixon administrations; inflation, corruption, government control, sources of funds, sociological factors; impressions of Stewart McDonald, Guy Hollyday, Leon Keyserling.

398 pp. *Permission required to cite or quote.* 1975. Papers.

COLEMAN, Henry. *See* Columbia Crisis of 1968.

COLER, Bird S. *Discussed in* John A. Heffernan.

COLETTE. *Discussed in* Roger W. Straus.

COLLADO, Emilio Gabriel (1910–   ) *See* Marshall Plan.

COLLBOHM, Franklin Rudolf (1907–   ) *See* Aviation Project. *Micro II.*

COLLINS, Joseph (1866–1950) Neurologist, writer.
NY medicine and psychiatry, 1888–1912; publishers and authors, 1912–30; Sir William Osler; Henry James; James Joyce.

62 pp. *Permission required to cite or quote.* 1949. *Micro I.* Papers: 5 Henry James letters; 36 other letters; 23 clippings.

COLLINS, Michael. *Discussed in* Sean Keating.

COLLINS, Oscar E. *See* Continental Group.

COLOM, Eduardo. *See* Argentina.

COLP, Ralph (1893–1974) *See* Mt. Sinai Hospital. *Micro IV.*

COLUMBIA CRISIS OF 1968

In this series of interviews, almost all conducted on campus in May, 1968, participants and observers of every hue—student activists (conservative, independent, and radical), junior and senior faculty, administrators, supporting staff, and parents—describe and discuss the many phases of the crisis that resulted in the occupation of five Columbia buildings by students April 23 and 24, the suspension of classes, fruitless negotiations, police intervention on April 30, a campuswide strike, a lesser eruption May 21–22, and the eventual restructuring of the University. Factors behind the crisis are examined and weighed in tones ranging from analytical detachment to passionate concern. A researcher for the Archibald Cox Fact Finding Commission read a small fraction of this material, with the explicit permission of the contributor in each instance. The project was conducted independently by the Oral History Office.

Participants and pages: Jacques Barzun, 17; Lawrence Berger, 43; Bureau of Applied Social Research Study, 46; John D. Cannon, 86; Thomas S. Colahan, 49; Henry S. Coleman, 46 *(permission required to cite or quote; certain pages closed);* Columbia Concerned Parents Meeting, 72; Cathleen Cook, 45; William Cumming, 58; Herbert A. Deane, 34; William T. de Bary, 29; Jay Facciolo, 59; Mark Flanigan, 95; Robert Fogelson, 44; Joel Frader, 48 *(permission required to cite or quote);*

James Goldman, 24; James Grossman, 38; Marvin Harris, 50 *(permission required to cite or quote);* Richard Hofstadter, 30 *(permission required to cite or quote);* Terence Hopkins, 74 *(open);* International Journalism Students, 41; Jeffrey Kaplow, 59; Peter Kenen, 73 *(permission required to cite or quote);* Grayson Kirk, 40; Polykarp Kusch, 33; Robert Masters, 47; Seymour Melman, 37; Walter Metzger, 33; Barbara and David Nasaw, 97 *(permission required to cite or quote);* Alexander B. Platt, 41; Project Planners Meeting, 57;

Orest Ranum, 49 *(open except for specified pages);* David Rothman, 68; Frank Safran, 156; Howard Schless, 10; James P. Shenton, 8; Bruce Smith, 74; Lionel Trilling, 78; David B. Truman, 83; Paul Vilardi, 90; Immanuel Wallerstein, 265 *(permission required to cite or quote).*

2,426 pp. *Permission required, except as*

noted. 1968. *Supporting papers. Underwritten by the Edward W. Hazen Foundation, New Haven, Connecticut.*
See also Walter Gellhorn, Part II.

COLUMBIA UNIVERSITY *See* Erik Barnouw; Douglas Black; Elizabeth Blake; Nicholas Murray Butler Project; Harry Carman; Hollis Caswell; Columbia Crisis of 1968; Theodosius Dobzhansky; Alphonse R. Dochez; Leslie C. Dunn; Dwight D. Eisenhower; Luther Evans; Frank D. Fackenthal; William Fondiller; George B. Ford; Friends of the Columbia Libraries; Walter Gellhorn; James Gutmann; Frank H. Hankins; Richard Hofstadter Project; Douglass Hunt; Philip C. Jessup; Alvin Johnson; Isaac L. Kandel; Abram Kardiner; William H. Kilpatrick; Polykarp Kusch;

Paul F. Lazarsfeld; Otto Luening; Millicent McIntosh; Robert M. MacIver; Harold R. Medina; Richard B. Morris; David S. Muzzey; Allan Nevins; Marjorie Nicolson; John K. Norton; Edmund A. Prentis; Carlton C. Qualey; I.I. Rabi; R. Bruce Raup; Benjamin H. Reese; Lindsay Rogers; Sir George Sansom; Herbert W. Schneider; Maurice F. Tauber; Vladimir Ussachevsky; Rudolph Von Bernuth; Herbert Wechsler; Constance M. Winchell.

COLVIN, Fred Herbert (1867–1965) *See* McGraw-Hill.

COMBS, George Hamilton, Jr. (1899–1977) Lawyer, congressman, news analyst.
Kansas City: Thomas J. Pendergast machine; Congress, 1927–29; election of 1932; NYC politics and Tammany Hall, 1932–50; NY election of 1950; Estes Kefauver investigation.
191 pp. *Permission required to cite or quote.* 1951.
See also New York Political Studies (C).

COMDEN, Betty (1919–   ) and Adolph Green. *See* Popular Arts. *Micro II.*

COMMAGER, Henry Steele (1902–   ) *See* American Historians.
Discussed in Richard B. Morris.

COMMINS, Dorothy Berliner (Mrs. Saxe) Editorial career of Saxe Commins at Live-

right and Random House; Modern Library. Impressions of Mr. Commins' relationship with authors, especially Eugene O'Neill and William Faulkner.
181 pp. *Closed during lifetime.* 1962.

COMMINS, Saxe. *Discussed in* Dorothy B. Commins.

COMMONS, John R. *Discussed in* Arthur Altmeyer; Ewan Clague; Paul and Elizabeth Raushenbush; Social Security.

COMMUNICATIONS *See* Joseph Barnes; Erik Barnouw; Children's Television Workshop; Ted Cott; Clifford J. Durr; Thomas A. Edison Project; Ed Edwin; Federal Communications Commission; James Lawrence Fly Project; William Fondiller; Dan Golenpaul; Morton Gould; James C. Hagerty; Eva von Baur Hansl; Carl Haverlin; Quincy Howe; Paul Lazarsfeld; Goddard Lieberson; Ralph Lowell; Sig Mickelson; William S. Paley; Radio Pioneers; Raymond Scherer; Frank Stanton; Goodwin Watson; Sir Robert Watson-Watt.

COMMUNIST PARTY *See* Herbert Benjamin; Earl Browder; James Carey; Fidel Castro; Joseph Curran; John W. Edelman; John P. Frey; William Jansen; Ernest R. McKinney; H.L. Mitchell; Frances Perkins; Lee Pressman; George Schuyler; Max Shachtman; Socialist Movement; Benjamin Stolberg; Charles E. Taylor; Rolland J. Thomas.

COMPTON, Arthur. *Discussed in* American Association of Physics Teachers.

COMPTON, Karl. *Discussed in* American Association of Physics Teachers.

COMSTOCK, Anthony. *Discussed in* Alfred A. Knopf.

CONANT, Frederick Warren (1892–   ) *See* Henry H. Arnold Project.

CONANT, James Bryant (1893–1978) *See* Carnegie Corporation.
Discussed in Hollis Caswell; Edward D. Churchill; W. H. Cowley; Lawrence A. Cremin; John K. Norton.

CONCEPCION, Alfredo. *See* Argentina.

CONDON, John Pomeroy (1911–   ) *See* Marine Corps.

CONGER, Clement (1912–   ) *See* Eisenhower Administration.

CONKLIN, Chester (1888–1971) *See* Popular Arts.

CONNELL, David. *See* Children's Television Workshop. *Micro IV.*

CONNELLY, Marc (1890–   ) *See* Popular Arts.

CONNORTON, John V. *See* New York Political Studies (B).

CONOLLY, Richard L. (1892–1962) Naval officer.
Early education and training at Annapolis; junior naval officer experiences aboard destroyers and battleships; WWI; Washington, Geneva, and London Conferences; naval training schools, 1920's and 1930's; Pearl Harbor; wartime experiences in the Pacific; Joint Chiefs of Staff in Washington; invasion of North Africa; assault on Sicily; Operation Avalanche (assault on Salerno); cooperation with the British; Guam, Saipan, and the Philippines; Paris Peace Conference, 1946; Commander US Fleet in Eastern Atlantic and Mediterranean; 6th Fleet; struggle over unification of the armed forces; President US Naval War College.
411 pp. *Open.* 1959.

CONRAD, Frank. *Discussed in* Radio Pioneers.

CONSERVATION OF NATURAL RESOURCES *See* Horace M. Albright; Continental Group; Clarence Davis; Wesley D'Ewart; Newton Drury; Forest History Society; Independence Park; Jackson Hole Preserve; Percy M. Lee; Walter C. Lowdermilk; Stewart Ogilvy; Lithgow Osborne; Whitney North Seymour, Sr.; Weyerhaeuser Timber Company.

CONSUMER REPORTING *See* Journalism Lectures (B).

CONTINENTAL GROUP, INC.
This project spans seventy years (1904–1974) of Continental Can Company (now The Continental Group, Inc.) history as told by 226 retired and active employees from all job and management categories. Semi-skilled factory workers and chief executive officers alike discuss corporate and industrial development in a variety of packaging fields embraced by Continental: metal cans, crowns and closures, glass and plastic containers, folding and corrugated cartons, fiber drums, grocery and multi-wall bags, paper cups and tubs, and flexible packaging. Manufacturing operations are described in detail, particularly in can plants and paper mills. Prominent themes are technological change through research and engineering, labor relations, mergers and acquisitions, corporate strategies and organization, international business, and government relations. Individual careers are followed, illustrating employee morale, the work ethic, opportunity and mobility in an industrial corporation, the role of personalities in management, the decision-making process, company loyalty, and corporate social responsibility. The wider context of American life is brought out in many of the interviews, and readers will find material on WWI, the Great Depression, and WWII among other social, economic, and political subjects.

Participants and pages: Alfred J. Abplanalp, 75; Claude M. Adams, 109; William M. Allin, 94; Charles Altier, 53; George M. Ambrose, 112; Joseph P. Arrigo, 89; Ed Askew, 87; John L. Badinelli, 94; Robert W. Baer, 89; Matthew V. Barbieri, 69; George H. Barker, 111; Gregory J. Barry, 67; Jess L. Belser, 68; Harold A. Bergstrom, 90; Bernard D. Bloser, 88; Louis G. Bohs, 94; Walter Elder Bond, 125; Lewis Bozell, 131; Thomas F. Brady, 76; Edward H. Broadwell, 95; John R. Brown, 73; Stephen L. Brown, 95; Frank W. Burns, 274;

Allan Cameron, 70; William M. Cameron, 77; Leonard G. Cannella, 97; Lee A. Carey, 121; Albert H. Carle, 78; James V. Carlson, 114; Richard L. Carlton, 107; Clarence E. Carrel, 112; Howard B. Chadwick and Anthony J. Civitello, 188; Wayne T. Chiappe, 159; Mary F. Clair, 51; Lucius D. Clay, 92;

Walter J. Coker, Jr., 118; Oscar E. Collins, 90; Patrick J. Coyne, 102; Walter C. Curtiss, Jr., 105; Mary T. Daly, 77; Neil C. Darrach, 70; George Davis, 130; John H. Dennis, 115; Oscar De Sylva, 120; Merton L. Dodge, 85; James I. Donahue, 45; George E. Dyke, 116;

George Edmonds, 67; Charles E. Eggerss, 56; Peter E. Fagan, 86; John Fedosky, Jr., 109; Harvey H. Fell, 72; Alfred H. Fisher, 72; Raymond G. Fisher, 163; Sylvester L. Flugge, 83; Thomas C. Fogarty, 153; Robert C. Foss, 77; Andrew E. Fox, 60; Joseph Frain, 52; Floyd E. Franklin, 94; Rose Frost, 78; E. Ewart Fry, 57; Gladys Gallagher, 80; John E. Gallagher, 149; James M. Gibb, 100; Arleigh D. Gifford, 78; Bruce B. Gordon, 95; Arthur Graf and L. Virgil Jones, 111; Edwin H. Graves, 95; Jacob Greco, 79; Henry J. Hagan, 85; Hans A. Hanel, 77; Lowell K. Hanson, 99; James J. Harris, 87; Robert S. Hatfield, 103; Martin L. Haupt, 58; Charles B. Hayes, 114; Warren J. Hayford, 59; Ellison L. Hazard, 228;

Robert D. Heaviside, 88; John M. Heinen, Jr., 93; John L. Heinlein, 127; Robert L. Heitman, 141; John Henchert, 95; Louis F. Henneke, 123; Raymond L. Hicks, 85; M.A. Higdon, 99; Paul E. Hile, 72; Fred S. Hinkle, 109; Mrs. William Hodgson, 9; Frederick J. Hoffman, 77; Edward J. Holder, 71; Fred W. Hoover, 83; Charles S. Huestis, 102; Fred E. Hummel, 54; T. Merritt Hunter, 77; Otto F. Hunziker, 134; Richard H. Ireland, 178; Oliver G. Jakob, 60; Frank E. Johnson, 113; Helmer R. Johnson, 107; Scott R. Johnson, 161; William H. Kaiser, 49; Mary H. Kalamar, 71; Louis F. Kalmar, 91; Roy G. Kennedy, 110; Thomas P. Keogh, 129; James F. Kinlock, 79; Joseph A. Kissinger, 84; Alfred W. Kitselman, 76; Walter E. Klint, 51; Genevieve Kuzma, 71; Warren A. Lacke, 77; Robert E. Lambert, 91; George K. Landon, 57; Jerrold E. Landon, 48; Wilson B. Larkin, 74; Burford LaTouche, 77; Robert A. Lehman, 139; Leroy W. Leiter, 73; Howard G. Lewis, 110; William J. Lobrovich, 86; Edward J. Lynn, 69;

Orren R. McJunkins, 69; Thomas McLaughlin, 107; Leighton McLendon, 90;

Robert M. McPherson, 82; Edward H. Marshall, 113; Vido Matich, 84; Ralph M. Mero, 83; Robert B. Mesrobian, 72; Robert C. Meyers, 75; Kenneth G. Michel, 92; James P. Morgan, 172; John W. Morris, Sr., 112; Hans Herbert Munte, 102; Walter Murray, 72; George H. Muth, 144; William I. Myers, 70; Charles A. Nash, 119; Wilbur K. Neuman, 90; Charles J. O'Connor, 95; Eugene J. O'Connor, 103; Gene P. Oehlberg, 96; Vera R. Oehlberg, 89; Iver J. Olsen, 93; James H. O'Neil, 62; Seymour Oppenheimer, 107; Robert A. Penk, 133; Reuben Perin, 185; Louis G. Petree, 108; Lewis B. Pitts, 59; C. Rogers Pollack, 72; Robert D. Post, 79; George E. Prokupek, 79; William H. Puschel, 110;

Arl S. Rapp, 87; Jerome R. Roberts, 99; Morris O. Roberts, 84; Frank A. Rockwell, 66; John L. Rowe, 104; Herbert S. Ruekberg, 83; Howard P. Ryan, 141; Edgar L. Sauters, 112; Earl C. Savage, 31; Jerome J. Schneewind, 93; Edward A. Schrader, 24; Harry A. Scott, 97; Edward W. Seibert, 108; Evelyn Norton Seiler, 47; Jack Selbiger, 115; Joseph J. Sennello, 83; Richard G. Shaughnessy, 111; Fred B. Shaw, 89; Anne Siroky, 89; A. Gerald Skibbe, 97; S. Bruce Smart, 115; Isaac L. Smith, 123; Jimmie H. Smith, 107; Wyatt Speight, 109; Leslie T. Stansbury, 87; Charles B. Stauffacher, 127; Sidney R. Steele, 57; Alois Steiner, 78; Arthur E. Stevenson, 82; James A. Stewart, 83; Woodrow Stillwagon, 100; Donald W. Stitt, 145; Clarence L. Stone, 107; Dean Stout, 35; Robert V. Swartz, 54; Harry Swideck, 80; John C. Swift, 85;

Frederick A. Tennant, 134; Bernard ter Haar, 97; Mary Ellen Tewksbury, 82; Roque Torrea, 112; Lester Tripp, 111; Bon H. Trullinger, 60; Allan Trumbull, 71; Robert E. Tucker, 87; Frances A. Tyler, 79; Clark A. Valentiner, 203; Charles E. Valiant, 63; Camiel F. Vanderbush, 104; Aubrey W. Vaughan, Jr., 91; Allen P. Vining, 164; Charles E. Wallace, 66; Everett A. Weathers, 96; Richard D. Weinland, 159; Archie L. Wenrich, 73; Colin L. Westerbeck, 100; William Wheelis, 96; Philip O'Connell White, 66; Robert P. White, 69; Ralph L. Whittall, 80; Lawrence Wilkinson, 141; David and Patricia Wilson, 112; Roger V. Wilson, 112; James Wirsta, 62;

Peter Wojtul, 149; Alphonse Wunsch, 100; Armand R. Zazueta, 85; Donald H. Zipper, 87.
  21,306 pp. *Permission required.* 1974–75. *Underwritten by The Continental Group, Inc.*

COOK, Cathleen. *See* Columbia Crisis of 1968.

COOK, Charles D. (1924–   ) Lawyer.
EISENHOWER ADMINISTRATION
Education and training in Michigan; US Navy, 1943–47: V-12 program, Saipan; Columbia University: Law School, School of International Affairs; US Mission to UN, 1950–62: UN civil service, the Secretary Generalship, UN diplomacy, relations with US State Department, Uniting for Peace resolution, admission of new members, voting, various crises; Henry Cabot Lodge, John Foster Dulles, Adlai Stevenson, Dwight Eisenhower, Krishna Menon.
  658 pp. *Permission required.* 1964.

COOK, Constance (1919–   ) *See* Women's History and Population Issues.

COOK, Howard Alexander (1915–   ) *See* Eisenhower Administration. *Micro III.*

COOK, Richard W. (1907–   ) *See* Eisenhower Administration.

COOKE, Jesse. *Discussed in* Omar T. Pfeiffer.

COOLEY, Albert Dustin (1900–1976). *See* Marine Corps.

COOLIDGE, Calvin. *Discussed in* Horace M. Albright; Guy Emerson; Claude M. Fuess; H. V. Kaltenborn; Eugene Meyer; James T. Williams, Jr.

COOLIDGE, Charles Allerton (1894–   ) Lawyer.
EISENHOWER ADMINISTRATION
Special Assistant to the Secretary of Defense, 1955–58; reorganization of the Defense Department and disarmament policy under President Eisenhower.
  35 pp. *Permission required to cite or quote.* 1967. *Micro III.*

COONEY, Joan Ganz. *See* Children's Television Workshop. *Micro IV.*

COOPER, David. *See* Vietnam Veterans.

COOPER, Jackie (1922–   ) *See* Popular Arts.

COOPER, William G., Jr. *See* Eisenhower Administration. *Micro III.*

COPE, Sidney Raymond (1907–   ) *See* World Bank.

COPELAND, Lammot du Pont. *See* Longwood Gardens.

COPLAND, Aaron (1900–   ) Composer.
Childhood, education, early compositions, teachers; Paris, 1921–24, studying composition with Nadia Boulanger; return to US; League of Composers, assistance from Serge Koussevitzky, lecturing and teaching, MacDowell and Yaddo Colonies; Copland-Sessions Concerts, analysis of own compositions, discussion of methods, commissions; trips to Mexico, 1926–28; Norton Professorship at Harvard; Tanglewood and Boston Symphony, 1937–62; Hollywood, composition for films; problems of publication, choice of titles; dance compositions for Martha Graham, Eugene Loring, Agnes de Mille; Pulitzer Prize, 1945; radio music, recording contracts, McCarthy hearings; conducting at home and abroad from 1957; vocal works; vignettes of Roger Sessions, Leonard Bernstein, Igor Stravinsky, many other musicians and critics.
  573 pp. *Permission required.* 1976. *Acquired from Yale University School of Music Oral History Project.*
Discussed in Otto Luening.

COPSEY, Robert L. (1896–   ) *See* Air Force Academy.

CORBIN, Hazel (1895–   ) Nurse.
Description of her work for better maternity care through Maternity Center Association (1918–65): prenatal care, maternity institutes, training public health nurses, certification program for nurse-midwives, teaching aids; health legislation and federal agencies; WHO.

78 pp. *Permission required to cite or quote.* 1970. *Micro II.*
Underwritten by friends of Miss Corbin; contributed by Ruth Watson Lubic, New York City.

CORCORAN, Thomas and Anna Chennault. *See* Flying Tigers.

CORCORAN, Thomas Gardiner (1900–) *See* James Lawrence Fly Project.
Discussed in John Steelman.

CORCUNDALE, Thomas. *See* Flying Tigers.

CORDIER, Andrew Wellington (1901–1975) UN official, educator.
Executive assistant to UN Secretary-General, 1946; comprehensive discussion of UN: as a propaganda arena, role of small nations, administration and duties of officers, rules of procedure, staffing, effect of press, General Assembly, Security Council, early development of Secretariat; impressions of Russian leaders: Nikita Khrushchev, Andrei Gromyko, and deputies; comparison of Trygve Lie, Dag Hammarskjold, and U Thant; discussion of Hammarskjold's personality with anecdotal illustrations; plane crash in Ndola. Detailed description of UN handling of Korean prisoner problem, Congo, Suez, Hungary, and Lebanon crises.
532 pp. *Permission required to cite or quote.* 1964. *Micro IV.*
See also Dag Hammarskjold Project *and* International Negotiations.
Discussed in Douglass Hunt.

CORELLI, Franco. *Discussed in* Schuyler Chapin.

CORI, Carl Ferdinand (1896–) *See* Nobel Laureates.

CORLEY, James H. Administrator.
Experiences at University of California at Berkeley 1927–64: Comptroller, Vice President, representative of University at State Legislature and in Washington, D.C.
113 pp. *Permission required to cite or quote.* 1969. Papers. *Memoir obtained by Regional Oral History Office, University of California, Berkeley.*

CORNELL, Katharine (1893–1974) *See* Popular Arts.

CORSO, Gregory Nunzio (1930–) *See* Poets on their Poetry.

CORT, William Walter (1887–1971) Parasitologist.
Education, Colorado College, University of Illinois; Professor, Johns Hopkins School of Hygiene and Public Health, 1919–53; work on hookworm and other parasites in southern US, China, Puerto Rico, Panama, Trinidad, and Egypt; recollections of biologists.
31 pp. *Open.* 1966.

CORWIN, Norman (1910–) Writer, director, producer.
RADIO PIONEERS
Early days in radio; WQXR; "Twenty-six by Corwin" radio program on WCBS; reaction of radio industry, advertising agencies, and the public to *Red Channels.*
100 pp. *Closed during lifetime.* 1966.
See also James Lawrence Fly Project.

CORYELL, Charles DuBois (1912–1971) Chemist.
Education in California and Germany; political philosophy; Manhattan Project, Chicago and Oak Ridge; security restrictions and problems; relationships with Army and DuPont Company; tension among scientists; emotional and scientific impact of bomb and its use; attempts to inform and influence public opinion and Congress; Smyth report; Europe and Israel sojourn; Robert Oppenheimer case; impressions of many prominent atomic scientists.
441 pp. *Permission required to cite or quote.* 1960. *Micro II.*

COSIO VILLEGAS, Daniel (1898–1976) Lawyer, educator.
Family background, education; interior of Mexico, 1905–06; Mexican Revolution, 1914; National Student Federation; University of Mexico; Mexican politicians and intellectuals during the 1920's; Law School; teaching at the University of Mexico and formation of its School of Economics; founding of publishing house, *Fondo de Cultura Economica,* 1933; Financial Counselor, Mexican Embassy in Washington,

1936; chargé d'affaires, Lisbon; Spanish Civil War. The memoir is in Spanish.
297 pp. *Permission required to cite or quote.* 1963.

COSTELLO, Jerry and John Vivian. *See* Flying Tigers.

COSTIKYAN, Edward (1924–) Politician.
Part I: Childhood and education, NYC: Horace Mann, Columbia, 1949; Army Infantry: Okinawa and Korea, 1943–45; NYC politics: New Democratic Club, 1951–66; NY County Democratic leader, 1964; Robert Wagner as Mayor; Wagner-Carmine De Sapio feud; relationships with Reform leaders and other political figures, including anecdotes of Adlai Stevenson, Eleanor Roosevelt, Herbert Lehman, James Farley, Averell Harriman, Robert F. Kennedy. Detailed analysis and description of NYC mayoralty campaign and election, 1965.
677 pp. *Permission required.* 1966.

Part II: NY State Democratic Party politics, 1966–70; breakdown of district leader-captain relationships; Constitutional Convention; national Democratic politics: 1968 preconvention, convention, and campaign; Robert Kennedy, Eugene McCarthy, and others.
76 pp. *Permission required.* 1970.

Discussed in Justin N. Feldman.

COTT, Ted (1917–1973) Radio and television executive.
Radio interest during high school and college; WNYC and Mayor Fiorello La Guardia; early radio techniques and programming; Radio Code; independent stations and networks; FCC; sponsorship, spot announcements; television pioneering; political broadcasting; educational television; National Talent Associates; Nikita Khrushchev interview on "Open End"; censorship; pay television.
297 pp. *Permission required to cite or quote.* 1961. *Micro II.*
See also Journalism Lectures.

COTTON, Thomas (–1964) *See* Flying Tigers.

COTTONE, Benedict Peter (1909–) *See* James Lawrence Fly Project.

COUCH, William Terry (1901–) Publisher.
SOUTHERN INTELLECTUAL LEADERS (A) Childhood and education, rural Virginia; University of North Carolina; University of North Carolina Press, Associate Director, 1926–32 and Director, 1932–45; freedom of the press in the South; problems of tenant farmers and the FSA; Southern Policy Committee; Southern Conference for Human Welfare; Federal Writers Project, Regional Director, 1937–39; *These Are Our Lives;* University of Chicago Press, Director, 1945–50; *Collier's Encyclopedia,* editor-in-chief, 1952–59; *Oxford Junior Encyclopedia,* editor, 1959–63; William Volker Foundation; impressions of the Nashville Agrarians, Henry G. Alsberg, Clarence Carson, Harry Woodburn Chase, Jonathan Daniels, Frank P. Graham, Robert M. Hutchins, Herman C. Nixon, Howard W. Odum, and others.
571 pp. *Permission required.* 1970. Papers.
Discussed in Rupert B. Vance.

COUDERT, Frederic Rene (1871–1955) Lawyer.
Recollections of his father; early political impressions, notably the "Cross of Gold" speech; Spanish-American War; Insular cases; NY politics, John P. Mitchel; legal adviser to British Government regarding legal controversies involving US, especially British blockade and problems of international maritime law, 1915–20; impressions of Woodrow Wilson, Sir Cecil Spring-Rice, Robert Lansing, Alexis Carrel, Benjamin Cardozo, Cornelius Clifford, Boris Bakhmeteff, Henri Bergson, Simon Flexner; Columbia University and Nicholas Murray Butler.
170 pp. *Permission required to cite or quote.* 1950. *Micro I.* Papers.
Discussed in Boris Bakhmeteff.

COUGHLIN, Edward. *See* Federated Department Stores.

COUNTS, George. *Discussed in* Joseph Jablonower; Isaac L. Kandel; William H. Kilpatrick; Goodwin Watson.

COUPER, Richard W. (1922–   )
KIRKLAND COLLEGE
Hamilton College trustee, chairman long-range planning committee, 1959, Vice President, 1962; the founding of Kirkland; higher education in the 1950's, Deputy Commissioner of Higher Education, NY; Chief Executive NY Public Library since 1971.
15 pp. *Permission required.* 1977.

COURNAND, Andre F. (1895–   ) *See* Nobel Laureates.

COURTS *See* Judiciary.

COUSINS, Norman (1912–   ) *See* Journalism Lectures *and* International Negotiations.

COWAN, Charles S. *See* Forest History Society.

COWAN, Louis G. (1909–1976) Communications executive.
RADIO PIONEERS
Early interest in communications; University of Chicago; radio work in Chicago in the 1930's; various early productions, including "Quiz Kids"; work during WWII: Director, Voice of America and OWI NYC office; programs for War Department, including "Command Performance," "Chaplain Jim"; Louis G. Cowan radio and television productions, 1946–55; transition from radio to television; Negroes in broadcast industry; use of broadcasting and television in Adlai Stevenson 1952 Presidential campaign; Peabody and other broadcast awards; CBS network role.
225 pp. *Permission required to cite or quote.* 1967. *Micro IV.*

COWAN, Thomas H. (1884–   ) Radio station executive.
RADIO PIONEERS
Family background; pioneer work in radio, WJZ, Newark, 1921; milestones in the history of WNYC from 1924; work with various NYC mayors. Impressions of Thomas A. Edison and various radio figures.
119 pp. *Open.* 1951.

COWELL, Henry (1897–1965) Composer.
Early compositions; tone clusters, influence on other composers; travel and study in Europe and US; teaching; OWI; folk music; Oriental music; music publishing; lectures; Columbia, New School; anecdotes of notable musicians, especially Charles Ives.
142 pp. *Open.* 1963.

COWLES, Gardner, Jr. *Discussed in* George H. Gallup.

COWLES, William Sheffield. *See* Theodore Roosevelt Association. *Micro IV.*

COWLEY, William Harold (1899–1978) Educator.
Brooklyn childhood and education; American Steel and Wire Company; YMCA work, night school, Mt. Hermon, Clark School; Dartmouth, 1920–24; Western Electric Company; graduate work, Chicago, 1925–27; Board of Vocational Guidance and Placement, 1927; Ohio State University, Bureau of Educational Research, 1929–38; editing *Journal of Higher Education;* residential housing study, administering NYA, state educational conferences, bibliographic work; Carnegie Corporation; student personnel work; American Council on Education; President, Hamilton College, 1938–44; admissions and curriculum studies; Washington, 1942, role of education in war effort; Air Force programs at Hamilton; Professor of Higher Education, Stanford, from 1945; work with graduate students, fundamental concepts. Impressions of noted educators, including W. W. Charters, Robert Hutchins, Frederick Keppel, J. L. Morrill, James B. Conant, Harold Dodds.
768 pp. *Permission required to cite or quote.* 1962. Papers.

COX, Sir Harold Roxbee (1902–   ) *See* Aviation Project. *Micro II.*

COX, Joseph Aloysius (1896–   ) Judge.
Early life, WWI; CCNY; teaching; Fordham Law School; NYC politics; attorney for Public Administrator; law practice; detailed description of notable cases, including Ida Wood, Mabel Greer, Collyer brothers, heir chasing, undue influence; State Supreme Court, 1952; Judicial Conference; Appellate Division; Surrogate of NY County, 1956.
407 pp. *Closed during lifetime.* 1962.

COX, Otto T. (1885–1972) *See* Marine Corps.

COYNE, Patrick J. (1908–   ) *See* Continental Group.

CRABB, Jarred V. (1902–   ) Air Force officer.
AIR FORCE ACADEMY
Peacetime Air Corps training and morale; Kelly and Selfridge Fields; bomb sight maintenance; 14th Reconnaissance Squadron, Gander, 1941; communications training, 1941–42; South Pacific Theater, 1943–46: 5th Air Force and 5th Bomber Command; bombing tactics; Philippines, 1948–49; FEAF staff, 1949–52; Korea air operations; Air Defense Command, 1952–54; recollections of WWII colleagues, especially Gen. George C. Kenny, Douglas MacArthur, Ennis C. Whitehead, and Thomas D. White.
150 pp. *Open.* 1970.

CRAIG, Edward Arthur (1896–   ) *See* Marine Corps.

CRAIG, Malin. *Discussed in* Ira C. Eaker.

CRAIG, Robert (1920–   ) *See* McGraw-Hill.

CRAIGIE, Laurence C. (1902–   ) *See* Air Force Academy *and* Aviation Project, *Micro II.*

CRANE, Burton (–1963) *See* Occupation of Japan. *Micro II.*

CRANE, Esther. *See* Occupation of Japan. *Micro II.*

HART CRANE PROJECT
Impressions of Hart Crane and the literary scene in Ohio and NYC during the 1920's; includes a WBAI radio program transcript with reminiscences by friends.
Participants and pages: Mrs. Margaret Babcock, 50; Waldo Frank, 53; Fredrica Crane Lewis, 17; Samuel Loveman, 46; Allen Tate, 35 *(closed during lifetime).*
WBAI broadcast: Nathan Ashe, Peggy Baird, Solomon Grundberg, Samuel Loveman, John Unterecker, 24.
225 pp. *Permission required except as*

noted. 1963. *Contributed by John Unterecker, Honolulu.*

CRANSTON, Earl (1895–1970) *See* China Missionaries.

CRANSTON, Mildred Welch. *See* China Missionaries.

CRARY, Albert P. (1911–   ) Geophysicist, oceanographer.
Seismic and geologic explorations, oceanography and geophysics; oil exploration in Colombia and Venezuela; early loran and sofar; Maurice Ewing; air acoustics and balloons; Alamogordo; Arctic and Antarctic glaciology; IGY.
87 pp. *Permission required to cite or quote.* 1962. *Micro I.*

CRAWFORD, Edward. *See* Alaskan Pioneers.

CRAWFORD, Kenneth Gale (1902–   ) Journalist.
EISENHOWER ADMINISTRATION
Eisenhower's relations with the press as General and President; impressions of Eisenhower administration.
26 pp. *Permission required to cite or quote.* 1967. *Micro III.*

CREELEY, Robert. *Discussed in* Tom Clark.

CREMIN, Lawrence Arthur (1925–   ) Educator.
CARNEGIE CORPORATION
Contacts with the Carnegie Corporation; TC; *The Transformation of the School;* National Academy of Education, 1964–65; Behavioral Science Center, Stanford University, 1963; Carnegie grant for a history of American education, 1964; Institute of Philosophy and Politics of Education, 1964. Impressions of Lloyd Morrisett, James B. Conant, and others.
107 pp. *Permission required.* 1968.

CRENA DE IONGH, Daniel (1888–1970) *See* World Bank.

CRIPPS, Sir Stafford. *Discussed in* Sir Robert Watson-Watt.

CRITE, Allan Rohan (1910–   ) Artist.
Family background; education, art train- -

ing, Boston Fine Arts Museum School, 1936; illustrations of spirituals; slide-tape history presentations with third-world perspective; impressions of South End and Roxbury sections of Boston, 1920's–'70's.
64 pp. *Permission required to cite or quote.* 1977.

CROFT, Frank Cornelius (1903–   ) *See* Marine Corps.

CROHN, Burrill Bernard (1884–   ) *See* Mt. Sinai Hospital.

CROLY, Herbert. *Discussed in* Alvin Johnson.

CROMWELL, John (1887–   ) *See* Popular Arts.

CROSS, Robert Dougherty (1924–   ) *See* American Historians.

CROSS, Rowland McLean (1888–   ) *See* China Missionaries.

CROSS, Wilbur. *Discussed in* Raymond Baldwin.

CROSSFIELD, Albert Scott (1921–   ) *See* Aviation Project.

CROSSMAN, John. *See* McGraw-Hill.

CROWDER, Walter (1907–   ) *See* McGraw-Hill.

CROWELL, Benedict. *Discussed in* Goldthwaite H. Dorr.

CROWELL, Paul (1891–1970) *See* New York Political Studies (A).

CROWLEY, Daniel F. (1915–   ) *See* McGraw-Hill.

CROWTHER, Bosley (1905–   ) *See* Popular Arts.

CRUGER, Bertram D. (1893–1952) Secretary to John Purroy Mitchel.
The Mitchel administration, NYC.
33 pp. *Permission required to cite or quote.* 1950. *Micro IV.*

CRUIKSHANK, Nelson Hale (1902–   ) Labor economist.
SOCIAL SECURITY
War Manpower Commission; AFL office for Social Security, 1944; Advisory Committee to the Senate Finance Committee, 1949; chairman, labor staff coordinating committee on Medicare, 1959–60; Commission on Church and Economic Life; staff executive officer, AFL Committee on Social Security; AFL-CIO efforts toward national health insurance: 1956 disability bill and Medicare bill and its precursors, 1957–65; AMA opposition to Medicare, support of Medicare by National Council of Churches and National Council of Senior Citizens; drafting AFL-CIO constitution. Impressions of Andrew Biemiller, Wilbur Cohen, John F. Kennedy, George Meany, Walter Reuther, Abraham Ribicoff.
506 pp. *Permission required to cite or quote; certain pages closed.* 1967. *Micro III. Discussed in* Ray Henry; James C. O'Brien; Elizabeth Wickenden; Kenneth Williamson.

CRUMP, Edward H. *Discussed in* Gordon Browning.

CUBBERLEY, Elwood. *Discussed in* John K. Norton.

CUDAHY, Sheila. *Discussed in* Roger W. Straus.

CULLMAN, Lewis Benjamin (1919–   ) Financier.
Family background, education; WWII, meteorological experience; founding of weather service in Boston; NYC and investment banking, 1948–54; Cullman Brothers, 1954–61; setting up investment advisory business in NYC, 1962; Canadian investment business, Incubation Group, Ltd., 1963; description of negotiations leading to acquisition of Orkin Exterminating, 1964, and Allied Graphic Arts, 1966; formation of holding company, Cullman Ventures, Inc., 1969; Keith Clark negotiations.
245 pp. *Permission required.* 1978.

CUMBERLAND, William Wilson (1890–1955) Economist.
Early life; research in Mexico on economic conditions, 1917; Paris Peace Conference with John Foster Dulles: economic decisions, personalities; economic adviser to

State Department: post WWI economic conditions in US and Europe; mandated territories; economies of Peru, Haiti, Nicaragua; stock market and US economy; NRA, 1933; consultant, UN conference, 1945.

286 pp. *Permission required to cite or quote.* 1951. *Micro I.*

CUMMING, William. *See* Columbia Crisis of 1968.

CUMMINGS, Homer. *Discussed in* Gordon Dean.

CUMMINGS, Martin M. *See* Health Sciences.

CUMMINGS, Willis N. (1894–   ) Harlem dentist.
Black and white genealogy; college years at Fisk and the University of Pennsylvania, in particular as a member of the latter's cross country and track teams, 1917–19, vs. Columbia, the Naval Academy, others; experiences as first Black captain of an Ivy League varsity.
57 pp. *Permission required to cite or quote.* 1974. Papers.

CUNNINGHAM, Merce. *Discussed in* Valda Setterfield.

CUPP, Roderick B. *See* Radio Pioneers.

CURLEY, Michael. *Discussed in* Eddie Dowling.

CURRAN, Joseph (1906–   ) Labor union executive.
Early life; National Maritime Union, president, 1931; influence of Communist party in unions; vice president, AFL-CIO.
193 pp. *Closed during lifetime.* 1964. *Discussed in* M. Hedley Stone.

CURTIS, Albert B. (1903–   ) Chief fire warden.
WEYERHAEUSER TIMBER COMPANY
Work with Fire Protection Association, Idaho, from 1918; early years in fire protection, Weyerhaeuser Co.; Cattle Grazers Association, 1935; air control. Impressions of J. P. Weyerhaeuser, Theodore Fohl.
103 pp. *Permission required.* 1956.

CURTIS, Donald (1896–   ) *See* Marine Corps.

CURTIS, James Freeman (1878–1952) Lawyer.
Childhood; education at Harvard; early law practice; Assistant Attorney General, Assistant District Attorney, Massachusetts, 1906–09; Assistant Secretary of the Treasury, Customs Bureau, 1909–13; establishment of Federal Reserve System, 1914–19; Liberty Loan; private legal practice in NY, 1919–51; impressions of Franklin MacVeagh, Boies Penrose, William Howard Taft, T. E. Lawrence, and Efrem Zimbalist; personal experiences in financial speculation, travels; avocations; philosophy of life.
334 pp. *Permission required to cite or quote.* 1951. *Micro I.*

CURTIS, Thomas B. (1911–   ) *See* Eisenhower Administration. *Micro III.*

CURTISS, Walter C., Jr. (1915–   ) *See* Continental Group.

CUSHING, Harvey. *Discussed in* Edward D. Churchill.

CUSHMAN, Thomas Jackson (1895–1972) *See* Marine Corps.

CUSTER, Benjamin Scott (1905–   ) Naval officer.
Family background, childhood; Naval Academy; early cruises; Pensacola, flight training; flying boat squadron, Alaska; teaching at Annapolis; Caribbean Sea Frontier, Adm. John Hoover; executive officer, *Croatan;* Adm. John Vest; command of the *Norton Sound;* WWII: Atlantic and Pacific theaters; atomic bomb; Flight Safety Board, Pay Board; Naval Attaché to Canada; Northwest cruise to Hudson's Bay; Floyd Bennett Field; Strauss Commission; Princeton. Impressions of contemporaries in the Navy and of government officials; discussion of strategy and battle plans, World Wars I and II.
1,022 pp. *Permission required.* 1965.

CUTLER, Elliot. *Discussed in* Edward D. Churchill.

CUYLER, Lewis. *See* Association for the Aid of Crippled Children.

D

DABNEY, Virginius (1901–   ) Newspaper editor.
SOUTHERN INTELLECTUAL LEADERS (B)
Family background, education, University of Virginia, 1921; Virginia and national politics, 1920's–70's; role of Harry Byrd, Sr. in state politics; involvement in race problems of 1930's–40's; editor, Richmond *Times-Dispatch;* author: *Liberalism in the South* (1932), *Below the Potomac* (1942), others; current status of American journalism.
273 pp. *Permission required to cite or quote.* 1975.

DA COSTA GOMES, Francisco. *Discussed in* Stuart N. Scott.

DA COSTA, Morton (1914–   ) *See* Popular Arts.

DAHL, Perry J. *See* Air Force Academy.

DALE, Harry (–1962) *See* Book-of-the-Month Club. *Micro IV.*

DALEY, Richard J. *Discussed in* Elizabeth S. Ives; Carl McGowan.

DALLY, A. B., Jr. *See* Benedum and The Oil Industry.

DALY, Charles Ulick (1927–   ) *See* Social Security *Micro III.*

DALY, Edward J. (1898–   ) *See* Thomas A. Edison Project.

DALY, Mary T. (1907–   ) *See* Continental Group.

DAMROSCH, Walter. *Discussed in* Radio Pioneers.

DANAHER, John Anthony (1899–   ) Judge.
EISENHOWER ADMINISTRATION
Early career; Republican Party and National Committee; Director, Division of Special Activities, 1952 campaign.
58 pp. *Permission required to cite or quote.* 1968.

DANCE *See* Aaron Copland; Morton Gould; Max Rabinoff; William Schuman; Valda Setterfield; Carl Van Vechten.

DANDISON, Basil Gray (1900–   ) *See* McGraw-Hill.

DANGERFIELD, George (1904–   ) *See* American Historians.

DANIEL, E. Clifton, Jr. (1912–   ) *See* Journalism Lectures.

DANIEL, Price. *Discussed in* D.B. Hardeman.

DANIELIAN, Noobar R. (1906–1974) *See* Eisenhower Administration.

DANIELS, Alfred Harvey (1912–   ) *See* Federated Department Stores.

DANIELS, Bebe. *Discussed in* Albert E. Sutherland.

DANIELS, Jonathan Worth (1902–   ) Journalist.
SOUTHERN INTELLECTUAL LEADERS (A)
Childhood in North Carolina; education, University of North Carolina; writer for *Fortune;* editor, *The News and Observer;* politics and race relations in North Carolina; *A Southerner Discovers the South;* As-

sistant Director, US Office of Civilian Defense; Administrative Assistant, later Press Secretary, to President Franklin D. Roosevelt; racial problems during WWII; senatorial campaign of Frank Porter Graham, 1950; Democratic Party since 1945. Impressions of Josephus Daniels, Henry Luce, Eleanor Roosevelt, Harry S. Truman, Thomas Wolfe, and leading southern journalists.

176 pp. *Permission required to cite or quote.* 1972.
See also Adlai E. Stevenson Project. *Micro III.*
Discussed in William T. Couch.

DANIELS, Josephus. *Discussed in* Walter S. Anderson; Jonathan W. Daniels; James T. Williams, Jr.

DANUSSI, Luis (1913–   ) *See* Argentina.

DARBY, Harry (1895–   ) Senator.
EISENHOWER ADMINISTRATION
Republican Party and politics; pre-convention moves to encourage Eisenhower to run in 1952; impressions of Robert A. Taft.

73 pp. *Permission required.* 1967.

DARRACH, Neil C. (1917–   ) *See* Continental Group.

DAURAT, Didier. *See* Aviation Project.

DAVENPORT, Frederick Morgan (1866–1956) Politician.
Childhood and education; NY State legislature; Theodore Roosevelt; Bull Moose Party; NY State Republican politics; US House of Representatives; National Institute of Political Affairs.

101 pp. *Permission required to cite or quote.* 1952. *Micro II.*

DAVES, Delmer Lawrence (1904–1977) *See* Popular Arts.

DAVID, Alvin. *See* Social Security.

DAVIDSON, Ben (1900–   ) Politician.
Childhood in Pittsburgh; education, Carnegie Institute of Technology, Columbia, 1921; early involvement with labor unions, 1920's–'30's; NYC public school teaching

career; Director, Worker's School, 1925–29; political movements, 1920's–'40's; Director, American Labor Party, 1943–44; Executive Director, Liberal Party of NY State, 1944–77: founding convention, organizational development, fund raising, relationship of Democratic, Conservative and Liberal Parties in NYC and state; legal actions against Liberal Party; detailed chronological account of city, state, and national campaigns 1944–77. Impressions of Franklin D. Roosevelt, Jr., Robert F. Wagner, Herbert H. Lehman, Rudolph Halley, Alex Rose, John Lindsay, many others.

857 pp. *Permission required to cite or quote.* 1978. Papers.

DAVIDSON, Donald. *Discussed in* Robert Penn Warren.

DAVIDSON, Howard Calhoun. *See* Air Force Academy.

DAVIDSON, Robert. *See* Children's Television Workshop. *Micro IV.*

DAVIE, Eugenie Mary (Mrs. Preston) (1895–1975) *See* Robert A. Taft Project.

DAVIS, Benjamin. *Discussed in* George S. Schuyler.

DAVIS, Benjamin O. *See* Air Force Academy.

DAVIS, Gen. and Mrs. Benjamin O. *See* Air Force Academy.

DAVIS, Chester Charles (1887–1975) Agriculturist.
Newspaper work in South Dakota and Montana; Commissioner of Agriculture and Labor in Montana, 1921–23; Illinois Agricultural Assolciation; AAA; Federal Reserve System; WFA, 1943.

537 pp. *Permission required to cite or quote.* 1953. *Micro I.*
Discussed in Cully A. Cobb; Jerome N. Frank; Frederick W. Henshaw; Marvin Jones; M.L. Wilson.

DAVIS, Clarence Alba. Lawyer.
EISENHOWER ADMINISTRATION
Education; early political career in Nebraska; Under Secretary of Interior, 1954–

60; fisheries, water conservation, electric power.
106 pp. *Permission required.* 1967.

DAVIS, Doreen. *See* Flying Tigers.

DAVIS, Elmer Holmes (1890–1958) Writer.
The Henry Ford Peace Ship, 1915.
34 pp. *Permission required to cite or quote.* 1955. *Micro I.*

DAVIS, George (1914–   ) *See* Continental Group.

DAVIS, James J. *Discussed in* John P. Frey.

DAVIS, Joel. *See* Vietnam Veterans.

DAVIS, John Warren (1888–   ) Educator.
Georgia childhood; University of Chicago; YMCA administrator, 1917–19; history of black colleges in Atlanta; evolution of segregated land-grant colleges in West Virginia; President, West Virginia State College, 1919–50: faculty recruitment, building program, establishment in North Central Association, 1926, ROTC for black colleges; black masonic lodges; first black member of NEA; American Technical Assistance to Liberia, role of Firestone in diplomatic relations; NAACP Legal Defense and Educational Fund, 1954–   ; impressions of Ralph Bunche, Mary McLeod Bethune, Roy Wilkins, Whitney Young, Carter Woodson, Harry S. Truman, Thurgood Marshall.
629 pp. *Permission required to cite or quote.* 1976.

DAVIS, John William (1873–1955) Lawyer.
Early life and law practice in Clarksburg, W. Va.; Solicitor General of the US; 1924 campaign for President; comments on the Supreme Court, President, Cabinet and Washington, D.C.; ambassador to Great Britain; exchange and treatment of prisoners in WWI; law practice.
172 pp. *Permission required to cite or quote.* 1954. *Micro I.*
Discussed in Will Clayton; David Dean Johnson; Charles Poletti; Allen Wardwell.

DAVIS, Kenneth S. (1912–   ) *See* Adlai E. Stevenson Project.

DAVIS, Malcolm Waters (1889–   ) Internationalist.
Early life, education, training in journalism; Springfield *Republican,* 1911–13; relief work and USIS, Russia, 1917–19; October Revolution; NY *Evening Post;* Council on Foreign Relations; Yale University Press; Carnegie Endowment for International Peace, League of Nations, 1931–39; impressions of Nicholas Murray Butler; Germany and National Socialism; International Red Cross, 1939–40, European leaders, WWII; OSS, 1941–45; San Francisco UN Conference, 1945.
435 pp. *Permission required to cite or quote.* 1950. Papers. *Micro II.*
See also United Nations Conference.

DAVIS, Margaret E. (1892–   ) *See* Benedum and the Oil Industry.

DAVIS, Michael Marks (1879–1971) *See* Social Security.

DAVIS, William Hammatt (1879–1964) Labor mediator.
Work as Deputy Administrator and Compliance Director of NRA; NY State Mediation Board; work as Chairman of National Defense Mediation Board and WLB; impressions of James Byrnes, John L. Lewis, Herbert Lehman, George Meany, Robert Wagner, and Robert Taft.
205 pp. *Permission required to cite or quote.* 1958. *Micro I.* Papers.

DAVISON, Frederick Trubee (1896–1974) Lawyer, public official.
Family background and early life; Groton; Yale and the Yale Unit; Columbia Law School; NY politics, 1920–26; Crime Commission, 1926; Assistant Secretary of War for Air, 1926–32; American Museum of Natural History; election of 1940; Air Force and WWII.
280 pp. *Closed until November 14, 1984.* 1951.
See also Theodore Roosevelt Association.

DAVISON, Wilbert Cornell (1892–   ) Physician.
JAMES B. DUKE PROJECT
Family background, childhood, education; Princeton, 1909–13, Rhodes scholar, Oxford, 1913; WWI: volunteer in France

and Yugoslavia, 1914; Johns Hopkins Medical School, 1914; First Army Unit, Europe, 1918; Dean, Duke Medical School: construction of School and hospital, opening of School in 1930, furnishing library, selection of staff; trustee of Duke Endowment, 1960. Impressions of Doris Duke and numerous academic figures.
153 pp. *Permission required.* 1963.

DAWES, Charles G. *Discussed in* James M. Barker.

DAWSON, Marion Lindsay (1905–   ) *See* Marine Corps.

DAY, Clarence. *Discussed in* Alfred A. Knopf.

DAY, Edmund E. *Discussed in* Flora M. Rhind; J.P. Warburg.

DAY, James Edward (1914–   ) *See* Adlai E. Stevenson Project.

DAY, Karl Schmolsmire (1896–1973) *See* Marine Corps.

DAYAL, Rajeshwar (1909–   ) *See* International Negotiations.

DEAKIN, Harold Osborne (1913–   ) *See* Marine Corps.

DEAN, Gordon Evans (1905–1958) Lawyer. Education at Duke University; journalism; legal education at University of Southern California; teaching law at Duke and early practice; Criminal Division of Department of Justice; work with Homer Cummings, Frank Murphy, Robert H. Jackson and Thurman Arnold.
146 pp. *Permission required to cite or quote.* 1954. *Micro I.*

DEANE, Herbert A. *See* Columbia Crisis of 1968.

DEARING, Warren Palmer (1905–   ) *See* Health Sciences.

DEARY, William. *Discussed in* Weyerhaeuser Timber Company.

DE BAKEY, Michael. *Discussed in* Edward D. Churchill.

DE BARY, William Theodore (1919–   ) *See* Columbia Crisis of 1968.

DEBS, Eugene V. *Discussed in* A. Philip Randolph; Max Shachtman; Socialist Movement; John Spargo.

DEBYE, Peter Joseph William (1884–1967) *See* Nobel Laureates.

DE CAPRILES, Miguel (1906–   ) Administrator.
NEW YORK UNIVERSITY
Washington Square College, 1924–28; NYU Law School; early athletics program; effects of Depression on NYU; Hofstra-NYU affiliation; NYU Law School administration, 1930's, '40's; university development program; 1953, Director of Instructional Research and Educational Planning; Dean, NYU Law School, 1964–67; Heald, Newsom, Hester administrations; budgetary problems of 1970's; role as NYU legal counsel.
117 pp. *Permission required to cite or quote.* 1976.

DE CARLO, Charles. *Discussed* in Esther Raushenbush.

DECKER, Peter. *See* Rare Books (B).

DE CSEPEL, Baron Alfons Weiss. *See* Hungarian Project.

DEETERS, Jasper. *Discussed in* Sol Jacobson.

DE FLOREZ, Luis. *See* Aviation Project. *Micro II.*

DE FOREST, Lee (1873–1961) *See* Radio Pioneers.

DE GAULLE, Charles. *Discussed in* Joseph C. Baldwin; Michel Gordey; James C. Hagerty; Amory Houghton.

DE KIEWIET, Cornelis Willem (1902–   ) Historian.
CARNEGIE CORPORATION
Carnegie Corporation program for educa-

tion in developing African nations; British participation. Impressions of Alan Pifer, Stephen Stackpole, Whitney Shepardson, Charles Dollard, and John Gardner.
117 pp. *Permission required.* 1968

DE LA **CHAPELLE**, Clarence E. (1897–) Physician.
Education and medical training; NYU and Bellevue Hospital Medical College as teacher and administrator, 1924–62; teaching pathology, Medical Examiner system, police work; consultant practice; aviation and aerospace medicine; unusual patients; postgraduate medical education; medical training during WWII and postwar; women in medicine; research and clinical investigation; Heart Associations, socialized medicine and AMA.
461 pp. *Permission required to cite or quote.* 1962. *Micro II.*
See also New York Political Studies (A).

DELACORTE, Alfred. *See* Popular Arts.

DELANO, William Adams (1874–1960) Architect.
Education at Yale and Columbia School of Architecture; early practical work; study abroad; notable buildings and clients; Washington experiences; Board of Design for NY World's Fair, 1936; LaGuardia and Idlewild airports; West Point; charitable work.
94 pp. *Permission required to cite or quote.* 1950. *Micro I.*

DE LEON, Daniel. *Discussed in* John Spargo.

DeLONG, Edmund (1900–) Journalist.
Crime reporting on the NY *Sun;* Hall-Mills murder case; Philip Musica and his F. Donald Coster impersonation; Lindbergh kidnapping and the trial of Bruno Richard Hauptmann.
198 pp. *Permission required to cite or quote.* 1962. *Micro I.*

DEL **RIO**, Jorge. *See* Argentina.

DEL **VALLE**, Pedro Augusto (1893–1978) *See* Marine Corps.

DEMARCHI, Virginio. *See* Argentina.

DEMAREST, William (1892–) *See* Popular Arts.

DE **MILLE**, Agnes. *Discussed in* Aaron Copland.

DE **MILLE**, Cecil Blount (1881–1959) *See* Popular Arts.

DEMOCRATIC PARTY *See* Herman Badillo; Claude Bowers; Edward Costikyan; Jonathan W. Daniels; Marion Dickerman; Paul Douglas; Eisenhower Administration; James A. Farley; Justin N. Feldman; Edward J. Flynn; James W. Gerard; Florence J. Harriman; Edward I. Koch; Arthur Krock; Herbert Lehman; Katie Louchheim; Marshall Plan; Robert B. Meyner; Ferdinand Pecora; Herbert C. Pell; Frances Perkins; Charles Poletti; Joseph M. Proskauer; Lindsay Rogers; Terry Sanford; Adlai E. Stevenson Project; Frank Thompson, Jr.; Robert F. Wagner; Henry A. Wallace; Burton K. Wheeler.
See also New Deal.

DEMUTH, Richard Holzman (1910–) International official.
WORLD BANK
Prior experience and appointment to World Bank; relationship between directors and staff; Meyer and McCloy presidencies; creation of Development Advisory Service and Economic Development Institute; negative pledge clause; survey missions; political loans; development banks; project loans; balance of payment loans; lines of credit.
91 pp. *Permission required to cite or quote.* 1961.

DENFELD, Louis. *Discussed in* James L. Holloway, Jr.

DENHAM, Reginald (1894–) *See* Popular Arts.

DENNIS, John H. (1907–) *See* Continental Group.

DENNIS, Lawrence (1893–) Writer, banker.
Childhood; education, Exeter and Harvard; military experiences; diplomatic service to 1927: Haiti, Rumania, Honduras, Nicaragua; banking experiences with Seligmans;

theories of government; isolationism; *The Coming American Fascism; Appeal to Reason;* impressions of Adolf Hitler, Benito Mussolini, Hermann Goering, Joseph Goebbels; WWII; Vietnam; trial for sedition.
90 pp. *Permission required to cite or quote.* 1967. *Micro II.*

DENNY, Charles Ruthven (1912–) *See* James Lawrence Fly Project.

DENNY, George. *Discussed in* Selma W. Warner.

DENNY, Reginald Leigh (1891–1967) *See* Popular Arts.

DEPARTMENT OF DEFENSE *See* William A.M. Burden; Carter Burgess; Charles A. Coolidge; James H. Douglas, Jr.; Gordon Gray; Najeeb Halaby; Karl G. Harr, Jr.; Roger W. Jones; James R. Killian, Jr.; Neil H. McElroy; Earl McGrath; Marine Corps; Naval History; John S. Patterson; Robert P. Patterson Project; Kenneth C. Royall; Murray Snyder; Mansfield D. Sprague; Nathan F. Twining.
See also US Air Force; US Army; US Navy.

DEPEW, Chauncey. *Discussed in* Beverley R. Robinson.

DEPRESSION OF THE 1930's *See* Barbara Armstrong; Eleanor Arnold; Will Barnet; Herbert Benjamin; Adolf Berle; Holger Cahill; Paul Douglas; John W. Edelman; John Clellon Holmes; Ernest Rice McKinney; Milton Meltzer; Frances Perkins; Louis H. Pink; Jacob S. Potofsky; Paul and Elizabeth Raushenbush; Jackson E. Reynolds; Rexford G. Tugwell; Walter Wyatt.

DE SAPIO, Carmine. *Discussed in* Edward Costikyan; Justin N. Feldman; Herman S. Greitzer; Edward I. Koch; Ludwig Teller; Robert F. Wagner.

DESSEZ, Lester Adolphus (1896–) *See* Marine Corps.

DE SYLVA, Oscar (1909–) *See* Continental Group.

DEVEREUX, James Patrick Sinnott (1903–) Marine Corps officer.

Family background; duty in Nicaragua, 1926–29; China, 1930–32; WWII: defense of Wake Island, prisoner of war, liberation; experiences as a member of Congress from 1951.
208 pp. *Open.* 1970.

D'EWART, Wesley Abner (1889–1973) Government official.
EISENHOWER ADMINISTRATION
Experiences as Assistant Secretary of the Interior: water policy and development, national parks, public lands, Indian affairs.
136 pp. *Permission required to cite or quote.* 1967. *Micro III.*

DEWEY, Godfrey (1887–1977) Educator and author.
Simplified spelling movement in US and Britain, 1876–1971.
38 pp. *Open.* 1971. Papers. *Contributed by Benjamin D. Wood, New York.*

DEWEY, John (1859–1952) Philosopher.
Ninetieth birthday interview and tribute.
8 pp. *Open.* 1949. *Contributed by Oliver Reiser, Pittsburgh.*
Discussed in Harold F. Clark; Charlotte Garrison; James Gutmann; Isaac L. Kandel; William H. Kilpatrick; John K. Norton; R. Bruce Raup; Herbert W. Schneider; Goodwin Watson.

DEWEY, Thomas Edmund (1902–1971) Lawyer, governor.
Family background, childhood in Michigan, music; legal education, University of Michigan and Columbia; early legal experience; Chief Assistant US Attorney, 1931–33; George Z. Medalie; political experience, 9th and 10th Assembly Districts, NYC; US Attorney; Young Republican Club; Fiorello La Guardia; 1932 campaign, NY State; income tax and Samuel Seabury investigation; labor gangster cases; private practice, 1934; special prosecutor, 1935; rackets investigation and "Lucky" Luciano; NY County District Attorney, 1937: procedural changes, blue ribbon juries, Hines Case; campaigns 1938, 1939, 1940; USO campaign, 1942.
659 pp. *Permission required to cite or quote.* 1959.

EISENHOWER ADMINISTRATION
Recollections of the Eisenhower administration.
43 pp. *Permission required to cite or quote.* 1970.

Discussed in Sherman Adams; William H. Allen; Raymond Baldwin; David Dressler; Stanley Fuld; Stanley M. Isaacs; Edwin A. Lahey; Warren Moscow; David W. Peck; Francis R. Stoddard; Robert F. Wagner.

DE WILDE, John C., Gerald Alter and Harold Larsen. *See* World Bank.

DEWSON, Mary W. *Discussed in* Eveline Burns.

D'HARNONCOURT, Rene (1901–1968)
Museum director.
CARNEGIE CORPORATION
Relations of Carnegie Corporation and American Federation of Art.
65 pp. *Permission required.* 1968.

DIAMOND, Sigmund (1920–   ) *See* American Historians.

DIAMOND, William (1917–   ) and Michael Hoffman. *See* World Bank.

DIAZ DE VIVAR, Joaquin. *See* Argentina.

DICK, Jane (Mrs. Edison) (1906–   )
ADLAI E. STEVENSON PROJECT
Recollections of Adlai Stevenson during 1920's and 30's; Ellen Borden Stevenson; Stevenson's religious beliefs; views on capital punishment; Stevenson's gubernatorial campaign and nomination for President; 1952 campaign; Stevenson as UN Ambassador; reaction to Cuba missile crisis.
102 pp. *Permission required to cite or quote.* 1969.

DICKER, Edward T. *See* Eisenhower Administration. *Micro III.*

DICKERMAN, Marion (1890–   ) Educator.
WWI; friendship with Franklin and Eleanor Roosevelt; Todhunter School; Valkill Industries; Alfred E. Smith; opposition to Tammany Hall; Democratic conventions, 1924–32; reminiscences of Hyde Park,

Campobello, Warm Springs; Eleanor Roosevelt: childhood, interest in women's suffrage and West Virginia mine workers, travels in Tennessee, Kentucky, Illinois; 74th Congress, 1935–36; visiting royalty; international conferences; death of President Roosevelt; of Mrs. Roosevelt; recollections of Roosevelt children, Louis Howe, Sumner Welles, Marguerite Le Hand, Harry Hopkins, and many others.
345 pp. *Permission required.* 1971.

DICKEY, James (1923–   ) *See* Poets on their Poetry.

DICKINSON, Edwin Walter (1891–1978)
Artist.
Family background, childhood and early education; studies with William Chase and Charles W. Hawthorne; experiences as an art student; views on art and experiences as a professional painter; illustrated discussion of a number of his paintings.
227 pp. *Permission required to cite or quote.* 1958. *Micro II.*

DICKINSON, Robert L. *Discussed in* Emily H. Mudd.

DICKINSON, Thorold and Joanna. *See* Robert J. Flaherty Project.

DICKMAN, Frank. *See* McGraw-Hill.

DICKMANN, Emilio. *See* Argentina.

DICKSTEIN, Samuel (1885–1954) Lawyer, congressman.
Early 20th-century NY politics; House Un-American Activities Committee; Dickstein Nationality Act and immigration.
74 pp. *Permission required to cite or quote.* 1950. *Micro I.*

DIEHL, Walter Stuart (1893–   ) Naval officer.
Pensacola; MIT, 1917; work in aerodynamics, aeronautics, 1918–46; designing and testing Navy planes, World Wars I and II; Taylor Model Basin.
93 pp. *Permission required.* 1965.

DIEM, Ngo Dinh. *Discussed in* Leo Cherne.

DIERINGER, John W. (1899–) *See* Benedum and the Oil Industry.

DIES, Martin. *Discussed in* Thomas I. Emerson.

DIGGINS, John P. *See* Herbert W. Schneider.

DILL, Sir John. *Discussed in* James Fife.

DILLINGER, John. *Discussed in* Edwin A. Lahey.

DILLON, Clarence Douglas (1909–) Government official, financier.
EISENHOWER ADMINISTRATION
Ambassador to France, 1953–57; Suez crisis, Indochina; Deputy Under Secretary, later Under Secretary of State, 1957–61: international economic policy, Secretaries John Foster Dulles and Christian Herter, Latin American policy, Inter-American Bank, Treasury Secretaries George Humphrey and Robert B. Anderson, U-2 incident, NSC, AID, foreign assistance, Congo, 1960 gold crisis, EDC; evaluation of Eisenhower administration; administrative transition, 1961; appointment as Treasury Secretary, 1961.
94 pp. *Permission required; certain pages closed.* 1972.

DIONNE, Joseph (1933–) *See* McGraw-Hill.

DIPLOMACY/INTERNATIONAL AF-FAIRS *See* Dean Acheson; Sherman Adams; Winthrop W. Aldrich; George V. Allen; Dillon Anderson; Hilda Anderson; Sir Norman Angell; Paul Appleby; John Badeau; Boris Bakhmeteff; Roger N. Baldwin; James W. Barco; Adolf Berle; Hugh Borton; Claude Bowers; Chester Bowles; Spruille Braden; Hilarion N. Branch; Ellis Briggs; William A. M. Burden; Candler Cobb; Charles Cook; Andrew Cordier; Daniel Cosio Villegas; Frederic R. Coudert; W.W. Cumberland; John W. Davis; Lawrence Dennis; C. Douglas Dillon; Goldthwaite Dorr; Eleanor L. Dulles; Donald Dumont; Ethnic Groups and American Foreign Policy; James W. Gerard; Andrew J. Goodpaster; Lloyd C. Griscom; Ernest A. Gross;

John Hightower; Robert C. Hill; Alger Hiss; Amory Houghton; International Negotiations; F. Peterson Jessup; Philip C. Jessup; Joseph E. Johnson; Nelson T. Johnson; Joseph J. Jova; Walter H. Judd; Brij Mohan Kaul; Henry J. Kellerman; Bruno Lasker; League of Nations Project; John Davis Lodge; Clare Boothe Luce; Thomas C. Mann; Marshall Plan; Livingston T. Merchant; Allan Nevins; David R. Nimmer; Occupation of Japan; Lithgow Osborne; Jan Papanek; Herbert C. Pell; William Phillips; DeWitt Clinton Poole;

Arthur F. Raper; Ogden R. Reid; Walter S. Robertson; Nelson A. Rockefeller; George Rublee; Roy R. Rubottom, Jr.; Aleksander W. Rudzinski; Sir George Sansom; Francis B. Sayre; Stuart N. Scott; Adlai E. Stevenson Project; Anna Lord Strauss; Henry A. Wallace; James P. Warburg; Leslie A. Wheeler; John C. White; World Bank; William Yale; Sir Muhammad Zafrulla Khan. *See also* North Atlantic Treaty Organization; United Nations.

DIXON, J. Curtis (1894–) Educator.
Family background, early schooling; Mercer and Columbia Universities; WWI; career as teacher, principal, businessman, school superintendent in Richland, Georgia; State Supervisor of School Administration and Finance; county schools survey; State agent for Negro schools; graduate work, TC; General Education Board; Rosenwald Fund; rural education conferences; Jeanes teachers; Vice Chancellor, University of Georgia, 1940–42; Vice President, Mercer University, 1942–46; Southern Education Foundation, 1945–65: moving headquarters to Atlanta, staff, financing, programs, travel, charter; analysis of Negro educational institutions; training for principals; effect of 1954 desegregation decision.
513 pp. *Permission required to cite or quote.* 1967. *Underwritten by the Rockefeller Foundation.*

DIXON, Sherwood (1896–) *See* Adlai E. Stevenson Project.

DIZNEY, Helen (1894–) *See* China Missionaries.

DMYTRYK, Edward (1908–   ) *See* Popular Arts.

DOAN, Richard K. *See* Radio Pioneers.

DOBZHANSKY, Theodosius (1900–1975) Geneticist.
Part I: Childhood and education in Russia; early interest in genetics; experiences during revolutionary and postrevolutionary years; training in genetics in Russia; Rockefeller fellowship to work in US, 1928; California Institute of Technology, 1930–40; professor of zoology, Columbia University, 1940. Detailed descriptions of work with T.H. Morgan, A. H. Sturtevant, and C. B. Bridges.
Part II: Problems of artificial selection; racism; Zoology Department, Columbia University, 1940–62; research in California, Mexico, Brazil; Latin American scientists; travels to New Guinea, Australia, Egypt, India, Indonesia. Impressions of noted scientists.
637 pp. *Permission required to cite or quote. 1962. Micro II.*
Discussed in Leslie C. Dunn.

DOCHEZ, Alphonse Raymond (1882–1964) Physician.
Undergraduate work at Johns Hopkins; work at Rockefeller Institute, 1907–19 (pneumococcus and hemolytic streptococcus); work in 1920's on scarlet fever and early experiments on common cold; reflections on P&S during the 1920's and 1930's; WWII: OSRD.
165 pp. *Permission required to cite or quote. 1955. Micro IV.* Papers: Bibliography and 3 papers.

DODD, Frank H. *Discussed in* S. Phelps Platt.

DODDS, Harold W. (1889–   ) University president.
Princeton University during his Presidency, 1933–57; Peruvian-Chilean dispute and Tacna-Arica Plebiscite Commission, 1925–26; President's Commission on Universal Military Training, 1947.
292 pp. *Permission required.* 1966.
See also Carnegie Corporation.
Discussed in W. H. Cowley.

DODGE, Cleveland E. (1888–   ) *See* Mining Engineers.

DODGE, Grace. *Discussed in* Charlotte Garrison.

DODGE, Homer Levi (1887–   ) *See* American Association of Physics Teachers.

DODGE, Merton L. *See* Continental Group.

DODSON, James. *See* Aviation Project.

DOERSCHUK, Beatrice. *Discussed in* Esther Raushenbush.

DOHENY, Edward L. *Discussed in* Michael L. Benedum; Hilarion N. Branch.

DOHERTY, William Charles (1902–   ) Union official.
National Letter Carriers' Union during the late 1930's; efforts of the Union to improve wages and working conditions through legislation; autobiographical details.
57 pp. *Permission required to cite or quote. 1956. Micro IV.*

DOISY, Edward Adelbert (1893–   ) *See* Nobel Laureates.

DOLAN, Charles. *See* Air Force Academy.

DOLAN, Henry P. *See* New York Political Studies (A).

DOLBERG, Glen. *See* Radio Pioneers.

DOLGER, Henry. *See* Mt. Sinai Hospital.

D'OLIVE, Charles. *See* Air Force Academy.

DOLLARD, Charles (1907–1977) Foundation executive.
CARNEGIE CORPORATION
Career with Carnegie Corporation; assistant to president, 1938–45; executive associate, 1945–47; Vice President, 1947–48; President, 1948–54; grants in social sciences; Commonwealth program; discussion of policies, program, and personnel. Impressions of Frederick Keppel, Devereux Josephs, John Gardner, Florence Anderson, and others.

329 pp. *Permission required.* 1966.
See also Association for the Aid of Crippled Children.
Discussed in Florence Anderson; Cornelis W. de Kiewiet; Caryl P. Haskins; Gunnar Myrdal; Frederick Osborn; John M. Russell; Stephen Stackpole.

DOLLFUS, Charles. *See* Aviation Project.

DOMENECH, Jose. Labor leader.
ARGENTINA
Detailed account of experiences as union leader, 1909–43: early work on railroads, local union official, founding of railway union, 1922; national labor official, 1926–43; Argentine representative to Latin American labor groups; political activity.
192 pp. *Open except for specified pages.* 1970.
Discussed in Ernesto Janin; Juan Rodriguez.

DOMJAN, Joseph (1907–   ) *See* Hungarian Project.

DONAHUE, James I. (1901–   ) *See* Continental Group.

DONAHUE, P.J. *Discussed in* John T. Hettrick.

DONAHUE, Richard. *See* Social Security.

DONALD, David (1920–   ) *See* American Historians.

DONOVAN, Hedley Williams (1914–   ) Publishing executive.
AMERICAN CULTURAL LEADERS
Boyhood, Minneapolis; University of Minnesota and Oxford University, 1930–36; experiences as *Washington Post* reporter, 1937–42; *Fortune* writer and editor, 1945–51; editorial procedures and management structure, *Time*, Inc., 1951–67.
184 pp. *Permission required.* 1967.

DONOVAN, Robert John (1912–   ) Journalist.
EISENHOWER ADMINISTRATION
Washington Bureau Chief, NY *Herald Tribune,* 1957–63; *Eisenhower: The Inside Story;* impressions of Eisenhower and his administration.

51 pp. *Permission required to cite or quote.* 1968. *Micro IV.*

DONOVAN, William. *Discussed in* James Fife.

DOOLEY, Thomas. *Discussed in* Leo Cherne.

DOOLITTLE, James Harold (1896–   ) Aviator.
Childhood interest in aviation; flight training, years as instructor; promoting aviation after WWI; early stunts, air shows; Gen. Billy Mitchell; WWII bombing missions; DH-4 flight across US; Snyder Cup races; acceleration and wind gradients research; full-flight lab work; test piloting, development of instrumentation.
160 pp. *Permission required to cite or quote.* 1973. *Micro III. Contributed by Robert S. Gallagher, LaCrosse, Wisconsin.*
See also Air Force Academy *and* Aviation Project. *Micro II.*

DOOMAN, Eugene (1890–1969) Diplomat.
OCCUPATION OF JAPAN
Background, early experiences as language student in Japan; US Embassy, Tokyo, 1921–31; Manchurian question; London, 1931–33; State Department, 1933–37; Counselor, US Embassy, Tokyo, 1937–41; detailed analysis of US-Japanese relations prior to Pearl Harbor; impressions of Japanese officials, Joseph Grew, Cordell Hull.
171 pp. *Permission required to cite or quote.* 1962. *Micro III.* Papers.
Discussed in Joseph Ballantine.

DORR, Goldthwaite Higginson (1876–1977) Lawyer.
Harvard, European travel; early law practice; assistant US Attorney; War Department, 1917–19; renegotiating war contracts, conversion to peace; law practice, NY; travels in Middle East, 1931; WWII, special assistant to Secretary of War; Hoover Commission on Law Observance, 1930–31; Cotton Textile Code and early days of NRA, 1932–33; Cabinet Committee to prepare joint plan with British for solution to Palestine problem, 1947; International Refugees and Displaced Persons Bills, 1947; IRO, 1948; problems of European migration, Migration Conference,

1950; representative of Defense Department at Council of Foreign Ministers meeting in Paris, 1949; travels; Joseph McCarthy era. Impressions of Presidents Theodore Roosevelt, William H. Taft, Herbert Hoover, Franklin D. Roosevelt, Harry Truman; of Henry L. Stimson, Robert P. Patterson, Benedict Crowell, Hugh Johnson, and many other political figures.

647 pp. *Permission required.* 1962. Papers.

DOUBLEDAY, Frank N. *Discussed in* Alfred A. Knopf; May Massee; Arthur W. Page.

DOUGLAS, Donald Wills (1892–   ) Aircraft manufacturer.
HENRY H. ARNOLD PROJECT
Family background; Naval Academy, MIT; aeronautical design; chief engineer, Martin Co., Los Angeles, 1915–16, Cleveland, 1917–20; chief, aeronautical engineering, US Signal Corps, 1916–17; Davis-Douglas Co., 1920; Douglas Co., 1921–28; Douglas Aircraft Co., 1928 to present. Comments on early aviation, planes, engines, changes in the aircraft industry, relations with government and military agencies; early designs, DC1–3, B-19; recollections of Gen. H. H. Arnold, Glenn Martin, Harry Chandler, Howard Hughes, and other pioneers in aviation.

137 pp. *Permission required.* 1959.

DOUGLAS, James Henderson, Jr. (1899–   ) *See* Eisenhower Administration. *Micro IV.*

DOUGLAS, Lewis (1894–1974) Government official.
EISENHOWER ADMINISTRATION
Amherst College; MIT; Arizona state legislator, 1923–25; Congressional Representative, 1926–34; Director of the Budget, 1933–34; economic advisor to President Eisenhower; impressions of Adlai E. Stevenson, President Eisenhower, John Foster Dulles.

56 pp. *Permission required to cite or quote.* 1972. *Micro IV.*
See also Marshall Plan. *Micro IV.*
Discussed in James P. Warburg.

DOUGLAS, Melvyn (1901–   ) *See* Popular Arts.

DOUGLAS, Paul H. (1892–1976) Senator.
Relationships with Harry S. Truman, Adlai E. Stevenson; Chicago alderman, 1939–42, investigation of corruption; federal patronage, government appointments for Democrats in Illinois; Great Depression, economic cycles, proposed methods of stabilization.

52 pp. *Open.* 1975.
See also Herbert H. Lehman Project.
Discussed in Lawrence Irvin.

DOUGLAS OF KIRTLESIDE, Lord (William Sholto Douglas) (1893–1969) *See* Aviation Project.

DOUTHIT, George. *See* Eisenhower Administration. *Micro III.*

DOW, Arthur. *Discussed in* Max Weber.

DOWLING, Eddie (1894–1976) Actor, producer, director.
Family background; childhood and education, Rhode Island; early vaudeville career; 1919–20 *Follies;* Actors' strike, 1919; early plays: *Sally, Irene, and Mary; Honeymoon Lane; Sidewalks of New York;* Chrysler-Ziegfeld Radio Follies; NYC Democratic politics: William F. Kenny's Tiger Room; national and state campaigns, 1926–40, organization and finances; Banking Crisis; 1932 Federal Theater Project; organizer and first president, USO Camp Shows, WWII; Tennessee Williams, *The Glass Menagerie;* Eugene O'Neill, *The Iceman Cometh;* comments on many people in the theater, Hollywood, business, finance and politics, including L. B. Mayer, Marcus Loew, Sarah Bernhardt, Boris Said, George Jean Nathan, Alfred E. Smith, J. J. Raskob, Tim Mara, Henry Morgenthau, Frank Hague, Joseph P. Kennedy, Michael Curley.

838 pp. *Permission required to cite or quote.* 1963. *Micro III.*

DOWNS, Alletta Laird. *See* Longwood Gardens.

DOXIADIS, Constantinos A. (1913–1975) Architect, city planner.

Man's increasing alienation from his urban habitat; from urbanization to universal city; need for new conceptions of functions of the city; need to move from static to continuous planning; connection of esthetics to kinetics.
41 pp. *Open.* 1964.

DRAPER, Warren Fales (1883–1970) *See* Health Sciences.

DRAPER, William H., Jr. (1894–1974) *See* Eisenhower Administration. *Micro III.*

DREISER, Theodore. *Discussed in* Ellen C. Masters; Carl Van Vechten.

DRESSLER, David (1907–) Social worker, writer.
Childhood and education; training as a social worker; service on Parole Board in NY; law enforcement in NYC; impressions of Thomas Dewey, Fiorello La Guardia, Herbert Lehman, Louis Valentine.
185 pp. *Permission required to cite or quote.* 1961. *Micro I.*

DREYFUS, John. *Discussed in* Helen Macy.

DRINKER, Cecil. *Discussed in* Edward D. Churchill.

DRUMMOND, Sir Eric. *Discussed in* Thanassis Aghnides; Pablo de Azcarate; Branko Lukac.

DRUMMOND, Roscoe (1902–) Columnist.
EISENHOWER ADMINISTRATION
Christian Science Monitor Washington Bureau, 1940–53; NY *Herald Tribune,* 1953–55; foreign policy under Eisenhower; John Foster Dulles, Richard Nixon.
32 pp. *Permission required to cite or quote.* 1967. *Micro III.*

DRURY, Newton Bishop (1889–1978) Conservationist.
Secretary to University of California president Benjamin Ide Wheeler; Drury Brothers Advertising Agency; Save-the-Redwoods League; creation of California State Park system; National Park Service, 1940–51; Jackson Hole acquisition and other controversies; administration of California

State Park system, 1951–59; first World Conference on National Parks; establishment of Redwood National Park; comments on campaigns, California legislators, state and federal officials, conservation leaders, and lobbying.
651 pp. *Permission required to cite or quote.* 1972. Papers. *Acquired from the Regional Oral History Office, University of California, Berkeley.*

DRURY, Newton and Horace M. Albright. *See* Horace M. Albright.

DRYDEN, Hugh Latimer (1898–1965) *See* Aviation Project. *Micro II.*

DRYDEN, Kenneth Wayne (1947–) Athlete.
Montreal Summer Olympics, 1976; Canadian National Hockey Team; impressions of Moscow, Leningrad, 1969; Soviet Army-Philadelphia Flyers incident; Soviet Sport Institute.
58 pp. *Permission required to cite or quote; certain pages closed.* 1976.

DUARTE, Hector (1914–) *See* Argentina.

DuBOIS, Eugene. *Discussed in* Joseph C. Aub.

DU BOIS, William Edward Burghardt (1868–1963) Author, educator.
Family background, childhood and education; Fisk University; Harvard and graduate work in Germany; teaching at Wilberforce University; sociological studies for Wharton School; teaching and annual conferences at Atlanta University; Niagara Movement; Booker T. Washington.
191 pp. *Permission required to cite or quote.* 1960. *Micro I.*
Discussed in Arthur B. Spingarn.

DUBOS, Rene Jules (1901–) Bacteriologist.
Part I: Development of his work in bacteriology to 1943, and, more particularly, his thinking about his work; childhood and early training; polysaccharide of pneumococcus; Oswald T. Avery; tyrocidine, streptomycin and gramicidin; Harvard University and the war years.

Part II: Development of his work in bacteriology since 1945; and in particular his concern with the physiological, biochemical, and metabolic aspects of tuberculosis research; writing of *Louis Pasteur, The White Plague, The Biochemical Determinants of Disease,* and *Bacterial and Mycotic Infections in Man;* scientific papers; Rockefeller Institute.

1,541 pp. *Permission required to cite or quote.* 1957.

DUER, Caroline King (1865-1956) Poet, writer.
NY society; hospital work in World Wars I and II; personal recollections of Henry James, Edith Wharton, and other writers.
76 pp. *Permission required to cite or quote.* 1950. *Micro IV.* Papers: letters from France during WWI (microfilm).

DUFFUS, Robert Luther (1888-1972) Author, journalist.
Youth and education; San Francisco journalism, 1911-19; NY *Globe* and *Herald,* 1919-24; free-lance writing, 1924-37; editorial board NY *Times,* 1937-51.
134 pp. *Permission required to cite or quote.* 1951. *Micro I.*

DUGGER, Ronnie (1930-   ) *See* American Cultural Leaders.

DUKE, Doris. *Discussed in* Wilbert C. Davison; Edward S. Hansen; Thomas L. Perkins.

JAMES B. DUKE PROJECT
Through a series of interviews, the origins and subsequent activities of the Duke Endowment are set forth, with particular focus upon the personality and career of the founder. Associates of James B. Duke (1857-1925) and persons active in his manifold interests provide personal reminiscences, anecdotes, and comments on the Duke family, the career of Duke, the development of the Duke Power Company and various other business ventures designed to advance the Piedmont region of North Carolina, his early interest in southern education, in particular Trinity College (now Duke University), and developments since his death. A number of the memoirs also contain firsthand material on life in the Piedmont in the early years of the century and the economic and social changes brought by industrialization, which followed hard upon the provision of dependable power. Others discuss the establishment of Duke University, with much material on the faculty and presidents during the Trinity College era. Recent efforts of the Endowment in education, religion and hospital work in the South are considered.
Participants and pages: Mildred Baldwin, 49; Bernard Baruch, 51; Clarence E. Buchanan, 31; E. R. Bucher, 35; Charles A. Cannon, 45; Norman Cocke, 204; Wilbert C. Davison, 153; Mary Few, 285; John Fox, 68; Bennette Geer, 94; Mary Glassen, 33; Edward S. Hansen, 176; Philip B. Heartt, 62; Christy Hibberd, 13; Leon E. Hickman, 7; Tom F. Hill, 18; Roy A. Hunt, 39; Thomas D. Jolly, 34; Marvin Kimbrell, 24; Carl Lee, 93; Mrs. E. C. Marshall, 54; Grier Martin, 73; Robert Mayer, 69; Mr. and Mrs. E. R. Merrick, 70; Thomas L. Perkins, 126; Rufus P. Perry, 75; Richard Pfaehler, 20; John L. Plyler, 78; Grady Rankin, 41; Watson S. Rankin, 87; Charles S. Reed, 38; William Robinson, 20; Frank W. Rounds, Jr., 5; Mary Semans, 150; Hersey Spence, 78; Kenneth C. Towe, 168; C. T. Wanzer, 54; Edward Williams, 42; Mrs. John Williams, 64; Bunyan Snipes Womble, 81.
2,907 pp. *Permission required.* 1966. *Underwritten by the Duke Endowment.*

DULANY, George William, Jr. (1877-   ) *See* Forest History Society.

DULLES, Allen. *Discussed in* Eleanor Dulles; F. Peterson Jessup.

DULLES, Eleanor Lansing (1895-   ) Economist.
EISENHOWER ADMINISTRATION
Family background; childhood in NY State; Bryn Mawr; refugee work, Paris, 1917-19; graduate training, industrial management; factory employment manager; London School of Economics, 1921-22; Radcliffe and Harvard; European study and travel; teaching, Bryn Mawr, 1932-36; University of Pennsylvania; Social Security Board; BEW, 1942; State Department, 1942-62: UNRRA, Morgenthau Plan, displaced persons, Bretton Woods Confer-

ence, security investigations, occupation of Austria and treaty negotiations, currency reform and monetary conversion. Impressions of Robert Lansing, John Foster Dulles, Allen Dulles, and many others.
973 pp. *Permission required.* 1967.

EISENHOWER ADMINISTRATION
Recollections of brother John Foster Dulles, his duties, crises faced as President Eisenhower's Secretary of State.
41 pp. *Permission required.* 1970.

EISENHOWER ADMINISTRATION
Critique of Leonard Mosley's *Dulles: A Biography of Eleanor, Allen, and John Foster Dulles and Their Family Network.*
93 pp. *Permission required.* 1978.

See also John F. Kennedy Project.

DULLES, John Foster (1888–1959) *See* New York Political Studies (C.)
Discussed in Elie Abel; Sherman Adams; H. Meade Alcorn, Jr.; George V. Allen; Dillon Anderson; James W. Barco; Robert R. Bowie; Ellis O. Briggs; Prescott Bush; Charles D. Cook; W.W. Cumberland; C. Douglas Dillon; Lewis Douglas; Roscoe Drummond; Eleanor L. Dulles; Milton S. Eisenhower; Ernest Gross; John Hightower; Robert C. Hill; Alger Hiss; Amory Houghton; Walter H. Judd; Clare Boothe Luce; Carl W. McCardle; Livingston T. Merchant; Flora M. Rhind; Chalmers M. Roberts; Walter S. Robertson; James R. Shepley; James P. Warburg.

DUMONT, Donald A. (1911–   ) *See* Eisenhower Administration.

DUNCAN, Donald (1896–1975) Naval officer.
Education, Michigan and Naval Academy; WWI; naval aviation, Pensacola, 1920; experience in ordnance, communication; Fleet Aviation Officer, 1930–31; training aviation unit, Naval Academy; Plans Division, Bureau of Aeronautics, 1933; carrier duty, air tactics, group tactics; development of auxiliary carriers: the *Long Island;* WWII: Adm. Ernest King's staff, Tokyo raid, commanding *Essex,* War Plans Officer for Adm. King, detailed description of Joint Chiefs of Staff and Combined Chiefs

of Staff, Harry Hopkins, Quebec and Yalta conferences, Pacific carrier task groups; postwar chief of staff to Commander-in-Chief, Pacific; atom bomb tests; reorganization; Deputy Chief for Air, 1947; National Advisory Committee for Aeronautics; missiles; Naval air bases; 2nd Task Fleet; Korean War; Vice Chief of Naval Operations, 1951–56.
981 pp. *Closed until Sept. 8, 1980.* 1964.

DUNCAN, Robert. *See* Poets on their Poetry.

DUNN, Leslie Clarence (1893–1974) Geneticist.
Training in the biological sciences in the US from 1905; history of genetics in the US, Great Britain, Germany, and Russia; developmental genetics, interdisciplinary symposia, "Growth Symposia"; influence of genetics on pathological and biochemical researches; impressions of Soviet science and scientists: trip to Russia, 1927, Genetics Congress meeting at Columbia, 1932; plant breeding in Russia; demise of Gorki Institute of Medico-Genetics and of some Soviet scientists during 1938 crisis; Lysenko school versus the Mendelist-Morganist-Weissmanist school; American-Soviet Science Society; scientific debates in Russia, 1936, 1938–39, 1948. The Jackson Laboratory; experimental studies of wild mice; cytogenetics; population genetics and evolution; work in population genetics in Sweden; Institute for the Study of Human Variation; genetics studies in Japan; bacterial genetics; Nevis Biological Station; radiation and genetics; scientists and government; Columbia's Department of Zoology; chronological summary of developments in genetics. Impressions of William Castle, Thomas H. Morgan, William Bateson, Richard Goldschmidt, Alexander Serebrovskii, Nikolai Vavilov, Theodosius Dobzhansky, H. J. Muller, Trofim Lysenko, and others.
1,086 pp. *Permission required to cite or quote.* 1960. *Micro IV.*

DUNN, Loula Friend. *See* Social Security.
Discussed in Charles I. Schottland.

DUNN, William R. *See* Air Force Academy.

DUNNING, John Ray (1907–1975) *See* Journalism Lectures (A).

DU PONT, Pierre S. *Discussed in* Longwood Gardens; John K. Jenney.

DURANT, Helen Van Dongen. *See* Robert J. Flaherty Project.

DURDEN, Dennis. *See* Federated Department Stores.

DURDIN, Frank Tillman (1907–   ) *See* International Negotiations.

DURMENT, T. S. *See* Weyerhaeuser Timber Company.

DURR, Charles W. *See* Thomas A. Edison Project.

DURR, Clifford Judkins (1899–1975) Lawyer.
Family history and Southern tradition; legal practice; RFC; Government Reorganization Act; Defense Plant corporation; development programs; FCC; Communication Act of 1934; House Committee on Un-American Activities; FBI loyalty programs; broadcast license renewal considerations; academic freedom issue; Montgomery civil rights practice; impressions of Jesse Jones, Hugo Black, Aubrey Williams, others in New Deal Washington.
328 pp. *Permission required to cite or quote.* 1974. *Micro III.*
See also James Lawrence Fly Project.

DURR, Virginia Foster (Mrs. Clifford) Civil rights worker.

Family history and background, Birmingham society; Hugo Black; marriage and move to Washington,; recollections of New Deal Washington; RFC, poll tax, unions, La Follette Committee hearings; Southern Conference for Human Welfare in Birmingham; Brown decision; Internal Security Sub-Committee, Dies Committee; 1948 campaign and Henry A. Wallace; return to Alabama, 1951 civil rights activities, bus boycott, freedom riders, Selma march, Black Power movement; Southern issues, Southern women. Impressions of many Washington figures, including Lyndon Johnson, Justice Brandeis, James Eastland.
373 pp. *Permission required to cite or quote.* 1974. *Micro III.*

DURSTINE, Roy Sarles (1886–1962) Advertising executive.
Election of 1912; William Howard Taft; Bruce Barton; advertising, 1912–49.
49 pp. *Permission required to cite or quote.* 1949. *Micro III.*

DU VIGNEAUD, Vincent (1901–1978) *See* Nobel Laureates.

DUYVENDAK, J.J.L. *Discussed in* L. Carrington Goodrich.

DYER, Edward Colston (1907–1975) *See* Marine Corps.

DYER, Rolla Eugene (1886–1971) *See* Health Sciences.

DYKE, George E. (1892–   ) *See* Continental Group.

E

EAGLE, Arnold. *See* Robert J. Flaherty Project.

EAKER, Ira C. (1896–   ) Manufacturing executive.
HENRY H. ARNOLD PROJECT
Early interest in aviation; participation in races; hemispheric flight, 1926–27; transcontinental blind flight; Mitchell court martial case; Army Air Corps and air mail, 1934; Long Beach earthquake; pressure for a separate Air Force; Air Force intelligence; George C. Marshall and air power; relation of Gen. Arnold and Gen. Malin Craig; Winston Churchill and around-the-clock bombing; 8th Air Force Bomber Command, England from 1942: transfer of units to England, relations with RAF, critique of operations; Ploesti and Tokyo raids; pro- and anti-Air Force interests in government in early 1960's; impressions of Gens. Frank Andrews, and Carl Spaatz.
184 pp. *Permission required.* 1959.
See also Air Force Academy.

EARHART, Amelia. *Discussed in* Jacqueline Cochran; Muriel E. Morrissey.

EARLE, Genevieve Beavers (Mrs. William P.) (1883–1956) Social worker, politician.
NYC politics, 1917–50; NYC Charter Revision Committee, 1935; Fiorello H. La Guardia.
126 pp. *Permission required to cite or quote.* 1950. *Micro IV.* Papers.

EARLEY, Elisabeth (1917–   ) *See* Richard Hofstadter Project.

EASTLAND, James. *Discussed in* Virginia Durr.

EASTMAN, George. *Discussed in* Rouben Mamoulian; Otto Luening.

EASTMAN, Max. *Discussed in* John Spargo.

EATON, Clement (1898–   ) *See* American Historians.

EBERSTADT, Ferdinand (1890–1969) *See* Robert P. Patterson Project.

ECHEVERRIA, Luis. *Discussed in* Joseph J. Jova.

ECONOMICS *See* Sherman Adams; Louis Bean; Adolf Berle; Percival F. Brundage; Arthur E. Burns; Eveline M. Burns; Harold F. Clark; Miles Colean; W.W. Cumberland; C. Douglas Dillon; Eleanor L. Dulles; Mordecai Ezekiel; Gabriel Hauge; Neil Jacoby; Lewis L. Lorwin; Isador Lubin; Raymond Saulnier; Herman Somers; Rexford G. Tugwell; Jacob Viner; James P. Warburg; Aryness Wickens; W. Walter Williams; Leo Wolman; World Bank.
See also New Deal.

EDEL, Leon (1907–   ) Writer.
Immigrant parents, early life in Yorktown, Canada; recollections of student life, McGill University, 1923–27; journalist with Montreal *Star;* impressions of Paris as student and journalist, 1928–32; WWII, military intelligence unit in France; discussion of his work on Henry James; impressions of Edith Wharton, Henry James.
230 pp. *Permission required.* 1976.

EDELMAN, John W. (1893–1971) Labor representative.

Education; early experiences on fringes of Socialist movement; condition of hosiery workers in New Jersey and Pennsylvania during the late 1920's and Depression: role of hosiery workers union in the AFL; AFL conventions; beginnings of Textile Workers Union of America; its role in the CIO; influence of Communist Party in the CIO; merger of the CIO and the AFL; impressions of men and women prominent in the labor movement.

247 pp. *Permission required to cite or quote.* 1957. *Micro II.*
See also Social Security.

EDELSTEIN, Julius C.C. *See* Herbert H. Lehman Project, *Micro II, and* New York Political Studies (B).

EDEN, Anthony. *Discussed in* James Fife; Robert C. Hill; Livingston T. Merchant.

EDER, Phanor James (1880–1971) Lawyer.
Education; early experiences in law; banking and law in Latin America; Gold Clause case and others; writings.

110 pp. *Permission required to cite or quote.* 1965. *Micro I.*

EDISON, Charles (1890–1969) Industrialist.
Family background, childhood, and education; Thomas A. Edison, Inc., its various enterprises, organization, personnel relations; Thomas Alva Edison.

294 pp. *Permission required to cite or quote.* 1953. *Micro II.*
Discussed in Francis A. Jamieson; Henry Williams.

EDISON, Theodore M. *See* Thomas A. Edison Project.

EDISON, Thomas Alva. *Discussed in* Thomas H. Cowan; Charles Edison.

THOMAS ALVA EDISON PROJECT
Interviews with family members and associates of Thomas Alva Edison (1847–1931) illuminate his character, personality, and motivation. The appearance and arrangement of the family home and the laboratory in West Orange, New Jersey, are described, and specific projects carried on in the laboratory are recalled. Earlier record-

ings prepared by the Edison National Historic Site are included.

Participants and pages: Harold S. Anderson, 44; Edward K. Cary, 19; John C.F. Coakley, 27; John C.F. and Thelda Coakley, 68; Edward J. Daly, 38; Charles W. Durr, 64; Theodore Edison, 206; Karl Ehricke, 30; Samuel Gardner, 39; Thomas Halstrom, 31; William H. Hand, 39; A.E. Johnson, 53; P. Kasakove, 47; Roderic Peters, 47; Madeleine Edison Sloane, 76; Norman R. Speiden, 90; Ernest L. Stevens, 47; Lillian P. Warren, 80.

1,045 pp. *Permission required.* 1972–73. Papers. *Underwritten by the Eastern National Park and Monument Association, Philadelphia.*

EDMONDS, George (1905–) *See* Continental Group.

EDSALL, David. *Discussed in* Joseph C. Aub; Edward D. Churchill.

EDUCATION *See* Air Force Academy; Will Alexander; James E. Allen; American Cultural Leaders; American Association of Physics Teachers; U H'tin Aung; John Badeau; Thomas H. Bender; Algernon Black; Samuel Brownell; Lyman Bryson; Agnes Burke; Harry Carman; Carnegie Corporation; William G. Carr; Hollis Caswell; Children's Television Workshop; Harold F. Clark; Kenneth Clark; Wilbur Cohen; James Corley; Daniel Cosio Villegas; W.H. Cowley; Ben Davidson; John Warren Davis; Godfrey Dewey; J. Curtis Dixon; Harold Dobbs; W.E.B. Du Bois; James B. Duke Project; Guy Stanton Ford; Claude M. Fuess; Charlotte Garrison; Walter Gellhorn; Harry D. Gideonse; Albert Giesecke; Willard E. Givens; Leland Goodrich; Frank P. Graham; James Gutmann;

J. George Harrar; Frederick G. Hochwalt; Willi Hoffer; Richard Hofstadter Project; Robert M. Hutchins; Francis A.J. Ianni; Joseph Jablonower; William Jansen; Arthur T. Jersild; Alvin Johnson; Guy B. Johnson; Isaac L. Kandel; William H. Kilpatrick; Kirkland College; Kenneth Koch; Theodore F. Kuper; Gerda Lerner; Milton E. Loomis; Ralph Lowell; Helen Lynd; Earl J. McGrath; Millicent McIntosh; Robert M.

MacIver; Frederick C. McLaughlin; Harold C. Martin; Geoffrey Matthews; Pearl Max; Lucy Sprague Mitchell; Thomas S. Moorman; Richard B. Morris; Henry Neumann; New York University; Marjorie Nicolson; John K. Norton;

Houston Peterson; Kathryn S. Phillips; I.I. Rabi; R. Bruce Raup; Esther Raushenbush; Flora M. Rhind; Max J. Rubin; Arthur M. Schlesinger; Herbert W. Schneider; Southern Intellectual Leaders; Wesley J. Streater; Maurice R. Tauber; Ordway Tead; John J. Theobald; Katherine A. Towle; Charles H. Tuttle; Ralph W. Tyler; Goodwin Watson; James M. Wood.
See also Columbia University.

EDWARDS, Idwal. See Air Force Academy.

EDWARDS, John R. Discussed in John H. Hoover.

EDWIN, Ed (1922–   ) Author, journalist.
American Forces Network in Germany and military news policy and censorship, 1945–48; US Foreign Service Resident and Information Officer, 1949–53; television and radio coverage of national and local (including NYC) elections, 1954–70; media reaction to rise of black militancy in northern ghettos from 1958, with recollections of interviews with its leaders; the writing of Adam Clayton Powell and the Politics of Race; population problem and related environmental issues, 1966–72; oral history projects.
185 pp. Permission required to cite or quote. 1972.
See also Eisenhower Administration.

EDWIN, Edward S. (1889–   ) Physician.
Recollections of his professional and social relationship with Charles M. Russell, the artist.
17 pp. Permission required. 1967.

EGGERSS, Charles E. (1891–   ) See Continental Group.

EGNER, Frank (1892–1957) See McGraw-Hill.

EHRICKE, Karl. See Thomas A. Edison Project.

EINSTEIN, Albert. Discussed in William Fondiller; Max Schuster.

EISENHOWER, Dwight David (1890–1969) Army officer, President.
EISENHOWER ADMINISTRATION
President of Columbia University, 1948–52; President of the US, 1953–61; labor unions and leaders; state vs. federal controls; China; Cuba; Vietnam; Suez Canal; Open Skies policy; inflation; impressions of Gen. George C. Marshall, Robert A. Taft, Harry Truman, Richard Nixon.
114 pp. Permission required to cite or quote. 1967.
Discussed in Barry Bingham; Eisenhower Administration; Frank D. Fackenthal; William M. Fechteler; John Fetzer; James Gutmann; John L. Hall, Jr.; Roswell B. Perkins; Kenneth C. Royall; Charles I. Schottland; William A. Sullivan; Lloyd Taft.

EISENHOWER, Edgar N. (1889–1971) Lawyer.
EISENHOWER ADMINISTRATION
Family and religious background; personal recollections of Dwight Eisenhower and his Presidency; Supreme Court; Sherman Adams, Richard Nixon.
117 pp. Closed until 1980. 1967.

EISENHOWER, John Sheldon David (1922–   ) Army officer.
EISENHOWER ADMINISTRATION
Anecdotes and personal recollections of Dwight Eisenhower's military career and Presidency; Korea; inauguration, 1953; development of military weapons; Geneva Conference.
144 pp. Permission required. 1967.
See also additional interview in Eisenhower Administration.

EISENHOWER, Mamie. Discussed in Bertha Adkins; Henry Aurand; Robert C. Hill; Katherine G. Howard.

EISENHOWER, Milton Stover (1899–   ) Government official.
EISENHOWER ADMINISTRATION
Latin American relations; Eisenhower

brothers; President Eisenhower and his administration; White House staff and organization; Gen. Eisenhower's decisions to run in 1952 and 1956; 1960 campaign; Republican Critical Issues Council; impressions of Harry S. Truman, Richard Nixon, Joseph R. McCarthy, Lyndon B. Johnson, John Foster Dulles, Fidel Castro.

115 pp. Permission required to cite or quote. 1967. *Micro III.*

EISENHOWER ADMINISTRATION
Dwight D. Eisenhower as president; decision to run, 1952 convention; Nixon as vice-presidential candidate, selection of cabinet; Senator Joseph McCarthy, public sentiment; military-industrial complex.

55 pp. *Permission required to cite or quote.* 1969.
Contributed by Herbert S. Parmet, New York.

Discussed in J. Clifford Folger.
See also additional interview in Eisenhower Administration.

EISENHOWER ADMINISTRATION
This project has gathered firsthand testimony from those who played major roles in the Eisenhower Administration (1953–61), as well as the recollections of observers and of those knowledgeable about special aspects. In addition to Gen. Dwight D. Eisenhower and members of his family, the list of participants below includes members of the White House staff, cabinet members, political advisers, members of Congress, administrators, scientists, journalists, ambassadors, military and civilian specialists, and others in a position to testify about trends and events of the period.

Among topics well documented in material presently available are the Republican conventions and campaigns of 1952 and 1956, the functioning of White House advisers and staff, the President's relations with his cabinet, the functioning of the Bureau of the Budget and various independent agencies, relations with the press, scientific developments, and other special aspects too numerous to mention, the whole interlaced with anecdotes about major and minor episodes in public life in the 1950's. A series of interviews done in Little Rock, Arkansas on the school integration crisis there is of particular interest.

In addition to memoirs done under Columbia's aegis, the series includes fourteen donated by Professor Herbert S. Parmet, who conducted them in preparing his *Eisenhower and the American Crusades* (Macmillan, 1972), and seventy-one thus far acquired from the Eisenhower Library through an exchange agreement whereby both institutions share oral history transcripts about Eisenhower, his family, career and administration, under identical restrictions. These acquisitions explain the fact that, in the listing that follows, some names are repeated with different page numbers (and in some instances different restrictions) after each.

Participants and pages: Elie Abel, 45; Helen Ackenhausen, 57; Sherman Adams, 268; Sherman Adams, 50 *(permission required);* Bertha S. Adkins, 72; George D. Aiken, 31; H. Meade Alcorn, 159; Winthrop W. Aldrich, 38; T. Dale Alford, 115 *(permission required);* George V. Allen, 213; Joseph Alsop, 19; Dillon Anderson, 130; Jack Z. Anderson, 64; Robert B. Anderson, 27 *(permission required);* J. Sinclair Armstrong, 125 *(permission required);* Levy J. Asper, 18; Allen V. Astin, 57 *(permission required);* Evan P. Aurand, 138; Henry S. Aurand, 34; Frederick W. Babbel, 169; James W. Barco, 1,061 *(closed until 1984);* Ray W. Barker, 97; Rollin D. Barnard, 60;

Edward L. Beach, 470 *(permission required);* J. Bill Becker, 33; Earl C. Behrens, 44; Jack L. Bell, 31; Stephen Benedict, 137 *(permission required);* Stephen Benedict, 33 *(permission required);* Charles E. Bennett, 18; Ezra Taft Benson, 13; Andrew H. Berding, 38; John A. Bird, 39; J.W. Bishop, 115; Richard M. Bissell, 48; Douglas M. Black, 53; Harold Boeschenstein, 24; Charles E. Bohlen, 25; Robert R. Bowie, 51; Omar N. Bradley, 23; C.L. Brainard, 77; Karl Brandt, 69 *(permission required);* Wiley A. Branton, 61 *(permission required);* Vivion Brewer, 45; John W. Bricker, 40 *(permission required);* Ellis O. Briggs, 139; Wallace R. Brode, 51; Herbert Brownell, 347; Herbert Brownell, 16; Herbert Brownell, 47; Samuel Brownell, 83; Percival F. Brundage, 52;

Wiley T. Buchanan, Jr., 178 *(closed until 1993);* E. LaMar Buckner, 18; William A.M. Burden, 81 *(closed during lifetime);* Carter Burgess, 40; Arleigh A. Burke, 249; James V. Burke, Jr., 52; Arthur E. Burns, 45; Prescott Bush, 454; Richard C. Butler, 46; Earl L. Butz, 51; Ralph Cake, 78; O. Hatfield Chilson, 54; Mark W. Clark, 91; Lucius D. Clay, Sr., 1,101; Lucius D. Clay, Sr., 113; Lucius D. Clay, Sr., 39 *(permission required);* Lucius D. Clay, Jr., 25; Jacqueline Cochran, 257; Wilbur J. Cohen, 45; Roy Cohn, 15 *(permission required);* Clement Conger, 25 *(permission required);* Charles D. Cook, 658 *(closed until 1979);* Howard A. Cook, 16; Richard W. Cook, 73; Charles A. Coolidge, 35; William G. Cooper, Jr., 48;

Kenneth Crawford, 26; Thomas B. Curtis, 46; John A. Danaher, 58; Noobar R. Danielian, 51; Harry Darby, 73 *(permission required);* Clarence A. Davis, 106 *(permission required);* Wesley D'Ewart, 136; Thomas E. Dewey, 43; Edward T. Dicker, 32; C. Douglas Dillon, 94 *(permission required; certain pages closed);* Robert J. Donovan, 51; James H. Douglas, Jr., 53; Lewis Douglas, 56; George Douthit, 48; William H. Draper, Jr., 18; Roscoe Drummond, 32; Eleanor L. Dulles, 973 *(permission required);* Eleanor L. Dulles, 41 *(permission required);* Eleanor L. Dulles, 93 *(permission required);* Donald A. Dumont, 76 *(permission required);*

Ed Edwin, 47 *(permission required);* Dwight D. Eisenhower, 114 *(certain pages closed);* Edgar N. Eisenhower, 117 *(closed until 1980);* John S.D. Eisenhower, 144 *(permission required);* John S.D. Eisenhower, 147; Milton S. Eisenhower, 115; Milton S. Eisenhower, 55; Milton S. Eisenhower, 54; Edward L. Elson, 293; Ford Q. and Anita M. Elvidge, 47; Harold Engstrom, 61; Luther H. Evans, 34; Orval Faubus, 135; Robert H. Finch, 69 *(permission required);* Leonard Firestone, 15; Ivan M. Fitzwater, 59; Ralph Flanders, 51; J. Clifford Folger, 42; Edward Folliard, 72; Marion B. Folsom, 163; Abram Forney, 18; Clarence Francis, 37; William B. Franke, 50; Howard Funk, 12 *(permission required);*

Thomas S. Gates, Jr., 59; Thomas S. Gates, Jr., 38; James M. Gavin, 36 *(permission re-*

quired); Robert O. Gemmill, 87; Barry Goldwater, 85 *(closed during lifetime);* Andrew J. Goodpaster, 137; Arthur Gray, Jr., 32; Gordon Gray, 338 *(permission required);* Gordon Gray, 58; Robert K. Gray, 38; Howard C. Green, 100; Peter Grimm, 32; Nat R. Griswold, 84; Ernest Gross, 984; Alfred M. Gruenther, 97 *(permission required);* Homer Gruenther, 107; Amis Guthridge, 27; L. Richard Guylay, 90; Louis M. Hacker, 38; James C. Hagerty, 569 *(permission required);* James C. Hagerty, 109 *(permission required);* Najeeb E. Halaby, 32; Leonard Hall, 59 *(closed during lifetime);* Leonard Hall, 24 *(permission required);* Charles A. Halleck, 35; Robert E. Hampton, 57 *(permission required);* John W. Hanes, Jr., 27; D.B. Hardeman, 146 *(permission required);* Raymond A. Hare, 114 *(permission required);* Bryce N. Harlow, 144 *(permission required);* Karl G. Harr, Jr., 41 *(permission required);* Wilson Harwood, 52; Gabriel Hauge, 130; Gabriel Hauge, 28 *(permission required);* Brooks Hays, 165;

Leonard D. Heaton, 80; Loy W. Henderson, 51; Hans von Herwarth, 4; Stephen Hess, 41; John Hightower, 41; Robert C. Hill, 105; Luther H. Hodges, 39; Eric Hodgins, 162; Leo A. Hoegh, 95 *(permission required);* John B. Hollister, 52; Amory Houghton, 96 *(permission required);* A.F. House, 44; Patricia House, 46; Katherine G. Howard, 600; Elizabeth Huckaby, 75; George M. Humphrey, 62 *(permission required);* Joe Ingraham, 58; Joe Ingraham and H. Jack Porter, 177; Nettie Stover Jackson, 43; Albert Jacobs, 38; Neil H. Jacoby, 141; Jacob Javits, 15; F. Peterson Jessup, 105 *(permission required);* Jesse C. Johnson, 36; Roger W. Jones, 73; Len B. Jordan, 65; Walter H. Judd, 149;

James T. Karam, 29 *(permission required);* Kenneth B. Keating, 126; Henry J. Kellerman, 29; David W. Kendall, 85 *(permission required);* Gordon Kidd, 108; James R. Killian, Jr., 375 *(closed until 1985);* Arthur A. Kimball, 104; Helen S. King, 29; George Kinnear, 47; Grayson Kirk, 59; Herbert G. Klein, 39 *(permission required);* Goodwin J. Knight, 94 *(permission required);* William F. Knowland, 170; Walter Kohler, Jr., 52; Robert L. Kunzig, 40; William S.B. Lacy, 20; James M. Lambie, Jr., 49; Alvin H. Lane, 39; Alvin H. Lane, 49; Sigurd S. Larmon, 92; William H. Lawrence, 37; J. Bracken Lee, 70; William L. Lee, 482; Barry Leithead, 52; Lyman Lemnitzer, 64; John W. Leonard, 107; Orme Lewis, 54; R.A. Lile, 31; John Davis Lodge, 195; Mrs. Robert J. Long, 5; Mary Pillsbury Lord, 428; Robert A. Lovett, 21; Clare Boothe Luce, 108; John Luter, 79; Eugene J. Lyons, 90;

Charles V. McAdams, 62; Edward A. McCabe, 171; Kevin McCann, 158; Carl W. McCardle, 48; Nancy J. McCarty, 58; John J. McCloy, 47; John J. McCloy, 16; John A. McCone, 16; Alvin McCoy, 35; James McCrory, 19 *(permission required);* John F. McDonnell, 59; Neil McElroy, 88; Edward Perkins McGuire, 97; Theodore R. McKeldin, 78; Sidney McMath, 31; Henry R. McPhee, Jr., 59; Clarence Manion, 98; Thomas C. Mann, 60 *(permission required);* Thomas C. Mann, 90; Henry J. Matchett, 42; Earl Mazo, 52 *(permission required);* Clifton L. Mears, 73; Livingston T. Merchant, 86; Robert E. Merriam, 209; Henry L. Miller, 58; L. Arthur Minnich, 34; J. Bradshaw Mintener, 65 *(permission required);* William L. Mitchell, 84; John A. Moaney, 138; Ray Moore, 45; Malcolm Moos, 41 *(permission required);* Edward P. Morgan, 53 *(permission required);* Gerald D. Morgan, 133 *(permission required);* E. Frederic Morrow, 175; E. Frederic Morrow, 32 *(permission required);* True D. Morse, 114;

Robert D. Murphy, 45; Robert D. Murphy, 21; Ancher Nelsen, 34; Arthur Nevins, 87; Herschel D. Newsom, 108; Kenneth D. Nichols, 100 *(permission required);* Roderic O'Connor, 144 *(permission required);* Mr. and Mrs. Floyd Oles, 122; Dennis O'Rourke, 41; Don Paarlberg, 164; Hugh A. Parker, 76; Bradley H. Patterson, Jr., 65; Hugh Patterson, Jr., 85 *(permission required);* John S. Patterson, 54; G.R. Pearkes, 53; Charles H. Percy, 33; Wilton B. Persons, 161; Howard C. Petersen, 68; Lelia G. Picking, 24; Richard M. Pittenger, 37; Sir Charles Portal, 11; H. Jack Porter, 47 *(permission required);* H. Jack Porter, 53; Terrell E. Powell, 34; Wesley Pruden, 33 *(permission required);* Howard Pyle, Jr.

and Charles Masterson, 134 *(permission required);*

Elwood R. Quesada, 88; Maxwell Rabb, 38; Maxwell Rabb, 23 *(permission required);* Ogden R. Reid, 22; Ralph W.E. Reid, 51; Edward E. Rice, 73; Chalmers Roberts, 36; Charles Roberts, 35 *(permission required);* Clifford Roberts, 878 *(closed until 1997);* Walter S. Robertson, 194; Nelson A. Rockefeller, 40 *(closed until 1997 or death, whichever is later);* William P. Rogers, 51 *(permission required);* Robert V. Roosa, 153 *(permission required);* Richard H. Rovere, 44; Roy R. Rubottom, Jr., 95 *(permission required);* Stanley M. Rumbough, Jr., 39; Harrison E. Salisbury, 48; Irving Salomon, 39; Leverett Saltonstall, 151; Irene Samuel, 49; Howland Sargeant, 26; Raymond J. Saulnier, 71; J. Earl Schaefer, 37; Leonard Scheele, 44; Raymond Scherer, 54; G. David Schine, 20; Robert L. Schulz, 293 *(closed until 1993);* Fred C. Scribner, Jr., 83;

Stephen Shadegg, 30 *(permission required);* Bernard M. Shanley, 123; Dudley C. Sharp, 67; James Sheldon, 186 *(permission required);* Joseph S. Sheldon, 28; Joseph S. Sheldon, 59; William T. Shelton, 35; James R. Shepley, 39; Robert Lee Sherrod, 52; Allan Shivers, 58; David M. Shoup, 29; Rocco Siciliano, 91; William H. Simpson, 127; Ellis D. Slater, 38; Ilene Slater, 58 *(permission required);* Bromley Smith, 36 *(permission required);* Howard K. Smith, 44; Merriman Smith, 79; William J. Smith, 90; Robert E. Smylie, 72; Orin Snider, 52; Murray Snyder, 66; Mansfield D. Sprague, 57; Elmer B. Staats, 59; James R. Stack, 132; John H. Stambaugh, 102; Maurice H. Stans, 83 *(closed during lifetime);* Harold Stassen, 68 *(closed until 1985);* John R. Steelman, 89 *(closed until 1990);* Thomas E. Stephens, 98 *(permission required);* Robert G. Storey, 65; Lewis L. Strauss, 177 *(closed until 1985);* Theodore Streibert, 35; Arthur Summerfield, 93 *(permission required);* Glenn W. Sutton, 45; D. Walter Swan, 95; Joseph Swing, 76 *(permission required);*

Robert H. Thayer, 44; Walter N. Thayer, 52; Jessie W. Thornton, 41 *(permission required);* Edward J. Thye, 76; Webster B.

Todd, 88 *(permission required);* Thor C. Tollefson, 82; Janet Tourtellotte and Edith Williams, 68; Everett Tucker, Jr., 62 *(permission required);* Elbert Tuttle, 113 *(closed during lifetime);* Nathan F. Twining, 250 *(permission required);* Wayne Upton, 64; James J. Wadsworth, 248; David W. Wainhouse, 33; Abbott M. Washburn, 91 *(closed during lifetime);* Arthur V. Watkins, 98; Sinclair Weeks, 172; Sinclair Weeks, 54 *(permission required);* Anne Wheaton, 178; Francis O. Wilcox, 63; E. Grainger Williams, 65; W. Walter Williams, 103 *(permission required);* Charles F. Willis, Jr., 50; Ray I. Witter, 41; Henry Woods, 56; Henry Wriston, 51; Charles R. Yates, 34; Milton R. Young, 31 *(permission required);* Frederick A. Zaghi, 12.

35,597 pp. *Permission required to cite or quote except as noted.* 1962– . Papers. *Many of the memoirs are available in microform; consult individual entries.*

Underwritten in part by grants from the National Endowment for the Humanities and the National Archives.

EISLER, Georg (1928–) *See* Austrian Project.

EIZENSTAT, Stuart. *See* Ethnic Groups and American Foreign Policy.

ELDREDGE, Inman F. *See* Forest History Society.

ELEGANT, Robert S. (1928–) *See* International Negotiations.

ELIOT, Charles Norton. *Discussed in* Felix Franfurter.

ELIOT, Martha May (1891–1978) Physician.
SOCIAL SECURITY
Origins of Public Health Service, Children's Bureau, and Social Security Administration; AMA's role in medical care and insurance programs; public health legislation; Committee on Costs of Medical Care, 1920's; Committee on Economic Security, 1930's; Social Security Act; Wagner-Murray-Dingell health insurance bills; Hill-Burton Bill; first National Health Conference, 1938.

115 pp. *Permission required to cite or quote.* 1966. *Micro IV.*

WOMEN'S HISTORY AND POPULATION ISSUES
Family background, education, medical training; rickets study and early association with Children's Bureau; Title V of Social Security Act; maternal and child health services in Europe before and during WWII; OFRRO, UNRRA, UNICEF; tours for WHO, 1949–51; history of Children's Bureau, 1912–73; Professor, Maternal and Child Health, Harvard, 1957–60.

454 pp. *Permission required to cite or quote.* 1974.

Discussed in Charles I. Schottland.

ELIOT, T.S. *Discussed in* Roger W. Straus.

ELIOT, Thomas Hopkinson (1907–)
See Social Security. *Micro III.*
Discussed in Bernice Bernstein; Jack B. Tate; Alanson Willcox.

ELKINS, Stanley (1925–) *See* American Historians.

ELLICKSON, Katherine.
SOCIAL SECURITY
Labor efforts toward federal old age, survivors, and Medicare legislation since 1953; drafts of legislation and amendments; AFL-CIO relations with HEW and with Ways and Means Committee.

285 pp. *Permission required to cite or quote.* 1967. *Micro IV.* Papers inserted in memoir.

ELLIMAN, Douglas Ludlow (1882–1972) Real estate broker.
NYC real estate, 1900–68; development of Park Avenue.

180 pp. *Open.* 1968.

ELLIS, David. *See* Kirkland College.

ELLISON, Ralph (1914–) *See* James Agee. *Discussed in* Jean B. Hutson.

ELSON, Edward Lee Roy (1906–)
Clergyman.
EISENHOWER ADMINISTRATION
Childhood; experiences as 7th Army chap-

lain, WWII; relationship of Presidents Harry S. Truman and Dwight Eisenhower with Presbyterian Church; personal knowledge of Middle Eastern countries and leaders; establishment of American Friends of the Middle East; Eisenhower funeral; election as Chaplain of the Senate.
293 pp. *Permission required to cite or quote.* 1969.

ELVIDGE, Ford Q. (1892–) and Anita M. *See* Eisenhower Administration.

EMERSON, Guy (1886–1969) Lawyer, banker.
Episcopal Church Pension League; Roosevelt Non-Partisan League; Liberty Loan campaign; National Hoover League; American Bankers Association convention; Calvin Coolidge campaign; Reserve City Bankers Association.
249 pp. *Permission required to cite or quote.* 1951. *Micro I.*

EMERSON, Haven (1874–1957) Physician.
NYC politics and the health program; WWI medical corps; national public health and socialized medicine.
103 pp. *Permission required to cite or quote.* 1950. *Micro I.* Papers.

EMERSON, Mary. *Discussed in* Richard Gordon.

EMERSON, Thomas Irwin (1907–) Lawyer.
Part I: Family, early youth and high school, Yale College; Yale Law School and *Law Journal;* law practice, NYC; Depression and election of 1932; NRA, 1933–34; drafting National Labor Relations Act; Garrison Board in 1934 textile strikes; cases testing the National Labor Relations Act; Social Security Board and John Winant; formation of National Lawyers Guild; legislative aspects of NLRB; duties as special assistant to Attorney General Francis Biddle; FBI; Martin Dies; Smith Committee; social life in Washington; OPA law enforcement problems; loyalty problems; policy decision of OES; death of Franklin D. Roosevelt; VE Day; Office of War Mobilization and Reconversion; drafting of Atomic Energy Act; teaching at Yale Law School, 1946; political associations; Public

Affairs Committee; PAC of CIO; formation of Progressive Party, campaign of 1948.
2,227 pp. *Permission required.* 1953.

Part II: 1953 loyalty cases; Smith Act cases; Owen Lattimore case; research on segregation cases; New Haven branch of ACLU; civil liberties in England, 1955.
279 pp. *Permission required.* 1955.

EMERY, Carlos. *See* Argentina.

EMERY, John (1930–) *See* McGraw-Hill.

EMIGRATION *See* Immigration/Emigration.

EMMERICH, Andre (1924–) and Nancy Graves. *See* New York's Art World.

EMMET, Jessie (Mrs. Richard) *See* Association for the Aid of Crippled Children.

EMMONS, Delos Carleton (1888–1965) *See* Aviation Project.

EMSPAK, Julius (1904–1962) Union official.
Comments on labor unionism; early life; development of United Electrical, Radio and Machine Workers from 1936: RCA strike, relations with CIO and Association of Catholic Trade Unionists; labor and government during WWII; Communism and labor movement; labor during the cold war.
363 pp. *Permission required to cite or quote.* 1960. *Micro I.*

ENDICOTT, Kenneth M. (1916–) *See* Health Sciences.

ENGINEERING *See* William Fondiller; Mining Engineers; Adelaide Oppenheim; Samuel M. Robinson; Gerard Swope.

ENGLE, Lavinia. Government official.
SOCIAL SECURITY
Field Secretary, National American Women's Suffrage Association; executive director, Maryland League of Women Voters; 1932 presidential campaign; member of Maryland legislature until 1932; Frank Bane in Social Security Administration; chief, Social Security division of field opera-

tions until WWII; regional director, District of Columbia area; decentralization of Social Security programs; Anna Rosenberg. 184 pp. *Open.* 1967.

ENGSTROM, Harold. *See* Eisenhower Administration. *Micro III.*

ENNIS, Thomas G. (1904–   ) *See* Marine Corps.

EPSTEIN, Abraham. *Discussed in* Henriette Epstein; Reinhard A. Hohaus; Maurine Mulliner.

EPSTEIN, Henriette.
Husband Abraham Epstein's activities: emigration from Russia to US; involvement with the workers' education movement, 1920; impressions of Russia, 1921; research director for Pennsylvania Old Age Commission, 1920–27; founding of American Association for Old Age Security, 1927; fight for old age pension laws in various states; Social Security Act of 1935.
   120 pp. *Permission required.* 1976.

ERLANGER, Joseph (1874–1965) *See* Nobel Laureates.

ERNST, Morris Leopold (1888–1976) *See* Socialist Movement. *Discussed in* Osmond K. Fraenkel.

ERSKINE, Graves Blanchard (1897–1973) Marine Corps officer.
Family background, education; WWI, France; sea and foreign duty, 1921–30; Peking, 1935–37; WWII, Attu, Kiska operations, 1941–43; Kwajalein operation; Gen. Holland M. Smith; Saipan, Iwo Jima, Guam, 1944–45; Administrator, Retraining and Reemployment Administration, Department of Labor, 1945–47; Special Joint State-Defense Survey mission to Southeast Asia, 1950; CG, Fleet Marine Force, Atlantic: planning, involvement with NATO.
   573 pp. *Open.* 1970.
Discussed in Robert E. Hogaboom.

ERSKINE, Helen W. (Mrs. W. H. H. Cranmer) (1896–   ) Author.
Early life in Denver, Colorado and NYC; Paris, 1925; NY *World* and *World-Tele-*

gram, 1926–31; Professor John Erskine. 223 pp. *Closed during lifetime.* 1957.

ERSKINE, John. *Discussed in* Melville H. Cane; Helen W. Erskine.

ESPENSCHIED, Lloyd. *See* Radio Pioneers. *Micro IV.*

ESSELSTYN, Caldwell (1903–1975) *See* Social Security.

ETHNIC GROUPS AND AMERICAN FOREIGN POLICY
This series of interviews is being conducted by Dr. Judith Goldstein to document the impact of American ethnic groups on the formulation of American foreign policy and their interaction with Congress in the Nixon, Ford, and Carter administrations. The collection includes interviews with members of the executive branch, senators, representatives, legislative assistants, scholars, journalists, lobbyists, and members of ethnic organizations. The project examines the history, foreign policy objectives, and methods of operation of individuals and organizations vis-a-vis specific international issues and events.

Participants and pages: Morris B. Abram, 23 *(open);* Morris B. Abram, 24 *(permission required);* Morris Amitay, 289 *(permission required);* George W. Ball, 42 *(permission required);* Jonathan Bingham, 22 *(open);* Hyman Bookbinder, 123 *(closed until 1981);* Stuart Eizenstat, 18 *(closed until 2003);* Leonard Garment, 65; Bernard Gwertzman, 18 *(permission required);* Clifford Hackett, 63 *(open);* Ernest Hamburger, 58; Rita Hauser, 35 *(permission required);* Daniel K. Inouye, 18; Jacob Javits, 3 *(open);* Isaiah L. Kenen, 98 *(closed until 1980);* Gordon Kerr, 45 *(permission required);* Sol M. Linowitz, 42 *(closed until 1980);* Robert Lipshutz, 31 *(permission required);* Richard Maass, 47 *(closed until 1980);* Israel Miller, 26; Richard Perle, 115 *(permission required);* Norman Podhoretz, 153 *(permission required);* Benjamin S. Rosenthal, 13 *(open);* Eugene Rossides, 45 *(permission required);* Alex Schindler, 31 *(permission required);* Mark Siegel, *(in process);* Terence Smith, 43 *(permission required);* Stephen Solarz, 16 *(open);* Mark

Talisman, 36 *(permission required);* Laurence Tisch, 35 *(open);* Michael Van Dusen, 27 *(permission required);* Kenneth Wollack, 266 *(permission required);* Harriet Zimmerman, 45 *(permission required).*

1,915 pp. *Closed until 1996 except as noted.* 1974–   . *Underwritten by private contributors.*

EURICH, Alvin. *See* International Negotiations.

EVANS, Carol. *See* Adlai E. Stevenson Project.

EVANS, Clifford. *See* New York Political Studies (A).

EVANS, Eli and Alan Pifer. *See* Carnegie Corporation.

EVANS, Francis (–1974) *See* Aviation Project. *Micro II.*

EVANS, James C. *See* Air Force Academy.

EVANS, Luther Harris (1902–   ) Educator, librarian.
Early life and education: University of Texas, Stanford, Yale, Pennsylvania Military College; instructor at NYU, Dartmouth, Princeton; WPA, 1935–39; director of Historical Records Survey; director of Legislative Reference Service; Librarian of Congress, 1945–53; new projects, programs; establishment of Council of National Library Association; UNESCO: US National Commission, 1946; Executive Board, 1949, director-general, 1953, delegate to General Conference, 1947–51; UNESCO program development: education, agriculture, mass communication, financial aid; Brookings Institution; NEA; automation project; US Commission for Refugees; ACLU. Impressions of Harry Hopkins, Archibald MacLeish, Torres Bodet, Henry Cabot Lodge, Dag Hammarskjold, Lyndon Johnson.

844 pp. *Permission required to cite or quote.* 1965. *Micro I.*

EISENHOWER ADMINISTRATION
WPA, Historical Records Survey; Library of Congress, 1939 and 1945; UNESCO, 1949–58; first meeting with Dwight D. Eisenhower as President of Columbia University.
34 pp. *Permission required to cite or quote.* 1970. *Micro III.*

EVANS, Robley. *Discussed in* Joseph C. Aub.

EVANS, Rudolph Martin (1890–1956) Agriculturist.
Early life; farmer and livestock raiser, 1921–33; corn-hog program, 1933–36; assistant to the Secretary of Agriculture, 1936–38; AAA, 1938–42.
261 pp. *Permission required to cite or quote.* 1953. *Micro I.*
Discussed in Carl Hamilton.

EVANS, Walker (1903–   ) *See* James Agee.

EVANS, Walter C. *See* Radio Pioneers.

EWEN, John W. *See* Robert A. Taft Project.

EWING, Maurice. *Discussed in* Albert P. Crary.

EWING, Oscar Ross (1889–   ) *See* Social Security. *Micro III.*

EZEKIEL, Mordecai Joseph Brill (1899–1974) Agricultural economist.
Department of Agriculture and Federal Farm Board; economic adviser to Henry Wallace and Claude Wickard; WPB; FAO of the UN; economic aspects of the New Deal.
137 pp. *Permission required to cite or quote.* 1956. *Micro I.* Papers.

EZZARD, Richard. *See* Vietnam Veterans.

F

FABIAN, Bela (1889–1967) Hungarian politician.
Youth and education in Hungary; newspaper work in Budapest, 1907–14; concentration camp experiences, 1914–18; escape to Petrograd; Russia and Hungary in 1918; Hungarian political experiences 1919–39; trip to Spain, 1934; WWII; Hungarian underground, 1940–44; arrest and deportation, 1944.
447 pp. *Permission required to cite or quote.* 1951. *Micro I.* Papers.

FABIAN, Harold Pegram (1885–1975) Lawyer.
JACKSON HOLE PRESERVE
Law practice, Salt Lake City, 1910; Jackson Hole National Park: acquisition of land, opposition, Senate investigation; impressions of John D. Rockefeller, Jr. and Horace M. Albright.
106 pp. *Permission required.* 1966.

FACCIOLO, Jay. *See* Columbia Crisis of 1968.

FACKENTHAL, Frank Diehl (1883–1968) University administrator.
Childhood and education; administrative work at Columbia University, 1902–48; Nicholas Murray Butler and Dwight D. Eisenhower as university presidents.
57 pp. *Permission required to quote.* 1956.

FADIMAN, Clifton (1904–   ) *See* Book-of-the-Month Club. *Micro II.*
Discussed in Dan Golenpaul.

FAGAN, Peter E. (1889–   ) *See* Continental Group.

FAHY, Charles (1892–   ) Lawyer, judge.
Family background; law practice, Washington, D. C., 1914–24, and New Mexico, 1924–33; experiences as WWI naval aviator; Indian affairs and oil in Department of Interior, 1933–35; New Deal; NRA; NLRB; experiences as Assistant Solicitor General and Solicitor General, 1940–45, including London Base-Lease negotiations, 1941; adviser to US delegation, San Francisco Conference, 1945; legal adviser, US military government of Germany, 1945–46; legal adviser, Department of State, 1946–47; Legal Committee, UN General Assembly, 1946; alternate US representative, UN General Assembly, 1947 and 1949; judge, US Court of Appeals for District of Columbia, 1949–
451 pp. *Permission required.* 1958.

FAIR, Clinton (1909–   ) *See* Social Security.

FAIRBANK, John (1907–   ) *See* International Negotiations.

FAIRBANKS, Douglas, Sr. *Discussed in* Popular Arts.

FAIRFIELD, Leslie and Mary. *See* China Missionaries.

FALCONBERG, Paul. *See* Robert J. Flaherty Project.

FALK, Isidore Sydney (1899–   ) Public health specialist, medical economist.
SOCIAL SECURITY
Early interest in health insurance; teaching at University of Chicago and service on

Chicago Board of Health, 1923–29; Committee on Costs of Medical Care; effect of recommendation for group practice and group payment; voluntary vs. compulsory insurance; New Deal and background of Social Security legislation; Technical Committee and Advisory Council, Committee on Economic Security; Social Security Board, 1936; National Health Survey, 1935–36; National Health Conference, 1938; Technical Committee on Medical Care; legislative efforts to explore and expand role of federal government in health insurance. Impressions of Franklin D. Roosevelt, Harry Hopkins, Frances Perkins, Arthur Altmeyer, Edgar Sydensticker, and many others.

289 pp. *Permission required to cite or quote.* 1968. *Micro III.* Papers.
See also Health Sciences.
Discussed in Arthur Altmeyer; William Reidy.

FALL, Albert B. *Discussed in* Horace M. Albright.

FALL, Helen Williamson (1910–   )
Impressions, reminiscences of Dr. William Carlos Williams, her children's pediatrician in Rutherford, NJ, 1940's.

40 pp. *Permission required to cite or quote.* 1977. *Contributed by James E. Fall, NYC.*

FARINTOSH, Ernest. *Discussed in* James Campbell.

FARLEY, Edward Philip (1886–1956) Shipping executive.
USSB; EFC; US shipping, 1924–50.
44 pp. *Open.* 1949. Papers.

FARLEY, James Aloysius (1888–1976) Politician.
Political activities, 1912–44, with emphasis on his years as National Chairman of the Democratic Party, 1932–40 and Chairman of the NY State Democratic Party, 1930–44; personal impressions of Franklin D. Roosevelt, Wendell L. Willkie, Charles McNary, William E. Borah, and others.

400 pp. *Permission required to cite or quote.* 1958.
See also Herbert H. Lehman Project.

Discussed in Edward Costikyan; Joseph C. O'Mahoney.

FARM HOLIDAY ASSOCIATION
Farm Holiday Association pressure on the New Deal in 1933–34, as recalled by participants, with descriptions of riots and violence, threats of a farm strike, demands for mortgage relief, and impressions of Milo Reno. The memoirs also include material dealing with the United Farmers League and other Communist-sponsored rivals of the Farm Holiday Association.
Participants and pages: John Bosch, 56; Richard Bosch, 27; Homer Hush, 56; Dale Kramer, 23; Donald Murphy, 32.
194 pp. *Open.* 1960–61.
Contributed by Lowell Dyson, Spirit Lake, Iowa.

FARMAN, Maurice (–1964) *See* Aviation Project.

FAROUK, King. *Discussed in* John Badeau; James M. Landis.

FARR, Barclay H. *See* Theodore Roosevelt Association.

FARRELL, Glenda (1904–   ) *See* Popular Arts.

FARRELL, Walter Greatsinger (1897–   ) Marine Corps officer.
Family background, father's experiences with H. H. Kitchener in the Sudan; early Boy Scout movement in US; WWI: France and German occupation, 1918–19; Haiti, 1919–20; US Olympics swimming champion; aviation duty, China and Guam, 1928–30; Bureau of Aeronautics, 1930–33; Naval War College; inventor of rubber landing boat; WWII, Middle East observer, 1941; Commander, Marine Aircraft, Hawaiian area, 1944; major USMC aviation tactical developments.
846 pp. *Permission required.* 1970.

FARWELL, Margaret M. (Mrs. John V. III). *See* Adlai E. Stevenson Project.

FAUBUS, Orval Eugene (1910–   ) Governor of Arkansas.
EISENHOWER ADMINISTRATION
Detailed history of the integration of Little

Rock High School; integration of institutions of higher education in the South; National Guard; meeting with President Eisenhower in Newport; federal troops; Arkansas elections of 1958; attitude of the press toward Faubus and the school crisis. Impressions of Dwight Eisenhower, Virgil Blossom, Brooks Hays, Dale Alford.

135 pp. *Permission required to cite or quote.* 1971.
Discussed in Brooks Hays.

FAULKNER, Cyril. *See* China Missionaries.

FAULKNER, William. *Discussed in* Dorothy B. Commins; Donald S. Klopfer.

FAUNCE, Sarah Cushing and Beverly Pepper. *See* New York's Art World.

FAURI, Fedele Frederick (1909–   ) *See* Social Security. *Micro III.*

FAX, Elton C. (1909–   ) Book illustrator, writer.
Family background, childhood in Baltimore; Syracuse University, 1927–31; NYC in 1936: illustrating, WPA teaching at Harlem Cultural Center; work with children; life in Morelia, Mexico to 1956; trips for State Department, cultural exchange program; lecture circuit; books published.
161 pp. *Permission required to cite or quote.* 1976.

FECHTELER, William Morrow (1896–1967) Naval officer.
Education, Naval Academy, training cruises, Yangtze River Patrol; teaching at Naval Academy; Hawaii, 1940–42, Pearl Harbor; Bureau of Naval Personnel; Pacific operations; demobilization problems; Hook Commission; Commander in Chief, Atlantic Fleet, 1951; Chief of Naval Operations, 1951; unification; NATO relationships; impressions of Winston Churchill, Dwight Eisenhower, Dan Kimball, and Forrest Sherman.
266 pp. *Permission required.* 1962.

FEDERAL COMMUNICATIONS COMMISSION
A series of interviews on the FCC during the 1950's and early sixties, focusing on issues, policies, and personalities. Participants and pages: Frederick W. Ford, 73; E. William Henry, 53; Robert E. Lee, 48; Newton Minow, 76; Frank Stanton, 53.
303 pp. *Permission required.* 1978. *Contributed by James L. Baughman.*

FEDERATED DEPARTMENT STORES
This project comprises a series of interviews with those who built the largest department store organization in the US, Federated Department Stores. Changes over the years in Federated's policies, methods, and objectives, changes in consumer tastes and buying habits, and the evolution of the organization are traced. There are also interviews with the family and friends of Fred Lazarus, Jr., founder and board chairman.

Participants and pages: Edward Coughlin, 33; Alfred H. Daniels, 46; Dennis Durden, 44; Abe Fortas, 9; Robert Fuoss, 58; Alfred Gruenther, 38; George Hammond, 38; George C. Hayward, 58; Walter Heymann, 22; Harold D. Hodgkinson, 27; Gray Hussey, 18; Mrs. Gray Hussey, 10; Joseph Kasper, 45; Bernard S. Klayf, 42; Herbert Landsman, 81; Celia R. Lazarus, 99; Charles Lazarus, 21; Eleanor and Margaret Lazarus, 47; Fred Lazarus, Jr., 1,039; Fred Lazarus III, 42; Irma M. Lazarus, 40; Jeffrey Lazarus, 32; Maurice Lazarus, 59; Ralph Lazarus, 54; Mrs. Ralph Lazarus, 22; Robert Lazarus, 32; Simon Lazarus, 44; John F. Lebor, 56; Robert Lenhart, 28;

Paul Mazur, 59; Leonard Minster, 26; Alfred Neal, 38; Mrs. Jesse Evans Ross, 34; Lewis Saille, 28; Oral Scheaf, 40; Ann Lazarus Schloss, 47; Trent Sickles, 37; Myron Silbert, 99; William Snaith, 46; Sidney Solomon, 42; Herbert Stein, 29; J. Paul Sticht, 55; Frank Sulzburger, 20; Ann Visconti, 51; George Whitten, 42; Charles Wiedemer, 12; John C. Wilson, 22.
2,911 pp. *Permission required.* 1965.
Underwritten by the children of Fred Lazarus, Jr.

FEDOSKY, John, Jr. (1893–   ) *See* Continental Group.

FEIKER, Frederick Morris (1881–1967) *See* McGraw-Hill.

FEIL, Helen R. *See* Book-of-the-Month Club.

FEIS, Herbert. *Discussed in* James P. Warburg.

FEJOS, Paul (1897–1963) Anthropologist.
Childhood and education in Hungary; medical training; to US, 1923; Rockefeller Institute, 1924–26; film industry, Hollywood and Europe, during the late 1920's and early 1930's; ethnographic work for Swedish film industry, 1937–40; work with primitive tribes, Madagascar, Seychelles; shipwreck on Komodo Island; archaeology and anthropology in Peru, 1940, with Axel Wenner-Gren; Army Specialized Training Unit, Stanford University, 1943–44; Director, Wenner-Gren Foundation; use of technical aids in anthropology; Yale, 1950–51; Columbia, 1951; international symposia in Austria; *Anthropology Today.*
244 pp. *Permission required.* 1962. Papers.
Discussed in Albert Giesecke.

FELDMAN, George J. *See* Benjamin A. Javits Project.

FELDMAN, Justin N. (1919–   ) Lawyer, politician.
Education: NYC, Columbia; NYC Democratic politics, 1948–65; Mayors William O'Dwyer and Robert F. Wagner; 1960 gubernatorial campaign, with emphasis on roles of Averell Harriman, Franklin Roosevelt, Jr., Eleanor Roosevelt, Carmine De Sapio; county and district leaders; reform movement; Herbert Lehman; Edward Costikyan; Adam Clayton Powell; 1962 state convention; campaign manager for Robert Morgenthau; reapportionment.
330 pp. *Closed during lifetime.* 1968.

FELDMAN, Lew David. *See* Rare Books (A).

FELDMAN, Myer (1917–   ) *See* Social Security.

FELDMAN, Paul. *See* Socialist Movement.

FELICANI, Aldino (1891–1967) Publisher.
A detailed account of the work of the Sacco-Vanzetti Defense Committee, plus some

background material on the Italian-American radical press in the first quarter of the 20th century.
160 pp. *Open.* 1954. *Micro IV.*

FELIX, Edgar. *See* Radio Pioneers.

FELIX, Robert H. (1904–   ) *See* Health Sciences.

FELL, Harvey H. (1910–   ) *See* Continental Group.

FERENCZI, Sandor. *Discussed in* Sandor Rado.

FERGUSON, Frances Hand (1907–   ) *See* Women's History and Population Issues.

FERGUSON, Homer (1889–   ) *See* Robert A. Taft Project.

FERMI, Enrico. *Discussed in* Norman Ramsey.

FERNANDEZ, Jesus. *See* Argentina.

FERRELL, Conchata. Actress.
Childhood, West Virginia; Marshall University; Circle Repertory Theatre Company, NYC Theatre World Award; acting experience.
59 pp. *Permission required to cite or quote.* 1974.

FERRELL, Robert (1921–   ) *See* American Historians.

FERRER, José Vicente (1912–   ) *See* Popular Arts.

FERRO, Edward (1895–1968) Immigration inspector.
Early life and education in Italy; emigration to US; life on Lower East Side of Manhattan, early 1900's; immigration interpreter on Ellis Island; immigration procedures, experiences as immigration inspector.
76 pp. *Permission required to cite or quote.* 1968.
Contributed by Harry Kursh, Lakeland Schools, Mohegan Lake, New York.

FERTIG, Wendell H. (1901–1975) *See* Air Force Academy.

FETZER, John Earl (1901–1966) Radio, television executive.
RADIO PIONEERS
Experiments in radio from 1911; license, 1918; early stations in Michigan; controversy with FCC; Broadcasters Victory Council, 1940; radio censorship, 1944; work in Europe for US government, 1945. Impressions of Gen. Dwight D. Eisenhower, various radio personalities.
91 pp. *Permission required to cite or quote.* 1951. *Micro II.*

FEW, Mary Reamey Thomas (Mrs. William Preston).
JAMES B. DUKE PROJECT
Family background in Virginia; education, Trinity College, North Carolina, 1902; friendship with Duke family; graduate studies, Columbia University, 1908; life as wife of president of Trinity College, later Duke University; James B. Duke and Duke University: founding of the university, 1924; Republican National Committeewoman. Impressions of various academic and political figures.
285 pp. *Permission required.* 1963.

FEYER, George (1908–   ) *See* Hungarian Project.

FIDANZA, Alfredo. *See* Argentina.

FIELD, Betty (1918–1973) *See* Popular Arts.

FIELD, Ruth (Mrs. Marshall) (1907–   ) *See* Adlai E. Stevenson Project.

FIELDS, Dorothy (1905–1974) *See* Popular Arts.

FIELDS, Gracie (1898–   ) *See* Popular Arts.

FIELDS, Lewis J. (1909–   ) Marine Corps officer.
Education, St. John's College; Maryland National Guard, 1925–32; South Pacific, Australia, New Zealand, 1942–44; Aide to USMC Commandant, 1945–47; postwar demobilization; SHAPE, 1954–56; Director of Personnel, HQMC, 1962–65; Vietnam.
289 pp. *Open.* 1971.

FIELDS, W.C. *Discussed in* Popular Arts.

FIFE, James (1897–1975) Naval officer.
Background and education, Naval Academy; convoy duty, WWI; submarine school, 1918, Yangtze River patrol; fleet problems and training; merchant marine inspections; Director, Submarine School, New London, 1938–40; submarine observer in England, 1940; London Blitz, Portsmouth and Coventry damage; Mediterranean mission, submarine patrol; impressions of Gen. Archibald Wavell, Col. William Donovan, Anthony Eden, Sir John Dill; General Board, Washington, 1941; Pearl Harbor; Philippines, Adm. Thomas Hart, Corregidor; submarine operations, Australia and South Pacific; Battle of Java Sea; Gen. Douglas MacArthur; Task Force 42; Solomons campaign; impressions of Adms. William Leahy, Chester Nimitz, Alan Kirk, Arthur Hepburn, Ernest King, Robert Ghormley, Arthur Carpender, Thomas Kinkaid, Charles Lockwood, and Fairfax Leary.
617 pp. *Permission required to cite or quote.* 1962. *Micro I.*

FILM *See* James Agee; Erik Barnouw; Aaron Copland; Paul Fejos; Robert J. Flaherty Project; John Houseman; Sol Lesser; William S. Paley; Popular Arts; Upton Sinclair; Sheba Skirball; Phyllis Cerf Wagner.

FINANCE/BANKS AND BANKING *See* James Barker; Daniel W. Bell; Henry Bruere; Prescott Bush; Miles Colean; James F. Curtis; Lawrence Dennis; C. Douglas Dillon; Phanor J. Eder; Guy Emerson; Bernard L. Gladieux; Brenton Harries; Joseph J. Klein; R. McAllister Lloyd; Edward Merkle; Eugene Meyer; Chester Morrill; Roy Neuberger; Allan Nevins; Ferdinand Pecora; William Prendergast; William A. Read; Jackson Reynolds; Walter E. Sachs; Hokan B. Steffanson; Lewis L. Strauss; Jesse W. Tapp; Hobart Taylor, Jr.; TIAA-CREF; James P. Warburg; George Whitney; World Bank; Walter Wyatt.

FINBERG, Barbara. *See* Children's Television Workshop. *Micro IV.*

FINCH, Edward R. *Discussed in* Hokan B. Steffanson.

FINCH, Robert Hutchison (1925–)
Government official.
EISENHOWER ADMINISTRATION
Early association with Richard M. Nixon, 1950 senatorial campaign; California politics; chairman, Los Angeles County Republican Committee; 1960 Presidential primary and campaign.
69 pp. *Permission required.* 1967.

FINE, Benjamin (1905–1975) *See* Journalism Lectures.

FINLETTER, Thomas Knight (1893–)
See Adlai E. Stevenson Project.

FINLEY, John H. *Discussed in* Charles Henry Tuttle.

FINNEY, Burnham (1899–) *See* McGraw-Hill.

FINNEY, Thomas Dunn, Jr. (1925–1976) *See* Adlai E. Stevenson Project.

FINUCANE, Peter (1891–1962) *See* Robert P. Patterson Project.

FIORILLO, Albert. *See* Joseph M. Proskauer Project.

FIRESTONE, Leonard Kimball (1907–) *See* Eisenhower Administration. *Micro III.*

FISCHER, John. *Discussed in* Will W. Alexander; Evan Thomas, II.

FISHER, Adrian S. *See* International Negotiations.

FISHER, Alfred H. *See* Continental Group.

FISHER, Dorothy Canfield (1879–1958)
Author.
BOOK-OF-THE-MONTH CLUB
Member, first selection committee of Book-of-the-Month Club; comments on committee members and book selection policies; notable books reviewed, 1926–49; relationship of selection committee to management of club.
129 pp. *Permission required to cite or quote.* 1955. *Micro I.*

FISHER, Edwin Shelton (1911–) *See* McGraw-Hill.

FISHER, Oliver David (1875–1967) *See* Weyerhaeuser Timber Company.

FISHER, Raymond G. (1911–) *See* Continental Group.

FISHER, Walter Taylor (1892–) *See* Adlai E. Stevenson Project. *Micro III.*

FITCH, Lyle C. (1913–) *See* New York Political Studies (B.)

FITCH, William Kountz (1889–) Government official.
SOCIAL SECURITY
Director, HEW Office of the Aging, 1956; staff director, White House Conference on Aging; executive director, National Retired Teachers Association and American Association of Retired Persons.
100 pp. *Open.* 1966.

FITTS, William Cochran, Jr. (1905–)
See James Lawrence Fly Project.

FITZ GERALD, Alice (Mrs. William) *See* Association for the Aid of Crippled Children.

FITZGERALD, F. Scott. *Discussed in* Carl Van Vechten.

FITZPATRICK, William. *See* New York Bar.

FITZWATER, Ivan M. *See* Eisenhower Administration.

ROBERT J. FLAHERTY PROJECT
Friends and associates discuss Robert Joseph Flaherty (1884–1951) and his extraordinary accomplishments as a film maker. The memoirs include material on his philosophy in making documentary films, his lack of preconception, his sense of industrial landscape, and his treatment of ordinary

people in their work. The making of *Louisiana Story* (1946–48) is described in detail. There is material also on *Nanook of the North, Man of Aran, The Land,* and *Moana of the South Seas.* Several respondents weigh his technical contributions and his influence on other film makers. Flaherty's warmth in personal relationships and gifts as raconteur are apparent in all the accounts.

Participants and pages: Bill Alexander, 22; Edgar Anstey, 34; Edgar and Daphne Anstey, 39; Michael Balcon, 17; Julien Bryan, 31; Ellsworth Bunker, 19; Edmund Carpenter, 23; Thorold and Joanna Dickinson, 30; Helen Van Dongen Durant, 66; Arnold Eagle, 38; Paul Falconberg, 20; Lewis Jacobs, 53; Richard Leacock, 49; Lucy Lemann, 19; Jay Leyda, 21; Carl Maas, 78; Chris Marker, 9; John Monck, 67; Elodie Osborn, 5; Henry Persons, 11; Hans Richter, 13; Ralph Rosenblum, 88; Paul Rotha, 14; Edward Sammis, 55; Charles Siepmann, 48; Sidney Smith, 70; Cecile Starr, 18; Judy Steele, 20; George Stoney, 13; John Taylor, 70; Virgil Thomson, 19; Willard Van Dyke, 9; Michael Voysey, 20; Harry Watt, 12; Eddy Weetaltuk, 27; Basil Wright, 53.

1,200 pp. *Permission required.* 1973–74. *Contributed by Bruce Harding and International Film Seminars, Inc.*

FLANDERS, Ralph Edward (1880–1969) Senator.
EISENHOWER ADMINISTRATION
Senate investigation of Senator Joseph McCarthy; McCarthy and his effect on the nation and on the Republican Party.
51 pp. *Permission required to cite or quote.* 1967. *Micro IV.*

FLANIGAN, Mark. *See* Columbia Crisis of 1968.

FLATH, August William (1898–1969) Police inspector.
Career in NYC Police Department; technical improvements; Prohibition; recreation; immigrants; press.
91 pp. *Open.* 1959.

FLEESON, Doris. *See* Doris Fleeson Kimball.

FLEISCHMAN, Harry (1914–   ) *See* Socialist Movement.

FLEISCHMAN, Raoul. *Discussed in* Gardner Botsford.

FLEMMING, Arthur S. *See* Health Sciences.

FLETCHER, Arthur. *Discussed in* Wesley J. Streater.

FLEXNER, Abraham (1866–1959) Educator.
The career of Simon Flexner; Rockefeller Institute; leaders in American medical history, particularly Doctors William Halsted, Howard Kelly, and William Welch.
36 pp. *Permission required to cite or quote.* 1954. *Micro I.*

FLEXNER, Carolin A. *See* Herbert H. Lehman Project.

FLEXNER, Simon. *Discussed in* Frederic R. Coudert; Abraham Flexner.

FLUGGE, Sylvester L. (1906–   ) *See* Continental Group.

FLY, James Harold. *See* James Agee.

JAMES LAWRENCE FLY PROJECT
Friends and associates recall James L. Fly (1898–1966), particularly his chairmanship of the FCC, 1939–44.
Participants and pages: Thurman Arnold, 16; Edward Brecher, 35; Marcus Cohn, 39; Thomas Corcoran, 29; Norman Corwin, 49; Benedict Peter Cottone, 24; Charles R. Denny, 28; Clifford J. Durr, 32; William C. Fitts, Jr., 52; Abe Fortas, 11; Fred W. Friendly, 14; Lucien Hilmer, 16; Rosel H. Hyde, 19; Leonard H. Marks, 25; Neville Miller, 33; Charles S. Murphy, 13; John Lord O'Brian, 14; Harry Plotkin, 36; Paul A. Porter, 30; Joseph Rauh, 35; James Rowe, 9; Pete Shuebruk, 36; Telford Taylor, 60.
655 pp. *Closed until January 1, 1982.* 1967. *Contributed by Sally Fly Connell, New York.*

FLYING TIGERS
At the Flying Tiger reunion at Ojai, California, in 1962, pilots, mechanics, radiomen, administrative, and ground crew personnel reminisced of their experiences with Chen-

nault's American Volunteer Group in Burma and China, and with the China National Aviation Corps, during and after WW II. They detail adventurous days in Rangoon, Toungoo and Kunming, retreating over the Burma Road, flying P-40's against Japanese bombers and Zeros, and operating the Mukden shuttle before the fall of Shanghai in 1949. The natural focus of those days was Claire Chennault, and these men and women recount anecdotes and impressions of him. While informal and unstructured, these interviews provide source material on a thinly documented phase of WW II, and the lore that has grown around it.

Participants and pages: Mrs. Anna Chennault and Thomas Corcoran, 4; Thomas Corcundale, 16; Jerry Costello and John Vivian, 12; Tom Cotton, 31; Doreen Davis, 47; Tex Hill, 23; Joe Jordan, 38; Gayle McAlister, 13; Robert Neale, 60; Charley Older, 38; Bob Prescott, 43; Doc Richardson and Bob Blyer, 21; Don Rodewald and Wilfred Schaper, 40; Don Rodewald, Harvey Wirta and Wilfred Schaper, 57; Bob Smith, 38; Tom Trumble, 78; John Vivian, 24.

583 pp. *Permission required to cite or quote.* 1962.

FLYNN, Edward Joseph (1892–1953) Politician.
Democratic Party politics, 1922–40.
24 pp. *Permission required to cite or quote.* 1950. *Micro I.*
Discussed in William O'Dwyer.

FOGARTY, Thomas C. (1905–   ) *See* Continental Group.

FOGELSON, Robert. *See* Columbia Crisis of 1968.

FOHL, Theodore. *Discussed in* Albert B. Curtis.

FOLEY, Adrian, Jr. (1922–   ) Lawyer, politician.
Democratic and Republican parties in New Jersey, 1954–   ; Clean Government Group, 1960; Constitutional Convention, 1966.
32 pp. *Open.* 1975.

FOLGER, John Clifford (1896–   ) Investment banker.
EISENHOWER ADMINISTRATION
Citizens' movement; financing 1956 and 1960 Republican campaigns; Milton Eisenhower, Leonard Hall; Ambassador to Belgium.
42 pp. *Permission required to cite or quote.* 1968. *Micro IV.*

FOLKS, Homer (1867–1963) Social worker.
American social work; Children's Aid; NYC politics and social work, 1900–35.
98 pp. *Permission required to cite or quote.* 1949. *Micro I.*

FOLLIARD, Edward Thomas (1899–   ) Newspaperman.
EISENHOWER ADMINISTRATION
President Eisenhower and the press; problems of presidential press coverage; relations between Presidents Harry Truman and Dwight Eisenhower.
72 pp. *Permission required to cite or quote.* 1967. *Micro III.*

FOLSOM, Marion Bayard (1893–1976) Executive, government official.
SOCIAL SECURITY
Beginnings of voluntary social security at Eastman Kodak Company; development of philosophy leading to social security program and Medicare.
207 pp. *Permission required to cite or quote.* 1965. *Micro III.*

EISENHOWER ADMINISTRATION
Early career; Under Secretary of the Treasury, 1953–55; tax legislation; Secretary of HEW, 1955–58; problems, policies, personalities; National Defense Education Act; Social Security.
163 pp. *Permission required to cite or quote.* 1968. *Micro III.*

See also Health Sciences.
Discussed in Charles I. Schottland.

FONDA, Henry (1905–   ) *See* Popular Arts.

FONDILLER, William (1885–1975) Engineer.

Career with Bell System; recollections of Michael Pupin and Albert Einstein.
18 pp. *Permission required.* 1970.

FONER, Eric (1943–) *See* Richard Hofstadter Project.

FOOT, Hugh Mackintosh (Baron Caradon) (1907–) *See* International Negotiations.

FORAND, Aime Joseph (1895–1972) *See* Social Security. *Micro IV.*

FORD, Ford Maddox (1873–1939) Author.
Impressions of Ford during his later years by family and others including Robert Lowell, Ezra Pound, Louise Bogan, Alan Tate, Matthew Josephson, Harold Loeb, Joseph Brewer and Edward Namberg, Jr. Radio program written and produced by WBAI, NY.
23 pp. *Open.*

FORD, Frederick W. (1909–) *See* Federal Communications Commission.

FORD, George Barry (1885–1978) Priest, student counselor.
Columbia University, 1927–45; personalities in the Roman Catholic Community; NYC political figures; American reaction to the Spanish Civil War; Morningside Heights development.
126 pp. *Permission required to cite or quote.* 1956. *Micro I.*

FORD, Gerald R. *See* International Negotiations.
Discussed in Theodore R. Kupferman.

FORD, Guy Stanton (1873–1962) Historian.
Early life and education; University of Wisconsin, 1892–95 and 1898–99; teaching at Wisconsin Rapids, 1895–98; European travel, 1899–1905; Columbia University, 1900–01; Yale University; illness, 1906; University of Illinois, 1906–13; Dean, University of Minnesota, 1913; sabbatical at Harvard, 1916; Committee on Public Information, 1917–18; *AHR;* SSRC; mission for Rockefeller Foundation, 1924; return to Minnesota; Commission for the Investiga-

tion of Social Studies in the Schools; Acting President, University of Minnesota, 1931–32; Stanford University, 1933; Commission of Inquiry on National Policy in International Economic Relations, 1934; achievements at the University of Minnesota as Dean of the Graduate School, 1913–38, Acting President, 1937–38, President, 1938–41; Executive Secretary, AHA; WWII.
963 pp. *Permission required to cite or quote.* 1955. *Micro I.*

FORD, Henry. *Discussed in* Clarence B. Kelland; Radio Pioneers.

FORD, John. *Discussed in* Albert E. Sutherland.

FORD, Katherine. *See* Carnegie Corporation.

FORDYCE, Alice (1905–) Foundation officer.
Use of BCG vaccine for tuberculosis in US and in other countries; isoniazid; Lasker Foundation Awards for Medical Journalism.
128 pp. *Permission required to cite or quote.* 1964. *Micro II.*

Medical profession's continued resistance to use of BCG.
14 pp. *Permission required to cite or quote.* 1974.

FOREMAN, Carl (1914–) *See* Popular Arts.

FOREST HISTORY SOCIETY
These interviews on forestry and logging contain material on conservation, woods safety, fire-fighting and the development of protective associations, old Minnesota logging camps, logging methods and machinery, and the development of the Paul Bunyan legends. Impressions of H. L. Mencken are included, as are impressions of George S. Long and other lumbermen.
Participants and pages: Charles S. Cowan, 54; George W. Dulany, 37; Inman F. Eldredge, 12; Royal S. Kellogg, 55; Donald MacKenzie, 17; Maggie Orr O'Neill, 19;

P. J. Rutledge, 10; James Stevens, 33. 237 pp. *Permission required to cite or quote.* 1957.

Contributed by the Forest History Society, Inc., Santa Cruz, California.

FORESTER, C.S. *Discussed in* D. Angus Cameron.

FORNEY, Abram. *See* Eisenhower Administration.

FORRESTAL, James V. *Discussed in* Joseph J. Clark; Thomas C. Hart; James L. Holloway, Jr.; Kenneth C. Royall; Eugene E. Wilson.

FORTAS, Abe (1910–   ) *See* Federated Department Stores *and* James Lawrence Fly Project.

FOSDICK, Harry Emerson. *Discussed in* Willard E. Givens.

FOSDICK, Raymond. *Discussed in* Flora M. Rhind; Warren Weaver.

FOSS, Robert C. (1924–   ) *See* Continental Group.

FOSSA, Manuel. *See* Argentina.

FOSSA, Mateo (1897–   ) *See* Argentina.

FOSTER, Paul F. (1889–1972) Naval officer.
Family background, Oklahoma and the land rush, Utah, Idaho; Naval Academy, cruises; gunnery and fire control; occupation of Vera Cruz, 1914; submarine service; Navy recruiting; engineering duty; resignation from Navy, 1929; Wall Street, adventures in business; Naval service WWII: Panama, Alaska, Puerto Rico, Assistant Naval Inspector General, Navy Manpower Survey Board; merchandising, Mandel Brothers, 1946–50; World Bank, 1950–54; AEC, Atoms for Peace Program, Operations Coordinating Board, general manager, AEC; US representative International Atomic Energy Agency, 1959. Impressions of Adm. Thomas Hart, Lewis L. Strauss, John McCone, Vyacheslav Molotov, and many others.
373 pp. *Permission required.* 1966.

FOSTER, William Z. *Discussed in* John Brophy.

FOULOIS, Benjamin D. (1879–1967) *See* Aviation Project. *Micro IV.*

FOUNDATION FOR CHILD DEVELOP-MENT *See* Association for the Aid of Crippled Children.

FOUNDATIONS *See* Philanthropy.

FOWLER, Donald. *See* World Bank.

FOX, Andrew E. (1921–   ) *See* Continental Group.

FOX, John. *See* James B. Duke Project.

FOX, William. *Discussed in* Upton Sinclair.

FOX, William T. R. (1912–   ) *See* Carnegie Corporation *and* United Nations Conference.

FRADER, Joel. *See* Columbia Crisis of 1968.

FRAENKEL, Osmond K. (1888–   ) Lawyer.
Harvard, 1904–08; Columbia Law School; early law practice; Soviet cases; Norris, Patterson, Trop, and Leyra cases; ACLU; National Lawyer's Guild; obscenity, civil liberties, equal rights, communism in US; publications; impressions of Arthur Garfield Hays, Morris Ernst, Alger Hiss, US Supreme Court Justices.
144 pp. *Permission required to cite or quote.* 1974. *Micro IV.*

FRAIN, Joseph (1914–   ) *See* Continental Group.

FRANCIS, Clarence (1888–   ) Corporation executive.
Eisenhower Administration
Early career; inter-agency division for disposition of agricultural surpluses.
37 pp. *Permission required to cite or quote.* 1967. *Micro III.*

FRANCO, Francisco. *Discussed in* John Davis Lodge.

FRANK, Jerome New (1889–1957) Judge.
Education at the University of Chicago; law practice in Chicago and NY; general counsel of AAA; NRA; impressions of Henry A. Wallace, Chester Davis, George Peek, Rexford G. Tugwell, Harry Hopkins, Alger Hiss, and Hugh Johnson.
194 pp. *Permission required to cite or quote.* 1952. *Micro II.*
Discussed in Cully A. Cobb; Gardner Jackson.

FRANK, Waldo (1889–1967) *See* Hart Crane Project.

FRANKE, William Birrell (1894–   ) *See* Eisenhower Administration. *Micro III.*

FRANKEL, Charles (1917–   ) *See* Journalism Lectures (C.)

FRANKFURTER, Felix (1882–1965) Supreme Court Justice.
Life in NYC as an immigrant; Harvard Law School, influence of Professors Samuel Williston and John C. Gray; comments on beginning of legal education; C. C. Langdell, Charles Eliot; association with Henry L. Stimson: US Attorney's Office, NY; War Department; anti-trust activity; minimum wage laws.
337 pp. *Permission required to cite or quote.* 1955. *Micro I.*
Discussed in Marquis W. Childs; Edward S. Greenbaum; Learned Hand; Gardner Jackson; James M. Landis; David A. Morse; Henry A. Wallace; Charles Wyzanski, Jr.

FRANKLIN, Floyd E. (1901–   ) *See* Continental Group.

FRANKS, Robert. *Discussed in* Carnegie Corporation.

FRASER, Phyllis. *Discussed in* Bennett Cerf.

FREDRICKSON, A. N. *See* Weyerhaeuser Timber Company.

FREED, Arthur (1894–1973) *See* Popular Arts.

FREEDMAN, Max. *See* Journalism Lectures.

FREEMAN, Douglas S. *Discussed in* George H. Gallup; Broadus Mitchell.

FREEMAN, Edward M. *Discussed in* J. George Harrar.

FREIDEL, Frank (1916–   ) *See* Richard Hofstadter Project.

FREUD, Anna. *Discussed in* Willi Hoffer; Joseph Sandler.

FREUD, Sigmund. *Discussed in* Edward L. Bernays; Psychoanalytic Movement; Theodor Reik.

FREUND, Paul. *Discussed in* David A. Morse.

FREY, John Philip (1871–1957) Union official.
Family background, early life; *Molders' Journal*, 1903–27; Milwaukee Foundry strike, 1906; Thomas Mooney and James McNamara cases; WWI labor and manpower problems; labor consultant to European allies, 1918; Socialist Party; IWW; Metal Trades Department, AFL, 1927–50; relations of AFL with Labor Department; Frances Perkins as Secretary of Labor; NRA; 1934 Wages & Hours Bill and Roosevelt administration; NLRB; Anaconda Copper strike, 1935; 1935 AFL convention; formation of the CIO; Communist Party and the labor movement; Martin Dies Committee; San Francisco strike, 1941; International Association of Machinists; WWII manpower and production; NAM; mobilization in World Wars I and II; relations of labor with political parties and Catholic Church; craft unionism; organizing Negroes. Impressions of Harry Bridges, James J. Davis, Samuel Gompers, William Green, Herbert Hoover, John L. Lewis, Theodore Roosevelt, Franklin D. Roosevelt, William H. Taft.
752 pp. *Permission required to cite or quote.* 1955. *Micro II.*

FRIEDLICH, Herbert Aaron (1893–   ) *See* Robert P. Patterson Project.

FRIEDMAN, Samuel. *See* Socialist Movement.

FRIENDLY, Fred W. (1915–   ) *See* James Lawrence Fly Project *and* Radio Pioneers, *Micro II.*
Discussed in Frank Stanton.

FRIENDLY, Henry Jacob (1903–   ) *See* Aviation Project. *Micro II.*

FRIENDS OF THE COLUMBIA LIBRARIES
Selected speakers at dinner meetings of The Friends of the Columbia Libraries, generally on literary topics.
Participants and pages: Robert Halsband, 19; Rockwell Kent, 20; Hellmut Lehman-Haupt, 36; Ogden Nash, 20.
95 pp. *Permission required to cite or quote.* 1960–1972.

FRILLMAN, Paul W. (1912–1972) Missionary.
Missionary experiences, China; Japanese occupation, 1936–41; with Gen. Claire Chennault and the Flying Tigers to Burma and China, 1941; protecting Burma Road and Rangoon; evacuation of Rangoon; Kunming; disbanding of Flying Tigers, 1942; US Army Air Corps, 1942; Combat Intelligence with Chennault and 14th Air Force in China, 1943; OSS; postwar China; USIS.
416 pp. *Permission required to cite or quote.* 1962. *Micro I.*

FRINK, W.H. *Discussed in* Abram Kardiner.

FRITCHEY, Clayton. *See* Adlai E. Stevenson Project.

FRODING, Oskar. *Discussed in* Hokan B. Steffanson.

FROST, Robert. *Discussed in* Dorothy Baker; William S. Braithwaite.

FROST, Rose. *See* Continental Group.

FRY, E. Ewart (1916–   ) *See* Continental Group.

FRY, Guy S. *See* John Robert Gregg Project.

FRY, Luther. *Discussed in* Paul F. Lazarsfeld.

FRYE, Helene. *See* McGraw-Hill.

FUESS, Claude Moore (1885–1963) Educator.
Preparatory school teaching; headmastership at Andover: abolition of fraternities, distinguished Andover graduates; literary recollections and impressions; comments on historians; impressions of Alfred Stearns, Henry Cabot Lodge, Endicott Peabody, Calvin Coolidge, Henry L. Stimson.
285 pp. *Permission required to cite or quote.* 1962. *Micro I.*

FULBRIGHT, James William (1905–   ) Senator.
Childhood and education; Oxford University; Washington, D.C.; University of Arkansas; the Fulbright Act; the House of Representatives and the US Senate.
128 pp. *Permission required to cite or quote.* 1957.

FULD, Stanley H. (1903–   ) Judge.
NEW YORK BAR
Education, Columbia University Law School; law practice, NYC, 1926–1935; appointment by Thomas E. Dewey to NY rackets investigation and to head Appeals Bureau, 1938–1944; NY Court of Appeals, 1946–1973; notable decisions, including definition of pornography and adoptive parent custody issues; views on roles, obligations, and duties of judges and lawyers, judicial review systems, precedent reversal, courtroom media coverage, and other legal issues; work on national commission dealing with copyright revision.
190 pp. *Permission required to cite or quote.* 1977. Papers.

FULLER, Glen V. *See* China Missionaries.

FULLER, Robert. *See* Radio Pioneers.

FULLINGTON, Wayland. *See* Radio Pioneers.

FUNK, Howard. *See* Eisenhower Administration.

FUOSS, Robert (1912–   ) *See* Federated Department Stores.

G

GABLER, Milton. *See* Popular Arts.

GALLAGHER, Buell. *Discussed in* Charles H. Tuttle.

GALLAGHER, Gladys (1904–) *See* Continental Group.

GALLAGHER, John E. (1914–) *See* Continental Group.

GALLOWAY, Judith. *See* Air Force Academy.

GALLUP, George Horace (1901–) Public opinion statistician.
Family background and education; early newspaper readership surveys; journalism teaching 1929–32; principles of effective advertising; magazine publishing: *Literary Digest, Reader's Digest, Saturday Evening Post, Look,* etc.; postcard polling; Gallup polls from 1933; impressions of Gardner Cowles, Jr., Raymond Rubicam, Douglas Southall Freeman.
    158 pp. *Permission required to cite or quote.* 1962. *Micro III.*
See also Book-of-the-Month Club. *Micro III.*

GALPIN, Perrin Comstock (1889–1973) Educator.
Education; Belgium and WWI; impressions of Brand Whitlock, Hugh Gibson, Herbert Hoover, and others.
    40 pp. *Permission required to cite or quote.* 1956. *Micro I.*

GAMBLE, Clarence. *Discussed in* Women's History and Population Issues.

GAMBLING, John (1897–1974) *See* Radio Pioneers. *Micro IV.*

GAMBOA, Javier. *See* Argentina.

GANDHI, Mohandas K. *Discussed in* Frank W. Rounds, Jr.; Sir Muhammad Zafrulla Khan.

GANNETT, Lewis. *Discussed in* Arthur B. Spingarn.

GANS, Hiram Selig (1905–) *See* New York Political Studies (C).

GARBER, Paul. *See* Air Force Academy.

GARBO, Greta. *Discussed in* Rouben Mamoulian.

GARDINER, Muriel (1901–) Psychoanalyst.
PSYCHOANALYTIC MOVEMENT
Childhood, education; college political activities; analysis with Ruth Mack Brunswick; medical studies in Vienna; work as school psychiatrist in New Jersey; underground political activities in Vienna, 1942–45.
    179 pp. *Permission required.* 1978.

GARDNER, Grandison. *See* Henry H. Arnold Project.

GARDNER, John William (1912–) Foundation executive.
CARNEGIE CORPORATION
First impressions of Carnegie Corporation, 1946; area studies; Harvard Russian Research Center; Afro-American Institute; President of Carnegie Corporation, 1955–

67: relations with trustees, other Carnegie organizations, staff selection; evaluation of foundation work. Impressions of Corporation officers and trustees.

221 pp. *Permission required.* 1969.

GARDNER, Roy and W. B. Lane. *See* Benedum and the Oil Industry.

GARDNER, Samuel (1891–   ) *See* Thomas A. Edison Project.

GAREY, Woodrow Wilson. *See* McGraw-Hill.

GARMENT, Leonard. *See* Ethnic Groups and American Foreign Policy.

GARMES, Lee (1898–   ) *See* Popular Arts.

GARNER, Robert Livingston (1894–1975) International banker.
WORLD BANK
Role of Bank's management and directors, 1947–49; policy developments; history of various loans; staff; organization of Bank and its role as mediator.

100 pp. *Permission required to cite or quote.* 1961.

GARRISON, Charlotte (1881–1972) Educator.
Education, TC, 1906–08; Director, Horace Mann Kindergarten, 1908–28; parents' associations; educational toys; progressive education; Manhattanville Nursery; Russia, 1929; impressions of James E. Russell, Grace Dodge, Patty Hill, Agnes Burke, and John Dewey.

58 pp. *Permission required to cite or quote.* 1967. *Micro II.*

GARRISON, Lloyd Kirkham (1897–   ) Lawyer, government official.
Chairman of NLRB, 1934: establishment of board, personnel, procedures; problem of sanctions; regional boards; relationship with Department of Labor, Frances Perkins; colleagues; Smith Committee hearings; evaluation of NLRB; Gen. Hugh Johnson.

63 pp. *Permission required to cite or quote.* 1969.

Acquired from the Labor-Management Documentation Center, Cornell University.

GARTNER, William. *See* McGraw-Hill.

GARVEY, Marcus. *Discussed in* A. Philip Randolph; George S. Schuyler.

GASSER, George. *See* Alaskan Pioneers.

GATES, Thomas Sovereign, Jr. (1906–   ) Cabinet member.
EISENHOWER ADMINISTRATION
Experiences in WWII; Under Secretary and Secretary of the Navy, 1953–59; Deputy Secretary and Secretary of Defense, 1959–60.

59 pp. *Permission required to cite or quote.* 1967.
See also additional interview in Eisenhower Administration.

GAUSS, Christian. *Discussed in* Harold R. Medina.

GAVAGAN, Joseph Andrew (1892–1968) Politician, judge.
NY State politics, 1922–29; Congress, 1929–43; NYC politics in 1950.

70 pp. *Permission required to cite or quote.* 1950. *Micro I.*

GAVIN, James M. (1907–   ) Army officer.
EISENHOWER ADMINISTRATION
Eisenhower as General and President: decisions, management ability, relations with Gens. George Patton and Walter B. Smith and with Marshal Bernard Montgomery; missiles.

36 pp. *Permission required.* 1967.

GAY, Luis F.   Labor leader.
ARGENTINA
Telephone Workers' union; development of unions during 1920's, political maturing; power of General Confederation of Workers; effect of Depression, rise of Adolf Hitler and Benito Mussolini; Peron's relationship with organized labor, especially 1944–45; formation and dissolution of Labor Party.

107 pp. *Open.* 1971.

GAYNOR, Janet (1906–   ) *See* Popular Arts.

GAYNOR, William A. *Discussed in* William A. Prendergast; Lawrence Veiller.

GEER, Bennette Eugene (1873–1964) *See* James B. Duke Project.

GELLES, Gerry. *See* Socialist Movement.

GELLHORN, Alfred (1913–   ) Physician, educator.
Research on nitrogen mustard and treatment for shock, teaching activities, Columbia, 1943–68; cancer research and treatment at Delafield Hospital, 1949–68; Director, University of Pennsylvania Medical Center, 1968–73; concerns as Director, Center for Biomedical Education, CCNY, from 1974; controversy concerning ethnic distribution, reverse discrimination in admissions policies of biomedical program; related difficulties in program accreditation, funding, curriculum development; push for community medicine; work with Council of International Organizations of the Medical Sciences on bio-ethical issues, human rights, internationalization of drug research, development.
735 pp. *Permission required.* 1978.

GELLHORN, Edna (Mrs. George) (1879–1970)
League of Women Voters, 1919–54: organization, concern with federal and state laws, leaders.
17 pp. *Open.* 1954.

Women's Suffrage League of St. Louis, 1919; early suffragists.
6 pp. *Open.* 1964.

GELLHORN, Walter (1906–   ) Lawyer.
Part I: Experiences as student and later faculty member at Columbia University; clerkship with Justice Harlan Stone; Washington, D.C. in the early 1930's; Social Security Board; Attorney General's Committee on Administrative Procedure; OPA; WLB, Region 2.
590 pp. *Permission required to cite or quote.* 1955.

Part II: Angelo Herndon case; postwar years at Columbia Law School: impressions of deans, faculty members, Columbia presidents; ACLU activities, 1940's–50's; NAACP Legal Defense Fund activities, from 1940's; McCarthy investigations; 1951 British National Health Service study; 1952 study of families and children in courts; 1957 study on revision of New York State Constitution; visiting professorships: Tokyo, Harvard and others; legal educational standards work for Association of American Law Schools; presidency, AALS, 1963; research on citizen grievance-handling mechanisms, especially ombudsmanship; 1969 study on eligibility of church-related institutions for state funds; 1968 Columbia student demonstrations; women and blacks in legal education and profession; contract and grievance arbitration since 1936; establishment of National Legal Services Corporation; activities as trustee of Amherst College, 1960–72.
603 pp. *Permission required to cite or quote.* 1977.

GEMMILL, Robert O. *See* Eisenhower Administration.

GENTELE, Goeran. *Discussed in* Schuyler Chapin.

GEORGE, Harold Lee (1893–   ) and Haywood Hansell. *See* Air Force Academy.

GEORGE, Walter F. *Discussed in* Cully A. Cobb.

GERARD, James Watson (1867–1951) Lawyer, diplomat.
Democratic party and elections, 1902–40; experiences as ambassador to Germany, 1913–17; impressions of Woodrow Wilson, Walter Hines Page, and others.
96 pp. *Permission required to cite or quote.* 1950. *Micro I.*

GERSHWIN, George. *Discussed in* Popular Arts.

GERSTER, John Carl Arpad (1882–1974) *See* Mt. Sinai Hospital.

GETTY, Jean Paul (1892–1976) Oil executive.
Family background; childhood; personal life, travels abroad; experiences in oil business; Mission Corporation and Tidewater Oil; WWII aircraft factory; general comments on business and work; art collecting; J.P. Getty Museum; tour of Sutton Place; world oil shortage.
332 pp. *Permission required to cite or quote.* 1974. Papers.

Contributed by Somerset de Chair, Essex, England.

GHIOLDI, Americo (1900–   ) *See* Argentina.

GHORMLEY, Robert. *Discussed in* James Fife, DeWitt Peck.

GIBB, James M. (1896–   ) *See* Continental Group.

GIBBONS, Katherine Clark
ADLAI E. STEVENSON PROJECT
Reminiscences of meetings and correspondence with Stevenson, 1952–65.
73 pp. *Permission required.* 1969.

GIBSON, Edwin T. (1886–1959) Corporation executive.
Development of frozen foods; General Foods organization; defense mobilization in Washington; MSA; American Assembly; Eisenhower Exchange Fellowships.
83 pp. *Permission required to cite or quote.* 1956. *Micro I.*

GIBSON, Hugh. *Discussed in* Perrin C. Galpin.

GIBSON, Mary Bass (1905–   ) Editor.
Family background, childhood in Mexico, college life, publicity work; marriages, motherhood and career; *Ladies Home Journal,* 1939–1962: work with Bruce and Beatrice Gould, editorial policies, philosophy, "How America Lives" series, "What the Women of America Think" polls, Kinsey report; WWII coverage and feature articles; plotting readership appeal; advertising, magazine rivalry, 1955–65; financial crisis, Curtis Publishing Co.; *Seventeen* magazine book editing; lecture series; *Family Circle* "Careers at Home" series; MacDowell Colony.
549 pp. *Permission required.* 1975.

GIDDINGS, Franklin H. *Discussed in* Frank H. Hankins.

GIDEONSE, Harry David (1901–   )
College president.
Experiences as President of Brooklyn College; relationship with NYC Board of Higher Education, Mayor's Office, and presidents of other city colleges; investiga-

tions; Russell case, Rapp-Coudert Committee.
118 pp. *Permission required.* 1961.

GIESECKE, Albert Anthony (1883–1970)
Educator, archeologist.
Youth and education; Ministry of Education in Peru, 1909; Rector of University of Cuzco, 1910–23; Director General of Education of Peru, 1923–31; educational problems and policies in Latin America, student strikes; archeological discoveries and collections; Inter-American Conferences; American Embassy in Lima from 1931; Tacna-Arica Plebiscite Commission, 1925–26. Impressions of Hiram Bingham, Axel Wenner-Gren, Paul Fejos, Gen. John J. Pershing, and many others.
438 pp. *Permission required to cite or quote.* 1962. *Micro II.*

GIFFORD, Arleigh D. (1904–   ) *See* Continental Group.

GIGLI, Beniamino. *Discussed in* Gabor Carelli.

GILBERT, James L. *See* McGraw-Hill.

GILBERT, John. *Discussed in* Popular Arts.

GILBERT, Louis Wolfe (1886–1970) *See* Popular Arts.

GILBERT, Wells. *See* Weyerhaeuser Timber Company.

GILDERSLEEVE, Virginia C. (1877–1969) *See* Nicholas Murray Butler Project.

GILE, Elizabeth. *See* McGraw-Hill.

GILES, Bascom. *See* Benedum and the Oil Industry.

GILLIAM, Franklin. *See* Rare Books (B).

GILMAN, Elizabeth. *Discussed in* Broadus Mitchell.

GILMAN, Mildred (Mrs. Robert Wohlforth)
Heywood Broun's activities and friends in the 1920's and '30's: Sacco-Vanzetti case, NY *World,* Algonquin Round Table,

Newspaper Guild, *Connecticut Nutmeg;* Ruth Hale, Sherwood Anderson, Robert Benchley, H. L. Mencken.
82 pp. *Permission required to cite or quote.* 1969. *Micro II.* Papers.

GILPIN, Brooke, Virginia Morgan and Charles Mason. *See* Longwood Gardens.

GIMENEZ, Ovidio. *See* Argentina.

GINGELL, George. *See* Radio Pioneers.

GINOCCHIO, Rafael. *See* Argentina.

GINSBERG, Allen. *Discussed in* John Clellon Holmes.

GINZBERG, Leon. *See* Mt. Sinai Hospital. *Micro II.*

GIROUX, Robert. *Discussed in* Roger W. Straus.

GISSEN, Max. Journalist.
Childhood and education; book reviewing for *New Republic;* Edmund Wilson; book reviewing for *Time;* Whittaker Chambers, T. S. Matthews, Henry Luce; background of cover stories on Louis Armstrong, J. P. Marquand.
298 pp. *Closed during lifetime.* 1963.

GIUSTI, Roberto F. *See* Argentina.

GIVENS, Willard Earl (1886–1971) Educator.
Early life and education, Columbia, 1915, Union Theological Seminary, 1916; teaching experiences in Hawaii; Superintendent of Schools, Oakland, California, 1925–27; NEA, Executive Secretary, 1935–52. Impressions of Harry Emerson Fosdick, Henry Sloane Coffin.
64 pp. *Permission required to cite or quote.* 1968. *Micro IV.*

GLADIEUX, Bernard Louis (1907–   )
Government official, management consultant.
Early life and education, Oberlin College and Maxwell School, Syracuse University; administrative consultant in federal government, 1936–40; Chief, special staff on war organization, Bureau of the Budget, 1939–

42; administration and budgetary management of the executive branch in wartime; preparation of executive orders for president; formation, operation, and budgets of OPM, BEW, SPAB, WPB, CIAA, ODT, OSS, OCD, OWI, OES; wartime production and manpower problems; leadership and operational evaluations; later work in WPB, 1943–44; UNRRA, 1944; Department of Commerce, 1945–50; Ford Foundation, 1950–51.
744 pp. *Permission required to cite or quote.* 1951. *Micro II.*

GLASER, Milton (1929–   ) *See* New York's Art World.

GLASS, Carter. *Discussed in* Walter Wyatt.

GLASSEN, Mary (Mrs. William H.) *See* James B. Duke Project.

GLASSFORD, Pelham. *Discussed in* Frances Perkins.

GLEASON, Henry. *See* New York Botanical Garden.

GLIMCHER, Arnold (1938–   ) *See* Louise Nevelson, New York's Art World.

GLOVER, Edward (–1972) Psychoanalyst.
PSYCHOANALYTIC MOVEMENT
History of psychoanalysis; techniques of analysis; research; British Psychoanalytic Society; training analysts; evaluation of Sigmund Freud, Carl Jung, and other analysts; personal background.
137 pp. *Permission required.* 1965.

GODDARD, Esther C. (Mrs. Robert H.) *See* Aviation project.

GOEBBELS, Joseph. *Discussed in* Lawrence Dennis.

GOELL, Theresa. Archeologist.
Early life and education; archeological expedition to Turkey, Numrad Dag; Hartley Lehman.
54 pp. *Permission required.* 1965.
Contributed by Frederick P. Latimer, Jr.

GOERING, Hermann. *Discussed in* Lawrence Dennis.

GOETHALS, George. *Discussed in* Gerard Swope.

GOFF, Stan. *See* Vietnam Veterans.

GOLDBERG, Arthur Joseph (1908–   ) Labor lawyer, mediator.
INTERNATIONAL NEGOTIATIONS
Multilateral and bilateral negotiation techniques; changing functions of US ambassadors; "demonstrative diplomacy"; impressions of Cyrus Vance, W. Averell Harriman, and William P. Rogers.
51 pp. *Permission required.* 1970.

GOLDBERG, Jacob. *See* Joseph M. Proskauer Project.

GOLDBLOOM, Maurice. *See* Socialist Movement.

GOLDFINE, Bernard. *Discussed in* Edward A. McCabe.

GOLDMAN, James. *See* Columbia Crisis of 1968.

GOLDMAN, John. *See* John Monck.

GOLDSCHMIDT, Richard. *Discussed in* Leslie C. Dunn.

GOLDSMITH, Sadja (1930–   ) *See* Women's History and Population Issues.

GOLDSTEIN, Jonah J. (1886–1967) Judge.
Early life in NYC, NYU Law School, 1909; Educational Alliance, Grand Street Boys; Secretary for Alfred E. Smith, 1911; numerous Jewish philanthropies; administering relief program, Palestine, 1929; NYC Judge: accounts of court cases and work for court reform, 1931–56; Republican candidate for mayor, 1945; relationships with Felix Warburg, Senators Robert F. Wagner and Herbert Lehman, Mayors James Walker, Fiorello La Guardia, William O'Dwyer.
686 pp. *Open.* 1966.

GOLDWATER, Barry Morris (1909–   )
Senator.
EISENHOWER ADMINISTRATION

Presidency of Dwight Eisenhower; Senate Campaign Committee; Republican Party; impressions of Sherman Adams, Richard Nixon, Lyndon Johnson, Robert Taft, William Knowland.
85 pp. *Closed during lifetime.* 1967.
Discussed in H. Meade Alcorn, Jr.; Stephen Shadegg; F. Clifton White.

GOLENPAUL, Dan (1900–1974) Radio producer.
Information Please Almanac; genesis and production of "Information Please"; Heywood Broun, Oscar Levant, Clifton Fadiman, John Kieran, and others on the program; relations with advertising agencies and sponsors.
205 pp. *Permission required to cite or quote.* 1964.

GOMEZ MORALES, Alfredo. *See* Argentina.

GOMPERS, Samuel. *Discussed in* John Brophy; John P. Frey; Socialist Movement; Florence Thorne; Eva M. Valesh.

GOOD, George Franklin, Jr. (1901–   )
See Marine Corps.

GOODE, James P. *See* Air Force Academy.

GOODING, Ralph. *See* Hood River Blackie.

GOODMAN, Benny (1909–   ) *See* Popular Arts.

GOODMAN, Harry. *See* Radio Pioneers.

GOODMAN, Saul (1906–   ) Timpanist.
Silent movie accompaniment; Newport Casino, 1926; New York Philharmonic, 1926–76; conducting and rehearsing skills; Beethoven centennial concerts, 1927; Philharmonic tour, 1930; orchestra unionization, pension plans; teaching, Juilliard School, Conservatory of Montreal; experience with Martha Graham; views of avant-garde music; impressions of Bruno Walter, Arthur Judson, Leonard Rose, Fritz Reiner, Leopold Stokowski; Arturo Toscanini; Dmitri Mitropoulos, Arthur Rodzinski.
212 pp. *Permission required to cite or quote.* 1976.

GOODPASTER, Andrew Jackson (1915–) Army officer.
EISENHOWER ADMINISTRATION
White House Staff Secretary, 1954–61: liaison officer with NSC; relations with Russia, Latin America, Middle East, and Asia during Eisenhower administration.
137 pp. *Permission required to cite or quote.* 1967. *Micro III.*

GOODRICH, Lawrence Keith (1906–1968) *See* McGraw-Hill.

GOODRICH, Leland Matthew (1899–) Professor of international relations.
Childhood and education in Maine; Bowdoin and Harvard, 1916–25; Brown University; Commission for Belgian Relief, 1923–25; Lafayette University; World Peace Foundation; Columbia University.
151 pp. *Permission required to cite or quote.* 1967. *Micro II.*
See also United Nations Conference.

GOODRICH, Lloyd (1897–) Museum officer and art historian.
AMERICAN CULTURAL LEADERS
Government and foundation support of arts; Whitney Museum; art criticism; White House, 1961–63; visual arts in US.
86 pp. *Permission required.* 1967.

GOODRICH, Luther Carrington (1894–) Sinologist.
Early life in China; PUMC after WWI; training in sinology, Columbia University; impressions of Paul Pelliot, J. J. L. Duyvendak and others; research problems of *The Literary Inquisition of Ch'ien-Lung.*
159 pp. *Permission required to cite or quote.* 1959. *Micro II.*

GOODWIN, Kathryn. *See* Social Security.

GORDEY, Michel (1913–) Journalist.
Journalistic experiences, especially in OWI during WWII and in Budapest during Hungarian revolt in 1956. Impressions of Nikita Khrushchev and Gen. Charles de Gaulle.
106 pp. *Permission required.* 1962.

GORDON, Bruce B. (1906–) *See* Continental Group.

GORDON, David. *Discussed in* Valda Setterfield.

GORDON, Dorothy (1889–1970)
RADIO PIONEERS
Childhood and education; concert singer, marriage; children's concerts, 1923; early experience in radio; CBS "Children's Corner," 1930; NBC children's programs; "Yesterday's Children"; Youth Forums for NY *Times* from 1943; impressions of radio personalities and public figures.
168 pp. *Permission required to cite or quote.* 1951. *Micro II.*

GORDON, Joseph. *See* Occupation of Japan. *Micro II.*

GORDON, Richard (1882–1956) Actor.
Childhood in Connecticut; playing in stock companies throughout US, 1902–16; impressions of Corse Peyton, Maude Adams, Francis Wilson, William Hodge, Mary Emerson, Anne Sutherland, Thomas Meighan, Frances Ring, Philip H. Lord, Mildred Holland.
203 pp. *Permission required to cite or quote.* 1951. *Micro IV.*

GORE, Albert Arnold (1907–) Politician.
SOUTHERN INTELLECTUAL LEADERS (B)
Childhood; education, University of Tennessee, 1932; Tennessee politics 1938–70's; assessment of national political figures; campaigns for Congress, Senate, 1938–70; civil rights, Vietnam, the cold war.
103 pp. *Permission required to cite or quote.* 1976.

GORMAN, Carl. *See* Marine Corps.

GORNEY, Jay (1896–) *See* Popular Arts.

GOULD, Bruce Charles (1898–) and Beatrice. Editors.
Both describe family backgrounds, childhoods and meeting at State University of Iowa in 1920's; she discusses teaching, newspaper work, short story writing; he discusses General Film Co., college humor magazine, newspaper reporting, Army Air Service 1918–19, playwriting

and reviewing, associate editorship of *Saturday Evening Post;* marriage, 1923; New York scene in 1920's, Prohibition; joint editors of *Ladies Home Journal,* 1935–62: staff and format, health campaigns, reader polls, important articles, series, literary pieces; difficulties and decline of Curtis Publishing Company; impressions of George Horace Lorimer, Eleanor Roosevelt, others.

726 pp. *Permission required to cite or quote.* 1976.
Discussed in Mary Bass Gibson.

GOULD, Morton (1913–   ) Composer, conductor.
Family background, early music; Institute of Musical Art; Woodstock; vaudeville, Radio City Music Hall; marriages, family and friends; WOR radio series; WWII government radio broadcasts; commissioned works; ballet music; work routine; impressions of Fritz Reiner, Leopold Stokowski, Arturo Toscanini, Dmitri Mitropoulos, Milton Katims.
201 pp. *Permission required.* 1975.

GOULTER, Oswald John. *See* China Missionaries.

GOVERNMENT *See* Politics and Government.

GRAEBEL, Richard (–1976) *See* Adlai E. Stevenson Project. *Micro III.*

GRAF, Arthur (1905–   ) and L. Virgil Jones. *See* Continental Group.

GRAF, Irene and Terry Walter. *See* Air Force Academy.

GRAFF, Henry F. (1921–   ) *See* Richard Hofstadter Project.

GRAHAM, Bruce (1925–   ) *See* Ludwig Mies van der Rohe.

GRAHAM, Evarts. *Discussed in* Edward Churchill.

GRAHAM, Frank Porter (1886–1972) University president.
University of North Carolina during presidency, 1930–49.

38 pp. *Permission required to cite or quote.* 1961.
See also Social Security.
Discussed in William T. Couch; Jonathan W. Daniels; Arthur F. Raper; Terry Sanford; Rupert B. Vance.

GRAHAM, Martha. *Discussed in* Aaron Copland; Saul Goodman.

GRAHAM, Sheilah. *See* Popular Arts.

GRANGER, Lester B. (1896–1976) Social worker.
Background and education; experiences as a Negro soldier in WWI; early encounters with discrimination and segregation; extension work, counselling, social work; Urban League, studies of employment structure and placement facilities; racial questions in labor unions; National Negro Congress; segregation in armed forces; Community Relations projects; approaches to leaders of industry; American Association of Social Work; International Conferences; Negroes in international relations; CORE; sit-in movements; Dr. Martin Luther King, Jr., NAACP; Negro nationalism; new African leadership; federal record on equal rights in employment.
326 pp. *Open.* 1960.

GRANT, John B. (1890–1962) Public health officer.
Education in China, Nova Scotia, University of Michigan, Johns Hopkins; IHB; work on hookworm in North Carolina, China; foundation and early years of PUMC; Peking Health Station; setting up first Ministry of Health in China, 1929; political problems and relationships; public health organization in Japan; Rockefeller Foundation program; Institute of Public Health in Tokyo, 1932; public health work in Yugoslavia; rural reconstruction in China and India; problems of social medicine in US, Europe, and Canada; international organizations. Impressions of Victor Heiser, Joseph Mountin, Selskar Gunn, Roger Greene, and Wickliffe Rose.
1,223 pp. *Permission required to cite or quote.* 1961. *Micro III.*
Underwritten by the Rockefeller Foundation.

GRANVILLE, Bonita (1923–   ) *See* Popular Arts.

GRAUER, Alvin.
OCCUPATION OF JAPAN
Experience in advertising; Army Industrial Services during WWII; public relations for occupation forces in Yokohama and Tokyo, 1945; Visitors Bureau, 1946; American soldier in Japan: attitude of Japanese, fraternization; Gen. Douglas MacArthur.
  139 pp. *Permission required to cite or quote.* 1961. *Micro II.*

GRAUER, Ben (1908–1977) Radio reporter.
RADIO PIONEERS
Early days of radio; experiences as radio reporter.
  65 pp. *Permission required to cite or quote.* 1968. *Micro II.*

GRAVES, Edwin H. (1910–   ) *See* Continental Group.

GRAVES, Nancy S. (1940–   ) and Andre Emmerich. *See* New York's Art World.

GRAY, Arthur Jr. (1922–   ) Investment broker.
EISENHOWER ADMINISTRATION
Chairman of special events, Citizens for Eisenhower-Nixon, 1952; 1952 convention and campaign.
  32 pp. *Permission required to cite or quote.* 1967. *Micro III.*

GRAY, Gordon (1909–   ) Government official.
EISENHOWER ADMINISTRATION
Education, University of North Carolina, Yale Law School; early legal practice; publishing; North Carolina State Senate, 1938–42, 1946–47; service in WWII; Assistant Secretary and Secretary of the Army, 1947–50; unification of services, civilian control of Department of Defense; Special Assistant to President Harry Truman, 1950; President, University of North Carolina, 1950–55; Assistant Secretary of Defense for International Security Affairs, 1955–57; service intelligence operations; Director, Office of Defense Mobilization, 1957–58; Special Assistant to President Eisenhower for National Security Affairs, 1958–61; Robert Oppenheimer Case and

Personnel Security Board for AEC, 1954; National Trust for Historic Preservation; Commission for Financing Hospital Care; Research Triangle Institute.
  338 pp. *Permission required.* 1967. Papers.
See also additional interview in Eisenhower Administration.

GRAY, Gordon (1921–   ) *See* Radio Pioneers.

GRAY, John C. *Discussed in* Felix Frankfurter.

GRAY, Robert Keith (1923–   )
EISENHOWER ADMINISTRATION
Background of *Eighteen Acres Under Glass;* impressions of President Eisenhower, Richard Nixon, Sherman Adams.
  38 pp. *Permission required to cite or quote.* 1970. *Micro III.*

GREB, Gordon (1921–   ) *See* Radio Pioneers. *Micro IV.*

GRECO, Jacob (1906–   ) *See* Continental Group.

GREEN, Adolph (1915–   ) and Betty Comden. *See* Popular Arts. *Micro II.*

GREEN, Howard C. *See* Eisenhower Administration.

GREEN, Paul (1894–   ) Playwright.
SOUTHERN INTELLECTUAL LEADERS (B)
Childhood, family background; education, University of North Carolina, 1921, Cornell, 1923; influences on his writing; WWI experiences, Berlin in the 1920's; teaching at Chapel Hill, late 1920's; development of symphonic drama; Group Theater, Hollywood, 1930's; strikes, civil rights efforts.
  258 pp. *Permission required to cite or quote.* 1975.

GREEN, William. *Discussed in* John Brophy; John P. Frey; Albert J. Hayes; Boris Shishkin.

GREENBAUM, Edward Samuel (1890–1970) Lawyer.
Family background, education, NYC; Williams College; Columbia Law School; NYC

practice, Greenbaum, Wolff & Ernst from 1915; WWI; Johns Hopkins Institute of Law and survey of litigation in NY, 1930's; impressions of legal and political figures, including Felix Frankfurter, Henry Morgenthau, Sr., and Herman Oliphant.
266 pp. *Permission required to cite or quote.* 1965. *Micro II.*
See also Robert P. Patterson Project.

GREENBERG, Jack (1924–   ) Director, Counsel for NAACP Legal Defense Fund. NYC family background; education and naval duty; Law Revision Commission; history of Legal Defense Fund; NAACP Legal Defense Fund, 1949–   : important cases, staff problems, conflicts; Miranda case, racial discrimination in jury selection and housing, capital punishment, welfare rights; sit-ins and Freedom Rides; contributions of SNCC and CORE to civil rights movement; Mexican-American Legal Defense Fund; working relationship of Legal Defense Fund with Supreme Court; impressions of Thurgood Marshall, James Meredith, others.
404 pp. *Permission required.* 1975.

GREENE, Jack P. *See* American Historians.

GREENE, Roger. *Discussed in* John B. Grant.

GREENE, Rosaline. *See* Radio Pioneers. *Micro IV.*

GREENEWALT, Crawford Hallock (1902–   ) *See* Longwood Gardens.

GREENOUGH, William C. (1914–   ) Chairman, TIAA-CREF.
TIAA-CREF PROJECT
Childhood, Indiana; education; development of TIAA's life insurance services for college faculty; experiences of Carnegie Free Pensions, and development of transferable and self-supporting pensions; legislative impact of TIAA activities over the years; establishment of CREF, idea of variable annuities; relationship of TIAA-CREF to Social Security retirement systems.
In process.

GREENSTEIN, Robert (1924–   ) Architect.

Work with Charles Le Corbusier on Unity House, Marseilles.
40 pp. *Permission required to cite or quote.* 1950. *Micro I.*

GREER, Mabel. *Discussed in* Joseph A. Cox.

GREGERSON, Halfdan. *See* Benjamin A. Javits Project.

GREGG, Alan (1890–1957) Physician.
Early life and education at Harvard College and Harvard Medical School; internship at MGH; experiences in WWI; work for Rockefeller Foundation as a public health officer in Brazil, 1919–22; work in Division of Medical Sciences, NY, 1923–25; survey of medical needs of Colombia, 1924; beginnings of survey of medical education in Italy, 1925; Rockefeller Foundation; legal medicine.
259 pp. *Permission required to cite or quote.* 1956. *Micro I.*

JOHN ROBERT GREGG PROJECT
This is a compilation of interviews with friends and associates of John Robert Gregg (1867–1948), the man who developed the Gregg shorthand system.
Participants and pages: Guy S. Fry, 46; W.W. Lewis, 23; Louis Pfeiffer, 17; Margaret Richards Shimko and Charles Lee Swem, 82.
168 pp. *Permission required.* 1956. *Underwritten by Mrs. Alfred C. Howell, New York.*

GREITZER, Herman S. (1919–   ) Lawyer, politician.
NYC politics; detailed account of his candidacy for Democratic District Leader, First Assembly District South, Manhattan, in 1957, against incumbent, Carmine De Sapio.
101 pp. *Permission required to cite or quote.* 1962. *Micro II.*

GRENFELL, Wilfred. *Discussed in* Joseph C. Aub; Francis B. Sayre.

GREW, Joseph C. *Discussed in* Joseph Ballantine; Eugene Dooman; Walter Johnson.

GRIFFITH, D. W. *Discussed in* Popular Arts.

GRIFFITH, Samuel Blair II (1906–   )
See Marine Corps.

GRIFFITH, William Morris (1897–   )
See Benedum and the Oil Industry.

GRIMM, Peter (1886–   ) Real estate executive.
Family background, growing up in NYC;
Columbia College, 1911; beginnings in
NYC real estate; WWI, balloon training;
William A. White and Sons; John D. Rockefeller, Jr.
181 pp. *Permission required.* 1972.
See also Eisenhower Administration.

GRISCOM, Clement. *Discussed in* Lloyd C.
Griscom.

GRISCOM, Lloyd Carpenter (1872–1959)
Diplomat.
Business and political association of Clement Griscom with steamship transportation, the Pennsylvania Railroad, Theodore
Roosevelt, Marcus A. Hanna, and others;
diplomatic experiences, 1893–1909; NYC
politics, 1910–11; subsequent career as
newspaper proprietor.
123 pp. *Permission required to cite or
quote.* 1951. *Micro I.* Papers: 13 letters
(copies).

GRISWOLD, Estelle. See Women's History
and Population Issues.

GRISWOLD, Nat R. See Eisenhower Administration. *Micro III.*

GROGAN, Thomas (1922–   ) See
McGraw-Hill.

GROMYKO, Andrei. *Discussed in* Andrew
W. Cordier.

GROPIUS, Walter (1883–1969) Architect.
ARCHITECTURE PROJECT
Influence of technical inventions and social
developments on architectural field; establishment of Bauhaus School of Design; need
for cooperative architectural, environmental planning work; projects of the Architects Collaborative, including University
of Baghdad, US Embassy in Athens,
Gropius town in Germany.
32 pp. *Open.* 1961.

GROSS, Calvin. *Discussed in* Frederick C.
McLaughlin.

GROSS, Ernest A. (1906–   ) Lawyer.
EISENHOWER ADMINISTRATION
Family background; Harvard, Oxford,
Harvard Law School; counsel to various
government agencies, 1933–47; Deputy Assistant Secretary of State for Occupied
Areas, 1946; State Department legal adviser
and Assistant Secretary of State for Congressional Relations, 1947–49; Deputy representative to UN, 1949; drafting of Marshall Plan and Economic Cooperation Act;
full account of UN and other activities, including NATO, Military Assistance Program, India-Pakistan dispute, 1965; Korea;
reminiscences of Dean Rusk, John Foster
Dulles, Trygve Lie, and others.
984 pp. *Permission required to cite or
quote.* 1968. *Micro II.*
See also Dag Hammarskjold Project.

GROSS, Robert Ellsworth (1897–1961) See
Henry H. Arnold Project.

GROSSETTA, Anthony. See Air Force
Academy.

GROSSMAN, James. See Columbia Crisis
of 1968.

GROVES, Harold. *Discussed in* Paul and
Elizabeth Raushenbush.

GROVES, Leslie A. (1896–1970) See Robert P. Patterson Project. *Discussed in* Norman Ramsey.

GRUENTHER, Alfred M. (1899–   )
Army officer.
EISENHOWER ADMINISTRATION
Recollections of Gen. Eisenhower; Operation Torch; NATO; pre-campaign discussions and New Hampshire primary, 1952;
SHAPE.
97 pp. *Permission required.* 1967.
See also Federated Department Stores.

GRUENTHER, Homer H. (1900–1977) See
Eisenhower Administration. *Micro IV.*

GRUNDBERG, Solomon. See Hart Crane
Project.

GUARDO, Ricardo. *See* Argentina.

GUFFEY, Joseph. *Discussed in* Michael L. Benedum.

GUGGENHEIM, Harry. *Discussed in* Emory S. Land.

GUINNESS, Sir Alec. *Discussed in* Helen Macy.

GUINZBURG, Thomas. *Discussed in* Marshall Best.

GUION, Connie Myers (1882–1971) Physician.
Family background and childhood; education; internship at Bellevue; experiences as assistant to Dr. James Babcock and Dr. Frank S. Meara; Cornell Pay Clinic, 1922–32; Cornell Medical College, 1932–41; the Family Comprehensive Care Program.
260 pp. *Permission required to cite or quote.* 1956. *Micro I.* Papers.

GULICK, Luther Halsey (1892–) City administrator.
Reorganization of NYC government, 1950–56; origin, development and comment upon the Mayor's Committee on Management Survey; personal observations as City Administrator.
90 pp. *Permission required to cite or quote.* 1956. Papers.
See also New York Political Studies (B).

GUNN, Selskar. *Discussed in* John B. Grant.

GUNZENDORFER, Wilton. *See* Radio Pioneers.

GUSTAFSON, John Kyle (1906–) *See* Mining Engineers.

GUSTAFSON, Phyllis. *See* Adlai E. Stevenson Project.

GUTHRIDGE, Amis. *See* Eisenhower Administration.

GUTHRIE, Virgil B. (1886–1968) *See* McGraw-Hill.

GUTMANN, James (1897–) Educator.
Early life in NYC: Columbia University student, 1914–18, student and teacher at Ethical Culture Society School; preparing directory of war services, Washington, 1917; teaching philosophy at Columbia, 1920–62; Director, University Seminars, 1970–76; reflections on people and events at Columbia through the Butler, Fackenthal, Eisenhower, Kirk, and Cordier administrations; impressions of Nicholas Murray Butler, Dwight Eisenhower, John Dewey, Reinhold Niebuhr, Felix Adler, many members of the Columbia faculty.
284 pp. *Permission required to cite or quote.* 1977. Papers.

GUTTMACHER, Lenore (Mrs. Alan F.) *See* Women's History and Population Issues.

GUY, Raymond Frederick (1899–) *See* Radio Pioneers.

GUYLAY, L. Richard (1913–) Public relations counselor.
EISENHOWER ADMINISTRATION
Robert A. Taft; 1952 Republican Convention; Fair Play Amendment; Dwight D. Eisenhower; public relations in campaign of 1956.
90 pp. *Permission required to cite or quote.* 1967. *Micro III.*
See also Robert A. Taft Project.

GWERTZMAN, Bernard. *See* Ethnic Groups and American Foreign Policy.

H

HAAGEN, Jorge F. *See* Argentina.

HAAS, Richard. *See* New York's Art World.

HAAS, Robert K. (1890–1964) *See* Book-of-the-Month Club. *Micro IV.*

HAAS, Victor H. (1909–   ) *See* Health Sciences.

HABER, William (1899–   ) *See* Social Security.

HABIAGUE, Esteban (1893–1972)
ARGENTINA
Experiences in journalism and politics; account of Alberto Barcelo and his political control in Avellaneda; illustrative anecdotes of Argentine development, 1910–45.
147 pp. *Open.* 1971.

HACKER, Louis Morton (1899–   ). *See* Eisenhower Administration.

HACKETT, Albert (1900–   ) *See* Popular Arts.

HACKETT, Clifford. *See* Ethnic Groups and American Foreign Policy.

HACKETT, Francis. *Discussed in* Ben W. Huebsch.

HADLEY, Morris (1894–1979) *See* Carnegie Corporation. *Discussed in* Frederick Osborn.

HAEFFNER, Joseph Anthony (1907–   ) *See* Radio Pioneers.

HAGAN, Henry J. (1911–   ) *See* Continental Group.

HAGEN, Beulah W.
Family background, teaching experiences; marriage, life in NYC during Depression; Harper & Brothers, 1935–75, duties as assistant to Cass Canfield, relationships with Harper authors, wartime, historical series, fellowships, prize-winning publications, employee unionization, archival work.
235 pp. *Permission required to cite or quote.* 1976. *Micro IV.*

HAGER, Kolin. *See* Radio Pioneers. *Micro IV.*

HAGERTY, James C. (1909–   ) Journalist.
EISENHOWER ADMINISTRATION
1952 convention and campaign; trip to Korea; effect of television on politics, campaigns, and press conferences; relations with news media and press conferences; advance trips and travels with President Eisenhower in US and abroad; elections of 1954, 1956, 1960; President Eisenhower's heart attack; Sherman Adams; impressions of Winston Churchill, Nikita Khrushchev, Charles de Gaulle; cabinet meetings; impressions of Eisenhower's associates and aides.
569 pp. *Permission required.* 1968.

EISENHOWER ADMINISTRATION
Experiences as President Eisenhower's press secretary; recollections of the President, his relationship with staff and associates, issues faced: desegregation, McCarthyism, the cold war, Korea; Rich-

ard Nixon's 1960 presidential campaign. 109 pp. *Permission required.* 1969.

HAGUE, Frank. *Discussed in* Eddie Dowling; Francis A. Jamieson; Robert B. Meyner.

HALABY, Najeeb E. (1915–   ) *See* Eisenhower Administration. *Micro III.*

HALDANE, Richard. *Discussed in* Sir Robert Watson-Watt.

HALE, Ruth. *Discussed in* Mildred Gilman.

HALL, Elizabeth. *See* New York Botanical Garden.

HALL, John Lesslie Jr. (1891–1978) Naval officer.
William and Mary, Naval Academy, athletics; early cruises; instructor, Naval Academy; Naval War College 1937–40; North African campaign 1942–43; Commander Amphibious Forces, landings in North Africa, Sicily, Italy; invasion of Normandy, Omaha Beach, 1944; commands in Pacific, 1945; Okinawa; Commandant, Armed Forces Staff College 1948–51. Impressions of military leaders, especially Adms. Ernest King and Thomas Hart and Gens. George Patton, Dwight Eisenhower, and Omar Bradley.
338 pp. *Permission required to cite or quote.* 1963. *Micro I.*
Discussed in William A. Sullivan.

HALL, Leonard (1900–   ) Politician.
EISENHOWER ADMINISTRATION
Republican Party politics; chairman of National Republican Committee; campaigns of 1956 and 1964.
59 pp. *Closed during lifetime.* 1965.
Contributed by James Cannon, New York.

EISENHOWER ADMINISTRATION
Campaigns of 1956 and 1964; President Eisenhower's public image, character.
24 pp. *Permission required.* 1969.

Discussed in H. Meade Alcorn, Jr.; J. Clifford Folger.

HALL, Samuel Stickney, Jr. (1894–   ) Financial consultant.

CARNEGIE CORPORATION
Father's role in teachers' insurance program of Carnegie Foundation; Assistant Treasurer, TIAA, 1919; investment officer for Carnegie philanthropies, 1921–40; impressions of Mrs. Andrew Carnegie and various associates.
115 pp. *Permission required.* 1967.

HALLANAN, Walter Simms (1890–1962) *See* Benedum and the Oil Industry.

HALLECK, Charles A. (1900–   ) Congressman.
EISENHOWER ADMINISTRATION
1952 Republican Convention and campaign; President Eisenhower's relations with Congress.
35 pp. *Permission required to cite or quote.* 1967.

HALLER, Edouard de, Pablo de Azcarate and W. Van Asch Van Wijck. *See* Pablo de Azcarate, League of Nations Project.

HALLEY, Rudolph. *Discussed in* Ben Davidson; New York Political Studies.

HALSBAND, Robert. *See* Friends of the Columbia Libraries.

HALSEY, William. *Discussed in* Robert B. Carney; Samuel E. Morison. DeWitt Peck; Frank W. Rounds, Jr.; Felix B. Stump.

HALSTED, Anna Roosevelt (1906–1975)
Family life at Hyde Park and Washington, D.C.; relationship of parents, Eleanor and Franklin Roosevelt; effects of father's paralysis; 1928, 1932 political campaigns; White House life, work during father's administrations; his relationships with Louis Howe, Missy Le Hand, Lucy Mercer; Yalta conference; Franklin Roosevelt's death.
55 pp. *Permission required to cite or quote.* 1973. *Micro IV.*

HALSTED, William. *Discussed in* Abraham Flexner.

HALSTROM, Thomas. *See* Thomas A. Edison Project.

HAMBURGER, Ernest. *See* Ethnic Groups and American Foreign Policy.

HAMILTON, Carl (1914–) Agricultural journalist.
Early life in rural Iowa; move to Wisconsin, life of Moneta community; 4-H work; Iowa State College; journalistic activity; AAA information work, New Deal; assistant to Secretary of Agriculture, Claude Wickard, 1940–42; 1939 "corn problem"; assistant to Food Administrator, 1942–43; assistant on REA matters, 1943–45; impressions of Henry A. Wallace, M.L. Wilson, Harry Brown, Rudolph Evans, Paul Appleby, Milo Perkins, Joe Storm; discussion of relationship between Claude Wickard and Franklin D. Roosevelt.
735 pp. *Permission required to cite or quote.* 1953. *Micro II.* Papers.

HAMILTON, Thomas F. *Discussed in* Eugene E. Wilson.

HAMMARSKJOLD, Dag. *Discussed in* Thanassis Aghnides; James W. Barco; Andrew Cordier; Luther H. Evans; Dag Hammarskjold Project.

DAG HAMMARSKJOLD PROJECT
Colleagues recall their association with Dag Hammarskjold, his personal qualities, his training and experience in Sweden and elsewhere in Europe, his abilities and interests, and his approach to the administrative and executive challenges of the post of Secretary General of the UN, particularly staffing the Secretariat, the Congo crisis, and the Russian troika proposal.
Participants and pages: Sven Ayman, 11; Andrew Cordier, 22; Ernest Gross, 100; C.V. Narasimhan, 48, Oscar Schacter, 24; Brian E. Urquhart, 25.
230 pp. *Permission required to cite or quote.* 1962.
Underwritten by the Institute for International Order, New York.

HAMMERSTEIN, Oscar II (1895–1960) *See* Popular Arts.
Discussed in Richard Rodgers.

HAMMOND, George. *See* Federated Department Stores.

HAMMOND, John (1910–) Musician.
Recording and promoting jazz artists in NYC; integrating black and white artists; early record companies.
21 pp. *Permission required to cite or quote.* 1975.

HAMMONS, Earle Wooldridge (1886–1962) *See* Popular Arts.

HAMPTON, Robert Edward (1922–) Government official.
EISENHOWER ADMINISTRATION
White House staff; processing Presidential appointments; Civil Service Commission.
57 pp. *Permission required.* 1967.

HAND, Augustus. *Discussed in* Learned Hand; Telford Taylor; Harrison Tweed.

HAND, Learned (1872–1961) Judge.
Family background and childhood; Harvard College and Law School; impressions of Augustus Hand, Louis D. Brandeis, Felix Frankfurter, and others; views on politics, world events, religion, history, and the law.
169 pp. *Permission required to cite or quote.* 1957. *Micro I.*
Discussed in Harold R. Medina; Harrison Tweed.

HAND, William H. *See* Thomas A. Edison Project.

HANDLER, Milton (1903–) Lawyer.
Drafting New Deal legislation, 1933; National Labor Board: General Counsel, 1933, regional boards, opinion writing; NRA, Section T; Wagner Act, 1935; NLRB; Weirton Steel case; impressions of Senator Robert F. Wagner, Hugh S. Johnson, Leo Wolman.
42 pp. *Permission required to cite or quote.* 1973. *Micro II. Contributed by Cornell University.*
See also Benjamin A. Javits Project.

HANDOVER, Dennis. *See* Aviation Project. *Micro IV.*

HANDSFIELD, Hugh (1911–) *See* McGraw-Hill.

HANEL, Hans A. (1905–) *See* Continental Group.

HANES, John Wesley, Jr. (1925–   ) *See* Eisenhower Administration. *Micro III.*

HANKINS, Frank Hamilton (1877–1969) Sociologist.
Columbia University during early 1900's; Franklin H. Giddings; Sociology Department.
20 pp. *Open.* 1968.
Contributed by Neal De Nood, Northampton, Massachusetts.

HANNA, Marcus A. *Discussed in* Lloyd C. Griscom.

HANSELL, Haywood Shepherd. *See* Air Force Academy.

HANSEN, Alvin Harvey (1887–1975) *See* Social Security.

HANSEN, Clifford Peter (1912–   ) *See* Jackson Hole Preserve.

HANSEN, Edward S. (1889–   )
JAMES B. DUKE PROJECT
Childhood in Norway, arrival in US, 1909; footman and butler for the Duke family; description of mansion, daily household routine, parties; impressions of Mr. and Mrs. James B. Duke, Doris Duke.
176 pp. *Permission required.* 1963.

HANSER, Richard Frederick (1909–   ) Writer.
RADIO PIONEERS
WWII; OWI, psychological warfare unit; Normandy after D-Day; *Frontpost;* capture of Radio Luxembourg; *Fieldpost;* "Tom Jones" radio program; Battle of the Bulge; SHAEF; "This is America"; "Victory at Sea."
32 pp. *Permission required to cite or quote.* 1967. *Micro II.*

HANSL, Eva von Baur (1889–1978) Journalist.
WOMEN JOURNALISTS
Barnard College, 1909; *New York Evening Star,* 1909–13; *Parents* magazine, 1917; teacher, Columbia University School of Journalism; *The Bulletin;* research, writing about continuing education; NBC radio program about career women.
54 pp. *Open.* 1974.

HANSON, Lowell K. (1903–   ) *See* Continental Group.

HARBACH, Otto (1873–1963) *See* Popular Arts.

HARDEMAN, D. B.
EISENHOWER ADMINISTRATION
Texas politics; Tidelands issue; Adlai Stevenson Campaigns, 1952 and 1956; 1960 Democratic Convention; impressions of Adlai Stevenson, Sam Rayburn, Estes Kefauver, Lyndon Johnson, Price Daniel, Allan Shivers.
146 pp. *Permission required.* 1970.

HARDING, Warren G. *Discussed in* Horace M. Albright; Alan Kirk; Eugene Meyer; James T. Williams, Jr.

HARDMAN, J.B.S. (1882–1968) Labor leader.
Early life in Vilna; Russia, 1900–10; Social Democratic Party Conference, 1907; Leon Trotsky; union organization; Amalgamated Clothing Workers.
83 pp. *Open.* 1962.

HARDY, Oliver. *Discussed in* Albert E. Sutherland.

HARE, Raymond Arthur (1901–   ) *See* Eisenhower Administration.

HARKNESS, William E. (1873–   )
RADIO PIONEERS
Network radio; educational radio; advertisers, sales; radio and music rights; patent infringements; recorded programs; recollections of many early radio figures.
99 pp. *Open.* 1951.

HARLAN, John Marshall (1899–1972) *See* Adlai E. Stevenson Project.

HARLOW, Bryce Nathaniel (1916–   ) Government official.
EISENHOWER ADMINISTRATION
White House staff and organization under President Eisenhower; a typical week in the White House; press conferences; preparation of State of the Union messages and other speeches; relations with Congress.
144 pp. *Permission required.* 1967.

HARMON, Mrs. H.R. *See* Air Force Academy.

HARMON, Lewis. *See* Sol Jacobson.

HAROLD, John. *See* Occupation of Japan. *Micro II.*

HARPER, Fowler. *Discussed in* Jack B. Tate.

HARR, Karl Gottlieb, Jr. (1922–   ) Lawyer.
EISENHOWER ADMINISTRATION
Deputy Assistant Secretary of Defense; National Security Planning Board; special assistant to President Eisenhower for security operations coordination; Operations Coordinating Board.
41 pp. *Permission required.* 1967.

HARRAR, J. George (1906–   ) Foundation executive.
Early life and family; education, Oberlin and Iowa State College; University of Puerto Rico, 1929–30; impressions of University of Minnesota department of plant pathology under Edward M. Freeman and E. C. Stakman; corn smut and wheat rusts; teaching at Virginia Polytechnic Institute and Washington State College; reflections on education in US; origins of Rockefeller Foundation agriculture program; experiences of Rockefeller research team, Mexico, 1943–46.
In process.
Discussed in Flora M. Rhind; E.C. Stakman.

HARRIES, Brenton (1928–   ) *See* McGraw-Hill.

HARRIMAN, Florence Jaffray (Mrs. J. Borden) (1870–1967) Politician, diplomat.
Democratic Party politics, 1912–45.
40 pp. *Permission required to cite or quote.* 1950. *Micro I.*
Discussed in Katie Louchheim.

HARRIMAN, W. Averell (1891–   ) Government official.
INTERNATIONAL NEGOTIATIONS
Extensive discussion of process of international negotiations with illustrations from his diplomatic career, especially the test ban agreement, WWII conferences, Vietnam peace talks; effects of national and world opinion; roles of the military, Congress, and the press; choice of negotiating personnel, training for professional diplomats; assessment of the use of the Presidency in international affairs, 1933–69; "Good officer" experiences: Iran oil concession case and India-Pakistan disputes. Many vignettes of international leaders.
353 pp. *Permission required.* 1969.

Campaign for governor of NY, 1954; Governor, NY, 1955–58: appointments, policies, programs, and problems; candidate for Democratic presidential nomination, 1952, 1956; Democratic politics, 1950's, national convention, 1956.
In process.

See also Henry H. Arnold Project.
Discussed in Prescott Bush; Edward Costikyan; Justin N. Feldman; Arthur J. Goldberg; James P. Warburg.

HARRINGTON, Donald S. (1914–   ) Minister, political activist.
Childhood; education: Antioch College, Meadville Theological School, 1938; travels in Europe during Nazi period; religious career in Chicago and NYC as Unitarian-Universalist minister; activities in international peace organizations; activist political development: Socialist Party to Liberal Party, 1930's to present; impressions of Alex Rose, NYC, state, national politics in 1960's, '70's; 1977 NYC mayoral campaign; search for new State leadership, Liberal Party.
319 pp. *Permission required.* 1977.

HARRIS, Sir Arthur Travers (1892–   ) *See* Henry H. Arnold Project.

HARRIS, James J. (1908–   ) *See* Continental Group.

HARRIS, Joseph. *See* Social Security. *Micro III.*

HARRIS, Julie (1925–   ) *See* Popular Arts.

HARRIS, Marguerite.
Deciphering, editing Boswell journals and

papers, 1927–29; impressions of Colonel Ralph Isham; Geoffrey Scott.
33 pp. *Permission required to cite or quote.* 1975.

HARRIS, Marvin (1927–   ) *See* Columbia Crisis of 1968.

HARRIS, Roy. *Discussed in* William Schuman.

HARRISON, Sir Geoffrey Wedgwood (1908–   ) *See* International Negotiations.

HARRISON, Wallace K. (1895–   ) Architect.
Childhood, Worcester, Mass.; education; work with McKim, Mead & White, NYC; experiences with Navy, WWI; architectural studies in France; Penn Power & Light design project; design for 1939 World's Fair; evaluation of atelier system of architectural education; teaching experiences at Columbia University; architectural design work on Radio City Music Hall, Rockefeller Center complex, Metropolitan Opera, United Nations facilities.
412 pp. *Permission required.* 1978.
Discussed in Francis Jamieson.

HART, Fred J. and Ira D. Smith. *See* Radio Pioneers.

HART, Herschell. *See* Radio Pioneers.

HART, John Neely (1902–1970) *See* Marine Corps.

HART, Lorenz. *Discussed in* Henry Myers; Richard Rodgers.

HART, Thomas Charles (1877–1971) Naval officer.
Childhood and education; Spanish-American War; ordnance, teaching, submarines; Army War College; command of *Mississippi;* submarine command; Superintendent, Naval Academy, 1931–34; heavy cruisers, 1934–36; General Board, 1936–39 and 1942–45; Asiatic Fleet, 1939–41; Hart Investigation of Pearl Harbor; Senator from Connecticut, 1945–47. Impressions of many political and military figures, including Theodore Roosevelt, Franklin Roose-

velt, Frank Knox, James Forrestal, Gen. Douglas MacArthur and Adms. William Leahy, Harry Ervin Yarnell, Ernest King, Arthur Hepburn, Chester Nimitz, and Harold Stark.
284 pp. *Permission required to cite or quote.* 1962. *Micro I.* Papers.
Discussed in James Fife; Paul F. Foster; John L. Hall, Jr.; Felix B. Stump.

HARTE, Houston (1893–1971) *See* Benedum and the Oil Industry.

HARTMANN, Heinz (1894–1970) Psychoanalyst.
PSYCHOANALYTIC MOVEMENT
Early education, Vienna; development of interest and training in psychoanalysis in Berlin and Vienna; analysis by Sigmund Freud; early associations with leading figures in European and American psychoanalytic movement; *Ego Psychology and the Problem of Adaptation,* 1939; effect of ego metapsychological writings on current psychoanalytic theory and technique; New York Psychoanalytic Institute; collaborative work with Drs. Rudolph Loewenstein and Ernest Kris.
145 pp. *Open except for specified pages.* 1963.
Discussed in Rudolph M. Loewenstein.

HARVEY, George. *Discussed in* Candler Cobb.

HARWOOD, Wilson (1912–   )
EISENHOWER ADMINISTRATION
National Science Foundation; National Bureau of Standards; McCarthyism and scientific community; meetings with President Eisenhower.
52 pp. *Permission required to cite or quote.* 1968. *Micro III.*

HASKINS, Caryl Parker (1908–   ) Educator, scientist.
CARNEGIE CORPORATION
History of Carnegie Institution of Washington; Carnegie Corporation grant for psychophysical research, 1948; consultant for Carnegie Corporation, 1950, trustee, 1955; President, Carnegie Institution, 1956; evaluation of grants and programs; views on Andrew Carnegie; relations between Institution and Corporation; impressions of

Devereux Josephs, Charles Dollard, John Gardner, and other Carnegie officers and trustees.
251 pp. *Permission required.* 1967.

HASS, Eric. *See* Socialist Movement.

HASSIALIS, Menelaos D. (1909–   ) and John G. Palfrey.
A joint lecture on nuclear energy.
38 pp. *Open.* 1958.

HASSNA, Steve. *See* Vietnam Veterans.

HATFIELD, Robert S. (1916–   ) *See* Continental Group.

HAUBERG, John Henry (1916–   ) Lumber company executive.
WEYERHAEUSER TIMBER COMPANY
History of Denkmann and Weyerhaeuser families from 1860; Mississippi River Logging Company, Southern Lumber Company.
127 pp. *Permission required.* 1949.

HAUGE, Gabriel (1914–   ) Economist.
EISENHOWER ADMINISTRATION
Preconvention activity and 1952 campaign; President Eisenhower's cabinet appointments; economic policies; Council of Economic Advisors; Departments of Agriculture and Interior; Arthur Burns.
130 pp. *Permission required to cite or quote.* 1967.

EISENHOWER ADMINISTRATION
Preconvention research; President Eisenhower's early speeches; speech-writing; duties as economic advisor.
28 pp. *Permission required.* 1968.

Discussed in Sherman Adams; Stephen Benedict.

HAUKAA, Runa. *See* Alexandra Kollontai Project.

HAUPT, Martin L. (1902–   ) *See* Continental Group.

HAUPTLI, Albert (1894–1964)
McGRAW-HILL
Magazine work, McGraw-Hill, from 1920: paid vs. free circulation publications; growth of advertising agencies, role of salesmen, special media publications; *American Machinist, Product Engineering;* automation.
103 pp. *Permission required.* 1956.

HAUPTMANN, Bruno R. *Discussed in* Edmund DeLong.

HAUSER, Rita. *See* Ethnic Groups and American Foreign Policy.

HAUSMAN, Louis (1906–   ) *See* Children's Television Workshop. *Micro IV.*

HAVENS, Beckwith (–1969) *See* Aviation Project. *Micro IV.*

HAVERLIN, Carl (1899–   ) Radio executive.
Early years in the Southwest; touring with a theatrical troupe, 1916–17; radio in Los Angeles in the 1920's.
38 pp. *Closed during lifetime.* 1955.
See also Allan Nevins Project.

HAWKES, John (1925–   ) *See* American Cultural Leaders.

HAWKINS, Laurence Ashley (1877–1958) *See* Radio Pioneers.

HAWTHORNE, Charles W. *Discussed in* Edwin W. Dickinson.

HAY, Marley Fotheringham (1880–1963) Naval architect.
Submarine construction and warfare in WWI.
19 pp. *Open.* 1950.

HAYAKAWA, Sessue (1890–1973) *See* Popular Arts.

HAYDEN, Philip M. *See* Nicholas Murray Butler Project.

HAYES, Albert John (1900–   ) Labor union executive.
Early life; International Association of Machinists; NIRA; formation of CIO; merger of AFL-CIO; Ethical Practices Committee, AFL-CIO; Truman Commission on Health; impressions of John L. Lewis, William Green, Arthur Wharton.

216 pp. *Permission required to cite or quote.* 1957. *Micro I.*

HAYES, Carlton J. H. (1882–1964) *See* Nicholas Murray Butler Project.

HAYES, Charles B. (1918–   ) *See* Continental Group.

HAYES, Charles Harold (1906–   ) Marine Corps officer.
Education; early assignments; WWII: Guadalcanal, Green Island, Emirau, Leyte, Luzon, Palau, 1943–45; occupation of Japan; Korea; Assistant USMC Commandant, 1961–65.
239 pp. *Permission required to cite or quote.* 1970.

HAYES, Edward Pearce (1895–   ) *See* China Missionaries.

HAYES, Egbert M. *See* China Missionaries.

HAYES, George Francis (1885–1969) *See* Popular Arts.

HAYFORD, Warren J. (1929–   ) *See* Continental Group.

HAYS, Arthur Garfield. *Discussed in* Osmond K. Fraenkel.

HAYS, Brooks (1898–   ) Congressman, lawyer.
EISENHOWER ADMINISTRATION
Early career; Little Rock school crisis; Newport meeting with President Eisenhower and Orval Faubus.
165 pp. *Permission required to cite or quote.* 1970. *Micro IV.*
Discussed in Orval E. Faubus.

HAYWARD, George C. *See* Federated Department Stores.

HAYWOOD, William D. *Discussed in* Roger N. Baldwin; John Spargo.

HAZARD, Ellison Lockwood (1911–   ) *See* Continental Group.

HAZEN, Allen T. (1904–1977) *See* Rare Books (A).

HEACOX, E. F., C. S. Martin and C. Davis Weyerhaeuser. *See* Weyerhaeuser Timber Company.

HEALD, Henry. *See* Ludwig Mies van der Rohe.

HEALTH *See* Medicine.

HEALTH SCIENCES
A study of the US Public Health Service, its contribution to the formation and growth of the National Institutes of Health. Those interviewed include administrators and researchers within the NIH as well as heads of related government agencies and university professors in the bio-medical field. Such issues as the changing role of the federal government in relation to research and training in the health field, the transition from service to research within the USPHS, and the value of epidemiological fieldwork are discussed. Note is made of the development of categorical institutes within the NIH, the bureaucratization and specialization of research, and the political underpinnings of the expansion of the health sciences.
Participants and pages: Ernest M. Allen, 61; Howard B. Andervont, 108; Carl Baker, 191; William R. Bryan, 75; Leroy E. Burney, 68; G. Robert Coatney, 119; Lowell T. Coggeshall, 63; Martin M. Cummings, 47; W. Palmer Dearing, 96; Warren F. Draper, 59; Rolla E. Dyer, 46; Kenneth M. Endicott, 53; Isidore S. Falk, 79; Robert H. Felix, 73; Arthur S. Flemming, 44; Marion B. Folsom, 123; Victor H. Haas, 149; John R. Heller, Jr., 58; Herman Hilleboe, 130; Vane M. Hoge, 42; Mark Hollis, 72; James M. Hundley, 76;

Carlyle Jacobsen, 59; Charles V. Kidd, 68; Lawrence Kolb, 73;
Alexander D. Langmuir, 57; Esmond R. Long, 96; Jack Masur, 32; Leonard Mayo, 76; Joseph S. Murtaugh, 53; Thomas Parran, 133; George S. Perrott, 73; David E. Price, 36; Leonard A. Scheele, 70; William Henry Sebrell, Jr., 56; James A. Shannon, 67; Murray J. Shear, 190; William P. Shepard, 53; Wilson George Smillie, 61; Roscoe Spencer, 117; Harold L. Stewart, 58; Frederick L. Stone, 35; Norman Topping, 58; Cassius J. Van Slyke, 74.

3,427 pp. *Permission required to cite or quote.* 1962–67.
Underwritten by the National Institutes of Health.

HEARST, William Randolph. *Discussed in* Claude Bowers; Keats Speed; Emily S. Warner.

HEARTT, Philip Brewster (1896–) *See* James B. Duke Project.

HEATON, Leonard D. (1902–) *See* Eisenhower Administration.

HEAVISIDE, Robert D. (1917–) *See* Continental Group.

HECHINGER, Fred. *Discussed in* John B. Oakes.

HECHT, Ben (1894–1964) *See* Popular Arts.

HECKSCHER, August (1913–) City official, journalist.
Childhood, education: St. Paul's, Yale, Harvard; editor *Citizen Advertiser,* Auburn, NY; chief editorial writer, *Herald Tribune,* 1948–56; executive head, Twentieth Century Fund, 1956–67; Commissioner of Parks, Recreation, NYC, 1966–73; philosophy of park use; impressions of John Lindsay and his mayoralty.
78 pp. *Permission required to cite or quote.* 1978.

HEDGES, William Saxby (1895–1978) Radio executive.
RADIO PIONEERS
Early experiences in radio; formation of National Association of Broadcasters, code of decency, 1928; channel allocations; NBC from 1930's: relations of network companies and affiliates, planning and development, soap operas, television; President, NBC Integrated Services Department.
123 pp. *Open.* 1951.

HEFFERNAN, John A. (1871–1952) Newspaperman.
Impressions of Bird S. Coler; Brooklyn politics, 1900–20.
87 pp. *Permission required to cite or quote.* 1950. *Micro IV.*

HEIDEN, Jim. *See* Vietnam Veterans.

HEIFETZ, Jascha. *Discussed in* Schuyler Chapin.

HEIGHT, Dorothy I. (1912–) Social worker.
Childhood and education, Virginia, NYC; affiliation with National Council of Negro Women, 1937–74; career with YWCA, interracial education, leadership training, 1938– ; Harlem in the 1930's and 40's; work on advisory committee on women in the Services, 1952–55; visiting professor, Delhi School of Social Work, India, 1952; civil rights work: school desegregation, War on Poverty, Head Start, voter registration in the South; women's organizations; travels in Latin America; International Women's Year Conference, 1975; impressions of Eleanor Roosevelt, Mary McLeod Bethune.
461 pp. *Closed until February, 1981.* 1976.
Contributed by Schlesinger Library, Radcliffe College, Cambridge, Mass.

HEILBRONER, Robert (1919–) *See* American Historians.

HEIN, Marjorie. *See* Robert A. Taft Project.

HEINEN, John M., Jr. (1916–) *See* Continental Group.

HEININGER, Alfred Dixon. *See* China Missionaries.

HEINLEIN, John L. (1901–) *See* Continental Group.

HEISER, Victor. *Discussed in* John B. Grant.

HEISKELL, Marian (Mrs. Andrew) (1918–) *See* Adlai E. Stevenson Project. *Micro III.*

HEITMAN, Robert L. (1918–) *See* Continental Group.

HELD, Adolph. *See* Socialist Movement.

HELLER, John Roderick, Jr. (1905–) *See* Health Sciences.

HEMPLE, Wayne. *See* Vietnam Veterans.

HENCHERT, John (1896–   ) *See* Continental Group.

HENDERSON, Deirdre. *See* John F. Kennedy Project.

HENDERSON, Harold Gould (1889–1974) *See* Occupation of Japan. *Micro II.*

HENDERSON, Loy Wesley (1892–   ) *See* Eisenhower Administration. *Micro III.*

HENDERSON, Ralph Ernest (1899–   ) Editor.
Early years of *Reader's Digest,* from 1925, DeWitt Wallace and its guiding principles; vignettes of early editors; inception of Condensed Book Club, editorial selection and editing process; family background. Impressions of DeWitt and Lila Bell Wallace, Kenneth Payne, many other *Digest* editors and executives.
256 pp. *Closed until 1984.* 1977. The memoir includes supporting documents.

HENDERSON, Ray (1896–1971) *See* Popular Arts.

HENDRICK, Burton Jesse (1870–1949) Writer, editor.
Magazine publishing, 1900–20; S. S. McClure, Ida Tarbell and the "muckrakers"; Walter Hines Page, Andrew Carnegie.
59 pp. *Permission required to cite or quote.* 1949. *Micro I.*

HENNEKE, Louis F. (1910–   ) *See* Continental Group.

HENNEY, Keith. *See* McGraw-Hill.

HENRIKSON, Carl H., Jr. (1899–   ) Business executive.
Lumbering in Minnesota; WWI naval service.
145 pp. *Permission required to cite or quote.* 1955. *Micro I.*

HENRY, Emil William (1929–   ) *See* Federal Communications Commission.

HENRY, Ray.
SOCIAL SECURITY

Drive for Medicare legislation: publications, consultation with Congressmen, encounters with AMA members. Impressions of Blue Carstenson, Nelson Cruikshank, Zalman J. Lichtenstein.
135 pp. *Closed during lifetime.* 1966.
Discussed in James C. O'Brien.

HENRY, S.T. (1882–1957) *See* McGraw-Hill.

HENSHAW, Frederick W. (1898–1953) Journalist.
Youth and education; Michigan State; Detroit *News,* 1923–28; *Magazine of Michigan,* 1929–33; Division of Information, AAA, 1933–38; George Peek; Henry Wallace; Chester Davis; Alfred Stedman; Howard R. Tolley; Franklin Roosevelt; BEW, 1940; *US News.*
175 pp. *Permission required to cite or quote.* 1953. *Micro IV.*

HEPBURN, Arthur. *Discussed in* James Fife; Thomas C. Hart.

HERBERT, Victor. *Discussed in* Popular Arts.

HERGESHEIMER, Joseph. *Discussed in* Alfred A. Knopf.

HERMLE, Leo David (1890–1976) *See* Marine Corps.

HERNDON, Angelo. *Discussed in* Walter Gellhorn; Whitney North Seymour, Sr.

HERRING, Edward Pendleton (1903–   ) Educator.
CARNEGIE CORPORATION
Carnegie Corporation and social sciences; American Political Science Association; case study method in public administration; investigation of polling procedures following 1948 election; impressions of Devereux Josephs and James T. Shotwell.
129 pp. *Permission required.* 1967.

HERSEY, John. *See* John F. Kennedy Project.

HERTER, Christian. *Discussed in* C. Douglas Dillon; Robert C. Hill.

HERVE, Lucien (1910–   ) *See* Hungarian Project.

HERWARTH, Hans von. *See* Eisenhower Administration.

HERZ, Otto (1894–1976) *See* Hungarian Project.

HERZFELD, Willie. *See* Civil Rights in Alabama.

HESS, Arthur E.
SOCIAL SECURITY
Bureau of Old Age and Survivors' Insurance; efforts toward disability legislation.
102 pp. *Permission required to cite or quote.* 1966. *Micro III.*

HESS, Stephen (1933–   ) *See* Eisenhower Administration. *Micro IV.*

HESS, Thomas (1920–1978) *See* New York's Art World.

HESTER, James M. *See* New York University.

HETTRICK, John T. (1868–n.d.) Newspaperman, lawyer.
Leading figures on Brooklyn *Eagle,* NY *World,* NY *Times,* 1889–1900; NY sporting life; NYC under Mayor Robert Van Wyck; NYC subways, building and development; secretary to August Belmont, 1900–15; Lockwood Investigating Committee; impressions of Theodore Roosevelt, John W. Keller, P. J. Donahue.
202 pp. *Permission required to cite or quote.* 1949. *Micro IV.* Papers.

HEURTAUX, A. *See* Aviation Project.

HEWITT, F.W. *See* Weyerhaeuser Timber Company.

HEWITT, H. Kent (1887–1972) Naval officer.
Youth and education, Naval Academy; world cruise, 1907; teaching at Naval Academy; hydrographic survey work; Cuban Revolution, 1917; destroyer duty, 1918; Naval Institute; War College; President Franklin Roosevelt's trip to Buenos Aires, 1936; fleet exercises, ammunition depot, Bremerton; Panama Canal Zone; Pearl Harbor; neutrality patrol; amphibious training; training for combined operations, London; Operation Torch; Commander US Naval Forces, Mediterranean, 1943; Operation Husky; Salerno. Impressions of many political and military figures.
478 pp. *Permission required to cite or quote.* 1961. *Micro I.*
Discussed in John J. Ballentine; Charles J. Moore.

HEYMAN, Lee. *See* Vietnam Veterans.

HEYMANN, Walter M. (1892–   ) *See* Federated Department Stores.

HIBBERD, Christy. *See* James B. Duke Project.

HICKENLOOPER, Bourke Blakemore (1896–1971) *See* Robert A. Taft Project.

HICKERSON, John D. (1907–   ) *See* International Negotiations.

HICKMAN, Harry B. (1889–   ) *See* Benedum and the Oil Industry.

HICKMAN, Leon Edward (1907–   ) *See* James B. Duke Project.

HICKS, Raymond L. (1910–   ) *See* Continental Group.

HIDALGO SOLA, Hector. *See* Argentina.

HIGDON, M.A. (1914–   ) *See* Continental Group.

HIGGINS, Joe. *See* Popular Arts.

HIGGINS, Juanda. *See* Adlai E. Stevenson Project.

HIGHET, Gilbert Arthur (1906–1978) *See* Book-of-the-Month Club. *Micro II.*

HIGHTOWER, John Murmann (1909–   ) Newspaperman.
EISENHOWER ADMINISTRATION
Foreign policy under Eisenhower; John Foster Dulles.
41 pp. *Permission required to cite or quote.* 1968.

HILE, Paul E. (1909–   ) *See* Continental Group.

HILL, Frank Ernest (1888–1969) Journalist, author.
Family background and boyhood in California; Stanford University and Columbia, 1913–17; editorial writer, NY *Globe* and NY *Sun,* literary editor *Sun,* 1925; editor, Longmans, Green Company, 1925–31: authors, manuscripts, NYC literary and publishing circles; *The Winged Horse,* 1927; adult educational programs, CBS; lecturing and freelance writing, poetry and prose; *Westward Star, The Canterbury Tales,* texts and young people's books; collaboration with Allan Nevins on biographies of Rockefeller and Ford; Radio Pioneers project for the Oral History Research Office. Comments on publishing, books, and authors, especially Allan Nevins, Don Marquis, Edwin Markham, Vachel Lindsay, Carl Sandburg.
605 pp. *Permission required to cite or quote.* 1961. *Micro I.*

HILL, George Washington. *Discussed in* Albert D. Lasker.

HILL, Harry W. (1890–1971) Naval officer.
Naval Academy; early cruises, gunnery training; WWI: Scapa Flow, German Fleet surrender; Navy Department reorganization; arms limitation, naval budget, congressional liaison; Hoover good will cruise to South America, 1928; Naval War College, 1937; War Plans Division, 1940; WWII: US-Canada Joint Board Armed Defense, convoys and patrols, Murmansk, Iceland; Pacific theater commands: detailed analysis of amphibious assault at Tarawa; operations at Saipan, Tinian, Iwo Jima, Okinawa; plans for assault on Japan; National War College, Naval Academy superintendent; Naval Home. Accounts of Gens. Douglas MacArthur and Holland M. Smith; Adms. Ernest King, Chester Nimitz, Raymond Spruance, Kelly Turner, and other military, naval, and political figures.
964 pp. *Permission required to cite or quote.* 1967. *Micro II.* Papers.

HILL, Jerome. *Discussed in* Will Clayton.

HILL, John A. *Discussed in* McGraw-Hill.

HILL, John E. *See* Radio Pioneers.

HILL, Lister (1894–   ) Senator.
Boyhood and early political experiences in Alabama.
18 pp. *Closed during lifetime.* 1958.

HILL, Patty. *Discussed in* Charlotte Garrison.

HILL, Robert Charles (1917–1978) Ambassador.
EISENHOWER ADMINISTRATION
Vice consul, Calcutta, India, 1943; Chicago convention, 1952; Ambassador to Costa Rica, El Salvador; Richard Nixon's visit to El Salvador; Special Assistant, State Department, 1955; Assistant Secretary of State, 1956; Ambassador to Mexico, 1957; Eisenhower's visits to Mexico; President Lopez Mateos' visit to US; impressions of President and Mrs. Eisenhower, John Foster Dulles, Herbert Hoover, Christian Herter, Anthony Eden, Richard Nixon.
105 pp. *Permission required to cite or quote.* 1972.

HILL, Tex. *See* Flying Tigers.

HILL, Tom F. *See* James B. Duke Project.

HILLEBOE, Herman Ertresvaag (1906–1974) *See* Health Sciences.

HILLMAN, Sidney. *Discussed in* Will Alexander; Heber Blankenhorn; John Brophy; Abraham Kazan; Jacob Potofsky; Lee Pressman.

HILLQUIT, Morris. *Discussed in* Benjamin McLaurin; John Spargo.

HILMER, Lucien. *See* James Lawrence Fly Project.

HINES, Earl Kenneth Fatha (1905–   ) *See* Jazz Project.

HINGLE, Pat (1924–   ) *See* Popular Arts.

HINKLE, Fred S. (1912–   ) *See* Continental Group.

HINTON, Milton (1910–   ) *See* Jazz Project.

HIRSCHHORN, Kurt. *See* Mt. Sinai Hospital.

HISS, Alger (1904–   ) Lawyer.
Role in, impressions of conferences at Yalta, Dumbarton Oaks, San Francisco; details and consequences of the "Pumpkin papers case"; political philosophy; opinions on the New Deal, cold war, McCarthyism, parallel trials (Ellsberg, Berrigan, Chicago Seven), books written about his trials; impressions of Justice Holmes, other Supreme Court justices, New Deal personalities, John Foster Dulles, Adlai Stevenson.
280 pp. *Permission required.* 1975.

CARNEGIE CORPORATION
Carnegie Endowment for International Peace and its relations with Carnegie Corporation; role of trustees; impressions of Russell Leffingwell, Arthur Page, Whitney Shepardson.
67 pp. *Permission required.* 1968.

Discussed in Osmond K. Fraenkel; Jerome N. Frank; Gardner Jackson; Devereux Josephs; Frederick Osborn; Henry M. Wriston.

HISTORY *See* American Historians; Frank M. Anderson; Thomas H. Bender; Claude Bowers; Solon J. Buck; Civil War Centennial; Guy Stanton Ford; Richard Hofstadter Project; Walter Johnson; Waldo G. Leland; Dumas Malone; Broadus Mitchell; Samuel E. Morison; Richard B. Morris; David Muzzey; Allan Nevins; Allan Nevins Project; Arthur M. Schlesinger; James T. Shotwell; Philip Taft.

HITLER, Adolf. *Discussed in* Sidney Alderman; Lawrence Dennis; Luis F. Gay; H.V. Kaltenborn; Henry A. Wallace.

HO, Franklin L. *See* Chinese Oral History. *Microform available.*

HOBBY, Ovetta Culp. *Discussed in* Roswell B. Perkins; Leonard A. Scheele; Charles I. Schottland.

HOBOES *See* Hood River Blackie; Philip Taft.

HOBSON, Wilder. *See* James Agee.

HOCHWALT, Frederick George (1909–1966) Priest.
Administrator, Cincinnati parochial schools, 1940's; federal aid to education; National Catholic Education Association; UNESCO.
47 pp. *Permission required to cite or quote.* 1962. *Micro IV.*

HOCTOR, Alice. *See* Carnegie Corporation.

HODGE, William. *Discussed in* Richard Gordon.

HODGES, Luther Hartwell (1898–1974) Cabinet member.
EISENHOWER ADMINISTRATION
Southern Governors' Conference, 1957; Little Rock crisis; visit to Russia; Governor of North Carolina; Secretary of Commerce; Adlai E. Stevenson; President Eisenhower.
39 pp. *Permission required to cite or quote.* 1968. *Micro IV.*

HODGINS, Eric (1899–1971) Author.
EISENHOWER ADMINISTRATION
Paley Commission; speech writing for Adlai Stevenson campaign, 1952; education, early experience in journalism: *Youth's Companion,* 1920's; *Fortune* in the 1930's; *Time* during WWII; Henry R. Luce; writing of the *Blandings* books and *Episode.*
162 pp. *Permission required to cite or quote.* 1969. *Micro IV.*

HODGKINSON, Harold Daniel (1890–   ) *See* Federated Department Stores.

HODGSON, John G. *Discussed in* Mrs. William Hodgson.

HODGSON, Mrs. William. *See* Continental Group.

HOEGH, Leo Arthur (1908–   ) Lawyer, politician.
EISENHOWER ADMINISTRATION
Iowa politics; 1952 Republican Convention; Director of Civil and Defense Mobilization, 1958–61; relations with President Eisenhower; 1960 and 1964 elections.
95 pp. *Permission required.* 1968.

HOEY, Jane Margueretta (1892–1968) Government official.
SOCIAL SECURITY
Assistant Director of Welfare Council, NYC; experiences as federal director of Public Assistance, 1936–54.
102 pp. *Permission required to cite or quote.* 1965. *Micro IV.*
Discussed in Jack B. Tate.

HOFFA, James. *Discussed in* Dave Beck; Victor Rabinowitz; Mary H. Varse.

HOFFER, Willi (1897–1967) Psychoanalyst.
PSYCHOANALYTIC MOVEMENT
Creating a children's home; analysis by H. Nunberg, 1921–22; use of play in education; remedial educator; emigration to London, 1938; scientific journals; behaviorism; case histories; ego, defense, and other problems of psychoanalysis; impressions of Anna and Sigmund Freud.
116 pp. *Permission required to cite or quote.* 1965.

HOFFMAN, Abbie. *Discussed in* Herbert Sacks.

HOFFMAN, Frederick J. (1918–) *See* Continental Group.

HOFFMAN, Michael Lindsay (1915–) and William Diamond. *See* World Bank.

HOFFMAN, Paul Gray (1891–1974) Government official, industrialist.
Family background, education in Illinois; early interest in automobiles; Studebaker salesman, California, 1912; regional manager, 1917; OTC, WWI; establishment of own company to distribute automobiles, 1920–25; vice president, Studebaker, 1925; receivership, 1933, and reorganization; Studebaker in WWII; new designs, labor relations, merger with Packard.
100 pp. *Permission required.* 1963.

HOFSTADTER, Richard (1916–1970) *See* American Historians *and* Columbia Crisis of 1968. *Discussed in* Richard Hofstadter Project.

RICHARD HOFSTADTER PROJECT
This project brings together the recollections of students, faculty colleagues, and others who knew Richard Hofstadter, for the most part during his years at Columbia (1946–70), where he became DeWitt Clinton Professor of American History. Contributors recall him as teacher, social observer, writer, and friend, tracing the intellectual development of a major scholar. Specifics include comment on *Social Darwinism in American Thought, The American Political Tradition, The Age of Reform, Anti-Intellectualism in American Life,* and other works, as well as insights into the mind and character of the man.
Participants and pages: Daniel Bell, 42; Elisabeth Earley, 24; Eric Foner, 21; Frank Freidel, 22; Henry F. Graff, 35; H. Stuart Hughes, 23; Alfred Kazin, 28; Walter Metzger, 29; Arthur M. Schlesinger, Jr., 14.
238 pp. *Permission required to cite or quote.* 1972.

HOFSTADTER, Robert L. (1915–) *See* Nobel Laureates.

HOGABOOM, Robert Edward (1902–) Marine Corps officer.
Family background, education; early duty in Nicaragua, Shanghai; Sino-Japanese War; amphibious warfare doctrine, 1939–42; WWII: Attu and Kiska operations, Marianas, Iwo Jima, preparations for invasion of Japan; reminiscences of Gens. Holland Smith and Graves Erskine, Adm. Kelly Turner; staff, National War College; CG, NATO exercises, phase-out operations in Korea; Deputy Chief of Staff (Plans) and Chief of Staff, HQMC, 1955–59.
357 pp. *Permission required to cite or quote.* 1970.

HOGE, Alicia (Mrs. Michael Arlen). *See* Adlai E. Stevenson Project.

HOGE, Vane M. (1902–1970) *See* Health Sciences.

HOHAUS, Reinhard Arthur (1896–) Actuary.
SOCIAL SECURITY
Apprentice actuary, Metropolitan Life Insurance, 1921; Committee on Economic Security; chairman, Advisory Council on Social Security, 1953; social adequacy concept; actuarial science, experience rating, other concepts of social insurance legislation; impressions of Vincent Miles,

Abraham Epstein, John Winant.
141 pp. *Closed during lifetime.* 1965.

HOLCOMB, Bankson Taylor, Jr. (1908–
) *See* Marine Corps.

HOLDER, Edward J. (1917–   ) *See* Continental Group.

HOLDER, Wesley McD. (1897–   ) Administrative assistant.
Education in British Guiana; immigration to US, 1920; service on the WPB, 1942–46; Brooklyn editor, *Amsterdam News;* politics and black politicians in NYC; Congresswoman Shirley Chisholm; activities of the 12th District Congressional office, Brooklyn.
45 pp. *Permission required to cite or quote.* 1973.

HOLLAND, Kenneth (1907–   ) *See* Carnegie Corporation.

HOLLAND, Lawrence La Motte (1895–
) *See* Radio Pioneers.

HOLLAND, Mildred. *Discussed in* Richard Gordon.

HOLLANDER, Jacob. *Discussed in* Broadus Mitchell.

HOLLANDER, Louis. *See* Journalism Lectures (A).

HOLLEMAN, Clarence H. (1890–   ) *See* China Missionaries.

HOLLIS, Mark D. (1908–   ) *See* Health Sciences.

HOLLISTER, John Baker (1890–1979) Congressman, lawyer.
EISENHOWER ADMINISTRATION
Service in House, 1931–36; Senator Robert A. Taft; ICA, 1955–57; visit to Vietnam, 1955.
52 pp. *Permission required to cite or quote.* 1970. *Micro III.*
See also Robert A. Taft Project.

HOLLOWAY, James Lemuel, Jr. (1898–
) Naval officer.
Education, Naval Academy; convoy duty, WWI; Atlantic Fleet; WWII, exercises off

Puerto Rico, Operation Torch; Bermuda training exercises; Director of Training, 1943–44; Holloway Plan for Naval Academy; Superintendent Naval Academy; Chief of Naval Personnel; reserve officers; relationship with Congress; impressions of Harry Truman, James Forrestal, Adm. Louis Denfeld.
187 pp. *Permission required.* 1962.

HOLLYDAY, Guy. *Discussed in* Miles Colean.

HOLM, Celeste (1919–   ) *See* Popular Arts.

HOLM, Jeanne (1921–   ) *See* Air Force Academy.

HOLMAN, Charles William (1886–1971) Agriculturist.
Childhood, family background and education; early newspaper work; National Conference on Marketing and Farm Credit; farmers' cooperatives; Herbert Hoover in Woodrow Wilson's WFA.
69 pp. *Permission required to cite or quote.* 1953. *Micro II.*

HOLMES, John Clellon (1926–   ) Author.
The Depression's influence on values and ethics; WWII: Medical Corps, GI Bill; Columbia University; the Beat Generation, Allen Ginsberg, Jack Kerouac; Eastern and Western philosophies.
111 pp. *Permission required to cite or quote.* 1976.

HOLMES, Lulu.
OCCUPATION OF JAPAN
Adviser to SCAP on Higher Education for Women in Japan, 1946–48.
54 pp. *Permission required to cite or quote.* 1966. *Contributed by the Regional Oral History Office, University of California, Berkeley.*

HOLMES, Oliver Wendell, Jr. *Discussed in* Chauncey Belknap; Alger Hiss; James M. Landis; John L. O'Brian.

HONEY, John C. *See* Carnegie Corporation.

HOOD, Bob. *See* Vietnam Veterans.

HOOVER, Fred W. (1918–) *See* Continental Group.

HOOVER, Herbert Clark (1874–1964)
RADIO PIONEERS
Role in developing policy on radio broadcasting as Secretary of Commerce, 1921–27; annual radio conference, 1922–25; allocation of wave lengths, problems of monopoly, censorship, commercial use; Federal Radio Act, 1927; Aimee Semple McPherson; Federal Radio Commission; amateur operators.
21 pp. *Permission required to cite or quote.* 1950. *Micro II.*
Discussed in Horace M. Albright; Raymond Baldwin; Harvey Bundy; Goldthwaite H. Dorr; John P. Frey; Perrin C. Galpin; Robert C. Hill; Charles Holman; Eugene Meyer; Jackson E. Reynolds; H. Alexander Smith; Lewis L. Strauss; Harold C. Train; John C. White; James T. Williams, Jr.

HOOVER, J. Edgar. *Discussed in* Robert H. Jackson; Harold C. Train; Keyes Winter.

HOOVER, John Howard (1887–1970)
Naval officer.
Family background; Annapolis; US Navy of 1910–30; early cruises, torpedo training, destroyer duty; growth of naval aviation; WWI duty at Channel ports and in eastern Mediterranean; submarine training, Submarine Desk, 1923–28; the *Lexington* and carrier duty; naval air stations, San Diego and Norfolk; WWII and Caribbean Sea Frontier, 1941–43; convoying and anti-submarine efforts; impressions of Adms. Ernest King, John R. Edwards, Raymond Spruance, and Henry Wilson.
432 pp. *Permission required to cite or quote.* 1964. *Micro I.*
Discussed in Ben Custer.

HOPKINS, Harry. *Discussed in* John R. Alison; Frank Bane; Lucius D. Clay; Marion Dickerman; Donald Duncan; Luther H. Evans; Isidore Falk; Jerome N. Frank; Florence Kerr; Emory S. Land; Katharine Lenroot.

HOPKINS, Joseph G.E. *See* Rare Books (A).

HOPKINS, Terence K. *See* Columbia Crisis of 1968.

HOPPOCK, Robert (1901–) *See* Carnegie Corporation.

HORD, Stephen Y. (1897–) *See* Adlai E. Stevenson Project. *Micro III.*

HORNBLOW, Arthur, Jr. (1893–1976) *See* Popular Arts.

HORNER, H. Mansfield (1903–) *See* Aviation Project. *Micro II.*

HOTZ, Robert (1914–) *See* McGraw-Hill.

HOUDINI, Harry. *Discussed in* Melville H. Cane.

HOUGH, Henry Beetle. *Discussed in* Charles Ascher.

HOUGHTON, Amory (1899–) Ambassador, executive.
EISENHOWER ADMINISTRATION
Ambassador to France during President Eisenhower's visits; Charles de Gaulle; NATO; aborted summit meeting; relations with State Department; impressions of John Foster Dulles.
96 pp. *Permission required.* 1968.

HOUSE, A. F. *See* Eisenhower Administration. *Micro IV.*

HOUSE, Patricia. *See* Eisenhower Administration. *Micro IV.*

HOUSEMAN, John (1902–) Producer, director.
Experiences as film producer, writer, actor.
50 pp. *Open.* 1974.

HOUSING *See* Urban Development/Housing.

HOUSTON, Lyda Suydam (1891–) *See* China Missionaries.

HOVING, Walter. *Discussed in* William Lusk.

HOWARD, Ben Odell (1904–1970) *See* Aviation Project. *Micro IV.*

HOWARD, Ernest (1910–) AMA official.

AMA since 1948; mission to Peru, 1946–48; AMA positions on: national health, public health insurance program; Congressional hearings; involvement in political campaigns; disability legislation; Forand bill; impact of President Kennedy's assassination; Kerr-Mills bill; votes on health bills; AMA support from American Farm Bureau, Blue Shield; Madison Square Garden rally; civil rights and Medicare; analysis of Senators' positions on health legislation; 1964 campaign.

302 pp. *Closed during lifetime.* 1967.

HOWARD, Katherine Graham (Mrs. Charles P.) (1898–   )
EISENHOWER ADMINISTRATION
Republican National Committee; 1952 Republican Convention; Deputy Civil Defense Administrator; NATO Civil Defense Committee; Eisenhower campaign, 1952; vignettes of Gen. and Mrs. Eisenhower.

600 pp. *Permission required to cite or quote.* 1971.

HOWE, Harold II. *Discussed in* Children's Television Workshop.

HOWE, Louis. *Discussed in* Marion Dickerman; Anna Roosevelt Halsted; James P. Warburg.

HOWE, Quincy (1900–1977) Journalist.
Childhood and education; *The Living Age, Atlantic Monthly, Atlas;* radio broadcasting. Impressions of A. Lawrence Lowell and Ellery Sedgwick.

127 pp. *Permission required to cite or quote.* 1962. *Micro I.*

HOWELL, William F. *See* World Bank.

HOWSON, Albert Sidney (1881–1960) *See* Popular Arts.

HU, C. T. *See* International Negotiations.

HU Shih. *See* Chinese Oral History. *Microform available.*

HUANG, Shen I-yun. *See* Chinese Oral History.

HUCKABY, Elizabeth. *See* Eisenhower Administration.

HUDGENS, Robert Watts (1896–   ) Government official.
Early life; Citadel College; religious, economic, and political conditions in the South; RA and FSA; important New Deal personalities, policies, and problems.

290 pp. *Permission required to cite or quote.* 1954. *Micro II.*

HUEBSCH, Ben W. (1876–1964) Publisher.
NYC in the 1890's; schooling; apprenticeship with a lithographer; work as a printer; early ventures in publishing; Gelett Burgess; Francis Hackett; first US publication of Sherwood Anderson and James Joyce; friendship with Joyce, Franz Werfel, Stefan Zweig; editing and publishing *The Freeman;* correspondence with D. H. Lawrence, 1916–23; Henry Ford Peace Expedition, 1915–16; genesis of Viking Press; H. G. Wells; Hendrik Willem Van Loon; origins of ACLU; correspondence with John Quinn on Joyce and others; letters from H. L. Mencken; general comments on book publishing.

492 pp. *Permission required to cite or quote.* 1955. *Micro I.*
Discussed in Marshall Best.

HUESTIS, Charles S. (1906–   ) *See* Continental Group.

HUFFMAN, Roy. *See* Weyerhaeuser Timber Company.

HUGHES, Charles Evans. *Discussed in* Chauncey Belknap; Meier Steinbrink; Frederick C. Tanner; Allen Wardwell.

HUGHES, Emmett. *Discussed in* Sherman Adams.

HUGHES, Everett Cherrington (1897–   ) *See* Carnegie Corporation.

HUGHES, H. Stuart (1916–   ) *See* Richard Hofstadter Project.

HUGHES, Howard. *Discussed in* Jacqueline Cochran; Donald W. Douglas.

HUGHES, Langston. *Discussed in* Raoul Abdul; Jean B. Hutson.

HULL, Albert Wallace (1880–1966) Physicist.

RADIO PIONEERS
Early life; General Electric Laboratory, dynatron and magnetron; development of tubes during WWII; cathodes; Irving Langmuir, Willis R. Whitney.
31 pp. *Open.* 1951.

HULL, Cordell. *Discussed in* Joseph Ballantine; Spruille Braden; Eugene Dooman; James P. Warburg.

HUMMEL, Fred E. (1896–1975) *See* Continental Group.

HUMPHREY, Bruce. *See* Vietnam Veterans.

HUMPHREY, George M. (1890–1970) *See* Eisenhower Administration.
Discussed in C. Douglas Dillon; Neil H. Jacoby.

HUMPHREY, Hubert Horatio, Jr. (1911–1978) *See* John F. Kennedy Project *and* Herbert H. Lehman Project.
Discussed in Edward R. Annis; Elizabeth S. Ives; Carl McGowan.

HUNDLEY, James Manson (1915–   )
See Health Sciences.

HUNGARIAN PROJECT
This project contains personal recollections of Hungarian immigrants active in the arts, politics and international relations. The experience of immigration to the U.S. and adjustment to the American cultural milieu is discussed; their contributions to the arts, as well as commercial and professional accomplishments are enumerated. Impressions of teachers and colleagues such as Bela Bartok, Zoltan Kodaly, and Beniamino Gigli offer a picture of their European heritage. Participants and pages: Gabor Carelli, 119 *(permission required to cite or quote)*; Alfons Weiss de Csepel, 29; Joseph Domjan, 16; George Feyer, 39; Lucien Herve, 49; Otto Herz, 112: Abel Lajtha, 47; Marian Mikolajczyk, 24; Remig A. Papp, 29 *(permission required to cite or quote)*; Laszlo Pathy, 52; Gyorgy Sandor, 43; Alexander Szent Ivanyi *(in process)*; Bela Varga, 219 *(permission required)*; Mrs. Lajos Zilahy, 56 *(closed until ten years after death)*.
834 pp. *Open except as noted.* 1974—
Contributed by Mrs. Rose Stein, NYC.

HUNSAKER, Jerome Clarke (1886–   )
Aeronautical engineer.
AVIATION PROJECT
Naval Academy, 1904–08; naval architecture, MIT; research in Europe, stability analysis and wind tunnels; Navy duty, WW I: flying boat, Material Division; first aircraft carrier, 1922; non-rigid air ships; Zeppelins; Goodyear, 1929–30; coordinator of research for Navy, 1940; impressions of Gen. William Mitchell, Adm. William Moffett.
112 pp. *Permission required to cite or quote.* 1960. *Micro IV.*

HUNT, Douglass (1924–   ) Lawyer, financier.
Columbia University, 1969–73: Deputy to President for Governmental Affairs; controller's office, payroll reorganization; Andrew Cordier as President of the University.
95 pp. *Closed during lifetime.* 1973.

HUNT, Robert W. *See* Weyerhaeuser Timber Company.

HUNT, Roy Arthur (1881–1966) *See* James B. Duke Project.

HUNTER, Marjorie. *See* Social Security. *Micro III.*

HUNTER, T. Merritt (1905–   ) *See* Continental Group.

HUNZIKER, Otto F. (1915–   ) *See* Continental Group.

HURLEY, Patrick. *Discussed in* Walter S. Robertson.

HUSAIN, Sir Fazle. *Discussed in* Sir Muhammad Zafrulla Khan.

HUSH, Homer. *See* Farm Holiday Association.

HUSSEY, George Frederick, Jr. (1894–   ) Naval officer.
Background and education; Naval Academy; *Pennsylvania*, 1920; courses in ordnance, ballistics; Australian cruise, 1925; Bureau of Ordnance, Armor and Projectile Section, Proof Officer, Naval Proving Ground; Gunnery Officer *Salt Lake City*,

destroyer command; command of Mine Division and Mine Squadron; command offshore patrol, Pearl Harbor, December, 1941—April, 1942; Bureau of Ordnance: Director of Production, Assistant Chief, later Chief of Bureau until September, 1947; contractor-operated ordnance plants; basis for postwar ordnance research; many military and naval vignettes.

582 pp. *Permission required to cite or quote.* 1965. *Micro II.*

HUSSEY, Gray. *See* Federated Department Stores.

HUSSEY, Mrs. Gray. *See* Federated Department Stores.

HUSTON, John (1906–   ) *See* James Agee.

HUTCHINS, Louise Gilman (1911–   ) *See* Women's History and Population Issues.

HUTCHINS, Robert Maynard (1899–1977) University president.
Election as President of University of Chicago, 1929; concept of a university; relationships with faculty, students, trustees, alumni, and the general public; experiments: Great Books courses, divisions, liberal arts college; professional schools and the university; Rush Medical College; attacks on University of Chicago program; effect of WWII nuclear research; *Encyclopedia Britannica;* Gen. Robert E. Wood; William Benton.

110 pp. *Permission required to cite or quote.* 1967. *Micro II.*
Contributed by Donald McDonald, Center for the Study of Democratic Institutions, Santa Barbara, California.
Discussed in William T. Couch; W. H. Cowley.

HUTSON, Jean B. (1914–   ) Librarian.
Childhood in Maryland; radical and black student politics, 1930's; positions with Schomburg Center for Research in Black Culture: curator (1948–72), Chief Librarian from 1972; role of Schomburg Center in Harlem Renaissance; associations with Arthur Schomburg, Langston Hughes, Richard Wright, Ralph Ellison, Paul Robeson.

65 pp. *Permission required to cite or quote.* 1978.

HUTSON, John B. (1890–1964) Government official.
Education; University of Kentucky; problems of the South; tobacco farming; AAA; Agricultural Adjustment Acts, 1933 and 1938; BAE; AAA tobacco program; Kerr Tobacco Control Act; Bankhead Cotton Control Act; Soil Conservation; CCC; private farm organizations; WWII; OPA; parity; Steagall Amendment; Production and Marketing Administration; Office of Agricultural Defense Relations; price stabilization; WFA; UN Secretariat; Tobacco Associates, Inc.

559 pp. *Permission required to cite or quote.* 1954. *Micro I.*

HUTTON, William R. Public relations counsellor.
SOCIAL SECURITY
Public relations work with Master Newspaper Syndicate; information director, National Council of Senior Citizens for Health Care; efforts toward Medicare legislation.

113 pp. *Permission required to cite or quote.* 1966. *Micro IV.*

HUXLEY, Aldous. *Discussed in* Cass Canfield.

HUXLEY, Julian. *Discussed in* Charles Ascher; Cass Canfield.

HYDE, Edd. *See* Adlai E. Stevenson Project. *Micro III.*

HYDE, Rosel Herschel (1900–   ) *See* James Lawrence Fly Project.

HYLAN, John. *Discussed in* Ferdinand Pecora; Lawrence Veiller.

HYLBERT, Ethel Lacey. *See* China Missionaries.

HYLE, Gordon. *See* Book-of-the-Month Club.

HYMAN, Abraham. *See* Mt. Sinai Hospital.

HYMAN, Harold M. (1924–   ) *See* Civil War Centennial.

I

IANNI, Francis A. J. (1926–   ) Educator.
Office of Education, 1960–65, particularly Bureau of Research; new developments under Commissioners Sterling McMurrin and Francis Keppel: team research and development, curriculum reform, cognitive psychology; effects of Sputnik and of civil rights movement on education; Elementary and Secondary Education Act, 1965.
66 pp. *Permission required to cite or quote.* 1967. *Micro II.*

IBARGUREN, Carlos. *See* Argentina.

ICKES, Harold. *Discussed in* Horace M. Albright; Charles Ascher; Lucius D. Clay.

IKENBERRY, Ernest L. *See* China Missionaries.

ILIFF, Sir William Angus Boyd (1898–1972) Banker.
WORLD BANK
Background in finance; World Bank, 1948; divisions of Bank; Bank dealings with India and Egypt: Aswan Dam, Suez Canal, Kashmir, and Indus water dispute.
76 pp. *Permission required to cite or quote.* 1961.

IMMIGRATION/EMIGRATION   *See* Austrian Project; Herbert Brownell; Leo Cherne; Samuel Dickstein; Goldthwaite H. Dorr; Henriette Epstein; Edward Ferro; August W. Flath; Edward S. Hansen; Hungarian Project; Bernard G. Richards; George Rublee; Gerhart H. Seger; Sheba Skirball; Joseph Swing; Arthur V. Watkins.

IMPELLITTERI, Vincent. *Discussed in* Frederick C. McLaughlin; Pearl Max.

IMSDAHL, John. *See* Vietnam Veterans.

INDEPENDENCE NATIONAL HISTORICAL PARK
The story of the Independence Hall Association from 1942 and the development of the Independence National Historical Park are recounted by those who played the major parts, in particular Judge Edwin O. Lewis. Accounts of the ensuing urban redevelopment, and of historic preservation and restoration in Philadelphia explore the legal, financial, architectural, and procedural problems and how they were surmounted. Park historians and superintendents describe the role of the National Park Service.

Participants and pages: Medford O. Anderson, 38; Roy Appleman, 27 *(permission required to cite or quote);* Edmund Bacon, 47; Lysbeth Borie, 27; Michael J. Bradley, 27; Mrs. Joseph Carson, 22; Herbert Kahler, 13 *(permission required to cite or quote);* Arthur Kaufmann, 21 *(permission required to cite or quote);* Dennis Kurjack, 58 *(permission required to cite or quote);* Roy Larson, 39 *(permission required to cite or quote);* Edwin O. Lewis, 70; M. Joseph McCosker, 33; Isidor Ostroff, 40; Charles Peterson, 47; Edward Riley, 40 *(permission required to cite or quote);* Leon Sacks, 14; Hardy Scott, 11.
574 pp. *Permission required except as noted.* 1970. *Underwritten by the Eastern National Park and Monument Association, Philadelphia.*

INDIANA, Robert (1928–   ) *See* New York's Art World.

INDIANS *See* American Indians.

INDUSTRIAL WORKERS OF THE WORLD *See* Roger N. Baldwin; Herbert Benjamin; John P. Frey; Philip Taft; Mary Heaton Vorse.

INGERSOLL, C. Jared. *See* Longwood Gardens.

INGERSOLL, Royal E. (1883–1976) Naval officer.
Naval Academy; early cruises; Paris Peace Conference; War Plans Division, 1935; London Naval Conference, 1935; Commander in Chief, Atlantic Fleet, 1942–44; Operation Torch; Atlantic convoys.
126 pp. *Permission required to cite or quote.* 1964. *Micro II.*

INGRAHAM, Joe (1903–   ) *See* Eisenhower Administration.

INGRAM, Charles H. (1892–   ) *See* Weyerhaeuser Timber Company.

INOUYE, Daniel Ken (1924–   ) *See* Ethnic Groups and American Foreign Policy.

INSURANCE *See* Samuel S. Hall, Jr.; Devereux Josephs; Louis H. Pink; Social Security; TIAA-CREF Project.

INTEGRATION/SEGREGATION *See* Sherman Adams; Air Force Academy; T. Dale Alford; Samuel Battle; J. Bill Becker; Wiley A. Branton; Vivion Brewer; Earl Browder; Herbert Brownell; Richard C. Butler; William G. Cooper, Jr.; Benjamin Davis; George Douthit; Virginia Durr; Harold Engstrom; James P. Goode; Nat R. Griswold; Amis Guthridge; Brooks Hays; Luther H. Hodges; A.F. House; Patricia House; Elizabeth Huckaby; Daniel James, Jr.; James Karam; John Lewis; R.A. Lile; Anthony C. McAuliffe; Sidney McMath; Jack Marr; Harold C. Martin; Hughie E. Mathews; Constance B. Motley; James M. Nabrit, III; Hugh Patterson, Jr.; Terrell E. Powell; Wesley Pruden; Maxwell M. Rabb; Kenneth C. Royall; Irene Samuel; George

S. Schuyler; William T. Shelton; William J. Smith; Everett Tucker, Jr.; Wayne Upton; J. Waties Waring; Roy Wilkins; E. Grainger Williams; Henry Woods.

INTERNAL SECURITY INVESTIGATIONS *See* Hilda Anderson; Kenneth Bainbridge; Erik Barnouw; William Benton; Algernon D. Black; D. Angus Cameron; Aaron Copland; Norman Corwin; Charles D. Coryell; Lawrence Dennis; Samuel Dickstein; Goldthwaite Dorr; Clifford J. Durr; Virginia Durr; Milton S. Eisenhower; Thomas I. Emerson; Federal Communications Commission; Ralph E. Flanders; John P. Frey; Walter Gellhorn; Gordon Gray; Najeeb Halaby; Wilson Harwood; Alger Hiss; Philip Jessup; Arthur Kinoy; Corliss Lamont; Percy M. Lee; Herbert H. Lehman; Helen Lynd; Carl W. McCardle; Kenneth D. Nichols; John L. O'Brian; Frances Perkins; Victor Rabinowitz; Norman Ramsey; Esther Raushenbush; Edwin Seaver; Elie Siegmeister; Anna Lord Strauss; Arthur Watkins; Goodwin Watson.

INTERNATIONAL AFFAIRS *See* Diplomacy/International Affairs.

INTERNATIONAL NEGOTIATIONS
Edward W. Barrett, director of the Communications Institute of the Academy for Educational Development, conducted a series of interviews with practitioners in the field of international negotiations and mediation of disputes. The interviews are preserved by the Oral History program and will be drawn on in delineating guidelines that may be useful to those mediating and negotiating international differences in the future. The work is part of a continuing study of international negotiation and mediation conducted by the Academy under a grant from Dr. and Mrs. John S. Schweppe of Chicago.
Participants and pages: Theodore C. Achilles, 43; Frederik Arkhurst, 60; George W. Ball, 19; Lucius D. Battle, 51; Manlio Brosio, 24; W. Randolph Burgess, 29; Norman Cousins, 23; Rajeshwar Dayal, 35; Hugh Mackintosh Foot (Baron Caradon) 62; Gerald R. Ford, 34; Arthur Goldberg, 51; W. Averell Harriman, 353; Sir Geoffrey Harrison, 34; John D. Hickerson,

36; Max Jakobson, 51; Philip C. Jessup, 49; Joseph E. Johnson, 120; Khwaja Kaiser, 29; Theodore W. Kheel, 43; Robert Lovett, 28; John J. McCloy, 24; George C. McGhee, 48; Livingston T. Merchant, 41; Robert D. Murphy, 35; Kenneth Rush, 9; J. Robert Schaetzel, 59; Dirk Spierenberg, 39; Llewellyn Thompson, 29; Ernst Van der Beugel, 51; Vladimir Velebit, 80; Sir Alan Watt, 67; Charles W. Yost, 21.
1,677 pp. *Permission required.* 1970—

Round table discussion of their roles in international negotiations; Paris Peace talks; SALT talks; Arab-Israeli discussions; Russian diplomacy; UN role in mediation.
Participants: Edward W. Barrett, Andrew Cordier, Alvin Eurich, Adrian S. Fisher, Joseph E. Johnson, Henry Cabot Lodge, others.
104 pp. *Permission required.* 1973.

The Academy has also canvassed academic and journalistic specialists for their views on future relations between countries, particularly in the Far East, in interviews by Professor Frederick T. C. Yu of Columbia. The interviews include recorded conversations with the following:
John M. Allison, 23; Davis Bobrow, 41; Emerson Chapin, 25; Theodore Chen, 26; Tillman Durdin, 20; Robert S. Elegant, 33; John Fairbank, 25; C. T. Hu, 18; Harold Isaacs, 9; T. B. Koh, 28; Daniel Lerner, 15; John Lindbeck, 18; Sidney Liu, 28; Ithiel de Sola Pool, 20; Lucien Pye, 32; Milton Sacks, 26; Sol Sanders, 52; Ezra Vogel, 23.
462 pp. *Permission required.* 1970.
Contributed by the Academy for Educational Development, New York.

IRAZUSTA, Julio. *See* Argentina.

IRELAND, Richard H. (1894–   ) *See* Continental Group.

IRVIN, Lawrence.
ADLAI E. STEVENSON PROJECT
Patronage system; Democratic Party in Illinois, 1952; relationship between Adlai Stevenson and Paul Douglas; Stevenson and party politics; Stevenson as governor.
72 pp. *Permission required.* 1969.

IRVIN, Leslie LeRoy (1895–1966) *See* Aviation Project. *Micro II.*

IRWIN, David. *See* Mining Engineers.

IRWIN, Leo (1917–   ) *See* Social Security. *Micro III.*

IRWIN, R. E. *See* Weyerhaeuser Timber Company.

ISAACS, Harold (1910–   ) *See* International Negotiations.

ISAACS, Julius (1896–   ) Lawyer, politician.
NYC politics during the Fiorello La Guardia administration.
28 pp. *Permission required to cite or quote.* 1949. *Micro II.*
See also New York Political Studies (C).

ISAACS, Norman E. (1908–   ) Journalist.
Indianapolis Star; St. Louis Star-Times; ethics investigation for Sigma Delta Chi, 1953; chairman, ethics committee, New England Society of Newspaper Editors; President, American Society of Newspaper Editors; creation, 1973, chairman, 1976, National News Council; ethical dilemmas in journalism; Council members and advisors; relationship of journalists to CIA, FBI; future of News Council.
68 pp. *Permission required to cite or quote.* 1977.

ISAACS, Stanley Myer (1882–1962) Lawyer, Politician.
Columbia University, New York Law School, 1905; settlement house work; Republican political activity, 1900–12; fusion movement; Theodore Roosevelt and National Progressive Party, 1912, Convention, 1916; Draft Board, War Department under Secretary Newton D. Baker, 1917–18; Republican platform, 1920; NY real estate, 1919–37: mortgage participation, Lockwood Committee investigation, Tenement House Law, United Neighborhood Houses; campaign manager for Congresswoman Ruth Pratt, 1928, '30; La Guardia mayoralty campaigns, 1929, '33;

Samuel Seabury investigation; State Constitutional Convention, 1938; Manhattan Borough President, 1938–41; East River Drive, acquisition of riparian rights; Robert Moses, WPA; City Council from 1941; NYC mayoralty election, 1945; NY election, 1949. Recollections of Herbert Parsons, Ogden Mills, Kenneth Simpson, Irving Ives, Fiorello La Guardia, Thomas Dewey, William O'Dwyer, Newbold Morris.

260 pp. *Permission required to cite or quote.* 1950. *Micro I.*
See also Theodore Roosevelt Association. *Micro IV.*
Discussed in Theodore R. Kupferman.

ISHAM, Ralph. *Discussed in* Marguerite Harris.

ITURBE, Alberto. *See* Argentina.

IVES, Charles. *Discussed in* Henry Cowell; Elie Siegmeister.

IVES, Elizabeth Stevenson (Mrs. Ernest) (1898–   )
ADLAI E. STEVENSON PROJECT

Last year of Stevenson's life; Cuba missile crisis; 1960 Democratic Convention; family homes, Libertyville and Bloomington; evaluation of brother's biographers; 1948 Illinois gubernatorial campaign; governorship, 1949–53; 1956 campaign; UN mission, 1961–65; family anecdotes and childhood recollections; impressions of Stevenson's personal friends and recollections of his relationships with John F. Kennedy and Robert F. Kennedy, Richard J. Daley, Hubert H. Humphrey, Lyndon B. Johnson, William McCormick Blair, Jr., Willard Wirtz, and others.

309 pp. *Permission required to cite or quote.* 1969. Papers: 68-page critique of *Adlai Stevenson of Illinois,* by John B. Martin.

IVES, Ernest (1887–1972) *See* Adlai E. Stevenson Project.

IVES, Irving. *Discussed in* Stanley M. Isaacs.

IVY, James W. *Discussed in* George S. Schuyler.

J

JABARA, James (–1966) *See* Aviation Project. *Micro IV.*

JABLONOWER, Joseph (1888–1971) Educator.
Childhood in Austria; NYC, Lower East side, 1896; Teachers Union, 1916; Ethical Culture School, 1919; influence and development of Ethical Culture; views on WWI; Vienna, 1932–33; teachers union, 1930's; Communist influence; Board of Examiners,

NYC Board of Education, 1940–59; choosing teachers, salaries, state control vs. autonomy, underprivileged neighborhoods, strikes; progressive education. Impressions of Felix Adler, David Muzzey, George Counts.

379 pp. *Permission required to cite or quote.* 1965. *Micro II.*

JACK, Samuel Sloan (1905–   ) *See* Marine Corps.

JACKSON, C.D. *Discussed in* Stephen Benedict; Abbott M. Washburn.

JACKSON, Charles. *Discussed in* Roger W. Straus.

JACKSON, Frederick Herbert (1919–   )
CARNEGIE CORPORATION
Carnegie Corporation, 1955–64; mathematics program, university self-studies, honors programs, Chinese and Japanese language programs; evaluation of grants, daily routine, board of trustees; role of foundation officer; Negro education; administrator at NYU, 1964. Impressions of John Gardner, James Perkins, Florence Anderson.
305 pp. *Permission required.* 1967.

JACKSON, Gardner (1896–1965) Public official.
Youth, family background, education; newspaper reporter, Boston and Washington; Sacco-Vanzetti defense; Mooney report; Bonus Army; AAA; New Deal; liberalism in the 1930's, labor movement; impressions of Henry Wallace, Claude Wickard, Herbert Parisius, John L. Lewis, Felix Frankfurter, Louis D. Brandeis, Jerome Frank, Alger Hiss, Drew Pearson, Arthur Schlesinger.
786 pp. *Permission required to cite or quote.* 1955. *Micro I.*
See also La Follette Civil Liberties Committee.
Discussed in Samuel B. Bledsoe.

JACKSON, Nettie Stover. *See* Eisenhower Administration.

JACKSON, Sir Robert G. A. (1911–   )
International administrator.
British Royal Navy, coordinating defense of Malta, 1937–41; Middle East Supply Center, 1941–44: maximum efficiency of resources; UNRRA: assistant to Director General Herbert Lehman, 1944, organizational and financial problems, personalities, Lehman's resignation, 1946; Dean Acheson, Will Clayton and the end of UNRRA, 1947; relationship with Herbert and Edith Lehman; impressions of many British and American WWII figures.
308 pp. *Permission required to cite or quote.* 1978. Papers.

JACKSON, Robert Houghwout (1892–1954) Supreme Court Justice.
Lawyer, upper NY State; General Counsel, Bureau of Internal Revenue; Assistant Attorney General, Tax Division and Anti-Trust Division of the US Department of Justice; Solicitor General; Attorney General; Justice of the US Supreme Court; US Prosecutor at Nuremberg War Crimes Trials.
1,672 pp. *Closed until June 1, 1980.* 1952.
Discussed in Marquis Childs; Gordon Dean.

JACKSON HOLE PRESERVE
This project relates the history of Jackson Hole Preserve, describing the Rockefeller family's interest in preserving and protecting the area and problems encountered in acquiring the land which was eventually added to the National Park System. Included are memoirs of people who knew Jackson Hole as their home and who have experienced the transformation of the area since it became part of the National Park System in the 1940's.
Participants and pages: Horace M. Albright, 238; Mrs. Struthers Burt, 91; Kenneth Chorley, 160; Harold Fabian, 106; Clifford P. Hansen, 53; Harry E. Klissold, 50; W. C. Lawrence, 51; Leslie A. Miller, 122; Homer C. Richards, 53; Laurance Rockefeller, 42; Conrad L. Wirth, 76; Mike Yokel, 38.
1,080 pp. *Permission required.* 1966.
Underwritten by Jackson Hole Preserve, Inc.

JACOBS, Albert Charles (1900–1976) *See* Eisenhower Administration. *Micro III.*

JACOBS, Lewis. *See* Robert J. Flaherty Project.

JACOBSEN, Carlyle (1902–   ) *See* Health Sciences.

JACOBSON, Sol (1912–   ) Press agent.
Early interest in journalism; theatrical press agent for Jasper Deeters, Lee and J.J. Shubert, George Abbott, Guthrie McClintic; recollections of actors, writers, producers. Lewis Harmon participants in parts of the interview.

37 pp. *Permission required to cite or quote.* 1975.

JACOBY, Neil H. (1909–) Economist.
EISENHOWER ADMINISTRATION
University of Chicago, 1937–42; Dean, College of Business Administration, University of California, 1948; Council of Economic Advisors, 1953–55: functions, personnel, philosophy, goals; relationship with UN Department of Economic Affairs; US representative to UNESCO, 1957; comments on Federal Reserve system, Commodity Credit Corporation, agricultural economics, social legislation. Impressions of President Eisenhower, Arthur Burns, Raymond Saulnier, Walter Stewart, George Humphrey.
141 pp. *Permission required to cite or quote.* 1970. *Micro III.*

JACQUITH, James. *See* Civil Rights in Alabama.

JAKOB, Oliver G. (1892–) *See* Continental Group.

JAKOBSON, Max. *See* International Negotiations.

JAMES, Daniel, Jr. (1920–1978) *See* Air Force Academy.

JAMES, E. P. H. *See* Radio Pioneers.

JAMES, George (1915–1972) *See* Mt. Sinai Hospital.

JAMES, Henry (1843–1916) *Discussed in* Joseph Collins; Caroline K. Duer; Leon Edel.

JAMES, Henry (1879–1947) *Discussed in* Carnegie Corporation; George E. Johnson, Jr.; R. McAllister Lloyd.

JAMIESON, Francis Anthony (1904–1960) Newspaperman.
Reporter in Albany; Lindbergh kidnapping; New Jersey politics during Frank Hague's rule and Charles Edison's governorship; work in the NY office of the AP and founding of the Newspaper Guild; public relations adviser, Office of Inter-American Affairs under Nelson Rockefeller; ad-

mission of Argentina to the UN; role of the Rockefeller family in locating the UN in NYC.
205 pp. *Permission required.* 1952.

JANIN, Ernesto. Labor leader.
ARGENTINA
Socialists, syndicalists, Communists, and anarchists in Argentine labor during 1930's: influence, strength, shifting alliances, organization of new unions; strikes, increase in union membership; Angel Borlenghi and Jose Domenech.
57 pp. *Open.* 1970.

JANIS, Eddie. *See* Radio Pioneers.

JANSEN, William (1887–1968) Educator.
Early years and education; teacher, principal, assistant superintendent, superintendent of schools in NYC, 1947–58; impressions of William Kilpatrick, George Strayer, and other TC professors; Communist purge in NYC schools; Bronx Park experiment; banning of the *Nation.*
163 pp. *Permission required to cite or quote.* 1963. *Micro I.*
Discussed in Frederick C. McLaughlin.

JAPAN *See* Hugh Borton; John B. Grant; Charles H. Hayes; Occupation of Japan; John D. Rockefeller 3rd; Sir George Sansom.

JARDINE, William. *Discussed in* Howard R. Tolley.

JASON, Hillard. *See* Mt. Sinai Hospital.

JAURETCHE, Arturo. *See* Argentina.

BENJAMIN A. JAVITS PROJECT
A series of interviews with friends, associates and family of Benjamin A. Javits (1894–1973). Topics discussed include his politico-economic ideas for the future of modern capitalism in the direction of widely expanded ownership.
Participants and pages: George J. Feldman *(in process);* Halfdan Gregerson, 26; Milton Handler, 18; Jacob Javits, 30; Leon Keyserling, 65 *(permission required to cite or quote);* Roger Mazlen, 73; Lillian Poses, 24; Dorothy Seghers, 51 *(permission required to cite or quote).*

287 pp. *Permission required except as noted.* 1978– . *Underwritten by a friend of the University.*

JAVITS, Jacob Koppel (1904–) *See* Eisenhower Administration, *Micro III;* Ethnic Groups and American Foreign Policy; Benjamin A. Javits Project; *and* Social Security, *Micro III.*
  Discussed in Richard Aurelio; Ben Davidson; Frank Thompson, Jr.

JAZZ PROJECT
This series of interviews with musicians focuses on social conditions on Chicago's Southside in the 1920's and '30's and their effects on the development of jazz. Specific topics include relations between black and white musicians and their respective union locals, social status of the jazz musician, Prohibition, organized crime and the Depression. Participants discuss their individual careers and compare the New York and Chicago jazz scenes.
  Participants and pages: Ralph E. Brown, 21; Scoville Browne, 19 *(permission required to cite or quote);* Earl Fatha Hines, 18 *(permission required to cite or quote);* Milton Hinton, 33 *(permission required to cite or quote);* Willie Randall, 30; William E. Samuels, 21; Red Saunders, 15; Leon Washington, 23.
  180 pp. *Permission required except as noted.* 1971. *Contributed by John Lax.*

JEFFORD, Jack. *See* Aviation Project.

JENNEY, John K. (1904–) DuPont executive.
  Childhood in Syracuse; education, Princeton; DuPont diversification, decentralization, 1920's; research emphases, including development of synthetic ammonia, cellophane, synthetic rubber; duPont family, generational differences in business philosophy; formation of DuPont Foreign Relations Department; American and European chemical industry in the 1920's, related legal agreements; effects of Common Market; reorganization, International Department.
  375 pp. *Permission required to cite or quote.* 1975.
  Underwritten by The Eleutherian Mills-Hagley Foundation, Wilmington, Delaware.

JENSEN, Oliver (1914–) Editor, writer.
  Career as a picture book publisher; editor, *Life* magazine; founding *American Heritage;* impressions of Joseph J. Thorndike and James Parton.
  29 pp. *Open.* 1959.

JEROME, William Travers. *Discussed in* William J. Schieffelin.

JERSILD, Arthur T. (1902–) Psychologist, educator.
  Education, South Dakota and Nebraska; TC, 1929; consulting psychologist to CBS, 1935–48; Institute for Educational Leadership in Japan, 1948–49; school consultant; impressions of educators James Russell and William Russell, William H. Kilpatrick, and Edward G. Thorndike.
  255 pp. *Permission required to cite or quote.* 1967. *Micro I.*

JERVEY, Huges. *Discussed in* Adolf A. Berle.

JESSEL, George. *Discussed in* Samson Raphaelson.

JESSUP, Frederick Peterson (1920–) Government official.
  EISENHOWER ADMINISTRATION
  The politics and growth of intelligence operations, 1946–72, with reference to CIA; Germany in the 1950's; US diplomatic personnel, Switzerland and Israel, 1957–63; NSC staff work, 1963–72; US-Israeli relations; impressions of Robert A. McClure, Lucian Truscott, Allen Dulles, McGeorge Bundy, Walt Rostow, Henry Kissinger, and others.
  105 pp. *Permission required.* 1972.

JESSUP, Philip Caryl (1897–) Diplomat, scholar.
  Early years and education; teaching international law at Columbia University; State Department; research on neutrality; setting up Naval School of Military Government and Administration at Columbia; work with Herbert Lehman organizing OFRRO and later UNRRA; international conferences (UNRRA, Bretton Woods, San Francisco); US delegation to the UN; impressions of personalities in American

government; Joseph McCarthy charges and Senate investigations.
388 pp. *Permission required.* 1958.
See also Journalism Lectures (A) *and* International Negotiations.
Discussed in James W. Barco.

JESSUP, Walter A. *Discussed in* Carnegie Corporation.

JEWISH ISSUES *See* Ethnic Groups and American Foreign Policy; Jonah Goldstein; Bernard G. Richards; Gerhard H. Seger; Sheba Skirball.

JOFRE, Emilio (1907–) Politician.
ARGENTINA
Lawyer, joined Democratic Party, 1931; economics and politics of Mendoza, Argentina; relation of provincial and national governments; foreign agricultural workers, sharecropping, viniculture; petroleum development; Peronism; Governor Ricardo Videla.
40 pp. *Open.* 1971.

JOHANSEN, John. *See* John F. Kennedy Project.

JOHNS, S. P., Jr. *See* Weyerhaeuser Timber Company.

JOHNS, Thomas Chris. *See* Vietnam Veterans.

JOHNSON, A. E. *See* Thomas A. Edison Project.

JOHNSON, Alfred Wilkinson (1876–1963) Naval officer.
Naval family background; Annapolis; Spanish-American War; early cruises; naval inventions; instructor at Naval Academy 1907–10.
88 pp. *Permission required to cite or quote.* 1962. *Micro I.*

JOHNSON, Allen. *Discussed in* Dumas Malone.

JOHNSON, Alvin (1874–1971) Writer, educator.
Early years in the Middle West; education; teaching at Columbia; impressions of Nicholas Murray Butler and faculty members;

New Republic and impressions of Walter Lippmann and Herbert Croly; New School.
195 pp. *Permission required to cite or quote.* 1960. *Micro I.*

JOHNSON, Ben H. (1891–) *See* Air Force Academy.

JOHNSON, Charles S. *Discussed in* Rupert B. Vance.

JOHNSON, David Dean (1899–) *See* Benedum and the Oil Industry.

JOHNSON, Frank E. (1913–) *See* Continental Group.

JOHNSON, George E., Jr. (1905–) Counsellor.
TIAA-CREF PROJECT
Vision difficulties in early life; father's activities with radio and aviation; relationship between Carnegie Corporation and TIAA; complementary arrangements between TIAA-CREF and Social Security; McClintock Contracts; experiences with Henry James.
57 pp. *Closed until 1983.* 1977.

JOHNSON, Guion Griffis (Mrs. Guy B.) (1900–) Historian.
SOUTHERN INTELLECTUAL LEADERS (B)
St. Helena Island project; evolution of publications by Dr. Johnson; University of North Carolina History Department, 1920's; activities as Executive Secretary of Georgia Conference on Social Welfare, 1943–47.
175 pp. *Permission required to cite or quote.* 1974.
See also Carnegie Corporation.

JOHNSON, Guy Benton (1901–) Sociologist.
SOUTHERN INTELLECTUAL LEADERS (A)
Childhood and education in rural Texas; graduate work, University of Chicago, University of North Carolina; research on race relations in the South; St. Helena Island Study, 1928–29; teaching career, University of North Carolina; research associate, *An American Dilemma;* Director, Southern Regional Council, 1945–47; trustee, Howard University. Impressions of Gunnar Myrdal and Howard W. Odum.

171 pp. *Permission required to cite or quote.* 1972.
See also Carnegie Corporation.

JOHNSON, Helmer R. (1913–) *See* Continental Group.

JOHNSON, Hiram. *Discussed in* Horace M. Albright.

JOHNSON, Hugh S. *Discussed in* Goldthwaite Dorr; Jerome N. Frank; Milton Handler; Lloyd K. Garrison; Frances Perkins; Henry A. Wallace; James P. Warburg.

JOHNSON, James Weldon. *Discussed in* George S. Schuyler; Carl Van Vechten.

JOHNSON, Jesse Charles (1894–) *See* Eisenhower Administration. *Micro III.*

JOHNSON, John B. *Discussed in* William O'Dwyer.

JOHNSON, Joseph Esrey (1906–) Professor of History.
Activities in Latin American diplomacy; Dumbarton Oaks Conference; Division of International Security Affairs.
58 pp. *Closed during lifetime.* 1951.
See also Carnegie Corporation, International Negotiations, *and* United Nations Conference.

JOHNSON, Lydia (1893–) *See* China Missionaries.

JOHNSON, Lyndon Baines. *Discussed in* Edward R. Annis; Wilbur Cohen; Virginia Durr; Milton S. Eisenhower; Luther H. Evans; Barry Goldwater; D.B. Hardeman; Elizabeth S. Ives; Newton Minow; John Sharon; Frank Stanton; Hobart Taylor, Jr.; Marietta Tree; Elizabeth Wickenden.

JOHNSON, Nelson Trusler (1887–1954) Diplomat.
Family background and early life; experiences as student interpreter for Consular Service in China, 1907; Battle of the Concessions, Open Door Policy; Manchuria, 1909–10; concession railways; Taiping rebellion; Revolution of 1911; Yale-in-China activities; Chinese social life and attitudes, early 1900's; recall to Washington and preparations for the Washington Conference; appointment as inspection officer in China, 1923.
730 pp. *Permission required to cite or quote.* 1954. *Micro I.*

JOHNSON, Nunnally (1897–1977) *See* Popular Arts.

JOHNSON, Philip C. (1906–) Architect.
NEW YORK'S ART WORLD
Organization of International Exhibit of Modern Architecture and establishment of international style; Director, Dept. of Architecture, Museum of Modern Art, 1930–36, '46–54; design of MOMA annex and courtyard, Glass House (1947), Seagram Building; questions of preservation, modernization; processional and monumental elements in architectural design.
64 pp. *Permission required.* 1978.
See also Ludwig Mies van der Rohe.

JOHNSON, Robert S. *See* Aviation Project. *Micro II.*

JOHNSON, Scott R. (1895–) *See* Continental Group.

JOHNSON, Virginia. *Discussed in* Emily H. Mudd.

JOHNSON, Walter (1915–) Historian.
Family background; Massachusetts childhood; Dartmouth; association with Adlai E. Stevenson: 1948 gubernatorial campaign, 1952 draft, 1953 world trip, and 1956 campaign; editing Stevenson papers; Yalta project with Edward Stettinius; Joseph C. Grew project; race for Chicago alderman, 1943; establishment of Independent Voters of Illinois.
191 pp. *Permission required to cite or quote.* 1976. *Micro IV.*
See also Adlai E. Stevenson Project. *Micro III.*

JOHNSTON, Eric A. (1896–1963) *See* Popular Arts.

JOLLY, Thomas David (1891–) *See* James B. Duke Project.

JOLSON, Al. *Discussed in* Radio Pioneers; Samson Raphaelson.

JONES, Caswell S., Thomas J. Newlin and Alex U. McCandless. *See* Benedum and the Oil Industry.

JONES, Charles Sherman (1894–1976) *See* Aviation Project. *Micro IV.*

JONES, Francis Price (1890–   ) *See* China Missionaries.

JONES, Hilary P. *Discussed in* Harold C. Train.

JONES, J. Raymond. *Discussed in* James E. Booker.

JONES, Jesse. *Discussed in* Will Clayton; Clifford J. Durr; Emory S. Land.

JONES, L. Virgil and Arthur Graf. *See* Continental Group.

JONES, Louis Reeder (1895–1973) *See* Marine Corps.

JONES, Lucille Williams (Mrs. Francis) (1889–   ) *See* China Missionaries.

JONES, Marvin (1882–1976) Jurist, legislator.
Youth and education; early law practice in Amarillo, Texas; US Congress; WWI; legislative organization and procedure; farm legislation; Farm Bureau; National Grange; Farmers' Union; McNary-Haugen Bill; House Agricultural Committee; state and national elections, 1928–40; Agricultural Adjustment Act; Franklin D. Roosevelt and the New Deal; Emergency Farm Mortgage Act; Farm Credit Act; Federal Farm Bankruptcy Act; Soil Conservation and Domestic Allotment Act; RA; OES; WFA; President, Hot Springs Food Conference, 1943; WFA, 1943–45; US Court of Claims; impressions of Henry A. Wallace, George Peek, James F. Byrnes, Claude Wickard, Chester Davis, and others.
1,453 pp. *Permission required to cite or quote.* 1953. *Micro I.*

JONES, Roger Warren (1908–   ) Government official.

EISENHOWER ADMINISTRATION
WWII experience with Combined Chiefs of Staff; Bureau of the Budget; US Civil Service Commission; legislation and personnel in the Eisenhower administration.
73 pp. *Permission required to cite or quote.* 1967. *Micro III.*

JONES, W.A. (Pete) *Discussed in* Clifford Roberts.

JONES, William J. *See* Benedum and the Oil Industry.

JORALEMON, Ira Beaman (1884–1975) *See* Mining Engineers.

JORDAHL, Russell Nelton (1903–   ) *See* Marine Corps.

JORDAN, Joseph. *See* Flying Tigers.

JORDAN, Len B. (1899–   ) *See* Eisenhower Administration.

JOSEPHS, Devereux Colt (1893–1977) Executive.
CARNEGIE CORPORATION
Personal background; vice president, later president, of TIAA, 1939–45; president, Carnegie Corporation, 1946–48; philosophy of Corporation; projects, selection of staff; Alger Hiss; impressions of trustees and staff.
150 pp. *Permission required.* 1967.
Discussed in Morse A. Cartwright; Charles Dollard; Caryl P. Haskins; Edward P. Herring; Robert M. Lester; R. McAllister Lloyd.

JOSEPHSON, Matthew (1899–1978) *See* Ford Maddox Ford.

JOSEPHSON, Matthew and Robert Wohlforth. *See* La Follette Civil Liberties Committee.

JOUANICOT, Maxwell. *See* Vietnam Veterans.

JOURNALISM *See* Elie Abel; Maxwell Anderson; Richard Aurelio; Joseph Barnes; Earl Behrens; S. Michael Bessie; Heber Blankenhorn; Bruce Bliven; James E. Booker; Gardner Botsford; Anne Braden;

Sevellon Brown; Nicolas Chatelain; Marquis Childs; Virginius Dabney; Jonathan Daniels; Chester Davis; Malcolm Davis; Edmund DeLong; Hedley Donovan; Robert J. Donovan; Roscoe Drummond; Robert L. Duffus; Leon Edel; Ed Edwin; Helen W. Erskine; Aldino Felicani; Edward T. Folliard;

George H. Gallup; Mary Bass Gibson; Max Gissen; Michel Gordey; Bruce and Beatrice Gould; Ben Grauer; James C. Hagerty; Richard F. Hanser; Albert Hauptli; August Heckscher; Burton J. Hendrick; Frederick W. Henshaw; John T. Hettrick; Frank Ernest Hill; Eric Hodgins; Quincy Howe; Norman Isaacs; Francis A. Jamieson; Journalism Lectures; Jill Krementz; Arthur Krock; Edwin A. Lahey; William L. Laurence; William H. Lawrence; James D. LeCron; Walter Lippmann; T.S. Matthews; Eugene Meyer; Sig Mickelson; Edward P. Morgan; Allan Nevins;

John B. Oakes; Robert Lincoln O'Brien; J. Hamilton Owens; Arthur W. Page; James Parton; Joseph Pulitzer, Jr.; Radio Pioneers; Benjamin H. Reese; Chalmers Roberts; Cleveland Rodgers; Frank W. Rounds, Jr.; Richard Rovere; Raymond L. Scherer; M. Lincoln Schuster; George S. Schuyler; Edwin Seaver; Gerhart H. Seger; John Seigenthaler; Howard K. Smith; George E. Sokolsky; Sigmund Spaeth; Keats Speed; J. David Stern; Roger W. Straus; Frank Sullivan; Charles E. Taylor; Eva M. Valesh; Carl Van Vechten; Selma Warner; Stanley Washburn; Roy Wilkins; James T. Williams, Jr.; Women Journalists.

JOURNALISM LECTURES
Guest lecturers at the Graduate School of Journalism of Columbia University occasionally provide firsthand accounts of pivotal events. Benjamin Fine's account of the integration crisis of Central High School in Little Rock and Harrison Salisbury's description of Nikita Khrushchev's visit to the US and the "Battle of Coon Rapids" are examples. Other lectures grouped under this heading range from Watson Berry's on NYC journalism in the 1890's to discussions of the role of the news media from the 1950's on.

Participants and pages: Dean Acheson, 39; Brooks Atkinson, 29; Hanson Baldwin, 17; Ross Barnett, 23; Watson Berry, 25; Herbert Block, 34; Robert Briscoe, 24; Ted Cott, 36; Norman Cousins, 26; Clifton Daniel, 76; Benjamin Fine, 25; Max Freedman, 29; John V. Lindsay, 22; Walter Lippmann, 58; Samuel Lubell, 127; Malcolm X, 38; Lester Markel, 46; Herbert Mayes, 29; Sig Mickelson, 31; James Reston, 46; William Rusher, 66; Harrison Salisbury, 65; David Schoenbrun, 46; Harry S. Truman, 13.

970 pp. *Permission required to cite or quote.*

A. BASIC ISSUES IN THE NEWS
In these lectures, given at the Graduate School of Journalism each scholar has undertaken to tell newsmen something of what they need to know in his area of specialization.

Participants, topics, and pages: Adolf Berle on economics, 29; John Ray Dunning on nuclear energy, 104; Louis Hollander on the labor movement, 58; Philip Jessup on the national state and the international community, 85; Polykarp Kusch on physics, 17; Wallace Sayre on the problems of the city, 136.

429 pp. *Permission required.* 1959–63.

B. CONSUMER REPORTING
Two conferences at the Graduate School of Journalism examined problems facing journalists in covering the consumer movement. Aspects of reporting product analysis, consumer research, and ecological questions are discussed.

982 pp. *Permission required to cite or quote.* 1971–72.

C. FORUMS
Two Columbia forums assess American journalism in the 1960's, the first from the several vantage points of learned observers, the second from those of professionals in the field.

Forum I: Grayson Kirk, moderator; Charles Frankel, Polykarp Kusch, Margaret Mead, Leo Rosten.

Forum II: Edward W. Barrett, moderator; Hodding Carter, Max Lerner, Marya Mannes, Michael J. Ogden, Eric Sevareid.

105 pp. *Permission required to cite or quote.* 1963.

JOVA, Joseph John (1916–   ) Ambassador.

Family background; United Fruit Company farm overseer, Guatemala, 1938–41; WWII Navy experiences; Foreign Service diplomatic assignments in Iraq, Morocco, Portugal, Chile; functions of an ambassador and his wife; Chilean politics during Kennedy administration; US Ambassador to Honduras, 1965–69: economic and social issues, El Salvador-Honduras Soccer War, 1969; Ambassador to OAS: schism in Roman Catholic clergy, territorial and trade disputes, Castro's Cuba; Ambassador to Mexico, 1974–77: drug traffic, prisoner exchange, Henry Kissinger and Latin American relations; impressions of Luis Echeverria, other Mexican officials.
In process.

JOYCE, George J. *See* New York Political Studies (A).

JOYCE, James. *Discussed in* Joseph Collins; Ben W. Huebsch.

JUDD, Walter H. (1898–   ) Physician, Congressman.
EISENHOWER ADMINISTRATION
Personal background, religion; University of Nebraska, 1916, Medical School, 1919; missionary doctor in China, 1925–31, 1934–38; lecturing against Communism, 1938–40; Congressman from Minnesota,

1943; Chiang Kai-shek and Nationalist government; Marshall Plan; nomination of Dwight D. Eisenhower; Geneva Conference, 1955; State Department; US foreign policy. Impressions of John Foster Dulles, Richard Nixon, John F. Kennedy.
149 pp. *Permission required to cite or quote.* 1970. *Micro IV.*

JUDICIARY *See* Raymond Baldwin; Joseph A. Cox; Charles Fahy; Felix Frankfurter; Stanley H. Fuld; Jonah Goldstein; Learned Hand; Robert H. Jackson; Marvin Jones; Theodore R. Kupferman; James M. Landis; Joseph W. Madden; Thurgood Marshall; Harold R. Medina; Edith Miller; Constance B. Motley; Robert P. Patterson Project; David W. Peck; Joseph M. Proskauer; Stanley F. Reed; Benno C. Schmidt, Jr.; Meier Steinbrink; Thomas D. Thacher; Elbert P. Tuttle; J. Waties Waring; Charles E. Wyzanski, Jr.; Sir Muhammad Zafrulla Khan.

JUDSON, Arthur (1881–1975) *See* Radio Pioneers.
Discussed in Howard Barlow; Saul Goodman.

JUNG, Carl. *Discussed in* Edward Glover.

JUSTO, Agustin P. *Discussed in* Jose Luis Pena; Dario Sarachaga.

K

KADES, Charles Louis (1906–   ) *See* Occupation of Japan.

KAHLER, Herbert. *See* Independence Park.

KAILO, Meyer. *See* New York Political Studies (B).

KAISER, Khwaja. *See* International Negotiations.

KAISER, William H. (1897–   ) *See* Continental Group.

KALAMAR, Mary H. (1892–   ) *See* Continental Group.

KALAND, William J. *See* Radio Pioneers.

KALBFUSS, Edward. *Discussed in* Charles J. Moore.

KALMAR, Louis F. (1918–   ) *See* Continental Group.

KALTENBORN, Hans V. (1878–1965) Editor, radio commentator.
RADIO PIONEERS
Childhood and early occupations; Harvard; Brooklyn *Eagle;* radio broadcaster with several NYC stations and CBS and NBC networks, 1921–50; organized Association of Radio News Analysts, 1942; views on past and future roles of radio; visits to Russia, 1926, 1929; impressions of Adolf Hitler, Calvin Coolidge, and others.
248 pp. *Permission required to cite or quote.* 1950. *Micro I.*

KAMARCK, Andrew Martin (1914–   ) *See* World Bank.

KANDEL, Isaac Leon (1881–1965) Educator.
Education in US and abroad; TC, 1913–46: comparative, permissive, and progressive education; foreign students, travel, pensions. Impressions of John Dewey, W. H. Kilpatrick, George Counts, and other educators.
85 pp. *Permission required to cite or quote.* 1962. *Micro I.*

KAPLAN, Joseph (1892–   ) Physicist.
National Academy of Science; government support and influence for basic research facilities; IGY, National Committee: panels, chairman's role, international program, space questions, use of IGY information.
82 pp. *Permission required.* 1960.

KAPLOW, Jeffrey. *See* Columbia Crisis of 1968.

KAPP, Dave. *See* Popular Arts.

KARAM, James. *See* Eisenhower Administration.

KARCH, Frederick Joseph (1917–   ) *See* Marine Corps.

KARDINER, Abram (1891–   ) Psychoanalyst.
PSYCHOANALYTIC MOVEMENT
Early childhood and education in NYC; Cornell Medical College; analysis by Sigmund Freud; Vienna in the 1920's, association with leading figures in the psychoanalytic movement; work with Drs. W. H. Frink, A. A. Brill, Otto Rank, Franz Alexander; New York psychoanalytic movement, 1920's and 1930's; activities and associations as lecturer in anthropology, Columbia University; chairman of Columbia Psychoanalytic Clinic's research seminar on comparative analysis of cultures, 1939–51; director, 1955–57; development as practicing psychoanalyst, interest in anthropology; research in the relation of psychiatry and the social sciences; discussion of his major books.
712 pp. *Open except for specified pages.* 1963.

KARK, Alan Eugene (1921–   ) *See* Mt. Sinai Hospital.

KARTVELI, Alexander (1896–1974) *See* Aviation Project. *Micro IV.*

KASAKOVE, P. *See* Thomas A. Edison Project.

KASPER, Joseph Phillip (1897–   ) *See* Federated Department Stores.

KATIMS, Milton. *Discussed in* Morton Gould.

KATZ, Alex. *See* New York's Art World.

KAUFMAN, Boris. *See* Popular Arts.

KAUFMAN, Ralph. *See* Mt. Sinai Hospital.

KAUFMANN, Arthur. *See* Independence Park.

KAUL, Brij Mohan (–1972) Indian Army officer.
Education, Royal Military College, Sandhurst, 1933; Rajputana Rifles; Secretary, Nationalization Committee, India, 1946–47; India's Military Attaché, Washington,

D.C., 1947; adviser, Indian delegation to UN Security Council, 1948; fought in the Kashmir War till the end of 1948; commander, infantry brigade and division, 1948–56; Chief of Staff, Neutral Nations Repatriation Commission, Korea, 1953–54; visits to Peking and other parts of China, 1954; Quartermaster General, 1959–61; Chief of the General Staff, Indian Army, 1961–62; Chinese invasion of India, 1962; premature resignation from the Indian Army, December, 1962; impressions of Jawaharlal Nehru, Krishna Menon, and many others.

445 pp. *Permission required.* 1964.

KAZAN, Abraham (1889–1971) Labor leader.
Early life; immigration to US; ILGWU; Union Welfare Fund; ILGWU Cooperative Ventures; union housing; problems in cooperative housing; Twin Lake Cooperative Farm; United Housing Foundation; self help in cooperatives. Recollections of Sidney Hillman, Robert Moses, Jacob Potofsky.

554 pp. *Permission required to cite or quote.* 1968. *Micro II.*

KAZIN, Alfred (1915–   ) *See* James Agee, American Historians *and* Richard Hofstadter Project.

KEATING, Kenneth B. (1900–1975) Senator, ambassador.
EISENHOWER ADMINISTRATION
Service in House and Senate; President Eisenhower's relations with Congress; 1958 NY Senate campaign; Judiciary and Space Committees.

126 pp. *Permission required to cite or quote.* 1968. *Micro III.*

KEATING, Sean (1903–   ) Government official.
Experiences in Ireland with Irish Republican Army, 1920; prisoner of British, 1920–21; NYC Department of Licenses, 1949; assistant to Mayor Robert F. Wagner, 1958–61; regional director of US Post Office; impressions of Michael Collins, William and Paul O'Dwyer, John and Robert Kennedy.

67 pp. *Permission required.* 1974.

KEATON, Buster (1896–1966) *See* Popular Arts.
Discussed in Albert E. Sutherland.

KEENEY, Barnaby (1914–   ) *See* American Cultural Leaders.

KEEZER, Dexter Merriam (1896–   ) *See* McGraw-Hill.

KEFAUVER, Estes (1903–1963) *See* Herbert H. Lehman Project.
Discussed in Barry Bingham; Gordon Browning; D.B. Hardeman; William O'Dwyer; John Sharon.

KELLAND, Clarence Budington (1881–1964) Author, politician.
Family background; life in Michigan in 1900; Henry Ford and the Ford Motor Company; writer, editor of *American Boy,* publicity director of the YMCA in France, WWI; beginnings in politics; presidential conventions, especially 1952; experiences in Arizona as Republican National Committeeman.

164 pp. *Open.* 1952.

KELLER, John W. *Discussed in* John T. Hettrick.

KELLERMAN, Henry Joseph (1910–   ) *See* Eisenhower Administration. *Micro III.*

KELLEY, Florence. *Discussed in* George W. Alger.

KELLEY, Nicholas (1885–1965) Lawyer.
Family background; Harvard College and Law School; experiences at Cravath, Henderson & De Gersdorff and other firms; war loan staff of the Department of the Treasury during WWI; business reorganization work; trip to Peru as head of mission on behalf of American banking interests; reorganization of the Maxwell Company into the Chrysler Corporation; detailed description of the Chrysler Corporation, including production, finances and labor; Automobile Labor Board during the New Deal; Chrysler strikes in 1937 and 1939; anti-trust action against the automobile industry in 1937; Chrysler's war contracts; philanthropic activities.

522 pp. *Permission required to cite or quote.* 1953. *Micro I.* Papers.
Discussed in Carnegie Corporation.

KELLOGG, Claude Rupert. *See* China Missionaries.

KELLOGG, Royal S. (–1965) *See* Forest History Society.

KELLY, Barry. *See* Vietnam Veterans.

KELLY, Frank. *Discussed in* New York Political Studies.

KELLY, Gene Curran (1912–) *See* Popular Arts.

KELLY, Howard. *Discussed in* Abraham Flexner.

KELLY, Hugh Joseph (1905–) *See* McGraw-Hill.

KELSO, Winchester (1895–) *See* Benedum and the Oil Industry.

KEMPER, John Mason (1912–1971) Army officer, educator.
Family background, education; West Point.
113 pp. *Permission required to cite or quote.* 1963. *Micro II.*

KENDALL, David Walbridge (1903–)
See Eisenhower Administration.

KENDALL, Edward Calvin (1886–1972)
See Nobel Laureates.

KENDRICK, John B. *Discussed in* Joseph C. O'Mahoney.

KENEN, Isaiah L. (1905–) *See* Ethnic Groups and American Foreign Policy.

KENEN, Peter B. (1932–) *See* Columbia Crisis of 1968.

KENNAN, George. *Discussed in* Frank W. Rounds, Jr.

KENNEDY, Elsie Parsons (Mrs. John D.) (1903–1966)
Recollections of parents and grandparents; Newport and NY society; Republican Con-

vention, 1920; real estate developments, NYC, 1920's.
50 pp. *Permission required to cite or quote.* 1962. *Micro II.*

KENNEDY, Jacqueline. *Discussed in* Cass Canfield.

KENNEDY, John F. *Discussed in* Edward Annis; Roger N. Baldwin; Barry Bingham; Roger Blough; Chester Bowles; Nelson Cruikshank; Elizabeth S. Ives; Walter H. Judd; Sean Keating; John F. Kennedy Project; Carl McGowan; A.S. (Mike) Monroney; Ivan A. Nestingen; Richard Neustadt; Charles Odell; John Seigenthaler; John Sharon; James Sheldon; Howard K. Smith; Frank Thompson, Jr.; Marietta Tree; Elizabeth Wickenden; Kenneth Williamson; Irwin Wolkstein; Wilson W. Wyatt.

JOHN F. KENNEDY PROJECT
A series of interviews with friends and associates of President Kennedy, conducted during preparation of a biography.
Participants and pages: Eleanor L. Dulles, 32; Deirdre Henderson, 71; John Hersey, 24; Hubert Humphrey, 21; John Johansen, 21; Lawrence P. O'Brien, 43; David F. Powers, 55; James A. Rousmaniere, 34; Seymour St. John, 23; R. Sargent Shriver, 44; Theodore C. Sorensen, 56; Frank Thompson, Jr., 19.
443 pp. *Closed pending publication.* 1976– . *Contributed by Herbert S. Parmet, NYC.*

KENNEDY, Joseph P. *Discussed in* Eddie Dowling; Alan Kirk; Emory S. Land; James M. Landis; James A. Rousmaniere.

KENNEDY, Ken. *See* Radio Pioneers.

KENNEDY, Robert F. *Discussed in* Edward Costikyan; Elizabeth S. Ives; Sean Keating; John Seigenthaler; Hobart Taylor, Jr.

KENNEDY, Roy G. (1905–) *See* Continental Group.

KENNERLEY, Mitchell. *Discussed in* Alfred A. Knopf.

KENNY, George C. *Discussed in* Jarred V. Crabb.

KENNY, William F. *Discussed in* Eddie Dowling.

KENT, Rockwell (1882–1971) *See* Friends of the Columbia Libraries.

KEOGH, Eugene James (1907–   ) Congressman.
NY State politics, 1930–36; national politics, 1937–50.
82 pp. *Permission required to cite or quote.* 1950. *Micro I.*

KEOGH, Thomas P. (1904–   ) *See* Continental Group.

KEPPEL, Francis (1916–   ) *See* Carnegie Corporation.
Discussed in Francis A. J. Ianni.

KEPPEL, Frederick P. *Discussed in* Carnegie Corporation; W. H. Cowley.

KERN, Jerome. *Discussed in* Popular Arts.

KEROUAC, Jack. *Discussed in* John Clellon Holmes.

KERR, Barbara. *See* Adlai E. Stevenson Project.

KERR, Florence (1890–1975) WPA Administrator.
Chicago Midwest Regional Director, Women's and Professional Projects, WPA, 1935–38; Washington Assistant Commissioner, WPA, 1939; Assistant Commissioner, Federal Works Administration, 1942–45; unskilled women's projects; Arts Project; Harry Hopkins; relationship with Franklin D. Roosevelt, 1939; impressions of many New Deal figures.
110 pp. *Permission required to cite or quote.* 1974. *Micro III.*

KERR, Gordon. *See* Ethnic Groups and American Foreign Policy.

KERR, Robert. *Discussed in* Frederick B. Arner; Herman M. Somers.

KEYNES, John Maynard. *Discussed in* Ansel F. Luxford.

KEYSERLING, Leon H. (1908–   ) Lawyer, economist, government official.
Legal assistant to Senator Robert Wagner, 1933; drafting of NIRA, constitutional challenge, Schechter case; Senator Wagner as chairman of original Labor Board, 1933; analysis of Wagner Act, its passage, creation of NLRB, 1935; Smith Committee hearings; Senator Wagner's disapproval of Taft-Hartley Act.
65 pp. *Permission required to cite or quote.* 1969. *Acquired from the Labor-Management Documentation Center, Cornell University.*
See also Benjamin A. Javits Project.
Discussed in Miles Colean.

KHEEL, Theodore Woodrow (1914–   ) Lawyer, mediator.
INTERNATIONAL NEGOTIATIONS
General philosophy of mediation; examples from his career.
43 pp. *Permission required.* 1969.

KHRUSHCHEV, Nikita S. (1894–1971) Premier of the Soviet Union.
In late 1966 or early 1967, at the state-owned dasha outside Moscow to which he had been consigned after his fall from power in 1964, Nikita Khrushchev began the series of tape-recorded monologues that make up this archive. He continued, with one four-month interruption because of illness, until a few days before his death, dictating without benefit of interviewer, papers, or a reference library. Spanning his entire career, the memoirs detail early steps up the Party ladder; first impressions of Stalin; the failures of collectivization; the years of the purges; campaigns of WWII; Stalin's behavior in post-war years; the state of Party leadership after Stalin's death; Khrushchev's exposure of Stalin's crimes in the secret speech at the Twentieth Party Congress; and a topic-by-topic discussion of foreign and domestic affairs in the years that followed, generously sprinkled with earthy anecdotes and vignettes of Soviet leaders.
How these tapes came into the hands of Time, Inc. remains undisclosed, but they furnished the grist for two volumes that

were translated and edited by Strobe Talbott, *Khrushchev Remembers* (1970) and *Khrushchev Remembers: A Last Testament* (1974). The front matter of these provides all that is available as to provenance; but this archive, which includes detailed topical outlines in addition to completely new transcriptions of the tapes, in Russian, offers a much fuller record of what Khrushchev had to say. These transcriptions and the outlines have been furnished by the University's Russian Institute on a grant supplied by the donors, Time, Inc. An English translation is in the offing. Also included is a report of the voice-printing analyses to which the tapes were subjected to verify their authenticity.

2,516 pp. *Permission required.* 1966–71. *Discussed in* George V. Allen; Evan Aurand; James W. Barco; Chester Bowles; Andrew W. Cordier; Ted Cott; Michel Gordey; James C. Hagerty; W. Averell Harriman; John Luter; Harrison Salisbury.

KIDD, Charles Vincent (1914–   ) *See* Health Sciences.

KIDD, Gordon. *See* Eisenhower Administration.

KIEFFER, Jarold Alan (1923–   ) *See* Social Security. *Micro III.*

KIERAN, John. *Discussed in* Dan Golenpaul.

KILLIAN, James R., Jr. (1904–   ) Scientist.
EISENHOWER ADMINISTRATION
Special Assistant to President Eisenhower for Science and Technology; President's Science Advisory Committee; Technological Capabilities Panel; Department of Defense; State Department; CIA; NSC; National Science Foundation; relations with President Eisenhower; effect of Sputnik; science and government; influence and limitations of a science adviser; Defense Communications Agency; Advanced Research Projects Agency; Geneva Conference on nuclear test detection.
375 pp. *Closed until 1985.* 1970. *Contributed by Stephen White, New York.*

KILPATRICK, William Heard (1871–1965) Educator.
Georgia during Reconstruction; Mercer University; Johns Hopkins; John Dewey and theories of teaching; board of trustees, Bennington College; General Education Board; Lincoln and Horace Mann Schools; education experiments at TC; impressions of William Russell and James Russell, Edward Thorndike, Nicholas Murray Butler, Harold Rugg, George Counts, John Childs, Montessori system; project method.
212 pp. *Open.* 1961.
Discussed in Harold F. Clark; William Jansen; Arthur T. Jersild; Isaac L. Kandel; John K. Norton; R. Bruce Raup; Goodwin Watson.

KIMBALL, Arthur Alden (1908–   ) Government official.
EISENHOWER ADMINISTRATION
Early career; International Information Administration; Senator Joseph McCarthy; USIA; President's Advisory Committee on Government Organization.
104 pp. *Permission required to cite or quote.* 1967. *Micro IV.*

KIMBALL, Dan. *Discussed in* William M. Fechteler.

KIMBALL, Doris Fleeson (1901–1970) *See* Adlai E. Stevenson Project. *Micro IV.*

KIMBRELL, Marvin. *See* James B. Duke Project.

KIMMEL, Husband. *Discussed in* Ralph C. Parker; Omar T. Pfeiffer; Harold C. Train.

KINDELBERGER, James Howard (1895–1962) *See* Henry H. Arnold Project.

KING, Ernest Joseph. *Discussed in* Orvil A. Anderson; Walter S. Anderson; John J. Ballentine; Joseph J. Clark; Donald Duncan; James Fife; John Lesslie Hall, Jr.; Thomas C. Hart; Harry W. Hill; John H. Hoover; Omar T. Pfeiffer; William A. Read; William A. Sullivan; Eugene E. Wilson.

KING, Helen S. *See* Eisenhower Administration.

KING, Jimmy, Sr. *See* Marine Corps.

KING, Martin Luther, Jr. *Discussed in* Lester B. Granger; John Lewis; E. Frederic Morrow; Constance B. Motley.

KINGMAN, Harry L. (1892–   ) Lobbyist.
Youth in China and America; education; professional baseball; army service, WWI; 1916–57, Stiles Hall (University YMCA, Berkeley); 1921–27, International YMCA, China; Shanghai Incident; 1943–45, Director, West Coast Fair Employment Practice Commission; with Ruth Kingman, Citizens' Lobby: 1957–70 in Washington, from 1970 in Berkeley; 1960 Kennedy presidential campaign; civil rights, peace.
248 pp. *Permission required to cite or quote.* 1972. Papers.
Contributed by the Regional Oral History Office, University of California, Berkeley.

KINGMAN, Ruth (Mrs. Harry L.) *Discussed in* Harry L. Kingman.

KINKAID, Thomas Cassin (1888–1972) Naval officer.
Education, Naval Academy; world cruise, 1908; Turkey, burning of Smyrna; Geneva Conference, 1932; Naval Attaché, Rome and Belgrade, 1938–41; Benito Mussolini, Galeazzo Ciano, Bernard Berenson, Spanish royal family; destroyer squadron, convoy duty; Pearl Harbor, 1941; Task Force II, carrier operations, Coral Sea, Midway, Guadalcanal, Eastern Solomons; Commander North Pacific Fleet, Aleutians; combat intelligence; preparations for Philippine campaign; detailed description of Leyte Gulf and subsequent operations; Yellow Sea and Korea; Shanghai, Chungking; impressions of Gen. Douglas MacArthur, Chiang Kai-shek, many prominent naval and political figures.
450 pp. *Permission required.* 1961.
Discussed in James Fife.

KINLOCK, James F. (1906–   ) *See* Continental Group.

KINNEAR, George. *See* Eisenhower Administration.

KINOY, Arthur (1920–   ) Lawyer.
Harvard College, Marxist activist; Columbia Law School, 1947; Rosenberg and Sobell case; US vs. US District Court wiretap case, 1972; House Un-American Activities Committee subpoena cases; Puerto Rican Solidarity Committee activities; United Electrical Workers cases, particularly Evansville, Indiana.
268 pp. *Permission required.* 1975. Papers.

KINSEY, Alfred. *Discussed in* S. Michael Bessie; Emily H. Mudd.

KIRCHHOFER, Alfred Henry (1892–   ) *See* Radio Pioneers. *Micro IV.*

KIRK, Alan Goodrich (1888–1963) Naval officer.
Background and education, Naval Academy; European cruises, Asiatic Fleet, Canton, 1911, Sun Yat Sen; WWI, fleet exercises; Naval Proving Ground, testing ordnance; Presidential yacht *Mayflower,* Warren G. Harding; Bureau of Ordnance; Australia, 1925; fleet gunnery officer; Naval War College, 1928–29; Naval Attaché, London, 1939–41; Joseph P. Kennedy; Director of Naval Intelligence, 1941; codes and war plans; Atlantic Fleet; naval mission to London, 1942–43; Mediterranean; amphibious force, 1943; John Mason Brown; North African landings; Operation Husky; planning for Normandy; impressions of many outstanding naval and political figures.
386 pp. *Permission required to cite or quote.* 1961. *Micro I.*
Discussed in James Fife; Frank W. Rounds, Jr.; William A. Sullivan.

KIRK, Grayson Louis (1903–   ) *See* Columbia Crisis of 1968, Eisenhower Administration *and* United Nations Conference.

KIRKLAND, Edward Chase (1894–   ) *See* American Historians.

KIRKLAND COLLEGE
The life and death of a small liberal arts college for women. Subjects discussed include early planning (1962–63), the role of Robert W. McEwen, President of Hamilton College (Kirkland's coordinate institution) from 1949 to 1966, exploration by the McIntosh Committee of definitions for the

new college, debates on coordinate institutions versus co-education and on the function of women's education, development of Kirkland's educational program, staff and campus, and the use of architecture to express educational values.

Participants and pages: Samuel F. Babbitt, 74 *(permission required to cite or quote);* Walter Beinecke, 43; William Bolenius *(in process);* Ursula J. Colby *(in process);* Richard W. Couper, 15; David Ellis, 21; Marjorie McEwen, 39 *(permission required to cite or quote);* Millicent McIntosh, 44; Debbie Moskowitz, 32; Inez Nelbach, 32 *(permission required to cite or quote);* Ruth Rinard, 30; Carl Schneider, 32; Connie Strellas, 39.

401 pp. *Permission required except as noted.* 1977– . *Contributed by Kirkland College, Clinton, NY.*

KIRKPATRICK, Sidney Dale (1894–1973) *See* McGraw-Hill.

KISSINGER, Henry. *Discussed in* F. Peterson Jessup; Joseph J. Jova; Stuart N. Scott.

KISSINGER, Joseph A. (1907–) *See* Continental Group.

KITCHENER, H.H. *Discussed in* Walter G. Farrell.

KITCHENS, A. W. (1918–) *See* McGraw-Hill.

KITSELMAN, Alfred W. (1916–) *See* Continental Group.

KLAYF, Bernard Spencer (1921–) *See* Federated Department Stores.

KLEEGMAN, Sophia. *Discussed in* Emily H. Mudd.

KLEIN, Herbert George (1918–) Newspaper editor.
EISENHOWER ADMINISTRATION
Richard M. Nixon's elections to the House and Senate; 1952 campaign and election; Nixon fund.
39 pp. *Permission required.* 1967.

KLEIN, Joseph J. (1884–1975) Accountant.
Recollections of CCNY as student, teacher,

member of NYC Board of Higher Education; Council for National Defense and Internal Revenue Service, WWI; career as accountant: certification, founding of Klein, Hines, and Fink; taxation work; Ivar Kreuger International Match Co. case. Impressions of Julius Rosenthal, Felix Warburg, Morris Raphael Cohen.
193 pp. *Permission required to cite or quote.* 1969.

KLEIN, Samuel. *See* Mt. Sinai Hospital.

KLEIN, Solomon A. Lawyer.
NEW YORK POLITICAL STUDIES (A)
Immigration to US; education, Cornell College, Harvard Law School; association with Harry G. Anderson, 1935–39; Kings County District Attorney's office from 1940; chief of Appeal Bureau; views on religion, ethics, politics; Manton case; organized crime; Murder, Inc. cases; blue ribbon juries; selection of jurors. Impressions of William O'Dwyer, Burton Turkus, Samuel Liebowitz.
160 pp. *Permission required to cite or quote.* 1962. *Micro II.*

KLEMPERER, Otto. *Discussed in* Roger H. Sessions.

KLINGENSTEIN, Percy (1896–) *See* Mt. Sinai Hospital. *Micro II.*

KLINT, Walter E. (1919–) *See* Continental Group.

KLISSOLD, Harry E. *See* Jackson Hole Preserve.

KLOPFER, Donald Simon (1902–) Publisher.
William Faulkner's funeral in Oxford, Mississippi.
11 pp. *Open.* 1962.

United Diamond Works; Modern Library with Bennett Cerf; publishing during the Depression; *Ulysses;* growth of Random House; changes in market, paperbacks; associations with authors; Russia.
113 pp. *Closed during lifetime.* 1975.

Discussed in Bennett Cerf.

KLOPSTEG, Paul Ernest (1889–   ) *See* American Association of Physics Teachers.

KLUCKHOHN, Clyde. *Discussed in* Carnegie Corporation.

KNAPP, James. *See* Mining Engineers.

KNAPP, Joseph Burke (1913–   ) *See* World Bank.

KNIGHT, Goodwin J. (1896–1970) Government official.
EISENHOWER ADMINISTRATION
California politics; Presidential campaigning; Republican Party politics, 1950's; Elephant-Eagle Mine. Recollections of Richard M. Nixon, Dwight D. Eisenhower, William F. Knowland, Earl Warren.
94 pp. *Permission required.* 1967.

KNIGHT, Kirk. Program manager.
RADIO PIONEERS
Early days in radio announcing at WJBK, Ypsilanti, and WEXL, Detroit; television programing from 1948, WWJ, Detroit.
34 pp. *Open.* 1951.

KNOERR, Alvin. *See* McGraw-Hill.

KNOPF, Alfred A. (1892–   ) Publisher.
Early life in NYC; Columbia College; years with Doubleday, Page & Co. and Mitchell Kennerley; founding of own firm, 1915; notable early publications; Anthony Comstock and other book censors; H. L. Mencken, George Jean Nathan, and the *American Mercury;* book design; growth of the firm; vignettes of Charles A. Beard, Willa Cather, Clarence Day, Joseph Hergesheimer, Thomas Mann, Katherine Mansfield, and others.
325 pp. *Permission required.* 1961.
Discussed in D. Angus Cameron.

KNOPF, Blanche. *Discussed in* D. Angus Cameron.

KNOWLAND, William Fife (1908–1974) Senator, publisher.
EISENHOWER ADMINISTRATION
1952 convention; California delegation; Nixon fund; President Eisenhower's relations with Congress; domestic legislation; foreign policy; Richard M. Nixon and the 1956 convention; 1960 campaign; Senator Knowland's career; 1958 gubernatorial campaign; California politics; "right to work" issue; relations with President Eisenhower: appointments, role of Senate Majority Leader, president as party leader; Senator Joseph McCarthy; Joint Committee on Atomic Energy.
170 pp. *Permission required to cite or quote.* 1970. *Micro III.*
Discussed in Earl C. Behrens; Barry Goldwater; Goodwin J. Knight.

KNOX, Frank. *Discussed in* Walter S. Anderson; Thomas C. Hart; Edwin A. Lahey; Henry Williams.

KNUDSEN, William S. *Discussed in* Lawrence D. Bell; Emory S. Land.

KOBAK, Edgar (1895–1962) Business consultant.
MCGRAW-HILL
McGraw-Hill from 1916; business manager of *Electrical World;* aviation, electronics, and nucleonics; stock participation; corporate building erected during Depression; NBC vice president.
120 pp. *Permission required.* 1956.

KOCH, Edward I. (1924–   ) Politician.
Village Independent Democrats; Tamawa Club; 1962 Assembly race; NYC reform movement; 1963 district leader race; corruption and crime, NYC; bussing and racial balance, Forest Hills controversy; southern voter registration; Small Business Administration; Israel; relations with Carmine De Sapio, Richard Kuh, Robert Morgenthau, Bella Abzug, John Lindsay, others; constituency: racial composition, ethnic politics; 1966 City Council race; Congressman, 1968–1976: National Labor Caucus, ERA, gay rights, pornography, rent stabilization, amnesty, privacy, marijuana legislation; congressional committees, NY caucus.
617 pp. *Closed until Feb. 19, 1996.* 1976.

KOCH, Kenneth (1925–   ) *See* Poets on their Poetry.

KOCH, Rudolf. *Discussed in* Warren Chappell.

KODALY, Zoltan. *Discussed in* Otto Herz; Abel Lajtha.

KOENIG, Robert P. (1904–   ) Engineer, geologist, executive.
Education; early experience in mining in Latin America, 1925–35; Lehman Brothers and Electric Shovel Corporation, 1935–39.
121 pp. *Closed during lifetime.* 1964.
See also Mining Engineers.

KOENIG, Samuel S. (1872–1955) Lawyer, politician.
NY politics, 1905–35: state elections, Republican nominations, and party background.
53 pp. *Permission required to cite or quote.* 1950. *Micro I.*

KOH, T. B. *See* International Negotiations.

KOHLER, Walter Jodok, Jr. (1904–1976) *See* Eisenhower Administration. *Micro IV.*

KOHLMAN, Edwina. *See* Book-of-the-Month Club. *Micro IV.*

KOHN, Louis A. (1907–   ) *See* Adlai E. Stevenson Project.

KOKOSCHKA, Oskar. *Discussed in* Georg Eisler.

KOLB, Lawrence (1881–1972) Psychiatrist, administrator.
HEALTH SCIENCES
Family, educational background; PHS work with NY Psychiatric Institute; medical director on Ellis Island, 1913–19; 1920's drug and alcohol addiction study, Hygienic Laboratory; administration of narcotics hospital, research lab, Kentucky; Director, Division of Mental Hygiene, USPHS, 1938–44; push for NIMH, community centers; role of World Wars in medical research; aging and mental health study.
73 pp. *Permission required to cite or quote.* 1963.

KOLB, Lawrence Coleman (1911–   ) Psychiatrist.
PSYCHOANALYTIC MOVEMENT
Education; work in neurology with Adolf Meyer; work with war neurosis as Navy psychiatrist, WWII; analysis with Frieda Reichmann; director of research, NIMH, 1946–49; teaching activities and psychotherapeutic work with amputees, Mayo Clinic, 1949–54; development of theory of personality sets; association with NY Psychiatric Institute; establishment of Washington Heights Community Mental Health project; beginnings of Columbia Psychoanalytic Clinic, its training program; expansion of psychoanalytic influence in medical schools; student unrest, 1960's, at Columbia Presbyterian Medical Center; impressions of Harry Stack Sullivan, Frederick Peterson, David Levy, Kevin Cahill.
In process.

ALEXANDRA KOLLONTAI PROJECT
This series of interviews on the life and career of Alexandra Kollontai (1872–1952) was undertaken by Sonya Baevsky as part of a larger project on the Russian revolutionary and diplomat, involving also a documentary film. Some of the taped interviews are with persons who knew Mme. Kollontai; others discuss the significance of her career for Russian history, revolutionary movements, and women's history.
Participants and pages: Erik Boheman, 3; Barbara Clements, 110; Runa Haukaa, 5; Meridal Lessueur, 61; Just Lippe, 4; Alva Myrdal, 7; Eva Palmaer, 15; Margit Palmaer-Walden, 11; Margit Palmaer-Walden and Alva Myrdal, 2; Kenneth Rexroth, 9; Gloria Steinem, 26; Aksel Zachariassen, 6.
259 pp. *Permission required.* 1978.
Underwritten by the Joe and Emily Lowe Foundation, NYC.

KOO, Vi Kyuin Wellington (1888–   ) *See* Chinese Oral History. *Microform available.*

KOREAN WAR *See* Air Force Academy; Aviation Project; Mark Clark; John S. D. Eisenhower; Ernest A. Gross; Marine Corps; Naval History.

KORNBERG, Arthur (1918–   ) *See* Nobel Laureates.

KOUSSEVITZKY, Serge. *Discussed in* Aaron Copland; William Schuman.

KRAFT, Alice E. *See* McGraw-Hill.

KRAMER, Dale (–1966) *See* Farm Holiday Association.

KRAMER, Kenneth (1904–) *See* McGraw-Hill.

KRANTZ, Aron (1897–1974) *See* Aviation Project.

KRASNER, Lee. *See* New York's Art World.

KREMENTZ, Jill (1940–) Photo-journalist, author.
Photography background; early professional assignments, Harlem riots, Vietnam, 1965–66; children's books, text and photography; rights of photographers, copyright litigation.
75 pp. *Permission required.* 1977. Papers.

KREUGER, Ivar. *Discussed in* Joseph J. Klein; Hokan B. Steffanson.

KRIS, Ernst. *Discussed in* Heinz Hartmann; Rudolph M. Loewenstein.

KROCK, Arthur (1887–1974) Newspaperman.
NY Democratic Party, 1920's; Charles F. Murphy; NY *World,* 1923–27; NY *Times,* 1927; reporting Washington politics for NY *Times,* 1932–50: campaigns of 1932 and 1936, Brain Trust, NRA, foreign policy, preparations for war; Pearl Harbor, Yalta Conference; impressions of many political figures.
102 pp. *Permission required to cite or quote.* 1950. *Micro I.*

KROLL, Leon (1884–1974) Artist.
Family background and early education in NYC; studies in Europe; experiences exhibiting and teaching; associations with the McDowell group; technique and philosophy of painting; work as a muralist; illustrated discussion of 158 of his paintings, drawings, and murals.
259 pp. *Permission required to cite or quote.* 1957. *Micro II.* Papers.

KRULAK, Victor Harold (1913–) Marine Corps officer.
Education; early assignments, Shanghai, 1937–39, Sino-Japanese War; Aide to Gen.

Holland M. Smith; Okinawa operation and Tsingtao occupation; unification fight; Korea: Inchon landing, Chosin reservoir operation; Secretary of the General Staff, HQMC, 1951–55, Lemuel Shepherd Commandancy; Special Assistant for Counter-insurgency Matters to Secretary of Defense Robert McNamara, 1962–64; CG, Fleet Marine Force, Pacific, 1964–68; reminiscences of USMC personalities.
269 pp. *Permission required.* 1970.

KRULEWITCH, Melvin Levin (1895–1978) *See* Marine Corps.

KU KLUX KLAN *See* Will Alexander; Civil Rights in Alabama; Weyerhaeuser Timber Company.

KUH, Richard. *Discussed in* Edward I. Koch.

KUME, Ai. *See* Occupation of Japan.

KUNG, Hsiang-hsi (1881–1967) *See* Chinese Oral History.

KUNZIG, Robert Lowe (1918–) *See* Eisenhower Administration. *Micro III.*

KUPER, Theodore Fred (1886–) Lawyer.
Education, NYU Law School; early practice, NYC; oil business; Thomas Jefferson Memorial Foundation, 1923–32; acquisition of Monticello; efforts to preserve other Virginia antiquities; consultant to NYC Board of Education, 1927–43. Impressions of Fiorello La Guardia and Claude G. Bowers.
186 pp. *Permission required to cite or quote.* 1963. *Micro I.*

The 1911 insurgency in NY Legislature.
17 pp. *Permission required to cite or quote.* 1968. *Micro II.*

Creation of the Fashion Institute of Technology and Educational Foundation for the Fashion Industry.
16 pp. *Permission required to cite or quote.* 1971. *Micro II.*

KUPFERMAN, Theodore R. (1920–) Lawyer, judge.

NYC legal and political career: 1948–49 law secretary to Justice D. W. Peck, NY Supreme Court; 1943–59, legal departments of Warner Bros., NBC, Cinerama; private law practice; NY Law School professorship 1959–64; counsel to minority leader of City Council, Stanley Isaacs, 1958–62; City Councilman, 1962–65; Congressman, 1966–68; NY State Supreme Court Justice, 1969–70, associate justice Appellate Division, 1971–   ; impressions of NYC politicians, Gerald Ford.

105 pp. *Permission required to cite or quote.* 1976.

KURJACK, Dennis. *See* Independence Park.

KUSCH, Polykarp (1911–   ) Physicist.
Part I: Family background and early education; Cleveland Public Library; Case Institute and University of Illinois; research assistant, University of Minnesota, 1936; Columbia University, 1937–41; Westinghouse Electric, 1941–42; Columbia Radiation Laboratory, 1942–44; Bell Telephone Laboratories; Columbia University, from 1946; research program, head of Physics Department and Radiation Laboratory; description of receiving the Nobel Prize, 1955.

212 pp. *Permission required.* 1962.
Part II: Account of experiences as Executive Vice President for Academic Affairs and Provost of Columbia University, 1969–71.

297 pp. *Permission required.* 1972.
See also Columbia Crisis of 1968, Journalism Lectures (A *and* C) *and* Nobel Laureates.

KUZMA, Genevieve (1910–   ) *See* Continental Group.

KYLE, Wood Barbee (1915–   ) Marine Corps officer.
Education, Texas A & M, 1932–36; Shanghai, 1937–39; WW II: Tulagi-Guadalcanal, Tarawa, and Saipan operations, Command and General Staff School, Fort Leavenworth; Fleet Marine Force, Pacific, 1947–49; mobilization of reserves for Korea; Army War College; Joint Plans Branch, 1958–61; Lebanon.

226 pp. *Open.* 1969.

L

LABOR RELATIONS *See* Arthur Altmeyer; Argentina; Heber Blankenhorn; John Brophy; James Carey; Cyrus Ching; Continental Group; William H. Davis; John P. Frey; Lloyd K. Garrison; Milton Handler; Paul G. Hoffman; Nicholas Kelley; Leon H. Keyserling; Arthur Kinoy; La Follette Civil Liberties Committee; Edwin A. Lahey; Thomas C. Mann; James C. O'-Brien; Frances Perkins; Esther Peterson; Lindsay Rogers; John Steelman; Philip Taft; Ludwig Teller; Norman Thomas; Florence Thorne; Nathan Witt; Charles E. Wyzanski, Jr.
See also Unions; AFL-CIO.

LACKE, Warren A. (1909–   ) *See* Continental Group.

LACY, William Sterling Byrd (1910–   ) *See* Eisenhower Administration.

LAEMMLE, Carl. *Discussed in* Popular Arts.

LA FOLLETTE, Robert M., Jr. *Discussed in* Barbara Armstrong; Bernice Bernstein; La Follette Civil Liberties Committe.

LA FOLLETTE CIVIL LIBERTIES COMMITTEE
These interviews deal with labor and civil

liberties during the New Deal, with discussion of the roles of the NLRB and the CIO, anti-union practices in industry and agriculture, the functioning of the committee, and recollections of Senator Robert M. La Follette, Jr. (1895–1953).
Participants and pages: John J. Abt, 16; Gardner Jackson, 24; Carey McWilliams, 20; Luke Wilson, 28; Robert Wohlforth and Matthew Josephson, 75.
163 pp. *Permission required to cite or quote.* 1963.
Contributed by Jerold S. Auerbach, Wellesley, Mass.

LAGOS, Julio A. *See* Argentina.

LA GUARDIA, Fiorello H. *Discussed in* William H. Allen; George Baehr; Samuel Battle; Paxton Blair; Mrs. Walter Bunzl; Harry Carman; Ted Cott; Thomas E. Dewey; David Dressler; Genevieve B. Earle; Jonah Goldstein; Julius Isaacs; Stanley M. Isaacs; Theodore Kuper; Marie M. La Guardia; James M. Landis; Reuben A. Lazarus; Walter S. Mack, Jr.; Pearl Max; Newbold Morris; Paul O'Dwyer; William O'Dwyer; Dorothy Rosenman; Sigmund Spaeth; Francis R. Stoddard; Emily S. Warner; Paul Windels.

LA GUARDIA, Marie M. (Mrs. Fiorello H.) (1896–)
Mayor Fiorello La Guardia: some personal reminiscences.
56 pp. *Permission required to cite or quote.* 1950. *Micro I.*

LA GUARDIA, Marie M. and Newbold Morris. *See* New York Political Studies (C).

LAHEY, Edwin A. (1906–1969) Columnist.
Early days on the Chicago *Daily News;* Frank Knox; Al Capone and John Dillinger cases; work as labor specialist and relations with Philip Murray; impressions of Lee Pressman, James Carey, John L. Lewis, Robert A. Taft, and Thomas E. Dewey.
161 pp. *Permission required to cite or quote.* 1959. *Micro I.*
See also Robert A. Taft Project.

LAHM, Frank Purdy (1877–1963) *See* Henry H. Arnold Project.

LAIDLER, Harry Wellington (1884–1970) *See* Socialist Movement.

LAIRD, Allison W. *Discussed in* William L. Maxwell.

LAIRD, William Winder. *See* Longwood Gardens.

LAJTHA, Abel (1922–) *See* Hungarian Project.

LAMBERT, Robert E. (1911–) *See* Continental Group.

LAMBIE, James McClurg, Jr. (1914–) Executive.
EISENHOWER ADMINISTRATION
Eisenhower Headquarters Committee, 1952 campaign; Advertising Council; CARE; impressions of President Eisenhower and his administration.
49 pp. *Permission required to cite or quote.* 1968. *Micro III.*

LAMONT, Corliss (1902–) Author, teacher.
Childhood and education; interest in civil liberties and ACLU; conflicts with Congressional committees; passport difficulties; visits to Russia; Senator Joseph McCarthy; contempt citation; humanism.
165 pp. *Permission required.* 1960.
Discussed in Charles Poletti.

LAND, Emory Scott (1879–1971) Naval officer.
Naval Academy, athletics; early cruises; naval architecture, MIT; Bureau of Ships, Bureau of Aeronatutics; Harry Guggenheim and air research; Charles A. Lindbergh; Fleet Naval Construction, 1930–32; Chief, Bureau of Ships, 1933–37; Maritime Commission, 1937; Joseph Kennedy; Merchant Marine Academy; shipbuilding for National Defense Agency; William Knudsen; Liberty Ships; War Shipping Administration; Air Transport Association, 1946–53. Impressions of Theodore Roosevelt, Franklin D. Roosevelt, Harry Hopkins, Bernard Baruch, Jesse Jones.
227 pp. *Permission required to cite or quote.* 1963. *Micro I.*
See also Aviation Project. *Micro IV.*
Discussed in Henry Williams.

LANDIS, James McCauley (1899–1964) Lawyer, government official.
Family background; childhood and education in Japan and US; Harvard Law School; early legal writings; secretary to Justice Louis Brandeis; professor, Harvard, 1926–34; government service, 1933–37; Dean, Harvard Law School, 1937–46; later government service: Civil Defense, WWII, Civil Aeronautics Board; Middle East; government studies and reports, 1953–60; 1956 and 1960 campaigns, elections; presidential adviser. Comments on Justices Felix Frankfurter, Oliver W. Holmes, and Benjamin Cardozo; Samuel Williston, Roscoe Pound, Franklin Roosevelt, Joseph P. Kennedy, John L. Lewis, Fiorello La Guardia, King Farouk, Lord Moyne.
685 pp. *Permission required to cite or quote.* 1964. *Micro II.*

LANDON, Alfred Mossman (1887–   )
See Robert A. Taft Project.
Discussed in Raymond Baldwin; Marvin Jones; M.L. Wilson.

LANDON, George K., Jr. (1925–   ) *See* Continental Group.

LANDON, Jerrold E. (1935–   ) *See* Continental Group.

LANDSMAN, Herbert Samuel (1918–   )
See Federated Department Stores.

LANE, Alvin Huey (1895–   ) Lawyer, business executive.
EISENHOWER ADMINISTRATION
Texas delegation to 1952 Republican Convention; Republican Party in Texas.
39 pp. *Permission required to cite or quote.* 1969.
See also additional interview in Eisenhower Administration.

LANE, Burton (1912–   ) *See* Popular Arts.

LANE, Chester Tevis (1905–1958) Lawyer.
Childhood and early education; Harvard Law School; Milbank, Tweed, Hope and Webb, 1930–35; corporate trusteeship NYC; General Counsel's office of the SEC, 1935–42; drafting Securities Act; relationship between SEC General Counsel, Attor-

ney General, and Solicitor General; Transamerica Corporation cases; special assistant to the Attorney General, 1942–45; war policies unit, War Division, Justice Department; Solicitor General's office; legal consultant, Army-Navy Liquidation Commission; Lend-Lease administrator and deputy foreign liquidation commissioner, 1946–47.
869 pp. *Permission required to cite or quote.* 1951. *Micro I.*

LANE, Franklin K. *Discussed in* Horace M. Albright.

LANE, W. B. (1898–   ) and Roy Gardner. *See* Benedum and the Oil Industry.

LANG, Chester Henry (1893–1961) Corporation official.
RADIO PIONEERS
Early life and education; WWI; traveling auditor for General Electric, 1919; WGY, Schnectady; memorable broadcasts; impressions of David Sarnoff, Martin P. Rice, Owen D. Young, Harry S. Truman.
29 pp. *Open.* 1951.

LANGDELL, C. C. *Discussed in* Felix Frankfurter.

LANGDON, Harry. *Discussed in* Popular Arts.

LANGDON, Jesse (1881–1975) Rough Rider.
THEODORE ROOSEVELT ASSOCIATION
Enlistment in the Rough Riders; San Antonio, Tampa; crossing from Florida to Cuba; landing at Daiquiri; Kettle Hill; San Juan Hill; postwar experiences; Philippine action; Storey-Langdon Foundation.
67 pp. *Permission required to cite or quote.* 1970.

LANGMUIR, Alexander Duncan (1910–   ) *See* Health Sciences.

LANGMUIR, Irving. *Discussed in* Albert W. Hull.

LANING, Clair. *See* Holger Cahill.

LANSDALE, Edward G. *See* Air Force Academy.

LANSING, Robert. *Discussed in* Frederic R. Coudert; Eleanor L. Dulles.

LARGE, Arlen. *See* Social Security. *Micro III.*

LARKIN, Wilson B. (1905–   ) *See* Continental Group.

LARMON, Sigurd Stanton (1891–   ) *See* Eisenhower Administration. *Micro III.*

LARRABEE, Eric (1922–   ) Editor, writer.
CARNEGIE CORPORATION
Carnegie Corporation's African studies program; music and art in West Africa; American studies program; American Shelf Project; European Unity Conference in Italy; International Education Act; foundation policies.
89 pp. *Permission required.* 1967.

LARSEN, Harold. *See* World Bank.

LARSON, Arthur (1910–   ) *See* Social Security. *Micro III.*

LARSON, August (1904–   ) *See* Marine Corps.

LARSON, Roy Frank (1893–1973) *See* Independence Park.

LASKER, Albert Davis (1880–1952) Advertising executive.
Early adventures as a newspaper reporter; career in advertising; George Washington Hill and others; reorganization of professional baseball, 1920; Republican politics, 1918–30; USSB.
180 pp. *Open.* 1950. Papers.

LASKER, Bruno (1880–1965) Social researcher.
Early life in Germany, England, and US; University Settlement, Manchester, England; social work in England and US from 1916; Seebohm Rowntree and the Rowntree Trust; "The Inquiry," WWI; Henry Street Settlement, 1916; *The Survey* and *The Survey Graphic;* Service Bureau for International Relations; IPR; Southeast Asia Institute; travels in Southeast Asia; 50 years of political, social, and charitable endeavor.

543 pp. *Permission required to cite or quote.* 1956. *Micro I.* Papers.

LASKER, Mary (Mrs. Albert D.) (1900–   ) Promoter of medical research, philanthropist.
Part I: Family background, University of Wisconsin, Radcliffe; interest in fine arts; European travel, study at Oxford; art dealer; Hollywood dress pattern business; interest in and promotion of Planned Parenthood Federation, other voluntary agencies in the field of health; fund-raising: American Cancer Society, American Heart Association; attempts to secure adequate appropriations to implement existing legislation for medical research; US Public Health Service: National Science Foundation; formation and development of national institutes for cancer, heart, arthritis, mental health, neurological diseases, blindness; aid to medical education; interest in psychoanalysis; medical research in NY; large scale clinical trials through Veterans Administration; activities of Lasker Foundation to promote health through medical research; health insurance; HIP in NY; Presidential Health Commission; support of performing arts; art collection. Impressions of many statesmen, legislators, and medical and scientific pioneers.
1,157 pp. *Closed until 25 years after death.* 1965.

Part II: A continuing account, bringing up to date the major activities described in Part I: federal aid to medical research, development of regional medical centers, Cancer, Heart and Stroke Commission, NIH appropriations; beautification: plans for National Horticultural Park and Garden, activities in NY, District of Columbia, and elsewhere; visits to Johnson ranch; Medal of Freedom; health and medical research, from 1968: national health insurance, family planning, alcoholism, passage of 1971 cancer bill; Kennedy Center for the Performing Arts; restoration of Versailles.
679 pp. *Closed until 25 years after death.* 1972–   . Papers.

LASSWELL, Alva Bryan (1905–   ) *See* Marine Corps.

LATHROP, John Howland (1880–1967) Clergyman.
Ministry in Massachusetts, California, and Brooklyn; commission to investigate minority rights in Rumania; travels in India; Unitarian Service Missions to Czechoslovakia, Hungary, Yugoslavia, and the Middle East.
330 pp. *Permission required to cite or quote.* 1953. *Micro I.*

LATIMER, Mary Lee. *See* China Missionaries.

LATIMER, Murray Webb (1901–) *See* Social Security.
Discussed in J. Douglas Brown.

LATIN AMERICA *See* Argentina; Claude Bowers; Spruille Braden; Hilarion N. Branch; Ellis O. Briggs; Fidel Castro; Daniel Cosio Villegas; W.W. Cumberland; Harold Dodds; Phanor J. Eder; Milton S. Eisenhower; Elton C. Fax; Paul Fejos; Albert Giesecke; Alan Gregg; J. George Harrar; Robert C. Hill; John K. Jenney; Joseph J. Jova; Luis Machado; Thomas C. Mann; William O'Dwyer; Nelson A. Rockefeller; George Rublee; Roy R. Rubottom, Jr.; Edward L. Tinker; Henry A. Wallace; John C. White.

LaTOUCHE, Burford (1928–) *See* Continental Group.

LATTIMORE, Owen. *Discussed in* Joseph Ballantine; Thomas I. Emerson.

LAUREL, Stanley. *Discussed in* Albert E. Sutherland.

LAURENCE, William Leonard (1888–1977) Science editor.
Part I: Early years in Czarist Russia and Germany; dreams of flying; arrival in US, 1905, and first jobs; experience at Harvard as student and tutor, 1908–17; WWI experiences.
148 pp. *Permission required to cite or quote.* 1954. *Micro I.*

Part II: Experiences in NYC journalism: NY *World*, 1926–30; science reporter, NY *Times*, 1930–64; notable stories covered, including discovery of neutron, new ele-

ments, Harvard 300th Anniversary Conference; coverage of development of atomic energy: Manhattan Project, tests, dropping of bomb; Pulitzer Prizes, medical reporting.
395 pp. *Permission required to cite or quote.* 1964. *Micro I.*

LAURENS, Jean. *Discussed in* Max Weber.

LAW *See* Sidney Alderman; George Alger; Thurman Arnold; Adolf Berle; Bernice Bernstein; Paxton Blair; Albert Blumenthal; Henry Breckinridge; Herbert Brownell; Harvey Bundy; Charles C. Burlingham; Melville H. Cane; Thomas G. Chamberlain; Candler Cobb; Frederic Coudert; James F. Curtis; John W. Davis; Gordon Dean; Thomas E. Dewey; Clifford J. Durr; Phanor J. Eder; Thomas I. Emerson; Harold P. Fabian; Charles Fahy; Osmond K. Fraenkel;
Walter Gellhorn; Edward S. Greenbaum; Jack Greenberg; Ernest A. Gross; Alger Hiss; Robert H. Jackson; Benjamin A. Javits Project; Philip C. Jessup; Nicholas Kelley; Leon H. Keyserling; Arthur Kinoy; Theodore R. Kupferman; Chester T. Lane; Edward A. McCabe; Langdon P. Marvin; Thurgood Marshall; Gerald D. Morgan; David A. Morse; James M. Nabrit III; New York Bar; John Lord O'Brian; Paul O'Dwyer;
Robert P. Patterson Project; Ferdinand Pecora; Thomas L. Perkins; Lee Pressman; Joseph M. Proskauer Project; Victor Rabinowitz; Max J. Rubin; George Rublee; Martin Saxe; Eustace Seligman; Morris L. Strauss; Laurence A. Tanzer; Hobart Taylor, Jr.; Telford Taylor; Ludwig Teller; Thomas D. Thacher; Charles H. Tuttle; Harrison Tweed; William H. Wadhams; Robert F. Wagner; Allen Wardwell; Charles Warren; Herbert Wechsler; Nathan Witt; John E.F. Wood.
See also Judiciary; Law—Education.

LAW—EDUCATION *See* John Harlan Amen; Miguel de Capriles; Thomas I. Emerson; Jerome Frank; Felix Frankfurter; Walter Gellhorn; Arthur Kinoy; James M. Landis; Harold R. Medina.

LAWRENCE, D.H. *Discussed in* Ben W. Huebsch.

LAWRENCE, Don. *See* Weyerhaeuser Timber Company.

LAWRENCE, Ernest. *Discussed in* Warren Weaver.

LAWRENCE, Gertrude. *Discussed in* Richard Rodgers.

LAWRENCE, T.E. *Discussed in* James F. Curtis.

LAWRENCE, W. C. *See* Jackson Hole Preserve.

LAWRENCE, William Howard (1916–1972) Journalist.
EISENHOWER ADMINISTRATION
President Eisenhower and the news media; impressions of Eisenhower, Richard Nixon, Sherman Adams, Harold Talbot, and others.
37 pp. *Permission required to cite or quote.* 1967.

LAWRENCE, William Van Duser. *Discussed in* Esther Raushenbush.

LAZARSFELD, Paul Felix (1901–1976) Sociologist.
Vienna during and after WWI; instructor in social psychology, University of Vienna, 1927; empirical studies; Rockefeller Foundation traveling fellowship in US, 1933–35; University of Newark Research Center, 1935; Director, Rockefeller Princeton Radio Project, 1937; Columbia, 1940; Bureau of Applied Social Research, 1941; market research; impressions of Hadley Cantril, Frank Stanton, Samuel Stouffer, Robert Lynd, Luther Fry.
377 pp. *Permission required.* 1962.
Discussed in Frank Stanton.

LAZARUS, Celia Rosenthal (Mrs. Fred, Jr.) *See* Federated Department Stores.

LAZARUS, Charles. *See* Federated Department Stores.

LAZARUS, Eleanor and Margaret. *See* Federated Department Stores.

LAZARUS, Fred, Jr. (1884–1973) Merchandising executive.
FEDERATED DEPARTMENT STORES
Family background; F. & R. Lazarus Co., Shillito's; philosophy of retailing and merchandising; development of Federated Department Stores; Filene's; Committee on Economic Development; Ohio Retail Merchants' Council; American Retail Federation; US Chamber of Commerce; detailed discussion of operation of a department store: personnel, customer service, selling, layout, design of fixtures, credit, stock, service departments, discount houses, special sales, night and Sunday shopping, computerization, area research, resources, retail accounting and applied statistical procedures, business forecasting, revolving credit, unionization, family financing; charitable and philanthropic undertakings; Retail Research Association; Associated Merchandising; Red Cross, American Jewish Committee.
1,039 pp. *Permission required.* 1965.

LAZARUS, Fred III (1912–   ) *See* Federated Department Stores.

LAZARUS, Irma Mendelson (Mrs. Fred III) *See* Federated Department Stores.

LAZARUS, Jeffrey L. (1894–   ) *See* Federated Department Stores.

LAZARUS, Maurice (1915–   ) *See* Federated Department Stores.

LAZARUS, Paul N., Jr. (1913–   ) *See* Popular Arts.

LAZARUS, Ralph (1914–   ) *See* Federated Department Stores.

LAZARUS, Mrs. Ralph. *See* Federated Department Stores.

LAZARUS, Reuben Avis (1895–1971) Lawyer.
NYC and State politics including the administrations of Mayors James Walker, Fiorello La Guardia, and William O'Dwyer, 1926–49; NY State legislature; the Liberal Party; rent control; election of 1950; the Senate crime investigation.
502 pp. *Permission required to cite or quote.* 1951. *Micro II.*
See also New York Political Studies (C).

LAZARUS, Robert (1890–1973) *See* Federated Department Stores.

LAZARUS, Simon. *See* Federated Department Stores.

LEACOCK, Richard. *See* Robert J. Flaherty Project.

LEAGUE OF NATIONS *See* Malcolm Davis; League of Nations Project; Lewis L. Lorwin; Herbert Louis May; Geoffrey Parsons; James W. Wadsworth.

LEAGUE OF NATIONS PROJECT
These recollections by former officers of the League of Nations were recorded through the cooperation of the Carnegie Endowment for International Peace. The interviews, obtained in Geneva, describe the early days of organizing the League Secretariat and record many international problems and negotiations.

Participants and pages: Thanassis Aghnides, 506 *(permission required);* Pablo de Azcarate, 80; Pablo de Azcarate with Edouard de Haller, and W. Van Asch Van Wijck, 156; Branko Lukac, 124.
866 pp. *Permission required to cite or quote except as noted.* 1966–69.

LEAGUE OF WOMEN VOTERS *See* Lavinia Engle; Edna Gellhorn; Percy M. Lee; Anna L. Strauss.

LEAHY, William. *Discussed in* James Fife; Thomas C. Hart.

LEAR, William Powell (1902–1978) *See* Aviation Project. *Micro II.*

LEARNED, William S. *Discussed in* Carnegie Corporation.

LEARY, Fairfax. *Discussed in* James Fife.

LEBOR, John Francis (1906–   ) *See* Federated Department Stores.

LeBOUTILLIER, Oliver C. *See* Air Force Academy.

LE CORBUSIER, Charles-Edouard (1887–1965) Architect, city planner.
Architecture Project
The evolution from radiocentric cites of exchange to linear cities of the industrial age.
8 pp. *Open.* 1961.
Discussed in Robert Greenstein.

LeCRON, James D. (1885–1961) Government official.
Childhood and education; Des Moines *Register & Tribune,* 1913–33; US Department of Agriculture, 1934–40; the "purge"; election of 1940; Agricultural Marketing Service, 1940–42; Institute of Inter-American Affairs, 1942–43, Henry A. Wallace, 1913–48.
181 pp. *Open.* 1953.

LEE, Carl. *See* James B. Duke Project.

LEE, Don. *Discussed in* William S. Paley.

LEE, Frances Glessner. *Discussed in* Percy M. Lee.

LEE, Joseph Bracken (1899–   ) Government official.
Eisenhower Administration
Governor of Utah; Mayor of Salt Lake City; 1952 Republican Convention; impressions of Dwight D. Eisenhower, Robert A. Taft, and others; Republican Party; John Birch Society.
70 pp. *Permission required to cite or quote.* 1967. *Micro III.*

LEE, Lila (1905–1973) *See* Popular Arts.

LEE, Percy Maxim (Mrs. John Glessner Lee) (1906–   ) Former President, League of Women Voters.
League of Women Voters activities in Connecticut, election to National Board, 1942; OPA support, 1941; refugee children; Carrie Chapman Catt Memorial Foundation, later Overseas Education Fund of LWV and Institute for Foreign Visitors; relationship of local, state and national Leagues; President, LWV, 1950–58: McCarthyism and Freedom Agenda, policy on Brown decision (1954), support for UN, relations with State Department; member, College Grants Advisory Committee of Ford Foundation; water management efforts in Con-

necticut, 1955; reminiscences of family members, including Hiram Percy Maxim; Frances Glessner Lee, police work, "Nutshell Studies"; impressions of Anna Lord Strauss and other LWV leaders.

559 pp. *Permission required to cite or quote.* 1973. *Micro IV.*

LEE, Robert E. (1912–) *See* Federal Communications Commission.

LEE, Robert M. *See* Air Force Academy.

LEE, Stephen D. *Discussed in* Cully A. Cobb.

LEE, Tsung-Dao (1926–) *See* Nobel Laureates.

LEE, Warren Isbell (1874–1955) Congressman.
Brooklyn Republican politics, 1900–22.
20 pp. *Open.* 1950.

LEE, William L. (1903–1976) *See* Eisenhower Administration.

LEFFINGWELL, Russell C. *Discussed in* Carnegie Corporation.

LE HAND, Marguerite (Missy) *Discussed in* Marion Dickerman; Anna Roosevelt Halsted.

LEHMAN, Edith (Mrs. Herbert) *Discussed in* Sir Robert Jackson.

LEHMAN, Hartley. *Discussed in* Theresa Goell.

LEHMAN, Herbert Henry (1878–1963) Governor, Senator.
HERBERT H. LEHMAN PROJECT
Family background, boyhood in NYC; Williams College; Lehman Brothers; textile business; WWI, Army and Navy Quartermaster Corps; Lillian Wald, UJA, ORT; Alfred E. Smith; election in 1928 as Lieutenant Governor under Franklin D. Roosevelt; Governorship of NY, 1932–42: Prohibition and Repeal, crime investigation, public housing, labor and social welfare, relations with Tammany Hall, significant legislation, gubernatorial campaigns, Geoghan trial, Druckman case. Director Gen-

eral, UNRRA and post WWII problems. NY Reform movement; election to US Senate, 1949, and fight against McCarthyism; impressions of many public figures. This memoir has a full topical index.

785 pp. *Permission required to cite or quote.* 1961. *Micro I.*
See also New York Political Studies (C).
Discussed in Edward Costikyan; Ben Davidson; William H. Davis; David Dressler; Justin N. Feldman; Jonah Goldstein; Sir Robert Jackson; Philip C. Jessup; Katie Louchheim; Charles Poletti.

HERBERT H. LEHMAN PROJECT
Herbert Lehman's own memoir, described above, is supplemented by a series of interviews with persons who were closely associated with him through various stages of his career.
Participants and pages: Helen Altschul, 13; Emanuel Celler, 3; Paul Douglas, 22; Julius Edelstein, 28; James A. Farley, 44; Carolin Flexner, 67; Hubert Humphrey, 25; Estes Kefauver, 12; George Meany, 13; Henry Morgenthau, Jr., 8; Wayne Morse, 29; Charles Poletti, 32; Eleanor Roosevelt, 17; Anna M. Rosenberg, 14; Samuel I. Rosenman, 23; Marc Tanenbaum, 38; Roy Wilkins, 26.

414 pp. *Permission required to cite or quote.* 1959.
Some memoirs are available in microform; consult individual entries.

LEHMAN, Maxwell. *See* New York Political Studies (B).

LEHMAN, Robert A. (1914–) *See* Continental Group.

LEHMAN-HAUPT, Hellmut (1903–) *See* Friends of the Columbia Libraries.

LEITER, Leroy W. (1913–) *See* Continental Group.

LEITHEAD, Barry T. (1907–1974) Business executive.
EISENHOWER ADMINISTRATION
Fund raising in the 1952 and 1956 campaigns; personal associations with President Eisenhower.
52 pp. *Permission required to cite or quote.* 1968.

LELAND, Waldo Gifford (1879–1966) Historian.
AHA and *AHR;* state and regional historical societies; Public Archives Commission; International Committee of Historical Sciences; origin of the ACLS and of the *DAB.*
63 pp. *Permission required to cite or quote.* 1955. *Micro I.*

LE MAISTRE, George. *See* Civil Rights in Alabama.

LEMANN, Lucy Benjamin. *See* Robert J. Flaherty Project.

LEMAY, Curtis E. (1906–   ) *See* Air Force Academy.

LEMKE, Al. *See* Vietnam Veterans.

LEMMON, Jack (1925–   ) *See* Popular Arts.

LEMNITZER, Lyman L. (1899–   ) *See* Eisenhower Administration. *Micro IV.*

L'ENGLE, Madeleine (Mrs. Hugh Franklin) (1918–   ) Author.
Childhood, education, family; theological studies and religious influences; writing career, the inception of various of her books.
69 pp. *Permission required.* 1976.

LENHART, Robert (1913–   ) *See* Federated Department Stores.

LENROOT, Katharine Fredrica (1891–   ) Social worker.
SOCIAL SECURITY
Family background, childhood in Wisconsin, University of Wisconsin, 1912; Wisconsin Industrial Commission, 1913–14; US Children's Bureau from 1915: studies on infant mortality and child labor, early Mother's Aid laws, development of Social Security Act, Bureau's relations with states and Congress; Reorganization Act, 1945; Bureau under Social Security Administration. Impressions of Emma Lundberg, Edwin Witte, Frances Perkins, Harry Hopkins, Eleanor Roosevelt, and others.
173 pp. *Permission required to cite or quote.* 1965. *Micro III.*
Discussed in Charles I. Schottland.

LEONARD, John W. (1890–1974). *See* Eisenhower Administration.

LEOPOLD, Richard W. (1912–   ) *See* American Historians.

LERNER, Daniel (1917–   ) *See* International Negotiations.

LERNER, Gerda (1920–   ) Women's historian, educator.
Education in Vienna, emigration to US; legitimizing women's history as a scholarly discipline: reflections on past progress and present status.
In process.

LERNER, Max (1902–   ) *See* Journalism Lectures (C).

LESLIE, Edgar. *See* Popular Arts.

LESSER, Allen. *See* Social Security. *Micro IV.*

LESSER, Leonard (1898–1974) *See* Social Security. *Micro IV.*

LESSER, Sol (1890–   ) Motion picture executive.
San Francisco earthquake and fire, 1906; early days in motion picture industry: film exchange and distribution, dealer in feature films, financing, production, laboratory, ownership of a studio; foreign markets; theater circuits; consultant; anecdotes of many industry personalities; relationship of producer and author: Thornton Wilder and *Our Town;* Edgar Rice Burroughs and *Tarzan* series; seminar at University of Southern California.
154 pp. *Permission required to cite or quote.* 1970. *Micro II.*
Contributed by Theodore Fred Kuper, Los Angeles.

LESSUEUR, Meridal. *See* Alexandra Kollontai Project.

LESTER, Robert MacDonald (1889–1969) Foundation executive.
CARNEGIE CORPORATION
Detailed account of operations, personnel policies, relationships of Carnegie Corporation, 1926–54. Impressions of Andrew

Carnegie, Walter A. Jessup, Devereux Josephs, Nicholas Murray Butler, Frederick Keppel, and many other prominent educators and public figures.
872 pp. *Permission required.* 1967. Papers.
Discussed in Roberta Capers.

LEUCHTENBURG, William Edward (1922–   ) *See* American Historians.

LEVANT, Oscar. *Discussed in* Dan Golenpaul.

LEVENSALER, Lewis. *See* Mining Engineers.

LEVENSTEIN, Aaron J. (1910–   ) *See* Socialist Movement.

LEVENTHAL, Harold (1915–   ) *See* Stanley Reed.

LEVINE, Jack (1915–   ) Artist.
Childhood and early training; life of an artist; philosophy of art; painting techniques; the creative process; illustrated commentary on some of his own work; etchings, drawings; abstract art.
150 pp. *Permission required to cite or quote.* 1956. *Micro I.*

LEVINE, Manuel. *See* Social Security. *Micro IV.*

LEVINGSTON, Roberto Marcelo. *See* Argentina.

LEVY, David. *Discussed in* Lawrence C. Kolb.

LEWIS, Edwin Owen (1879–   ) *See* Independence Park.

LEWIS, Fredrica Crane. *See* Hart Crane Project.

LEWIS, Freeman (1908–1976) and Leon Shimkin. Publishers.
The founding of Pocket Books, Inc., and observations on the publishing trade, literacy, and economics of retailing paperbound books.
63 pp. *Permission required to cite or quote.* 1955. *Micro II.*

LEWIS, Howard G. (1913–   ) *See* Continental Group.

LEWIS, John. Civil rights leader.
SNCC, 1960–66: voter registration campaigns, relations with Justice Department and other civil rights organizations; Mississippi delegation, Democratic Convention, 1964; March on Washington; Selma; role of white sympathizers during 1960's; Martin Luther King, Jr.
38 pp. *Permission required.* 1970.
Contributed by Steven F. Lawson, NYC.

LEWIS, John L. *Discussed in* Dave Beck; John Brophy; William H. Davis; John P. Frey; Albert J. Hayes; Gardner Jackson; Edwin A. Lahey; James M. Landis; Lee Pressman; Boris B. Shishkin; M. Hedley Stone.

LEWIS, Katherine Handy (Mrs. Homer) *See* Popular Arts.

LEWIS, Kathryn (1911–   ) *See* Adlai E. Stevenson Project.

LEWIS, Mort. Author.
ALLAN NEVINS PROJECT
Recollections of Allan Nevins, especially after 1960; anecdotes of Nevins at the Huntington Library and at the Pen Club; methods of work; associates in California.
110 pp. *Permission required.* 1970.

LEWIS, Orme (1903–   ). *See* Eisenhower Administration.

LEWIS, Robert (1909–   ) *See* Popular Arts. *Micro II.*

LEWIS, Sinclair. *Discussed in* Melville H. Cane; Helen Macy.

LEWIS, W. W. *See* John Robert Gregg Project.

LEYDA, Jay. *See* Robert J. Flaherty Project.

LI Han-hun. *See* Chinese Oral History. *Microform available.*

LI Huang (1895–   ) *See* Chinese Oral History. *Microform available.*

LI Shu-hua (1890–   ) *See* Chinese Oral History. *Microform available.*

LI Tsung-jen (1890–   ) *See* Chinese Oral History.

LIBBY, Willard Frank (1908–   ) *See* Nobel Laureates.

LIBERAL PARTY OF NEW YORK STATE *See* Ben Davidson; Donald Harrington; Reuben A. Lazarus.

LIBERMAN, Alex. *See* New York's Art World.

LIBRARIES *See* Richard Couper; Luther H. Evans; Friends of the Columbia Libraries; Jean B. Hutson; May Massee; Isadore G. Mudge; Rare Books; Sheba Skirball; Harold Spivacke; Maurice F. Tauber; Constance M. Winchell.

LICHTENFELD, Leon. *See* Radio Pioneers.

LICHTENSTEIN, Roy (1923–   ) and Leo Castelli. *See* New York's Art World.

LICHTENSTEIN, Zalman J. *Discussed in* Ray Henry; Elizabeth Wickenden.

LIE, Trygve. *Discussed in* Thanassis Aghnides; Andrew W. Cordier; Ernest A. Gross.

LIEBERSON, Goddard (1911–1977) Composer, business executive.
AMERICAN CULTURAL LEADERS
Early life, Seattle; Eastman School of Music; Columbia Recording Corporation and Columbia Records, 1940–66; US recording industry.
   95 pp. *Permission required.* 1966.
Discussed in Frank Stanton.

LIEBOWITZ, Samuel. *Discussed in* Solomon A. Klein.

LIEUALLEN, James. *See* Vietnam Veterans.

LILE, R. A. *See* Eisenhower Administration.

LIND, John. *Discussed in* Association for the Aid of Crippled Children.

LINDBECK, John (1915–1971) *See* International Negotiations.

LINDBERG, Jaffet. *See* Mining Engineers.

LINDBERGH, Anne. *Discussed in* Marjorie Nicolson.

LINDBERGH, Charles A. *Discussed in* Aviation Project; William Benton; Emory S. Land; Marjorie Nicolson; Eugene E. Wilson.

LINDEMAN, Eduardo. *Discussed in* Roger N. Baldwin.

LINDEMANN, Frederick (Lord Cherwell). *Discussed in* Sir Robert Watson-Watt.

LINDSAY, John V. (1921–   ) *See* Journalism Lectures.
Discussed in Richard Aurelio; Ben Davidson; August Heckscher; Edward I. Koch; I. D. Robbins; Robert F. Wagner.

LINDSAY, Samuel McCune (–1959) *See* Theodore Roosevelt Association.

LINDSAY, Vachel. *Discussed in* Frank Ernest Hill; Ellen C. Masters; John Wheelock.

LINK, Arthur S. (1920–   ) *See* American Historians.

LINOWITZ, Sol Myron (1913–   ) *See* Ethnic Groups and American Foreign Policy.

LIPMANN, Fritz Albert (1899–   ) *See* Nobel Laureates.

LIPPE, Just. *See* Alexandra Kollontai Project.

LIPPMANN, Walter (1889–1974) Editor, author.
Early years in journalism; Treaty of Versailles; Harvard; the Fabian Socialists; outbreak of WWI; psychological warfare; politics and journalism in the 1920's; Franklin D. Roosevelt's candidacy for President;

outbreak of WWII; US-Britain-Russia and the peace; books.

265 pp. *Permission required to cite or quote.* 1956. *Micro II.* Papers: typescript of diary of Mr. Lippmann's journeys to Europe and India, 1948 and 1949 (169 pp. *Permission required*).
See also Journalism Lectures.
Discussed in Ralph Albertson; Alvin Johnson; Allan Nevins.

LIPSHUTZ, Robert. *See* Ethnic Groups and American Foreign Policy.

LITTAUER, Kenneth (–1968) *See* Aviation Project. *Micro II.*

LITTLE, Donald G. (1893–   ) Business executive.
RADIO PIONEERS
Family background, education; amateur radio work in Kalamazoo, Michigan; US Signal Corps; radio engineering at Westinghouse; work with Dr. Frank Conrad; broadcast of 1920 election; station KDKA; short wave and FM broadcasting; studio techniques.
101 pp. *Open.* 1951. Papers.

LITVAK, Michael Anatole (1902–1974) *See* Popular Arts.

LIU, J. Heng (1890–1961) *See* Chinese Oral History.

LIU, Sidney. *See* International Negotiations.

LLOYD, Glen Alfred (1895–1975) and Mrs. Lloyd. *See* Adlai E. Stevenson Project. *Micro III.*

LLOYD, Harold Clayton (1893–1971) *See* Popular Arts.
Discussed in Albert E. Sutherland.

LLOYD, R. McAllister (1898–   ) Foundation executive.
TIAA-CREF PROJECT
Education; early banking career; appointment as President, TIAA, 1945; Carnegie Investment Office activities, development of new investment policies; development of CREF; Harvard participation in TIAA program; association with Henry James, Devereux Josephs.

In process.
See also Carnegie Corporation.

LLOYD, Trevor (1906–   ) Geographer.
CARNEGIE CORPORATION
Founding of the Canadian Association for Adult Education; Arctic Institute of North America at McGill University. Impressions of Whitney Shepardson and Morse Cartwright.
45 pp. *Permission required.* 1968.

LOBOS, Roberto. *See* Argentina.

LOBROVICH, William J. (1901–   ) *See* Continental Group.

LOCKWOOD, Charles A. (1890–1967) Naval officer.
Youth in Missouri, Naval Academy, early cruises; Asiatic Fleet, submarine duty and command; Philippines, Command of 1st Asiatic Submarine Division, 1917; Japan, 1918; New London submarine base; captured German submarines; interwar training cruises and submarine experiences; fleet operations; Naval Mission, Rio de Janeiro, 1929; *Squalus* rescue operations; Naval Attaché, London, 1941; Commander Submarines, Pacific Fleet, 1943; wolfpack techniques, sonar and radar, periscope photography, rescue operations; postwar career; nuclear propulsion, development of atomic submarine.
720 pp. *Permission required to cite or quote.* 1965.
Discussed in James Fife.

LODGE, Henry Cabot (1850–1924) *Discussed in* Claude M. Fuess.

LODGE, Henry Cabot (1902–   ) *See* International Negotiations.
Discussed in Charles D. Cook; Luther H. Evans.

LODGE, John Davis (1903–   ) Government official.
EISENHOWER ADMINISTRATION
WWII experiences; member of Congress; Governor of Connecticut; 1952 Republican Convention; Ambassador to Spain; impressions of Gen. Francisco Franco.
195 pp. *Permission required to cite or quote.* 1969.

LOEB, Harold. *See* Ford Maddox Ford.

LOEB, Robert. *Discussed in* Dana W. Atchley; Jules Stahl.

LOEMKER, Dorothy Rowden. *See* Carnegie Corporation.

LOENING, Grover (1888–1976) Aircraft engineer.
Recollections of Wilbur Wright; early days in aviation.
   43 pp. *Permission required to cite or quote.* 1967. *Contributed by E. W. Robischon, Washington, D. C.*
See also Air Force Academy.

LOEW, Marcus. *Discussed in* Eddie Dowling.

LOEWENSTEIN, Rudolph Maurice (1898–1976) Psychoanalyst.
PSYCHOANALYTIC MOVEMENT
Childhood; studies at the Universities of Zurich, Berlin, Paris; Berlin Psychoanalytic Institute, 1923–25; analysis by Dr. Hans Sachs; founding of Paris Psychoanalytic Society, 1926; collaboration with Princess Marie Bonaparte in translating Freud's five case histories into French, 1935; New York Psychoanalytic Institute since 1943; work with Drs. Heinz Hartmann and Ernst Kris; theory and technique of psychoanalysis.
   149 pp. *Open.* 1963. Papers.
Discussed in Heinz Hartmann.

LOFTUS, John Joseph. *See* China Missionaries.

LOHF, Kenneth A. *See* Rare Books (A).

LOMAX, Alan. *Discussed in* Harold Spivacke.

LOMAX, John. *Discussed in* Harold Spivacke.

LONG, E. B. *See* Civil War Centennial *and* Allan Nevins Project.

LONG, Esmond Ray (1890–   ) *See* Health Sciences.

LONG, George S. *Discussed in* Forest History Society; Weyerhaeuser Timber Company.

LONG, George S., Jr. *See* Weyerhaeuser Timber Company.

LONG, Huey. *Discussed in* Gordon Browning; Burton K. Wheeler.

LONG, Mrs. Robert J. *See* Eisenhower Administration.

LONGWOOD GARDENS
Recollections of friends and associates of Pierre S. du Pont (1870–1954) concerning his development of and association with Longwood Gardens, Kennett Square, Pennsylvania.
Participants and pages: Lammot du Pont Copeland, 41; Alletta Laird Downs, 23; Crawford H. Greenewalt, 30; Jared Ingersoll, 7; William W. Laird, 24; Rosa McDonald, 30; Sophie du Pont May, 29; Virginia Morgan, Brooke Gilpin, Charles Mason, 32; Wilhelmina du Pont Ross, 28; Edgar Scott, 8.
   252 pp. *Permission required.* 1974–75.
Underwritten by Longwood Gardens, Inc.

LONGWORTH, Alice Lee Roosevelt (1884–   ) *See* Theodore Roosevelt Association.

LOOMIS, Francis Butler, Jr. (1903–   )
See Marine Corps.

LOOMIS, Milton Early (1887–1973) Educator.
NYU School of Education and Washington Square College, 1916–39; Associate Commissioner of Education, NY State, 1939–40.
   63 pp. *Permission required to cite or quote.* 1966. *Micro II.*

LOOS, Anita (Mrs. John Emerson) (1893–   ) *See* Popular Arts.

LOPEZ MATEOS, Adolfo. *Discussed in* Robert C. Hill.

LORD, Henry Gardner (1865–1961) *See* McGraw-Hill.

LORD, Mary Pillsbury (Mrs. Oswald B.) (1904–1978) Government official.
EISENHOWER ADMINISTRATION
Citizens for Eisenhower; NATO; years with UN; refugee problems; Planned Parenthood Association; travels; political and social conditions in Africa, Middle East; experiences in Iron Curtain countries; Atlantic Institute; Ethiopia uprising of 1960; student riots in Paris; impressions of prominent women.
428 pp. *Permission required to cite or quote.* 1969. *Micro IV.*

LORD, Philip H. *Discussed in* Richard Gordon.

LORIMER, George Horace. *Discussed in* Bruce and Beatrice Gould.

LORING, Eugene. *Discussed in* Aaron Copland.

LORWIN, Lewis L. (1883–1970) Economist.
Professor of economics, University of Montana, 1918; mine tax study and resignation, 1920; survey of Russia, 1921–23; Chicago *Daily News;* Brookings Institution, 1925–35; National Planning Association; Franklin D. Roosevelt administration; chief economist, ILO, 1935; ILO and League of Nations, 1935–39; BEW, 1943–45; IPR; recollections of John Winant.
479 pp. *Permission required.* 1961.

LOUCHHEIM, Katie Scofield (1903–   ) Political activist.
ADLAI E. STEVENSON PROJECT
Office of Foreign Relief and Rehabilitation, 1942; creation of UNRRA; Atlantic City and Montreal conferences; tour of DP camps in Europe; Democratic National Convention, 1948; Democratic National Committeewoman, 1952; Director of Women's Activities, Democratic Party, 1953; Adlai Stevenson presidential campaigns 1952, 1956; impressions of Adlai Stevenson, Herbert H. Lehman, Daisy Harriman.
198 pp. *Permission required to cite or quote.* 1973. *Micro IV.*

LOUCKHEIM, Jerome. *Discussed in* Howard Barlow.

LOVE, Edgar J. (1905–   ) *See* Radio Pioneers.

LOVEJOY, Arthur. *Discussed in* Marjorie Nicolson.

LOVELACE, William R. II (1907–1965) *See* Aviation Project. *Micro II.*

LOVEMAN, Amy (1881–1955) *See* Book-of-the-Month Club. *Micro IV.*

LOVEMAN, Samuel A. (1885–1976) *See* Hart Crane Project.

LOVETT, Robert Abercrombie (1895–   ) *See* Henry H. Arnold Project, Eisenhower Administration *and* International Negotiations.

LOWDERMILK, Walter Clay (1888–1974) Conservationist.
Childhood and education; Forest Service, 1915–17; Lumberjack Regiment, 1917–20; Forest Service, Missoula, Montana, 1920–22; China, 1922–27: studies of erosion, Nanking incident; Soil Erosion Service, Washington, 1933–35; Soil Conservation Service, 1935–37; consultant on soil, forest, and water conservation and reclamation in China, Israel, Africa, and US.
684 pp. *Permission required to cite or quote.* 1968.
Acquired from the Regional Oral History Office, University of California, Berkeley.

LOWELL, A. Lawrence. *Discussed in* Quincy Howe.

LOWELL, Amy. *Discussed in* William S. Braithwaite.

LOWELL, Ralph (1890–1978) Foundation executive.
History of Lowell Institute; trustee, 1938 on; public lectures, University Extension Courses; Lowell Institute School at MIT; educational radio station; Cooperative Broadcasting Council, 1946; National Educational Television and Ford Foundation.
98 pp. *Permission required to cite or quote.* 1964. *Micro I.*

LOWELL, Robert (1917–   ) *See* Ford Maddox Ford.

LOWRY, W. McNeil (1913–   ) Foundation executive.
AMERICAN CULTURAL LEADERS
Childhood and education; service in OWI, domestic branch, 1942–43; political correspondent, Washington, 1947–52; career as program director and vice president, humanities and the arts, Ford Foundation, 1957–1967.
296 pp. *Permission required.* 1967.

LOY, Myrna (1905–   ) *See* Popular Arts.

LUBELL, Samuel (1911–   ) *See* Journalism Lectures.

LUBIN, Isador (1896–1978) Economist.
Early life; Missouri University and Thorstein Veblen; statistical branch of the WIB in WWI; the Brookings Institution; Bureau of Labor Statistics, 1939–44; other wartime federal posts, impressions of associates, New Deal legislation; UNESCO.
168 pp. *Permission required to cite or quote.* 1957. *Micro I.*
See also Social Security. *Micro III.*
Discussed in Ewan Clague; John Roy Steelman.

LUBITSCH, Ernst. *Discussed in* Popular Arts.

LUCE, Clare Boothe (Mrs. Henry R.) (1903–   ) Government official.
EISENHOWER ADMINISTRATION
Impressions of President Eisenhower; 1952 campaign; foreign service; Ambassador to Italy; Trieste; Ambassador to Brazil; Republican Party; John Foster Dulles.
108 pp. *Permission required to cite or quote.* 1968. *Micro IV.*

LUCE, Henry R. *Discussed in* Raymond Baldwin; Jonathan W. Daniels; Max Gissen; Eric Hodgins; Thomas S. Matthews.

LUCIANO, Charles (Lucky). *Discussed in* Thomas E. Dewey.

LUCKEY, Robert Burneston (1905–1974) Marine Corps officer.
Education, University of Maryland, 1923–27; expeditionary duty, Nicaragua, 1929; early assignments, artillery training; US Embassy Guard, Peking, 1936–38; aide to

Gen. James Breckinridge, 1938–39; WWII: Guadalcanal, Cape Gloucester, and Okinawa operations, occupation of Tsingtao; USMC in interwar period; postwar assignments: Marine Barracks, Washington, D.C., 1949–51; USMC Schools, Quantico; Hogaboom Board, 1953–54; Fleet Marine Force, Atlantic, 1954–55; amphibious warfare operations; USMC Recruit Depots, Parris Island, 1957–59; 3d Marine Division, 1959–60; Far Eastern situation; Camp Lejeune, 1960–61; CG, Fleet Marine Force, Atlantic, 1961–63; contingency planning.
228 pp. *Permission required.* 1969.

LUENING, Otto (1900–   ) Composer.
Family background; early life in Madison, Wisconsin; musical education in Munich, 1912–17; composing, performing and acting in Europe during WWI; Chicago, 1920–25; executive director, opera department, Eastman School of Music, 1925–28; teaching at University of Arizona; Yaddo; organization of American Composers Alliance; Barnard College Music Department, 1944–47; professor of music, Columbia University, 1949–   ; electronic workshop at Columbia, development of electronic music; meetings of National Institute of Arts and Letters; impressions of Aaron Copland, Leonard Bernstein, Randall Thompson, John Cage, and others.
607 pp. *Permission required.* 1976.
Discussed in Vladimir Ussachevsky.

LUHAN, Mabel Dodge. *Discussed in* Carl Van Vechten.

LUKAC, Branko. League of Nations official.
LEAGUE OF NATIONS
Role of Secretary General and leaders in League of Nations before WWII; Manchuria, Germany's entrance; relations with Switzerland as host country; Russo-Finnish War, fall of France; detailed analysis of use of sanctions in Ethiopia conflict, 1935; impressions of Sir Eric Drummond and Joseph Avenol. The memoir is in French.
124 pp. *Permission required to cite or quote.* 1966.

LUMBARD, Joseph Edward, Jr. (1901–   ) Judge.

NEW YORK BAR
NYC childhood; Harvard College and Law School, 1925; special Assistant Attorney General NY State during Queens sewer scandal and prosecution of Maurice Connelly, 1936; Drukman murder; cases from career as attorney and justice in NY State courts, private defense counsel, and Chief Judge, US Court of Appeals, 2nd district counsel, 1959– ; comparisons and impressions of US legal studies, practice, systems, 1930's–70's.
331 pp. *Permission required to cite or quote.* 1977.

LUMBER INDUSTRY *See* Continental Group; Forest History Society; Carl H. Henrikson, Jr.; Weyerhaeuser Timber Company.

LUMET, Sidney (1924–) *See* Popular Arts. *Micro IV.*

LUMUMBA, Patrice. *Discussed in* James W. Barco.

LUNDBERG, Emma. *Discussed in* Katharine Lenroot.

LUNTZ, Jerome (1923–) *See* McGraw-Hill.

LUSHBAUGH, Robert E. and James C. Thomas. *See* James C. Thomas, Air Force Academy.

LUSK, William (1901–1978) Corporation executive.
Tiffany and Lusk family background; education, Groton, and Yale; Tiffany and Co., 1837–1955: expansion of manufacturing and retail trade, personnel, effects of Depression, closing of Paris office, 1955 stock sale and reorganization under Walter Hoving, upgrading of various departments, franchises for sale of Tiffany silver, publicity innovations, synthetic gems, buying trips to Europe after WWII, memorable sales; *The Tiffany Touch.* Impressions of many figures in Tiffany's history including Louis Moore, Walter Hoving.
395 pp. *Closed until March 5, 1998.* 1972.

LUTER, John (1919–) *See* Eisenhower Administration. *Micro III.*

LUTES, Leroy (1890–) *See* Henry H. Arnold Project.

LUXFORD, Ansel Frank (1911–) Lawyer.
WORLD BANK
Early experience with Bank; Bretton Woods Conference planning; relationship with other financial organizations; John Maynard Keynes' attitude toward Bank; Savannah conference; internal organization.
61 pp. *Permission required to cite or quote.* 1961.

LYNCH, John J. *See* New York Political Studies (A).

LYNCH, Warren (1915–1977) *See* Book-of-the-Month Club. *Micro IV.*

LYND, Helen M. (1896–) Educator, writer.
Early life, education, family background; married life, details of working with her husband, Robert Lynd, on *Middletown;* her children; teaching at Sarah Lawrence; McCarthy hearings.
290 pp. *Permission required.* 1973.

LYND, Robert. *Discussed in* Paul F. Lazarsfeld; Helen Lynd.

LYNN, Edward J. (1918–) *See* Continental Group.

LYONS, Eugene J. *See* Eisenhower Administration.

LYONS, Ruth. *See* Radio Pioneers.

LYSENKO, Trofim. *Discussed in* Leslie C. Dunn.

M

McADAMS, Charles V. (1892–   ). *See* Eisenhower Administration.

McADOO, William G. *Discussed in* Hilarion N. Branch.

McALISTER, Gayle. *See* Flying Tigers.

McANENY, George (1869–1953) Banker, civic leader.
NYC history; subway construction; rewriting the city charter; zoning law; Negro education; historical monuments; NY World's Fair, 1939–40.
102 pp. *Permission required to cite or quote. 1949. Micro I.*

MacARTHUR, Douglas. *Discussed in* Eleanor Arnold; Joseph Ballantine; John J. Ballentine; Hugh Borton; Robert B. Carney; Leo Cherne; Lucius D. Clay; Jarred V. Crabb; James Fife; Thomas C. Hart; Harry W. Hill; Thomas C. Kinkaid; Occupation of Japan; Kenneth C. Royall; Lemuel C. Shepherd, Jr.; H. Alexander Smith; Oliver P. Smith; William A. Sullivan.

McAULIFFE, Anthony C. (1898–1975) Army officer.
Childhood and education; West Point; early Army training; Command and General Staff School, War College; General Staff, Research and Development, Service of Supply; OSRD; origins of "dukw" and jeep; WWII: 101st Airborne Division, 1942; gliders; training in US and Europe; Normandy; Arnhem; Battle of the Bulge, Bastogne and "Nuts" reply to demand for surrender, Korea; atomic tests at Bikini; General Staff, 1946; Japan, 1948; Chief of Chemical Corps, G-1; Army integration;

Deputy Chief of Staff, 1951–53; 7th Army, Commander US Forces in Europe; American Cyanamid, 1956–63.
267 pp. *Open.* 1963.

McCABE, Edward Aeneas (1917–   ) Lawyer.
EISENHOWER ADMINISTRATION
Early career; general counsel, House Committee on Education and Labor, 1953–55; associate counsel, later administrative assistant to the President, 1956–61; coordinating interests of executive and legislative branches; Eisenhower and legislation, 1958–60; Landrum-Griffin Act; transition period, 1960; campaigns of 1960 and 1964; Sherman Adams and Bernard Goldfine; impressions of the President and White House staff.
171 pp. *Permission required to cite or quote.* 1967. *Micro III.*

McCALLUM, James H. *See* China Missionaries.

McCAMMAN, Dorothy. *See* Social Security.

McCANDLESS, Alex U. (–1954) *See* Benedum and the Oil Industry.

McCANN, Kevin (1904–   ) Author.
EISENHOWER ADMINISTRATION
Impressions of Dwight Eisenhower, Sherman Adams; evaluation of the influence of White House aides, staff, Cabinet, friends, and other associates on President Eisenhower.
158 pp. *Permission required to cite or quote.* 1966. *Micro III.*

McCANN, Richard H. *See* Robert P. Patterson Project.

McCARDLE, Carl Wesley (1904–1972) Government official.
EISENHOWER ADMINISTRATION
Journalism background; Assistant Secretary of State for Public Affairs, 1953–57; impressions of John Foster Dulles and President Eisenhower; SEATO; Senator Joseph McCarthy and State Department.
48 pp. *Permission required to cite or quote.* 1967. *Micro III.*

McCARTHY, Eugene. *Discussed in* Edward Costikyan.

McCARTHY, James P. *See* Air Force Academy.

McCARTHY, Joseph R. *Discussed in* Kenneth Bainbridge; Raymond Baldwin; Stephen Benedict; William Benton; Edward L. Bernays; Herbert Brownell; Prescott Bush; Leo Cherne; Milton S. Eisenhower; Ralph E. Flanders; Arthur A. Kimball; William F. Knowland; Corliss Lamont; Carl W. McCardle; Carl McGowan; Norman Ramsey; Arthur V. Watkins; Alexander Wiley.

McCARTHY, Mary. *Discussed in* Roger W. Straus.

McCARTHY HEARINGS *See* Internal Security Investigations.

McCARTY, Nancy Jensen (1940–   ). *See* Eisenhower Administration.

McCLELLAN, George. *Discussed in* Lawrence Veiller.

McCLELLAND, George F. *Discussed in* Radio Pioneers.

McCLINTIC, Guthrie. *Discussed in* Sol Jacobson.

McCLINTOCK, Charles Arbuthnot (1883–1968) *See* Benedum and the Oil Industry.

McCLOY, John Jay (1895–   ) *See* Eisenhower Administration, *Micro III,*

and International Negotiations.
Discussed in World Bank.

McCLURE, Robert A. *Discussed in* F. Peterson Jessup.

McCLURE, S. S. *Discussed in* Burton J. Hendrick.

McCOMAS, Gail. *See* Air Force Academy.

McCONE, John A. (1902–   ) *See* Eisenhower Administration.
Discussed in Paul F. Foster.

McCONNELL, John P. (1908–   ) *See* Air Force Academy.

McCONNELL, Thomas Raymond (1901–   ) *See* Carnegie Corporation.

McCOOEY, John. *Discussed in* New York Political Studies.

McCORD, Robert. *See* American Cultural Leaders.

McCORMICK, Kenneth D.   Editor.
Childhood, college life; writing, Doubleday bookstores; promotion manager, Garden City; editorial work; WWII, Office of Flying Safety; recollections of authors, literary popularity; scouting authors; nuisance suits; titles, illustrations, jacket design; screenplays; unsolicited manuscripts; Freedom to Read Committee.
379 pp. *Permission required.* 1975.

McCORMICK, Sr. Mary Colmcille. *See* China Missionaries.

McCOSKER, M. Joseph. *See* Independence Park.

McCOY, Alvin. *See* Eisenhower Administration.

McCRAY, Ossie, Jr. *See* Vietnam Veterans.

McCREA, Joel (1905–   ) *See* Popular Arts.

McCRORY, James. *See* Eisenhower Administration.

McCUE, Constance. *See* Carnegie Corporation.

McCULLERS, Carson. *Discussed in* Dorothy Baker.

McDERMOTT, Robert Francis (1920–) Air Force officer.
AIR FORCE ACADEMY
Experiences as vice dean, later dean of faculty, USAF Academy, 1954–68; with detailed discussions of his relations with the superintendents, commandants of cadets, and faculty serving at the Academy during this period.
207 pp. *Permission required.* 1972.

McDONALD, George. *Discussed in* Hokan B. Steffanson.

MacDONALD, Jeanette (1907–1965) *See* Popular Arts.

McDONALD, (Mrs.) Rosa Packard Laird Hayward. *See* Longwood Gardens.

McDONALD, Stewart. *Discussed in* Miles Colean.

McDONNELL, John F. *See* Eisenhower Administration.

McDOUGAL, Edward Dickinson, Jr. (1896–) *See* Adlai E. Stevenson Project.

McDOUGAL, Katherine (Mrs. Edward) *See* Adlai E. Stevenson Project. *Micro III.*

McDOWALL, Roddy (1928–) *See* Popular Arts.

McDOWELL, David. *See* James Agee.

McELROY, Neil Hoosier (1904–1972) Business executive.
EISENHOWER ADMINISTRATION
White House Conference on Education, 1954–56; Secretary of Defense, 1957–59; Senate Preparedness Subcommittee; missiles and satellites; 1958 Defense Reorganization Bill.
88 pp. *Permission required to cite or quote.* 1967. *Micro III.*

McEVOY, Nan. *See* Adlai E. Stevenson Project.

McEWEN, Marjorie. *See* Kirkland College.

McEWEN, Robert W. *Discussed in* Kirkland College.

McFARLAND, Emily (Mrs. Ross). *See* Association for the Aid of Crippled Children.

McGHEE, George C. (1912–) *See* International Negotiations.

McGOUGH, Charles J. *See* Weyerhaeuser Timber Company.

McGOWAN, Carl (1911–) Judge.
ADLAI E. STEVENSON PROJECT
Youth in Chicago, WWII naval service; Stevenson as Governor of Illinois: divorce, recruitment of staff, relationship with Democratic Party, patronage system; 1952 campaign; Elks Club group; Stevenson's speeches; press relations; 1956 campaign; UN. Recollections of John F. Kennedy, Hubert Humphrey, Joseph McCarthy, Richard Nixon, Richard Daley, and others.
252 pp. *Permission required to cite or quote.* 1969. *Micro IV.*

McGRATH, Earl James (1902–) Educator.
Childhood and education; teaching and administration, University of Buffalo, 1928–45; War Manpower Commission, 1942; education program for naval personnel; trimester college program; teacher quality and qualifications; US Commissioner of Education, 1949–53.
145 pp. *Permission required to cite or quote.* 1963. *Micro II.*

CARNEGIE CORPORATION
Relations with the Carnegie Corporation, 1933–67; University of Buffalo; American Council on Education, 1938; University of Kansas City, 1953–56; Institute for Higher Education, TC, 1956–67: selection of staff, fiscal problems, research programs, study of Negro colleges. Impressions of John Gardner and other Corporation officials.
107 pp. *Permission required.* 1967.

McGRAW, Donald C. (1897–1974) *See* McGraw-Hill.

McGRAW, Donald C., Jr. (1925–) *See* McGraw-Hill.

McGRAW, Mrs. Donald C. (1900–) *See* McGraw-Hill.

McGRAW, Harold Whittlesey, Jr. (1918–) *See* McGraw-Hill.

McGRAW, James A. (1886–1973) *See* McGraw-Hill.

McGRAW, James H. *Discussed in* McGraw-Hill.

McGRAW, John L. (1930–) *See* McGraw-Hill.

McGRAW-HILL

The development of McGraw-Hill, Inc. and its part in educational, industrial, and technical development in the US and abroad are traced in a series of interviews beginning with the lives of James H. McGraw (1860–1948) and John A. Hill (1858–1912). Associates recall the career of each as a publisher of trade and technical magazines. Others deal with the merger of the book publishing activities of the two companies as the McGraw-Hill Book Co., 1909, and the purchase of the Hill interest in trade magazines by McGraw to form the McGraw-Hill Publishing Company in 1916. Interviews continue the story of the company's expansion through the acquisition of the F. W. Dodge Corporation, 1961, which brought the firm into the field of information services, the purchase of such periodicals as *House & Home* and *Modern Packaging,* and the acquisition of the Webster Publishing Co.

Editors of McGraw-Hill trade, educational, and business publications discuss editorial and circulation policy, standards of responsibility in dealing with readers and advertisers, and new functions and fields for the company's publications and instructional materials.

Special phases include: changes in the writing and publishing of college textbooks, textbooks for courses in vocational education; elementary and high school materials, visual education aids, programmed books, and text films; Whittlesey House and trade book publishing, paperback books, technical writing, training manuals for the US armed forces, and international aspects of book publishing such as translation, licensing, and international editions of textbooks. Interviewees give background on such McGraw publications as the *Catholic Encyclopedia,* the *Encyclopedia of World Art,* and *Science and Technology* as well as more recent corporate developments. The project is brought up to date periodically.

Participants and pages: Russell Anderson, 47; Fred Annett, 65; Edward C. Aswell, 49; Moses Baker, 23; Walter Bara, 23; Robert Beard, 38; William K. Beard, 35; Curtis G. Benjamin, 78; James Blackburn, 33; C. Presby Bliss, 43; Robert F. Boger, 23; Nelson Bond, 26; Edward Booher, 84; Waldo Bowman, 35; Harold Veatch Bozell, 56; Mason Britton, 56; Emerson Brown, 17; Herbert Buhrow, 32; John P. Burke, 27; William Buxman, 70; John Callaham, 43; Lillian Charlton, 25; Willard Townshend Chevalier, 129; Maud Clark, 27; Carl Coash, 51; Fred Herbert Colvin, 21; Robert Craig, 24; John Crossman, 29; Walter Crowder, 59; Basil Dandison, 35; Frank Dickman, 29; Frank Egner, 68; Frederick Morris Feiker, 45; Burnham Finney, 23; Shelton Fisher, 45; Helene Frye, 24;

Woodrow Wilson Garey, 84; William Gartner, 35; James L. Gilbert, 39; Elizabeth Gile, 26; Thomas Grogan, 39; Virgil B. Guthrie, 41; Hugh Handsfield, 28; Albert Hauptli, 103; Keith Henney, 22; S.T. Henry, 61; Robert Hotz, 42; Dexter Keezer, 19; Hugh Kelly, 27; Hugh Joseph Kelly, 62; Sidney Dale Kirkpatrick, 31; Alvin Knoerr, 100; Edgar Kobak, 120; Alice E. Kraft, 45; Kenneth Kramer, 30; Henry Gardner Lord, 71; Jerome Luntz, 41; Donald C. McGraw, 27; Mrs. D.C. McGraw, 34; Harold W. McGraw, 29; James A. McGraw, 47; Alice McMullin, 52; George MacMurray, 23; Howard Mateer, 51; Edward J. Mehren, 53; Paul Montgomery, 25; Arch Morris, 36; L.C. Morrow, 75; Malcolm Muir, 25; Matthew Murphy, 43;

Carl Nagel, 29; Bela Reiter, 46; Margaret Richards, 32; A.J. Rosenberg, 36; Richard Rowden, 31; Louis Rowley, 74; George Sears, 15; H.W. Shaw, 14; Willard T. Shoener, 39; Robert Slaughter, 39; Ralph Smith, 24; John C. Spurr, 32; Alfred W. Staehle, 101; Philip William Swaine, 32; John Taylor, 27; George Clinton Tenney, 41; James Stacy Thompson, 80; Angelo Venezian, 58; William Weidig, 33; John E. Welle, 32; Joseph Vandenburg Wight, 58; John Wilhelm, 89; Lawrence Wray, 40; Norman Wynkoop, 45.
4,170 pp. *Permission required.* 1956.

Paul Abbott, 20; Curtis G. Benjamin, 51; Edward E. Booher, 57; Edwin Shelton Fisher, 69; Lawrence Keith Goodrich, 22; Hugh J. Kelly, 29; Donald C. McGraw, 7; Harold W. McGraw, Jr., 39; Wallace Traendly, 30; Harry Waddell, 30; John Wilhelm, 66.
420 pp. *Permission required.* 1964.

Joseph H. Allen, 85; Edward Booher, 65; Daniel F. Crowley, 50; Joseph Dionne, 52; John Emery, 35; Brenton Harries, 50; A.W. Kitchens, 45; Donald C. McGraw, Jr., 29; Harold W. McGraw, Jr., 47; John L. McGraw, 15; Fred Stahl, 16; Wallace Traendly, 36; Norman Walt, 67; Theodore Weber, 46.
638 pp. *Permission required.* 1973. *Underwritten by McGraw-Hill, Inc.* 1956–

MacGREGOR, Frank (1897–1971) Publisher.
Family background and education, Nova Scotia and New England; Harvard; head of college department at Harper & Bros. from 1924; reminiscences of authors and publishers.
374 pp. *Permission required to cite or quote.* 1966. *Micro III.*

McGREGOR, James Murray.
Impressions of Tracy McGregor.
86 pp. *Open.* 1954.

McGREGOR, Tracy. *Discussed in* James M. McGregor; William J. Norton.

McGUIRE, Edward Perkins (1904–   ) *See* Eisenhower Administration.

McHARG, Ormsby (1871–n.d.) Lawyer, politician.
Frontier life in Dakota Territory; North Dakota politics, 1899–1900; Congressional personalities, 1900–12; New Mexico land fraud litigation, 1907–08; Republican national politics, 1908–12.
126 pp. *Permission required to cite or quote.* 1951. *Micro I.*

McHUGH, James F. (1894–1969) *See* Popular Arts.

McINTOSH, Millicent Carey (1898–   ) Educator.
Family, youth, and education; Bryn Mawr School; Bryn Mawr College; Newnham College, Cambridge; career at Brearley School; changes in curriculum and methodology; trends in progressive education; comments on women's education; graduate school, Johns Hopkins, 1926–30; Barnard College, president; development of religion and education programs at Barnard; attitudes toward advanced placement; social work and community activities; reflections on changes in manners and morals and the generation gap; impressions of prominent educators.
695 pp. *Permission required.* 1966.
See also Kirkland College.

McINTYRE, Alfred. *Discussed in* D. Angus Cameron

MacIVER, Robert Morrison (1882–1970) Sociologist.
Education in Scotland and at Oxford; teaching political science and sociology at Aberdeen University, 1907–11; University of Toronto, 1915–27; Barnard College, 1927–36; Columbia University, 1929–50; Russell Sage Foundation; "The Inquiry"; youth studies for NYC; report on Jewish community relations agencies.
99 pp. *Permission required to cite or quote.* 1962. *Micro IV.*

McJUNKINS, Orren R. (1907–   ) *See* Continental Group.

McKEAN, Josephine. *See* Occupation of Japan. *Micro III.*

McKELDIN, Theodore Roosevelt (1900–1974) Government official.
EISENHOWER ADMINISTRATION
Nominating speech for Eisenhower, 1952 convention; correspondence with Eisenhower; Mayor of Baltimore; Governor of Maryland.
78 pp. *Permission required to cite or quote.* 1968. *Micro III.*

McKELLAR, Kenneth. *Discussed in* Gordon Browning.

MacKENNA, Kenneth (1899–) *See* Popular Arts.

MacKENZIE, Donald. *See* Forest History Society.

McKINLEY, William. *Discussed in* Hobart S. Bird.

McKINNEY, Ernest Rice (1886–) Organizer.
Development of the National Unemployed League, Depression days; organizing steel workers for CIO, and as a member of the Workers' Socialist Party; upgrading Negroes in industry; Working Men's Welfare Committees; Workers Party of the United States (Trotskyist Group) and its relationship to Communist and Socialist Parties; resignation from Workers Party.
116 pp. *Permission required to cite or quote.* 1961. *Micro II.*

McKITTRICK, Thomas Harrington (1889–1970) Banker.
Childhood and education, Hackley School, Tarrytown, and Harvard; impressions of friends and teachers.
43 pp. *Permission required to cite or quote.* 1952.

McLAIN, George. *Discussed in* Charles Odell.

McLAUGHLIN, Frederick Charles (1905–) Educator.
Part I: Childhood and education in Midwest; TC; US Army Air Force; Superintendent of Schools, NYC, hiring problems; Queens College case; Junior Red Cross Director; student volunteer workers in city hospitals; head of Public Education Association: activities, relationship with Board of Education and other organizations, public events. Impressions of Mayors William O'Dwyer, Vincent Impellitteri, and Robert F. Wagner; and Superintendents William Jansen, John Theobald, and Calvin Gross; comments on desegregation, busing, community relations in school issues.
531 pp. *Permission required to cite or quote.* 1964. *Micro II.*

Part II: Young Plan to establish state university; Sviridoff Human Relations Study; issue of minimum days for school attendance; School 201 incident; Griffith Study; More Effective Schools program; Bundy report on decentralization; Ocean Hill-Brownsville project; teachers strike; impressions of personalities connected with NYC public education.
630 pp. *Permission required to cite or quote.* 1966. *Micro II.*

McLAUGHLIN, Kathleen. Journalist.
WOMEN JOURNALISTS
Atchison Daily Globe; Chicago Tribune, 1924; *New York Times* reporting on Eleanor Roosevelt; war and post-war correspondent, 1945–52; UN coverage for National Catholic News Service, 1970.
44 pp. *Open.* 1974.

McLAUGHLIN, Thomas (1900–) *See* Continental Group.

McLAURIN, Benjamin. Labor organizer.
Childhood and education, Florida; Edward Water College; labor school at University of Wisconsin, Brookwood Labor College; Pullman Company, organization of Brotherhood of Sleeping Car Porters; Railway Labor Act amendment; A. Philip Randolph; salaries, tips and pensions; FEPC; American Negro Labor Council; life in Harlem; International Ladies Auxiliary; company unions, AFL-CIO relationships; American Labor Party; Morris Hillquit; Urban League, NAACP; organizing in the South; March on Washington, 1941.
353 pp. *Permission required to cite or quote.* 1960. *Micro I.*

MacLEISH, Archibald. *Discussed in* Luther H. Evans.

McLENDON, Leighton (1915–   ) *See* Continental Group.

McLOUGHLIN, Donald. *See* Mining Engineers.

MacMAHON, Aline (1899–   ) *See* Popular Arts.

McMATH, Sidney Sanders (1912–   ) *See* Eisenhower Administration. *Micro III.*

McMILLAN, Edwin Mattison (1907–   ) *See* Nobel Laureates.

McMULLIN, Alice (1902–   ) *See* McGraw-Hill.

MacMURRAY, George (1881–1961) *See* McGraw-Hill.

McMURRIN, Sterling. *Discussed in* Francis A.J. Ianni.

McNAIR, W. K. *See* Weyerhaeuser Timber Company.

McNAMARA, James. *Discussed in* John P. Frey.

McNAMARA, Patrick. *Discussed in* Harold Sheppard; Irwin Wolkstein.

McNAMARA, Robert. *Discussed in* Victor Krulak; William Reidy; Margaret Slaymaker.

McNARY, Charles. *Discussed in* James A. Farley.

McNERNEY, Walter James (1925–   ) *See* Social Security. *Micro III.*

McNUTT, Paul. *Discussed in* Jack B. Tate.

McPEAK, William. *Discussed in* Association for the Aid of Crippled Children.

McPHEE, Henry Roemer, Jr. (1925–   ) *See* Eisenhower Administration.

McPHERSON, Aimee Semple. *Discussed in* Herbert C. Hoover.

McPHERSON, Robert M. (1897–   ) *See* Continental Group.

McQUAID, Kay. *See* Adlai E. Stevenson Project.

McQUEEN, John Crawford (1899–   ) *See* Marine Corps.

McREYNOLDS, David (1929–   ) *See* Socialist Movement.

MacVEAGH, Franklin. *Discussed in* James F. Curtis.

McWILLIAMS, Carey (1905–   ) *See* La Follette Civil Liberties Committee.

MAAS, Carl. *See* Robert J. Flaherty Project.

MAASS, Richard. *See* Ethnic Groups and American Foreign Policy.

MACARTNEY, R. R. *See* Weyerhaeuser Timber Company.

MACHADO, Luis (1899–   ) Diplomat.
WORLD BANK
Bretton Woods; early years of Bank; loan policies; Latin American relations.
35 pp. *Permission required to cite or quote.* 1961.

MACK, Walter Staunton, Jr. (1895–   ) Executive.
Republican politics in NYC, 15th Assembly District; state senatorial campaign, 1932; election fraud investigation, 1933; Fusion Committee for election of Fiorello La Guardia.
74 pp. *Permission required to cite or quote.* 1950. *Micro I.*

MACREADY, John A. *See* Aviation Project. *Micro II.*

MACY, George. *Discussed in* Helen Macy.

MACY, Helen (1904–1978) Publishing executive.
Life and career of her husband, George Macy (1900–1956): Columbia College 1921, Macy Macius Publishing Co., Limited Editions Club books, illustrators, typographers; travels for Limited Editions

Club; social life in NYC; other publishing ventures; Heritage Club; Reader's Club; impressions of John Dreyfus, Sinclair Lewis, Alec Guinness.

605 pp. *Permission required to cite or quote.* 1974.

MADDEN, Joseph Warren (1890–1972) Judge.
Family and rural life; Freeport years; education and teaching; NLRB; Roscoe Pound and the administrative process; US Court of Claims; legal division of the military government of Germany.

170 pp. *Permission required to cite or quote.* 1957. *Micro II.*

MADIGAN, Michael J. (1894–   ) *See* Robert P. Patterson Project.

MAGGI, Juan. *See* Argentina.

MAGINNIS, Harry. *See* Robert A. Taft Project.

MAGINNIS, Patricia. Social activist.
WOMEN'S HISTORY AND POPULATION ISSUES
Experiences in WACs; studies at San Jose State; petitioning for Knox Bill; public education efforts; founding, activities of Society for Humane Abortion; abortion referral service; politics of abortion laws; the "San Francisco Nine" Eunice Shriver Conference; fight against San Francisco Police Code; establishment of free pre- and post-abortion care clinic; formation of National Association for Repeal of Abortion Laws.

162 pp. *Permission required to cite or quote.* 1975.

MAGNES, Judah. *Discussed in* Bernard G. Richards.

MAGNUSON, Paul Budd (1884–1970) and Mrs. Magnuson (–1968) *See* Adlai E. Stevenson Project.

MAHLER, Margaret. Psychoanalyst.
PSYCHOANALYTIC MOVEMENT
Youth, education in Hungary and Germany; work with von Pirquet and Moll Clinics, Vienna; undergoing analysis; association with second generation psychoanalysts; acceptance in Vienna Psy-

choanalytic Institute, 1933; Rorschach studies; establishment of first psychoanalytic child guidance clinic, 1933; Nazi oppression, escape to NYC; work with NY Psychiatric Institute; child development, analysis and psychosis studies.

116 pp. *Permission required to cite or quote; certain pages closed.* 1974.

MAHONEY, Jeremiah T. (1878–1970) Lawyer.
Education; NYC and State affairs: Board of Education, Banking Commission, Commission of Accounts, Democratic Party, Court of General Sessions of the Supreme Court; impressions of prominent NY politicians.

198 pp. *Permission required to cite or quote.* 1949. *Micro IV.*

MAHONEY, Margaret. *See* Carnegie Corporation.

MAILER, Norman. *Discussed in* D. Angus Cameron.

MALACCORTO, Ernesto. *See* Argentina.

MALAMUD, Bernard. *Discussed in* Roger W. Straus.

MALCOLM X (Malcolm Little) (1925–1965) Black nationalist.
Description of police attack on mosque in Los Angeles. Radio program produced by WBAI, NY.

9 pp. *Open.* 1962.
See also Journalism Lectures.
Discussed in Kenneth Clark.

MALHERBE, Ernst G. *See* Carnegie Corporation.

MALKAMES, Don. *See* Popular Arts.

MALLORY, Leslie. *See* Weyerhaeuser Timber Company.

MALONE, Dumas (1892–   ) Historian.
Editing the *DAB;* impressions of Allen Johnson and others.

46 pp. *Permission required to cite or quote.* 1954. *Micro I.*

MAMOULIAN, Rouben (1897–   ) Stage and motion picture director.

POPULAR ARTS
Director in London, 1919; directing opera in Rochester, NY; interviews with George Eastman; Theatre Guild in NYC; films: *Applause, Queen Christina, Becky Sharp;* stage productions of *Porgy and Bess* and *Carousel;* move from major studios to more individualized production units; impressions of Eugene O'Neill, Greta Garbo.
115 pp. *Closed during lifetime.* 1958.

MANATOS, Mike N. *See* Social Security.

MANHEIM, Sylvan (1897–   ) *See* Mt. Sinai Hospital. *Micro II.*

MANION, Clarence (1896–   ). *See* Eisenhower Administration.

MANKIEWICZ, Joseph Leo (1909–   ) *See* Popular Arts.

MANN, Delbert (1920–   ) *See* Popular Arts. *Micro II.*

MANN, Thomas. *Discussed in* D. Angus Cameron; Alfred A. Knopf.

MANN, Thomas Clifton (1912–   ) Government official.
EISENHOWER ADMINISTRATION
Diplomatic service: Greece, 1953; Guatemala, 1955; El Salvador, 1955–57; Mexico, 1961–63; Assistant Secretary of State for economic affairs, 1957–60; Latin American affairs during Eisenhower administration; foreign aid; Fidel Castro; impressions of President Eisenhower.
60 pp. *Permission required.* 1968.
See additional interview in Eisenhower Administration.

MANNES, Marya (1904–   ) *See* Journalism Lectures (C).

MANNING, Helen Herron Taft (1891–   ) *See* Robert A. Taft Project.

MANNING, Stanley Rutter (1891–   ) *See* Radio Pioneers.

MANSEAU, Benjamin. *Discussed in* William A. Sullivan.

MANSFIELD, Katherine. *Discussed in* Alfred A. Knopf.

MANSHIP, Paul (1885–1966) Sculptor.
Family background and youth; art education; study in Europe; professional career.
71 pp. *Permission required to cite or quote.* 1956. *Micro II.*

MAO Tse-Tung. *Discussed in* Walter S. Robertson; Frank W. Rounds, Jr.

MARA, Tim. *Discussed in* Eddie Dowling.

MARBURY, William Luke (1901–   ) *See* Robert P. Patterson Project.

MARCANTONIO, Vito (1902–1954) *See* New York Political Studies (C). *Discussed in* Paul O'Dwyer.

MARCUS, Morris M. (1891–   )
Iran oil leases, 1952–53 and negotiations with Mohammed Mossadegh.
43 pp. *Closed during lifetime.* 1953.

MARCUS, Sarah (1894–   ) *See* Women's History and Population Issues.

MARGOLIES, Joseph A.   Bookseller.
Rhine School; career at Brentano's, 1913–51; anecdotes of NYC publishers and bookstores.
38 pp. *Permission required to cite or quote.* 1971.

MARGUEIRAT, Raul. *See* Argentina.

MARINE CORPS
This series of memoirs by retired Marines, begun in 1966, is a continuing program of the Historical Branch of the US Marine Corps. Together the interviews provide a picture of the development of the Marine Corps in the twentieth century. Personal experiences and anecdotes highlight events of WWI, duty in China and the Caribbean, the development of amphibious warfare in WWII, Marine aviation, the postwar unification struggle, and Korea. An example of material of special interest is the series of interviews with Marine Navajo code talkers conducted in 1971 in Window Rock, Arizona.

Participants and pages: Chester R. Allen, 383; Charles L. Banks, 47; Robert O. Bare, 141; William F. Battell, 306; Fred D. Beans, 119; Sidney Bedoni, 13; John Benally, 32; James P. Berkeley, 481; Ion M. Bethel, 115 *(permission required to cite or quote);* Wilfred Billey, 13; Robert Blake, 117 *(permission required to cite or quote);* Paul Blatchford, 27; Thomas E. Bourke, 44; Alpha L. Bowser, 434 *(permission required to cite or quote);* William O. Brice, 96; Wilburt S. Brown, 314; William W. Buchanan, 115; Joseph C. Burger, 377; Henry W. Buse, Jr. *(in process);*

Clifton B. Cates, 254; George H. Cloud, 115; John P. Condon, 171; Albert D. Cooley, 32; Otto T. Cox, 99; Edward A. Craig, 201; Frank C. Croft, 167 *(permission required);* Donald Curtis, 117; Thomas J. Cushman, 31; Marion L. Dawson, 140; Karl S. Day, 86; Harold O. Deakin, 101 *(permission required to cite or quote);* Pedro del Valle, 245 *(permission required to cite or quote);* Lester A. Dessez, 255; James P.S. Devereux, 208; Edward C. Dyer, 293 *(permission required to cite or quote);* Thomas G. Ennis, 141; Graves B. Erskine, 573; Walter G. Farrell, 846 *(permission required);* Lewis J. Fields, 289;

George F. Good, Jr., 141; Carl Gorman, 3; Samuel B. Griffith II, 205 *(permission required);* John N. Hart, 192; Charles H. Hayes, 239 *(permission required to cite or quote);* Leo D. Hermle, 94; Robert E. Hogaboom, 357 *(permission required to cite or quote);* Bankson T. Holcomb, Jr., 86; Samuel S. Jack, 80; Louis R. Jones, 163; Russell N. Jordahl, 202; Frederick J. Karch, 93; Jimmy King, Sr., 36; Victor H. Krulak, 269 *(permission required);* Melvin L. Krulewitch, 125; Wood B. Kyle, 226; August Larson, 225 *(permission required);* Alva B. Lasswell, 62 *(permission required to cite or quote);* Francis B. Loomis, Jr., 149; Robert B. Luckey, 228 *(permission required);*

John C. McQueen, 161; John H. Masters, 193; Vernon E. Megee, 236; Ivan W. Miller, 69; Ralph J. Mitchell, 30; Francis P. Mulcahy, 169; John C. Munn, 106; David R. Nimmer, 199 *(permission required);* Alfred H. Noble, 111; Henry R. Paige, 128; Don

V. Paradis, 274; DeWitt Peck, 162; Omar T. Pfeiffer, 461; Edwin A. Pollock, 326 *(permission required);* Carson A. Roberts, 128; Ray A. Robinson, 139; Ford O. Rogers, 108; William W. Rogers, 99; George A. Roll, 196; Ronald D. Salmon, 278; Lawson H.M. Sanderson, 63; Christian Schilt, 136; Alan Shapley, 163; Samuel R. Shaw, 495 *(permission required);* Lemuel C. Shepherd, Jr., 517; Merwin H. Silverthorn, 479 *(permission required to cite or quote);*

Julian C. Smith, 354 *(permission required to cite or quote);* Oliver P. Smith, 337; Edward W. Snedeker, 122; Joseph L. Stewart, 112; Gerald C. Thomas, 989 *(permission required to cite or quote);* Daniel W. Torrey, Jr., 81; James L. Underhill, 204; William J. Wallace, 127; Donald M. Weller, 266 *(permission required);* Frederick L. Wieseman, 236 *(permission required);* Alex Williams, 21; Dean Wilson, 20; Louis E. Woods, 354 *(permission required to cite or quote);* Thomas A. Wornham, 127; William A. Worton, 328 *(permission required to cite or quote).*
   19,816 pp. *Open except as noted.* 1966— *Contributed by the Marine Corps Oral History Program, Historical Division, USMC.*

MARION, Frances L. (1886–1973) *See* Popular Arts.

MARKEL, Lester (1894–1977) *See* Journalism Lectures.

MARKER, Chris. *See* Robert J. Flaherty Project.

MARKHAM, Edwin. *Discussed in* Frank Ernest Hill.

MARKS, Herbert Hilliard (1913–1960) *See* Popular Arts.
Discussed in David A. Morse.

MARKS, Leonard Harold (1916–) *See* James Lawrence Fly Project.

MARQUAND, John Phillips (1893–1960) *See* Book-of-the-Month Club. *Micro II.* *Discussed in* Max Gissen.

MARQUIS, Don. *Discussed in* Frank Ernest Hill.

MARR, Jack. *See* Air Force Academy.

MARSH, Mae. *See* Popular Arts.

MARSHALL, Mrs. E. C. *See* James B. Duke Project.

MARSHALL, Edward H. (1906–   ) *See* Continental Group.

MARSHALL, George C. *Discussed in* Orvil A. Anderson; Eleanor Arnold; Chauncey Belknap; Stephen Benedict; Harvey H. Bundy; Will Clayton; Ira C. Eaker; Dwight D. Eisenhower; Walter S. Robertson; Kenneth C. Royall; James T. Williams, Jr.

MARSHALL, John (with Charlotte T.) Foundation officer.
Childhood, education, travel to Europe; Medieval Academy of America, ACLS, 1920's; to Rockefeller Foundation as assistant director for Humanities, 1933; support of humanities projects: film, broadcasting, drama, foreign studies; world travels for Foundation, funding European libraries, conserving Middle Eastern antiquities; director, Villa Serbelloni, Bellagio, Italy, 1959–70, conference center and residence for visiting scholars. Mrs. Marshall recounts her experiences at the Villa.
1,053 pp. *Permission required.* 1974. Papers. *Underwritten by the Rockefeller Foundation, NYC.*

MARSHALL, Louis. *Discussed in* Joseph M. Proskauer; Bernard G. Richards.

MARSHALL, S. L. A. (1900–1977) *See* Air Force Academy.

MARSHALL, Thurgood (1908–   ) Supreme Court Justice.
Childhood in Baltimore; education, Lincoln University, 1930, Howard University Law School, 1933; 1936–61, assistant first counsel, Special Counsel, NAACP; impressions of civil rights cases, 1940's–70's, many judges, political figures, race riots; black press, leaders, civil rights organizations; Kenyan and Nigerian nationalism; 1961–65, US circuit judge; 1965, appointment as Solicitor General by President Johnson; 1967, as Supreme Court Justice; landmark civil rights cases.

193 pp. *Permission required.* 1977. *Discussed in* John Warren Davis; Jack Greenberg.

MARSHALL PLAN
This group of memoirs gathers together material on the genesis and development of the Marshall Plan in the Department of State, and describes in particular the role played by Will Clayton.
Participants and pages: Dean Acheson, 5; Will Clayton, 32; Emilio G. Collado, 14; Lewis W. Douglas, 2; Livingston Merchant, 3; Norman Ness, 5; Paul Nitze, 8; Arthur Stevens, 4; James Stillwell, 5; Leroy Stinebower, 6; Ivan White, 19.
103 pp. *Permission required to cite or quote.* 1947–61. *Contributed by Ellen Garwood, Austin, Texas.*

MARSTON, James. *See* Ludwig Mies van der Rohe.

MARTIN, Ben. *See* Air Force Academy.

MARTIN, C. S., E. F. Heacox and C. Davis Weyerhaeuser. *See* Weyerhaeuser Timber Company.

MARTIN, George and Emil Pattberg. *See* World Bank.

MARTIN, Glenn. *Discussed in* Lawrence D. Bell; Donald W. Douglas.

MARTIN, Grier. *See* James B. Duke Project.

MARTIN, Harold C. (1916–   ) Educator.
Union College President, 1965–74; integration of black students, anti-war demonstrations, alumni, faculty-student administrative emergency council.
39 pp. *Open.* 1976.

MARTIN, Malachi. *Discussed in* Roger W. Straus.

MARTINEZ, Jose Heriberto (1895–   ) *See* Argentina.

MARTINEZ PAIVA, Celina de. *See* Argentina.

MARVEL, William. Educator.
CARNEGIE CORPORATION
Changes in focus of the Corporation; area studies versus comparative studies; relationship of the government and foundations; Council on Higher Education in the American Republics; University Service Center, Hong Kong.
278 pp. *Permission required.* 1967.

MARVIN, Langdon Parker (1876–1957) Lawyer.
Alaska Boundary Tribunal; Leonard Wood; Franklin D. Roosevelt as a friend and law partner.
80 pp. *Permission required to cite or quote.* 1949. Papers. *Micro I.*

MASON, Charles. *See* Longwood Gardens.

MASON, L. Randolph (1886–   ) *See* Robert A. Taft Project.

MASON, Max. *Discussed in* Warren Weaver.

MASSEE, May (1889–1966) Editor.
Education, Wisconsin Library School; early library work: Armour Institute and Buffalo Library; organizer and editor of children's book department at Doubleday; impressions of publishers, including Frank Doubleday.
96 pp. *Permission required to cite or quote.* 1966. *Micro I.*

MASTERS, Edgar Lee. *Discussed in* Ellen C. Masters; John Hall Wheelock.

MASTERS, Ellen Coyne (Mrs. Edgar Lee) (1899–   )
Anecdotes of Edgar Lee Masters' early life; courtship and marriage, NYC, 1920's; husband's personality and creative approach; discussion of specific works, especially *Spoon River Anthology* and *Domesday Book;* girlhood in Kansas City, Panama, and Missouri Ozarks; University of Chicago; Abbey Theatre, 1924; recollections of Theodore Dreiser, Vachel Lindsay, H. L. Mencken.
208 pp. *Permission required.* 1971.

MASTERS, John H. (1913–   ) Marine Corps officer.

Education; early training and assignments; North Atlantic convoy duty; Sino-American Cooperative Organization in China, 1942–44; Gen. Tai Li and Commander Milton Miles; Gens. Clifton Cates and Alexander Vandegrift; Legislative Assistant, 1960–62; USMC relationships with Congress.
193 pp. *Open.* 1971.

MASTERS, Robert. *See* Columbia Crisis of 1968.

MASTERS, William. *Discussed in* Emily H. Mudd.

MASTERSON, Charles Francis (1917–   ) *See* Howard Pyle, Eisenhower Administration.

MASUR, Jack (1908–   ) *See* Health Sciences.

MATCHETT, Henry J. *See* Eisenhower Administration.

MATEER, Howard (1894–   ) *See* McGraw-Hill.

MATHEWS, Hughie E. *See* Air Force Academy.

MATHOV, Arturo. *See* Argentina.

MATICH, Vido (1910–   ) *See* Continental Group.

MATISSE, Henri. *Discussed in* Max Weber.

MATTHEWS, Geoffrey (1917–   ) Educator.
Experiences as director, Nuffield project in mathematics teaching: choice of staff and pilot areas, curriculum, design of books and films, collaboration with Jean Piaget; Madison Project.
116 pp. *Permission required to cite or quote.* 1968.

MATTHEWS, Thomas Stanley (1901–   ) Editor.
Early career and associates on the *New Republic,* 1925–29; association with *Time,* as books editor, managing editor, and editor, including discussion of *Time's* develop-

ment, staff and the projected *Time-in-Britain;* Henry R. Luce.
  136 pp. *Permission required to cite or quote.* 1959. *Micro II.*
See also Adlai E. Stevenson Project.
Discussed in Max Gissen.

MATTHIESSEN, F.O. *Discussed in* Dorothy Baker.

MAUBORGNE, Joseph O. (1881–1971) *See* Air Force Academy.

MAUZEY, Peter. *Discussed in* Vladimir Ussachevsky.

MAVERICK, Maury, Jr. *See* Adlai E. Stevenson Project. *Micro III.*

MAX, Pearl (Mrs. Louis W.) (1904–   ) Educator.
Administration of NYC Board of Higher Education, 1938–1961; relationships between city administrations and city colleges; Russell case; Rapp-Coudert Committee; Strayer Committee; policies and personalities in NYC higher education; impressions of Mayors Fiorello La Guardia, Vincent Impellitteri, and Robert F. Wagner.
  185 pp. *Permission required to cite or quote.* 1961. *Micro I.*

MAXIM, Hiram Percy. *Discussed in* Percy M. Lee.

MAXWELL, William L. Auditor, controller.
WEYERHAEUSER TIMBER COMPANY
Potlatch Lumber Company from 1906: excise tax law requiring separate accounting for land and timber values, Potlatch Village, 1910 forest fires at Elk River, IWW, eight-hour day, blister rust, group insurance plan for Potlatch employees. Impressions of William Deary, Allison W. Laird, Andrew Bloom, Frederick and Charles A. Weyerhaeuser.
  112 pp. *Permission required.* 1956.

MAY, Ernest Richard (1928–   ) *See* American Historians.

MAY, Herbert Louis (1877–1966) Lawyer, diplomat.

International narcotics control, 1926–51; League of Nations and UN.
  92 pp. *Permission required to cite or quote.* 1951. *Micro I.*

MAY, I. Sophie du Pont (Mrs. Ernest) *See* Longwood Gardens.

MAYER, Arthur Loeb (1886–   ) *See* Popular Arts.

MAYER, Louis B. *Discussed in* Eddie Dowling; Popular Arts.

MAYER, Maria Goeppert (1906–1972) *See* Nobel Laureates.

MAYER, Robert. Director, NY State Council for the Arts.
NEW YORK'S ART WORLD
Establishment and workings of NY State Council for the Arts; its funding criteria; debate over elitist-populist funding; politics and funding of the arts; problems with funding of individual artists; importance and neglect of art education in the US.
  35 pp. *Permission required.* 1978.

MAYER, Robert A. *See* James B. Duke Project.

MAYES, Herbert Raymond (1900–   ) *See* Journalism Lectures.

MAYNOR, Dorothy (1910–   ) Singer.
Childhood in Virginia; music tours with Hampton Institute Choir; views on music education; founder and director of NYC School of the Arts, 1964–   ; impressions of Arturo Toscanini, Eugene Ormandy.
  62 pp. *Permission required.* 1976. *Contributed by Deena Rosenberg, NYC.*

MAYO, Leonard W. (1899–   ) *See* Association for the Aid of Crippled Children *and* Health Sciences.

MAZLEN, Roger. *See* Benjamin A. Javits Project.

MAZO, Earl (1919–   ) *See* Eisenhower Administration.

MAZUR, Paul Myer (1892–   ) *See* Federated Department Stores.

MEAD, Margaret (1901–1978) *See* Journalism Lectures (C).

MEADE, Edward, Jr. *See* Children's Television Workshop. *Micro IV.*

MEANY, George (1894–   ) *See* Herbert H. Lehman Project.
Discussed in Nelson Cruikshank; William H. Davis; Philip Taft.

MEARA, Frank S. *Discussed in* Connie M. Guion.

MEARS, Clifton L. (1907–   ). *See* Eisenhower Administration.

MEDALIE, George Z. *Discussed in* Thomas E. Dewey.

MEDICINE *See* George Baehr; David Barr; Frank B. Berry; Edward D. Churchill; Alphonse R. Dochez; Abraham Flexner; Alice Fordyce; Connie M. Guion; Walter H. Judd; Mount Sinai Hospital; Adaline P. Satterthwaite; Leonard A. Scheele; Jules Stahl; Ray E. Trussell.
See also Nursing; Public Health; Psychology/Psychiatry.

MEDICINE—EDUCATION *See* Dana W. Atchley; Wilbert C. Davison; Clarence de la Chapelle; Alfred Gellhorn; Mount Sinai Hospital; Isidor S. Ravdin.

MEDICINE—RESEARCH *See* Elizabeth Arnold; Association for the Aid of Crippled Children; Dana W. Atchley; Joseph C. Aub; George Baehr; George Chandler; Alphonse R. Dochez; Rene Dubos; Alfred Gellhorn; Health Sciences; Mary Lasker; Mount Sinai Hospital; Nobel Laureates; Ernest Lyman Scott.

MEDINA, Harold R. (1888–   ) Judge.
NEW YORK BAR
Family background, childhood in Brooklyn and Westhampton; education, Princeton, 1909, Columbia Law School, 1912; 1915–40, Columbia Law School professor; 1918, founded Medina & Sherpick, appellate practice; 1947–51, US District Court, South District NYC Judge; US Circuit Judge, Court of Appeals, 1951–58, senior circuit judge, 1958–   ; legal books, including

Judge Medina Speaks (1954) and *Anatomy of Freedom* (1959); public speaking career; discussion of the art of practicing law, judicial temperament; important cases argued or presided over; Anthony Kramer treason case, Corscadden mayoralty succession case, 1949 conspiracy trial of 11 Communists; private studies: Latin, Spanish, English literature, cryptology; book collecting, other hobbies. Impressions of Harlan F. Stone, Learned Hand, Christian Gauss, others.
696 pp. *Closed until July 1, 1981.* 1977.
Discussed in Walter E. Sachs.

MEEHAN, Tommy. *Discussed in* Albert E. Sutherland.

MEGEE, Vernon Edgar (1900–   ) *See* Marine Corps.

MEHREN, Edward J. (1884–1963) *See* McGraw-Hill.

MEIGHAN, Thomas. *Discussed in* Richard Gordon.

MEIN, William Wallace (1873–1964) *See* Mining Engineers.

MELLON, Andrew. *Discussed in* Candler Cobb; Garrard Winston.

MELLOR, William. *See* Popular Arts.

MELMAN, Seymour. *See* Columbia Crisis of 1968.

MELTZER, Milton (1915–   ) Author, historian.
Early life, education, Worcester, Mass.; NYC during the Depression; college experiences and radical political movements at New College, Columbia, 1932–36; beginnings as a writer; work for the WPA Federal Theater Project, 1936–39; *Violins and Shovels.*
75 pp. *Permission required to cite or quote.* 1978.

MENCKEN, August (1889–1967) Engineer, author.
H. L. Mencken: a brother's reminiscence, including parents, trust in doctors, relationship with various friends, daily routine,

wife's death, disposition of unpublished work; Mencken Room in Enoch Pratt Library, Baltimore.
Part I: 77 pp. *Open.* 1958.
Part II: 73 pp. *Closed until Jan. 1, 1980.* 1958.

MENCKEN, H. L. *Discussed in* Forest History Society; Mildred Gilman; Ben W. Huebsch; Alfred A. Knopf; Ellen C. Masters; August Mencken; J. Hamilton Owens; George S. Schuyler.

MENDELS, Morton M. (1908–   ) Lawyer.
WORLD BANK
Appointment to World Bank; organization, procedure for loan applications; International Monetary Fund; functions of executive directors; early loans, bond issues; Polish loan proposal; comparison of board functions in Fund and in Bank; weighted voting system.
76 pp. *Permission required to cite or quote.* 1961.

MENENDEZ, Santiago. *See* Argentina.

MENNIN, Peter (1923–   ) Composer.
Musical training, Eastman School, MA, 1945; director, Peabody Conservatory, 1958–62; Juilliard: teacher, 1947–58, president, 1962–   ; composing, influences on his work.
37 pp. *Permission required.* 1976.
Discussed in William Schuman.

MENON, Krishna. *Discussed in* Roger N. Baldwin; Charles D. Cook; Brij M. Kaul.

MERCER, Lucy. *Discussed in* Anna Roosevelt Halsted.

MERCHANT, Livingston Tallmadge (1903–1976) Government official.
EISENHOWER ADMINISTRATION
Career in State Department; Japan Peace Treaty, Assistant Secretary for European Affairs, 1953, organization and procedures; Bermuda Conference and EDC, Berlin Conference, 1954; presidential speech writers; press conferences. Impressions of President Eisenhower, Sir Winston Churchill, John Foster Dulles, Anthony Eden, Vyacheslav Molotov, and others.

86 pp. *Permission required to cite or quote.* 1967.
See also International Negotiations *and* Marshall Plan.

MEREDITH, James. *Discussed in* Jack Greenberg; Constance B. Motley.

MERITY, Gerald L. *See* Vietnam Veterans.

MERKLE, Edward Arrol (1909–   ) Financial executive.
Stock Exchange in the 1920's; financial structures, Europe and India; mutual funds, growth funds; SEC.
106 pp. *Permission required.* 1968.

MERO, Ralph M. (1896–   ) *See* Continental Group.

MERRIAM, Robert Edward (1918–   ) Business executive.
EISENHOWER ADMINISTRATION
Early political career in Chicago, Washington; WWII: combat historian, 1944, Battle of the Bulge; early relationship with Gen. Eisenhower; postwar housing in Chicago; Alderman, Chicago, 1947; Eisenhower administration; Adlai E. Stevenson; White House experiences; HOPE, People to People program; workings of Presidential office; Bureau of the Budget; deputy assistant to President for intergovernmental relations; Ad Hoc Committee on Metropolitan Area Problems; advisory committee on intergovernmental relations.
209 pp. *Permission required to cite or quote.* 1969. *Micro III.*

MERRICK, Mr. and Mrs. E. R. *See* James B. Duke Project.

MERRITT, Francis E. *See* Air Force Academy.

MERWIN, Loring Chase (1906–1972) *See* Adlai E. Stevenson Project.

MESERVE, Frederick Hill (1865–1962) Lincoln collector.
Early life and education; collecting photographs of the Civil War period.
96 pp. *Open.* 1953. Papers.

MESROBIAN, Robert B. (1924–   ) *See* Continental Group.

MESSER, Thomas M. *See* New York's Art World.

MESSERSCHMITT, Willy (1898–1978) *See* Aviation Project.

METZGER, Walter. (1922–   ) *See* Columbia Crisis of 1968 *and* Richard Hofstadter Project.

MEYER, Adolf. *Discussed in* Lawrence C. Kolb.

MEYER, Eugene (1875–1959) Financier, newspaper executive.
Childhood and education; early financial operations; farm credit during the 1920's; Federal Farm Loan Bureau; RFC and the Federal Reserve System during the banking crisis, 1933; *Washington Post*, 1933–53; World Bank and International Monetary Fund; impressions of Presidents Warren Harding, Calvin Coolidge, Herbert Hoover, and Franklin D. Roosevelt, and many other political and financial figures.
938 pp. *Permission required to cite or quote.* 1953. *Micro II.*
Discussed in World Bank.

MEYER, Joseph. *See* Popular Arts.

MEYERS, Robert C. (1921–   ) *See* Continental Group.

MEYNER, Robert Baumle (1908–   ) Governor.
Background; Lafayette College, Columbia Law School; New Jersey Democratic Party; Frank Hague, J. Parnell Thomas; minority leader, State Senate; court reform; Arthur T. Vanderbilt; gubernatorial campaign, 1953; governorship, 1954–61.
157 pp. *Closed during lifetime.* 1962.

MICHALS, Duane. Photographer.
Family background, childhood; University of Denver, art school; Army service in Germany; work at *Dance Magazine* and Time, Inc.; trip to Russia; free-lance photography 1959–   ; portrait and fashion work; working philosophy.
139 pp. *Permission required to cite or quote.* 1976. *Contributed by Richard Polsky, NYC.*

MICHEL, Kenneth G. (1928–   ) *See* Continental Group.

MICHELSON, Charles. *Discussed in* Joseph M. Proskauer.

MICKELSON, Sig (1913–   ) Journalist, broadcasting executive.
Childhood and education; School of Journalism, University of Minnesota; teaching; radio news work, WCCO, Minneapolis, 1943; documentaries; CBS, 1950; television coverage, special news events; news on film; *Time*, 1961.
122 pp. *Permission required to cite or quote.* 1961. *Micro IV.*
See also Journalism Lectures.

MIES VAN DER ROHE, Ludwig (1886–1969) Architect.
ARCHITECTURE PROJECT
Youth, beginnings in architectural field; influences on his work; design for Stuttgart Housing Exhibition, 1927; work at Bauhaus, Nazi harassment; design of Illinois Institute of Technology buildings; importance of structure vs. mechanical elements in architecture; relationships of architecture and civilization; rectangular vs. fluid space. Includes discussions with James Marston, Bruce Graham, Philip Johnson, and Henry Heald regarding Mies van der Rohe and their relationships with him.
78 pp. *Open.* 1961.

MIKOLAJCZYK, Marian (1926–   ) *See* Hungarian Project.

MILES, Milton. *Discussed in* John H. Masters.

MILES, Vincent. *Discussed in* A. Henry Aronson; Reinhard A. Hohaus; Maurine Mulliner.

MILLAY, Edna St. Vincent. *Discussed in* Cass Canfield.

MILLER, Arthur (1915–   ) *See* Popular Arts.

MILLER, Danforth P., Jr. *See* Air Force Academy.

MILLER, Dorothy Canning. *See* Holger Cahill.

MILLER, Edith (1930–   ) Judge.
Childhood, early education in NYC; Hunter College, 1946, St. John's Law School, 1954; political involvement, Riverside Democrats; social work experience; Family Court Judge, 1971–   : Domestic Relations Court, sitting judge, juvenile criminals, lack of judicial manpower, child abuse, social services in Family Court, crime against the elderly; media influence on juveniles; reflections on being a black woman and a judge; judicial appointment by Mayor Lindsay.
84 pp. *Permission required to cite or quote.* 1977.

MILLER, Henry L. (1912–   ) *See* Eisenhower Administration.

MILLER, Israel. *See* Ethnic Groups and American Foreign Policy.

MILLER, Ivan W. (1898–   ) *See* Marine Corps.

MILLER, Leslie A. (1886–   )
JACKSON HOLE PRESERVE
Experience in politics; early contact with Jackson Hole: purchase of land, forest-park feud, Congressional delegation, monument proclamation, local press; member of Board of Jackson Hole Preserve. Impressions of the Rockefeller family.
122 pp. *Permission required.* 1966.

MILLER, Mitchell William (1911–   ) *See* Popular Arts.

MILLER, Morton David (1915–   ) *See* Social Security. *Micro III.*

MILLER, Nathan. *Discussed in* Francis R. Stoddard.

MILLER, Neville (1894–   ) *See* James Lawrence Fly Project.

MILLER, Robert. *See* Popular Arts.

MILLER, Robert E. *Discussed in* Kenneth Chorley.

MILLES, Carl. *Discussed in* Hokan B. Steffanson.

MILLIKAN, Robert. *Discussed in* Warren Weaver.

MILLIKEN, Carl Elias (1877–1961) Governor.
Maine politics, 1905–27; Hays Office, 1927–47.
142 pp. *Permission required to cite or quote.* 1950. *Micro I.*

MILLING, Thomas D. (–1960) *See* Henry H. Arnold Project.

MILLS, Ogden. *Discussed in* Stanley M. Isaacs.

MILLS, Wilbur. *Discussed in* Sidney Saperstein; Kenneth Williamson; Irwin Wolkstein.

MILTON, Theodore R. (1915–   ) *See* Air Force Academy.

MINING. *See* Alaskan Pioneers; Horace M. Albright; Spruille Braden; John Brophy; John K. Jenney; Robert Koenig; Mining Engineers; Edmund A. Prentis.

MINING ENGINEERS
Brief interviews with notable mining engineers on salient phases of their careers. Consultants and executives of companies in widely scattered areas from Alaska to South Africa, they also provide information on the discovery and exploration of new mines.
Participants and pages: Robert Annan, 24; John Baragwanath, 30; Alan Bateman, 15; Arthur Bunker, 47; Henry Carlisle, 34; Louis Cates, 15; Cleveland Dodge, 25; John Gustafson, 40; David Irwin, 20; Ira B. Joralemon, 18; James Knapp, 27; Robert Koenig, 26; Lewis Levensaler, 12; Jaffet Lindberg, 35; Donald McLoughlin, 19; W. W. Mein, 18; Reno Sales, 28; Henry DeWitt Smith, 22; Comar Wilson, 21; William E. Wrather, 42.
518 pp. *Permission required to cite or quote.* 1961.

Contributed by Henry C. Carlisle, San Francisco.

MINKOFF, Nathaniel. *See* Socialist Movement.

MINNICH, Lawrence Arthur (1918–   ) Government official.
EISENHOWER ADMINISTRATION
Assistant White House Staff Secretary, 1953–60; preparing *The Public Papers of the President.*
34 pp. *Permission required to cite or quote.* 1968.

MINOW, Newton Norman (1926–   ) Lawyer.
ADLAI E. STEVENSON PROJECT
Education; Stevenson campaign, 1948; Stevenson staff, 1952; 1952 campaign; legal practice with Stevenson, 1954; 1956 campaign; Eisenhower's heart attack; Lyndon Johnson; relations with the Kennedys; 1960 campaign; Stevenson in the UN; Bay of Pigs; ambitions in 1964. Impressions of William McCormick Blair, Willard Wirtz, Arthur Schlesinger, Jr., and other Stevenson aides.
122 pp. *Permission required to cite or quote.* 1969.
See also Federal Communications Commission.

MINSTER, Leonard. *See* Federated Department Stores.

MINTENER, James Bradshaw (1902–   ) Lawyer.
EISENHOWER ADMINISTRATION
Youth; education, Yale and Oxford; first meetings with Gen. Eisenhower; Minnesota "write-in" primary, 1952.
65 pp. *Permission required.* 1968.

MISSIONS AND MISSIONARIES *See* China Missionaries; Paul W. Frillman; Walter H. Judd; John Howland Lathrop; Abbe Livingston Warnshuis.

MITCHEL, John Purroy. *Discussed in* Frederic R. Coudert; Bertram Cruger; Frances Perkins; Louis H. Pink; Morris L. Strauss.

MITCHELL, Broadus (1892–   ) Economic historian.

SOUTHERN INTELLECTUAL LEADERS (A)
Childhood and education; career of Samuel Chiles Mitchell, University of Richmond and University of South Carolina; graduate work and teaching, Johns Hopkins University; Socialist Party in Maryland; research on cotton textile industry; Baltimore Urban League; *Alexander Hamilton;* impressions of Elizabeth Gilman, Jacob Hollander, Douglas Southall Freeman, George S. Mitchell, Morris Mitchell, and Josiah Morse.
165 pp. *Permission required to cite or quote.* 1972.

MITCHELL, George S. *Discussed in* Broadus Mitchell.

MITCHELL, George Wilder (1904–   ) *See* Adlai E. Stevenson Project.

MITCHELL, Harry Leland (1906–   ) Union official.
Formation of the Southern Tenant Farmers Union; its eventual affiliation with the CIO; resistance to the Communist Party; reorganization with the AFL as the National Agricultural Workers Union; conditions among tenants and sharecroppers in Arkansas, Missouri, Oklahoma, and Mississippi.
191 pp. *Permission required to cite or quote.* 1957. *Micro I.*

MITCHELL, Lucy Sprague (1878–1967) Educator.
Dean of Women at University of California, 1906; marriage to Dr. Wesley Clair Mitchell and move to NY, 1912; interest in experimental education, founding of Bank Street School; teaching and writing for children.
167 pp. *Permission required to cite or quote.* 1960. *Conducted by Regional Oral History Office, University of California, Berkeley; contributed by Bank Street School of New York City.*

MITCHELL, Morris. *Discussed in* Broadus Mitchell.

MITCHELL, Ralph Johnson (1891–1970) *See* Marine Corps.

MITCHELL, Samuel Chiles. *Discussed in* Broadus Mitchell.

MITCHELL, Stephen Arnold (1903–1974) Lawyer.
ADLAI E. STEVENSON PROJECT
Family background; education; law practice in Chicago; activities in Democratic Party; WWII; Stevenson campaign, 1948; Stevenson's attitude towards politics; Ellen Borden Stevenson; pressures of public office; Chairman Democratic National Committee, 1952–55; 1952 campaign: Harry Truman, party unity; 1956 campaign: civil rights plank, the Kennedys; impressions of various political figures.
173 pp. *Permission required.* 1967.

MITCHELL, Wesley Clair. *Discussed in* Lucy Sprague Mitchell.

MITCHELL, William. *Discussed in* Henry A. Arnold Project; Aviation Project; Joseph J. Clark; James Doolittle; John F. Victory; Eugene E. Wilson.

MITCHELL, William Lloyd (1900–   ) *See* Social Security, *Micro IV, and* Eisenhower Administration, *Micro IV.*

MITROPOULOS, Dmitri. *Discussed in* Saul Goodman; Morton Gould.

MITSCHER, Marc. *Discussed in* Joseph J. Clark; William A. Read.

MOANEY, John A. (–1978) *See* Eisenhower Administration.

MOCK, Richard M. (1905–   ) *See* Aviation Project. *Micro II.*

MOFFETT, William A. *Discussed in* Joseph J. Clark; Jerome C. Hunsaker; Felix B. Stump; Eugene E. Wilson.

MOGABGAB, Winifred S. (1913–   ) Businesswoman.
Early life; move to Cyprus, 1972; recollections of 1974 Turkish invasion of Cyprus.
41 pp. *Permission required to cite or quote.* 1976.

MOISANT, Mathilde (–1964) *See* Aviation Project.

MOLEY, Raymond (1886–1975) *See* Social Security. *Micro IV.*
Discussed in Adolf A. Berle; James P. Warburg.

MOLINAS, Luciano F. *See* Argentina.

MOLOTOV, Vyacheslav. *Discussed in* Paul F. Foster; Livingston T. Merchant.

MONCK, John Goldman *See* Robert J. Flaherty Project.

MONRONEY, Aimer Stillwell Mike (1902–   ) Senator.
ADLAI E. STEVENSON PROJECT
First impressions of Stevenson; Speakers Bureau; whistlestop speeches; 1956 battle over the vice presidential candidate; "draft Stevenson" movement, 1960; John F. Kennedy; 1960 Democratic Convention; Stevenson's influence on younger politicians and the party.
128 pp. *Permission required.* 1969.

MONRONEY, Michael (1927–   ) *See* Adlai E. Stevenson Project. *Micro III.*

MONTGOMERY, Bernard. *Discussed in* James M. Gavin.

MONTGOMERY, Douglass (1912–   ) *See* Popular Arts.

MONTGOMERY, Paul (1892–   ) *See* McGraw-Hill.

MOON, S. G. and C. D. Moon. *See* Weyerhaeuser Timber Company.

MOONEY, Thomas. *Discussed in* Earl Browder; John P. Frey.

MOORE, Arthur. *See* Adlai E. Stevenson Project.

MOORE, Charles J. (1889–1974) Naval officer.
Family and early life; Naval Academy, early cruises; WWI convoys; Naval Overseas Transportation Service; teaching at Naval Academy, Navigation Department; Yorktown Sesquicentennial; Naval War College duty; Pacific Fleet: Gilberts campaign, attacks on Kwajalein, Truk, Saipan;

diversion of forces to the Marianas, Philippine Sea Battle; impressions of Adms. Chester Nimitz, Edward Kalbfuss, H. Kent Hewitt, Raymond Spruance, and others. 1,244 pp. *Open.* 1967.

MOORE, Louis. *Discussed in* William Lusk.

MOORE, Ray. *See* Eisenhower Administration.

MOORMAN, Atha Grace (Mrs. Thomas) *See* Air Force Academy.

MOORMAN, Thomas Samuel (1910–   ) Air Force officer.
AIR FORCE ACADEMY
Experiences as USAF Academy Superintendent, 1965–70: curriculum reform, athletics, honor code, 4th class system, recruitment among minorities, White Committee investigation and cadet morale, library, programs in military training and airmanship.
134 pp. *Open.* 1971.

MOOS, Malcolm Charles (1916–   ) *See* Eisenhower Administration.

MORA, F. Luis. *Discussed in* Elizabeth Blake.

MORELLO, Alberto. *See* Argentina.

MORGAN, Cary (–1960) *See* Popular Arts.

MORGAN, Edward P. (1910–   ) Writer, broadcaster.
EISENHOWER ADMINISTRATION
1952 and 1960 campaigns; Eisenhower's news conferences; impressions of Dwight Eisenhower and Richard Nixon; "Kitchen Debate."
53 pp. *Permission required.* 1967.

MORGAN, Gerald Demuth (1908–1976) Lawyer.
EISENHOWER ADMINISTRATION
Harvard Law School; legislative drafting, Legislative Counsel Office to 1945; legislative liaison staff, 1953; administrative assistant to President Eisenhower, 1955–58.
133 pp. *Permission required.* 1968.

MORGAN, Howard Waldron (1902–   ) *See* Weyerhaeuser Timber Company.

MORGAN, J. P. *Discussed in* Boris Bakhmeteff; William J. Schieffelin.

MORGAN, Jack. *See* Weyerhaeuser Timber Company.

MORGAN, James P. (1902–   ) *See* Continental Group.

MORGAN, Shepard Ashman (1884–1968) Banker.
Early life in Rochester, NY; Williams College; NY *Sun.*
63 pp. *Permission required to cite or quote.* 1950.

MORGAN, Thomas H. *Discussed in* Theodosius Dobzhansky; Leslie C. Dunn.

MORGAN, Virginia Mason. *See* Longwood Gardens.

MORGENTHAU, Henry, Sr. *Discussed in* Edward S. Greenbaum.

MORGENTHAU, Henry, Jr. (1891–1967) *See* Herbert H. Lehman Project. *Micro II. Discussed in* Eddie Dowling.

MORGENTHAU, Robert. *Discussed in* Justin N. Feldman; Edward I. Koch.

MORISON, Samuel E. (1887–1976) Writer, historian.
Naval historian; impressions of Admiral Halsey.
27 pp. *Permission required to cite or quote.* 1973. *Contributed by the US Naval Institute.*
Discussed in Adolf A. Berle; Ralph C. Parker.

MORLEY, Christopher. *Discussed in* Allan Nevins.

MORRILL, Chester (1885–   ) Lawyer, Administrator.
Childhood and education; Department of Agriculture, 1914–25: various activities in the agricultural fields of marketing and distribution, including the Grain Futures and the Packers and Stockyards Administra-

tions; WFC, 1925–31; Federal Farm Loan Bureau, 1927–31; Federal Reserve System, 1931–50; RFC, 1931–33; banking in Nationalist China, 1951.

311 pp. *Permission required to cite or quote.* 1952. *Micro II.*

MORRILL, J.L. *Discussed in* W. H. Cowley.

MORRIS, Arch (1889–1964) *See* McGraw-Hill.

MORRIS, Chester (1901–   ) *See* Popular Arts.

MORRIS, John W., Sr. (1898–   ) *See* Continental Group.

MORRIS, Newbold (1902–1966) Lawyer. NYC politics, 1934–49; Fiorello H. La Guardia.

94 pp. *Permission required to cite or quote.* 1950. *Micro II.*
See also New York Political Studies (C).
Discussed in Stanley M. Isaacs; William O'Dwyer.

MORRIS, Richard Brandon (1904–   ) Historian.
NYC childhood; education, City College, Columbia; Regional Director, Survey of Federal Archives, 1936–37; committee work with American historical associations, 1930's–   ; *A Treasury of Great Reporting, The Spirit of '76, Government and Labor in Early America, Fair Trial,* other writings; legal history; teaching at City College, 1927–49, Columbia, 1946–61, visiting professorships; editing John Jay papers; world travels delivering lectures, researching books, promoting scholarly cooperation for American Revolution Bicentennial commemoration; impressions of Allan Nevins, Henry Steele Commager, other historians.

288 pp. *Closed until 1987.* 1978. Papers: speech, "Fair Trial Revisited."
See also American Historians.

MORRISETT, Lloyd N. (1929–   ) Foundation executive.
CARNEGIE CORPORATION
First association with the Carnegie Corporation, 1957; experiences as staff member,

later vice president of Corporation, 1958–67: staff members; program areas; cognitive research; Educational Testing Service; daily routine. Impressions of Corporation officers and trustees.

214 pp. *Permission required.* 1967.
See also Children's Television Workshop. *Micro IV.*
Discussed in Lawrence A. Cremin.

MORRISSEY, Muriel E. *See* Aviation Project. *Micro II.*

MORROW, Dwight. *Discussed in* Boris Bakhmeteff; Hilarion N. Branch; George Rublee.

MORROW, Everett Frederic (1909–   ) Government official.
EISENHOWER ADMINISTRATION
Eisenhower campaign train, 1952; administrative officer, Special Projects, 1955–61; Eisenhower and civil rights; impressions of Sherman Adams, Martin Luther King, Jr., and others; field secretary, NAACP; CBS; staff advisor on race relations to Eisenhower administration.

175 pp. *Permission required to cite or quote.* 1968.

EISENHOWER ADMINISTRATION
NAACP; work in Eisenhower's 1952 campaign; Eisenhower's stand on FEPC, civil rights issues; impressions of Sherman Adams.

32 pp. *Permission required.* 1968.

MORROW, L. C. (1888–1971) *See* McGraw-Hill.

MORSE, Carlton Errol (1901–   ) *See* Radio Pioneers.

MORSE, David A. (1907–   ) Lawyer.
Parents' experiences as immigrants, London and NYC; boyhood, Somerville, New Jersey; faculty and students, Rutgers College and Harvard Law School; New Deal lawyers; Petroleum Labor Policy Board, 1934–35; Enid, Oklahoma strike; impressions of Paul Robeson, Felix Frankfurter, Herbert Marks, Paul Freund.

127 pp. *Permission required.* 1971.

MORSE, Josiah. *Discussed in* Broadus Mitchell.

MORSE, True Delbert (1896–   ) Agricultural official.
EISENHOWER ADMINISTRATION
Department of Agriculture during his years as Under Secretary, 1953–61: programs, relations with President and Congress, Rural Development Program; impressions of Eisenhower and others in the administration.
114 pp. *Permission required to cite or quote. 1967. Micro III.*

MORSE, Wayne Lyman (1900–1974) *See* Herbert H. Lehman Project.

MORTON, William Scott. *See* China Missionaries.

MOSCOW, Warren (1908–   ) Journalist. NY politics, 1940–50; William O'Dwyer; Thomas E. Dewey; Democratic National Convention, 1952.
83 pp. *Permission required to cite or quote. 1953. Micro I.*

MOSES, Grandma (Anna Mary Robertson) *Discussed in* S. Michael Bessie.

MOSES, Robert (1888–   ) Government official.
Transcription of NBC television program in which Mr. Moses was interviewed by Gilmore Clarke. Videotape available.
15 pp. *Open.* 1959.
Discussed in Stanley M. Isaacs; Abraham Kazan; Paul O'Dwyer; William O'Dwyer; Charles Poletti; Joseph M. Proskauer; I.D. Robbins; Dorothy Rosenman; Robert F. Wagner; Emily S. Warner.

MOSKOWITZ, Belle. *Discussed in* Dorothy Rosenman; Emily S. Warner.

MOSKOWITZ, Debbie. *See* Kirkland College.

MOSS, Maximilian. *Discussed in* William O'Dwyer.

MOSSADEGH, Mohammed. *Discussed in* Morris M. Marcus.

MOSSBAUER, Rudolf Ludwig (1929–   ) *See* Nobel Laureates.

MOTHERWELL, Robert (1915–   ) *See* New York's Art World.

MOTLEY, Constance Baker (1921–   ) US District Court Judge.
West Indian family background; childhood in New Haven; activities with New Haven Community Council, 1936; work with NYA, 1939; education at Fisk, NYU; Columbia Law School, 1944–46; discrimination and affirmative action in education; impact of Plessey, Brown, and Bakke cases; NAACP Legal Defense Fund work, 1945–65; restrictive covenant cases, 1948; James Meredith, 1961; judicial resistance to desegregation rulings; 1965 Selma to Montgomery march; march on Washington; right-to-counsel, freedom rider movement, sit-in cases; Civil Rights Act of 1964; Swain case on jury selection; urban renewal and fair housing programs in the courts; issues addressed as NY State Senator, 1964–65; Manhattan borough presidency, 1965–66, and work with NYC redevelopment programs, Morningside Urban Renewal conflict, community dispute mediations; US District Court Judge, NY, 1966–   ; the US court system and effects of Speedy Trial act; present direction of NAACP; impressions of Martin Luther King, Jr., Robert F. Wagner, Jr. and others.
801 pp. *Permission required to cite or quote.* 1978.

MOTT, Lucretia. *Discussed in* Anna Lord Strauss.

MT. SINAI HOSPITAL
A history of Mt. Sinai Hospital, NYC, with emphasis on staff contributions to medical knowledge, growth and development of specialized departments within the hospital, and comparison of modern medical training with earlier practices; brief description of establishment of Mt. Sinai Medical School. Transcripts of certain faculty meetings, investitures, and seminars are included.

Participants and pages: George Baehr, 36; Solomon Berson, 35 *(permission required);* Samuel Bloom, 24 *(permission required);* Bryan Brooke, 46 *(permission required);*

George Christakis, 29 *(permission required);* Ralph Colp, 22; B.B. Crohn, 11 *(permission required);* Henry Dolger, 34 *(permission required);* John Gerster, 21 *(permission required);* Leon Ginzberg, 31; Abraham Hyman, 33 *(permission required);* Hillard Jason, 49 *(permission required);* Samuel Klein, 44 *(permission required);* Percy Klingenstein, 29; Sylvan Manheim, 50; Hans Popper, 34; Coleman Rabin, 20; Martin Steinberg, 80; Joseph Turner, 37 *(permission required);* Peter Vogel, 17 *(permission required);* Edwin Weinstein, 27 *(permission required);* Harry Wessler, 15 *(permission required);* Asher Winkelstein, 23.

Faculty Meetings, 269 *(permission required);* Investitures: Morris P. Bender, 24; Kurt Hirschhorn, 24; George James, 26; Alan Eugene Kark, 24; Ralph Kaufman, 29; Hans Popper, 28; Memorial Dr. Garlock, 15; Seminars, 148 *(permission required).*

1,335 pp. *Permission required to cite or quote except as noted.* 1965– *. Some memoirs are available in microform; consult individual entries.*
Contributed by Dr. Albert S. Lyons, Mt. Sinai Hospital, NYC.

MOUNTIN, Joseph. *Discussed in* John B. Grant.

MOWRY, George. *See* American Historians.

MOYNE, Lord. *Discussed in* James M. Landis.

MUDD, Emily Hartshorne (1898–) Counselor, educator.
WOMEN'S HISTORY AND POPULATION ISSUES
Family background, education, marriage, children; pioneer work in development of professional marriage counseling; development of sex research in relation to marriage counseling; reform of abortion laws; Marriage Council of Philadelphia, founding, 1933, Director, 1936–37; founding member, President, American Association of Marriage and Family Counselors; professor, University of Pennsylvania Medical School; trip to Soviet Union, 1945–46; work with government agencies on sex education

and research; impressions of Robert L. Dickinson, Clarence Gamble, Virginia Johnson, Alfred Kinsey, Sophia Kleegman, William Masters, Abraham Stone, Hannah Stone.
291 pp. *Permission required to cite or quote.* 1974. Papers. *Contributed by the Schlesinger Library.*

MUDGE, Isadore Gilbert (1875–1957) *See* Nicholas Murray Butler Project.
Discussed in Constance M. Winchell.

MUGICA, Adolfo. *See* Argentina.

MUIR, Malcolm (1885–1979) *See* McGraw-Hill.

MULCAHY, Francis Patrick (1894–1973) *See* Marine Corps.

MULHEARN, Henry (1912–) Police officer.
Childhood in Brooklyn; teacher training; social work; NYC Police Department, 1936; Police Academy; Lower East Side, Chinatown; Brooklyn gang warfare, 1945–48; Juvenile Aid Bureau, 1949; Youth Board; Precinct Captain, 1956.
122 pp. *Permission required to cite or quote.* 1960. *Micro II. Contributed by John K. Kelly, Newark, Delaware.*

MULLER, H.J. *Discussed in* Leslie C. Dunn.

MULLER, Hermann Joseph (1890–1967) *See* Nobel Laureates.

MULLINER, Maurine.
SOCIAL SECURITY
Personal secretary to Senator Robert F. Wagner, 1932; technical adviser to Social Security Board, 1936; impressions of Abe Epstein, Arthur Altmeyer, John Winant, John Carson, Frances Perkins, Ellen Woodward, Vincent Miles.
303 pp. *Permission required to cite or quote.* 1967. *Micro III.*

MUMFORD, Lewis. *Discussed in* Charles Ascher.

MUNN, John Calvin (1906–) *See* Marine Corps.

MUNSEY, Frank. *Discussed in* Allan Nevins; Keats Speed.

MUNTE, Hans Herbert (1925–) *See* Continental Group.

MURKLAND, Lois. *See* Carnegie Corporation.

MURNAU, Frederic. *Discussed in* Popular Arts.

MURO DE NADAL, Francisco (1908–) *See* Argentina.

MURPHY, Charles F. *Discussed in* Arthur Krock; Ferdinand Pecora; Herbert C. Pell.

MURPHY, Charles Springs (1909–) *See* James Lawrence Fly Project.

MURPHY, Donald Ridgway (1895–) *See* Farm Holiday Association.

MURPHY, Frank. *Discussed in* Gordon Dean.

MURPHY, Jay. *See* Civil Rights in Alabama.

MURPHY, Katherine Prentis (1882–1969) Art collector.
Random reflections by a collector of early American furnishings.
 50 pp. *Open.* 1957.

MURPHY, Matthew J. (1920–) *See* McGraw-Hill.

MURPHY, Robert Daniel (1894–1978) *See* Eisenhower Administration, *Micro III, and* International Negotiations.

MURPHY, William Parry (1892–) *See* Nobel Laureates.

MURRAY, George Welwood. *Discussed in* Harrison Tweed.

MURRAY, James. *Discussed in* William Reidy.

MURRAY, James P. (1892–1972) *See* Aviation Project. *Micro II.*

MURRAY, Mae (1885–1965) *See* Popular Arts.

MURRAY, Philip. *Discussed in* John Brophy; Edwin A. Lahey; Lee Pressman.

MURRAY, Robert K. (1922–) *See* American Historians.

MURRAY, Walter (1895–) *See* Continental Group.

MURTAUGH, Joseph Stuart (1912–) *See* Health Sciences.

MUSEUMS *See* Roberta Capers; Edmund Carpenter; Frederick Davison; Rene d'Harnoncourt; J. Paul Getty; Lloyd Goodrich; Roy Neuberger; New York's Art World; Paul J. Sachs.

MUSIC *See* Rose Bampton; Howard Barlow; Gabor Carelli; Carnegie Corporation; Schuyler Chapin; Abram Chasins; Aaron Copland; Henry Cowell; George Feyer; Samuel Gardner; Benny Goodman; Saul Goodman; Morton Gould; Oscar Hammerstein II; John Hammond; Otto Harbach; Otto Herz; Jazz Project; Arthur Judson; Abel Lajtha; Katherine Lewis; Goddard Lieberson; Otto Luening; Jeanette MacDonald; Dorothy Maynor; Peter Mennin; Mitch Miller; Mary E. Peltz; Felix Popper; Max Rabinoff; Radio Pioneers; Claire Reis; John D. Rockefeller 3rd; Richard Rodgers; William Schuman; Roger Sessions; Elie Siegmeister; Madeline Smith; Sigmund Spaeth; Michael Tilson Thomas; Virgil Thomson; Vladimir Ussachevsky; Frederic Waldman; Andre Watts; Meredith Willson.

MUSICA, Philip. *Discussed in* Edmund DeLong.

MUSSER, Charles Riley (1911–) *See* Weyerhaeuser Timber Company.

MUSSOLINI, Benito. *Discussed in* Lawrence Dennis; Luis F. Gay; Thomas C. Kinkaid.

MUSTE, A. J. (1885–1967) Clergyman.
Childhood in Michigan; first contact with AFL; New Brunswick Theological Seminary; experiences, Lower East Side, NYC;

pastorates, NYC and Massachusetts; Socialist Party; Social Gospel Movement; WWI: pacifism, conscientious objectors; 1919 Lawrence strike; Amalgamated Textile Workers Union; Brookwood Labor College.

470 pp. *Permission required to cite or quote. Micro I.*
See also Socialist Movement.
Discussed in Max Shachtman.

MUTH, George H. (1898–   ) *See* Continental Group.

MUZZEY, David Saville (1870–1965) Historian.
Early life and education; Columbia University; Ethical Culture Society; writing American history.
44 pp. *Open.* 1956.
Discussed in Joseph Jablonower.

MYERS, Henry. Writer.
POPULAR ARTS
Early life, Columbia University; Larry Hart; early playwriting; press agent for Shuberts; Dmitri Tiomkin; first reactions to Hollywood; Clara Bow; "Writers Building," Paramount; *Million Dollar Legs;* writing for Columbia, Universal, MGM; comedy writing for films; *Destry Rides Again;* departure from Hollywood, 1950.
123 pp. *Open.* 1959.

MYERS, John. *See* Poets on their Poetry.

MYERS, Lonny (Caroline Rulon) (1922–   ) *See* Women's History and Population Issues.

MYERS, Robert Julius (1912–   ) Actuary.
SOCIAL SECURITY
Actuarial cost estimates for Social Security and allied legislation; Social Security Administration actuarial office; sources of data for cost estimates: American Hospital Association, Blue Cross, AFL-CIO, private insurance companies; legislative history of Medicare and the preceding insurance and assistance programs, 1900–67.
94 pp. *Permission required to cite or quote.* 1967. *Micro III.*

MYERS, Robin. *See* Socialist Movement.

MYERS, Theodore. *See* Adlai E. Stevenson Project.

MYERS, William I. (1891–   ) *See* Continental Group.

MYGATT, Tracy (1885–1973) *See* Frances Witherspoon.

MYRDAL, Alva. *See* Alexandra Kollontai Project.

MYRDAL, Gunnar Karl (1898–   ) Economist.
CARNEGIE CORPORATION
Origin of studies which resulted in *An American Dilemma: the Negro Problem and Modern Democracy,* 1944; impressions of Frederick Keppel, Charles Dollard, Arnold Rose, Ralph Bunche, Richard Sterner.
122 pp. *Permission required.* 1968.
Discussed in Guy B. Johnson; Arthur F. Raper.

N

NABRIT, James M. III (1932–   ) Lawyer.
Family background; Bates College, 1952, Yale Law School, 1955; spectator, Brown vs. Board of Education arguments; Army cryptographer, Paris, 1957–58; Legal Defense Fund 1959–   ; Virginia desegregation cases, Little Rock, Arkansas, 1957, sit-in strategy, equal employment cases, Boston desegregation, 1976, Selma voting rights, 1964, Evans vs. Newton, Birmingham march, busing cases.
330 pp. *Permission required to cite or quote.* 1976.

NADER, Ralph. *Discussed in* Roger N. Baldwin.

NAGEL, Carl (1920–   ) *See* McGraw-Hill.

NAGEL, Conrad (1897–1970) *See* Popular Arts.

NALDI, Nita (1902–1961) *See* Popular Arts.

NAMBERG, Edward, Jr. *See* Ford Maddox Ford.

NARASIMHAN, Chakravarthi V. (1915–   ) *See* Dag Hammarskjold Project.

NASAW, David (1945–   ) *See* Columbia Crisis of 1968.

NASH, Charles A. (1897–   ) *See* Continental Group.

NASH, Ogden (1902–1971) *See* Friends of the Columbia Libraries.
Discussed in D. Angus Cameron.

NASSER, Gamal Abdel. *Discussed in* John Badeau.

NATHAN, George Jean. *Discussed in* Eddie Dowling; Alfred A. Knopf.

NATHANSON, Ira. *Discussed in* Joseph C. Aub.

NATIONAL ASSOCIATION FOR THE ADVANCEMENT OF COLORED PEOPLE (NAACP) *See* Kenneth Clark; John Warren Davis; Walter Gellhorn; Lester B. Granger; Jack Greenberg; Benjamin McLaurin; Thurgood Marshall; E. Frederic Morrow; James M. Nabrit III; George S. Schuyler; Felice Schwartz; Arthur B. Spingarn; Hobart Taylor, Jr.; Roy Wilkins.

NAVAL HISTORY
This project, conducted with the cooperation of the Director of Naval History (Navy Department), covers many phases of modern naval history, among them training, procurement, logistics, ordnance, naval aviation, submarines, scientific development, salvage, and intelligence.
Operational strategy and tactics during WWI and in particular WWII are analyzed in detail; there is material also on Korea. Many political and military figures, American and foreign, appear, *passim,* along with fresh material on major battles.
Unification of the armed services and relationships in the Department of Defense are discussed.
Participants and pages: Walter S. Anderson, 290; John J. Ballentine, 758; Richard B. Black, 89; Robert B. Carney, 768 *(closed until July 1, 1989);* Joseph J. Clark, 840 *(permission required);* Richard

L. Conolly, 411; Benjamin S. Custer, 1,022 *(permission required);* Walter S. Diehl, 93 *(permission required);* Donald Duncan, 981 *(closed until September 8, 1980);* William M. Fechteler, 266 *(permission required);* James Fife, 617; Paul F. Foster, 373 *(permission required);* John L. Hall, Jr., 338; Thomas C. Hart, 284; H. Kent Hewitt, 478; Harry W. Hill, 964; James L. Holloway, Jr., 187 *(permission required);* John H. Hoover, 432; George F. Hussey, Jr., 582;
Royal E. Ingersoll, 126; Alfred W. Johnson, 88; Thomas C. Kinkaid, 450 *(permission required);* Alan G. Kirk, 386; Emory S. Land, 227; Charles A. Lockwood, 720; Charles J. Moore, 1,244; Chester W. Nimitz, 89; Ralph C. Parker, 146; William A. Read, 739 *(permission required);* Samuel M. Robinson, 56; Felix B. Stump, 364; William Sullivan, 1,784 *(permission required);* William T. Tarrant, 53; Harold C. Train, 451; Henry Williams, 251; Eugene E. Wilson, 974.
    17,921 pp. *Permission required to cite or quote except as noted. 1960–69. Some memoirs are available in microform; consult individual entries.*

NEAL, Alfred. *See* Federated Department Stores.

NEAL, Robert R. *See* Social Security. *Micro IV.*

NEALE, Robert. *See* Flying Tigers.

NEEDHAM, Paul. *See* Rare Books (A).

NEF, John Ulric (1899–   ) *See* Adlai E. Stevenson Project. *Micro III.*

NEGROES *See* Black Issues.

NEGULESCO, Jean (1900–   ) *See* Popular Arts.

NEHRU, Jawaharlal. *Discussed in* Roger N. Baldwin; James W. Barco; Barry Bingham; Chester Bowles; Brij Mohan Kaul; Walter S. Robertson; Sir Muhammad Zafrulla Khan.

NEICHIN, Steve. *See* Vietnam Veterans.

NEILSON, Isabelle. *See* Carnegie Corporation.

NELBACH, Inez. *See* Kirkland College.

NELSEN, Ancher (1904–   ) Congressman.
EISENHOWER ADMINISTRATION
REA under President Eisenhower.
    34 pp. *Permission required to cite or quote. 1970. Micro III.*

NELSON, Donald. *Discussed in* Chester Bowles.

NELSON, Richard. *See* Adlai E. Stevenson Project.

NEMHAUSER, Vivian Gilchrist (1919–   ) Pilot.
North Dakota childhood; Jamestown College, 1937–40; early pilot training, Jamestown, 1941, first solo flight in 1942; Columbia Teachers College, 1942–43; training for ground-school instructor rating in NYC, 1942; Women's Air Force Service Pilots training class of 1944.
    48 pp. *Permission required to cite or quote. 1977.*

NESS, Norman Theodore (1903–   ) *See* Marshall Plan.

NESTINGEN, Ivan Arnold (1921–1978) Government official.
SOCIAL SECURITY
John F. Kennedy campaign in Wisconsin, 1960; Under Secretary, HEW: budgets and administration, Medicare legislation.
    109 pp. *Permission required to cite or quote. 1965. Micro III.*
Discussed in Blue Carstenson.

NEUBERGER, Roy (1903–   ) Stock broker, art collector.
Childhood; education in NYC, NYU work in journalism; experiences as buyer, 1922–25, B. Altman & Co.; café life, art studies in Europe, 1925–29; broker, Halle & Stieglitz, NYC, 1929–1940; formation of Neuberger and Berman, 1940; economic perspectives of Wall St., US, 1920's–70's; financial workings, acquisition processes of US museums; history, functions of American Federation of Arts, involvement since

1946, president 1957–67; development of personal art collection, 1938–   , philosophy of acquisition, discussion of individual artists, works, loans, donations to museums; Neuberger Museum at Purchase, NY; trusteeship, Whitney Museum, Metropolitan Museum of Art; Board of Directors, City Center of Music and Drama, NYC, 1957–74; historical overview of American art.

512 pp. *Permission required to cite or quote.* 1977. *Micro IV.*

NEUMAN, Wilbur K. (1916–   ) *See* Continental Group.

NEUMANN, Henry (1882–1966) Educator. Founding of Ethical Culture Society; Dr. Felix Adler.

89 pp. *Permission required to cite or quote.* 1965. *Micro I.*

NEUSTADT, Richard Elliott (1919–   ) Political scientist.
Experiences as adviser to John F. Kennedy, 1960–61.

77 pp. *Permission required.* 1961.

NEVELSON, Louise (1900–   ) Sculptor.
NEW YORK'S ART WORLD
Commission for St. Peter's Church, NYC; origins of environmental art; discussion of the psyche of the artist.

43 pp. *Permission required.* 1977.
See additional interview in New York's Art World.

NEVINS, Allan (1890–1971) Author, historian.
Illinois farm life in the 1890's; family and neighbors; education, formal and informal: reading, the University of Illinois; Stuart Pratt Sherman; NYC and editorial work for the *Nation* and *Evening Post,* 1913–18: editorial conferences, Oswald Garrison Villard, Rollo Ogden, Simeon Strunsky; social and intellectual activities: the Strunsky circle; the *Literary Review,* book reviewing, Christopher Morley; sale of the *Post,* 1923; NY *Herald* and NY *Sun:* Frank Munsey; NY *World,* 1923–31: Walter Lippmann, Claude Bowers, Herbert B. Swope; Cornell, 1927: Carl Becker; early books and the legacy of journalism experience; Columbia, 1928–58: teaching; biographies of Cleve-

land and Fish; Oxford, 1940–41; for OWI to Australia and New Zealand, 1942; chief public affairs officer, London, for Department of State, 1946–47; founding of Oral History Research Office, 1948–49; *American Heritage,* 1950; business history: Hewitt, Rockefeller, Ford, and Weyerhaeuser studies; *Ordeal of the Union;* to California, 1958.

290 pp. *Permission required to cite or quote.* 1963. *Micro III.* Papers.
See also Allan Nevins Project *and* Edwin W. Pauley.
Discussed in Frank Ernest Hill; Richard B. Morris.

ALLAN NEVINS PROJECT
Associates of Allan Nevins during his long career at Columbia (1928–58) and later at the Huntington Library recall the historian and the man as they knew him. Many of the interviews, contributed by Mort Lewis, a California friend, deal largely with his last years. Included is a half-hour interview with Nevins in 1963, conducted by Owen Bombard on film, subsequently transferred to ¾-inch video cassette. Nevins discusses Henry Ford and his place in history. It was donated to the Collection by the company in 1978.
Participants and pages: Lillian Bean, 47; Ray Allen Billington, 40; William Cullen Bryant II, 21; Carl Haverlin, 25; Mort Lewis, 110; E. B. Long, 29; Allan Nevins, 61; Arthur Nevins, 17; Mary Nevins, 81; John Niven (with Hal Bridges), 43; Irving Stone, 37; Jean Stone, 11; James Thorpe, 3; Justin Turner, 11.

536 pp. *Permission required.* 1966–
Papers.

NEVINS, Arthur (1891–   ) Army officer.
EISENHOWER ADMINISTRATION
Early Army days; early recollections of Dwight D. Eisenhower; WWII; War Department; Eisenhower farm at Gettysburg.

87 pp. *Permission required to cite or quote.* 1970.
See also Allan Nevins Project.

NEVINS, Mary Fleming (Mrs. Allan) (1894–   ) *See* Allan Nevins Project.

NEW DEAL *See* Paul H. Appleby; Thurman W. Arnold; Charles Ascher; Solomon

Barkin; Daniel W. Bell; Adolf A. Berle, Jr.; Henry Breckinridge; Holger Cahill; John M. Carmody; Ewan Clague; Lucius D. Clay; William T. Couch; Clifford J. Durr; Virginia Durr; Thomas I. Emerson; James L. Fly Project; Jerome Frank; Felix Frankfurter; Bernard Gladieux; Milton Handler; Frederick W. Henshaw; Alger Hiss; Robert W. Hudgens; Gardner Jackson;
Florence Kerr; Leon Keyserling; Arthur Krock; La Follette Civil Liberties Committee; James M. Landis; Herbert H. Lehman Project; Isador Lubin; Eugene Meyer; David A. Morse; Frances Perkins; Jacob Potofsky; Stanley F. Reed; Samuel I. Rosenman; Morris S. Rosenthal; Social Security; Socialist Movement; John Steelman; Telford Taylor; Rexford G. Tugwell; Robert F. Wagner; James P. Warburg; Nathan Witt; Leo Wolman; Walter Wyatt.

NEW DEAL AGRICULTURAL POLICIES *See* Paul H. Appleby; Louis H. Bean; Samuel Bledsoe; Charles Brannan; Philip Cardon; Will Clayton; Cully A. Cobb; Chester C. Davis; Rudolph Evans; Mordecai Ezekiel; Farm Holiday Association; Carl Hamilton; John B. Hutson; Marvin Jones; James D. LeCron; H.L. Mitchell; Edward O'Neal; Herbert Parisius; Robert H. Shields; O.C. Stine; Louis Taber; Jesse W. Tapp; Henry C. Taylor; Howard R. Tolley; Henry A. Wallace; Leslie Wheeler; Claude Wickard; M.L. Wilson.

NEW YORK BAR
This series of memoirs from some of the outstanding members of the New York bench and bar is designed to preserve their observations and recollections of colleagues and significant cases for the general scholar as well as for historians of the law. The participants discuss their education, their views of courts and the law, and their concept of professional responsibility. Many vignettes of famous jurists appear in these pages.
Participants and pages: Chauncey Belknap, 58; Herbert Brownell, 141; William FitzPatrick *(in process);* Stanley Fuld, 190; J. Edward Lumbard, Jr., 331; Harold R. Medina, 696 *(closed until July 1, 1981);* David W. Peck *(in process);* Frank Raichle, 104; Whitney North Seymour, Sr., 71; John Van Voorhis, 65.

1,656 pp. *Permission required to cite or quote except as noted.* 1975–
Underwritten by the New York Bar Foundation.

NEW YORK BOTANICAL GARDEN
Personal accounts and recollections of the New York Botanical Garden in its early years. Contributors include curators, administrators, and horticultural specialists.
Participants and pages: Henry Gleason, 129; Elizabeth Hall, 169; Harold W. Rickett, 43; W.J. Robbins, 29; George Small, 21; Ralph Randle Stewart, 37; Lillian Weber, 20.
448 pp. *Permission required.* 1973–
Underwritten by The New York Botanical Garden.

NEW YORK CITY POLITICS *See* Charles Abrams; George W. Alger; William H. Allen; Martin C. Ansorge; Richard Aurelio; Herman Badillo; Samuel Battle; William S. Bennet; Robert S. Binkerd; Paxton Blair; Albert Blumenthal; Henry Bruere; Mrs. Walter Bunzl; Charles C. Burlingham; Harry Carman; Richard Childs; George H. Combs, Jr.; Edward Costikyan; Joseph A. Cox; Bertram Cruger; Ben Davidson; Eddie Dowling; Genevieve B. Earle; Douglas L. Elliman; Haven Emerson;
Justin N. Feldman; Edward Ferro; Homer Folks; Jonah Goldstein; Edward S. Greenbaum; Herman S. Greitzer; Peter Grimm; Luther Gulick; Donald Harrington; August Heckscher; John A. Heffernan; John T. Hettrick; Wesley McD. Holder; Julius Isaacs; Stanley M. Isaacs; Sean Keating; Elsie P. Kennedy; Edward I. Koch; Theodore Kuper; Theodore R. Kupferman; Reuben A. Lazarus; Warren I. Lee; George McAneny; Frederick C. McLaughlin; Walter S. Mack, Jr.; Pearl Max; Newbold Morris; New York Political Studies;
John F. O'Ryan; Ferdinand Pecora; Louis H. Pink; William A. Prendergast; Lawson Purdy; Claire Reis; Vincent Riccio; I.D. Robbins; Beverley R. Robinson; John D. Rockefeller 3rd; Cleveland Rodgers; Samuel I. Rosenman; Martin Saxe; William J. Schieffelin; Hokan B. Steffanson; Francis R. Stoddard; Nathan Straus; Anna Lord Strauss; Morris L. Strauss; Laurence A. Tanzer; Ludwig Teller; John J. Theobald; Charles H. Tuttle; Lawrence Veiller; Wil-

liam H. Wadhams; Phyllis Cerf Wagner; Robert F. Wagner; Leonard Wallstein; Paul Windels; Keyes Winter.

NEW YORK POLITICAL STUDIES

From the first, political developments in New York City and State have held the interest of Oral History at Columbia. More than 200 memoirs in this catalogue (see listings under New York City Politics and New York State Politics) attest to this. In addition, the three special projects described below offer material on particular aspects.

A. BROOKLYN POLITICS, 1930–50

Selected individuals recount their experiences in the Brooklyn politicla arena during these two decades. Journalists, lawyers and politicians describe the problems and achievements of the borough and its relationship to the Mayor and the city and state administrations. The office of the district attorney receives special attention, centering on William O'Dwyer and his incumbency. Mayors James Walker and Fiorello La Guardia, John McCooey, Frank Kelly, John Cashmore, Rudolph Halley and other local leaders appear in these pages. Accounts of police procedure, political club practices, and court room incidents abound.

Participants and pages: Oscar Bernstien, 79; Paul Crowell, 40; Clarence de la Chapelle, 56; Henry P. Dolan, 76; Clifford Evans, 141; George J. Joyce, 45; Solomon Klein, 160 *(permission required to cite or quote);* John J. Lynch, 98; Paul O'Dwyer, 245; William O'Dwyer, 1,783.

2,723 pp. *Permission required except as noted. 1960–62. Contributed by John K. Kelly of Newark, Delaware.*

B. CITIZENS BUDGET COMMISSION

Ten years after the establishment in NYC of the office of Deputy Mayor, a group of civic organizations undertook to sponsor a scholarly study of this office in its first decade. Participating organizations included the Citizens Budget Commission, the Citizens Union, the New York Chamber of Commerce, the Women's City Club, and the Commerce and Industry Association. Transcripts of these interviews became a basis for the report, *New York City's Deputy Mayor, City Administrator—Accomplish-*ments, Problems and Potentialities *by Professor Demetrios Caraley.*

Participants and pages: Demetrios Caraley, 41; Henry Cohen, 36; John V. Connorton, 34 *(permission required);* Julius C.C. Edelstein, 24 *(permission required);* Lyle C. Fitch, 28; Luther Gulick, 28; Meyer Kailo, 25; Maxwell Lehman, 33; Charles F. Preusse, 28; Mathias L. Spiegel, 67; Charles H. Tenney, 6; Robert F. Wagner, 29 *(permission required).*

379 pp. *Permission required to cite or quote except as noted. 1966. Contributed by the Citizens Budget Commission.*

C. NEW YORK ELECTION OF 1949

A series of interviews and speeches on the New York City and State elections of 1949 in an attempt to record history as it transpired and to cover all candidates and parties. Discussion of the issues of the campaign, including federal aid to education, Communism, municipal corruption, and minority problems is combined with analyses of political organization and techniques, voting of religious and nationality groups, and the effect of labor union support and newspaper coverage upon the election.

Participants and pages: Alger Baldwin Chapman, 14; George Hamilton Combs, 21; John Foster Dulles, 13; Hiram Selig Gans, 68; Julius Isaacs, 8; Marie M. (Mrs. Fiorello H.) La Guardia and Newbold Morris, 8; Reuben Avis Lazarus, 23; Herbert H. Lehman, 12; Vito Marcantonio, 7; Newbold Morris, 16; William Louis Pfeiffer, 9; Paul L. Ross, 35; David Sher, 4; Jane H. Todd, 23; Harry Uviller, 7; John A. Wells, 16; Abraham Zeitz, 7.

291 pp. *Permission required to cite or quote. 1949.*

NEW YORK STATE POLITICS See Richard Aurelio; Herman Badillo; William Bennet; Robert Binkerd; Albert Blumenthal; Alger B. Chapman; Edward Costikyan; Frederic R. Coudert; Bertram Cruger; Frederick M. Davenport; Ben Davidson; F. Trubee Davison; Thomas E. Dewey; Samuel Dickstein; Eddie Dowling; Justin N. Feldman; Joseph A. Gavagan; W. Averell Harriman; Donald Harrington; Jane M. Hoey; Wesley Holder; Eugene J. Keogh; Samuel S. Koenig; Theodore F. Kuper;

Theodore R. Kupferman; Reuben A. Lazarus; Herbert H. Lehman;
Walter S. Mack; Jeremiah Mahoney; Warren Moscow; Robert Moses; New York Bar; New York Political Studies; John L. O'Brian; Lithgow Osborne; Geoffrey Parsons; Ferdinand Pecora; Herbert C. Pell; Frances Perkins; Charles Poletti; William A. Prendergast; Lawson Purdy; I.D. Robbins; Beverley R. Robinson; Samuel I. Rosenman; Paul L. Ross; Martin Saxe; Meier Steinbrink; John S. Stillman; Francis R. Stoddard; Nathan Straus; Frederick C. Tanner; Laurence A. Tanzer; Ludwig Teller; Thomas D. Thacher; George S. Van Schaick; William H. Wadhams; James W. Wadsworth; Robert F. Wagner; Emily S. Warner.

NEW YORK UNIVERSITY
A group of interviews with administrators of NYU, conducted by Professor Bayrd Still, relating to the development of that institution.
Participants and pages: James W. Armsey, 64; Miguel de Capriles, 117; James M. Hester, 33.
   214 pp. *Permission required to cite or quote. 1976. Contributed by New York University.*

NEW YORK'S ART WORLD
Recorded sessions of "Inside New York's Art World," a course utilizing an interview format at the New School, NYC. Participants include directors and curators of New York's major art museums, gallery directors, architects, artists, and critics. Topics discussed include the evolution of New York's art museums, their function and future, galleries and the artist-dealer relationship, urban architectural design, as well as influences on and mechanics of the participating artists' styles. Interviews with gallery owner Leo Castelli, conducted outside the classroom, are included.
Participants and pages: Thomas N. Armstrong III, 55; Leo Castelli, 65; Christo and Jean-Claude Christo, 63; Chuck Close, 62; Milton Glaser, 39; Nancy Graves and Andre Emmerich, 55; Richard Haas, 45; Thomas Hess, 49; Robert Indiana, 46; Philip C. Johnson, 64; Alex Katz, 42; Lee Krasner, 46; Alex Liberman, 25; Roy Lichtenstein and Leo Castelli, 50; Robert

Mayer, 35; Thomas M. Messer, 41; Robert Motherwell, 45; Louise Nevelson, 43; Louise Nevelson and Arnold Glimcher, 48; Richard Oldenburg, 60; I. M. Pei, 55; Beverly Pepper and Sarah Cushing Faunce, 42; James Rosenquist and Leo Castelli, 45; George Segal, 40; Lisa Taylor, 49.
   1,209 pp. *Permission required. 1977– Contributed by Barbaralee Diamonstein, NYC.*

NEWBY, Ray. *See* Radio Pioneers.

NEWLIN, Thomas J. *See* Benedum and the Oil Industry.

NEWMAN, Paul (1925–   ) *See* Popular Arts.

NEWMAN, Pauline. *See* Socialist Movement.

NEWSOM, Herschel D. (1905–1970) *See* Eisenhower Administration. *Micro III.*

NICASTRO, Mike. *See* Vietnam Veterans.

NICHOLS, Kenneth David (1907–   )
EISENHOWER ADMINISTRATION
Deputy Director of Guided Missiles; Chief of Armed Forces Special Weapons Projects; General Manager AEC; Robert Oppenheimer case.
   100 pp. *Permission required. 1967.*

NICHOLS, Roy Franklin (1896–1973) *See* American Historians.

NICHOLS, Ruth Rowland (1901–1960) *See* Aviation Project. *Micro IV.*

NICOLSON, Marjorie (1894–   ) Educator.
Childhood and education in Nova Scotia; family experiences during WWI; University of Michigan, 1914; teaching in Saginaw, Michigan, 1914; graduate study at Yale, 1918–20; teaching at University of Michigan, 1920–22; reflections on teaching at Goucher College, the role of women's colleges; research work in England on Henry Moore, 1925–26; Smith College, 1926–41; Columbia University English Department, 1941–62; impressions of Nicholas Murray Butler, Mary Ellen Chase, William Allen

Nielsen, Arthur Lovejoy, Charles and Anne Lindbergh.
    482 pp. *Closed during lifetime.* 1975. *Contributed by Dr. J. William Wieler.*

NIEBUHR, Reinhold (1892–1971) Theologian.
    Early life and education; Yale Divinity School; Christianity in an industrial setting in Detroit; writings and views on religious thought.
    95 pp. *Permission required to cite or quote.* 1953. *Micro I.*
Discussed in James Gutmann.

NIELSEN, William Allen. *Discussed in* Marjorie Nicolson.

NIESS, Oliver K. *See* Air Force Academy.

NIKIRK, Robert. *See* Rare Books (A).

NIMITZ, Chester W. (1885–1966) Naval officer.
    Early life in Texas; family background; career at Naval Academy; early commands; reorganization of Pearl Harbor after Japanese attack.
    89 pp. *Permission required to cite or quote.* 1965. *Micro IV.* Papers.
Discussed in Walter S. Anderson; John J. Ballentine; Robert B. Carney; Joseph J. Clark; James Fife; Thomas C. Hart; Harry W. Hill; Charles J. Moore; Ralph C. Parker; Omar T. Pfeiffer.

NIMMER, David Rowan (1894–1975) Marine Corps officer.
    Early assignments; occupation duty in France and Germany, 1918–19; *Mississippi,* 1925–27; China, 1929; Russian language student; American Embassy, Moscow, 1934–35; missions to Warsaw, Helsingfors, Leningrad, Sevastopol; Quantico, 1939–42; Guadalcanal and South Pacific, 1942–43, Okinawa, 1945.
    199 pp. *Permission required.* 1970.

NIN, Anais. *Discussed in* Sharon Spencer.

NITZE, Paul Henry (1907–   ) *See* Marshall Plan.

NIVEN, John. *See* Allan Nevins Project.

NIXON, Herman C. *Discussed in* William T. Couch; Rupert B. Vance.

NIXON, Richard M. *Discussed in* Elie Abel; Sherman Adams; H. Meade Alcorn, Jr.; Earl C. Behrens; Stephen Benedict; Roscoe Drummond; Dwight D. Eisenhower; Edgar N. Eisenhower; Milton S. Eisenhower; Robert H. Finch; Barry Goldwater; Robert K. Gray; Robert C. Hill; Walter H. Judd; Herbert G. Klein; Goodwin J. Knight; William F. Knowland; William H. Lawrence; Carl McGowan; Edward P. Morgan; Nelson A. Rockefeller; William P. Rogers; Stephen Shadegg; James R. Shepley; Howard K. Smith; Maurice H. Stans; Walter N. Thayer.

NOBEL LAUREATES ON SCIENTIFIC RESEARCH
An intensive study of Nobel laureates in science with particular emphasis on their relations with co-workers. The interviews include information on their associations with Nobel prize winners and other eminent scientists who have played important roles in the discoveries for which they were awarded the prize. Each laureate was asked to describe the sequence of events leading to his discovery, and the parts played by others in this process. This project was supported by the National Science Foundation.

Participants and pages: Carl D. Anderson, 46; John Bardeen, 43; George Beadle, 46; Felix Bloch, 24; Walter H. Brattain, 54; Melvin Calvin, 12; Owen Chamberlain, 44; Carl Cori, 52; Andre Cournand, 54; Peter J.W. Debye, 62; E.A. Doisy, 30; Vincent du Vigneaud, 33; Joseph Erlanger, 30; Robert L. Hofstadter, 32; Edward C. Kendall, 62; Arthur Kornberg, 24; Polykarp Kusch, 49; T. D. Lee, 23; Willard F. Libby, 58; Fritz Lipmann, 41; Edwin M. McMillan, 49; Maria Goeppert Mayer, 51; Rudolf L. Mossbauer, 38; Hermann J. Muller, 57; William Parry Murphy, 37; Linus Pauling, 51; Edward Mills Purcell, 35; Isidor Isaac Rabi, 44; Dickinson W. Richards, 20; Frederick C. Robbins, 37; Glenn T. Seaborg, 20; Emilio Segre, 50; William Shockley, 51; Wendell Stanley, 36; Albert Szent-Gyorgyi, 49; Edward Lawrie Tatum, 32; Max Theiler, 42; Harold Urey, 44; Eugene P. Wigner, 60; Chen Ning Yang, 67.

1,689 pp. *Permission required.* 1964. *Contributed by Harriet Zukerman, NYC.*

NOBILE, Umberto (1885–1978) *See* Aviation Project. *Micro IV.*

NOBLE, Alfred Houston (1894–   ) *See* Marine Corps.

NOE, Felipe. *See* Argentina.

NORRIS, George. *Discussed in* Burton K. Wheeler.

NORTH ATLANTIC TREATY ORGANIZATION *See* Theodore C. Achilles; Graves B. Erskine; William M. Fechteler; Ernest A. Gross; Alfred M. Gruenther; Amory Houghton; Katherine G. Howard; Mary Pillsbury Lord; Norman Ramsey; Felix B. Stump; Arthur V. Watkins.

NORTHCLIFFE, Lord (Alfred Harmsworth). *Discussed in* Sir Norman Angell.

NORTON, John Kelley (1893–   ) Educator.
Education, Palo Alto and Stanford University; athletics; 1920 Olympics; early experiences in teaching and educational administration; NEA, 1922–30; Columbia University, 1930–58; Educational Policies Commission; India, 1958–60; analysis of problems, policies, and progress at TC. Impressions of Elwood Cubberley, Lewis Terman, John Dewey, W. H. Kilpatrick,

George Strayer, William Carr, and James B. Conant.
274 pp. *Permission required to cite or quote.* 1963. *Micro II.*

NORTON, William John (1883–   ) Social worker.
Goodrich House, Cleveland, 1915; social work movements in Cincinnati, Detroit; Community Union and Tracy McGregor.
67 pp. *Open.* 1954.

NOVAK, Robert. *See* Social Security.

NOYES, Blanche (1900–   ) *See* Aviation Project.

NUGENT, Elliott (1900–   ) *See* Popular Arts. *Micro II.*

NUGENT, Richard. *Discussed in* Occupation of Japan.

NUNBERG, H. *Discussed in* Willi Hoffer.

NURICK, Lester. *See* World Bank.

NURSING *See* Elizabeth Arnold; Hazel Corbin; Isabel M. Stewart.

NYE, Russel B. (1913–   ) *See* American Historians.

NYGAARD, Leonard H. *See* Weyerhaeuser Timber Company.

O

OAKES, John Bertram (1913–   ) News-paper editor.
Part I: Journalistic experiences at school and Princeton; Rhodes Scholar, Oxford University; British press; Russia, 1936; Trenton-Times papers; Washington *Post,* 1937–41; US Army, 1941; officers training; intelligence work; *NY Times:* 1946, "Re-view of the Week," 1949, to editorial staff, 1961, editor of editorial page.
    64 pp. *Permission required.* 1962.

Part II: Influence of *NY Times* in news, editorial comment, opinion columns; "Top-ics of the Times"; separation of news and editorial functions; editorial issues: national security, endorsement of candidates, recog-nition of China, supersonic aircraft.
    113 pp. *Permission required.* 1964.

Part III: Relationship of editor to pub-lisher; editorializing in news stories; pres-sures from special interest groups; fair trial *vs.* free press; *Behind the\Front Page;* devel-opment of special features; introduction of Op Ed page, 1971; retirement as editorial page editor, 1976. Impressions of Arthur O. Sulzberger, A.H. Raskin, Fred Hechinger.
    In process.

OATES, James Franklin, Jr. (1899–   )
See Adlai E. Stevenson Project. *Micro III.*

OBREGON, Alvaro. *Discussed in* Edward Larocque Tinker.

O'BRIAN, John Lord (1874–1973) Lawyer.
Early childhood and education; Harvard; public activities in Buffalo; law practice, 1900; Crapsey case; NY Assemblyman, 1907; NY State politics, 1898–1915; NY Constitutional Convention, 1915; election of 1916; US Attorney; Theodore Roosevelt-William Barnes libel suit; WWI: Von Rin-telen conspiracy case, 1917; War Emer-gency Division, Department of Justice, 1917–19; German espionage, First Amend-ment cases before the Supreme Court; "Red Raids" and A. Mitchell Palmer; Zimmer-mann Note, 1917; election of 1920, head of Anti-Trust Division, 1929–32; TVA; law practice in Washington; Republican Na-tional Convention, 1940; OPM; SPAB; WPB; impressions of Theodore Roosevelt, Elihu Root, Henry L. Stimson, Alfred E. Smith, Supreme Court Justices Louis Bran-deis, Oliver W. Holmes, and Benjamin Car-dozo.
    611 pp. *Permission required to cite or quote.* 1952. *Micro I.*
    See also James Lawrence Fly Project.

O'BRIEN, James Cuff. Labor official.
SOCIAL SECURITY
Volunteer labor organizer, 1948; full time labor organizer, 1952; *Senior Steelworker;* 1960 Senior Citizens for Kennedy-Johnson campaign; executive board of the National Council of Aging, NYC; National Council of Senior Citizens; impressions of Nelson Cruikshank, Blue Carstenson, Ray Henry.
    220 pp. *Permission required to cite or quote.* 1966.
    Discussed in Charles Odell; Elizabeth Wickenden.

O'BRIEN, John. *Discussed in* Morris L. Strauss.

O'BRIEN, Lawrence P. *See* John F. Kennedy Project.

O'BRIEN, Robert Lincoln (1865–1955)
Publisher.
Early life; Boston *Evening Transcript* and *Herald,* 1895–1928; Tariff Commission, 1928–37; Sacco-Vanzetti case; political observations.
177 pp. *Permission required to cite or quote.* 1951. *Micro I.*

OCCUPATION OF JAPAN
This project embraces the memoirs of various participants in the occupation of Japan and in the formulation of its Constitution. Within the overall discussions of occupation programs and policies are specific accounts of social, economic, agricultural, educational, and cultural developments, together with material on the purges and problems of civil rights. There are vivid descriptions of the drafting of the new Constitution and steps leading to the change in the role of the Emperor of Japan. Leading figures of SCAP and the Far Eastern Commission are portrayed in action, notably Gens. Douglas MacArthur, Courtney Whitney, Charles Willoughby, and Colonels Charles Kades and Richard Nugent.

Participants and pages: Lauren V. Ackerman, 28; Roger Nash Baldwin, 116; Joseph Ballantine, 271; Faubion Bowers, 56; Burton Crane, 74; Esther Crane, 58; Eugene Dooman, 171; Joseph Gordon, 31; Alvin Grauer, 139; John Harold, 54; Harold Henderson, 61; Lulu Holmes, 54; Charles Kades, 78; Mme. Ai Kume, 59; Josephine McKean, 79; Douglas Overton, 51; Cyrus H. Peake, 55; Harlan Youel, 53.
1,488 pp. *Permission required to cite or quote.* 1960–61.
Some memoirs are available in microform; consult individual entries.

O'CONNELL, Joseph J. (1892–   ) *See* Weyerhaeuser Timber Company.

O'CONNOR, Charles J. (1907–   ) *See* Continental Group.

O'CONNOR, Eugene J. (1898–   ) *See* Continental Group.

O'CONNOR, Roderick Ladew (1921–   ) *See* Eisenhower Administration.

ODELL, Charles
SOCIAL SECURITY
Syracuse University, 1937; intern, National Institute for Public Affairs; unemployment security; White House Conference on Aging, 1950; UAW, 1957; health insurance for the aged; National Council of Senior Citizens: John F. Kennedy and the Council, the aged as a political factor, Medicare; staff, rallies; 1964 election. Impressions of James O'Brien, George McLain, Blue Carstenson, Wilbur Cohen, and others.
117 pp. *Permission required to cite or quote.* 1966. *Micro IV.*
Discussed in Harold Sheppard; Elizabeth Wickenden.

ODOM, Will E. *See* Benedum and the Oil Industry.

O'DONNELL, Emmett, Jr. (1906–1971)
Air Force officer.
AIR FORCE ACADEMY
West Point; WWII and Korea; use of B-29's; SAC in a limited war environment.
48 pp. *Permission required.*

O'DONNELL, Philip Kenneth (1924–1977)
See Social Security.

ODUM, Howard W. *Discussed in* William T. Couch; Guy B. Johnson; Rupert B. Vance.

O'DWYER, Paul (1907–   ) Lawyer, politician.
NEW YORK POLITICAL STUDIES (A)
Childhood in Ireland, coming to US; early jobs, Fordham Law School; NY waterfront practice; NYC politics; William O'Dwyer and the District Attorney's Office; American Labor Party, impressions of Fiorello La Guardia, Robert Moses, Vito Marcantonio.
245 pp. *Permission required.* 1962.
Discussed in Sean Keating; Robert F. Wagner.

O'DWYER, William (1890–1964) City official.
NEW YORK POLITICAL STUDIES (A)
Early experiences and education in Ireland and Spain; Brooklyn, informal education, 1910; Brooklyn policeman, lawyer, magistrate; district attorney, 1940–42; Prohibition and organized crime; Murder, Inc.;

WWII, investigating government contracts for Air Force; War Refugee Board, Italy, 1944; Mayor of NYC, 1945–50; establishment of UN headquarters; Idlewild, transportation, housing, schools, gambling; illness, appointment as Ambassador to Mexico, 1950–52; reflections on NYC power structure, politics, the office of the mayor, judicial appointments, court reform, charter revisions, Tammany Hall, the American dream and opportunity, attitudes toward the law and democracy, metropolitan press; impressions of John B. Johnson, Edward Flynn, Fiorello La Guardia, Robert Moses, William Reed, Michael Quill, Newbold Morris, Maximilian Moss.

1,783 pp. *Permission required.* 1962. Papers: Typescript copies of personal records, newspaper articles; partial transcripts of court testimony and of Estes Kefauver hearings, with some commentary.
Discussed in Samuel Battle; Harry J. Carman; Justin N. Feldman; Jonah Goldstein; Stanley M. Isaacs; Sean Keating; Solomon A. Klein; Reuben A. Lazarus; Frederick C. McLaughlin; Warren Moscow; Paul O'Dwyer; Laurence A. Tanzer.

OEHLBERG, Gene P. (1906–   ) *See* Continental Group.

OEHLBERG, Vera R. (1908–   ) *See* Continental Group.

OGDEN, Michael J. (1911–   ) *See* Journalism Lectures (C).

OGDEN, Rollo. *Discussed in* Allan Nevins.

OGG, Oscar (1909–1971) *See* Book-of-the-Month Club. *Micro II.*
Discussed in Warren Chappell.

OGILVY, Stewart (1914–   ) Foundation executive.
Affiliation with Sierra Club, Atlantic Chapter; editing the *Argonaut* (1957–59); growth and decentralization of Sierra Club; its changing emphasis under Dave Brower; preservation projects, including Black Rock Forest, Great Swamp; establishment and concerns of Friends of the Earth.
39 pp. *Permission required to cite or quote.* 1978.

OGLE, Harold H. *See* Weyerhaeuser Timber Company.

O'HARA, John. *Discussed in* Phyllis Cerf Wagner.

O'HARE, John (1881–   ) Labor unionist. Unionism in the automobile industry in the 1920's; organizing the Tobacco Workers' International Union; attempts to organize Reynolds' plant.
108 pp. *Permission required to cite or quote.* 1957. *Micro I.*

OIL *See* Frank W. Abrams; Sherman Adams; Benedum and the Oil Industry; Hilarion N. Branch; Albert Crary; J. Paul Getty; Morris M. Marcus; David A. Morse; Nelson A. Rockefeller.

OLDENBURG, Richard (1933–   ) *See* New York's Art World.

OLDER, Charles. *See* Flying Tigers.

OLES, Mr. and Mrs. Floyd. *See* Eisenhower Administration.

OLIPHANT, Herman. *Discussed in* Edward S. Greenbaum.

OLIPHANT, Paul and F.C. Sowell. *See* Radio Pioneers.

OLIVER, Charles W. *See* Air Force Academy.

OLIVER, Jay Charles. *See* China Missionaries.

OLIVER, Juan Pablo. *See* Argentina.

OLIVER, Maria Rosa (1904–   ) *See* Argentina.

OLIVER, Ruth Law (1891–1970) *See* Aviation Project.

OLIVEY, Alexander P. (1866–n.d.) *See* Benedum and the Oil Industry.

OLMAN, Adolph. *See* Popular Arts.

OLSEN, Iver J. (1895–   ) *See* Continental Group.

O'MAHONEY, Joseph Christopher (1884–1962) Senator.
Boyhood in Massachusetts and NY; education at Columbia; work as journalist in Colorado and Wyoming; Wyoming politics; impressions of Senator John B. Kendrick and James A. Farley: the 1932 Presidential campaign.
57 pp. *Open.* 1958.

O'NEAL, Edward Asbury (1875–1958) Agriculturist.
Early years, farming in Alabama, 1899–1919; the Farm Bureau; Muscle Shoals; McNary-Haugen movement, 1919–32; AAA; TVA, 1932–52.
136 pp. *Permission required to cite or quote.* 1952. *Micro I.*

O'NEIL, James H. (1888–) *See* Continental Group.

O'NEILL, Eugene. *Discussed in* Dorothy B. Commins; Eddie Dowling; Rouben Mamoulian.

O'NEILL, Maggie Orr. *See* Forest History Society.

O'NEILL, Michael J. *See* Social Security. *Micro III.*

OPPENHEIM, Adelaide. Engineer.
Education, Cornell 1930–34; SUNY 1934–35; General Electric engineering lab, 1941, Heat Transfer Laboratory supervisor; Knolls Atomic Power Lab; courses on women in program management and PERT (program evaluation review technique) at the Graduate School and Continuing Education at Union College, Schenectady NY, 1974.
50 pp. *Permission required to cite or quote.* 1976. *Micro IV.*

OPPENHEIMER, J. Robert. *Discussed in* Kenneth Bainbridge; Charles D. Coryell; Gordon Gray; Kenneth D. Nichols; I. I. Rabi; Norman Ramsey.

OPPENHEIMER, Seymour (1905–) *See* Continental Group.

ORAL HISTORY *See* Ed Edwin; Frank Ernest Hill; Allan Nevins; Theodore Rosengarten; Frank W. Rounds.

ORDE, Alan Campbell (1898–) *See* Aviation Project. *Micro IV.*

ORDONEZ, Manuel. *See* Argentina.

ORMANDY, Eugene. *Discussed in* Dorothy Maynor.

O'ROURKE, Dennis (1914–) Corporation executive.
EISENHOWER ADMINISTRATION
Vice president and general counsel, Holly Sugar Co.; sugar legislation during Eisenhower administration.
41 pp. *Permission required to cite or quote.* 1967. *Micro III.*

OROZCO, Jose Clemente. *Discussed in* Thomas Hart Benton.

O'RYAN, John F. (1874–1961) Lawyer.
Education; military training; officer in Mexico, 1916; NYC Transit Commissioner, 1922–26; Police Commissioner, 1934.
136 pp. *Permission required to cite or quote.* 1950. *Micro I.*

OSBORN, Frederick (1889–) Corporation executive.
CARNEGIE CORPORATION
Trustee of Carnegie Corporation from 1936; impressions of other board members; role of the Corporation; WWII service; postwar foreign affairs programs; area studies; Alger Hiss; Congressional investigations; impressions of Russell Leffingwell, Morris Hadley, Charles Dollard, and others.
140 pp. *Permission required.* 1967.

OSBORN, Elodie. *See* Robert J. Flaherty Project.

OSBORNE, Lithgow (1892–) Diplomat.
Childhood and education; diplomatic service in Germany and Denmark, 1915–19; Treaty of Versailles; NY State Conservation Commissioner, 1933–42; Ambassador to Norway, 1944–46; OFRRO and UNRRA; impressions of prominent NY politicians.
228 pp. *Permission required to cite or quote.* 1953. *Micro I.*

OSLER, Sir William. *Discussed in* Joseph Collins.

OSTERHAUS, Hugo. *Discussed in* Walter S. Anderson.

OSTROFF, Isidor. *See* Independence Park.

OSWALD, Cornelio. *See* Argentina.

OTERO, Pedro. *See* Argentina.

OVERTON, Douglas. (1915–1978) *See* Occupation of Japan. *Micro II.*

OWEN, Chandler. *Discussed in* A. Philip Randolph; George S. Schuyler.

OWENS, J. Hamilton (1888–1967) Editor. Family background; early career in NY and Baltimore journalism; editor-in-chief, Baltimore *Sun* papers; colleague and friend of H. L. Mencken.
    70 pp. *Permission required to cite or quote.* 1958. *Micro II.*

OWINGS, Dorsey. *See* Radio Pioneers.

OWSLEY, Frank L. *Discussed in* Robert Penn Warren.

P

PAARLBERG, Don (1911–   ) Educator.
EISENHOWER ADMINISTRATION
Economic Advisor, later Assistant Secretary, Department of Agriculture, 1953–58: agricultural legislation; Department's relations with Congress, farm organizations, other departments, and the President; Special Assistant to the President and coordinator of Food-for-Peace, 1958–61; Rural Development Program; Sugar Act; Cabinet meetings. Impressions of Ezra Taft Benson, Dwight Eisenhower, and others.
    164 pp. *Permission required to cite or quote.* 1968. *Micro III.*

PACIFISM *See* Sir Norman Angell; Roger N. Baldwin; Albert Bigelow; Donald S. Harrington; A.J. Muste; Alice Paul; A. Philip Randolph; Eustace Seligman; William H. Wadhams; Frances Witherspoon and Tracy Mygatt.

PADEREWSKI, Ignace. *Discussed in* Hokan B. Steffanson.

PAEPCKE, Elizabeth (Mrs. Walter) *See* Adlai E. Stevenson Project.

PAGE, Arthur Wilson (1883–1960) Business consultant.
Editing *World's Work,* 1913–27; Walter Hines Page and Woodrow Wilson; War Department in WWII; Doubleday, Page & Company.
    77 pp. *Permission required to cite or quote.* 1956. *Micro I.*
Discussed in Carnegie Corporation.

PAGE, Geraldine (1924–   ) *See* Popular Arts.

PAGE, Walter Hines. *Discussed in* James W. Gerard; Burton J. Hendrick; Arthur W. Page.

PAHLAVI, Mohammed Reza. *Discussed in* John Badeau.

PAIGE, Henry Reid (1904–   ) *See* Marine Corps.

PAIN, Evelyn. *See* Popular Arts.

PALEY, William S. (1901–   ) Broadcasting executive.
Childhood and education in Chicago; cigar factory, Philadelphia; Wharton School; ad-

vertising manager, Congress Cigar Company; use of radio in advertising; CBS, 1928 on; programing, stations, financing; Don Lee, Paramount Pictures; Adolph Zukor; Columbia Artists, Community Concerts.

67 pp. *Closed during lifetime.* 1960. Papers.
Discussed in Radio Pioneers; Frank Stanton.

PALFREY, John G. (1919–   ) *See* Menelaos D. Hassialis.

PALMAER, Eva. *See* Alexandra Kollontai Project.

PALMAER-WALDEN, Margit. *See* Alexandra Kollontai Project.

PALMER, A. Mitchell. *Discussed in* John L. O'Brian.

PALMER, Frederic. *See* American Association of Physics Teachers.

PANDIT, Vijaya Lakshmi. *Discussed in* Roger N. Baldwin.

PANTALEONI,   Helenka   (1900–   ) Civic worker.
International relief work; vice chairman, Women United for the United Nations, 1946, president, US Committee for UNICEF, 1953–   ; details of liaison work between the Committee and UNICEF; history, development, objectives, mechanics of UNICEF; special programs, problems in fund-raising; impressions of Maurice Pate, other executive directors, administrative personnel.

252 pp. *Permission required to cite or quote.* 1977. *Underwritten by US Committee for United Nations Children's Fund.*

PANTELL, Kate. *See* Joseph M. Proskauer Project.

PAPANEK, D. Ernst (1900–1973) *See* Socialist Movement.

PAPANEK, Jan (1896–   ) Diplomat.
Czech legions in Italy, 1916–19; independence of Czechoslovakia; study in Paris; Czech Ministry of Foreign Affairs; secretary to Eduard Benes; UN Conference in

San Francisco, 1945; permanent representative to the UN, 1946–48; comments on Czech affairs, international politics, Czech-Soviet relations; National Committee of a Free Czechoslovakia.

374 pp. *Permission required to cite or quote.* 1951. *Micro II.*

PAPP, Remig A. (1901–   ) *See* Hungarian Project.

PARADIS, Don V. (1896–   ) *See* Marine Corps.

PARADO, Alan. *See* Popular Arts.

PARISIUS, Herbert W. (1895–   ) Government official.
Youth and education; ministry and teaching; FSA; Assistant Secretary of Agriculture; head of Food Production Board under Claude Wickard; in North Africa with UNRRA; Foreign Economic Administration; Department of Commerce.

226 pp. *Closed until 5 years after death.* 1954. Papers.
Discussed in Samuel B. Bledsoe; Gardner Jackson.

PARKER, Dorothy Rothschild (1893–1967) *See* Popular Arts. *Discussed in* Frank Sullivan.

PARKER, Horatio. *Discussed in* Roger Sessions.

PARKER, Hugh A. (1907–   ) *See* Eisenhower Administration.

PARKER, Ralph Chandler (1883–   ) Naval officer.
Education at Naval Academy and early cruises; destroyer duty, WWI convoys; Naval War College 1921–22; War Plans Division, 1929; cruiser duty; Command of Alaska Sector, 1941; Japanese attack on the Aleutians, 1942; training school at Princeton; Adm. Chester Nimitz's staff at Pearl Harbor. Impressions of Adm. Husband Kimmel and Samuel E. Morison.

146 pp. *Open.* 1963.

PARKIN, George Raleigh (1896–   ) Business executive.

CARNEGIE CORPORATION
Carnegie grants to Canada; Seigniory Club meeting in 1938; programs for libraries, museums, adult education, and travel grants; impressions of Frederick Keppel, John Russell, Stephen Stackpole, and Whitney Shepardson.
152 pp. *Permission required.* 1968.

PARODI, Delia. *See* Argentina.

PARRAN, Thomas (1892–1968) *See* Health Sciences.

PARRIOTT, Foster Brooks (1878–1957) *See* Benedum and the Oil Industry.

PARRISH, Noel F. *See* Air Force Academy.

PARSONAGE, Douglas. *See* Rare Books (B).

PARSONS, Geoffrey (1879–1956) Journalist, lawyer.
Woodrow Wilson and the League of Nations; NY politics.
26 pp. *Open.* 1949.

PARSONS, Herbert. *Discussed in* Stanley M. Isaacs; William A. Prendergast.

PARSONS, Louella O. (1881–1972) *See* Popular Arts.

PARSONS, Talcott (1902–   ) *See* Carnegie Corporation.

PARTON, James (1912–   ) Publisher, editor.
Time; American Heritage; editorial staff, NY *Herald Tribune.*
24 pp. *Open.* 1959.
Discussed in Oliver Jensen.

PARTRIDGE, Earle E. *See* Air Force Academy.

PATE, Maurice. *Discussed in* Helenka Pantaleoni.

PATHY, Laszlo (1897–   ) *See* Hungarian Project.

PATLIS, Leon. *See* Argentina.

PATT, John Francis (1905–1971) *See* Radio Pioneers. *Micro II.*

PATTBERG, Emil (1910–   ) *See* World Bank.

PATTERSON, Alicia. *Discussed in* Phyllis Cerf Wagner.

PATTERSON, Bradley H., Jr. *See* Eisenhower Administration. *Micro IV.*

PATTERSON, Hugh Baskin, Jr. (1915–   ) *See* Eisenhower Administration.

PATTERSON, John Sutton (1902–   ) Government official.
EISENHOWER ADMINISTRATION
Veterans Administration, 1953–57; Office of Civil and Defense Mobilization, 1958–61; impressions of President Eisenhower.
54 pp. *Permission required to cite or quote.* 1970. *Micro III.*

PATTERSON, Robert Porter. *Discussed in* Edward D. Churchill; Goldthwaite Dorr; Robert P. Patterson Project; Harrison Tweed.

ROBERT P. PATTERSON PROJECT
Interviews on the life of Judge Robert Porter Patterson (1891–1952) as related by his associates covering his career as a lawyer, US District and Circuit judge, Assistant Secretary of War, Under Secretary of War, and Secretary of War.
Participants and pages: Bernard Baruch, 19; Chauncey Belknap, 51; Robert R. Bowie, 30; Grenville Clark, 35; Ferdinand Eberstadt, 27; Peter Finucane, 21; Herbert Friedlich, 30; Edward S. Greenbaum, 56; Leslie A. Groves, 51; Richard H. McCann, 11; Michael Madigan, 47; William Marbury, 40; Howard Petersen, 25; Auguste Richard, 23; Elihu Root, Jr., 15; David Sarnoff, 9; Bayard Schieffelin, 22; Austin Scott, 3; George Spiegelberg, 20; Raymond Wilkins, 50.
585 pp. *Closed until Jan. 1, 1980.* 1960–61. *Underwritten by a gift of a Friend of the University.*

PATTON, George. *Discussed in* John J. Ballentine; James M. Gavin; John L. Hall, Jr.; Charles Poletti.

PAUL, Alice (1885–1977) Feminist.
Quaker background; Swarthmore College; social work, NYC; work with Pankhursts in England; return to US, PhD in economics, 1912; leadership of suffrage movement, National American Women's Suffrage Association, Congressional Union; Shafroth-Palmer amendment and split with NAWSA; campaigning methods: lobbying, presidential delegations, imprisonment; formation of National Woman's Party, President Wilson's endorsement, Senate struggle, ratification process; 1923, ERA: wording, lobbying, publicity methods; opposition from American Association of University Women, Women's Bureau; factions within NWP; equal nationality rights; impressions of Maud Younger, Eva Belmont, Anita Pollitzer, Mabel Vernon, Lucy Burns, Jeannette Rankin.
648 pp. *Permission required to cite or quote.* 1973. *Contributed by Regional Oral History Office, University of California, Berkeley.*

PAULEY, Edwin Wendell (1903–   ) Political leader.
Allan Nevins's account of his interview with Mr. Pauley regarding the Vice Presidential nomination on the Democratic ticket in 1944. Efforts to prevent the renomination of Henry Wallace; how Harry Truman was chosen.
11 pp. *Permission required.* 1957.

PAULI, Wolfgang. *Discussed in* I. I. Rabi.

PAULING, Linus Carl (1901–   ) *See* Nobel Laureates.
Discussed in Albert Bigelow; Warren Weaver.

PAYNE, Kenneth W. *Discussed in* Ralph E. Henderson.

PAZ, Hipolito J. *See* Argentina.

PEABODY, Endicott. *Discussed in* Claude M. Fuess.

PEACHIN, Jim. *See* Vietnam Veterans.

PEAKE, Cyrus Henderson (1900–   ) *See* Occupation of Japan. *Micro II.*

PEARKES, G.R. (1888–   ) *See* Eisenhower Administration.

PEARSON, Drew. *Discussed in* Gardner Jackson.

PECK, David W. (1902–   ) Lawyer.
NEW YORK BAR
Childhood, Indiana; education; changes in legal education; case work with US Attorney's office, NYC, 1925–28; development of litigation activity, Sullivan & Cromwell, 1934–43; NY State Supreme Court, 1943–57; association with Emory Buckner, Thomas Dewey; work to restructure NY court system; views on reform of criminal code, selection procedures for judges; issues involved in setting and adhering to precedent; return to private practice, 1958.
142 pp. *Permission required to cite or quote.* 1978.
Discussed in Theodore R. Kupferman.

PECK, DeWitt (1894–1973) Marine Corps officer.
Development of Marine Officers Training Schools; tactics of Marine operations; WWII in the Pacific; impressions of William Halsey, Richmond Turner, Robert Ghormley.
162 pp. *Open.* 1967.

PECK, Hoyt. *See* World Bank.

PECORA, Ferdinand (1881–1971) Judge.
Family background, boyhood in NYC, primary and high school education; New York Law School, 1903–05; legal experience; Progressive Party, NYC, 1912, convention, 1916; Counsel to Register of NY County; Assistant District Attorney, NY County, 1918–30; detailed description of District Attorney's office and relationship to other branches of government; NY County Democratic politics, 1919–30; law practice, 1930–33; Counsel for Senate Banking and Currency Committee, 1933; detailed description of "Pecora investigation." Impressions of prominent figures in NYC politics, including Charles Murphy and Mayors John Hylan and James Walker.
1,570 pp. *Permission required.* 1962.

PEEK, George. *Discussed in* Jerome N. Frank; Frederick W. Henshaw; Marvin Jones.

PEI, Ieoh Ming (1917–   ) Architect.
NEW YORK'S ART WORLD
Emigration from China, 1935; teaching at Harvard School of Design, 1945–48; work with William Zeckendorf in Webb & Knapp, 1948–55, on urban redevelopment design; design of Roosevelt Island buildings, John Hancock building, Kennedy Library, Dallas Municipal Administration Center, and National Gallery wing; issues in museum design.
55 pp. *Permission required.* 1978.

PELL, Herbert Claiborne (1884–1961) Congressman.
Early life, education; Tuxedo Park; Spanish-American War; Progressive era; European travel; election of 1912; Congressman from NY, 1919–21; NY State Democratic chairman, 1921–26; Syracuse convention, 1922; the Ruhr; Charles F. Murphy and the Democratic Convention of 1924; Italy and Fascism; Germany and Hitler's Reich; minister to Portugal, 1937–41; coming of WWII; refugees; minister to Hungary, 1941; Hitler's timetable; returning home, 1942; UN Commission for Investigation of War Crimes; wartime London; reflections on corruption, education, intelligence, and progress; hopes for the future.
658 pp. *Open.* 1951. *Micro I.*

PELLIOT, Paul. *Discussed in* L. Carrington Goodrich.

PELTZ, Mary Ellis (1896–   ) Music critic.
Family background, childhood in NYC; music critic for *Evening Sun,* 1920–24; lecturing for Metropolitan Opera Guild speakers' bureau; establishment of Metropolitan Opera archives; editing *Opera News,* 1936–57; opera translations; impressions of Metropolitan management.
82 pp. *Permission required to cite or quote.* 1977.

PENA, Jose Luis (1892–   ) Politician.
ARGENTINA
Socialist Party from 1912: Dr. Repetto, party organization and leaders, Dr. Agustin

Justo, political factionalism; National Chamber of Deputies, 1924–28, 1932–36: budget, railroads, banking, and finance; revolution of 1930; Roca-Runciman Treaty.
74 pp. *Open.* 1971.

PENDERGAST, Thomas J. *Discussed in* George H. Combs, Jr.

PENK, Robert A. (1913–   ) *See* Continental Group.

PENROSE, Boies. *Discussed in* James F. Curtis.

PEPPER, Beverly and Sarah Cushing Faunce. *See* New York's Art World.

PEPPER, Claude Denson (1900–   ) *See* Social Security. *Micro IV.*

PERCY, Charles Harting (1919–   ) Senator.
EISENHOWER ADMINISTRATION
First contact with Dwight Eisenhower; entrance into Republican politics; Commission on National Goals; Committee on Programs and Progress; party platforms; recession; Sputnik; National Defense Education Act.
33 pp. *Permission required to cite or quote.* 1970. *Micro III.*

PEREZ LEIROS, Francisco (1895–1971) *See* Argentina.

PEREZ PARDO, Osvaldo. *See* Argentina.

PERIN, Reuben (1904–   ) *See* Continental Group.

PERKINS, Frances (1882–1965) Government official.
An extended memoir dealing in particular with the following: Mt. Holyoke College; social work in Chicago and Philadelphia; NY: Consumers' League, 54-hour bill, Triangle fire, Factory Investigation Commission, 1909–10; woman's suffrage, 1905–10; NY State Legislature, 1910–13; Mayor John P. Mitchel's administration, 1913–17; art and literature; Committee on Safety; WWI; NY Industrial Commission; Democratic National Convention, 1920; Merchants Association; Spargo Wire Company

strike; Alfred E. Smith as Governor; Democratic National Convention, 1924; Mayor James Walker and Tammany Hall; workmen's compensation, 1922–28; NY election of 1926; labor unions and labor legislation; election of 1928; Alfred E. Smith and Franklin D. Roosevelt; NY Labor Department; unemployment, 1929–32; NY election of 1930; Samuel Seabury Investigation; election of 1932; women and careers; Secretary of Labor, 1933–45; inauguration, 1933; the cabinet; reorganizing the Department of Labor; press and congressional relations; Gen. Pelham Glassford and migrant labor; Black bill; relief; FERA, CCC, WPA; Russian recognition; NY election of 1934; background of NRA; Title II; NRA administrative committees; Section 7(a) and textile code; coal and steel codes; Atlanta speech; NLRB; Avondale strike; automobile workers; Toledo strike; Akron sit-down strike; General Motors strike, 1937; steel strike; San Francisco longshoremen's strike; election of 1936; Walsh-Healy Act; Schechter case; Supreme Court fight; Communist Party; outbreak of WWII; third term issue; election of 1940; cabinet reorganization; Department of Labor preparing for war; Advisory Commission to the Council for National Defense; Lend-Lease; Cabinet Propaganda Committee; Pearl Harbor; labor and manpower in wartime; President Harry Truman; Civil Service Commission; ILO.

5,566 pp. *Permission required to cite or quote.* 1955. *Micro III.* Papers.
Discussed in John Brophy; Ewan Clague; John P. Frey; Lloyd K. Garrison; Social Security; John R. Steelman; Russell G. Wagenet.

PERKINS, James Alfred (1911–   ) *See* Carnegie Corporation *and* TIAA-CREF.
Discussed in Frederick H. Jackson; Alan Pifer.

PERKINS, Jorge Walter. *See* Argentina.

PERKINS, Maxwell. *Discussed in* John Hall Wheelock.

PERKINS, Milo. *Discussed in* Carl Hamilton; Morris S. Rosenthal.

PERKINS, Roswell Burchard (1926–   ) Lawyer, government official.
SOCIAL SECURITY
Education; consultant with HEW, 1953; analysis of Social Security laws; Assistant Secretary, HEW, 1954; President Dwight Eisenhower on social security; politics behind legislation; dealing with the aged; evaluation of AMA; insurance companies' position; Forand Medicare bill; advising Governor Nelson Rockefeller on health legislation; impressions of Oveta Culp Hobby, Wilbur Cohen, others.

143 pp. *Permission required to cite or quote.* 1968. *Micro IV.*

PERKINS, Thomas Lee (1905–1973) Lawyer.
JAMES B. DUKE PROJECT
Family background; William Perkins as James B. Duke's private counsel and principal aide in drafting indenture for the Duke Endowment; own education and legal career: counsel for Duke family, trustee of Duke Endowment from 1948; impressions of Doris Duke and fellow trustees.

126 pp. *Permission required.* 1964.

PERKINS, William. *Discussed in* Thomas L. Perkins.

PERLBERG, William (1899–   ) *See* Popular Arts.

PERLE, Richard. *See* Ethnic Groups and American Foreign Policy.

PERON, Juan D. *Discussed in* Argentina.

PERRIN, Robert. *See* Social Security.

PERROTT, George St. John (1893–   ) *See* Health Sciences.

PERRY, Rufus P. *See* James B. Duke Project.

PERSHING, John J. *Discussed in* Albert Giesecke.

PERSONS, Henry Zivah. *See* Robert J. Flaherty Project.

PERSONS, Wilton Burton (1896–1977) *See* Eisenhower Administration. *Micro IV.*

PETERS, Roderic (1892–   ) *See* Thomas A. Edison Project.

PETERSEN, Howard Charles (1910–   ) *See* Eisenhower Administration, Robert P. Patterson Project, *and* Adlai E. Stevenson Project.

PETERSEN, Ray. *See* Aviation Project. *Micro IV.*

PETERSON, A.C. *See* Henry H. Arnold Project.

PETERSON, Charles Emil (1906–   ) *See* Independence Park.

PETERSON, Esther (1906–   ) Consumer Adviser.
Family background; Brigham Young University, 1927, TC, 1930; Bryn Mawr Summer School for Women Workers in Industry; development of political philosophy; organizing teachers' and garment workers' unions; federal legislative representation of unions, 1940's–60's; special assistant to the President for Consumer Affairs, Assistant Secretary of Labor, 1961–69; Truth in Packaging issue.
In process.

PETERSON, Frederick. *Discussed in* Lawrence C. Kolb.

PETERSON, Houston (1897–   ) Educator.
Account of lecture programs at Cooper Union Forum, 1938–46, with vignettes of speakers and analysis of audience reaction; brief history of Cooper Union; experiences as writer and teacher.
398 pp. *Permission required.* 1967.

PETERSON, Jay. *See* Vietnam Veterans.

PETERSON, Roger. *Discussed in* S. Phelps Platt.

PETREE, Louis G. (1904–   ) *See* Continental Group.

PETRIE, Daniel. *See* Radio Pioneers. *Micro IV.*

PEYTON, Corse. *Discussed in* Richard Gordon.

PFAEHLER, Richard. *See* James B. Duke Project.

PFEIFFER, Louis. *See* John Robert Gregg Project.

PFEIFFER, Omar Titus (1895–   ) Marine Corps officer.
WWI service; Santo Domingo, 1919–21; duties as legal officer; China, 1926–27; Quantico, 1937–41; attack on Pearl Harbor; WWII: USMC Pacific operations and Navy strategy; 7th Fleet, 1947; Fleet Marine Force, Western Pacific, 1947; rise of Chinese Communists; Camp Pendleton, 1948–50. Impressions of Adms. Husband Kimmel, Chester Nimitz, Ernest King, and Jesse Cooke; and Presidents Franklin D. Roosevelt and Harry Truman.
461 pp. *Open.* 1968.

PFEIFFER, William Louis (1907–   ) *See* New York Political Studies (C).

PHELAN, Lana Clarke (1920–   ) *See* Women's History and Population Issues.

PHILANTHROPY *See* Will Alexander; Association for the Aid of Crippled Children; Carnegie Corporation; James B. Duke Project; Nicholas Kelley; Mary Lasker; Fred Lazarus, Jr.; Ralph Lowell; W. McNeil Lowry; Roy Neuberger; Louis Rabinowitz; Rockefeller Foundation; John D. Rockefeller 3rd; Tom Slick; Frank Thompson, Jr.

PHILLIPS, Kathryn Sisson (1879–1968) Educator.
Childhood in Kansas and Nebraska; Ohio Wesleyan; YWCA Secretary; early experiences as Dean of Women; formation of National Association of Deans of Women; educational opinions and theories; Phillips Foundation.
98 pp. *Permission required to cite or quote.* 1962. *Micro I.*

PHILLIPS, William (1878–1968) Diplomat.
Youth and education; diplomatic career in China and Britain; Minister: Holland, Lux-

embourg, Canada; Ambassador: Belgium, 1924, Italy, 1936–41; wartime assignments; OSS, London; ambassadorial mission, India; Palestine; Assistant Secretary of State, 1914–20; Under Secretary of State, 1922–24, 1933–36.
165 pp. *Permission required to cite or quote.* 1951. *Micro I.*

PHILOSOPHY *See* James Gutmann; Reinhold Niebuhr; Herbert W. Schneider.

PHOTOGRAPHY *See* Art.

PHYSICS *See* American Association of Physics Teachers; Allen V. Astin; Kenneth Bainbridge; Lloyd Berkner; Albert W. Hull; Joseph Kaplan; Polykarp Kusch; I. I. Rabi; Norman Ramsey; Sir Robert Watson-Watt. *See also* Atomic Energy.

PIAGET, Jean. *Discussed in* Geoffrey Matthews.

PICKFORD, Mary (Mrs. Buddy Rogers) (1894–   ) *See* Popular Arts.

PICKING, Lelia Grace. *See* Eisenhower Administration.

PIFER, Alan (1921–   ) Foundation executive.
CARNEGIE CORPORATION
Introduction to the Carnegie Corporation; Commonwealth Program: Ashby Commission, travels, especially in Africa; vice president, 1963–67: relationships with board members and staff, decision-making, programs and ideas, Negro education, the disadvantaged, educational television; role of foundations; presidency; sketches of officers, particularly John Gardner, James Perkins, Stephen Stackpole.
273 pp. *Permission required.* 1967.
Discussed in Florence Anderson; Cornelis W. de Kiewiet; Arthur Singer; Stephen Stackpole.

PIFER, Alan and Eli Evans. *See* Carnegie Corporation.

PIKE, James Albert (1913–1969) *See* Radio Pioneers.

PINCHOT, Gifford. *Discussed in* Horace M. Albright; George Rublee.

PINCUS, Gregory. *Discussed in* Adeline Satterthwaite.

PINEDO, Federico (1895–1971) *See* Argentina.

PINK, Louis Heaton (1882–1955) Lawyer, government official.
Social work in NYC; Mayor John P. Mitchel and the Committee of 107; NY State Housing Board; urban redevelopment; rent control; NY State Insurance Department, 1932–42: Depression and mortgages, industrial insurance, hospital and medical insurance, rewriting the Insurance Law; the Philippines after the war.
233 pp. *Permission required to cite or quote.* 1949. *Micro I.*

PISTARINI, Pedro. *See* Argentina.

PITTENGER, Richard.
EISENHOWER ADMINISTRATION
Houston National Governors Conference, 1952; Republican Convention and campaign, 1952; anecdotes of the Eisenhower administration.
37 pp. *Permission required to cite or quote.* 1967. *Micro III.*

PITTMAN, Key. *Discussed in* James P. Warburg.

PITTS, Lewis B. (1910–   ) *See* Continental Group.

PLANT, Elton M. (1903–   ) *See* Radio Pioneers.

PLATT, Alexander B. *See* Columbia Crisis of 1968.

PLATT, Sherman Phelps, Jr. (1918–   ) Publisher.
Childhood, education, Yale 1940; career progression in Dodd, Mead & Co.: production manager to president; history of Dodd, Mead; changes in publishing since WWI; advice to young writers; impressions of Winston Churchill, Agatha Christie, Roger Peterson, Frank H. Dodd.
118 pp. *Permission required.* 1977.

PLIMPTON, Francis Taylor Pearsons (1900–) *See* Adlai E. Stevenson Project, *Micro III, and* TIAA-CREF.

PLOTKIN, Harry. *See* James Lawrence Fly Project.

PLYLER, John Laney (1894–) *See* James B. Duke Project.

PODHORETZ, Norman. *See* Ethnic Groups and American Foreign Policy.

POETS ON THEIR POETRY
In these interviews with modern American poets, they discuss the major influences, themes and philosophy of their works and give their impressions of the literary scene in the 1950's and '60's. Their teaching, editing and publishing activities are described. Participants and pages: John Ashbery, 30; Bill Berkson, 22; Tom Clark, 53; Gregory Corso, 131; James Dickey, 42 *(open);* Robert Duncan, 90; Kenneth Koch, 20; John Myers, 29; James Wright, 29 *(open).*
446 pp. *Permission required except as noted. 1971–75. Contributed by Michael Andre and Ken Donow.*

POFI, Louis A. *See* Vietnam Veterans.

POGUE, Forrest (1912–) *See* Air Force Academy.

POLETTI, Charles (1903–) Lawyer.
Childhood in Vermont, education, Harvard Law School; NY politics and legislation while counsel to Governor Lehman, 1933–37, on State Supreme Court, 1937, Lieutenant Governor, 1938–42, Governor, December 1942; WWII, administering liberated Italy; 1964 NY World's Fair, diplomatic problems; association with St. Lawrence Power Development Commission, 1930 to 1960's; impressions of John W. Davis, Corliss Lamont, Robert Moses, Herbert H. Lehman, Franklin Roosevelt, Gen. George Patton.
677 pp. *Permission required to cite or quote.* 1978.
See also Herbert H. Lehman Project. *Micro II.*

POLICE *See* Samuel Battle; Algernon D. Black; George Chandler; Clarence de la

Chappelle; August W. Flath; Henry Mulhearn; John F. O'Ryan; Arthur W. Wallander; William A. Worton.

POLITICAL PARTIES, U.S. *See* American Labor; Communist; Democratic; Liberal; Progressive (1912); Progressive (1948); Republican; Socialist.

POLITICS AND GOVERNMENT—NATIONAL *See* Martin C. Ansorge; Herman Badillo; Joseph Baldwin; Raymond Baldwin; William Stiles Bennet; William Benton; Robert Binkerd; Hobart Bird; Claude Bowers; Chester Bowles; Gordon Browning; Harvey Bundy; Leo Cherne; Wilbur Cohen; George H. Combs, Jr.; James F. Curtis; Virginius Dabney; John W. Davis; James Devereux; Thomas E. Dewey; Eisenhower Administration; Ethnic Groups and American Foreign Policy; J. William Fulbright; Joseph A. Gavagan; Bernard L. Gladieux; Albert Gore; Donald S. Harrington; Thomas C. Hart; Ernest Howard; Clarence B. Kelland; Eugene J. Keogh; Arthur Krock;
James M. Landis; Chester T. Lane; Mary Lasker; Herbert H. Lehman Project; Richard Neustadt; John Lord O'Brian; Alice Paul; Edwin W. Pauley; Ferdinand Pecora; Frances Perkins; Nelson A. Rockefeller; Theodore Roosevelt Association; H. Alexander Smith; Social Security; John Steelman; Adlai E. Stevenson Project; Henry L. Stimson; Nathan Straus; Robert A. Taft Project; Herman E. Talmadge; Norman Thomas; William H. Wadhams; James W. Wadsworth; Henry A. Wallace; Burton K. Wheeler; F. Clifton White; Claude Wickard; Aryness Wickens; Alexander Wiley; James T. Williams, Jr.
See also Diplomacy/International Affairs; Internal Security Investigations; Judiciary; New Deal; Political Parties, U.S.

POLITICS AND GOVERNMENT—STATE AND LOCAL *See* Raymond Baldwin; Franklin L. Bate; Chester Bowles; Dorothy Bowles; Gordon Browning; George H. Combs, Jr.; Virginius Dabney; Paul Douglas; Newton Drury; Lavinia Engle; Robert H. Finch; Adrian Foley, Jr.; Albert Gore; D. B. Hardeman; Lister Hill; Luther H. Hodges; Francis A. Jamieson; Walter Johnson; Goodwin J. Knight; Wil-

liam F. Knowland; John Davis Lodge; Ormsby McHarg; Robert B. Meyner; Carl E. Milliken; New York Political Studies; John Lord O'Brian; Joseph C. O'Mahoney; H. Jack Porter; Terry Sanford; Adlai E. Stevenson Project; Robert A. Taft Project; Herman E. Talmadge; Charles E. Taylor; James T. Williams, Jr.
See also New York State Politics; New York City Politics.

POLLACK, C. Rogers (1890–) *See* Continental Group.

POLLACK, Jerome. *See* Social Security.

POLLARD, Graham. *See* Rare Books (A).

POLLITZER, Anita. *Discussed in* Alice Paul.

POLLOCK, Edwin A. (1899–) *See* Marine Corps.

POLLOCK, William (1899–) Union official.
Origins and early development of the Textile Worker's Union; autobiographical details.
    74 pp. *Permission required to cite or quote.* 1957. *Micro I.*

POND, M. Allen. *See* Social Security. *Micro IV.*

PONTING, Herbert (1881–) *See* Radio Pioneers.

PONTON DE ARCE, Leroy. *See* Aviation Project.

POOL, Ithiel de Sola (1917–) *See* International Negotiations.

POOLE, DeWitt Clinton (1885–1952) Diplomat.
Early life and education; journalism; vice consul in Berlin, 1911–14; Paris; detailed account of Russia during the Revolution, 1917–18; Archangel, 1919; division of Russian Affairs, Department of State.
    490 pp. *Permission required to cite or quote.* 1952. *Micro I.*

POPPER, Felix (1908–) *See* Austrian Project.

POPPER, Hans (1903–) *See* Mt. Sinai Hospital. *Micro III.*

POPULAR ARTS
Material on the development of the performing arts in this century is provided here through interviews with producers, directors, writers, playwrights, scenarists, composers, lyricists, orchestra conductors, designers, cinematographers, film cutters, actors, dancers, advertising and promotion men, distributors, music publishers, song "pluggers," journalists, columnists, critics, and "fan" magazine editors.
    The development of the motion picture is described from early nickelodeon days: early studios and equipment in New York and New Jersey and acting, directing, and distributing techniques; the Hollywood mythology from the time the industry moved to California until the coming of sound; recollections of the emergence of slapstick comedy, the Mack Sennett Studios and others; scandals and provocative films; state censorship; pressure groups and the origin of the Motion Picture Code; analyses of artistic problems created by the Code, of European influences and of the appeal of the silent film; the effects of the introduction of sound; mechanical and technical innovations, new ideas in acting, writing and producing.
    The Hollywood of the 1930's is portrayed in comments on its social structure, life on the lot, and the life of a child actor, as well as in reflections on the intellectual, social, and political climate of the New Deal era, the California election of 1934, artistic problems, the economics of the industry, and block booking. Problems of the postwar period, in particular the impact of television and of charges of Communism upon the entertainment industry, are detailed together with other major changes: the arrival of new faces with training in other media, influence of the Motion Picture Code in the 1950's, and the decline of the studios with the rise of independent producers and agencies. Some of the films discussed are: *The Great Train Robbery, Intolerance, Sunrise, Safety Last, The Jazz Singer, A Day at the Races, San Francisco, Gone with the Wind,*

How Green Was My Valley, The Southerner, The Best Years of Our Lives, Marty, Twelve Angry Men, Mr. Roberts, and *The Three Faces of Eve.* Personalities discussed include D. W. Griffith, Douglas Fairbanks, Sr., John Gilbert, Rudolph Valentino, Carl Laemmle, Irving Thalberg, Louis B. Mayer, Frederic Murnau, Ernst Lubitsch, Harry Langdon, and W. C. Fields.

Interviews in the field of popular music cover Tin Pan Alley and the vaudeville circuits, techniques of publicizing songs, styles in popular songs, effects of the player piano, phonograph and radio, music and the movies, the era of the big bands, and more recent trends in popular music.

Interviews on the stage cover the theater of Victor Herbert, Jerome Kern and George Gershwin, the stock company as training ground, the road, the Group Theatre, the Stanislavsky method, new methods of acting and directing, Actors' Studio, changes in business methods, the role of the legitimate theater in contemporary life, artistic freedom, comparisons of stage with screen techniques, concentration of theater in NYC.

Participants and pages: Walter C. Abel, 41; Jean and Julius Aberbach, 33; Edward Albee and Alan Schneider, 86 *(permission required);* Willard Alexander, 34; G. M. Anderson, 35; Dana Andrews, 50; George K. Arthur, 22; Abel Baer, 23; Richard Barthelmess, 45; Ralph Bellamy, 31; Louis Bernstein, 22; Walter Bishop, 39; Sidney Blackmer, 50; Louis A. Bonn, 33; Richard A. Boone, 36; Charles Brackett, 25; Harry Brandt, 67; Irving Caesar, 32; James Cagney, 56; Frank Capra, 73; Morris Carnovsky, 55 *(permission required);* John Cassavetes, 28; Betty Comden and Adolph Green, 59; Chester Conklin, 22; Marcus Cook Connelly, 43; Jackie Cooper, 86; Katharine Cornell, 106 *(permission required to cite or quote);* John Cromwell, 45; Bosley Crowther, 32;

Morton Da Costa, 43; Delmer Daves, 66; Alfred Delacorte, 57; William Demarest, 62; Cecil B. De Mille, 24; Reginald Denham, 64; Reginald Leigh Denny, 34; Edward Dmytryk, 78; Melvyn Douglas, 29; Glenda Farrell, 61; Jose Ferrer, 70 *(permission required);* Betty Field, 49; Dorothy

Fields, 40; Gracie Fields, 49; Henry Fonda, 62; Carl Foreman, 44; Arthur Freed, 16; Milton Gabler, 69; Lee Garmes, 64; Janet Gaynor, 28; Louis Wolfe Gilbert, 19; Benny Goodman, 16; Jay Gorney, 42; Sheilah Graham, 21; Bonita Granville, 38;

Albert Hackett, 37; Oscar Hammerstein II, 34; Earle Wooldridge Hammons, 19; Otto Harbach, 48; Julie Harris, 31; Sessue Hayakawa, 95; George Francis Hayes, 60; Ben Hecht, 64; Ray Henderson, 19; Joe Higgins, 43; Pat Hingle, 74; Celeste Holm, 96; Arthur Hornblow, Jr., 49; Albert Howson, 42; Nunnally Johnson, 52; Eric Johnston, 23; Dave Kapp, 31; Boris Kaufman, 33; Buster Keaton, 39; Gene Kelly, 22; Burton Lane, 35; Paul N. Lazarus, Jr., 41; Lila Lee, 46; Jack Lemmon, 55; Edgar Leslie, 13; Katherine Handy (Mrs. Homer) Lewis, 27; Robert Lewis, 61; Anatole Litvak, 23; Harold Lloyd, 76;

Anita Loos, 37; Myrna Loy, 57; Sidney Lumet, 54; Joel McCrea, 30; Jeanette MacDonald, 61; Roddy McDowall, 58; James Francis McHugh, 82; Kenneth MacKenna, 44; Aline MacMahon, 28; Don Malkames, 23; Rouben Mamoulian, 115 *(closed during lifetime);* Joseph Mankiewicz, 47; Delbert Mann, 61; Frances Marion, 29; Herbert Marks, 35; Mae Marsh, 40; Arthur L. Mayer, 43; William Mellor, 43; Joseph Meyer, 25; Arthur Miller, 44; Mitch Miller, 86; Robert Miller, 18; Douglass Montgomery, 98; Cary Morgan, 21; Chester Morris, 34; Mae Murray, 28; Henry Myers, 123;

Conrad Nagel, 59; Nita Naldi, 22; Jean Negulesco, 21; Paul Newman, 66; Elliott Nugent, 85; Adolph Olman, 29; Geraldine Page, 97; Evelyn Pain, 37; Alan Parado, 30; Dorothy Parker, 20; Louella O. Parsons, 35; William Perlberg, 33; Mary Pickford, 94; Otto Preminger, 37; Martin Joseph Quigley, 26; Richard Quine, 35; Tony Randall, 63; Samson Raphaelson, 123 *(closed during lifetime);* Basil Rathbone, 49; Gottfried Reinhardt, 39; Jean Renoir, 23; Blanche Ring, 18; Leo Rosten, 116; Harry Ruby, 39; Charles Ruggles, 42;

Dore Schary, 87 *(closed during lifetime);* Arthur Schwartz, 20; Zachary Scott, 39; George Seaton, 46; David O. Selznick, 21;

Sigmund Spaeth, 52; Samuel and Bella Loebel Spewack, 49; Kim Stanley, 41; Maureen Stapleton, 79 *(permission required);* Rod Steiger, 87; Albert E. Sutherland, 188; Gloria Swanson, 50; Akim Tamiroff, 55; King Wallis Vidor, 49; Rocco Vocco, 31; Tommy Volando, 12; Jerry Wald, 66; Eli Wallach, 22; Hal Wallis, 40; Bert Wheeler, 36; Meredith Willson, 42; Carey Wilson, 90; Julius Witmark, 23; Joanne Woodward, 74; Teresa Wright, 47; Jack Yellen, 40; Max Youngstein, 52; Adolph Zukor, 37.

7,819 pp. *Open except as noted.* 1958–60. *Some memoirs are available in microform; consult individual entries. Contributed by Mr. and Mrs. Robert C. Franklin of New York and Professor Arthur B. Friedman of the University of California, Los Angeles.*

PORTAL, Sir Charles (1893–1971) *See* Eisenhower Administration.

PORTER, Cole. *Discussed in* Madeline P. Smith.

PORTER, Homa Jackson (1896–   ) Republican National Committeeman.
EISENHOWER ADMINISTRATION
Eisenhower movement in Texas, 1952; Republican Party and politics in Texas.
47 pp. *Permission required.* 1969.
See also additional interview in Eisenhower Administration.

PORTER, Paul Aldermandt (1904–   ) *See* James Lawrence Fly Project.

PORTOS, Jose Luis. *See* Argentina.

POSES, Lillian. *See* Benjamin A. Javits Project.

POST, C.W. *Discussed in* Marjorie M. Post.

POST, Langdon W. *Discussed in* Charles Abrams.

POST, Marjorie Merriweather (1887–1973) Businesswoman, philanthropist.
Family background, early life, Springfield, Illinois, Battle Creek, Michigan; education; C.W. Post; Post Cereal Co.; early travels.
34 pp. *Permission required to cite or quote.* 1964. *Micro II.*

POST, Robert D. (1897–   ) *See* Continental Group.

POST, Wiley. *Discussed in* Harry Bruno.

POTOFSKY, Jacob Samuel (1894–   ) Union official.
Family background and education in Russia; emigration to US, Chicago; first job in Hart, Schaffner and Marx; 1910 Chicago clothing worker strike; United Garment Workers; Sidney Hillman; arbitration agreements; formation of Amalgamated Clothing Workers of America; industrial unionism; union banking; experiments with unemployment insurance; cooperative housing; the Depression; the New Deal.
833 pp. *Permission required to cite or quote.* 1965. *Micro II.*
Discussed in Abraham Kazan.

POTTER, David Morris (1910–   ) *See* American Historians.

POTTS, Ramsay (1916–   ) *See* Aviation, Project. *Micro II.*

POUND, Ezra (1885–1972) *See* Ford Maddox Ford.

POUND, Roscoe. *Discussed in* James M. Landis; Joseph W. Madden.

POWELL, Adam Clayton, Jr. *Discussed in* James E. Booker; Herbert Brownell; Kenneth Clark; Mamie Clark; Ed Edwin; Justin N. Feldman; Arthur B. Spingarn; Hobart Taylor, Jr.

POWELL, Terrell. *See* Eisenhower Administration. *Micro III.*

POWER, Thomas S. (1905–1970) *See* Aviation Project.

POWERS, Daniel L. (1912–   ) Writer.
Farm life in Iowa from turn of century through 1930's; comments on father's diaries, inventions, writing activities; family relationships; country school system; changing agricultural methods; establishment of mixed feed business, 1933.
41 pp. *Permission required to cite or quote.* 1974. Papers. *Acquired from Iowa State Historical Society.*

POWERS, David F. (1912–) *See* John F. Kennedy Project.

PRATT, Robert L. *See* Radio Pioneers.

PRATT, Ruth. *Discussed in* Stanley M. Isaacs.

PREMINGER, Òtto (1906–) *See* Popular Arts.

PRENDERGAST, William Ambrose (1867–1954) Banker, politician.
Childhood on the East Side, NYC; business and finance; National Association of Credit Men, 1899–1905; national bankruptcy act, 1906; interest in politics, lecturing; NYC finances; the Office of Comptroller, 1909; NY State and City politics; Board of Estimate and Apportionment; Gaynor Charter; Progressive Party; 1912 Republican National Convention; new subway system, 1913; Mayor William Gaynor and NYC finances; Municipal Reference Library; NY State Constitutional Convention, 1915; Gary plan, 1915; legislative investigations, 1915–16; WWI; West Side improvement plan; "land deals," 1917; retrospections; impressions of prominent New Yorkers, including Theodore Roosevelt, Bainbridge Colby, Herbert Parsons, Henry L. Stimson.
995 pp. *Permission required to cite or quote.* 1951. *Micro I.* Papers. Memoir was written by Mr. Prendergast for the Oral History Research Office.

PRENTICE, Ezra Parmalee (1863–1955) *See* Theodore Roosevelt Association.

PRENTIS, Edmund Astley (1883–1969) Engineer, collector.
Columbia University School of Mines; mining experiences, Mexico and Peru; Spencer, White & Prentis; military construction; White House repairs; King's College Room, Columbia, furnishings and acquisitions; comments on antique collecting.
232 pp. *Permission required to cite or quote.* 1962.

PRESCOTT, Robert (1913–1978) *See* Flying Tigers.

PRESSMAN, Lee (1906–1969) Lawyer.
Education, Harvard; assistant general counsel AAA; RA; general counsel WPA, 1935–1936: general counsel CIO, 1936; sit down strikes; General Motors Detroit strike, 1936, U. S. Steel, 1937, Chrysler strike, Fansteel strike, 1938; power struggle and leadership in the UAW; Communist influence on CIO; cases before NLRB; portal to portal; anti-trust act, Clayton Act; power struggle in CIO: 1940 CIO convention, John L. Lewis' speech supporting Wendell Willkie; World Trade Union movement; CIO struggle for recognition and competition with AFL; impressions of John L. Lewis, Philip Murray, Sidney Hillman, Walter Reuther, James B. Carey and others.
475 pp. *Permission required to cite or quote.* 1958. *Micro II.*
Discussed in John Brophy; Edwin A. Lahey.

PREUSSE, Charles F. (1902–1977) *See* New York Political Studies (B).

PRIAULX, Arthur. *See* Weyerhaeuser Timber Company.

PRICE, David E. (1914–) *See* Health Sciences.

PRINZ, Leroy. *See* Aviation Project.

PRISONS *See* Albert Blumenthal; George Chandler; David Dressler; Francis B. Sayre.

PRITCHETT, Henry. *Discussed in* Carnegie Corporation.

PROGRESSIVE PARTY (1912) *See* Frederick M. Davenport; Stanley M. Isaacs; Ferdinand Pecora; William A. Prendergast; Theodore Roosevelt Association.

PROGRESSIVE PARTY (1948) *See* C.B. Baldwin; Bruce Bliven; D. Angus Cameron; Thomas I. Emerson; Morris Rosenthal; Henry A. Wallace.

PROHIBITION *See* William H. Anderson; Ella Boole; August W. Flath; William O'Dwyer; Bernard (Toots) Shor; William F. Varney; James W. Wadsworth; Emily Smith Warner.

PROKUPEK, George E. (1923–   ) *See* Continental Group.

PROSKAUER, Joseph M. (1877–1971) Judge.
Family background; influence of James Harvey Robinson, George Woodberry, teachers at Columbia; Columbia Law School; law practice; bench; NY State Crime Commission; Citizens Union; "Happy Warrior" speech; St. Lawrence water power; Liberty League; Charter Commission; American Jewish Committee; human rights and UN Conference at San Francisco; impressions of Alfred E. Smith, Franklin Delano Roosevelt, Charles Michelson, Robert Moses, Stephen Wise, Louis Marshall, Chaim Weizmann, Wendell Willkie.
141 pp. *Permission required.* 1961.

JOSEPH M. PROSKAUER PROJECT
Anecdotes and recollections from family, friends, and associates have been added to Judge Proskauer's own reminiscences, with a view to preparing a biography.
Participants and pages: Albert Fiorillo, 20; Jacob Goldberg, 26; Kate Pantell, 32; Joseph M. Proskauer, 141; James N. Rosenberg, 32; Abram S. Sacher, 21; Ruth Proskauer Smith, 27.
299 pp. *Permission required.* 1966. *Contributed by friends of Judge Joseph M. Proskauer.*

PRUDEN, Wesley. *See* Eisenhower Administration.

PRUSS, Max (–1960) *See* Aviation Project. *Micro IV.*

PSYCHIATRY *See* Psychology/Psychiatry.

PSYCHOANALYTIC MOVEMENT
The early history of psychoanalysis and its subsequent ramifications, as discussed by psychoanalysts and others closely associated with the movement in interviews with Dr. Bluma Swerdloff. The series includes interviews, in this country and abroad, with associates of Sigmund Freud and leading representatives of major schools of psychoanalytic theory. The project aims to provide anecdotal, subjective material that will shed new light on the pioneers of the psychoanalytic movement and its influence on contemporary society.
Participants and pages: Michael Balint, 78; Muriel Gardiner, 179 *(permission required);* Edward Glover, 137 *(permission required);* Heinz Hartmann, 145 *(certain pages closed);* Willi Hoffer, 116; Abram Kardiner, 712 *(certain pages closed);* Lawrence C. Kolb *(in process);* Rudolph Loewenstein, 149; Margaret Mahler, 116 *(certain pages closed);* Sandor Rado, 317; Joseph Sandler, 43 *(permission required),* Raymond de Saussure, 73 *(permission required);* René Spitz, 104 *(permission required).*
2,169 pp. *Permission required to cite or quote except as noted.* 1963–   . *Underwritten by the New-Land Foundation of New York City.*

PSYCHOLOGY/PSYCHIATRY *See* Karl Bowman; Kenneth Clark; Mamie Clark; Joseph Collins; Arthur T. Jersild; Psychoanalytic Movement; Theodor Reik; Frank Stanton; Goodwin Watson.

PUBLIC HEALTH *See* Hazel Corbin; William Cort; Haven Emerson; John B. Grant; Alan Gregg; Health Sciences; Ernest Howard; Mary Lasker; Social Security; Benjamin E. Washburn; Robert B. Watson; Women's History and Population Issues.

PUBLIC RELATIONS *See* Advertising/Public Relations.

PUBLISHERS *See* Books and Book Publishing; Journalists.

PULITZER, Joseph, Jr. (1885–1955) Editor.
Relations with his father; education at Harvard; early training on the NY *World* and the St. Louis *Post-Dispatch;* philosophy of journalism; publishing the *Post-Dispatch.*
193 pp. *Permission required to cite or quote.* 1954. *Micro II.*

PUPIN, Michael. *Discussed in* William Fondiller.

PURCELL, Edward Mills (1912–   ) *See* Nobel Laureates.

PURDY, Lawson (1863–1959) Lawyer, civic worker.
NYC and State social work, taxation and housing, 1900–30.
47 pp. *Permission required to cite or quote.* 1948. *Micro III.*

PUSCHEL, William H. (1902–   ) *See* Continental Group.

PYE, Lucien (1921–   ) *See* International Negotiations.

PYE, W. S. *Discussed in* Harold C. Train.

PYLE, Ernie. *Discussed in* Roger Straus.

PYLE, Howard (1906–   ) and Charles Masterson. Government agency executives.
EISENHOWER ADMINISTRATION
Pyle's early career, contacts with Dwight Eisenhower, fact papers, impressions of White House staff, political career in Arizona. Masterson's experiences with Citizens for Eisenhower, Interstate Defense Highway legislation, Bricker amendment. In a joint interview, Pyle and Masterson discuss fact papers and workings within the administration.
134 pp. *Permission required.* 1967.

Q

QUALEY, Carlton Chester (1904–   ) Historian, educator.
Relations between Bard College and Columbia University during the 1930's.
9 pp. *Permission required.* 1968. *Contributed by Lila Johnson, Minnesota Historical Society.*

QUESADA, Elwood Richard (1904–   ) *See* Henry A. Arnold Project; Aviation Project, *Micro III; and* Eisenhower Administration, *Micro III.*

QUIGG, Murray T. (–1956) *See* Theodore Roosevelt Association.

QUIGLEY, Martin Joseph (1890–1964) *See* Popular Arts.

QUILL, Michael. *Discussed in* William O'Dwyer; Robert F. Wagner.

QUINE, Richard (1920–   ) *See* Popular Arts.

QUINN, John. *Discussed in* Ben W. Huebsch.

R

RABB, Maxwell M. (1910–   ) Government official.
EISENHOWER ADMINISTRATION
Secretary of the Cabinet, 1953–58; civil rights under Eisenhower, desegregating naval bases and Veterans Hospitals; President's Contract Compliance Committee.
38 pp. *Permission required to cite or quote.* 1970. *Micro III.*

EISENHOWER ADMINISTRATION
Recollections of General Lucius Clay; 1952 campaign; opinions on members of Eisenhower's Cabinet.
23 pp. *Permission required.* 1971.

RABI, Isidor Isaac (1898–   ) Physicist.
Childhood and education, NYC; early interest and experiments in physical sciences; Cornell and first awareness of physics; return to NYC; Brooklyn Study Circle and intellectual ferment of the 1920's; dissertation, early papers; Europe 1927–29, especially Copenhagen and Hamburg; Columbia 1929 on; activity in theoretical and experimental physics; quantum theory, complementarity; students. Impressions of many scientists, including Niels Bohr, Wolfgang Pauli, Robert Oppenheimer.
In process.
See also Nobel Laureates.
Discussed in Norman Ramsey.

RABIN, Coleman Berley (1900–   ) *See* Mt. Sinai Hospital. *Micro II.*

RABINOFF, Max (1876–1966) Impresario.
Introduction of Russian ballet to US, 1909–1911; touring with Boston National Opera and Ballet Russe until 1917; opera production, Mexico, 1910; beginning of Chicago Opera Company; American Institute of Operatic and Allied Arts, 1925.
48 pp. *Open.* 1963.

RABINOWITZ, Louis (1887–1957) Manufacturer, philanthropist.
Early life and immigration to the US; hook-and-eye industry; philanthropy and its problems.
42 pp. *Permission required to cite or quote.* 1957. *Micro I.*

RABINOWITZ, Victor (1911–   ) Lawyer.
Family background, education; early legal work for trade unions, NYC; American Labor Party, 1936; Boudin, Cohn and Glickstein, 1938–42: association with Communist-influenced unions, national and state labor boards; foundation of own firm, 1942: effects of Taft-Hartley Act, internal security investigations, American Communications Association vs. Douds, Steve Nelson case; discussion of Judith Coplon and Rosenberg cases; Teachers Union, NYC, and Board of Education; Jimmy Hoffa; representing Castro government from 1960.
In process.

RACE RELATIONS *See* Will Alexander; Anne Braden; Virginius Dabney; Jonathan W. Daniels; Guy B. Johnson; Arthur F. Raper; Benno Schmidt, Jr.; George S. Schuyler; Herman E. Talmadge; Rupert B. Vance; Margaret B. Young.
See also Black Issues.

RADFORD, Arthur. *Discussed in* Joseph J. Clark; Felix B. Stump.

RADIO LIBERTY

In anticipation of the 50th anniversary of the Russian Revolution, Radio Liberty and the Institute for the Study of the Union of the Soviet Socialist Republics in Munich collected memoirs of participants in the events of 1917. The material presents a broad political, social, economic, and cultural panorama of Russia at that time. The 75 interviews, conducted in Europe in 1964–65, are in Russian; a list is available on request.

1,595 pp. *Permission required.* 1965. *Contributed by Radio Liberty Committee, New York.*

RADIO PIONEERS

A comprehensive record of the early history of radio contributed by engineers, station and network executives, government officials, writers, directors, and performers.

Scientific matters discussed include types of sending apparatus, early experiments with wireless, radio antennas, wireless and radio transmitters, the Alexanderson alternator, early experiments with television, transmitters for radio stations, mobile radio units, problems of engineering in network broadcasts, manufacturers' laboratory research, and the effects of WWII on radio engineering.

The growth of the radio business from the days of amateurs is described in accounts of manufacturing apparatus for the radio market (Westinghouse Electric Company, General Electric Corporation, and the Radio Corporation of America), wireless telegraphy and telephony on the Great Lakes, operating methods in early radio stations, establishing and financing a radio station in the 1920's, persuading advertisers to buy radio time, responses of and to the radio audience, broadcast ethics, and the impact of television with its new business and performing methods.

The growth of networks and network competition with local stations is detailed in accounts of the development of NBC, the Red and Blue networks and the outgrowth of the American Broadcasting Company from them, CBS, Mutual Broadcasting System, American Telephone & Telegraph Company, and the stations of General Electric and Westinghouse.

Radio's relations with government are dealt with in accounts of the Washington Conference assigning international wavelengths, 1927; Federal Radio Commission; FCC, radio law and legislation; government regulation and comparisons of radio in the US, Great Britain, and Canada; the British Broadcasting Corporation; patent-licensing and the Department of Justice, 1932; US censorship in WWII; postwar problems.

Impressions are given of Walter Damrosch, David Sarnoff, Bertha Brainerd, Frank Conrad, Al Jolson, Owen D. Young, Henry Ford, Fred Waring, William S. Paley, George F. McClelland, Merlin H. Aylesworth, and others. Erik Barnouw, Professor of Film at Columbia University, added to the original series a number of interviews conducted in connection with his three-volume history of broadcasting in the US.

Participants and pages: Ernst Frederick Werner Alexanderson, 61; Ed Allen, 7; Frank Atkinson Arnold, 101; Walter Ransom Gail Baker, 20; Harry Ray Bannister, 62; Howard Barlow, 213; Patrick Henry Barnes, 35; Joseph M. Barnett, 30; Gustave A. Bosler, 21; Everett L. Bragdon, 20; Harry P. Breitenbach, 10; William Wilbur Brown, 28; Lyman Lloyd Bryson, 254; Orestes Hampton Caldwell, 28; Joseph D. Cappa, 22; Phillips Carlin, 27; Abram Chasins, 89; Thomas Edward Clark, 38; Norman Corwin, 100 *(closed during lifetime);* Louis Cowan, 225; Thomas H. Cowan, 119; Roderick Cupp, 12; Lee De Forest, 9; Richard K. Doan, 26; Glen Dolberg, 8;

Lloyd Espenschied, 48; Walter Chew Evans, 65; Edgar Felix, 55; John Earl Fetzer, 91; Fred Friendly, 50; Robert Fuller, 13; Wayland Fullington, 24; John Gambling, 39; George Gingell, 14; Harry Goodman, 8; Dorothy Gordon, 168; Ben Grauer, 65; Gordon Gray, 2; Gordon Greb, 29; Rosaline Greene, 42; Wilton Gunzendorfer, 10; Raymond Frederick Guy, 78; Joseph Anthony Haeffner, 30; Kolin Hager, 36; Richard F. Hanser, 32; William E. Harkness, 99; Herschell Hart, 21; Laurence Ashley Hawkins, 28; William Saxby Hedges, 123; John E. Hill, 8; Lawrence LaMotte Holland, 25; Herbert Clark Hoover, 21; Albert Wallace Hull, 31;

E.P.H. James, 17; Eddie Janis, 25; Arthur Judson, 25; William J. Kaland, 7; H.V. Kaltenborn, 248; Ken Kennedy, 7; Alfred Henry Kirchhofer, 21; Kirk Knight, 34; Chester Henry Lang, 29; Leon Lichtenfeld, 22; Donald G. Little, 101; Edgar J. Love, 15; Ruth Lyons, 7; Stanley Rutter Manning, 16; Carlton Morse and Michael Rafetto, 18; Ray Newby, 38; Paul Oliphant and F.C. Sowell, 32; Dorsey Owings, 16; John F. Patt, 73; Daniel Petrie, 48; James A. Pike, 18; Elton M. Plant, 45; Herbert Ponting, 10; Robert L. Pratt, 7;

Harry Rasky, 42; Philip H. Reisman, 60; Lord John Reith, 25; Bruce Robertson, 15; Otis E. Robinson, 17; William N. Robson, 41; Manuel Rosenberg, 8; J. Harold Ryan, 7; Abel Alan Schechter, 33; William Edmund Scripps, 33; Robert L. Shayon, 41; John L. Slaton, 7; Robert Smiley, 18; Ira D. Smith and Fred J. Hart, 82; Sigmund Spaeth, 121; Jeff Sparks, 60; Davidson Taylor, 82 *(permission required);* Sybil True, 23; Edwin Lloyd Tyson, 32; Clyde D. Wagoner, 34; James Truman Ward, 10; Gene Waters, 8; Irving Reid Weir, 31; Grover A. Whalen, 27; Rex G. White, 19; William Cummings White, 20; Mark Woods, 120; William R. Yates, 50.

4,765 pp. *Permission required to cite or quote except as noted. 1950–   . Some memoirs are available in microform; consult individual entries. Underwritten by the Twenty Year Club (now Broadcast Pioneers).*

RADO, Sandor (1890–1972) Psychoanalyst. PSYCHOANALYTIC MOVEMENT
Early education, Hungary; M.D., 1915; education as a psychoanalyst; work with Sigmund Freud and Sandor Ferenczi; faculty member of Berlin Psychoanalytic Institute, 1923–31; Karl Abraham; managing editor, *Internationale Zeitschrift fuer Psychoanalyse* and *Imago;* the US and organization of a psychoanalytic institute on the Berlin model; educational director, NY Psychoanalytic Institute, 1931–41; comments on the evolution of psychoanalytic theory and technique.
317 pp. *Permission required to cite or quote. 1965.*

RAFETTO, Michael and Carlton Morse. *See* Radio Pioneers.

RAICHLE, Frank G. (1898–   ) Lawyer. NEW YORK BAR
Highlights from career as trial lawyer in Buffalo and NYC; white-collar crime, negligence; civil anti-trust cases; views on legal ethics, jurors and jury system; activities in bar organizations.
104 pp. *Permission required to cite or quote. 1977.*

RAILROADS *See* Transportation.

RAINER, Yvonne. *Discussed in* Valda Setterfield.

RAMICONE, Luis (1901–   ) *See* Argentina.

RAMSEY, Norman (1915–   ) Physicist. Education, Columbia; Depression; Cambridge University, England; research with I. I. Rabi, Enrico Fermi; NDRC radiation laboratory, MIT; England, 1941; security problems; radar; Manhattan Project, 1943; Los Alamos; discussions on use of bomb and possible targets; Trinity test; Tinian; estimates of damage, Hiroshima; Brookhaven; Harvard; Congressional investigations; Harold Velde and Joseph McCarthy hearings; area rule; appearance on "Meet the Press," subsequent meeting with Senator McCarthy; contempt citations; Kamen trial; Robert Oppenheimer case; Gray Board; science adviser, NATO; impressions of Gen. Leslie Groves, Adm. Lewis L. Strauss, Edward Teller.
358 pp. *Permission required to cite or quote. 1960. Micro IV.*

RAND, Ayn. *Discussed in* Phyllis Cerf Wagner.

RANDALL, Tony (1920–   ) *See* Popular Arts.

RANDALL, Willie (1911–   ) *See* Jazz Project.

RANDOLPH, Asa Philip (1889–   ) Labor leader.
Boyhood, Jacksonville, Florida: family, education; first experiences in NYC: west

side, CCNY; Socialist and pacifist opposition to WWI; Eugene Debs; postwar Harlem: Lafayette Theater, the *Messenger;* Chandler Owen, Marcus Garvey, Madame C.J. Walker; early union work.
283 pp. *Open.* 1972. *Underwritten by the Center for War/Peace Studies, New York. Discussed in* Benjamin McLaurin; George S. Schuyler.

RANDOLPH, Jennings (1902–   ) *See* Social Security.

RANK, Otto. *Discussed in* Abram Kardiner; Theodor Reik.

RANKIN, Jeannette. *Discussed in* Alice Paul.

RANKIN, Joseph T. *See* Rare Books (A).

RANKIN, R. Grady. *See* James B. Duke Project *and* Norman Cocke.

RANKIN, Watson Smith (1879–   ) *See* James B. Duke Project.

RANSOM, Harry Huntt (1908–1976) University chancellor.
AMERICAN CULTURAL LEADERS
Boyhood and early education, Texas and Tennessee; University of Texas, 1935–67; campus activism and academic freedom; educational administration in US.
87 pp. *Permission required.* 1967.

RANSOM, John Crowe. *Discussed in* Robert Penn Warren.

RANUM, Orest. *See* Columbia Crisis of 1968.

RAPER, Arthur Franklin (1899–   ) Sociologist.
SOUTHERN INTELLECTUAL LEADERS (A)
Boyhood; education, University of North Carolina and Vanderbilt; Commission on Interracial Cooperation, research and field secretary, 1926–42; Southern Commission on the Study of Lynching; Southern Conference for Human Welfare; Carnegie Corporation study of the American Negro, 1939–40; Department of State and AID, 1952–62; agricultural development work in Japan, the Middle East, and Taiwan; East

Pakistan; impressions of Will Alexander, Frank P. Graham, Gunnar Myrdal, and others.
161 pp. *Permission required to cite or quote.* 1971.

RAPHAELSON, Samson (1896–   ) Author.
POPULAR ARTS
Lower East Side NYC and Chicago; stage and film versions of *The Jazz Singer; Young Love;* move to Hollywood, 1929; scriptwriter; life in Hollywood; major motion picture studios; relations with producers, agents, directors, actors; censorship; impressions of Al Jolson, George Jessel, Harry Cohn, Ernst Lubitsch, Myron Selznick, Billy Wilder, Frank Capra, and others.
123 pp. *Closed during lifetime.* 1959.

RAPP, Arl S. (1893–   ) *See* Continental Group.

RARE BOOKS
A. THE WORLD OF RARE BOOKS
A series of interviews with significant figures in the world of rare books, conducted by Gerald Gottlieb of The Pierpont Morgan Library. Interviewees include directors of rare book libraries, curators of special collections, rare book librarians, private collectors, dealers, and executives of auction houses. Emphasis is placed not only on reminiscences but also on the participants' observations on current trends, institutional vs. private collectors, conservation and restoration, control of access to rare materials, collection development, availability, market trends, and forgeries. The project is a continuing one.
Participants and pages: Herbert Cahoon, 39; Lew David Feldman, 20; Allen T. Hazen, 49; Joseph G. E. Hopkins, 15; Kenneth A. Lohf, 105; Paul Needham, 48; Robert Nikirk, 44; Graham Pollard and Allen T. Hazen, 43; Joseph T. Rankin, 37; Donald Reiman, 47; Charles A. Ryskamp, 40; Benjamin Swann, 34; Lola L. Szladits, 67; Stephen Weissman, 81.
669 pp. *Permission required.* 1973–
Contributed by Gerald Gottlieb, NYC.

B. THE AMERICAN ANTIQUARIAN BOOK TRADE, 1920–45

A group of interviews with dealers, collectors, and librarians on the American antiquarian book trade during the period between the two world wars.
Participants and pages: Peter Decker, 70; Franklin Gilliam *(in process);* Douglas Parsonage, 32; John Scopazzi *(in process)*.
102 pp. *Permission required.* 1978–
Contributed by Denis Carbonneau, NYC.

RASKIN, A.H. *Discussed in* John B. Oakes

RASKOB, J.J. *Discussed in* Eddie Dowling.

RASKY, Harry (1928–   ) *See* Radio Pioneers.

RATHBONE, Basil (1892–1967) *See* Popular Arts.

RAUGHT, Al. *See* Weyerhaeuser Timber Company.

RAUH, Joseph L. (1911–   ) *See* James Lawrence Fly Project.

RAUP, R. Bruce (1888–1976) Educator.
Education and early teaching experiences in the Middle West; TC, 1920–54; *Social Frontiers;* social and philosophical foundations of education; relationship of TC and Columbia University. Impressions of John Dewey, W. H. Kilpatrick, E. L. Thorndike, James Russell and William Russell, Harold Rugg, and others.
230 pp. *Permission required to cite or quote.* 1963. *Micro I.*

RAUSHENBUSH, Esther (1898–   )
College president.
Part I: Family history; education, University of Washington, A.B. 1921, M.A. 1922; marriage; professional career at Wellesley, Barnard, Sarah Lawrence, 1923–   ; presidency, Sarah Lawrence, 1965–69, president emeritus, 1969–   ; educational philosophy; progressive education; implementation of social change, scholarship programs for minority group members; Whitney Foundation Scholarship; McCarthy era; Jenner Committee; Center for Continuing Education; impressions of Charles de Carlo, Beatrice Doerschuk, William Van Duser Lawrence, Harold Taylor, Harrison Tweed, Paul Ward, Constance Warren.

628 pp. *Permission required.* 1973.

Part II: Continuing Education for Women at Sarah Lawrence, beginnings, development, present status.
30 pp. *Permission required to cite or quote.* 1974.

RAUSHENBUSH, Paul and Elizabeth (Mrs. Paul).
SOCIAL SECURITY
Personal backgrounds; teaching at University of Wisconsin from early 1920's; Wisconsin's Unemployment Act and the AFL; Louis Brandeis' work in unemployment; Wagner-Lewis bill, 1933–34; administration of Wisconsin's State Unemployment Compensation; development of Social Security and federal unemployment bills; other work in unemployment and Social Security; recollections of Harold Groves, John R. Commons, Frances Perkins, Arthur Altmeyer, and others.
295 pp. *Permission required to cite or quote.* 1966. Papers.
Discussed in Herman M. Somers.

RAVDIN, Isidor Schwaner (1894–1972) Surgeon.
B.A. Indiana University; M.D. University of Pennsylvania; academic surgery; specific procedures in gastrointestinal surgery in early 1930's; impact of WWII; 20th General Hospital in the CBI; academic surgery at Pennsylvania after WWII.
555 pp. *Permission required to cite or quote.* 1962. *Micro II.*

RAY, Gordon Norton (1915–   ) *See* American Cultural Leaders.

RAYBURN, Sam. *Discussed in* Lucius D. Clay; D.B. Hardeman.

RAYMOND, Arthur Emmons (1899–   ) *See* Henry H. Arnold Project.

READ, William Augustus (1895–1976) Naval officer.
Harvard, National Guard Service; naval aviation; WWI, Pensacola; banking career, Dillon, Read; Hanover Bank; Naval Reserve from 1939; special assistant to Adm. John Towers, 1942; experiences with fast carrier task forces as Staff Officer to Adm.

Marc Mitscher: logistics, morale, air-sea rescue, buildup; death of Adm. Isoroku Yamamoto; operations in New Caledonia, Gilberts, Marshalls, Marianas, Saipan, Philippines, Formosa, Leyte Gulf; plans for Iwo Jima, Okinawa; kamikaze attacks; postwar naval activities; impressions of Adm. Ernest King.

739 pp. *Permission required.* 1964.

REAL, Juan Jose. *See* Argentina.

REARDY, Viola. *See* Adlai E. Stevenson Project.

REECE, J. Carroll. *Discussed in* Carnegie Corporation.

REED, Alice Clara (1890–   ) *See* China Missionaries.

REED, Charles S. *See* James B. Duke Project.

REED, Robert. *See* Adlai E. Stevenson Project.

REED, Stanley Forman (1884–   ) Supreme Court Justice.
Boyhood in Kentucky; education in US and abroad; Kentucky legislature; the farm problem in the Hoover administration; appointment as Solicitor General in the early New Deal; presenting cases before the Supreme Court; appointment to the Supreme Court; impressions of other members of the Court and members of the bar; cases presented before the Court; the role of the Court in the New Deal; impressions of men and events of the Roosevelt administration. The memoir includes brief contributions by Harold Leventhal and John Sapienza.

350 pp. *Closed during lifetime.* 1959.

REED, William. *Discussed in* William O'Dwyer.

REESE, Benjamin Harrison (1888–1974) Journalist.
Childhood; early years in journalism in Joplin, Missouri; St. Louis *Post-Dispatch,* 1913–51: impressions of associates, notable public service campaigns and news beats, the Pulitzer trust; American Press Institute, Columbia University; seminars, reflections on journalism.

200 pp. *Permission required to cite or quote.* 1954. *Micro I.*

REEVE, Robert. *See* Aviation Project. *Micro III.*

REEVES, Joseph M. *Discussed in* Eugene E. Wilson.

REFORM *See* Social Work/Reform.

REICH, Joseph. *See* Air Force Academy.

REICHMANN, Frieda. *Discussed in* Lawrence C. Kolb.

REID, Clement. *Discussed in* Association for the Aid of Crippled Children.

REID, Ogden Rogers (1925–   ) Congressman.
EISENHOWER ADMINISTRATION
Ambassador to Israel, 1959–1961.

22 pp. *Permission required to cite or quote.* 1967. *Micro III.*

REID, Ralph Waldo Emerson (1915–   ) *See* Eisenhower Administration. *Micro III.*

REIDY, William.
SOCIAL SECURITY
University of Wisconsin, 1934; FSA, California, 1940; health programs, group health contracts; health insurance adviser to Senator James Murray, 1945; health reforms during the Truman administration; AMA position on compulsory health insurance; Wagner-Murray bill; National Council of Senior Citizens; cooperation with Robert McNamara; impressions of Isidore Falk, Wilbur Cohen, and others.

101 pp. *Permission required to cite or quote.* 1966.
Discussed in Harold Sheppard.

REIK, Theodor (1888–1969) Psychoanalyst.
Protegé and friend of Sigmund Freud; recollections of Otto Rank and Hans Sachs; analysis with Dr. Karl Abraham; founding of National Association for Allied Psychoanalysts.

99 pp. *Permission required to cite or quote.* 1965. *Micro I.*
Discussed in Roger W. Straus.

REIMAN, Donald. *See* Rare Books (A).

REINER, Fritz. *Discussed in* Saul Goodman; Morton Gould.

REINHARDT, Gottfried. *See* Popular Arts.

REIS, Claire (1888–1978) Writer on music. Texas childhood; musical training, Berlin and Juilliard; role in opening Walden School, teaching; impressions of many modern composers, musical conductors and artists; involvement with People's Music League, 1912–22; formation, activities of League of Composers, tribute programs, use of radio and film, publication of *Modern Music,* support of contemporary and avant-garde music forms, international aspects; early electronic concerts; publications in music field, 1914–68; history of Women's City Club, activities; NYC Center of Music and Drama opening, 1943, expansion and activities.
320 pp. *Permission required to cite or quote.* 1977. *Acquired from Yale University School of Music Oral History Project.*

REISMAN, Philip H.
RADIO PIONEERS
Education; early experiences in radio, Pathé News; combat photography; producing programs and script materials; script editor, William Esty agency.
60 pp. *Permission required to cite or quote.* 1968. *Micro II.*

REITER, Bela Z. (1890–1957) *See* McGraw-Hill.

REITH, Lord John (–1971) *See* Radio Pioneers.

REITSCH, Hanna. *See* Aviation Project.

RELIGION *See* Ralph Albertson; Will Alexander; John Badeau; Arlene Carmen; China Missionaries; Edward L. Elson; George B. Ford; Frederick Hochwalt; Donald Harrington; John H. Lathrop; Madeleine L'Engle; A.J. Muste; Reinhold Nie-

buhr; James A. Pike; Athanasius Samuel; Louise H. Southwick.
See also Missions and Missionaries.

RENO, Milo. *Discussed in* Farm Holiday Association.

RENOIR, Jean (1894–1979) *See* Popular Arts.

RENTSCHLER, Frederick B. *Discussed in* Eugene E. Wilson.

REPUBLICAN PARTY *See* Thomas Chamberlain; Alger Chapman; Frederick Davenport; Thomas E. Dewey; Eisenhower Administration; Stanley M. Isaacs; Samuel S. Koenig; Albert D. Lasker; Ormsby McHarg; Walter S. Mack, Jr.; John L. O'-Brian; William A. Prendergast; Beverley R. Robinson; Theodore Roosevelt Association; Martin Saxe; H. Alexander Smith; Robert A. Taft Project; Frederick C. Tanner; Stanley Washburn; F. Clifton White; James T. Williams, Jr.

RESCH, Glenn (1948–   ) Hockey Goalie.
Childhood in Canada; education, University of Minnesota; impressions of Soviet hockey players and representatives; Canadian strategy compared to Soviet's.
52 pp. *Open.* 1976.

RESTON, James Barrett (1909–   ) *See* Journalism Lectures.

REUTHER, Walter. *Discussed in* Edward R. Annis; John Brophy; Nelson Cruikshank; Lee Pressman; M. Hedley Stone.

REVESTIDO, Miguel. *See* Argentina.

REXROTH, Kenneth. *See* Alexandra Kollontai Project.

REYES, Cipriano. *See* Argentina.

REYNOLDS, Jackson E. (1873–1958) Lawyer, banker.
Columbia University Law School, 1896–99; founding of the Bank for International Settlements; Bank Holiday, 1933; Herbert C. Hoover.
179 pp. *Permission required to cite or*

quote. 1949. *Micro I.* Papers: 148 letters and newspaper clippings about the Bank for International Settlements.

REYNOLDS, William. *See* Social Security.

RHEE, Syngman. *Discussed in* Walter S. Robertson.

RHIND, Flora Macdonald (1904–   ) Foundation officer.
Background and education; experience with General Education Board and Rockefeller Foundation, 1933–64: requests received, limitations on grants, procedures in handling, program meetings, docket conferences, trustee meetings, evaluation of programs; responsibilities of Secretary's office, relation with counsel; social science program; fellowships and grants-in-aid; evolution of general education program; Laura Spelman Rockefeller Memorial, Education Policies Commission, American Council on Education, American Youth Commission; development of southern program: Southern Fellowships Fund, Southern Regional Education Board, Southern Education Fund, George Peabody College, state agents for rural schools; European program; congressional investigations, travel in connection with programs; Villa Serbelloni; retirement. Impressions of Raymond Fosdick, John D. Rockefeller, Jr., John D. Rockefeller 3rd, Beardsley Ruml, George Vincent, Edmund E. Day, Dean Rusk, John Foster Dulles, J. George Harrar, many others.
1,520 pp. *Permission required.* 1969. *Underwritten by the Rockefeller Foundation, New York.*

RIBICOFF, Abraham. *Discussed in* Blue Carstenson; Nelson Cruikshank; Irwin Wolkstein.

RICCIO, Vincent (1919–   ) Youth worker.
Work with NYC Youth Board among juveniles in Brooklyn; gang warfare, customs, dress, and talk.
290 pp. *Permission required to cite or quote.* 1961. *Micro II. Contributed by John K. Kelly, Newark, Delaware.*

RICE, Edward E. (1909–   ) *See* Eisenhower Administration. *Micro III.*

RICE, Martin P. *Discussed in* Chester H. Lang.

RICHARD, Auguste (1890–   ) *See* Robert P. Patterson Project.

RICHARDS, Bernard G. (1877–1971) Jewish leader.
American Jewish community during 20th century; Zionist and Territorialist organizations; Peace Conference, 1919; impressions of Dr. Judah Magnes, Dr. Stephen S. Wise, Louis Marshall, Louis Brandeis, Israel Zangwill.
360 pp. *Permission required to cite or quote.* 1960. *Micro II.*

RICHARDS, Dickinson W. (1895–1973) *See* Nobel Laureates.

RICHARDS, Homer C. (1895–   ) *See* Jackson Hole Preserve.

RICHARDS, Margaret (1900–   ) *See* McGraw-Hill.

RICHARDSON, Doc. *See* Flying Tigers.

RICHARDSON, Elliot Lee (1920–   ) *See* Social Security. *Micro III.*

RICHARDSON, Holden C. (–1960) *See* Aviation Project.

RICHARDSON, Stephen A. *See* Association for the Aid of Crippled Children.

RICHTER, Hans. *See* Robert J. Flaherty Project.

RICHTMYER, F.K. *Discussed in* American Association of Physics Teachers.

RICKENBACKER, Edward Vernon (1890–1973) *See* Air Force Academy *and* Aviation Project, *Micro IV.*

RICKETT, Harold W. *See* New York Botanical Garden.

RICKOVER, Hyman. *Discussed in* Edward L. Beach.

RIESMAN, David (1909–   ) *See* Carnegie Corporation.

RILEY, Edward. *See* Independence Park.

RINARD, Ruth. *See* Kirkland College.

RING, Blanche (1872–1961) *See* Popular Arts.

RING, Frances. *Discussed in* Richard Gordon.

RIPLEY, William Z. *Discussed in* Adolf A. Berle.

RIPMAN, Hugh. *See* World Bank.

RISENER, Randy. *See* Vietnam Veterans.

RIST, Leonard Bernstein (1905–) Banker, economist.
WORLD BANK
Early organization of Bank and International Monetary Fund; economic department; evolution of credit standards; studies of internal fiscal policies of borrowing countries; commodity studies; Meyer, McCloy, and Black presidencies; reconstruction loans and development loans; loans for imports, education, and public health programs.
62 pp. *Permission required to cite or quote.* 1961.

RIVERA, Diego. *Discussed in* Ben Shahn.

RIZZUTO, David T. Army helicopter pilot. Impressions of Vietnam, the war, the Vietnamese people. The memoir consists of tape-recorded letters sent by Officer Rizzuto from Southeast Asia to his family at home.
148 pp. *Permission required to cite or quote.* 1969.

ROBB, Andrew Donaldson. *See* Benedum and the Oil Industry.

ROBBINS, Frederick Chapman (1916–) *See* Nobel Laureates.

ROBBINS, I.D. (1913–) Civic worker. NYC political system, politicians, media, 1930's–70's; 1952– , association with City Club of New York, president (1959), founding editor of *City Club Comments;* effect of Mitchell-Lama Act on establish-

ment of Big Six Towers apartments and Hunts Point Cooperative Market; essays, opinions published in *Daily News, Wall Street Journal, New York Times;* mayoralty nomination effort and withdrawal, 1965; impressions of John Lindsay, Robert Moses, Robert Wagner, other NYC leaders.
350 pp. *Permission required to cite or quote.* 1976. *Micro IV.*

ROBBINS, W.J. *See* New York Botanical Garden.

ROBERTS, Carson A. (1905–) *See* Marine Corps.

ROBERTS, Chalmers McGeagh (1910–) Journalist.
EISENHOWER ADMINISTRATION
Covering State Department and foreign affairs during the Eisenhower administration; John Foster Dulles.
36 pp. *Permission required to cite or quote.* 1967. *Micro III.*

ROBERTS, Charles Wesley (1916–) *See* Eisenhower Administration.

ROBERTS, Clifford (1893–1977) Business executive.
EISENHOWER ADMINISTRATION
Recollections of Dwight Eisenhower from 1948: hobbies, Presidency of Columbia University, NATO, 1952 and 1956 campaigns; Eisenhower's personal financial arrangements; Republican politics; impressions of Eisenhower's friends, family, aides, Cabinet; Eisenhower Citizens Committee; heart attack and ileitis operation; Augusta National Golf Club; impressions of W.A. (Pete) Jones, and others.
878 pp. *Closed until 1997.* 1972. Papers.

ROBERTS, Jerome R. (1918–) *See* Continental Group.

ROBERTS, Morris O. (1904–) *See* Continental Group.

ROBERTSON, Bruce. *See* Radio Pioneers.

ROBERTSON, Walter Spencer (1893–1970) Diplomat.
EISENHOWER ADMINISTRATION

Experiences as Far Eastern affairs expert in State Department; China with Gens. Patrick Hurley and George Marshall, 1945–6; Assistant Secretary of State for Far East, 1953–59; policies in South East Asia; SEATO; Korea; impressions of John Foster Dulles, President Eisenhower, Mao Tse-tung, Chou En-lai, Jawaharlal Nehru, Syngman Rhee.

194 pp. *Permission required to cite or quote.* 1967. *Micro III.*

ROBESON, Paul. *Discussed in* Jean B. Hutson; David A. Morse.

ROBINSON, Beverley Randolph (1876–1951) Lawyer.
Education at Harvard and Columbia Law School; Republican political scene in NYC, 1897–1906; NY legislature, 1907–09; impressions of Theodore Roosevelt, Chauncey Depew, and others; 1916 Republican convention and campaign.

95 pp. *Permission required to cite or quote.* 1949.

ROBINSON, Boardman. *Discussed in* Warren Chappell.

ROBINSON, Edwin Arlington. *Discussed in* William S. Braithwaite; John Hall Wheelock.

ROBINSON, Frederick B. *Discussed in* Charles H. Tuttle.

ROBINSON, Helen R. Roosevelt (–1962) *See* Theodore Roosevelt Association.

ROBINSON, James Harvey. *Discussed in* Joseph M. Proskauer.

ROBINSON, Otis E. *See* Radio Pioneers.

ROBINSON, Ovid Daniel (1885–) *See* Benedum and the Oil Industry.

ROBINSON, Ray Albert (1896–1976) *See* Marine Corps.

ROBINSON, Samuel Murray (1882–1972) Naval officer.
Naval engineering, electric ship propulsion; Puget Sound Navy Yard, 1927–31; Chief of

Bureau Engineering, 1931; development of high speed diesel engine; Chief of Bureau of Ships, 1940; Chief of Procurement and Material, 1942–46; Webb Institute of Naval Architecture, 1946–51.

56 pp. *Permission required to cite or quote.* 1963.
Discussed in Henry Williams.

ROBINSON, William Smith O'B., Jr. (1885–) *See* James B. Duke Project.

ROBSON, William N. *See* Radio Pioneers.

ROCKEFELLER, John D., Jr. *Discussed in* Horace M. Albright; Chauncey Belknap; Kenneth Chorley; Harold P. Fabian; Peter Grimm; Flora M. Rhind; Warren Weaver.

ROCKEFELLER, Mrs. John D., Jr. *Discussed in* Holger Cahill.

ROCKEFELLER, John Davison 3rd (1906–1978) Philanthropist.
Part I: Concept and development of Lincoln Center for the Performing Arts: private and public financing, city and state authorities and NY World's Fair, relationship with Metropolitan Opera, Philharmonic, Juilliard, NY Public Library, City Center. Interest in Asia: International House (Japan), Population Council, agricultural economics, Council on Economic and Cultural Affairs, Japan Society, Asia Society.

334 pp. *Permission required.* 1963.

Part II: The evolution and execution of Lincoln Center for the Performing Arts.

69 pp. *Permission required.* 1967.

Discussed in Flora M. Rhind.

ROCKEFELLER, Laurance S. (1910–) *See* Jackson Hole Preserve. *Discussed in* Association for the Aid of Crippled Children.

ROCKEFELLER, Nelson Aldrich (1908–1979) Government official.
Part I: Travel abroad, 1930–39; Creole Petroleum Corporation; entering government service, 1937–39; Office of the Coordinator of Inter-American Affairs; wartime economic cooperation in the Americas; anti-Axis measures; programs for economic de-

velopment, 1940–44; Institute for Inter-American Affairs; politics in Washington: Congress, Department of State, BEW, information programs; wartime relations with Argentina; developing a Latin American policy and the Mexico City Conference; recognition of Argentina and relations between Argentina and the UN; Russia and San Francisco Conference, 1945; retirement from State Department; Latin American political, economic, and social prospects and hopes.

730 pp. *Closed until 1997.* 1952.

Part II: Studies on domestic and international affairs during the 1950's: "Partners in Progress," Rockefeller Brothers Fund recommendations; campaigns and electoral experiences; Governor of NY, 1959–73; Vice President, 1974–76; vignettes of many political figures.

52 pp. *Closed until 1997.* 1978.

EISENHOWER ADMINISTRATION
President's committee for Government Organization; Special Assistant to the President on International Affairs; Geneva Conference; relations with President Eisenhower and Vice President Richard Nixon; the "Fourteen Points."

40 pp. *Closed until 1997.* 1967.

Discussed in Richard Aurelio; William Benton; Will Clayton; Justin Feldman; Bernard Gladieux; Francis A. Jamieson; Roswell B. Perkins; Charles I. Schottland; Henry A. Wallace; Kenneth Williamson.

ROCKEFELLER FOUNDATION
The memoirs in this series, each of which was obtained quite independently of the others across the years, nonetheless have this much in common: all are about significant careers—in public health, plant pathology, foundation administration, and other areas—with the Rockefeller Foundation. Beyond this, the memoirs vary widely in subject, scope, and style, and there are comparatively few inter-connections, each memoirist having been invited to respond in his own way. *See:* J. Curtis Dixon, John Grant, Alan Gregg, J. George Harrar, John Marshall, Flora Rhind, E.C. Stakman, Benjamin Washburn, Robert

Briggs Watson, and Warren Weaver.
Copies are on deposit also at the Rockefeller Foundation Archives.

ROCKWELL, Frank A. (1915–   ) *See* Continental Group.

RODEWALD, Don. *See* Flying Tigers.

RODGERS, Cleveland (1885–1956) Editor.
Childhood; experience as linotype operator; NYC theaters; city planning movement, 1916; Brooklyn *Eagle,* 1906–37: special writer, drama critic, editor; NYC Board of Education, 1919–23; NYC Planning Commission, 1938–50; interest in Walt Whitman.

288 pp. *Open.* 1950. Papers.

RODGERS, Richard (1902–   ) Composer.
Childhood; start in theater; role of Dramatists Guild in securing rights of playwrights; beginnings of the Music Theater of Lincoln Center; association with Lorenz Hart and Oscar Hammerstein II; impressions of George Balanchine, Gertrude Lawrence, Florenz Ziegfeld, Billy Rose, and others.

392 pp. *Permission required to cite or quote; certain pages closed during lifetime.* 1968.

RODRIGUEZ, Juan (1903–   ) Union and government official.
ARGENTINA
Railroad union funds, 1930 revolution, British management, work stoppages, organizing white collar workers; ILO, Geneva, 1945; candidacy for Secretary General of General Confederation of Workers, 1946; impressions of Juan D. Peron, Jose Domenech, Antonio Tramonti, and others.

70 pp. *Open.* 1971.

RODRIGUEZ, Luis Maria. *See* Argentina.

RODZINSKI, Arthur. *Discussed in* Saul Goodman.

ROGERS, Ford O. (1894–1972) *See* Marine Corps.

ROGERS, Ginger. *Discussed in* Phyllis Cerf Wagner.

ROGERS, Lela. *Discussed in* Phyllis Cerf Wagner.

ROGERS, Lindsay (1891–1970) Political scientist.
Part I: Nicholas Murray Butler; mediation commission for the garment industry in the 1920's; Democratic conventions of 1928 and 1932.
106 pp. *Open.* 1958.

Part II: Experiences as assistant director, ILO, Montreal; UN conference in San Francisco.
21 pp. *Open.* 1965.

ROGERS, T.Y. *See* Civil Rights in Alabama.

ROGERS, William P. (1913–   ) Government official.
EISENHOWER ADMINISTRATION
Counsel for Senate Investigating Subcommittee; contested delegate cases, 1952 Republican convention; campaigning with Richard Nixon, 1952; Nixon Fund; Deputy Attorney General.
51 pp. *Permission required.* 1968.
Discussed in Arthur J. Goldberg.

ROGERS, William Walter (1893–1976) *See* Marine Corps.

ROLL, George Arthur (1913–   ) *See* Marine Corps.

ROMERO, Jose Luis. *See* Argentina.

ROMNEY, Vernon (1896–   ) *See* Robert A. Taft Project.

ROOSA, Robert Vincent (1918–   ) *See* Eisenhower Administration.
Discussed in Prescott Bush.

ROOSEVELT, Eleanor (Mrs. Franklin D.) (1884–1964) *See* Herbert H. Lehman Project. *Micro II.*
Discussed in Charles Ascher; Roger N. Baldwin; Samuel Battle; Chester Bowles; Cass Canfield; Edward Costikyan; Jonathan W. Daniels; Marion Dickerman; Justin N. Feldman; Bruce and Beatrice Gould; Anna Roosevelt Halsted; Dorothy Height; Katharine Lenroot; Kathleen McLaughlin;

Dorothy Rosenman; Harold C. Train; Marietta Tree; Wilson W. Wyatt.

ROOSEVELT, Franklin D. *Discussed in* Horace M. Albright; Will Alexander; Orvil A. Anderson; Charles Ascher; Raymond Baldwin; Adolf A. Berle, Jr.; Edward L. Bernays; Chester Bowles; Cass Canfield; Lucius D. Clay; Jonathan W. Daniels; Marion Dickerman; Goldthwaite Dorr; Thomas I. Emerson; Isidore Falk; James A. Farley; John P. Frey; Anna Roosevelt Halsted; Carl Hamilton; Thomas C. Hart; Frederick W. Henshaw; H. Kent Hewitt; Marvin Jones; Florence Kerr; Emory S. Land; James M. Landis; Herbert H. Lehman; Walter Lippmann; Lewis L. Lorwin; Langdon P. Marvin; Eugene Meyer; Frances Perkins; Omar T. Pfeiffer; Charles Poletti; Joseph M. Proskauer; Dorothy Rosenman; Samuel I. Rosenman; Socialist Movement; John R. Steelman; Henry Stimson; Francis R. Stoddard; Norman Thomas; James P. Warburg; Emily S. Warner; Burton K. Wheeler; James T. Williams, Jr.; M.L. Wilson; Walter Wyatt.

ROOSEVELT, Franklin, Jr. *Discussed in* Ben Davidson; Justin N. Feldman.

ROOSEVELT, James. *Discussed in* Gerald C. Thomas.

ROOSEVELT, Theodore. *Discussed in* George W. Alger; Frederick M. Davenport; Goldthwaite Dorr; John P. Frey; Lloyd C. Griscom; Thomas C. Hart; John T. Hettrick; Stanley M. Isaacs; Emory S. Land; John L. O'Brian; William A. Prendergast; Beverley R. Robinson; Frederick C. Tanner; Theodore Roosevelt Association; Henry Williams; James T. Williams, Jr.

THEODORE ROOSEVELT ASSOCIATION
Friends and associates reminisce about Theodore Roosevelt (1858–1919) and the Roosevelt family and circle, with reappraisals of Theodore Roosevelt's impact upon American life. Some new light is thrown on the Bull Moose campaign.
Participants and pages: Karl Howell Behr, 19; William Merriam Chadbourne, 34; William Sheffield Cowles, 118; F. Trubee Davison, 7; Barclay H. Farr, 33; Stanley Myer

Isaacs, 28; Jesse Langdon, 67; Samuel McCune Lindsay, 49; Alice R. Longworth, 41; Ezra Parmalee Prentice, 5; Murray T. Quigg, 28; Helen R. Roosevelt Robinson, 35; William Savacool, 30; Henry R. Stern, 21.
515 pp. *Permission required to cite or quote. 1953–55. Some memoirs are available in microform; consult individual entries.*

ROOT, Elihu (1845–1937) *Discussed in* Carnegie Corporation; John L. O'Brian; Stanley Washburn.

ROOT, Elihu, Jr. (1881–1967) *See* Robert P. Patterson Project.
Discussed in Carnegie Corporation.

RORABACK, J. Henry. *Discussed in* Raymond Baldwin.

ROSE, Alex. *Discussed in* Ben Davidson; Donald Harrington.

ROSE, Arnold. *Discussed in* Gunnar Myrdal.

ROSE, Billy. *Discussed in* Richard Rodgers.

ROSE, Leonard. *Discussed in* Saul Goodman.

ROSE, Wickliffe. *Discussed in* John B. Grant.

ROSENBERG, A. J. (1909–) *See* McGraw-Hill.

ROSENBERG, Anna M. (Mrs. Paul Hoffman) (1902–) *See* Herbert H. Lehman Project. *Micro II. Discussed in* William Benton; Lavinia Engle.

ROSENBERG, James N. *See* Joseph M. Proskauer Project.

ROSENBERG, Julius and Ethel. *Discussed in* Herbert Brownell; Arthur Kinoy; Victor Rabinowitz.

ROSENBERG, Manuel (–1967) *See* Radio Pioneers.

ROSENBLUM, Ralph. *See* Robert J. Flaherty Project.

ROSENGARTEN, Theodore (1944–) Author.
Account of interviews with Ned Cobb for *All God's Dangers;* Tallapoosa County, Alabama; Sharecroppers' Union, tenant farmers' labor movements; oral history methodology and implications. A lecture followed by discussion.
34 pp. *Open.* 1976.

ROSENMAN, Dorothy R. (Mrs. Samuel I.) (1900–)
Housing reform, 1930's–40's: Citizens' Housing Council, National Committee on Housing, NY State housing constitutional amendment; National Urban League; vignettes of Samuel I. Rosenman, Franklin and Eleanor Roosevelt, Fiorello La Guardia, Robert Moses, Belle Moskowitz.
65 pp. *Permission required to cite or quote. 1976. Micro IV.*

ROSENMAN, Samuel Irving (1896–1973) Judge.
NYC and State politics in the 1920's; speech-writing for Franklin D. Roosevelt; Washington personalities in the New Deal; administrative work; reorganization of the executive branch during WWII.
233 pp. *Permission required to cite or quote. 1959. Micro II.*
See also Herbert H. Lehman Project. *Micro II.*
Discussed in Wilbur Cohen; Dorothy Rosenman.

ROSENQUIST, James (1933–) *See* New York's Art World.

ROSENSTEIN-RODAN, Paul (1902–) *See* World Bank.

ROSENTHAL, Benjamin S. (1923–) *See* Ethnic Groups and American Foreign Policy.

ROSENTHAL, Julius. *Discussed in* Joseph J. Klein.

ROSENTHAL, Morris Sigmund (1897–1958) Foreign trade consultant.
Family, youth and education; experience with Stein-Hall, Inc., importers; government service during the New Deal and after, especially BEW, 1941–43; views on

liberalism in business and government; PAC of the CIO; ADA; Progressive Party; North African campaign; Milo Perkins and Henry A. Wallace.

484 pp. *Permission required to cite or quote.* 1953. *Micro II.*

ROSENWALD, Julius. *Discussed in* Will Alexander; James M. Barker.

ROSIN, Axel G. (1907–   ) *See* Book-of-the-Month Club. *Micro I.*

ROSS, Harold. *Discussed in* Gardner Botsford.

ROSS, Mrs. Jesse Evans. *See* Federated Department Stores.

ROSS, Paul L. (1902–1978) Lawyer.
NYC politics; mayoralty election of 1949; "Peekskill Riots," 1949; American Labor Party; election of 1948; federal war agencies, WWII.

135 pp. *Permission required to cite or quote.* 1950. *Micro II.*
See also New York Political Studies (C).

ROSS, Wilhelmina du Pont (1906–   ) *See* Longwood Gardens.

ROSSIDES, Eugene Telemachus (1927–   ) *See* Ethnic Groups and American Foreign Policy.

ROSTEN, Leo Calvin (1908–   ) *See* Journalism Lectures (C) *and* Popular Arts.

ROSTOW, Walt. *Discussed in* F. Peterson Jessup.

ROTHA, Paul. *See* Robert J. Flaherty Project.

ROTHMAN, David. *See* Columbia Crisis of 1968.

ROUNDS, Frank W., Jr. (1915–1970) Journalist, author.
Childhood and education; Princeton, 1934–38; Harvard, 1947–50; White House correspondent, 1938–41; chief, China Bureau, 1946–47; WWII: press officer for Adm. William Halsey, South Pacific, 1941–46; attaché, US Embassy, Moscow, 1951–52;

travels in China, India, Africa; impressions of Ambassadors Alan Kirk and George Kennan, Mao Tse-tung, Mohandas Gandhi.

222 pp. *Permission required to cite or quote.* 1963. *Micro II.*
See also James B. Duke Project.

ROUSMANIERE, James A. *See* John F. Kennedy Project.

ROVERE, Richard Halworth (1915–   ) Writer, editor.
EISENHOWER ADMINISTRATION
Impressions of President Eisenhower and his administration; Eisenhower's relations with the press.

44 pp. *Permission required to cite or quote.* 1968. *Micro III.*

ROWDEN, Richard (1905–   ) *See* McGraw-Hill.

ROWE, James Henry, Jr. (1909–   ) *See* James Lawrence Fly Project.

ROWE, John L. (1906–   ) *See* Continental Group.

ROWE, Stanley and Mrs. Rowe. *See* Robert A. Taft Project.

ROWLEY, Grace May. *See* China Missionaries.

ROWLEY, Louis Napoleon, Jr. (1909–   ) *See* McGraw-Hill.

ROWNTREE, Seebohm. *Discussed in* Bruno Lasker.

ROYALL, Kenneth Claiborne (1894–1971) Public official.
Education; Harvard Law School and *Law Review;* German saboteurs case, 1942; head legal department, Fiscal Division of Army Service Forces, 1942–43; Special Assistant to Secretary of War, 1944–45; postwar congressional relations and investigating committees; Under Secretary of War, Secretary of War, Secretary of Army, 1945–49; unification of armed forces; 1948 Democratic presidential nomination; postwar crises: Turkey, Greece, Berlin blockade, Korea, Japan and Douglas MacArthur; integration

efforts in Army; rejection of suggested appointment, Nuremberg trials. Impressions of Presidents Harry Truman and Dwight Eisenhower, Gens. George Marshall and James Van Fleet, Secretaries James Forrestal and Stuart Symington, others.
347 pp. *Permission required.* 1963.

RUBICAM, Raymond. *Discussed in* George H. Gallup.

RUBIEN, Gerel. *See* Social Security. *Micro III.*

RUBIN, Jerry. *Discussed in* Herbert Sacks.

RUBIN, Max Jacob (1906–) Lawyer.
Education, NYC; NYU Law School; law practice from 1927; Board of Education, Great Neck, NY, 1948–52; salary scales; Board of Regents; Board of Education, NYC, 1961.
260 pp. *Permission required to cite or quote.* 1967. *Micro I.*

RUBLEE, George (1868–1957) Lawyer.
Early life and law career; Ballinger-Pinchot controversy; election of 1912; FTC; WWI government work; Dwight Morrow and US relations with Mexico, 1928–30; election of 1928; London Naval Conference, 1930; adviser to the Colombian government, 1930–32; Leticia dispute between Peru and Colombia, 1932; coal arbitrator, 1933; war debts; German refugee relief, 1938.
307 pp. *Permission required to cite or quote.* 1951. *Micro I.*

RUBOTTOM, Roy Richard, Jr. (1912–) Diplomat.
EISENHOWER ADMINISTRATION
Assistant Secretary of State for Inter-American Affairs under President Eisenhower; relations with Cuba and other Latin American nations.
95 pp. *Permission required.* 1969.

RUBY, Harry (1895–1974) *See* Popular Arts.

RUDZINSKI, Aleksander Witold (1900–) Diplomat.
Motives for his resignation from the Polish Foreign Service; structure and function of diplomatic service in Poland; accounts of

Polish Consulate General in NYC and Polish UN delegation, 1949–50.
221 pp. *Permission required. The memoir is a manuscript contributed by the author in 1970.*

RUEKBERG, Herbert S. (1915–) *See* Continental Group.

RUGG, Harold. *Discussed in* William H. Kilpatrick; R. Bruce Raup.

RUGGLES, Charles (1892–1971) Actor.
POPULAR ARTS
Early career; San Francisco earthquake, 1906; first acting experience in NYC; first movie; vaudeville; first talking film, 1929; impressions of early motion picture personalities; philosophy of the art of comedy; Ernst Lubitsch.
42 pp. *Open.* 1959.

RUMBO, Eduardo. *See* Argentina.

RUMBOUGH, Stanley Maddox, Jr. (1920–) Industrialist.
EISENHOWER ADMINISTRATION
Formation of Citizens for Eisenhower, Citizens for Eisenhower-Nixon; Commerce Department; Executive Branch Liaison Office.
39 pp. *Permission required to cite or quote.* 1967. *Micro III.*

RUML, Beardsley. *Discussed in* Carnegie Corporation; Flora M. Rhind.

RUSH, Kenneth (1910–) *See* International Negotiations.

RUSHER, William Allen (1923–) *See* Journalism Lectures.

RUSK, Dean. *Discussed in* Ernest A. Gross; Flora M. Rhind.

RUSK, Howard. *Discussed in* Association for the Aid of Crippled Children.

RUSSELL, Charles M. *Discussed in* Edward S. Edwin.

RUSSELL, George. *Discussed in* Milburn L. Wilson.

RUSSELL, James Earl (1864–1945) *Discussed in* Carnegie Corporation; Hollis Caswell; Charlotte Garrison; Arthur T. Jersild; William H. Kilpatrick; R. Bruce Raup; Isabel Stewart; Goodwin Watson.

RUSSELL, James Sargent (1903–   ) *See* Aviation Project. *Micro II.*

RUSSELL, John McFarlane (1903–   ) Foundation president.
CARNEGIE CORPORATION
Carnegie Corporation, 1930–39; journey to New Zealand, Australia, and South Africa, 1927; evaluation of educational systems in Dominions; description of Corporation office, officers, and trustees; daily routine; recollections of grants and special programs; Myrdal Study; Commonwealth Program; Harvard, 1940–42; Markle Foundation from 1945. Impressions of Frederick Keppel, Morse Cartwright, Charles Dollard, Florence Anderson, and others.
    290 pp. *Permission required.* 1967. *Discussed in* G. Raleigh Parkin.

RUSSELL, William Fletcher (1890–1956) *Discussed in* Carnegie Corporation; Hollis Caswell; Arthur T. Jersild; William H. Kilpatrick; R. Bruce Raup; Goodwin Watson.

RUSSIA *See* U.S.S.R.

RUST, Lawrence and Mrs. Rust. *See* Adlai E. Stevenson Project.

RUTHERFORD, Ernest. *Discussed in* Sir Robert Watson-Watt.

RUTLEDGE, P.J. *See* Forest History Society.

RYAN, Howard P. (1892–   ) *See* Continental Group.

RYAN, John Harold (1885–1961) *See* Radio Pioneers.

RYSKAMP, Charles A. *See* Rare Books (A).

S

SAADI, Vicente. *See* Argentina.

SAAVEDRA LAMAS, Carlos. *Discussed in* Spruille Braden.

SABERSON, R.E. *See* Weyerhaeuser Timber Company.

SACCO-VANZETTI CASE *See* Roger N. Baldwin; Aldino Felicani; Mildred Gilman; Gardner Jackson; Robert L. O'Brien; Arthur M. Schlesinger; James T. Williams, Jr.

SACHER, Abram. *See* Joseph M. Proskauer Project.

SACHS, Hans. *Discussed in* Rudolph M. Loewenstein; Theodor Reik.

SACHS, Paul Joseph (1878–1965) Professor of fine arts.
Childhood, early career as banker and subsequent work in fine arts at Harvard until 1930; impressions of scholars of art and science; print collecting; collectors and their purveyors; patrons of art in the 20th century; Fogg Art Museum; Museum of Modern Art; Harvard Museum course; cooperation with Princeton Department of Art and Archaeology; Bliss Collection at Dumbarton Oaks; Roberts Fine Arts Commission, WWII; American museums after WWII with particular reference to activities of for-

mer students; a retrospective look at art critics, dealers, training, and the development of art in America. The memoir is drawn in large part from Mr. Sachs' correspondence.
1,395 pp. *Permission required.* 1958. Papers.

SACHS, Walter Edward (1884–   ) Banker.
Part I: Early life in NYC; study at Harvard and abroad; career with Goldman, Sachs & Co. since 1910.
124 pp. *Permission required to cite or quote.* 1956. *Micro I.*

Part II: Description of the investment banking business in general and the operations of Goldman, Sachs in particular; antitrust trial before Judge Harold Medina.
230 pp. *Permission required to cite or quote.* 1964. *Micro I.*

SACKHEIM, Maxwell. *See* Book-of-the-Month Club. *Micro IV.*

SACKS, Herbert (1926–   ) Psychiatrist.
Account of Black Panthers rally, New Haven, May 1–3, 1970: Yale-community relations; roles of students, radical leaders Abbie Hoffman and Jerry Rubin, faculty, police, National Guard.
59 pp. *Permission required to cite or quote.* 1970. *Micro II.*

SACKS, I. Milton (1919–   ) *See* International Negotiations.

SACKS, Leon. *See* Independence Park.

AL-SADAT, Anwar. *Discussed in* John Badeau, S. Michael Bessie.

SAFRAN, Frank. *See* Columbia Crisis of 1968.

SAID, Boris. *Discussed in* Eddie Dowling.

SAILLE, Lewis. *See* Federated Department Stores.

ST. JOHN, Seymour. *See* John F. Kennedy Project.

SALADIN, Raymond. *See* Aviation Project.

SALES, Reno. *See* Mining Engineers.

SALISBURY, Harrison Evans (1908–   ) *See* Eisenhower Administration, *Micro III, and* Journalism Lectures.

SALMON, Ronald D. (1909–1974) *See* Marine Corps.

SALOMON, Irving (1897–1979) *See* Eisenhower Administration. *Micro III.*

SALTER, William. *Discussed in* Joseph C. Aub.

SALTONSTALL, Leverett (1892–   ) Senator.
Eisenhower Administration
1952 pre-convention period and campaign; transition period; Senate Armed Services Committee; Appropriations Committee; White House legislative conferences; Republican politics, 1952–60.
151 pp. *Permission required to cite or quote.* 1967. *Micro III.*
Discussed in Raymond Baldwin.

SAMMIS, Edward. *See* Robert J. Flaherty Project.

SAMUEL, Athanasius Yeshu (1907–   ) Archbishop.
Childhood in Syria; refugee, illness; orphanage and monastery care; St. Mark's monastery and seminary, Jerusalem; exploration of caves near Jericho and Jordan; Egypt; archaeological studies; St. Catherine's monastery at Mount Sinai; Archbishop and Metropolitan of Jerusalem, 1946; Dead Sea scrolls: discovery, problems of interpretation and authentication; US, 1949: lectures and exhibits; sale of scrolls, 1954; detailed description of scrolls, contents and significance.
183 pp. *Permission required to cite or quote.* 1961. *Micro II.*

SAMUEL, Irene (Mrs. John) (1915–   ) *See* Eisenhower Administration. *Micro IV.*

SAMUELS, William E. *See* Jazz Project.

SANCERNI GIMENEZ, Julian. *See* Argentina.

SANCHEZ, Hilario. *See* Argentina.

SANDBURG, Carl. *Discussed in* Frank Ernest Hill.

SANDERS, Bob. *See* Vietnam Veterans.

SANDERS, Sol (1926–   ) *See* International Negotiations.

SANDERSON, Lawson H.M. (1895–   ) *See* Marine Corps.

SANDLER, Joseph. Psychoanalyst.
PSYCHOANALYTIC MOVEMENT
Early interest in psychoanalysis; education; work at Hampstead Clinic; impressions of Anna Freud and others; views of psychoanalytic theories and child analysis.
43 pp. *Permission required.* 1967.

SANDOR, Gyorgy (1912–   ) *See* Hungarian Project.

SANFORD, Terry (1917–   ) University president, politician.
SOUTHERN INTELLECTUAL LEADERS (B)
Childhood; education, University of North Carolina, B.A. 1939, J.D. 1946; assessments of North Carolina politics and politicians, 1920's–70's; campaign managing for Kerr Scott, Frank Graham; issues during terms as senator (1953–54) and governor (1961–65): poverty program, civil rights, education; national Democratic politics, conventions; presidency of Duke University.
173 pp. *Permission required to cite or quote.* 1976.

SANGER, Grant (1908–   ) *See* Women's History and Population Issues.

SANGER, Margaret. *Discussed in* Roger N. Baldwin.

SANSOM, Sir George (1883–1965) Diplomat, orientalist.
Education; British foreign service in Japan; Japanese cultural life; WWII; peace terms; East Asian Institute, Columbia.
96 pp. *Permission required to cite or quote.* 1957. *Micro II.*

SANTANDER, Silvano (1895–1971) *See* Argentina.

SANTAYANA, George. *Discussed in* Herbert W. Schneider.

SAPERSTEIN, Sidney.
SOCIAL SECURITY
Columbia University, 1939; Federal Security Agency, 1941; drafting health insurance legislation; Murray-Wagner-Dingell bill; Social Security; Ways and Means Committee; relations between politicians; American Hospital Association and AMA positions on health legislation, 1960's; Medicare; impressions of Wilbur Mills, Irwin Wolkstein, Wilbur Cohen, and others.
122 pp. *Closed during lifetime.* 1967.

SAPIENZA, John. *See* Stanley Reed.

SARACHAGA, Dario (1901–   ) Lawyer, politician.
ARGENTINA
Gen. Agustin P. Justo as soldier and statesman: Minister of War, 1922, modernizing army, developing national munitions industry, President, 1932–38, administrative and economic reform, Roca-Runciman Treaty, railroads.
21 pp. *Open.* 1971.

SARGEANT, Howland (1911–   ) *See* Eisenhower Administration. *Micro III.*

SARNOFF, David (1891–1971) *See* Robert P. Patterson Project. *Discussed in* Chester H. Lang; Radio Pioneers.

SARTON, May. *Discussed in* Dorothy Baker.

SATTERTHWAITE, Adaline Pendleton. *See* Women's History and Population Issues.

SAULNIER, Raymond J. (1908–   ) Economist.
EISENHOWER ADMINISTRATION
Council of Economic Advisors as organized under President Eisenhower: functions, operations, relations with President, Congress, and other agencies; Advisory Board on Economic Growth; economic policies under Eisenhower.
71 pp. *Permission required to cite or quote.* 1967. *Micro III.*
Discussed in Neil H. Jacoby.

SAUNDERS, Red. *See* Jazz Project.

SAUSSURE, Raymond de (–1971) Psychoanalyst.
PSYCHOANALYTIC MOVEMENT
Studies of psychoanalysis, Berlin, Vienna, Paris; theories of psychoanalysis; impressions of other analysts.
73 pp. *Permission required.* 1965.

SAUTERS, Edgar L. (1890–) *See* Continental Group.

SAVACOOL, William. *See* Theodore Roosevelt Association. *Micro IV.*

SAVAGE, Earl C. (1891–) *See* Continental Group.

SAXE, Martin (1874–1967) Lawyer, politician.
Activities as NY State Senator; Republican Convention, 1915; law practice with Morris, Plante and Saxe; NYC and State politics, 1902–13.
40 pp. *Permission required to cite or quote.* 1949. *Micro I.* Papers.

SAYRE, E. Berthol. *See* Nicholas Murray Butler Project.

SAYRE, Francis Bowes (1885–1972) Diplomat.
Early life; Williams College; work in Labrador with Dr. Wilfred Grenfell; Harvard Law School; Woodrow Wilson; Massachusetts State Commissioner of Correction; foreign affairs adviser to Thailand, 1933; observations on Thailand and the Far East.
127 pp. *Permission required to cite or quote.* 1952. *Micro II.*

SAYRE, Wallace Stanley (1905–1972) *See* Journalism Lectures (A).

SCHACHT, Hjalmar. *Discussed in* James P. Warburg.

SCHACTER, Oscar. *See* Dag Hammarskjold Project.

SCHAEFER, J. Earl (1893–) *See* Eisenhower Administration.

SCHAEFER, Walter Vincent (1904–)
See Adlai E. Stevenson Project. *Micro III.*

SCHAETZEL, J. Robert. *See* International Negotiations.

SCHAPER, Wilfred. *See* Flying Tigers.

SCHARY, Dore (1905–) *See* Popular Arts.

SCHEAF, Oral. *See* Federated Department Stores.

SCHECHTER, Abel Alan (1907–) *See* Radio Pioneers.

SCHEELE, Leonard Andrew (1907–) Physician.
EISENHOWER ADMINISTRATION
Surgeon-General, 1948–56; Salk vaccine; impressions of Oveta Culp Hobby and other members of the Eisenhower administration.
44 pp. *Permission required to cite or quote.* 1968. *Micro III.*
See also Health Sciences.

SCHERER, Raymond Lewis (1919–) Journalist.
EISENHOWER ADMINISTRATION
President Eisenhower's news conferences; early use of television; relations with the press; impressions of Eisenhower and his administration.
54 pp. *Permission required to cite or quote.* 1968. *Micro III.*

SCHERMAN, Harry (1887–1969) Book club executive, author.
BOOK-OF-THE-MONTH CLUB
Childhood in Philadelphia; journalism, advertising, NYC, 1907–16; formation of Little Leather Library Corporation, 1916; inception of Book-of-the-Month Club idea, 1926; selection committee and the book selection process; characteristics and tastes of the committee and of Club subscribers; book-dividend, gift book, and premium systems; structure and administration of Club; most notable and most popular books, 1928–54; art reproductions and records; pressure groups and Club; book club movement in America; reflections on American culture.

367 pp. *Permission required to cite or quote.* 1955. *Micro I.*
Discussed in Phyllis Cerf Wagner.

SCHIEFFELIN, Bayard (1903–   ) *See* Robert P. Patterson Project.

SCHIEFFELIN, William Jay (1866–1955) Businessman, civic worker.
Investigations of corruption in NYC during the 1890's; Committee of 70, 1894; reform movements, Mayor William Strong and William Travers Jerome; president of the Citizens Union, 1908–41; Council on African Affairs and Negro leaders. Impressions of J.P. Morgan, Alfred E. Smith, Nicholas Murray Butler.
126 pp. *Permission required to cite or quote.* 1949. *Micro I.*

SCHILT, Christian Franklin (1895–   ) Marine Corps officer.
Family background and education; WWI service; pilot training; Haiti, 1920–21; Santo Domingo, 1921–22; early USMC aircraft; International Air Races, 1920's; Nicaragua, 1927–29; WWII, Guadalcanal operation; Commander, Marine Air Reserve Training, 1946–49; Korea, 1951–52; Director of Aviation, 1955–57.
136 pp. *Open.* 1969.
See also Aviation Project. *Micro IV.*

SCHINDLER, Alex. *See* Ethnic Groups and American Foreign Policy.

SCHINE, Gerard David (1927–   ) *See* Eisenhower Administration.

SCHLENCK, Hugo. *See* Weyerhaeuser Timber Company.

SCHLESINGER, Arthur Meier (1888–1965) Historian.
Early childhood; college experiences at Ohio State, 1909–13; graduate work, Columbia University; teaching at Ohio State during WWI; writing *Colonial Merchants and the American Revolution* and *New Viewpoints in American History;* liberal movement during WWI; University of Iowa, 1919–24; Harvard University from 1925, including Sacco-Vanzetti case, Harvard and academic freedom, graduate students; around the world trip, 1933; experi-

ences at the University of Leiden, 1948; freedom of the press investigation, 1943–45; editing the "History of American Life" series and the *Harvard Guide to American History;* leading personalities in the American historical profession from about 1915. The material includes much correspondence.
1,266 pp. *Permission required.* 1959. Papers.
Discussed in Gardner Jackson.

SCHLESINGER, Arthur Meier, Jr. (1917–   ) *See* American Historians; Richard Hofstadter Project, *Micro IV; and* Adlai E. Stevenson Project, *Micro IV.*
Discussed in Newton N. Minow.

SCHLESS, Howard. *See* Columbia Crisis of 1968.

SCHLOSS, Ann Lazarus. *See* Federated Department Stores.

SCHLOSSBERG, Joseph (1901–   ) *See* Socialist Movement.

SCHMIDT, Benno C., Jr. (1942–   ) Lawyer, professor.
Law clerk to Chief Justice Earl Warren, 1966; work routines: manner in which cases were reviewed and chosen, opinion-writing assigned to Justices, bench memos prepared; impressions of Chief Justice Warren: his temperament, working habits, judicial philosophy, political career, strengths, weaknesses; important cases reviewed by the Warren Court relating to race relations, criminal procedure, apportionment, constitutional amendment rights.
386 pp. *Permission required to cite or quote.* 1975.

SCHMIDT, Orvis Adrian. *See* World Bank.

SCHNEEWIND, Jerome J. (1896–   ) *See* Continental Group.

SCHNEIDER, Alan (1917–   ) and Edward Albee. *See* Popular Arts.

SCHNEIDER, Carl. *See* Kirkland College.

SCHNEIDER, Herbert W. (1892–   ) Philosopher.

Family background and education; psychological testing for Army Medical Corps; teaching at Columbia from 1919: Contemporary Civilization course, philosophy curriculum; impressions of George Santayana, John Dewey, other philosophers; UNESCO: SE Asian tour, publications; American Philosophical Association representative to France, 1950; lectures on political philosophy, analytical ontology; first director, Blaisdell Institute; *History of American Philosophy;* pragmatism and American philosophy. John P. Diggins participates in one interview.
246 pp. *Open.* 1976.

SCHOENBRUN, David F. (1915–   ) *See* Journalism Lectures.

SCHOENWERK, Otto C. *See* Weyerhaeuser Timber Company.

SCHOMBURG, Arthur. *Discussed in* Jean B. Hutson.

SCHORR, Lisbeth Bamberger.
SOCIAL SECURITY
Role of AFL-CIO in health insurance and social security programs from 1958; legislation in Eisenhower, Kennedy, and Johnson administrations; relationship with AMA.
105 pp. *Permission required to cite or quote.* 1967. *Micro IV.*

SCHOTTLAND, Charles Irwin (1906–   ) University dean.
SOCIAL SECURITY
Work with California State Relief Administration, Los Angeles Federation of Jewish Welfare Organizations, and US Children's Bureau, 1933–41; Gen. Dwight Eisenhower's staff, WWII; Director of Social Welfare, California, 1950; Commissioner of Social Security, 1952: relations with Children's Bureau, other agencies, executive and legislative branches; Medicare; "Thrift" speech, 1956; impressions of Katharine Lenroot, Martha Eliot, Oveta Culp Hobby, Marion Folsom, Loula Dunn, Nelson Rockefeller, Wilbur Cohen.
167 pp. *Permission required to cite or quote.* 1965. *Micro III.*

SCHRADER, Edward A. (1912–   ) *See* Continental Group.

SCHROEDER, Theodore. *Discussed in* Roger N. Baldwin.

SCHULZ, Robert L. (1907–   ) Army officer, presidential aide.
EISENHOWER ADMINISTRATION
Military transportation officer; military aide to President Eisenhower; details of Eisenhower's travels; personal recollections of the Eisenhowers.
293 pp. *Closed until 1993.* 1968.
Discussed in Edward L. Beach.

SCHUMAN, William Howard (1910–   )
Composer, administrator.
Childhood, education, career; conception, revision, performances of each of his major works; choral conducting, composition for film, for dance; innovations and conflicts as administrator of Juilliard School of Music, President, 1945–62, emeritus, 1962–   , and Lincoln Center, President, 1962–69, emeritus, 1969–   ; opinions and anecdotes of many figures in the performing arts, including Serge Koussevitzky, Roy Harris, Leopold Stokowski, Peter Mennin.
751 pp. *Permission required.* 1977. *Acquired from Yale University School of Music Oral History Project.*

SCHUSTER, Max Lincoln (1897–1970) Editor, publisher.
NYC childhood; copy boy, NY *Evening World,* 1913; Columbia School of Journalism, 1917; early literary and journalistic interests; intellectual ferment and radicalism; journalistic experience in Washington and NYC, 1917–24; formation of Simon and Schuster, 1924; crossword puzzle books; *Story of Philosophy.*
226 pp. *Permission required to cite or quote.* 1964. *Micro IV.*

SCHUYLER, George Samuel (1895–1977) Author, journalist.
Background, childhood, and education in Syracuse; job discrimination; enlistment US Army, 1912; military transports, commission, segregation within armed forces; Government civil service, 1919; Harlem; Marcus Garvey; *The Messenger; Pittsburgh Courier;* magazine supplement, Chicago; differences among Negro leaders; southern travels; Socialist Party activities; NAACP; *The Crisis;* Negroes in politics; housing; in-

terracial marriage; Liberia; consumer cooperatives; Ethiopia; American Negroes in WWII; race relations in Latin America; Negro journalism; Negroes and Jews; Negroes and Communist Party; National Negro Congress; March on Washington; impressions of Benjamin Davis, A. Philip Randolph, Chandler Owen, James W. Ivy, James Weldon Johnson, Roy Wilkins, H. L. Mencken, Walter White.
723 pp. *Permission required to cite or quote.* 1960. *Micro I.*

SCHWARTZ, Arthur (1900–   ) *See* Popular Arts.

SCHWARTZ, Felice N. (1925–   ) Civic worker.
Education, Smith College, 1942–45; work with NAACP, 1945–46; founder and director of National Scholarship Service and Fund for Negro Students, 1946–51; Vice-President of Etched Products, Corp., 1951–54; founding and work as president of Catalyst, women's employment organization, 1962–   .
51 pp. *Permission required to cite or quote.* 1971. *Contributed by Smith College, Northampton, Mass.*

SCIENCE AND SCIENTISTS *See* Wallace R. Brode; Charles Coryell; Albert P. Crary; Theodosius Dobzhansky; Rene Dubos; Leslie C. Dunn; Thomas A. Edison Project; Wilson Harwood; Caryl P. Haskins; Health Sciences; John K. Jenney; Joseph Kaplan; James R. Killian, Jr.; Polykarp Kusch; William L. Laurence; Nobel Laureates; I. I. Rabi; E.C. Stakman; Sir Robert Watson-Watt; Warren Weaver.
See also Atomic Energy; Medicine; Physics.

SCOFIELD, Frank H. *Discussed in* Harold C. Train.

SCOPAZZI, John. *See* Rare Books (B).

SCOTT, Agnes. *See* China Missionaries.

SCOTT, Austin Wakeman (1884–   ) *See* Robert P. Patterson Project.

SCOTT, Edgar (1899–   ) *See* Longwood Gardens.

SCOTT, Ernest Lyman (1878–1966) Scientist.
Insulin research.
11 pp. *Open.* 1964. Papers.

SCOTT, Geoffrey. *Discussed in* Marguerite Harris.

SCOTT, Hardy (1907–   ) *See* Independence Park.

SCOTT, Harry A. (1909–   ) *See* Continental Group.

SCOTT, Kerr. *Discussed in* Terry Sanford.

SCOTT, Roderick (1885–   ) *See* China Missionaries.

SCOTT, Stuart Nash (1907–   ) Lawyer, ambassador.
US Ambassador to Portugal, 1974–75: preparation in Washington, Lisbon under Tomaz-Caetano regime, signs of military unrest, military coup of April 25, 1974; administration of General Antonio de Spínola, his resignation, September 1974; presidency of Francisco da Costa Gomes; Secretary of State Kissinger's views on Portugal and circumstances of Ambassador Scott's recall.
62 pp. *Permission required to cite or quote.* 1975.

SCOTT, Zachary (1914–1965) *See* Popular Arts.

SCRIBNER, Charles. *Discussed in* John Hall Wheelock.

SCRIBNER, Fred C., Jr. (1908–   ) *See* Eisenhower Administration.

SCRIPPS, William Edmund (1882–1952) *See* Radio Pioneers.

SEABORG, Glenn Theodore (1912–   ) *See* Nobel Laureates.

SEARS, George (1887–1960) *See* McGraw-Hill.

SEATON, George (1911–   ) *See* Popular Arts.

SEAVER, Edwin (1900–   ) Writer, editor.
Childhood and education; *Harvard Monthly;* publicity work NYC, early 1920's; book reviews for *New Republic* and *Nation;* ACLU publicity work; *The Company,* 1930; Woodstock; editorial work: columns, Book-of-the-Month Club, Braziller; effects of cold war on literature; McCarthy Committee hearing; promotion department work for Little, Brown, 1949–59.
98 pp. *Permission required to cite or quote.* 1976. *Micro IV.*

SEBRELL, William Henry, Jr. (1901–   ) Public health officer.
HEALTH SCIENCES
Background in medicine; US Public Health Service, 1925–55; quarantine stations; NIH; nutritional research; administrative personnel and policies; Institute of Nutrition Sciences, Columbia University, from 1957.
56 pp. *Permission required to cite or quote.* 1962.

SEDGWICK, Ellery. *Discussed in* Quincy Howe.

SEGAL, George (1924–   ) Sculptor.
NEW YORK'S ART WORLD
Reaction to abstract expressionism; move to sculpting and use of plaster for life castings; attitudes to public art in US; work on FDR Memorial, Washington, D.C.
40 pp. *Permission required.* 1978.

SEGER, Gerhart Henry (1896–1967) Editor, author, lecturer.
Journalism in Germany and Europe, 1921–33; German Reichstag, 1930–33; concentration camp experiences and escape, 1933; immigration to the US; lecturing on international affairs.
154 pp. *Permission required to cite or quote.* 1950. *Micro I.*

SEGHERS, Dorothy. *See* Benjamin A. Javits Project.

SEGRE, Emilio (1905–   ) *See* Nobel Laureates.

SEIBERT, Edward W. (1907–   ) *See* Continental Group.

SEIGENTHALER, John Lawrence (1927–   ) Newspaper editor.
SOUTHERN INTELLECTUAL LEADERS (B)
Early life; experiences as investigative reporter for the Nashville *Tennessean; Tennessean* in the 1950's; work for John F. Kennedy's campaign and with Robert Kennedy until 1962; civil rights involvement; southern journalism; *Tennessean* attitudes on TVA and concern with southern issues; Robert Kennedy's campaign and assassination.
121 pp. *Permission required to cite or quote.* 1974.

SEILER, Evelyn Norton (1883–   ) *See* Continental Group.

SELBIGER, Jack (1900–   ) *See* Continental Group.

SELF, Sir Henry (1890–1975) *See* Henry H. Arnold Project.

SELIGMAN, Eustace (1889–1976) Lawyer.
Family background, influences; NYC childhood; education, Amherst College, 1910, law schools: Harvard, 1910–12, Columbia, LLB, 1914; corporate law practice with Sullivan and Cromwell, 1914–70; trusteeship, Amherst College, 1942–72, impressions of Amherst presidents, fellow trustees; WWI experiences as Judge Advocate trying conscientious objector cases; philosophy of education; development of political views.
270 pp. *Permission required to cite or quote.* 1975.

SELZNICK, David Oliver (1902–1965) *See* Popular Arts.

SELZNICK, Myron. *Discussed in* Samson Raphaelson.

SEMANS, Mary Duke Biddle Trent (Mrs. James H.) (1920–   ) *See* James B. Duke Project.

SENN, Milton (1902–   ) *See* Association for the Aid of Crippled Children.

SENNELLO, Joseph J. (1920–   ) *See* Continental Group.

SEREBROVSKII, Alexander. *Discussed in* Leslie C. Dunn.

SESSIONS, Roger Huntington (1896–   ) Composer.
New England background; early music lessons and first composition, 1909; Harvard *Musical Review,* 1913; Yale Music School, 1915–17: Horatio Parker; Smith College, 1919–21; teaching music theory, Roy Welch; Cleveland Conservatory, Ernest Bloch; fellowships and work abroad, 1925–33: Florence, Rome, Berlin; comments on his own compositions, as well as on techniques of composition, tonality, harmony, teaching young composers, and on many artists, especially Igor Stravinsky, Otto Klemperer.
309 pp. *Permission required to cite or quote.* 1962. *Micro II.*
Discussed in Aaron Copland.

SETTERFIELD, Valda (1935–   ) Dancer.
Early studies in England; work with choreographers James Waring, Merce Cunningham, David Gordon, Yvonne Rainer.
43 pp. *Permission required to cite or quote.* 1977.

SEVAREID, Eric Arnold (1912–   ) *See* Journalism Lectures (C) *and* Adlai E. Stevenson Project, *Micro III.*

SEWARD, Ralph Theodore (1907–   ) *See* Cyrus Ching. *Micro II.*

SEYMOUR, Whitney North, Sr. (1901–   ) Lawyer.
NEW YORK BAR
Family background; education, University of Wisconsin and Columbia Law School, 1920–1923; Angelo Herndon and other cases handled as attorney, Simpson, Thacher & Bartlett, 1924–   ; work with Landmarks Conservancy in NYC, other environmental and cultural organizations; American Bar Association activities, 1937–   ; discussion of professional standards, case presentation and tactics, selection process of judges, legal clinics and continuing legal education.

71 pp. *Permission required to cite or quote.* 1977.

SHACHTMAN, Max (1903–1972) Trotskyite.
Development of socialist and radical groups in the 1920's and '30's, particularly Communist Workers Party, Workers' Council, and Trotskyites; factional struggles; trips to Moscow, 1925, 1927; International Labor Defense group; publications and editorial work; expulsion from Communist Party; effects of international political events; Socialist Party; split over Nazi-Soviet alliance; visits to Leon Trotsky in Turkey, Norway, Paris, Mexico; Trotsky's assassination; Independent Socialist League, 1948–58. Impressions of Joseph Stalin, Norman Thomas, Eugene V. Debs, A.J. Muste, and many others.
522 pp. *Permission required to cite or quote.* 1963. *Micro I.*
See also Socialist Movement. *Micro I.*

SHADEGG, Stephen (1909–   ) Author.
EISENHOWER ADMINISTRATION
Campaigns of Dwight Eisenhower, Richard Nixon, Barry Goldwater; Charles Percy Committee.
30 pp. *Permission required.* 1967.

SHAH OF IRAN *See* Mohammed Reza Pahlavi.

SHAHN, Ben (1898–1969) Artist.
Early life in Lithuania and Brooklyn; training in lithography; painting experiences with Diego Rivera; WPA art project.
154 pp. *Permission required to cite or quote.* 1960.

SHANKER, Albert. *Discussed in* Philip Taft.

SHANLEY, Bernard M. (1903–   ) *See* Eisenhower Administration.

SHANNON, James A. (1904–   ) *See* Health Sciences.

SHAPLEY, Alan (1903–1973) *See* Marine Corps.

SHARON, John.
ADLAI E. STEVENSON PROJECT
Campaigns of 1952 and 1956; choosing the

1956 Democratic vice presidential nominee; draft-Stevenson movement, 1960; relationship of Stevenson with Harry Truman, Estes Kefauver, John F. Kennedy, and Lyndon Johnson; Stevenson at the UN.
148 pp. *Permission required to cite or quote.* 1969. *Micro III.*

SHARP, Dudley Crawford (1905–) Government official.
EISENHOWER ADMINISTRATION
Assistant Secretary, later Secretary, of the USAF: missiles, Department of Defense, Joint Chiefs of Staff; U-2 incident; relations with President Eisenhower.
67 pp. *Permission required to cite or quote.* 1969. *Micro III.*

SHATTUCK, Fred. *Discussed in* Joseph Aub.

SHATTUCK, Roger Whitney (1923–) *See* American Cultural Leaders.

SHAUGHNESSY, Richard G. (1908–) *See* Continental Group.

SHAW, Fred B. (1913–) *See* Continental Group.

SHAW, H. *See* Aviation Project.

SHAW, H.W. (1904–) *See* McGraw-Hill.

SHAW, Samuel Robert (1911–) *See* Marine Corps.

SHAWN, William. *Discussed in* Gardner Botsford.

SHAYON, Robert Lewis (1912–) *See* Radio Pioneers. *Micro IV.*

SHEAR, Murray J. (1899–) *See* Health Sciences.

SHEARON, Marjorie. *Discussed in* Elizabeth Wickenden.

SHEFFER, Eugene. *See* Nicholas Murray Butler Project.

SHEFFIELD, Frederick (1902–1971) *See* Carnegie Corporation.

SHELDON, A. O. *See* Weyerhaeuser Timber Company.

SHELDON, Bobby. *See* Alaskan Pioneers.

SHELDON, Edward. *Discussed in* John Hall Wheelock.

SHELDON, James (1907–) State government official.
EISENHOWER ADMINISTRATION
Stevenson campaigns, 1952, 1956; organizing and public relations, Nationalities Division of the Democratic National Committee; the John F. Kennedy campaign, 1960.
186 pp. *Permission required.* 1972.

SHELDON, Joseph S.
EISENHOWER ADMINISTRATION
Republican Party in Texas; Taft-Eisenhower contest, 1952; impressions of Eisenhower and his administration.
28 pp. *Permission required to cite or quote.* 1969.
See also additional interview in Eisenhower Administration.

SHELLWORTH, H. C. *See* Weyerhaeuser Timber Company.

SHELTON, Robert. *See* Civil Rights in Alabama.

SHELTON, William T. *See* Eisenhower Administration. *Micro III.*

SHENTON, James P. *See* Columbia Crisis of 1968.

SHEPARD, Frank B. (1888–) *See* Benedum and the Oil Industry.

SHEPARD, William P. (1895–) *See* Health Sciences.

SHEPARDSON, Whitney H. *Discussed in* Carnegie Corporation.

SHEPHERD, Lemuel Cornick, Jr. (1896–) Marine Corps officer.
Family background, education; WWI service, France; occupation of Germany; Aide to Gen. Lejeune, 1920–22; China, 1927–29; Haiti, 1930–34; Naval War College; WWII: Cape Gloucester, Guam, Okinawa opera-

tions; occupation of Tsing-tao; USMC Assistant Commandant, 1946–48; unification fight; Commandant, USMC schools, 1948–50; Korea: Inchon landing, Gen. Douglas MacArthur and the USMC; USMC Commandant, 1952–56: role in Joint Chiefs of Staff deliberations, outstanding developments during period; Chairman, Inter-American Defense Board, 1956–59.
517 pp. *Open.* 1967.
Discussed in Oliver P. Smith.

SHEPLEY, James Robinson (1917–)
Journalist.
EISENHOWER ADMINISTRATION
Impressions of President Eisenhower, John Foster Dulles, Richard Nixon; Eisenhower's relations with the press.
39 pp. *Permission required to cite or quote.* 1967. *Micro III.*

SHEPPARD, Harold.
SOCIAL SECURITY
Senate subcommittee on the problems of the aged, 1958; Patrick McNamara; relations with UAW; Kennedy administration and Social Security; senior citizens' groups; Senior Service Corps; impressions of Wilbur Cohen, Charles Odell, Sidney Spector, William Reidy.
104 pp. *Permission required to cite or quote.* 1967.

SHER, David (1908–) *See* New York Political Studies (C).

SHERMAN, Forrest. *Discussed in* William Fechteler.

SHERMAN, Stuart Pratt. *Discussed in* Allan Nevins.

SHERROD, Robert Lee (1909–) *See* Eisenhower Administration. *Micro III.*

SHERWIN, William R. *See* Alaskan Pioneers.

SHIELDS, Robert Hazen (1905–)
Agriculturist.
Early life; University of Nebraska; Harvard Law School; AAA; peanut program, 1935 "purge," sugar program, 1938 Agricultural Adjustment Act; Office of Solicitor, Department of Agriculture: AAA and conservation, crop insurance, regional problems, Commodity Credit Corporation; Office of the Secretary of Agriculture: prices, ceilings, and production in wartime, OPA, FSA, private farm organizations, Steagall amendment to 1938 Agricultural Adjustment Act, 1941 "Omnibus Bill," relations with wartime agencies; personalities in the Agriculture Department during the New Deal and early war years.
572 pp. *Permission required to cite or quote.* 1954. *Micro II.*

SHIKLER, Aaron (1922–) Painter.
Childhood, education; art training, Tyler School of Fine Arts, Temple University, 1948; army service; career as portrait artist; Kennedy portrait commissions, 1967; art scene of 1977, personal exhibits.
160 pp. *Permission required to cite or quote.* 1977.

SHIMKIN, Leon (1907–) *See* Freeman Lewis. *Micro II.*

SHIMKO, Margaret Richards. *See* John Robert Gregg Project.

SHISHKIN, Boris Basil (1906–) Economist.
Early life and education in Russia; WWI and the Russian Revolution; flight to Istanbul; Columbia University during the late 1920's; role of AFL in New Deal legislation; AFL conventions, 1933–36; impressions of William Green, John L. Lewis, Maurice Tobin, Matthew Woll, and other labor leaders.
872 pp. *Permission required to cite or quote.* 1957. *Micro II.*

SHIVERS, Allan (1907–) Governor.
EISENHOWER ADMINISTRATION
Tidelands issue; meeting with Adlai Stevenson; 1952 election; relations with President Eisenhower; Texas politics and the Eisenhower administration.
58 pp. *Permission required to cite or quote.* 1969. *Micro III.*
Discussed in D.B. Hardeman.

SHOCKLEY, William Bradford (1910–) *See* Nobel Laureates.

SHOENER, Willard T. *See* McGraw-Hill.

SHOR, Bernard (Toots) (1903–1977) Restaurateur.
Philadelphia childhood; sales work; bouncer, greeter for NYC speakeasies during Prohibition; construction, financing, management of two NYC restaurants, 1940–70; unionization of restaurant employees; impressions of celebrity friends; travels; Kefauver Committee Hearings, 1954.
216 pp. *Permission required to cite or quote.* 1975.

SHOTWELL, James Thompson (1874–1965) Historian.
Education in Canada; Columbia University, historical studies; 11th edition of *Encyclopaedia Britannica;* WWI; Creel Committee; "The Inquiry"; Paris Peace Conference; the "Big Four"; ILO; *Economic and Social History of the World War;* postwar problems; British Imperial Conference, 1921; Locarno Treaties.
230 pp. *Permission required to cite or quote.* 1952. *Micro I.*
See also Nicholas Murray Butler Project.
Discussed in Edward P. Herring.

SHOUP, David M. (1904–   ) *See* Eisenhower Administration. *Micro III.*

SHRIVER, R. Sargent. *See* John F. Kennedy Project.

SHROYER, Thomas. *See* Robert A. Taft Project.

SHUEBRUK, Pete. *See* James Lawrence Fly Project.

SICILIANO, Rocco (1922–   ) *See* Eisenhower Administration.

SICKLES, Trent. *See* Federated Department Stores.

SIDNEY, Sylvia. *Discussed in* Bennett Cerf.

SIEBACK, Julius. *Discussed in* Howard Barlow.

SIEGEL, Mark. *See* Ethnic Groups and American Foreign Policy.

SIEGMEISTER, Elie (1909–   ) Composer.
Family background, NYC, education; study with Nadia Boulanger, 1927–31; American Ballad Singers, 1939–46; jazz, folk, classical influences; symphonic and theater productions; Rally of Hope, 1943; organization of Soviet-American Music Society; elitist, nationalist and populist influences in American music; composition orchestration; American Composers' Alliance; effects of McCarthyism on US artists and art; writing opera, film scores, since 1950's; elements of musical style; conducting, teaching; Composers and Lyricists Guild of America; 1968 Composers for Peace Concert; importance of fashion, planned obsolescence in modern culture; Council of Creative Artists, Libraries and Museums; development of Second American School of Music.
459 pp. *Permission required.* 1975.

SIEPMANN, Charles. *See* Robert J. Flaherty Project.

SIKORSKY, Igor. *Discussed in* Eugene E. Wilson.

SILBERT, Myron. *See* Federated Department Stores.

SILVERTHORN, Merwin Hancock (1896–   ) Marine Corps officer.
Family background and education; WWI duty in France; Haiti, 1923–26; Gen. Smedley Butler; Guam, 1930–32; Naval War College; Staff, Adm. Ernest King, Pacific Fleet, 1941–43; preparations for invasion of Japan, occupations of Japan and North China; demobilization; reorganization of Marine units in Pacific; mobilization of reserves for Korea; Assistant Commandant, USMC, 1949–50; Chief of Staff, HQMC, 1950–52, the Clifton Cates Commandancy.
479 pp. *Permission required to cite or quote.* 1969.

SIMKIN, Margaret Timberlake. *See* China Missionaries.

SIMPSON, Kenneth. *Discussed in* Stanley M. Isaacs.

SIMPSON, William H. (1888–) *See* Eisenhower Administration.

SIMS, William. *Discussed in* Henry Williams.

SINATRA, Frank. *Discussed in* Phyllis Cerf Wagner.

SINCLAIR, Upton (1878–1968) Author.
Background, youth and education; early experiments in writing; comments on friends; *The Jungle* and other muckraking books; life in experimental communities and colonies, Helicon Hall; Lanny Budd books; Socialist Party; strikes and arrests; EPIC and campaign for California governorship, 1934; *Dead Hand* series; *Oil;* movie industry; William Fox; *The Brass Check;* self help cooperative; child labor. Impressions of many American writers.
363 pp. *Permission required to cite or quote. 1962. Micro I. Contributed by Ronald Gottesman, Highland Park, New Jersey.*
Discussed in Socialist Movement.

SINCLAIRE, Reginald.
AIR FORCE ACADEMY
Lafayette Escadrille, training in France for WWI.
58 pp. *Open.* 1969.

SINGER, Arthur. Foundation official.
CARNEGIE CORPORATION
Introduction to Carnegie Corporation; nature of a foundation officer's work; automation, job-training, programs for the disadvantaged; Commission on Public Television; Center for Urban Education; Alfred P. Sloan Foundation. Impressions of John Gardner, Alan Pifer, and others.
138 pp. *Permission required.* 1969.

SINGER, Herman. *See* Socialist Movement.

SINGER, Isaac Bashevis. *Discussed in* Roger W. Straus.

SINGSEN, Antone Gerhardt (1915–1977) *See* Social Security. *Micro III.*

SIROKY, Anne (1910–) *See* Continental Group.

SKIBBE, A. Gerald (1913–) *See* Continental Group.

SKIRBALL, Henry. *Discussed in* Sheba Skirball.

SKIRBALL, Sheba (1932–) Librarian.
Jewish immigrant family background; education, Brown University, 1955, Columbia University, 1970; husband, Henry Skirball's work with youth movement; emigration to Israel, library career in the Hebrew University of Jerusalem, Institute for Contemporary Jewry, Film Archives.
105 pp. *Permission required to cite or quote. 1976. Micro IV.*

SLATER, Ellis Dwinnell (1895–) *See* Eisenhower Administration. *Micro III.*

SLATER, Ilene.
EISENHOWER ADMINISTRATION
Secretary for Citizens for Eisenhower; secretary to Sherman Adams in the White House.
58 pp. *Permission required.* 1968.

SLATER, Robert James (1923–) *See* Association for the Aid of Crippled Children.

SLATON, John L. *See* Radio Pioneers.

SLAUGHTER, Robert (1910–) *See* McGraw-Hill.

SLAYMAKER, Margaret McNamara. Pilot.
Experiences as Women's Air Force Service Pilot; dissolution of WASP, 1944; reminiscences of brother, Robert McNamara.
19 pp. *Permission required. 1975. Contributed by Sally Van Wagenen Keil, NYC.*

SLICK, Thomas Baker (1916–1962) *See* Benedum and the Oil Industry.

SLESSOR, Sir John Cotesworth (1897–) *See* Henry H. Arnold Project.

SLOAN, Alfred P. *Discussed in* Warren Weaver.

SLOANE, Madeleine Edison (Mrs. John Eyre) *See* Thomas A. Edison Project.

SMALL, George. *See* New York Botanical Garden.

SMART, S. Bruce (1923–   ) *See* Continental Group.

SMATHERS, George. *Discussed in* Edward R. Annis.

SMILEY, Robert. *See* Radio Pioneers.

SMILLIE, Wilson George (1886–1971) *See* Health Sciences.

SMITH, Alfred E. *Discussed in* George Chandler; Marion Dickerman; Eddie Dowling; Jonah Goldstein; Herbert H. Lehman; John L. O'Brian; Frances Perkins; Joseph M. Proskauer; William J. Schieffelin; Francis Stoddard; Robert F. Wagner, Jr.; Emily S. Warner.

SMITH, Bromley. *See* Eisenhower Administration.

SMITH, Bruce. *See* Columbia Crisis of 1968.

SMITH, Charles (1842–   ) Black cowboy.
Reminiscences of his boyhood in Africa, abduction by a slavetrader, and sale in a New Orleans slave market; experiences as a slave and free man on the ranch of Charles Smith near Galveston, Texas.
52 pp. *Open. 1963. Contributed by Holland A. Kelley, Bartow, Florida.*

SMITH, Charlie. *See* Vietnam Veterans.

SMITH, Cyrus Rowlett (1899–   ) *See* Aviation Project. *Micro II.*

SMITH, Dean. *See* Aviation Project. *Micro II.*

SMITH, H. Alexander (1880–1966) Senator.
Boyhood in NYC; Princeton, Columbia Law School; Colorado practice, 1905; US Food Administration, Herbert Hoover, WWI; executive secretary, Princeton, 1920–30; Chairman, Republican Party, New Jersey, member Republican National Committee, 1939; US Senate ca-

reer, 1944–58: primaries and campaigns, labor reform legislation, party reorganization, refugee problems, Taft-Hartley Act, Voice of America, Smith-Mundt Act; extensive travel in Europe and Far East; Republican Policy Committee, 1951; Douglas MacArthur hearings; Japan Peace Treaty; Senate Labor Committee; SEATO, 1954; health legislation; civil rights; impressions of many political figures.
595 pp. *Permission required to cite or quote.* 1963. *Micro I.*

SMITH, Henry DeWitt. *See* Mining Engineers.

SMITH, Hermon Dunlap (1900–   ) and Mrs. Smith (1902–1977)
See Adlai E. Stevenson Project.

SMITH, Holland M. *Discussed in* Graves B. Erskine; Harry W. Hill; Robert E. Hogaboom; Victor Krulak.

SMITH, Howard Kingsbury (1914–   ) Journalist.
EISENHOWER ADMINISTRATION
Foreign and domestic policies under Eisenhower; Eisenhower and the press; first Richard Nixon-John Kennedy debate.
44 pp. *Permission required to cite or quote.* 1968. *Micro III.*

SMITH, Ira D. *See* Radio Pioneers.

SMITH, Isaac L. (1915–   ) *See* Continental Group.

SMITH, Jesse. *See* Air Force Academy.

SMITH, Jimmie H. (1929–   ) *See* Continental Group.

SMITH, Julian Constable (1885–1973) *See* Marine Corps.

SMITH, Madeline P.
Experiences and impressions as private secretary to Cole Porter, 1947–64.
102 pp. *Permission required to cite or quote.* 1977. *Micro IV.*

SMITH, Merle. *See* Aviation Project.

SMITH, Merriman (1913–1970) *See* Eisenhower Administration.

SMITH, Oliver Prince (1893–1977) Marine Corps officer.
WWI: Mare Island, Guam; Personnel Section, HQMC, 1924–28; Haiti, 1928–31; USMC Schools, Quantico, 1932–33; WWII: Iceland, Talasea, and Peleliu operations; postwar USMC; unification dispute; Cates Commandancy; CG, 1st Division, 1950–51; Korea: Inchon landing, Chosin reservoir; relations with Gens. Douglas MacArthur, Edward Almond, Lemuel Shepherd; CG, Camp Pendleton, 1951–53.
337 pp. *Open.* 1960.

SMITH, Ralph Bevin (1894–   ) *See* McGraw-Hill.

SMITH, Robert J. *See* Air Force Academy.

SMITH, Robert James (1899–   ) *See* Flying Tigers.

SMITH, Ruth Proskauer. *See* Joseph M. Proskauer Project.

SMITH, Sidney. *See* Robert J. Flaherty Project.

SMITH, Terence. *See* Ethnic Groups and American Foreign Policy.

SMITH, Walter B. *Discussed in* Carter Burgess; James M. Gavin.

SMITH, William J. (1908–   ) *See* Eisenhower Administration.

SMYLIE, Robert E. (1914–   ) *See* Eisenhower Administration.

SMYTH, Henry D. *Discussed in* Kenneth Bainbridge.

SMYTHE, Lewis S.C. *See* China Missionaries.

SMYTHE, Margaret Garrett. *See* China Missionaries.

SNAITH, William Theodore (1908–   ) *See* Federated Department Stores.

SNEDEKER, Edward Walter (1903–   ) *See* Marine Corps.

SNIDER, Orin. *See* Eisenhower Administration.

SNOW, Edgar. *Discussed in* Helen F. Snow.

SNOW, Helen Foster. Author.
To Shanghai in 1931 as assistant secretary for American Mining Congress; work, travel, writing in China through 1930's, marriage to Edgar Snow; visits to China, 1972 and '73: setting up industrial cooperatives, impressions of Maoist China, cultural and spiritual climate; influence of Snow books in China.
134 pp. *Permission required to cite or quote.* 1975.

SNYDER, Howard. *Discussed in* Edward D. Churchill.

SNYDER, Murray (1911–1969) Public·relations executive.
EISENHOWER ADMINISTRATION
Experiences as Assistant White House Press Secretary 1953–57; Assistant Secretary of Defense for Public Affairs, 1957–61.
66 pp. *Permission required to cite or quote.* 1967.

SOCIAL SECURITY
This project has the dual aim of presenting personal recollections about the origins and early years of Social Security in the US, and of exploring the legislative history of Medicare.
Pioneers in the social insurance movement tell about many who were prominent in its early years, including John B. Andrews, John R. Commons, and Frances Perkins. There are descriptions of the activities and personnel of the American Association for Labor Legislation and the American Association for Social Security. Special emphasis is given to experiences with the Committee on Economic Security and the growth and organization of the Social Security Board.
Recollections of early attempts to enact government health insurance, the work on the Committee on Costs of Medical Care and the Committee on Economic Security, the National Health Conference of 1938,

the Wagner Bill, 1939, the Wagner-Murray-Dingell Bill, and the Forand Bill, 1957, provide background about the precursors of the Medicare program. The bulk of the Medicare recollections focus on the period 1960–65. Included are memoirs of members of the Social Security Administration, the Kennedy entourage, organized labor, the National Council of Senior Citizens, the US Senate, the insurance industry, Blue Cross, the House Ways and Means Committee, the American Hospital Association, and AMA.

Participants and pages: Arthur Altmeyer, 231; Edward Annis, 84 *(closed during lifetime);* Barbara Armstrong, 317; Fred Arner, 51 *(closed during lifetime);* A. Henry Aronson, 173 *(closed during lifetime);* Robert M. Ball, 84 *(permission required);* Frank Bane, 121; Alexander Barkan, 10; Harry Becker, 40 *(closed during lifetime);* Bernice Bernstein, 125; Andrew J. Biemiller, 49 *(closed during lifetime);* Carter Bradley, 27; Howard Bray, 112 *(closed during lifetime);* James Brindle and Martin Cohen, 35; J. Douglas Brown, 148; Eveline M. Burns, 180; John Byrnes, 51; Winslow Carlton, 55; Blue Carstenson, 227; Ewan Clague, 152; Wilbur J. Cohen, 57; Nelson Cruikshank, 506 *(certain pages closed);* Charles U. Daly, 27; Alvin David, 27 *(closed during lifetime);* Michael M. Davis, 65; Richard Donahue, 74 *(closed during lifetime);* Loula F. Dunn, 73;

John Edelman, 99; Martha May Eliot, 115; Thomas H. Eliot, 81; Katherine Ellickson, 285; Lavinia Engle, 184; Caldwell Esselstyn, 43; Oscar Ewing, 90; Clinton Fair, 75 *(closed during lifetime);* Isidore Falk, 289; Fedele Fauri, 59; Myer Feldman, 29 *(closed during lifetime);* William K. Fitch, 100; Marion B. Folsom, 207; Aime Forand, 77; Kathryn Goodwin, 80; Frank P. Graham, 24; William Haber, 78 *(closed during lifetime);* Alvin Hansen, 28; Joseph Harris, 44; Ray Henry, 135 *(closed during lifetime);* Arthur Hess, 102; Jane Hoey, 102; Reinhard A. Hohaus, 141 *(closed during lifetime);* Marjorie Hunter, 26; William Hutton, 113; Leo Irwin, 76; Jacob Javits, 12; Jarold Kieffer, 21;

Arlen Large, 66; Arthur Larson, 54; Murray Latimer, 50 *(closed during lifetime);*

Katharine F. Lenroot, 173; Allen Lesser, 46; Leonard Lesser, 78; Manuel Levine, 34; Isador Lubin, 32; Dorothy McCamman, 79 *(permission required);* Walter McNerney, 34; Mike N. Manatos, 41 *(closed during lifetime);* Morton D. Miller, 61; William Mitchell, 140; Raymond Moley, 19; Maurine Mulliner, 303; Robert J. Myers, 94; Robert R. Neal, 46; Ivan Nestingen, 109; Robert Novak, 46 *(closed during lifetime);* James C. O'Brien, 220; Charles Odell, 117; Kenneth O'Donnell, 40; Michael J. O'Neill, 60; Claude D. Pepper, 61; Roswell Perkins, 143; Robert Perrin, 48 *(certain pages closed);* Jerome Pollack, 47 *(closed during lifetime);* M. Allen Pond, 88; Jennings Randolph, 15; Paul and Elizabeth Raushenbush, 295; William Reidy, 101; William A. Reynolds, 61 *(certain pages closed);* Elliot L. Richardson, 57; Gerel Rubien, 41;

Sidney Saperstein, 122 *(closed during lifetime);* Lisbeth B. Schorr, 105; Charles Schottland, 167; Harold Sheppard, 104; Antone G. Singsen, 20; Herman M. Somers, 199 *(closed during lifetime);* Sidney Spector, 57; Joseph Stetler, 58; Jack B. Tate, 119; R. Gordon Wagenet, 108; Elizabeth Wickenden, 211; Alanson Willcox, 140; Kenneth Williamson, 240; Edwin Winge, 48; Irwin Wolkstein, 255; Leonard Woodcock, 28.

10,696 pp. *Permission required to cite or quote except as noted.* 1965–68. Papers. *Some memoirs are available in microform; consult individual entries. Underwritten by the Social Security Administration.*

SOCIAL WORK/REFORM *See* George W. Alger; William H. Allen; Roger N. Baldwin; Algernon D. Black; David Dressler; Henriette Epstein; Homer Folks; Dorothy Height; Guion Johnson; Bruno Lasker; Katharine F. Lenroot; William J. Norton; Alice Paul; Frances Perkins; Louis Heaton Pink; Lawson Purdy; I.D. Robbins; Upton Sinclair; Social Security; Anna Lord Strauss; Eva MacDonald Valesh; Lawrence Veiller.
See also Black Issues.

SOCIALIST MOVEMENT
This project describes the genesis and development of the Socialist Party, primarily in the words of those actively involved in

the Party, past and present. It deals with the relationship of the Socialist Party to unions, the American Labor Party, the Trotskyist movement, the Communist Party, and other groups. Included are analyses of failure of the Socialist Party to thrive in this country, and of the impact of Franklin Roosevelt and the New Deal on the Party. Memoirists also describe the role Socialists have played in civil rights activities. There are recollections about Eugene V. Debs, Samuel Gompers, Upton Sinclair, Norman Thomas, and others.

Participants and pages: Irving Barshop, 27; Daniel Bell, 49; John Bennett, 30; Travers Clement, 39; Morris L. Ernst, 33; Paul Feldman, 23; Harry Fleischman, 38; Samuel Friedman, 54; Gerry Gelles, 50; Maurice Goldbloom, 37; Eric Hass, 33; Adolph Held, 28; Harry Laidler, 50; Aaron J. Levenstein, 43; David McReynolds, 34; Nathaniel Minkoff, 28; A. J. Muste, 26; Robin Myers, 53; Pauline Newman, 33; D. Ernst Papanek, 62; Joseph Schlossberg, 51; Max Shachtman, 76; Herman Singer, 23; Mark Starr, 42; Seymour Steinsapir, 24; Irwin Suall, 43; Paul Sweezy, 14; Norman Thomas, 25; Gus Tyler, 28; James Weinstein, 45.

1,141 pp. *Permission required to cite or quote.* 1965. *Contributed by Mrs. Betty Yorburg, Pelham, New York.*

SOCIALIST PARTY *See* Herbert Benjamin; John W. Edelman; John P. Frey; J.B.S. Hardman; Donald Harrington; Ernest R. McKinney; Broadus Mitchell; A.J. Muste; A. Philip Randolph; George S. Schuyler; Max Shachtman; Upton Sinclair; Socialist Movement; John Spargo; Norman Thomas.

SOCIOLOGY *See* W.E.B. Du Bois; Frank H. Hankins; Guy B. Johnson; Paul F. Lazarsfeld; Helen Lynd; Robert M. McIver; Rupert B. Vance.

SOKOLSKY, George Ephraim (1893–1962) Columnist, author.
Early life on the Lower East Side; Columbia; Russia; China, 1927: militarism, Chinese bandits, arms procurement, Chiang Kai-shek and political-military situation.
126 pp. *Permission required to cite or quote.* 1962. *Micro I.*

SOLA, Fernando (1906–   ) *See* Argentina.

SOLARZ, Stephen. *See* Ethnic Groups and American Foreign Policy.

SOLOMON, Sidney L. (1902–1975) *See* Federated Department Stores.

SOMERS, Herman Miles (1911–   ) Economist.
SOCIAL SECURITY
Experiences in Wisconsin with unemployment insurance and public welfare; discussion of Madison group: academic involvement in public affairs, economics as instrument for action; establishment of Social Security, contributions of Arthur Altmeyer and Wilbur Cohen; Medicare debate: proposed legislation, lobbying, AMA reaction; 1961 Task Force on Health and Social Security; White House Conference on Aged. Impressions of Edwin Witte, Paul Raushenbush, Robert Kerr.
199 pp. *Closed during lifetime.* 1968.

SOMMERS, Davidson. *See* World Bank.

SOPWITH, Sir Thomas Octave Murdoch (1888–   ) *See* Aviation Project. *Micro II.*

SORENSEN, Pablo Ove. *See* Argentina.

SORENSEN, Theodore Chaikin (1928–   ) *See* John F. Kennedy Project. *Discussed in* Wilbur Cohen.

SOUTH, U.S. *See* Sidney Alderman; Civil Rights in Alabama; James B. Duke Project; Clifford T. Durr; Virginia Durr; John H. Hauberg; Lister Hill; Robert W. Hudgens; John B. Hutson; William H. Kilpatrick; H. Jackson Porter; Flora M. Rhind; Theodore Rosengarten; Allen Shivers; Southern Intellectual Leaders; Elbert P. Tuttle; Roy Wilkins.
See also Black Issues.

SOUTHERN INTELLECTUAL LEADERS
A. This series of interviews with intellectual leaders in the South whose work fell predominantly in the period between the two World Wars deals with such topics as southern politics, race relations, the Fed-

eral Writers Project, journalism and southern traditions. All memoirs in both series are individually described in this catalogue. Participants and pages: William T. Couch, 571 *(permission required);* Jonathan Daniels, 176; Guy B. Johnson, 171; Broadus Mitchell, 165; Arthur Raper, 161; Rupert Vance, 106; Robert Penn Warren, 147.

1,497 pp. *Permission required to cite or quote except as noted. 1970–72. Contributed by Daniel Singal, Washington, DC.*

B. These interviews with southern journalists and public officials include discussions of politics and politicians, civil rights, poverty programs and educational issues. Participants and pages: Virginius Dabney, 273; Albert Gore, 103; Paul Green, 258; Guion Johnson, 175; Terry Sanford, 173; John Seigenthaler, 121; Herman E. Talmadge, 132; Capus M. Waynick, 64.

1,299 pp. *Permission required to cite or quote. 1974–76. Contributed by Southern Oral History Program, University of North Carolina, Chapel Hill.*

SOUTHWICK, Louise H.
History of Trinity Church's Chapel of the Intercession at 153rd St. and Broadway, NYC, and its vicarage; impressions of Dr. Gates, other rectors since 1911; building, preparation, description, consecration of new church, 1914; history of church activities, organizations, services; brief history of Washington Heights, 1700–1970's; integration of the congregation.

352 pp. *Permission required. 1974. Underwritten by the Chapel of the Intercession, NYC.*

SOWELL, F. C. (1904–   ) *See* Radio Pioneers.

SPAATZ, Carl (1891–1974) *See* Air Force Academy *and* Henry H. Arnold Project. *Discussed in* Ira C. Eaker.

SPAETH, Sigmund (1885–1965) Writer, musician, lecturer.
RADIO PIONEERS
Family background, childhood in Philadelphia; education, Haverford College, Princeton; music critic and sports writer for NY *Evening Mail* and NY *Times;* music and sports programs; reminiscences of broad-

casting at various stations in NY and throughout the country from 1921. Impressions of Woodrow Wilson, Fiorello La Guardia, and others.

121 pp. *Permission required to cite or quote. 1951. Micro IV.*
See also Popular Arts. *Micro IV.*

SPANISH-AMERICAN WAR *See* Frederic R. Coudert; Thomas C. Hart; Alfred W. Johnson; Jesse Langdon; Herbert C. Pell; William T. Tarrant; Henry Williams.

SPANISH CIVIL WAR *See* Heber Blankenhorn; Claude Bowers; Earl Browder; Daniel Cosio Villegas; Luis Danussi; George B. Ford.

SPARGO, John (1876–1966) British Socialist, author.
Youth; British Social Democratic Federation; growth and development of the British labor movement; socialism in America; impressions of Daniel De Leon, William Haywood, Morris Hillquit, Mrs. Rand, Max Eastman, Felix Adler, Victor Berger, Eugene Debs; break with Socialist Party to work with Woodrow Wilson in WWI; Versailles Treaty.

356 pp. *Permission required to cite or quote. 1950. Micro I.*
Discussed in Boris Bakhmeteff.

SPARKMAN, John (1899–   ) *See* Adlai E. Stevenson Project.

SPARKS, Jeff. *See* Radio Pioneers.

SPECTOR, Sidney. *See* Social Security. *Discussed in* Harold Sheppard.

SPEED, Keats (1879–1952) Newspaperman.
Newspaper experiences, 1898–1950; Frank Munsey; William Randolph Hearst; career with the NY *Sun.*

64 pp. *Permission required to cite or quote. 1950. Micro IV.*

SPEIDEN, Norman R. *See* Thomas A. Edison Project.

SPEIGHT, Wyatt (1914–   ) *See* Continental Group.

SPENCE, Hersey Everett (1882–   ) *See* James B. Duke Project.

SPENCE, Ralph. *Discussed in* Albert E. Sutherland.

SPENCER, Roscoe (1888–   ) *See* Health Sciences.

SPENCER, Sharon. Author.
 Beginnings as a writer; reminiscences of friendship with Anais Nin and Nin's relationships with artists and writers, battle against cancer, 1966–77, impact and influence on women's movement, *Collages, Diaries*.
  51 pp. *Permission required to cite or quote.* 1978.

SPEWACK, Samuel (1899–1971) and Bella L. (Mrs. Samuel) (1899–   ) *See* Popular Arts.

SPIEGEL, Mathias L. *See* New York Political Studies (B).

SPIEGELBERG, George Alfred (1897–   ) *See* Robert P. Patterson Project.

SPIERENBERG, Dirk. *See* International Negotiations.

SPINGARN, Arthur B. (1878–1971) Lawyer.
 Early development of NAACP; NAACP president, 1911–40; impressions of Adam Clayton Powell, Roy Wilkins, W. E. B. Du Bois, Lewis Gannett, and others.
  101 pp. *Permission required to cite or quote.* 1966. *Micro IV.*

SPINOLA, Antonio de. *Discussed in* Stuart N. Scott.

SPITZ, René (1887–1974) Psychoanalyst.
 PSYCHOANALYTIC MOVEMENT
 Introduction to psychoanalysis; early career; Vienna, Paris, and US; discussion of theories; research in the nature of the thought process; cross-cultural studies; psychoanalytic groups in the US.
  104 pp. *Permission required.* 1965.

SPIVACKE, Harold (1904–1977) Musicologist.

CARNEGIE CORPORATION
Relationship of Carnegie Corporation and the Music Division of the Library of Congress; impressions of John Lomax and Alan Lomax, Frederick P. Keppel.
  76 pp. *Permission required.* 1968.

SPIVEY, Delmar T. *See* Air Force Academy.

SPOON, Donald R. *See* Air Force Academy.

SPORTS *See* Athletics.

SPRAGUE, Mansfield Daniel (1910–   ) Lawyer.
EISENHOWER ADMINISTRATION
Work for Eisenhower in Connecticut, 1952; General Counsel, Department of Defense, 1955–57; Assistant Secretary of Defense, International Security Affairs, 1957–58; Chariman, President's Committee on Information Activities Abroad, 1960; Sprague Report; impressions of Charles E. Wilson, Dwight D. Eisenhower, and others.
  57 pp. *Permission required to cite or quote.* 1968. *Micro III.* Papers.

SPRING-RICE, Sir Cecil. *Discussed in* Frederic R. Coudert.

SPRUANCE, Raymond. *Discussed in* Joseph J. Clark; Harry W. Hill; John H. Hoover; Charles Moore.

SPURR, John C. (1900–   ) *See* McGraw-Hill.

SQUIER, George O. *Discussed in* John Victory.

STAATS, Elmer Boyd (1914–   ) Government official.
EISENHOWER ADMINISTRATION
Bureau of the Budget from 1939; Executive Officer, Operations Coordinating Board.
  59 pp. *Permission required to cite or quote.* 1967. *Micro III.*

STACK, James R. (1904–1973) *See* Eisenhower Administration.

STACKPOLE, Stephen. Foundation officer.
CARNEGIE CORPORATION

First contacts with the Carnegie Corporation, 1935; member of Corporation staff from 1940: impressions of office and employees; Army duty, 1940–45; educational testing program, 1946; Corporation's Commonwealth program, 1946–67: travel grants, selection of grantees, political complications, book sets, college and university programs, Anglo-American collaborations in Africa; African education program at TC; evaluation of Commonwealth program; impressions of Frederick Keppel, Charles Dollard, John Gardner, Alan Pifer, and others.
398 pp. *Permission required.* 1967.
Discussed in Cornelis W. de Kiewiet; G. Raleigh Parkin; Alan Pifer.

STAEHLE, Alfred W. (1895–1972) *See* McGraw-Hill.

STAHL, Fred (1904–   ) *See* McGraw Hill.

STAHL, Jules (1902–   ) Physician.
Alsatian childhood, medical training; US influence, work with Drs. Robert Loeb and Dana Atchley; return to France, 1935; Strasbourg during the German occupation; postwar medical developments. The memoir is in French.
61 pp. *Permission required to cite or quote.*

STAKMAN, Elvin C. (1885–1979) Plant pathologist.
Youth and early education; University of Minnesota: undergraduate, graduate school, and teaching career; Department of Agriculture; barberry eradication program; rust control and other agricultural problems; work in Germany, Mexico, India, Japan, and other countries; effects of WWI, the Depression, and WWII on agriculture; world food and hunger problems; Rockefeller Foundation; *Campaigns Against Hunger;* agricultural science in Russia and other Communist countries; work on numerous scientific boards, commissions, journals; philosophy of education; impressions of prominent plant pathologists and other academic and public figures.
1,687 pp. *Permission required.* 1970. *Underwritten by the Rockefeller Foundation. Discussed in* J. George Harrar.

STALIN, Joseph. *Discussed in* Max Shachtman.

STAMBAUGH, John H. (1905–   ) *See* Eisenhower Administration.

STANLEY, Kim (1921–   ) *See* Popular Arts.

STANLEY, Louise Hathaway. *See* China Missionaries.

STANLEY, Wendell Meredith (1904–   ) *See* Nobel Laureates.

STANS, Maurice Hubert (1908–   ) Investment banker, government official.
EISENHOWER ADMINISTRATION
Post Office Department; Bureau of the Budget; impressions of President Eisenhower, Richard Nixon, Arthur Summerfield.
83 pp. *Closed during lifetime.* 1968.

STANSBURY, Leslie T. (1909–   ) *See* Continental Group.

STANTON, Frank (1908–   ) Broadcasting executive.
AMERICAN CULTURAL LEADERS
Boyhood, Dayton, Ohio; psychology department, Ohio State University, 1931–35; psychological research among radio audiences; Center for Advanced Study in the Behavioral Sciences; Office of Radio Research; experiences as CBS president, 1946–68: corporate organization and executives, news and public affairs programs, "CBS Reports," Columbia Records, color television, scheduling procedures, public television, broadcast editorials, video recording. Impressions of Paul Lazarsfeld, Fred Friendly, Goddard Lieberson, William Paley, Lyndon Johnson.
330 pp. *Permission required.* 1968.
See also Federal Communications Commission.
Discussed in Paul Lazarsfeld.

STAPLETON, Maureen (1925–   ) *See* Popular Arts.

STAPP, John Paul (1910–   ) *See* Aviation Project. *Micro II.*

STARK, Harold. *Discussed in* Thomas C. Hart.

STARR, Cecile. *See* Robert J. Flaherty Project.

STARR, Mark (1894–) *See* Socialist Movement.

STASSEN, Harold Edward (1907–) Lawyer.
EISENHOWER ADMINISTRATION
Governor of Minnesota; drafting Eisenhower for Presidential candidacy; campaigning, 1951–52; appointment as director of MSA; foreign aid.
68 pp. *Closed until 1985.* 1967.
Discussed in H. Meade Alcorn, Jr.; Richard M. Bissell, Jr.

STATES, M. N. *See* American Association of Physics Teachers.

STAUFFACHER, Charles B. (1916–) *See* Continental Group.

STEARNS, Alfred. *Discussed in* Claude M. Fuess.

STEDMAN, Alfred. *Discussed in* Frederick W. Henshaw.

STEELE, Judy. *See* Robert J. Flaherty Project.

STEELE, Sidney R. (1912–) *See* Continental Group.

STEELMAN, John Roy (1900–) Labor administrator.
Boyhood and education; work as federal conciliator with emphasis on years as Director of US Conciliation Service; relationship of Conciliation Service to the Department of Labor; impressions of Frances Perkins, Isador Lubin, Franklin D. Roosevelt, Harry S. Truman, Thomas G. Corcoran, and others; labor adviser and special assistant to President Truman; Cabinet and White House staff meetings; relations with the leading members of both Houses of Congress; personalities and influences which helped to shape the major decisions of the Truman administration.
378 pp. *Closed until 1985.* 1957.

EISENHOWER ADMINISTRATION
White House staffs under Truman and Eisenhower; transition between administrations; impressions of the two Presidents, Sherman Adams, Robert A. Taft.
89 pp. *Closed until 1990.* 1968.

Discussed in Ewan Clague.

STEFFANSON, Hokan Bjornstrom (1883–1962) Financier and executive.
Early life, education, business experiences in Sweden; travel to US, 1909; business ventures, US and Canada; Kraft pulp, paper mills, oil, investments; business and finance during WWI and Depression; Swedish-American cultural and educational activities; NYC society and social life; experiences on *Titanic,* 1912; Metropolitan Club, Newport and Carlsbad; comments on Wall Street, investments and investing, estate management, Prohibition, antenuptial agreements; Pinchots and US aid to Finland, 1940; impressions of Ivar Kreuger, Oskar Froding, Hjalmar Branting; the Eno family; Mary Eno Steffanson, Carl Milles, George McDonald, Ignace Paderewski, Axel Wenner-Gren, Edward R. Finch.
1,997 pp. *Permission required to cite or quote.* 1960. *Micro IV.*

STEFFANSON, Mary Eno. *Discussed in* Hokan B. Steffanson.

STEIGER, Rod (1925–) *See* Popular Arts.

STEIN, Clarence. *Discussed in* Charles Ascher.

STEIN, Gertrude. *Discussed in* Carl Van Vechten.

STEIN, Herbert (1916–) *See* Federated Department Stores.

STEINBERG, Martin. *See* Mt. Sinai Hospital. *Micro III.*

STEINBRINK, Meier (1880–1967) Lawyer.
Accounts of the Brooklyn bench and bar; Charles Evans Hughes, Selective Service Board of Appeals; investigation of aircraft industry, 1917; NYC politics; notable cases, NY Supreme Court, 1932–50; associates.

234 pp. *Permission required to cite or quote. 1955. Micro II. Contributed by Mr. Steinbrink's family.*

STEINEM, Gloria (1936–   ) *See* Alexandra Kollontai Project.

STEINER, Alois (1887–   ) *See* Continental Group.

STEINSAPIR, Seymour. *See* Socialist Movement.

STEPHENS, Lafayette. *See* Weyerhaeuser Timber Company.

STEPHENS, Thomas E. (1903–   )
EISENHOWER ADMINISTRATION
Appointments secretary to Eisenhower as candidate and President; 1952 campaign; anecdotes and personal observations.
98 pp. *Permission required.* 1968.

STERN, Henry R. (–1966) *See* Theodore Roosevelt Association.

STERN, Julius David (1886–1971) Editor, publisher.
Experiences in publishing the New Brunswick *Times,* 1912–47; Springfield *News-Record,* 1914–47; Philadelphia *Record,* 1928–47; NY *Post,* 1933–39.
109 pp. *Permission required to cite or quote.* 1954. *Micro I.*

STERNER, Richard. *Discussed in* Gunnar Myrdal.

STETLER, C. Joseph (1917–   ) *See* Social Security. *Micro III.*

STETTINIUS, Edward (1865–1925) *Discussed in* Boris Bakhmeteff.

STETTINIUS, Edward (1900–1949) *Discussed in* Will Clayton; Walter Johnson.

STEURT, Marjorie Rankin (1888–1978) *See* China Missionaries.

STEVENS, Arthur Grant (1912–   ) *See* Marshall Plan.

STEVENS, Ernest L. (1903–   ) *See* Thomas A. Edison Project.

STEVENS, James Floyd (1892–1971) *See* Forest History Society.

STEVENS, James Floyd (1892–1971). *See* Weyerhaeuser Timber Company.

STEVENSON, Adlai E. *Discussed in* Chester Bowles; Cass Canfield; Charles D. Cook; Edward Costikyan; Ben Davidson; Lewis Douglas; Paul H. Douglas; D.B. Hardeman; Alger Hiss; Luther H. Hodges; Walter Johnson; Robert E. Merriam; James Sheldon; Allan Shivers; Adlai E. Stevenson Project; Elizabeth Wickenden.

ADLAI E. STEVENSON PROJECT
Friends and associates describe Governor Adlai Stevenson's life and career from a number of vantage points. Personal reminiscences and anecdotes recall his wit and contribute fresh material for a study of his personality. Political associates analyze and illuminate his career, particularly as Governor of Illinois (1949–53), as Democratic nominee for the Presidency (1952 and 1956), and as Ambassador to the UN (1961–65).

Participants and pages: Mr. and Mrs. Warwick Anderson, 35 *(permission required to cite or quote);* Jacob M. Arvey, 59 *(permission required to cite or quote);* William Attwood, 33 *(permission required to cite or quote);* Lauren Bacall, 76; George W. Ball, 29; Elizabeth Beale, 36; Robert S. Benjamin, 39 *(permission required to cite or quote);* Richard Bentley, 35 *(permission required to cite or quote);* William Benton, 40 *(permission required to cite or quote);* Barry Bingham, 117 *(permission required to cite or quote);* William McCormick Blair, Jr., 94; Joseph E. Bohrer, 46; John Brademas, 23 *(permission required to cite or quote);* John Paulding Brown, 24; Mrs. John Carpenter, 14; Marquis W. Childs, 35 *(permission required to cite or quote);* Jonathan W. Daniels, 19 *(permission required to cite or quote);* Kenneth S. Davis, 91; J. Edward Day, 40; Jane Dick, 102 *(permission required to cite or quote);* Sherwood Dixon, 87; Carol Evans, 74;

Margaret M. Farwell, 31; Ruth Field, 26; Thomas K. Finletter, 62; Thomas Finney, 33; Walter T. Fisher, 27 *(permission re-*

quired to cite or quote); Clayton Fritchey, 27; Katherine C. Gibbons, 73; Richard Graebel, 39 (permission required to cite or quote); Phyllis Gustafson, 44; John M. Harlan, 23; Marian Heiskell, 27 (permission required to cite or quote); Juanda Higgins, 41; Alicia Hoge, 51; Stephen Y. Hord, 41 (permission required to cite or quote); Edd Hyde, 24 (permission required to cite or quote); Lawrence Irvin, 72; Elizabeth S. Ives, 309 (permission required to cite or quote); Ernest Ives, 36; Walter Johnson, 37 (permission required to cite or quote); Barbara Kerr, 39; Doris Fleeson Kimball, 22 (permission required to cite or quote); Louis A. Kohn, 18;

Kathryn Lewis, 55; Mr. and Mrs. Glen A. Lloyd, 30 (permission required to cite or quote); Katie Louchheim, 198 (permission required to cite or quote); Edward McDougal, 67; Katherine McDougal, 42 (permission required to cite or quote); Nan McEvoy, 42; Carl McGowan, 252 (permission required to cite or quote); Kay McQuaid, 6; Mr. and Mrs. Paul B. Magnuson, 32; Thomas S. Matthews, 39; Maury Maverick, Jr., 24 (permission required to cite or quote); Loring C. Merwin, 55; Newton Minow, 122 (permission required to cite or quote); George W. Mitchell, 37; Stephen A. Mitchell, 173; A.S. Mike Monroney, 128; Michael Monroney, 50 (permission required to cite or quote); Arthur Moore, 13; Theodore Myers, 50; John U. Nef, 20 (permission required to cite or quote); Richard Nelson, 79; James F. Oates, 20 (permission required to cite or quote); Elizabeth Paepcke, 46 (closed until May 31, 2027); Howard C. Petersen, 69; Francis T.P. Plimpton, 74 (permission required to cite or quote);

Viola Reardy, 99; Robert Reed, 22; Mr. and Mrs. Lawrence Rust, 36; Walter V. Schaefer, 78 (permission required to cite or quote); Arthur M. Schlesinger, Jr., 43 (permission required to cite or quote); Eric A. Sevareid, 47 (permission required to cite or quote); John Sharon, 148 (permission required to cite or quote); Mr. and Mrs. Hermon Dunlap Smith, 58; John Sparkman, 43; Adlai E. Stevenson III, 75; Ed M. Stevenson, 60; John Fell Stevenson, 28; Nancy Anderson Stevenson, 47; Carroll Sudler, 35 (permission required to cite or quote); Jo-

seph Tally, 13; Mr. and Mrs. Chalmer C. Taylor, 41 (permission required to cite or quote); Marietta Tree, 161; Mr. and Mrs. Clifton Utley, 55; Mrs. A.L. Voigt, 70; Kenneth Walker, 35 (permission required to cite or quote); James A. Wechsler, 21; Harriet Welling, 26; Franklin Hall Williams, 13; Willard Wirtz, 87 (permission required to cite or quote); Samuel W. Witwer, 49; Wilson W. Wyatt, 161.

5,524 pp. Written permission required to see, except as noted. 1966–70. Some of the memoirs are available in microform; consult individual entries. Underwritten by the National Endowment for the Humanities and by friends of Adlai E. Stevenson.

STEVENSON, Adlai E. III (1930–   ) See Adlai E. Stevenson Project.

STEVENSON, Alexander (1916–   ) See World Bank.

STEVENSON, Arthur E. (1886–   ) See Continental Group.

STEVENSON, Ed M. See Adlai E. Stevenson Project.

STEVENSON, Ellen Borden. Discussed in Jane Dick; Stephen A. Mitchell.

STEVENSON, John Fell (1936–   ) See Adlai E. Stevenson Project.

STEVENSON, Nancy Anderson (Mrs. Adlai E. III) See Adlai E. Stevenson Project.

STEWART, Harold Leroy (1899–   ) See Health Sciences.

STEWART, Irvin. Discussed in Carnegie Corporation.

STEWART, Isabel Maitland (1878–1963) Professor of nursing.
Nursing education in Canada at the end of the 19th century, Winnipeg General Hospital; beginning of graduate nursing education at TC; Lillian Wald; attempts to standardize curricula and improve nursing education; nurses in WWI; travel in Europe and Asia; Goldmark Commission; Rockefeller Commission to investigate

curricula in 1927 and subsequently.
459 pp. *Permission required to cite or quote.* 1960. *Micro I.* Papers. *Underwritten by Teachers College, Columbia University.*

STEWART, James A. (1920–   ) *See* Continental Group.

STEWART, Joseph Lester (1915–   ) *See* Marine Corps.

STEWART, Ralph Randle. *See* New York Botanical Garden.

STEWART, Walter. *Discussed in* Neil Jacoby.

STICHT, J. Paul. *See* Federated Department Stores.

STILLER, Ernest A. (1897–   ) *See* Benedum and the Oil Industry.

STILLMAN, John S. (1918–   ) Politician.
NYC and State politics, 1948–50; special election for Congress, 20th Congressional District, NY, 1949.
40 pp. *Permission required to cite or quote.* 1949. *Micro I.*

STILLWAGON, Woodrow (1913–   ) *See* Continental Group.

STILLWELL, James (1906–   ) *See* Marshall Plan.

STIMSON, Henry Lewis (1867–1950) Secretary of War, Secretary of State.
Franklin D. Roosevelt; relations with the press; the atomic bomb.
23 pp. *Permission required to cite or quote.* 1949. *Micro I.*
Discussed in Harvey H. Bundy; Edward D. Churchill; Goldthwaite Dorr; Felix Frankfurter; Claude M. Fuess; John L. O'Brian; William A. Prendergast.

STINE, Oscar Clemen (1884–1974) Agricultural economist.
Family and early life; Ohio University; teaching in Ohio; Henry C. Taylor and the University of Wisconsin; Department of Agriculture, WWI; preparing data for national policy in price determination; exten-

sion of wheat production; Congressional inquiry into farm situation; BAE; outlook work and price forecasting; farm organizations and agricultural problems in the 1920's; National Agricultural Conference, 1922; International Institute of Agriculture; foreign travel; Department of Commerce and farm marketing problems; McNary-Haugen Bill; Farm Board; Russia, 1934; AAA; Agricultural Act of 1948.
434 pp. *Permission required to cite or quote.* 1952. *Micro I.*

STINEBOWER, Leroy Dean (1904–1976) *See* Marshall Plan.

STINSON, Katherine (Mrs. Miguel Otero) (1891–1977) *See* Aviation Project. *Micro IV.*

STITT, Donald W. (1909–   ) *See* Continental Group.

STOCKWELL, F. Olin. *See* China Missionaries.

STODDARD, Francis Russell (1877–1957) Lawyer, politician.
Republican Party district leader, Greenwich Village: campaigning, voting procedures; 1921 mayoralty campaign and rise of Fiorello La Guardia; NY Assemblyman, 1912–15; Deputy Superintendent of Insurance, NY, 1915–21; Superintendent, 1921–24; WWI: anti-aircraft artillery study, 1917; 10th Assembly District leader, 1919–27; military aide to Mayor La Guardia, WWII. Observations on political leaders, notably Franklin Roosevelt, Thomas E. Dewey, Alfred E. Smith, Charles Whitman, and Nathan Miller.
122 pp. *Open.* 1949.

STOKOWSKI, Leopold. *Discussed in* Saul Goodman; Morton Gould; William Schuman.

STOLBERG, Benjamin (1891–1951) Author, journalist.
National politics and Communism.
48 pp. *Permission required to cite or quote.* 1950. *Micro III.*

STONE, Abraham. *Discussed in* Emily H. Mudd.

STONE, Clarence L. (1886–) *See* Continental Group.

STONE, Frederick Logan (1915–) *See* Health Sciences.

STONE, Hannah. *Discussed in* Emily H. Mudd.

STONE, Harlan Fiske. *Discussed in* Charles Ascher; Adolf A. Berle; Marquis Childs; Walter Gellhorn; Harold Medina.

STONE, Irving (1903–) *See* Allan Nevins Project.

STONE, Jean (Mrs. Irving) *See* Allan Nevins Project.

STONE, M. Hedley (1897–1970) Labor leader.
Early experiences; International Seaman's Union; National Maritime Union: conditions of employment, hiring halls, injury cases, racial discrimination, dues collection, pensions; contrast between East and West Coast shipping; relations with International Longshoremen's Association; strikes in the 1930's; Congressional investigations; effects of NRA, Wagner Act, New Deal; foreign flag ships; Communist Party and the unions; founding of CIO, merger with AFL; establishment of PAC-CIO. Impressions of Joseph Curran, Harry Bridges, Walter Reuther, John L. Lewis.
411 pp. *Closed until 1988.* 1969.

STONE, Myra M. (Mrs. William S.) *See* Air Force Academy.

STONEY, George C. *See* Robert J. Flaherty Project.

STORDEUR, Rene. *See* Argentina.

STOREY, Robert Gerald (1893–) *See* Eisenhower Administration. *Micro IV.*

STORM, Joe. *Discussed in* Carl Hamilton.

STOUFFER, Samuel A. *Discussed in* Carnegie Corporation; Paul Lazarsfeld.

STOUT, Dean (1916–) *See* Continental Group.

STOWERS, Keith A. *See* Air Force Academy.

STRANGMAN, Henry W. *See* Henry H. Arnold Project.

STRAUS, Nathan (1889–1961) Businessman, publisher.
Childhood; early newspaper work on *Puck* and *Literary Digest;* NYC housing (Hillside Homes); NYC and State politics, 1920–33; national politics, 1932–44; USHA.
139 pp. *Permission required to cite or quote.* 1950. *Micro II.* Papers.

STRAUS, Roger W. (1917–) Publisher.
Family background; Hamilton College, 1935–6; journalism, University of Missouri, 1940; *White Plains Reporter; Current History and Forum;* Book Ideas, Inc.; Navy public relations, WWII; Guggenheim family experiences; establishment of Farrar and Straus, 1946; acquisition of Creative Age Press, 1950, other acquisitions; partnerships and contributions of Stanley Young, Sheila Cudahy; Robert Giroux becomes partner, 1955; consolidation as literary publishing house, purchase of Noonday Press, 1960. Impressions of many authors, editors, publishers, including Ernie Pyle, Theodor Reik, Evelyn and Alec Waugh, Charles Jackson, Colette, Malachi Martin, Marguerite Yourcenar, Nelson Algren, Mary McCarthy, T.S. Eliot, Bernard Malamud, Isaac Bashevis Singer.
In process.

STRAUSS, Anna Lord (1899–) Civic leader.
Girlhood, NYC; *Century Magazine;* Lucretia Mott and women's suffrage; NYC and State League of Women Voters, 1934–43; NYC politics; United Aircraft, 1943–44; league positions on Equal Rights Amendment, TVA, Civil Service reform, civil rights; FAO conference, 1945; National League President, 1944–50; foreign affairs programs; Town Meeting of the Air tour, 1949; atomic energy control; International Alliance of Women; Overseas Education Fund; Freedom Agenda; postwar anti-Communist agitation; President Harry Truman's Commission on Internal Security; UN Association; UN delegate, 1951–52; Committee for Economic Development;

USIA mission, Africa and Asia; women's position, US and abroad; impressions of colleagues in government and League.

571 pp. *Permission required to cite or quote.* 1972. *Micro II.*

Contributed by Mrs. Walter Gellhorn, New York.

Discussed in Percy M. Lee.

STRAUSS, Lewis Lichtenstein (1896–1974) Government official, financier.

EISENHOWER ADMINISTRATION

Family background; religious upbringing in Richmond, Virginia; shoe salesman in the South; Herbert Hoover and Belgian War Relief, Food Administration, 1917–19; Kuhn, Loeb, 1919–47; Jewish Agricultural Society; Navy, WWII; AEC, 1946–50 and 1953–58: May-Johnson Bill, security problems; Rockefeller Brothers Fund, 1950–53.

177 pp. *Closed until 1985.* 1973.

Discussed in Edward L. Beach; Paul F. Foster; Norman Ramsey.

STRAUSS, Morris Lincoln (1877–1953) Lawyer.

Columbia College and Law School; law practice in Queens County; experiences as a trial lawyer; attorney with the NYC Law Department, 1914; Mayor John P. Mitchel; August Belmont and rapid transit; Citizens Water Supply Rate case, 1921; assistant corporation counsel to Mayor John O'Brien; NY bench and bar; commentaries on the American scene.

436 pp. *Permission required to cite or quote.* 1952. *Micro IV.*

STRAVINSKY, Igor. *Discussed in* Aaron Copland; Roger Sessions.

STRAYER, George. *Discussed in* Hollis Caswell; William Jansen; John K. Norton; Goodwin Watson.

STREATER, Wesley J. (1945–   ) Foundation executive.

Education; Assistant Director of Communications, United Negro College Fund, Inc., 1972–73; Arthur Fletcher; UNCF *Newsletter;* Black colleges and higher education.

55 pp. *Permission required to cite or quote.* 1973.

STREIBERT, Theodore (1899–   ) *See* Eisenhower Administration. *Micro III.*

STRELLAS, Connie. *See* Kirkland College.

STRIKES *See* Heber Blankenhorn; Cyrus Ching; Nicholas Kelley; A. J. Muste; Frances Perkins; Lee Pressman; Upton Sinclair; M. Hedley Stone; Mary Heaton Vorse; Robert F. Wagner; Capus M. Waynick.

STROGANOFF-SCHERBATOFF, George (1898–1976) Naval Officer.

Childhood and education; Russian Naval General Staff, radio communications, 1916–17; 1917 Revolution, pre-revolutionary Russian society; family history; attempts to recover inheritance; US Naval officer, WWII; translator at Yalta, Potsdam, Paris Peace and Big Four Conferences; Soviet-US veterans exchange program, 1958–67.

252 pp. *Permission required to cite or quote.* 1974. *Underwritten by Mrs. Lloyd H. Smith, Houston, Texas.*

STRONG, William. *Discussed in* William J. Schieffelin.

STROTHER, Dean C. (1908–   ) *See* Air Force Academy.

STRUNSKY, Morris. *Discussed in* Charles Abrams.

STRUNSKY, Simeon. *Discussed in* Allan Nevins.

STUDENT ACTIVISM *See* Columbia Crisis of 1968; Jean B. Hutson; Lawrence C. Kolb; Mary Pillsbury Lord; T. R. McConnell; Harold C. Martin; Harry Ransom; Herbert Sacks; Katherine A. Towle.

STUMP, Felix Budwell (1894–1972) Naval officer.

Family background; Naval Academy; early cruises, Central and South America; naval aviation training, Pensacola, 1919; aeronautical engineering, 1922–24; shore and sea commands, 1924–40: cruiser duty, dive bombing squadron, war games, Naval Air Maintenance Procurement Division, Bureau of Aeronautics; executive officer, *En-*

terprise, 1940: ship organization manual; *Langley,* 1941; WWII: duty in Java, Australia, 1942; Captain of the new *Lexington,* 1943–44; the Marshalls, Truk; Commander, Carrier Division 24, 1944–45: operations in Western Pacific and Philippines areas, Leyte, air strikes; technical training command, Chief of Naval Air Technical Training, 1945–48; Korean War; Commander NATO striking fleet. Comments on naval colleagues, especially Adms. William Halsey, Hart, William Moffett, and Arthur Radford.

364 pp. *Permission required to cite or quote.* 1965. *Micro II.*

STURTEVANT, A.H. *Discussed in* Theodosius Dobzhansky.

SUALL, Irwin. *See* Socialist Movement.

SUDLER, Carroll. *See* Adlai E. Stevenson Project. *Micro III.*

SUEZ CRISIS *See* Winthrop W. Aldrich; Arleigh A. Burke; C. Douglas Dillon; Dwight D. Eisenhower.

SUKARNO, Achmed. *Discussed in* James W. Barco.

SULLIVAN, Frank (1892–1976) Journalist, author.
Algonquin Round Table personalities, NYC, 1920's: Alexander Woollcott, Dorothy Parker, others; experiences as NY *World* newspaper columnist.
69 pp. *Permission required to cite or quote.* 1974. *Contributed by James Gaines.*

SULLIVAN, Harry Stack. *Discussed in* Lawrence C. Kolb.

SULLIVAN, John L. *Discussed in* Joseph J. Clark.

SULLIVAN, William (1894–   ) Naval officer.
Education, MIT; Naval construction; Annapolis; Navy Yards in US; Philippines; Shanghai, 1934–37; Trans-Siberian Railroad; Model Basin, Washington Naval Gun Factory; salvage and admiralty law; diving; Merritt, Chapman & Scott; San Diego salvage depot; equipment and personnel, pro-

curement problems; Assistant Naval Attaché, London; British WWII salvage operations: training personnel, blocking channels, enemy interference, financial aspects of salvage and marine insurance, rescue tugs; Bureau of Ships, 1941, salvage branch, training personnel; Pearl Harbor: communications problems, Naval districts; salvage off US and Canadian coasts; clearing Cape Cod Canal; Chief of Navy Salvage, WWII; *Normandie* fire and sinking; salvage training exercises and school; divers; civilian training; development of equipment; salvage award claims; clearing Casablanca harbor after North African landings; salvage problems in Mediterranean Theater: Bizerte Channel, Ferryville, Tunis; Operation Husky; landings in Sicily, Salerno, Naples; plans for landing at Kwajalein; London, preparations for D-Day; Normandy landings: demolition teams, artificial harbors, mine-sweeping; operations at LeHavre, Marseilles; clearing Manila Harbor; impressions of Adms. Alan Kirk, John Hall, Ernest King, Benjamin Manseau, and Gens. Dwight Eisenhower and Douglas MacArthur, and many others.
1,784 pp. *Permission required.* 1965.

SULZBERGER, Arthur O. *Discussed in* John B. Oakes.

SULZBURGER, Frank L. (1887–   ) *See* Federated Department Stores.

SUMMERFIELD, Arthur (1899–1972) *See* Eisenhower Administration.
Discussed in Maurice H. Stans.

SUN Yat-sen. *Discussed in* Alan Kirk.

SUTHERLAND, Albert Edward (1897–1974) Director, actor.
POPULAR ARTS
Early career in Hollywood film making; Tommy Meehan; Mack Sennett and the Keystone Film Co.; Charlie Chaplin; Harold Lloyd; careers of many Hollywood celebrities; Buster Keaton; Laurel & Hardy; movie director, stunt man, propman; Ralph Spence; impressions of other comedy writers and directors; John Ford, Frank Capra; movies as escapism; Bebe Daniels; W. C. Fields; testifying against the Neeley bill before Senate Investigation Committee; West-

erns; unions; Douglas Fairbanks, Sr.; *International House.*
188 pp. *Permission required to cite or quote.* 1959. *Micro IV.*

SUTHERLAND, Anne. *Discussed in* Richard Gordon.

SUTTON, Glenn W. (1904–   ) *See* Eisenhower Administration.

SVARTZ, Nana. *See* Alexandra Kollontai Project.

SWAIN, George F. *Discussed in* James M. Barker.

SWAINE, Philip William (1889–1958) *See* McGraw-Hill.

SWAN, D. Walter. *See* Eisenhower Administration.

SWANN, Benjamin. *See* Rare Books (A).

SWANSON, Gloria (1899–   ) *See* Popular Arts.

SWARTZ, Robert V. (1913–   ) *See* Continental Group.

SWEEZY, Paul M. (1910–   ) *See* Socialist Movement.

SWEM, Charles Lee (–1956) *See* John Robert Gregg Project.

SWIDECK, Harry (1897–   ) *See* Continental Group.

SWIFT, John C. (1910–   ) *See* Continental Group.

SWING, Joseph (1894–   ) Army officer. EISENHOWER ADMINISTRATION
US Immigration Commissioner; illegal immigration from Mexico; Chinese immigration and the "confession program"; immigration legislation; relations with President Eisenhower and with Congress.
76 pp. *Permission required.* 1967.

SWINYARD, Chester A. *See* Association for the Aid of Crippled Children.

SWOPE, Gerard (1872–1957) Electrical engineer.
Family, youth and education; early work in Chicago; Hull House; work for Western Electric; Gen. George Goethals and the Division of Purchase, Storage and Traffic, 1918; International General Electric.
116 pp. *Permission required to cite or quote.* 1955. *Micro I.* Papers.

SWOPE, Herbert Bayard. *Discussed in* Allan Nevins.

SYDENSTICKER, Edgar. *Discussed in* Isidore Falk.

SYMINGTON, Stuart. *Discussed in* Kenneth C. Royall.

SZENT-GYÖRGYI, Albert (1893–   ) *See* Nobel Laureates.

SZENT IVANYI, Alexander (1902–   ) *See* Hungarian Project.

SZILARD, Leo. *Discussed in* Kenneth Bainbridge.

SZLADITS, Lola L. *See* Rare Books (A).

T

TABER, Louis John (1878–1960) Past Master National Grange.
Agricultural political problems, 1915–40, and an exposition of personal and official Grange positions on these problems.
437 pp. *Permission required to cite or quote.* 1952. *Micro I.* Papers: 78 pp. of supplementary notes.

TABOADA, Diogenes. *See* Argentina.

TAFT, Barbara (Mrs. William H. III) *See* Robert A. Taft Project.

TAFT, Charles P. (1897–   ) *See* Robert A. Taft Project.

TAFT, Horace D. (1925–   ) *See* Robert A. Taft Project.

TAFT, Lloyd (1923–   )
ROBERT A. TAFT PROJECT
Childhood in Cincinnati; impressions of Senator and Mrs. Taft and their relatives; family vacations, Murray Bay, Canada; picnics, fishing, daily routine; Yale College; father's political career; Republican Convention, 1952; father's relationship with President Dwight Eisenhower; mother's illness; father's death.
113 pp. *Permission required.* 1970.

TAFT, Philip (1902–1976) Labor historian.
Childhood, NYC and on the road: hostels, hobo jungles, migrant work, railroading; membership in IWW, 1917; University of Wisconsin, co-author *History of Labor in the United States;* IWW: importance of halls, extent of movement, nature of membership; federal and state arbitration experience since 1937, Rhode Island Wage Board,

panel member WLB; union discrimination against blacks, women; 1954–59 writing history of AFL; book on United Federation of Teachers; future of labor movement. Impressions of Roger N. Baldwin, George Meany, Albert Shanker.
164 pp. *Permission required to cite or quote.* 1976. *Micro IV.* Papers.

TAFT, Robert A. *Discussed in* Raymond Baldwin; William Benton; Prescott Bush; Ralph H. Cake; Harry Darby; William H. Davis; Dwight Eisenhower; Barry Goldwater; L. Richard Guylay; John B. Hollister; Edwin A. Lahey; J. Bracken Lee; Robert A. Taft Project; John Steelman.

ROBERT A. TAFT PROJECT
The life and career of Senator Robert A. Taft (1889–1953) are recounted by colleagues, friends, and family. Interviews describe his legal development and political growth, as a Republican, his activities in Ohio and in Washington, and his family relationships.
Participants and pages: Harold B. Alderson, 27; Leslie C. Arends, 21; Stanhope Bayne-Jones, 62; Jack L. Bell, 22; Mrs. Robert L. Black, 36; Katharine Kennedy Brown, 41; Eugenie Mary Davie, 69; John W. Ewen, 18; Homer Ferguson, 15; L. Richard Guylay, 136; Marjorie Hein, 27; Bourke B. Hickenlooper, 40; John B. Hollister, 58; Edwin A. Lahey, 66; Alfred M. Landon, 43; Harry Maginnis, 17; Helen Taft Manning, 83; L. Randolph Mason, 41; Vernon Romney, 43; Mr. and Mrs. Stanley Rowe, 64; Thomas Shroyer, 36; Barbara Taft, 79; Charles P. Taft, 55; Horace Taft, 81; Lloyd Taft, 113; Seth

Taft, 30; Clare M. Torrey, 22; Walter Trohan, 26; Paul Walter, 131; Howard Young, 24.

1,624 pp. *Permission required.* 1967–70. *Underwritten by the Robert A. Taft Institute of Government of New York City.*

TAFT, Seth. *See* Robert A. Taft Project.

TAFT, William Howard. *Discussed in* Sevellon Brown; Thomas Chamberlain; Candler Cobb; James F. Curtis; Goldthwaite Dorr; Roy Durstine; John P. Frey; Frederick C. Tanner.

TALBOT, Harold. *Discussed in* William H. Lawrence.

TALIAFERRO, Charles. *See* Vietnam Veterans.

TALISMAN, Mark. *See* Ethnic Groups and American Foreign Policy.

TALLY, Joseph. *See* Adlai E. Stevenson Project.

TALMADGE, Eugene. *Discussed in* Herman Talmadge.

TALMADGE, Herman Eugene (1914–) Politician.
SOUTHERN INTELLECTUAL LEADERS (B) Influence, remembrances of father Eugene's political career and personality; law practice; campaigns for governor and Senate, 1948–   ; assessments of Southern Black leaders, prominent Georgia Democrats, politicians, Presidents since Truman, Watergate witnesses' testimony; daily schedule; race, segregation issues in his campaigns.
132 pp. *Permission required to cite or quote.* 1975.

TAMIROFF, Akim (1901–1972) *See* Popular Arts.

TANENBAUM, Marc Herman (1925–) *See* Herbert H. Lehman Project. *Micro II.*

TANNENBAUM, Frank. *Discussed in* Will Alexander.

TANNER, Frederick Chauncey (1878– 1963) Lawyer.
Early background and interest in politics, NY politics; Chairman, NY State Republican Party, 1914–17; impressions of Charles Evans Hughes, Theodore Roosevelt, William Howard Taft, and many other political figures.
299 pp. *Permission required to cite or quote.* 1950. *Micro I.* Papers.

TANZER, Laurence Arnold (1874–1963) Lawyer.
Columbia Law School and legal practice, NYC: inception of Citizens Union, 1897; charter revision efforts, 1910 and 1936; proportional representation; home rule; legislative drafting for NY Factory Investigation Commission, 1912–13; NY income tax law, 1919; 1945 mayoralty campaign: William O'Dwyer. Observations on NY political leaders, 1900–1949.
73 pp. *Permission required to cite or quote.* 1949. *Micro I.*

TAPP, Jesse Washington (1900–1967) Agricultural economist.
Agriculture in the South before 1917; Department of Agriculture, 1920–39; agricultural economics since 1920; WFA; Bank of America, 1939–53.
225 pp. *Open.* 1953.

TARBELL, Ida. *Discussed in* Burton J. Hendrick.

TARR, Frank. *See* Weyerhaeuser Timber Company.

TARRANT, William Theodore (1878–1972) Naval officer.
Naval Academy; Spanish-American War; instructor, Naval Academy; cruises and engineering duty; troop transport, WWI; commands afloat and ashore; adviser to OSS, WWII.
53 pp. *Open.* 1963.

TATE, Allen (1899–1979) *See* Hart Crane Project *and* Ford Maddox Ford. *Discussed in* Robert Penn Warren.

TATE, Jack Bernard (1902–1968) Lawyer.
SOCIAL SECURITY
Assistant to Chief, later General Counsel,

Social Security Board, 1935–39: federal public assistance programs, hiring staff, relations with states, dealings with Congress and FBI; 1939 amendments; General Counsel, Federal Security Agency, 1939–47; development of Social Security. Impressions of Thomas Eliot, Jane Hoey, Arthur Altmeyer, Paul McNutt, Fowler Harper, John Winant, and others.
119 pp. *Open.* 1965. *Micro IV.*
Discussed in Bernice Bernstein; Alanson Willcox.

TATUM, Edward Lawrie (1909–1975) *See* Nobel Laureates.

TAUBER, Maurice F. (1908–   ) Librarian, University professor.
Education, Temple University, Columbia Library School, University of Chicago, MA 1938–39, PhD 1941; head cataloguer, University of Chicago Library; professor, Columbia School of Library Service, 1944–76; experiences conducting library surveys, writing books: *The University Library, Technical Services in Libraries,* others.
118 pp. *Permission required.* 1974.

TAUSSIG, Charles W. *Discussed in* Adolf A. Berle; J.P. Warburg.

TAUSSIG, Helen Brooke (1898–   ) *See* Women's History and Population Issues.

TAYLOR, Chalmer C. and Mrs. Taylor. *See* Adlai E. Stevenson Project. *Micro III.*

TAYLOR, Charles E. (1883–1967) Farm leader.
Family background; Progressive politics; publisher and editor, Plentywood, Montana, *Producers News,* 1918–31, 1935–37; Nonpartisan League leader, 1918–24; joins Communist Party, 1920; expulsion as a Trotskyite, 1934; Montana State Senator, 1922–30; National Farm Labor Party Convention, 1924; President, United Farmers League, and director, Farmers National Committee of Action, 1932–34.
248 pp. *Open.* 1967. *Contributed by Lowell K. Dyson, Blacksburg, Virginia.*

TAYLOR, Harold. *Discussed in* Esther Raushenbush.

TAYLOR, Henry. *Discussed in* Henry Williams.

TAYLOR, Henry Charles (1873–1969) Agricultural economist.
Department of Agriculture, 1919–25; appraisal of the work of Henry C. Wallace and Henry A. Wallace in the Department; International Institute of Agriculture.
170 pp. *Permission required to cite or quote.* 1952. *Micro II.* Papers: 8 bound volumes of an unpublished history of agricultural economics in the US *(open).*
Discussed in O. C. Stine.

TAYLOR, Hobart, Jr. (1920–   ) Lawyer.
Texas childhood and education; graduate studies, Howard University; University of Michigan Law School; clerk to Chief Justice of Michigan Supreme Court; Wayne County corporation counsel; establishment of President's Committee on Equal Employment Opportunity, 1961, executive vice chairman, 1962; Special Assistant to Vice President Johnson; Associate Counsel to President Johnson; development of NAACP Special Contributions program; director, Export-Import Bank of the United States, 1964–67; impressions of Robert Kennedy, Adam Clayton Powell.
In process.

TAYLOR, James Davidson (1907–   ) *See* Radio Pioneers.

TAYLOR, John. *See* Robert J. Flaherty Project.

TAYLOR, John Whitfield (1914–   ) *See* McGraw-Hill.

TAYLOR, Lisa. *See* New York's Art World.

TAYLOR, Nan. *See* James Agee.

TAYLOR, Telford (1908–   ) Lawyer.
Early life; Harvard Law School; clerk to Judge Augustus Hand, 1932–33; Department of Interior, 1933–34; AAA, 1934–35; Securities and Exchange Act; associate counsel to the Senate Committee on Interstate Commerce, railroad investigation, 1935–39; FCC, 1940–42.

501 pp. *Closed until 5 years after death.* 1956.
See also James Lawrence Fly Project.

TAYLOR, William L. Civil rights worker.
Experiences on staff of US Commission on Civil Rights, 1961–68.
30 pp. *Permission required.* 1970. *Contributed by Steven F. Lawson, New York.*

TEACHERS INSURANCE AND ANNUITY ASSOCIATION OF AMERICA— COLLEGE RETIREMENT EQUITIES FUND (TIAA-CREF PROJECT)
Board and staff members trace the history of TIAA from 1918, the transition from free to self-supporting pensions, and TIAA's contribution to pension activity in the US. The relationship of TIAA-CREF to the Social Security retirement system is detailed, as are post-WWII developments in investment policy, including the use of mortgages and shopping center financing. Included are discussions of the establishment of CREF, 1952, its early years and the testing of the idea of variable annuities.
Participants and pages: William C. Greenough *(in process);* George E. Johnson, Jr., 57; R. McAllister Lloyd, *(in process);* James A. Perkins, 25; Francis T.P. Plimpton, 16.
98 pp. *Closed until 1983.* 1977– . *Underwritten by TIAA-CREF, NYC.*

TEAD, Ordway (1891–1973) Editor, teacher.
Experiences on NYC Board of Higher Education: relationship with the mayor's office and State legislature, personnel policies, Bertrand Russell case, Strayer Committee report, curricula; impressions of persons and policies in NYC college system.
212 pp. *Permission required to cite or quote.* 1960. *Micro II.*

TEASDALE, Sara. *Discussed in* William S. Braithwaite; John Hall Wheelock.

TEDESCO, Mariano. *See* Argentina.

TELLER, Edward. *Discussed in* Norman Ramsey.

TELLER, Ludwig (1911–1965) Lawyer, politician.

Childhood and education; NYU Law School; labor relations, Navy, 1943–45; labor relations specialist, law practice; drafting Taft-Hartley Act; NYC West Side politics: Amsterdam Democratic Club, relationship of clubhouse to NY County Committee, role and function of district leader, reform movement; State Assemblyman; Congressman. Impressions of Carmine De Sapio.
571 pp. *Open.* 1962. *Micro IV.*

TEMPLEWOOD, Lord. *Discussed in* Sir Muhammad Zafrulla Khan.

TENNANT, Frederick A. (1918–) *See* Continental Group.

TENNEY, Charles Henry (1911–) *See* New York Political Studies (B).

TENNEY, George Clinton (1898–) *See* McGraw-Hill.

TER HAAR, Bernard (1912–) *See* Continental Group.

TERMAN, Lewis. *Discussed in* John K. Norton.

TEWKSBURY, Mary Ellen (1922–) *See* Continental Group.

THACHER, Thomas Day (1881–1950) Judge.
NY and national bench and bar; Supreme Court; Russia, 1917; work of the Solicitor General, 1928–31; NY politics and charter revision, 1935–38.
108 pp. *Closed until 2000.* 1949. Papers.

THALBERG, Irving. *Discussed in* Popular Arts.

THANT, U. *Discussed in* Thanassis Aghnides; Andrew Cordier.

THATCHER, Herbert B. *See* Air Force Academy.

THAYER, Robert Helyer (1901–) *See* Eisenhower Administration. *Micro III.*

THAYER, Walter Nelson (1910–) Lawyer, banker.

EISENHOWER ADMINISTRATION
1952 Citizens for Eisenhower Committee; 1960 Volunteers for Nixon and National Republican Citizens Committee; relations between President Eisenhower and Richard Nixon in 1960 campaign.
52 pp. *Permission required to cite or quote.* 1967.

THEATER *See* Raoul Abdul; Agnes Allen; Maxwell Anderson; Eddie Dowling; Conchata Ferrell; Richard Gordon; Paul Green; Carl Haverlin; Sol Jacobson; Milton Meltzer; Popular Arts; Cleveland Rodgers; Richard Rodgers.

THEILER, Max (1899–1972) *See* Nobel Laureates.

THEOBALD, John J. (1904–   ) Educator.
Career in public education; Professor and Dean of City and Queens Colleges; Deputy Mayor of NYC; Superintendent of NYC Schools.
229 pp. *Permission required.* 1966. Papers.
Discussed in Frederick C. McLaughlin.

THEUS, Lucius. *See* Air Force Academy.

THOMAS, Evan Welling II (1920–   ) Editor, Publisher.
Childhood, education, Kent School, 1933; Princeton; ambulance driver, American Field Service, 1941–43; US Navy, 1943–45, D-day; Harper and Brothers, 1945–68: trade department, editor-in-chief, executive vice president, discussion of books edited, including *Profiles in Courage, Death of a President;* W.W. Norton, 1968–   : review of books edited, philosophy of publishing, book clubs, reviewers; discussion of publishers. Impressions of Cass Canfield, John Fischer, S. Michael Bessie, George Brockway, many authors.
313 pp. *Permission required to cite or quote.* 1974.

THOMAS, G. Harris. *See* Weyerhaeuser Timber Company.

THOMAS, Gerald Carthrae (1894–   ) Marine Corps officer.

Family background, education; WWI service; Haiti, 1919–21; Washington Disarmament Conference; special mission to Middle East with James Roosevelt, 1941: observation of British operations; WWII: Guadalcanal and Bougainville operations; Alexander Vandegrift Commandancy, unification fight; Marine occupation of North China; Chinese Civil War; fighting in Central Korea; Army personalities.
989 pp. *Permission required to cite or quote.* 1966.

THOMAS, J. Parnell. *Discussed in* Robert B. Meyner.

THOMAS, James C. and Robert E. Lushbaugh.
AIR FORCE ACADEMY
Development of physical fitness standards and program for women cadets by the USAFA Department of Physical Education.
44 pp. *Open.* 1977.

THOMAS, Joseph. *See* Vietnam Veterans.

THOMAS, Michael Tilson (1944–   ) Conductor.
Childhood in California; University of Southern California, 1958–62; associate conductor, Boston Symphony Orchestra, 1969–71; discussion of different interpretations of music, experiences conducting and recording.
85 pp. *Permission required.* 1976. *Contributed by Deena Rosenberg, NYC.*

THOMAS, Norman Mattoon (1884–1968) Clergyman, politician.
Part I: Detroit Socialist Convention of 1950; autobiographical material; impressions of Franklin D. Roosevelt and Henry A. Wallace and many other contemporaries; Socialist Party politics, 1920–49.
217 pp. *Permission required to cite or quote.* 1950. *Micro I.*

Part II: Impressions of US Presidents, 1912–65; activities in support of socialist and labor organizations; newspaper career; early political campaigns; work for civil liberties: freedom of speech in Jersey City, sharecropper protection, defense of Japanese-Americans during WWII.

152 pp. *Permission required to cite or quote.* 1965. *Micro II.*

See also Socialist Movement. *Micro II.*
Discussed in Max Shachtman.

THOMAS, Rolland Jay (1900–1967) Union official.
Early life and experiences as a migrant worker; early days of the automobile industry; formation of the UAW; politics in election of officers; role of the Communist Party in the UAW; Walter Reuther supporters.
270 pp. *Permission required to cite or quote.* 1956. *Micro II.*

THOMPSON, Frank, Jr. (1918–   ) Congressman.
AMERICAN CULTURAL LEADERS
Boyhood, Trenton, New Jersey; federal support of the arts; Kennedy Center for the Performing Arts; New Jersey Democratic politics, 1928–50; creation of National Foundation on the Arts and the Humanities; impressions of John F. Kennedy, Jacob Javits.
138 pp. *Permission required.* 1967.
See also John F. Kennedy Project.

THOMPSON, James Stacy (1887–   )
See McGraw-Hill.

THOMPSON, Llewellyn (1904–1972) *See* International Negotiations.

THOMPSON, Mrs. Marshall. *See* American Cultural Leaders.

THOMPSON, Ralph (1904–   ) *See* Book-of-the-Month Club. *Micro II.*

THOMPSON, Randall. *Discussed in* Otto Luening.

THOMSON, Virgil (1896–   ) Composer, music critic.
Family background; childhood in Kansas City; study with Nadia Boulanger; comparison of university and conservatory-oriented musical education systems; the process of writing music, working methods; musical theater in the US; limitations of electronic music.

In process.
See also Robert J. Flaherty Project.

THORNDIKE, Edward Lee. *Discussed in* Arthur Jersild; William H. Kilpatrick; R. Bruce Raup; Goodwin Watson.

THORNDIKE, Joseph J. *Discussed in* Oliver Jensen.

THORNE, Florence Calvert (1878–1973) Aide to Samuel Gompers.
Education, University of Chicago; AFL and Samuel Gompers; prominent US labor leaders before WWI; growth of the research movement in the AFL, 1920's.
165 pp. *Permission required to cite or quote.* 1957. *Micro II.*

THORNTON, Jessie Willock (Mrs. Dan) (1912–   ) *See* Eisenhower Administration.

THORPE, James. *See* Allan Nevins Project.

THYE, Edward J. (1896–1969) Senator.
EISENHOWER ADMINISTRATION
1952 Republican Convention; Ezra Taft Benson; Republican politics; Northwest Airlines' air rights; Senate committee work.
76 pp. *Permission required to cite or quote.* 1967. *Micro IV.*

TIBBETS, Paul, Jr. *See* Aviation Project.

TIETZE, Sarah Lewit (1912–   ) and Christopher (1908–   ) *See* Women's History and Population Issues.

TIFFANY, Louis. *Discussed in* Elizabeth Blake; William Lusk.

TILL, Emmett. *Discussed in* Herbert Brownell.

TINKER, Edward Larocque (1881–1968) Author.
Adventures in Mexico with Alvaro Obregon and Pancho Villa; Latin American experiences.
41 pp. *Permission required to cite or quote.* 1964. *Micro II.*

TIOMKIN, Dmitri. *Discussed in* Henry Myers.

TISCH, Laurence. *See* Ethnic Groups and American Foreign Policy.

TIZARD, Henry. *Discussed in* Sir Robert Watson-Watt; Warren Weaver.

TOBIN, Dan *Discussed in* Dave Beck.

TOBIN, Maurice. *Discussed in* John Brophy; Boris Shishkin.

TODD, Jane H. (–1966) *See* New York Political Studies (C).

TODD, Webster Bray (1899–   ) *See* Eisenhower Administration.

TOKLAS, Alice B. *Discussed in* S. Michael Bessie.

TOLLEFSON, Thor C. (1902–   ) *See* Eisenhower Administration.

TOLLEY, Howard Ross (1889–1958) Agricultural economist.
Early life and teaching in Indiana; Office of Farm Management; development of bureaus in the Department of Agriculture; BAE, 1915–29, 1938–43; Division of Agricultural Engineering; tariff policy; farm organizations; Secretaries Henry A. Wallace and William Jardine; outlook work; Giannini Foundation, University of California, 1930–33, 1935–36; AAA, 1933–35, 1936–38; OPA; interim commission of the FAO.
703 pp. *Permission required to cite or quote.* 1954. *Micro II.*
Discussed in Frederick W. Henshaw.

TOOTELL, George Thomas (1886–   ) *See* China Missionaries.

TOPPING, Norman Hawkins (1908–   ) *See* Health Sciences.

TOPPING, William Hill (1888–   ) *See* China Missionaries.

TORBERG, Friedrich. *See* Austrian Project.

TORREA, Roque (1905–   ) *See* Continental Group.

TORRES BODET, Jaime. *Discussed in* Luther H. Evans.

TORREY, Clare M. (1891–1977) *See* Robert A. Taft Project.

TORREY, Daniel Wellington, Jr. (1904–   ) *See* Marine Corps.

TOSCANINI, Arturo. *Discussed in* Saul Goodman; Morton Gould; Dorothy Maynor.

TOURTELLOTTE, Janet (1899–   ) *See* Eisenhower Administration.

TOWE, Kenneth Crawford (1893–1978) Business executive.
JAMES B. DUKE PROJECT
Family background, childhood in North Carolina; Trinity College; WWI experiences; postwar career; American Cyanamid Co., 1926–58: history of the company, impressions of leading officers; connections with James B. Duke, Duke Endowment, Duke Power Co., Duke University.
168 pp. *Permission required.* 1966.

TOWERS, John H. *Discussed in* Joseph J. Clark; William A. Read.

TOWLE, Katherine A. (1898–   ) Administrator.
Family background; education, University of California at Berkeley; formation of women's branches of armed forces; USMC Women's Reserve during WWII, later, first Director of Women in regular services; Berkeley: Dean of Women, 1953–61, Dean of Students, 1961–65, Free Speech Movement on campus.
269 pp. *Permission required to cite or quote.* 1967. Papers. *Contributed by Regional Oral History Office, Berkeley.*

TOWNSEND, Francis. *Discussed in* Elizabeth Wickenden.

TRADE—RETAIL/IMPORT-EXPORT
See Edward P. Farley; Federated Department Stores; William Lusk; Robert E. Wood.

TRAENDLY, Wallace Francis (1910–   ) *See* McGraw-Hill.

TRAIN, Harold C. (1887–1967) Naval officer.
Naval Academy; South American cruise; Nicaraguan Revolution, 1912; Navy Department Communications Office, 1916–18; Washington Disarmament Conference, 1921; Geneva Naval Conference, 1927; Herbert Hoover's 1928 tour of Latin America; London Naval Disarmament Conference, 1930; WWII: counter-attack at Pearl Harbor, Director of Naval Intelligence, Commander Southeast Pacific Force and Panama Sea Frontier; Eleanor Roosevelt's Caribbean Cruise; Dumbarton Oaks Conference; 1945 Inter-American Conference; postwar career. Impressions of J. Edgar Hoover, Adms. Hilary P. Jones, H. E. Kimmel, W.S. Pye, Frank H. Scofield, and others.
451 pp. *Permission required to cite or quote.* 1965. *Micro II.*

TRAMONTI, Antonio. *Discussed in* Juan Rodriguez.

TRANSPORTATION *See* Sidney Alderman; Lloyd C. Griscom; John T. Hettrick; Emory Scott Land; John F. O'Ryan; Telford Taylor; Paul Windels.
See also Aviation.

TREE, Marietta (Mrs. Ronald)(1917–   )
Civic leader, diplomatic representative.
ADLAI E. STEVENSON PROJECT
Recollections of Adlai Stevenson; appointment to UN Human Rights Commission; US mission to the UN under Stevenson; Democratic Advisory Committee; Stevenson's relationship with Lyndon Johnson; 1952 campaign; press representation during the 1950's; 1956 campaign; Cuba missile crisis; NSC; Marine landing in Dominican Republic; last weeks of Stevenson's life and Stevenson funeral. Impressions of Eleanor Roosevelt, Harry S. Truman, George Ball, John F. Kennedy.
161 pp. *Permission required.* 1967.

TREES, Joseph. *Discussed in* Michael L. Benedum.

TRILLING, Lionel (1905–1975) *See* Columbia Crisis of 1968.

TRIPP, Lester (1905–   ) *See* Continental Group.

TROHAN, Walter (1903–   ) *See* Robert A. Taft Project.

TROOB, Lester (1912–   ) *See* Book-of-the-Month Club. *Micro IV.*

TROTSKY, Leon. *Discussed in* Cass Canfield; J.B.S. Hardman; Max Shachtman.

TROY, David S. *See* Weyerhaeuser Timber Company.

TRUE, Sybil. *See* Radio Pioneers.

TRULLINGER, Bon H. (1895–1974) *See* Continental Group.

TRUMAN, David Bicknell (1913)–   )
See Columbia Crisis of 1968.

TRUMAN, Harry S. (1884–1973) *See* Journalism Lectures.
Discussed in Chester Bowles; Jonathan Daniels; John Warren Davis; Goldthwaite Dorr; Paul H. Douglas; Dwight D. Eisenhower; Milton S. Eisenhower; Edward L. Elson; Edward Folliard; Gordon Gray; James L. Holloway, Jr.; Chester H. Lang; Stephen A. Mitchell; Edwin Pauley; Frances Perkins; Omar T. Pfeiffer; Kenneth Royall; John Sharon; John Steelman; Marietta Tree; Burton K. Wheeler; James T. Williams, Jr.; Wilson W. Wyatt.

TRUMBLE, Thomas *See* Flying Tigers.

TRUMBULL, Allan (1916–   ) *See* Continental Group.

TRUSCOTT, Lucian. *Discussed in* F. Peterson Jessup.

TRUSSELL, Ray Elbert (1914–   ) Physician.
Childhood and education; Hunterdon Medical Center, 1953; problems of medical care and hospital maintenance.
320 pp. *Permission required.* 1966.

TSIANG, Ting-fu Fuller (1895–1965) *See* Chinese Oral History. *Microform available.*

TSO Shun-sheng. *See* Chinese Oral History. *Microform available.*

TSUEI, Julia. *See* Women's History and Population Issues.

TUCKER, Everett, Jr. *See* Eisenhower Administration.

TUCKER, Robert E. (1924–) *See* Continental Group.

TUGWELL, Rexford Guy (1891–) Economist.
The Brain Trust, 1928–33; 1933 banking panic; Department of Agriculture and the NRA.
   75 pp. *Permission required to cite or quote.* 1950. *Micro I.*
Discussed in Will Alexander; Charles Ascher; Adolf A. Berle; Jerome N. Frank; James P. Warburg; Milburn L. Wilson.

TURKUS, Burton. *Discussed in* Solomon A. Klein.

TURNER, Art. *See* Vietnam Veterans.

TURNER, Joseph. *See* Mt. Sinai Hospital.

TURNER, Justin George (1898–) *See* Allan Nevins Project.

TURNER, Richmond Kelly. *Discussed in* John J. Ballentine; Harry W. Hill; Robert E. Hogaboom; DeWitt Peck.

TURNER, Roscoe (1895–1970) *See* Aviation Project. *Micro II.*

TUTT, Thayer. *See* Air Force Academy.

TUTTLE, Charles Henry (1879–1971) Lawyer.
Education, early legal and political activities, NYC; appointment, Board of Trustees, CCNY, 1913; US Attorney, Southern District of NY, 1927–30; formation of Board of Higher Education, 1926; NYC higher education in the 1930's: the city colleges, their presidents, relations between the Board, the college presidents, and the city government; tenure, civil ser-

vice coverage, free tuition. Impressions of John H. Finley, Frederick B. Robinson, Buell Gallagher.
   263 pp. *Permission required to cite or quote.* 1964. *Micro I.*

TUTTLE, Elbert Parr (1897–) Federal judge.
EISENHOWER ADMINISTRATION
Georgia Republican Party; national conventions, 1948 and 1952; General Counsel, Treasury Department, 1953–54; decisions of 5th Circuit, US Court of Appeals, 1954–70, especially on civil rights; federal judiciary in the South, 1954–70; history of Republican Party in the South; impressions of colleagues in executive and judiciary branches.
   113 pp. *Closed during lifetime.* 1970.

TWEED, Harrison (1885–1969) Lawyer.
Education at Harvard College and Law School; practice with various firms, NYC; American Law Institute; Legal Aid Society of NY; impressions of notable members of the NY bench and bar, including George Welwood Murray, Learned Hand and Augustus Hand, and Robert P. Patterson.
   128 pp. *Permission required to cite or quote.* 1967. *Micro I.*
Discussed in Esther Raushenbush.

TWINING, Nathan Farragut (1897–) Air Force officer.
EISENHOWER ADMINISTRATION
WWII experiences; downed in Coral Sea; dropping the atom bomb; Air Force Chief of Staff; Chairman, Joint Chiefs of Staff, 1957–60; relations with Secretaries of Defense, Congress, and Presidents.
   250 pp. *Permission required.* 1967.
See also Air Force Academy.

TYLER, Frances A. (1899–) *See* Continental Group.

TYLER, Gus. *See* Socialist Movement.

TYLER, Ralph Winfred (1902–) Educator.
CARNEGIE CORPORATION
First connections with the Corporation, 1934; Eight-Year Study; chairman, De-

partment of Education, University of Chicago, 1938; work for Corporation over the years; Center for Advanced Study in the Behavioral Sciences; Carnegie study of American education. Impressions of various academic figures.

139 pp. *Permission required.* 1967.

TYNAN, Kenneth. *Discussed in* S. Michael Bessie.

TYSON, Edwin Lloyd. *See* Radio Pioneers.

U

UNDERHILL, James Latham (1891–   ) *See* Marine Corps.

UNION OF SOVIET SOCIALIST REPUBLICS (U.S.S.R.) *See* Ralph Albertson; Boris Bakhmeteff; Joseph Barnes; Dave Beck; Earl Browder; Andrew Cordier; Malcolm Davis; Theodosius Dobzhansky; Kenneth Dryden; Leslie C. Dunn; Henriette Epstein; Osmond K. Fraenkel; J.B.S. Hardman; Nikita Khrushehev Alexandra Kollontai Project; Lewis L. Lorwin; David R. Nimmer; DeWitt Clinton Poole; Radio Liberty; Glenn Resch; Frank W. Rounds, Jr.; Max Shachtman; Boris Shishkin; George E. Sokolsky; Elvin C. Stakman; George Stroganoff-Scherbatoff; Thomas D. Thacher; Mary Heaton Vorse; Henry A. Wallace; Stanley Washburn; John C. White.

UNIONS *See* Argentina; Solomon Barkin; Erik Barnouw; Dave Beck; John Brophy; Cyrus Ching; Joseph Curran; Ben Davidson; William Doherty; Julius Emspak; J.B.S. Hardman; Louis Hollander; Joseph Jablonower; Abraham Kazan; Ernest R. McKinney; Benjamin McLaurin; A.J. Muste; John O'Hare; Esther Peterson; William Pollock; Jacob Samuel Potofsky; Lee Pressman; Victor Rabinowitz; A. Philip Randolph; Harold Sheppard; Elie Siegmeister; Socialist Movement; M.

Hedley Stone; Rolland J. Thomas. *See also* AFL-CIO; Industrial Workers of the World; Labor Relations; Strikes.

UNITED NATIONS *See* Theodore Achilles; Thanassis Aghnides; James W. Barco; Samuel M. Brownell; Lord Caradon; William Carr; Waldo Chamberlin; Charles D. Cook; Andrew Cordier; Malcolm Davis; Luther H. Evans; Charles Fahy; Dag Hammarskjold Project; Sir Robert G.A. Jackson; Neil H. Jacoby; Francis A. Jamieson; Philip C. Jessup; Herbert H. Lehman; Mary Pillsbury Lord; Katie Louchheim; Isador Lubin; Herbert L. May; Lithgow Osborne; Helenka Pantaleoni; Jan Papanek; Nelson A. Rockefeller; Herbert W. Schneider; Adlai E. Stevenson Project; Anna Lord Strauss; United Nations Conference; James J. Wadsworth; Henry A. Wallace; Sir Muhammad Zafrulla Khan.

UNITED NATIONS CONFERENCE, SAN FRANCISCO, 1945.
Group discussion among Malcolm W. Davis, William T.R. Fox, Leland Goodrich, Joseph E. Johnson, and Grayson Kirk on such topics as press coverage, language problems, structure of the UN and the Secretariat, Big Five, and the veto.

77 pp. *Open.* 1951.

U.S. AIR FORCE *See* Air Force Academy; Henry H. Arnold Project; Aviation Project; Harold F. Clark; Lucius D. Clay, Jr.; F. Trubee Davison; Dudley C. Sharp; Nathan F. Twining.
See also Department of Defense; Korean War; Vietnam War; World War I; World War II.

U.S. ARMY *See* Omar Bradley; Henry Breckinridge; Mark Clark; Lucius D. Clay; James M. Gavin; Alfred M. Gruenther; Anthony C. McAuliffe; Arthur Nevins; Kenneth D. Nichols; Robert P. Patterson Project; Kenneth C. Royall; Robert L. Schulz; George S. Schuyler; Vietnam Veterans.
See also Department of Defense; Korean War; Vietnam War; World War I; World War II.

U.S. NAVY *See* J. Sinclair Armstrong; Evan P. Aurand; Edward L. Beach; Arleigh A. Burke; Charles D. Cook; Thomas S. Gates, Jr.; Marley F. Hay; Jerome C. Hunsaker; Marine Corps; Samuel E. Morison; Naval History; Lewis L. Strauss; Ludwig Teller.
See also Department of Defense; Korean War; Vietnam War; World War I; World War II.

UNTERECKER, John (1922–   ) *See* Hart Crane Project.

UPINGTON, Gaylord M. *See* Weyerhaeuser Timber Company.

UPTON, Wayne. *See* Eisenhower Administration.

URBAN   DEVELOPMENT/HOUSING *See* Charles Abrams; Charles Ascher; Thomas Bender; Miles Colean; Independence Park; Stanley M. Isaacs; Abraham Kazan; Louis Pink; I.D. Robbins; Dorothy Rosenman; Wallace S. Sayre; Nathan Straus; Lawrence Veiller.
See also Architecture.

UREY, Harold Clayton (1893–   ) *See* Nobel Laureates.
Discussed in Warren Weaver.

URIBURU, Juan Carlos. *Discussed in* Roberto Ares; Carlos Ibarguren; Jose Martinez.

URQUHART, Brian E. *See* Dag Hammarskjold Project.

URZIDIL, Gertrude. *See* Austrian Project.

USSACHEVSKY, Vladimir (1911–   ) Composer.
Childhood experiences in China; education in US, Eastman School of Music, PhD in composition, 1939; teaching in California and Vermont; Columbia University, 1951, recording operas, supervising equipment; development of electronic music at Columbia; Otto Luening and Peter Mauzey, early concerts; detailed technical discussion of various compositions.
In process.

UTLEY, Clifton Maxwell (1904–1978) and Mrs. Utley. *See* Adlai E. Stevenson Project.

UVILLER, Harry (1897–1973) *See* New York Political Studies (C).

V

VALENTINE, Louis. *Discussed in* David Dressler.

VALENTINER, Clark A. (1904–   ) *See* Continental Group.

VALENTINO, Rudolph. *Discussed in* Popular Arts.

VALESH, Eva MacDonald (1874–1956) Journalist, labor leader, civic worker.
Education; labor work and journalism, Minnesota and NY; AFL; Samuel Gompers and the *AFL Magazine;* social work in NY; Democratic National Committee; persons in labor and social work.
    228 pp. *Permission required to cite or quote.* 1952. *Micro I.*

VALIANT, Charles E. (1899–   ) *See* Continental Group.

VAN ASCH VAN WIJCK, W., Pablo de Azcarate and Edouard de Haller. *See* Pablo de Azcarate, League of Nations Project.

VANCE, Cyrus. *Discussed in* Arthur J. Goldberg.

VANCE, Rupert B. (1899–1975) Sociologist.
SOUTHERN INTELLECTUAL LEADERS (A)
Childhood; education, Henderson-Brown College; graduate work, Vanderbilt and University of North Carolina; development of social science in the South; Southern race relations; Populist Party; agricultural life; Southern Sociological Society; impressions of the Nashville Agrarians, W. T. Couch, Frank Graham, Charles S. Johnson, Herman C. Nixon, Howard W. Odum, and others.

    106 pp. *Permission required to cite or quote.* 1971.

VANDEGRIFT, Alexander. *Discussed in* Joseph C. Burger; Donald Curtis; John H. Masters.

VANDENBURG, Arthur. *Discussed in* Raymond Baldwin; William Benton.

VAN DER BEUGEL, Ernst Hans (1918–   ) *See* International Negotiations.

VANDERBILT, Arthur T. *Discussed in* Robert B. Meyner.

VANDERBUSH, Camiel F. (1896–   ) *See* Continental Group.

VAN DONGEN, Helen. *See* Helen Van Dongen Durant.

VAN DUSEN, Michael. *See* Ethnic Groups and American Foreign Policy.

VAN DYKE, Willard. *See* Robert J. Flaherty Project.

VAN FLEET, James. *Discussed in* Kenneth C. Royall.

VAN HISE, Charles. *Discussed in* William H. Allen.

VAN LOON, Hendrik Willem. *Discussed in* Ben W. Huebsch.

VAN SCHAICK, George S. (1883–1968) Lawyer, public official.
NY State politics; State Insurance Department, 1931–35.

93 pp. *Open.* 1950. Papers: 8 letters (microfilm).

VAN SLYKE, Cassius James (1900–   )
See Health Sciences.

VAN VECHTEN, Carl (1880–1964) Writer, critic.
Childhood and education; Chicago, 1900–06; music criticism, NY *Times;* European travel, 1906–12; drama and literature, 1914–32; Negroes; photography; ballet; impressions of Mabel Dodge Luhan, Gertrude Stein, James Weldon Johnson, F. Scott Fitzgerald, Theodore Dreiser, Thomas Wolfe.
355 pp. *Open.* 1960. Papers.

VAN VOORHIS, John (1897–   ) *See* New York Bar.

VARGA, Bela (1903–   ) *See* Hungarian Project.

VARNEY, William Frederick (1884–1960) Prohibitionist.
Social and political aspects of Prohibition; Presidential canditate on Prohibition Party ticket, 1928.
37 pp. *Open.* 1958.

VAUGHAN, Aubrey W., Jr. (1910–   ) *See* Continental Group.

VAUGHAN, George A. *See* Aviation Project.

VAVILOV, Nikolai. *Discussed in* Leslie C. Dunn.

VEBLEN, Thorstein. *Discussed in* Isador Lubin.

VEILLER, Lawrence (1872–1959) Social worker.
Tenement house reform, NYC, 1892–1902; City Club and municipal reform, 1903–06; national movement for housing reform; Hoover Housing Conference, 1931–32; zoning and city planning; initiation of permanent population data in sample NYC blocks; traffic control and rapid transit problems; reforms in NYC courts: Magistrate's, Children's, and Domestic Relations; records systems. Relations with May-

ors George McClellan, William Gaynor, and John Hylan, and others.
299 pp. *Permission required to cite or quote.* 1949. *Micro IV.*

VELDE, Harold. *Discussed in* Norman Ramsey.

VELEBIT, Vladimir (1907–   ) *See* International Negotiations.

VENEZIAN, Angelo. *See* McGraw-Hill.

VERNON, Mabel. *Discussed in* Alice Paul.

VERVILLE, Alfred. *See* Aviation Project. *Micro II.*

VEST, John. *Discussed in* Ben Custer.

VICCHI, Adolfo. *See* Argentina.

VICTORY, John Francis (1892–   ) Lawyer.
AIR FORCE ACADEMY
National Advisory Committee for Aeronautics during WWI; Gens. George O. Squier and William Mitchell.
114 pp. *Closed during lifetime.* 1970.

VIDELA, Ricardo. *Discussed in* Emilio Jofre.

VIDOR, King Wallis (1895–   ) *See* Popular Arts.

VIETNAM VETERANS
A sympathetic civilian interviewer here debriefs black and white enlisted men and a few officers on every facet of life during the war in Vietnam. Interviewees range from infantry "grunts" to veterans involved in intelligence, interrogation, helicopter duty, and "the rear." Their tours of duty came in the late 1960's and early 1970's. They discuss search-and-kill missions, bombing raids and other combat operations, life in camp, hospital, and stockade, tactical and morale problems, impressions of the South Vietnamese and of the Vietcong. They speculate, months before the war ended, on how it would end and what it was about. The project provides a view of the war, by Americans who fought it, in barracks language.

Participants and pages: Lonnie Alexander, 109; Frank Benson, 167; Richard Blanchfield, 77; Tim Bluitt, 134; Ernie Boitano, 73; Steven Borrowman, 115; Danny Branham, 78; Peter Cameron, 64; Scott Camil, 95; Russell Campbell, 118; David Cooper, 60; Joel Davis, 133; Richard Ezzard, 230; Stan Goff, 458; Steve Hassna, 275; Jim Heiden, 66; Wayne Hemple, 87; Lee Heyman, 103; Bob Hood, 58; Bruce Humphrey, 70; John Imsdahl, 127 *(certain pages closed);* Thomas C. Johns, 91; Maxwell Jouanicot, 139; Barry Kelly, 69; Al Lemke, 71; James Lieuallen, 66; Ossie McCray, Jr., 67; Gerald Merity, 39; Steve Neichin, 81; Mike Nicastro, 80; Jim Peachin, 111; Jay Peterson, 83; Louis A. Pofi, 136; Randy Risener, 74; Bob Sanders, 180; Charlie Smith, 64; Charles Taliaferro, 121; Joseph Thomas, 36; Art Turner, 63; Jerry O. West, 151; Betty Wilkinson, 118.

   3,720 pp. *Closed until 1980; thereafter permission required to cite or quote.* 1973– *Contributed by Prof. Clark Smith, University of California, Berkeley.*

VIETNAM WAR *See* Elie Abel; Dillon Anderson; Lawrence Dennis; Lewis Fields; Jill Krementz; W. Averell Harriman; David Rizzuto; Vietnam Veterans.

VILARDI, Paul. *See* Columbia Crisis of 1968.

VILLA, Pancho. *Discussed in* Edward Larocque Tinker.

VILLARD, Oswald Garrison. *Discussed in* Allan Nevins.

VILLEGAS, Juan Fernandez. *See* Argentina.

VINCENT, George. *Discussed in* Flora M. Rhind.

VINER, Jacob (1892–1970) Economist.
  Treasury Department; recession of 1937–38; State Department; Tariff Commission; USSB; aid to China in WWII.
   61 pp. *Open.* 1953.

VINING, Allen P. (1898–   ) *See* Continental Group.

VISCONTI, Ann. *See* Federated Department Stores.

VIVIAN, John. *See* Flying Tigers.

VOCCO, Rocco (–1960) *See* Popular Arts.

VOGEL, Ezra Feivel (1930–   ) *See* International Negotiations.

VOGEL, Peter. *See* Mt. Sinai Hospital.

VOIGT, Mrs. A.L. *See* Adlai E. Stevenson Project.

VOISIN, Gabriel (1880–1973) *See* Aviation Project.

VOLANDO, Tommy. *See* Popular Arts.

VON BERNUTH, Rudolph Ludwig (1883–1969) Lawyer.
  Family background, NYC; Columbia College and Law School; continuing interest and activities in Columbia athletics: Athletic Committee, 1909–51, Baker Field, 1934 Rose Bowl; university administration, trustees, coaches, and athletes.
   99 pp. *Open.* 1963.

VON KARAJAN, Herbert. *Discussed in* Schuyler Chapin.

VON KARMAN, Theodore (1881–1963) *See* Aviation Project.

VORSE, Mary Heaton (Mrs. Albert White) (1881–1966) Author.
  Lawrence strike; Elizabethton, Tennessee, textile strike; anarcho-syndicalism; Soviet Russia; IWW.
   73 pp. *Permission required to cite or quote.* 1957. *Micro II.*

VOSHMIK, Roy. *See* Weyerhaeuser Timber Company.

VOUGHT, Chance M. *Discussed in* Eugene E. Wilson.

VOYSEY, Michael. *See* Robert J. Flaherty Project.

W

WADDELL, Harry W. (1911–   ) *See* McGraw-Hill.

WADE, Leigh. *See* Air Force Academy.

WADHAMS, William Henderson (1873–1952) Lawyer.
NYC and State and national politics, 1898–1912; League to Enforce Peace; international law.
   118 pp. *Permission required to cite or quote.* 1950. *Micro I.*

WADSWORTH, James J. (1905–   ) Government official.
EISENHOWER ADMINISTRATION
Early career; Economic Cooperation Administration; Civil Defense; Deputy Representative to the UN; workings of the UN; International AEC; disarmament conferences; nuclear test ban treaty meetings; relations with Russia; Chief Delegate to the UN.
   248 pp. *Permission required to cite or quote.* 1967. *Micro III.*

WADSWORTH, James Wolcott (1877–1952) Congressman.
Childhood and education; rural life in upstate NY; NY State Assembly, 1905–10; NY politics, 1910–15; US Senate, 1915–27; Republican National Convention, 1916; WWI; Newton Baker; European travel; League of Nations and Senate debate; Warren Harding era; 1920 National Defense Act; Prohibition; US House of Representatives, 1933–45; vignettes of political contemporaries.
   458 pp. *Permission required to cite or quote.* 1952. *Micro II.*

WAGENET, Russell Gordon (1890–   ) Government official.
SOCIAL SECURITY
Professional background; Director, Unemployment Insurance, Social Security, 1935: hiring staff, administration of law, merit rating, relations with Internal Revenue Service and state governments; Employment Service; Director, California Employment Agency, 1940. Impressions of Frances Perkins, Arthur Altmeyer.
   108 pp. *Open.* 1965.

WAGNER, Hayden. *See* Henry H. Arnold Project.

WAGNER, Phyllis Cerf (1916–   ) Writer.
Childhood, Missouri and Oklahoma; Hollywood, 1930's; writing for movie magazines; move to NYC, 1939; advertising and daytime serial writing for radio; marriage to Bennett Cerf, 1940; columnist for *Newsday,* 1947–58; support for Hollywood Ten; development of Beginner Books; Aesthetics Committee, Metropolitan Transportation Authority, 1978: program for improving subway stations, funding, other agencies involved, problems of graffiti and vandalism, concessionaires; sale of Random House; Christopher and Jonathan Cerf; illness and death of Bennett Cerf, 1971; meeting, courtship and marriage to Robert Wagner. Impressions of Truman Capote, John O'-Hara, Alicia Patterson, Ayn Rand, Ginger and Lela Rogers, Harry Scherman, Frank Sinatra.
   In process.

WAGNER, Robert F. (1877–1949) *Discussed in* Heber Blankenhorn; William H.

Davis; Jonah Goldstein; Milton Handler; Leon Keyserling; Maurine Mulliner; Robert F. Wagner.

WAGNER, Robert F. (1910–   ) Politician.
NYC childhood; family background, influence of father's political career; education; NY Assemblyman, 1937–41; campaigns, New Deal political climate, health and housing reform efforts; WWII Army and Air Force experiences; law practice; reform efforts, 1946–49, City Tax Commission, Commissioner of Housing and Building, City Planning Commission; campaign, presidency, borough of Manhattan, 1949–53; mayor, NYC, 1954–65; pension, career, salary plans for city workers; Board of Education and school building difficulties; fiscal problems and policies; creation of City Administrator's Office; revamping city tax structure; relationship of state politics and legislation to NYC affairs; Mitchell-Lama projects; rent control issues; establishment of Housing and Redevelopment Authority; transit, hospital, newspaper strikes and labor negotiations; creation of Department of Labor; 1965 NYC mayoralty campaign; impressions of union leaders and politicians, including Alfred E. Smith, Thomas E. Dewey, Paul O'Dwyer, Mike Quill, Abraham Beame, John Lindsay, Robert Moses, Carmine De Sapio.
In process.
See also New York Political Studies (B).
Discussed in Harry Carman; Edward Costikyan; Ben Davidson; Justin N. Feldman; Sean Keating; Frederick McLaughlin; Pearl Max; Constance B. Motley; I.D. Robbins; Phyllis Cerf Wagner.

WAGONER, Clyde D. (–1963) *See* Radio Pioneers. *Micro IV.*

WAHL, John A. *See* Weyerhaeuser Timber Company.

WAINHOUSE, David W. (1900–1976) *See* Eisenhower Administration. *Micro IV.*

WALD, Charles. *See* Aviation Project. *Micro II.*

WALD, Jerry (1912–1962) Motion picture producer.

POPULAR ARTS
Warner Brothers Studio; *Twenty Million Sweethearts;* films dealing with current problems; *On the Waterfront;* war films; changes in Hollywood, 1933–59; writing and producing films; *The Man who Came to Dinner;* location shooting; recollections of many Hollywood personalities.
66 pp. *Permission required to cite or quote.* 1959.

WALD, Lillian. *Discussed in* George W. Alger; Adolf A. Berle; Herbert H. Lehman; Isabel Stewart.

WALDMAN, Frederic (1903–   ) *See* Austrian Project.

WALKER, Edith. *See* Book-of-the-Month Club.

WALKER, James. *Discussed in* William H. Allen; Samuel Battle; Jonah Goldstein; Reuben A. Lazarus; New York Political Studies; Ferdinand Pecora; Frances Perkins; Emily S. Warner.

WALKER, Kenneth. *See* Adlai E. Stevenson Project. *Micro III.*

WALKER, Madame C.J. *Discussed in* A. Philip Randolph.

WALLACE, Charles E. (1914–   ) *See* Continental Group.

WALLACE, DeWitt and Lila Bell. *Discussed in* Ralph E. Henderson.

WALLACE, Henry Agard (1888–1965) Public official.
Part I: A memoir abundantly supported by diaries and correspondence. Childhood; *Wallace's Farmer;* impressions of Henry Cantwell Wallace; the McNary-Haugen fight; election of 1932; organizing the Department of Agriculture and AAA; Hugh Johnson, NRA and early New Deal personalities; RA; election of 1936; Supreme Court fight; New Deal and farm problems, 1937; Agricultural Adjustment Act of 1938; "Ever-Normal Granary"; recession, 1937–39; the "purge"; politics and the third term issue; Food Stamp plan; food administration; Forest Service controversy; election

of 1940; Mexican trip; WW II; stockpiling; SPAB; BEW; Vice-Presidency; "The Century of the Common Man" speech; US-British relations; invasion of North Africa; Latin American trip, 1943; Britain and Russia in wartime; Democratic Party politics, 1943; trip to Soviet Asia; election of 1944; Department of Commerce; UN; Export-Import Bank; Russia after the war; Palestine; resignation; Bernard Baruch atomic energy plan; *New Republic;* trips abroad; Progressive Party and the election of 1948; policies.

5,197 pp. *Permission required to cite or quote.* 1951. *Micro III.* Papers: 36 items (microfilm).

Part II: Random reflections in answer to questions based chiefly on his editorials in *Wallace's Farmer.*

323 pp. *Permission required to cite or quote.* 1953. *Micro III.*

Discussed in Will Alexander; Paul H. Appleby; C.B. Baldwin; Samuel B. Bledsoe; Bruce Bliven; Will Clayton; Cully A. Cobb; Virginia Durr; Mordecai Ezekiel; Jerome N. Frank; Carl Hamilton; Frederick Henshaw; Gardner Jackson; Marvin Jones; James D. LeCron; Edwin Pauley; Morris S. Rosenthal; Henry C. Taylor; Norman Thomas; Howard R. Tolley; M.L. Wilson.

WALLACE, Henry C. *Discussed in* Henry C. Taylor; Henry A. Wallace.

WALLACE, William Jennings (1895–1977) *See* Marine Corps.

WALLACH, Eli (1915–   ) *See* Popular Arts.

WALLANDER, Arthur William (1892–   ) Police officer.
NYC Police force, 1914–49; work as Commissioner.
41 pp. *Open.* 1950.

WALLERSTEIN, Immanuel. *See* Columbia Crisis of 1968.

WALLIS, Hal Brent (1899–   ) *See* Popular Arts.

WALLSTEIN, Leonard M. (1884–1968) Lawyer.
NYC politics and public investigations, 1914–40.
112 pp. *Permission required to cite or quote.* 1949. *Micro I.* Papers.

WALSH, Thomas. *Discussed in* Burton K. Wheeler.

WALT, Lewis W. *See* Air Force Academy.

WALT, Norman (1928–   ) *See* McGraw-Hill.

WALTER, Bruno. *Discussed in* Saul Goodman.

WALTER, Paul. *See* Robert A. Taft Project.

WALTER, Terry. *See* Air Force Academy.

WANG, Sharon. *See* Women's History and Population Issues.

WANZER, C.T. *See* James B. Duke Project.

WAR CRIMES TRIALS *See* Sidney Alderman; John H. Amen; Robert H. Jackson; Herbert C. Pell; Kenneth C. Royall.

WARBURG, Felix. *Discussed in* Jonah Goldstein; Joseph J. Klein.

WARBURG, James Paul (1896–1969) Banker.
Family, youth, education; AB Harvard, 1917; Navy Flying Corps, 1918; International Acceptance Bank, 1929–32; economic advisor to Roosevelt, 1932–33: planning for World Economic Conference (British debt group); plans for emergency circulation and economic stability; foreign exchange policies; stabilization fund, passive control measures; bimetallism and monetary policies; negotiations with foreign delegations; international gold standard; Hugh Johnson and NRA; tariff and import quota negotiations; reciprocal trade program; debt settlement plans; stimulation of capital goods industries vs. public works; Thomas Amendment controversy; Most Favored Nation status; Emergency Banking Act; preliminary meetings for London Economic Conference; financial advisor to

American delegation; conference politics, press leaks, US liaison, return to Washington, new domestic currency policy formulation; new gold pricing; commodity dollar proposal; Glass-Steagall Bill; mobilizing business and academic support for sound money, 1934–36; Chicago Committee on Monetary Policy; impressions of Raymond Moley, Bernard Baruch, Rexford Tugwell, William Bullitt, Herbert Feis, W. Averell Harriman, Lewis Douglas, Key Pittman, Hjalmar Schacht, Franklin D. Roosevelt, Cordell Hull, Dean Acheson. Account based in part on diary and correspondence.

1,873 pp. *Permission required to cite or quote.* 1952. *Micro IV.*

WARD, James Truman (1898–   ) *See* Radio Pioneers.

WARD, Katherine. *See* China Missionaries.

WARD, Paul. *Discussed in* Esther Raushenbush.

WARD, Robert E. *See* Carnegie Corporation.

WARD, Robertson Dwight (1905–   ) *See* Carnegie Corporation.

WARDWELL, Allen (1873–1953) Lawyer.
Family background; Yale; Harvard Law School; Stetson, Jennings and Russell; WWI financing; impressions of John W. Davis, Charles Evans Hughes, Joseph Choate; Legal Aid Society.

124 pp. *Permission required to cite or quote.* 1952. *Micro I.*

WARING, Fred. *Discussed in* Radio Pioneers.

WARING, James. *Discussed in* Valda Setterfield.

WARING, Julius Waties (1880–1968) Judge.
Career as attorney in Charleston, South Carolina; appointment to Federal District Court; South Carolina voting, bus segregation, school segregation cases and the community reaction to his decisions; non-racial cases.

449 pp. *Permission required to cite or quote.* 1957. *Micro I.* Papers.

WARNER, Emily Smith (Mrs. John).
Recollections of father, Alfred E. Smith: boyhood and education, career in NY State Assembly, terms as Governor, 1928 campaign, civil rights stands, Prohibition; Tammany Hall; 1927 Governors' Conference; Smith's differences with Franklin D. Roosevelt. Impressions of Belle Moskowitz, Robert Moses, William Randolph Hearst, and Mayors James Walker and Fiorello La Guardia.

118 pp. *Permission required to cite or quote.* 1967. *Micro II.*

WARNER, Selma Warlick (1907–   ) Lecture agent.
Family background, childhood, education; journalism, North Carolina; NYC journalism: *Eagle, Post, Sun;* promotional work for Colston Leigh Lecture Bureau, 1938–41: markets, audiences, fees, popular speakers; assistant to George Denny, Town Hall, 1941–46; history of Town Hall, publicity work, radio debates; Director, Lecture Division, National Concerts and Artists Corporation, 1946–52: college circuits, political speakers; Wide World Lecture Bureau, 1962–73: experiences with various chiefs of state, poets, other lecturers.

385 pp. *Permission required to cite or quote.* 1976.

WARNSHUIS, Abbe Livingston (1877–1958) Missionary secretary.
Missionary experiences in Amoy; wartime mission to Switzerland, 1944.

160 pp. *Permission required to cite or quote.* 1952. *Micro I.*

WARREN, Charles (1868–1954) Lawyer.
Education; teaching; law practice; important law cases in which he was involved. The manuscript includes 17 pp. of impressions of Grover Cleveland written in 1919 by Mr. Warren's father, Winslow Warren (1838–1930).

67 pp. *Open.*

WARREN, Constance. *Discussed in* Esther Raushenbush.

WARREN, Earl. *Discussed in* Sherman Adams; Earl C. Behrens; Goodwin J. Knight; Benno Schmidt, Jr.

WARREN, Lillian P. *See* Thomas A. Edison Project.

WARREN, Robert Penn (1905–) Writer.
SOUTHERN INTELLECTUAL LEADERS (A)
Family background and childhood in rural Kentucky; education at Vanderbilt, Berkeley and Yale; participation in the Agrarian movement; writing *John Brown, Night Riders, At Heaven's Gate, Proud Flesh,* and *All the King's Men;* editing the *Southern Review,* 1935–42; reflections on southern politics, violence and racial thought; impressions of John Crowe Ransom, Allen Tate, Frank L. Owsley, Donald Davidson and others.
147 pp. *Permission required to cite or quote.* 1974.
Discussed in Dorothy Baker.

WARREN, Winslow. *See* Charles Warren.

WASHBURN, Abbott McConnell (1915–)
EISENHOWER ADMINISTRATION
Eisenhower campaign, 1951–52; appointment as assistant to C.D. Jackson; USIA; People to People program.
91 pp. *Closed during lifetime.* 1967.

WASHBURN, Benjamin E. (1885–) Physician.
Early life, education, University of North Carolina, University of Virginia; internship, private practice; Rockefeller Sanitary Commission for the Eradication of Hookworm Disease; International Health Board of the Rockefeller Foundation, 1915–39; Health Editor, *Progressive Farmer,* 1940–53; District Health Officer, North Carolina, 1941–50.
156 pp. *Permission required to cite or quote.* 1971. *Contributed by the Rockefeller Foundation.*

WASHBURN, Stanley (1878–1950) Journalist, businessman.
Republican politics, 1890–1932; Russo-Japanese War; Russian correspondent, London *Times,* 1914–17; Stevens' railroad mission and Elihu Root diplomatic mission to Russia, 1917.
201 pp. *Permission required to cite or quote.* 1950. *Micro I.*

WASHINGTON, Booker T. *Discussed in* W.E.B. Du Bois.

WASHINGTON, Leon. *See* Jazz Project.

WATERS, Gene. *See* Radio Pioneers.

WATKINS, Arthur V. (1886–1973) Government official.
EISENHOWER ADMINISTRATION
Mormon background; Utah; Columbia Law School; US Senator, 1946–58; Taft-Hartley Act; NATO agreement; McCarran Act, immigration problems; censure of Senator Joseph McCarthy; projects for water development, Colorado River; head of Indian Claims Commission, 1959; Navajo School, Brigham City; Mexican wetbacks.
98 pp. *Permission required to cite or quote.* 1968. *Micro III.*

WATSON, Goodwin (1899–1977) Educator.
Childhood and education, Wisconsin; early teaching experiences; University of Wisconsin; Director of Religious Education, Denver and NYC; TC and Union Theological Seminary; interest in psychology and psychoanalysis; socialist orientation; New College; Foreign Broadcast Intelligence Service under FCC, 1941; Martin Dies Committee; Bureau of Applied Social Research, 1943–44; World Study tours; psychology of social change; National Training Laboratories; Newark State College; National Institute of Labor Education. Impressions of William H. Kilpatrick, George Counts, George Strayer, John Dewey, Edward Thorndike, and James Russell and William Russell.
237 pp. *Permission required to cite or quote.* 1963. *Micro I.*

WATSON, Robert Briggs (1903–1978) Physician.
Family background; education; medical officer, Norris Dam Project, TVA; malaria control in Tennessee Valley; malaria control in WWII; use of anti-malarial drugs in Pacific Theater; field staff of Rockefeller

Foundation, 1946; travels in Latin America; work with Chinese government on malaria control from 1946; Taiwan, 1948; work in Japan, Korea, Philippines, Macao; medical education in India and public health problems; work in Brazil and South America; fellowships and policy; training teachers for medical schools; role of foundations.

375 pp. *Permission required to cite or quote. 1968. Underwritten by the Rockefeller Foundation.*

WATSON, Spann. *See* Air Force Academy.

WATSON-WATT, Sir Robert Alexander (1892–1973) Radio physicist, meteorologist.
Part I: Childhood and education, Scotland; meteorological work, WWI; radio and static studies, direction finders; Department of Scientific and Industrial Research; studies of nature of atmospherics; simultaneity of technical developments; memorandum on detection of radiation, 1935; Baudsie Manor, training observers, operation research; political pressures; Air Ministry staff, 1936; airborne radar; recruiting young scientists; US interest in radar; planned position indicator; target finding, H₂S; "Window"; interallied intelligence missions; secondary radar devices; Telecommunications Research Establishment; V-1 and V-2 raids; Royal Commission on awards to inventors; impressions of many political and military figures, notably Winston Churchill, Clement Attlee, Stafford Cripps, Frederick Lindemann, Henry Tizard, Ernest Rutherford, Arthur Balfour, Richard Haldane.

568 pp. *Permission required to cite or quote. 1961. Micro IV.*

Part II: Consulting with US military leaders during WWII; post-war activities in civil aviation, marine navigation; scientific adviser to British government ministries; Pugwash conferences; travel; writings; Center for Study of Democratic Institutions.

121 pp. *Permission required to cite or quote. 1964. Micro IV.*

WATT, Sir Alan. *See* International Negotiations.

WATT, Harry. *See* Robert J. Flaherty Project.

WATTS, Andre (1946–   ) Concert pianist.
Childhood, musical education; maturation of technique and interpretive method; repertoire building; competition in the field; live vs. taped performances; discussion of genius; pressures of public life and career. Included is a dialogue between Watts and Leonard Bernstein during a recording session.

308 pp. *Permission required.* 1973.

WAUGH, Alec. *Discussed in* Roger W. Straus.

WAUGH, Evelyn. *Discussed in* Roger W. Straus.

WAVELL, Archibald. *Discussed in* James Fife.

WAYNICK, Capus M. (1889–   ) Politician.
SOUTHERN INTELLECTUAL LEADERS (B) North Carolina politics and politicians, 1930's–60's; labor strikes, 1930's; political offices held, notably Highway Commission chairmanship.

64 pp. *Permission required to cite or quote.* 1974.

WEATHERS, Everett A. (1906–   ) *See* Continental Group.

WEAVER, Warren (1894–1978) Mathematician, foundation executive.
Childhood and family background, Wisconsin; education, University of Wisconsin; WWI Signal Corps; graduate work and teaching; views on home, family, work, religion, collecting *Alice in Wonderland;* Division of Natural Sciences, Rockefeller Foundation, 1932; experimental biology programs; Paris office, Rockefeller Foundation; European travel; detailed discussion of foundation programs and procedures; WWII: NDRC, 1940–46: range finders, fuses, bomb sights, gun directors, electrical predictors, computers; Applied Mathematics Panel; England, 1941; sequential testing; machine translations; Rockefeller agricultural work in Latin America and India;

European refugee scientists; Vice President for Natural and Medical Sciences; Sloan-Kettering Institute; Sloan Foundation; security problems and procedures; science writing and reporting; impressions of Robert Millikan, Max Mason, John D. Rockefeller, Jr., Raymond Fosdick, Linus Pauling, George W. Beadle, Harold Urey, Ernest Lawrence, Henry Tizard, John Cockcroft, Norbert Wiener, Niels Bohr, Alfred P. Sloan.

783 pp. *Open, except for specified pages.* 1961. *Underwritten by the Rockefeller Foundation.*

WEBER, Lillian. *See* New York Botanical Garden.

WEBER, Max (1881–1961) Artist.
Career as a painter; studies with Arthur Dow, Jean Laurens, and Henri Matisse; travel in Europe; experiences with Alfred Stieglitz; art critics, juries, and galleries in US; views on paintings and painters, past and present. Includes 30 illustrations.

520 pp. *Permission required to cite or quote.* 1958. *Micro II.* Papers: illustrations and other supporting material; correspondence; exhibition catalogues; Weber's writings and speeches, including his unpublished poetry (225 pp.).

WEBER, Theodore (1924–   ) *See* McGraw-Hill.

WEBSTER, Bethuel Matthew (1900–   ) *See* Carnegie Corporation.

WEBSTER, David Locke (1888–1976) *See* American Association of Physics Teachers.

WECHSLER, Herbert (1909–   ) Lawyer, teacher.
Family background, father's law practice; CCNY; James Wechsler at Columbia College; Columbia Law School, 1928: legal philosophy, repudiation of common law as a closed system, curriculum, faculty members, *Law Review*.
In process.

WECHSLER, James A. (1915–   ) *See* Adlai E. Stevenson Project.

WEDDINGTON, Sarah (1945–   ) *See* Women's History and Population Issues.

WEDEMEYER, Albert Coady (1897–   ) *See* Air Force Academy.

WEEKS, Sinclair (1893–1972) Secretary of Commerce.
EISENHOWER ADMINISTRATION
Finance Chairman, Republican National Committee; 1952 campaign; Secretary of Commerce, 1953–58: departmental operations and Cabinet meetings.
172 pp. *Permission required to cite or quote.* 1967.

EISENHOWER ADMINISTRATION
Concerns as Secretary of Commerce: Federal Aviation Administration, reciprocal trade, highway programs, St. Lawrence Seaway, indirect wage and price controls.
54 pp. *Permission required.* 1969.

Discussed in Allen V. Astin.

WEETALTUK, Eddy. *See* Robert J. Flaherty Project.

WEIDIG, William J. (1884–   ) *See* McGraw-Hill.

WEINLAND, Richard D. (1910–   ) *See* Continental Group.

WEINSTEIN, Edwin (1909–   ) *See* Mt. Sinai Hospital.

WEINSTEIN, James (1926–   ) *See* Socialist Movement.

WEIR, Irving Reid (1897–   ) *See* Radio Pioneers.

WEISSMAN, Stephen. *See* Rare Books (A).

WEIZMANN, Chaim. *Discussed in* Joseph M. Proskauer.

WELCH, Roy. *Discussed in* Roger Sessions.

WELCH, William. *Discussed in* Abraham Flexner.

WELLE, John E. (1898–1962) *See* McGraw-Hill.

WELLER, Donald M. (1908–   ) *See* Marine Corps.

WELLES, Sumner. *Discussed in* Spruille Braden; Cass Canfield; Marion Dickerman.

WELLING, Harriet (Mrs. John) *See* Adlai E. Stevenson Project.

WELLS, H. G. *Discussed in* Ben W. Huebsch.

WELLS, John A. (1908–   ) *See* New York Political Studies (C).

WENNER-GREN, Axel. *Discussed in* Paul Fejos; Albert Giesecke; Hokan B. Steffanson.

WENRICH, Archie L. (1911–   ) *See* Continental Group.

WERFEL, Franz. *Discussed in* Ben W. Huebsch.

WERNER, Eric. *See* Austrian Project.

WERT, Robert Joseph (1922–   ) College president.
CARNEGIE CORPORATION
Graduate student, Stanford University; Carnegie Corporation staff, 1954–59; relations with college and university administrators; programs; report on education in the South; relations with other foundations and with Carnegie affiliates; "The American Shelf"; Committee on Education; return to Stanford. Impressions of various Corporation officers.
200 pp. *Permission required.* 1968.

WESSLER, Harry. *See* Mt. Sinai Hospital.

WEST, Jerry O. *See* Vietnam Veterans.

WESTERBECK, Colin L. (1907–   ) *See* Continental Group.

WESTOVER, Wendell. *Discussed in* Eleanor Arnold.

WEYERHAEUSER, C. Davis (1909–   ) *See* Weyerhaeuser Timber Company.

WEYERHAEUSER, Charles A. *Discussed in* William L. Maxwell.

WEYERHAEUSER, Frederick King (1895–1978) Industrialist.
WEYERHAEUSER TIMBER COMPANY
Historical data on formation of Mississippi River Logging Company and related lumber companies in Wisconsin and Minnesota, 1871–1890's; Weyerhaeuser Timber Company, 1900, and related firms in the Northwest; life in lumber camps; policies and personalities; competitive factors in the lumber industry.
167 pp. *Permission required.* 1956.
Discussed in William L. Maxwell.

WEYERHAEUSER, John Philip, Jr. (1899–1956) *See* Weyerhaeuser Timber Company.
Discussed in Albert B. Curtis.

WEYERHAEUSER   TIMBER   COMPANY
Materials on the development of the lumbering industry and the lumber regions based upon the recollections of executives and employees of the Weyerhaeuser Timber Company and of others in the industry.
Descriptions of lumbering practices include accounts of life in the Minnesota and Wisconsin woods; labor problems; immigrants; religious practices and conflicts (including some account of the Ku Klux Klan in Washington); camp sports; camp safety practices; fire-fighting in camp, mill and forest; CCC; reforestation, homesteading and land claims in Idaho about 1900; timber speculation; cooperation in the development of white and ponderosa pine stands in Idaho, Oregon, and Washington; and methods of forest transportation.
Corporate developments are described in accounts of early days of the Weyerhaeuser Timber Company and the Weyerhaeuser Sales Company, the Potlatch Lumber Company, and other related or competing firms, market changes and sales problems, advertising and public relations, exploitation of the Eastern market, development of intercoastal shipping and of Baltimore and other terminals for Eastern distribution, effects of the change from rail to truck lots in local sales.
There are impressions of members of the

Weyerhaeuser and Denkmann families, George S. Long, William Deary, and others prominent in lumbering.
Participants and pages: Vol. I: A.E. Aitchison, 85; John Aram, 98; David H. Bartlett, 59; Jack Bishop, 32; Ralph Boyd, 26; Hugh B. Campbell, 32; Norton Clapp, 32; R. V. Clute, 65; T. S. Durment, 45; O. D. Fisher, 73; A. N. Fredrickson, 71; John H. Hauberg, 127; E. F. Heacox, C. S. Martin and C. D. Weyerhaeuser, 98; F. W. Hewitt, 66; Robert W. Hunt, 85; C. H. Ingram, 12; R. E. Irwin, 40; S. P. Johns, Jr., 46; Don Lawrence, 66; George S. Long, Jr., 46; Charles J. McGough, 66; R. R. Macartney, 44; William L. Maxwell, 112; Howard Morgan, 54; C. R. Musser, 27; Leonard H. Nygaard, 49; Harold H. Ogle, 47; Arthur Priaulx and James Stevens, 75; Al Raught, 54; Otto C. Schoenwerk, 40; A. O. Sheldon, 41; H. C. Shellworth, 77; Frank Tarr, 17; G. Harris Thomas, 63; David S. Troy, 36; Roy Voshmik, 16; John A. Wahl, 18; Frederick K. Weyerhaeuser, 167; J. Philip Weyerhaeuser, 41; Maxwell W. Williamson, 38.

Vol. II: Earl R. Bullock, 32; Albert B. Curtis, 103; Wells Gilbert, 26; Roy Huffman, 68; W. K. McNair, 33; Leslie Mallory, 13; S. G. and C. D. Moon, 32; Jack Morgan, 43; J. J. O'Connell, 77; R. E. Saberson, 81; Hugo Schlenck, 113; Gaylord M. Upington and Lafayette Stephens, 75.
2,982 pp. *Permission required.* 1956. *Underwritten by the Weyerhaeuser Timber Company.*

WEYLAND, Otto P. (1902–) *See* Aviation Project.

WHALEN, Grover A. (1886–1962) *See* Radio Pioneers.

WHARTON, Arthur. *Discussed in* Albert J. Hayes.

WHARTON, Edith. *Discussed in* Cass Canfield; Caroline K. Duer; Leon Edel.

WHEATON, Anne W. (1892–1977)
EISENHOWER ADMINISTRATION
Assistant chief of press relations and head of publicity for the women's division, Republican National Committee, 1939–57; 1952 convention and campaign; associate

press secretary to the President; Eisenhower's press conferences; Cabinet meetings; impressions of the Eisenhowers; White House staff.
178 pp. *Permission required to cite or quote.* 1968. *Micro III.*

WHEELER, Benjamin I. *Discussed in* Newton B. Drury.

WHEELER, Bert (1895–1968) *See* Popular Arts.

WHEELER, Burton Kendall (1882–1975) Senator.
Montana politics, 1920; Nonpartisan League; Anaconda Company; US Senator, 1923–47: committee assignments, Teapot Dome investigations, silver bills, court-packing issue, war preparations; accounts of Democratic conventions and campaigns, 1924, 1932, 1940, 1944; European trip, 1945. Impressions of Franklin Roosevelt, Harry S. Truman; Senators William Borah, George Norris, Huey Long, and Thomas Walsh.
161 pp. *Permission required to cite or quote.* 1969.

WHEELER, Leslie Allen (1899–) Agriculturist.
Childhood and education; Department of Commerce, 1923–26; BAE, 1926–40; Foreign Agricultural Service, Office of Foreign Agricultural Relations, 1940–47; US Foreign Service, 1948–51.
532 pp. *Closed until 5 years after death.* 1952.

WHEELER, Raymond A. (1885–1974) *See* World Bank.

WHEELIS, William (1911–) *See* Continental Group.

WHEELOCK, John Hall (1886–1978) Author.
Family history and childhood; Harvard College; work on literary publications; career as editor for Charles Scribner's Sons, 1926–57: clients and staff; career as poet: influences, publications, evaluations of his own and others' work; anecdotes concerning Zoe Akins, Van Wyck Brooks, Vachel Lindsay, Edgar Lee Masters, Maxwell Per-

kins, Edwin Arlington Robinson, the Charles Scribner family, Edward Sheldon, Sara Teasdale, Oscar Williams, Thomas Wolfe, and many others.
478 pp. *Closed until 1990.* 1967.

WHITE, F. Clifton (1918–) Politician.
Early political interests; Young Republican Clubs; candidacy of Senator Barry Goldwater in 1964: primaries and state conventions, San Francisco convention, campaign and election; vignettes of Republican leaders.
222 pp. *Permission required.* 1964. *Contributed by James Cannon, New York.*

WHITE, Harry Dexter. *Discussed in* Stephen Benedict.

WHITE, Ivan Bertis (1907–) *See* Marshall Plan.

WHITE, John Campbell (1884–1967) Diplomat.
Diplomatic service in Russia, 1915–16; Royalist-Venizelist controversy, Greece, 1916–17; Far East; Poland, 1919–21: food distribution, Bolshevik advance on Warsaw; oil exploration rights in Venezuela, 1921–23; Argentina, 1928–33: President Herbert Hoover's 1928 visit, 1930 revolution; Nazi Germany, 1933–35; consular duty, Calcutta, 1936–40; Ambassador to Haiti, 1940–43, Peru, 1944–45. Impressions of many statesmen.
139 pp. *Permission required to cite or quote.* 1953. *Micro I.*

WHITE, John Francis (1917–) *See* Children's Television Workshop.

WHITE, Lawrence Grant (1887–1956) Architect.
Early life, family history, and education; experiences in World Wars I and II; career with McKim, Mead & White; interest in aviation; literary activities; personal anecdotes of many well-known figures.
161 pp. *Permission required to cite or quote.* 1956. *Micro I.*

WHITE, Philip O'Connell (1898–) *See* Continental Group.

WHITE, Rex G. (–1951) *See* Radio Pioneers.

WHITE, Robert M. (1924–) *See* Aviation Project.

WHITE, Robert P. (1923–) *See* Continental Group.

WHITE, Sam. *See* Alaskan Pioneers.

WHITE, Thomas D. *See* Aviation Project. *Micro IV.*
Discussed in Jarred V. Crabb.

WHITE, Walter. *Discussed in* George S. Schuyler; Roy Wilkins.

WHITE, William Cummings. *See* Radio Pioneers.

WHITEHEAD, Ennis C. *Discussed in* Jarred V. Crabb.

WHITLOCK, Brand. *Discussed in* Perrin C. Galpin.

WHITMAN, Charles S. *Discussed in* George F. Chandler; Francis R. Stoddard.

WHITNEY, Courtney. *Discussed in* Occupation of Japan.

WHITNEY, George (1885–1963) Banker.
Childhood, Boston; Groton and Harvard; private banking firms; partnership in J.P. Morgan firm, 1920; financing foreign and domestic loans; impressions of prominent bankers and financiers.
82 pp. *Permission required to cite or quote.* 1963. *Micro I.*

WHITNEY, Willis R. *Discussed in* Albert W. Hull.

WHITTALL, Ralph L. (1925–) *See* Continental Group.

WHITTEN, George Easton (1896–) *See* Federated Department Stores.

WHITTLE, Sir Frank. *See* Air Force Academy.

WICKARD, Claude Raymond (1893–1967) Government official.
Early life in Indiana; education; farming; observation of the farm revolt and the

McNary-Haugen movement in the 1920's; election to the Indiana Senate, 1932; Corn and Hogs Section of the AAA; Agricultural Conservation Program; the Depression and the Department of Agriculture; experience as Under Secretary, 1940, and Secretary, 1940–45, of Agriculture; WWII; Lend-Lease; inter-American conferences on agriculture; work with the REA.

3,992 pp. *Permission required to cite or quote.* 1953.
Discussed in Samuel Bledsoe; Mordecai Ezekiel; Carl Hamilton; Gardner Jackson; Marvin Jones; Herbert W. Parisius.

WICKENDEN, Elizabeth.
SOCIAL SECURITY
Education, Vassar; FERA, 1933; medical programs; representative for American Public Welfare Association; public welfare philosophy; social insurance legislation; interaction with politicians; consultant on health insurance to Adlai Stevenson, John F. Kennedy, Lyndon Johnson, and others; Medicare and AMA; insurance companies; senior citizens in politics, 1950's and '60's. Impressions of Wilbur Cohen, Nelson Cruikshank, Francis Townsend, James O'Brien, Charles Odell, Zalman Lichtenstein, Marjorie Shearon, and others.

211 pp. *Permission required to cite or quote.* 1966. *Micro IV.*

WICKENS, Aryness Joy (Mrs. David L.) (1901–) Government official, economist.
Department of Labor, Coolidge to Eisenhower; Bureau of Labor Statistics and its relation to the labor movement.

94 pp. *Permission required to cite or quote.* 1957. *Micro I.*

WIEDEMER, Charles. *See* Federated Department Stores.

WIEN, Noel (–1977) *See* Aviation Project.

WIENER, Jan.
Experiences in Czechoslovakia during WWII; escape, service in Allied forces; life in occupied countries.

58 pp. *Permission required to cite or quote.*

WIENER, Norbert. *Discussed in* Warren Weaver.

WIESEMAN, Frederick L. (1908–) *See* Marine Corps.

WIGHT, Joseph V. *See* McGraw-Hill.

WIGNER, Eugene Paul (1902–) *See* Nobel Laureates.

WILCOCKSON, A.S. (–1974) *See* Aviation Project. *Micro II.*

WILCOX, Francis O. (1908–) *See* Eisenhower Administration. *Micro III.*

WILDER, Billy. *Discussed in* Samson Raphaelson.

WILDER, Thornton. *Discussed in* Sol Lesser.

WILEY, Alexander (1884–1967) Senator.
Childhood, education; political experience; election to US Senate; WWII; Senator Joseph McCarthy.

63 pp. *Open.* 1964.

WILEY, Bell Irvin (1906–) *See* Civil War Centennial.

WILEY, Martha. *See* China Missionaries.

WILHELM, John Remsen (1916–) *See* McGraw-Hill.

WILKINS, Raymond Sanger (1891–1971) *See* Robert P. Patterson Project.

WILKINS, Roy (1901–) Publicist, administrator.
Family background, childhood, education, St. Paul and Minneapolis; job discrimination; journalism, Kansas City *Call;* discrimination in Kansas City; NAACP; Walter White; housing, NYC; travel; labor problems in the South; *The Crisis;* Negroes in government; anti-lynching bills; industrial integration; 1941 March on Washington; FEPC; Supreme Court desegregation decision, 1954.

130 pp. *Permission required to cite or quote.* 1960. *Micro I.*

See also Herbert H. Lehman Project. *Micro II.*
Discussed in John Warren Davis; George S. Schuyler; Arthur B. Spingarn.

WILKINSON, Betty. *See* Vietnam Veterans.

WILKINSON, Lawrence (1905–   ) *See* Continental Group.

WILLCOX, Alanson Work (1901–1978) Lawyer.
SOCIAL SECURITY
Drafting Social Security Act, 1935–36; legal adviser, Social Security Board, 1938; General Counsel, Federal Security Agency, 1947; Murray-Wagner-Dingell bill; philosophy of social security; evaluation of legislation; Medicare: positions of AMA, Blue Cross, and American Hospital Association. Impressions of Jack Tate, Tom Eliot, Wilbur Cohen, and others.
140 pp. *Permission required to cite or quote.* 1966. *Micro IV.*
Discussed in Kenneth Williamson.

WILLIAMS, Alex, Sr. *See* Marine Corps.

WILLIAMS, Aubrey. *Discussed in* Clifford J. Durr.

WILLIAMS, E. Grainger. *See* Eisenhower Administration. *Micro III.*

WILLIAMS, Edith. *See* Eisenhower Administration.

WILLIAMS, Edward Eugene (1892–   ) *See* James B. Duke Project.

WILLIAMS, Franklin Hall (1917–   ) *See* Adlai E. Stevenson Project.

WILLIAMS, Henry (1877–1973) Naval officer.
Naval Academy; Spanish-American War; graduate course in naval architecture, Paris, 1899–1901; naval construction specialist, 1901–33: launching problems, development of plastic ship bottom paint, submarine rescue chamber; Army Industrial College, 1933; administrative officer, Bureau of Ships, and later for Secretary of Navy, WWII; Munitions Board; Mari-

time Commission; allocation of strategic materials, laying up surplus vessels, disposal of shipyards. Accounts of Theodore Roosevelt, Charles Edison, Frank Knox, and Adms. William Sims, Henry Taylor, Samuel Robinson, and Emory Land.
251 pp. *Permission required to cite or quote.* 1963. *Micro I.*

WILLIAMS, James Thomas, Jr. (1881–1969) Editor.
Background; education; reporter in Washington for Columbia, South Carolina *State,* AP, and Boston *Evening Transcript,* 1902–08; Theodore Roosevelt and his Cabinet; 1908 election; Arizona cure; Frank Blighton libel case; Arizona statehood; Republican conventions of 1912 and 1920; campaigns of 1912, 1916, 1920, 1936; Boyd-Adair; Leonard Wood; Boston police strike; Warren Harding; Calvin Coolidge; Philippines, Nicaragua; Mexico; Herbert Hoover and the Crash; William R. Hearst organization; Franklin D. Roosevelt; J. Reuben Clark; Josephus Daniels; WWII; George C. Marshall, Harry S. Truman; Sacco-Vanzetti Case.
966 pp. *Permission required to cite or quote.* 1953. *Micro I.*

WILLIAMS, Mrs. John. *See* James B. Duke Project.

WILLIAMS, Oscar. *Discussed in* John Hall Wheelock.

WILLIAMS, T. Harry (1909–   ) *See* American Historians *and* Civil War Centennial.

WILLIAMS, Tennessee. *Discussed in* Eddie Dowling.

WILLIAMS, W. Walter (1894–   ) Banker.
EISENHOWER ADMINISTRATION
Chairman, Committee for Economic Development; Citizens for Eisenhower; Under Secretary of Commerce.
103 pp. *Permission required.* 1967.

WILLIAMS, William Carlos. *Discussed in* Helen W. Fall.

WILLIAMSON, Kenneth.
SOCIAL SECURITY
California health insurance program, 1930–33; work with Blue Cross and American Hospital Association; impressions of AMA leaders; Wagner-Murray bill; work with federal government, 1945–67; HEW; Public Health Service; Forand bill; Medicare; President John F. Kennedy's concern for health programs and aid to the aged; Special Committee on Aging. Impressions of Nelson Cruikshank, Andrew Biemiller, Nelson Rockefeller, Wilbur Cohen, Wilbur Mills, Alanson Willcox, and others.
240 pp. *Open.* 1967.

WILLIAMSON, Maxwell W. (1884–   )
See Weyerhaeuser Timber Company.

WILLINGDON, Lord. *Discussed in* Sir Muhammad Zafrulla Khan.

WILLIS, Charles Fountain, Jr. (1918–   ) Airline executive.
EISENHOWER ADMINISTRATION
Citizens for Eisenhower; Special Assistant, White House staff; presidential appointments.
50 pp. *Permission required to cite or quote.* 1968.

WILLIS, Harold B. *See* Aviation Project.

WILLISTON, Samuel. *Discussed in* Felix Frankfurter; James M. Landis.

WILLKIE, Wendell L. *Discussed in* James A. Farley; Lee Pressman; Joseph M. Proskauer.

WILLOUGHBY, Charles. *Discussed in* Occupation of Japan.

WILLSON, Meredith (1902–   ) *See* Popular Arts.

WILSON, Carey (1889–1962) *See* Popular Arts.

WILSON, Charles E. *Discussed in* Elie Abel; Mansfield D. Sprague.

WILSON, Comar (–1961) *See* Mining Engineers.

WILSON, David and Patricia. *See* Continental Group.

WILSON, Dean. *See* Marine Corps.

WILSON, Edmund. *Discussed in* Max Gissen.

WILSON, Eugene Edward (1887–1974) Naval aviator, industrialist.
Childhood and education, Montana; US Naval Academy; Navy Rifle Teams; engineering and gunnery service at sea; Engineering School, Columbia; WWI experiences with Grand Fleet at Scapa Flow; Aviation Mechanics School at Great Lakes; Bureau of Aeronautics; pilot training; Aircraft Squadrons Battle Fleet, 1927; development of carrier task force; resignation from Navy, 1929; United Aircraft Corporation; aircraft industry developments and problems; air-cooled engine; controllable angle propeller; new types of planes; helicopter; airmail contract cancellations; aircraft industry through WWII; postwar industry problems. Impressions of industrial, political, naval, and military leaders, notably Adms. William A. Moffett, Ernest J. King, and Joseph M. Reeves, Gen. William Mitchell, Chance M. Vought, Charles A. Lindbergh, Thomas F. Hamilton, Frederick B. Rentschler, Igor Sikorsky, William Boeing, and James Forrestal.
974 pp. *Permission required to cite or quote.* 1962. *Micro I.*

WILSON, Francis. *Discussed in* Richard Gordon.

WILSON, Gill Robb (1893–1966) See Aviation Project.

WILSON, Henry. *Discussed in* John H. Hoover.

WILSON, John C. *See* Federated Department Stores.

WILSON, Luke. *See* La Follette Civil Liberties Committee.

WILSON, Milburn Lincoln (1885–1969) Agriculturist.
Childhood, education; early farming experiences in Nebraska and Montana; dry-

farming; Nonpartisan League; grain cooperatives; McNary-Haugen Bill; Fairway Farms Corporation; Department of Agriculture, 1924; advisory trip to Russia, 1929; extension service; Grange, Farmers' Union; BAE; domestic allotment plans, writing agricultural speeches for Franklin D. Roosevelt, 1932; first hundred days; AAA; land resettlement, use of submarginal land; Division of Subsistence Homesteads in Interior Department, 1933; Arthurdale project; Cuban sugar survey; Assistant Secretary of Agriculture, 1934; shelter belts; FSA; Roerich expedition, Wallace mysticism; visits of George Russell; Dust Bowl and land use; Department of Agriculture purge; RA; soil conservation; 1936 campaign; Under Secretary of Agriculture, 1937; impressions of many prominent New Deal figures, especially Henry A. Wallace, Rexford Tugwell, Chester Davis.
2,165 pp. *Permission required to cite or quote.* 1956. *Micro II.*
Discussed in Carl Hamilton.

WILSON, Roger V. (1901–   ) *See* Continental Group.

WILSON, William B. *Discussed in* John Brophy.

WILSON, Woodrow. *Discussed in* Horace M. Albright; Boris Bakhmeteff; Henry Breckinridge; Frederic R. Coudert; James W. Gerard; Arthur W. Page; Geoffrey Parsons; Francis B. Sayre; Sigmund Spaeth; John Spargo.

WINANCE, Eleutherius. *See* China Missionaries.

WINANS, Pearl Fosnot (1891–   ) *See* China Missionaries.

WINANT, John. *Discussed in* A. Henry Aronson; Frank Bane; Bernice Bernstein; Eveline Burns; Ewan Clague; Thomas I. Emerson; Reinhard A. Hohaus; Lewis L. Lorwin; Maurine Mulliner; Jack B. Tate.

WINCHELL, Constance Mabel (1896–   ) Librarian.
Education, NY Public Library School, 1919; early library experiences; University of Michigan, 1920–23; reference work, inter-library loans; American Library in Paris, 1924; Columbia University Library from 1925: Reference Department, move from Low Library to Butler Library; library school; *Guide to Reference Books;* American Library Association. Impressions of Miss Isadore G. Mudge, President Nicholas Murray Butler.
246 pp. *Permission required to cite or quote.* 1963. *Micro II.*

WINCHELL, Oscar (1903–   ) Pilot.
ALASKAN PIONEERS
Flying at fairs in South Dakota; Pioneer Airlines and flying school; bush pilot in Alaska, 1931–52; description of planes, equipment, landing fields. Impressions of life among Alaskan miners.
159 pp. *Open.* 1965.

WINDELS, Paul (1885–1967) Corporation counsel.
NY State Bridge and Tunnel Commission; Holland Tunnel; NY Port Authority; NYC politics; La Guardia administration; Committee of Fifteen and NY transit; Rapp-Coudert Committee.
178 pp. *Permission required to cite or quote.* 1950. *Micro I.*

Fiorello H. La Guardia.
24 pp. *Permission requried to cite or quote.* 1953. *Micro I.*

WING, Daniel G. *Discussed in* James M. Barker.

WINGATE, Orde. *Discussed in* John R. Alison.

WINGE, Edwin. *See* Social Security.

WINKELSTEIN, Asher (1893–   ) *See* Mt. Sinai Hospital. *Micro II.*

WINSTON, Garrard Bigelow (1882–1955) Lawyer.
Impressions of Andrew Mellon.
13 pp. *Open.* 1949.

WINTER, Keyes (1878–1960) Judge.
NYC party politics, 1920–33.
259 pp. *Closed until 2010.* 1950.

WIRSTA, James (1911–   ) *See* Continental Group.

WIRTA, Harvey. *See* Flying Tigers.

WIRTH, Conrad Louis (1899–   ) *See* Jackson Hole Preserve.

WIRTZ, William Willard (1912–   ) *See* Adlai E. Stevenson Project. *Micro III.*
Discussed in Elizabeth S. Ives; Newton Minow.

WISE, Stephen S. *Discussed in* Joseph M. Proskauer; Bernard G. Richards.

WISLOCKI, George. *Discussed in* Joseph C. Aub.

WITHERSPOON, Frances (1886–1973) and Tracy Mygatt. Pacifists.
Girlhoods in New England and the South; education, Bryn Mawr College; support of pacifism and racial equality; opposition to US participation in WWI; War Resisters' League; *The Glorious Company;* NY Bureau of Legal Advice and defense of conscientious objectors and persons charged under the Espionage Act.
   53 pp. *Permission required to cite or quote.* 1966. *Micro I.* Papers.

WITHERSPOON, Milton E. *See* Benedum and the Oil Industry.

WITMARK, Julius. *See* Popular Arts.

WITT, Nathan (1903–   ) Government official, labor lawyer.
Childhood and education, Harvard Law School; NYC legal experience, 1932; New Deal Washington, AAA, 1933–34; NLRB, 1934–40: Assistant General Counsel in charge of Review Division to 1937, later Secretary; formation of NLRB, political climate, problems of social legislation, analysis of Wagner and Landrum-Griffin Acts; Smith Committee investigation; impressions of board members, other New Deal figures.
   200 pp. *Permission required to cite or quote.* 1969. *Acquired from Labor-Management Documentation Center, Cornell University, Ithaca, NY.*

WITTE, Edwin. *Discussed in* Arthur Altmeyer; Barbara Armstrong; J. Douglas Brown; Eveline Burns; Wilbur Cohen; Katharine Lenroot; Herman M. Somers.

WITTER, Ray I. *See* Eisenhower Administration.

WITWER, Samuel Weiler (1908–   ) Lawyer.
ADLAI E. STEVENSON PROJECT
Stevenson as Governor of Illinois; state constitutional reform under Stevenson.
   49 pp. *Permission required.* 1969.

WOHLFORTH, Robert. *See* La Follette Civil Liberties Committee.

WOJTUL, Peter (1909–1976) *See* Continental Group.

WOLFE, Kenneth B. (1896–1971) *See* Henry H. Arnold Project.

WOLFE, Thomas. *Discussed in* Melville H. Cane; Jonathan W. Daniels; Carl Van Vechten; John Hall Wheelock.

WOLKSTEIN, Irwin.
SOCIAL SECURITY
Assistant Chief, Coverage and Disability Branch, Social Security; early health insurance bills; development of legislation; background of Medicare; Subcommittee on the Aged; consultant to Senator Patrick McNamara; speech-writing; 1960 election; John F. Kennedy's stand on Medicare; relations with HEW, Ways and Means Committee, AFL-CIO, White House staff, Blue Cross, AMA; Congressional hearings. Impressions of Wilbur Cohen, Wilbur Mills, Abraham Ribicoff, and others.
   255 pp. *Permission required to cite or quote.* 1968. *Micro III.*
Discussed in Sidney Saperstein.

WOLL, Matthew. *Discussed in* Boris Shishkin.

WOLLACK, Kenneth. *See* Ethnic Groups and American Foreign Policy.

WOLMAN, Leo (1890–1961) Economist.
Boyhood, Baltimore; education, Johns

Hopkins; work as economist in federal agencies, WWI; negotiator and economist, 1920's; impressions of New School faculty members, 1920's; joining a government agency during the early days of the New Deal.

316 pp. *Open.* 1960. Papers.
Discussed in Milton Handler.

WOMBLE, Bunyan Snipes (1882–   ) *See* James B. Duke Project.

WOMEN *See* Bertha Adkins; Elizabeth Blake; Jacqueline Cochran; Clarence de la Chapelle; Lavinia Engle; Judith Galloway; Edna Gellhorn; Mary Bass Gibson; Irene Graf and Terry Walters; Connie Guion; Dorothy Height; Jeanne Holm; Lulu Holmes; Florence Kerr; Kirkland College; Alexandra Kollontai Project; Percy M. Lee; Gerda Lerner; Katie Louchheim; Helen Lynd; Millicent McIntosh; Vivian Nemhauser; Marjorie Nicolson; Adelaide Oppenheim; Alice Paul; Frances Perkins; Esther Peterson; Kathryn S. Phillips; Esther Raushenbush; Felice Schwartz; Margaret Slaymaker; Social Security; Sharon Spencer; Anna Lord Strauss; James C. Thomas and Robert E. Lushbaugh; Katherine A. Towle; Anne Wheaton; Women Journalists; Women's History and Population Issues; James M. Wood.
See also League of Women Voters.

WOMEN JOURNALISTS
Experiences of three pioneer women journalists, centering on education, suffrage, and career issues.
Participants and pages: Emma Bugbee, 31; Eva von Baur Hansl, 54; Kathleen McLaughlin, 44.
129 pp. *Open.* 1974. *Contributed by Jean E. Collins, NYC.*

WOMEN'S HISTORY AND POPULATION ISSUES
Schlesinger Library interviews with persons who have played significant roles in the birth control movement, the delivery of maternal and child health services, marriage counseling and sex education. Participants include women associated in various capacities with Planned Parenthood as well as some of those who brought the abortion issue before the

public and initiated legal change.
Participants and pages: Elizabeth Arnold, 84; Beatrice Blair, 94; Mary S. Calderone, 47; Loraine L. Campbell, 93; Arlene Carmen, 88; Florence Clothier, 24; Constance Cook, 85; Martha May Eliot, 454; Frances H. Ferguson, 70; Sadja Goldsmith, 33; Estelle Griswold, 49; Lenore Guttmacher, 32; Louise G. Hutchins, 36; Patricia Maginnis, 162; Sarah Marcus, 64; Emily Hartshorne Mudd, 291; Lonny Myers and Sharon Wang, 87; Lana C. Phelan, 41; Grant Sanger, 62; Adaline P. Satterthwaite, 57; Helen B. Taussig, 52; Sarah L. and Christopher Tietze, 65; Julia Tsuei, 32; Sarah Weddington, 61.
2,164 pp. *Permission required to cite or quote.* 1973–76. *Acquired from the Schlesinger Library, Cambridge, Mass.*

WOOD, Benjamin De Kalbe (1894–   ) College professor, author.
CARNEGIE CORPORATION
Educational background; teaching at Columbia College; NY experiment with modern language tests, 1925–27; Pennsylvania Study, 1927; Educational Records Bureau; Frederick Keppel and other Corporation officers; educational testing programs.
123 pp. *Permission required.* 1967. Papers.

WOOD, Ida. *Discussed in* Joseph A. Cox.

WOOD, James Madison (1875–1958) Educator.
Childhood and early experiences in the Ozarks; teaching; interest in farming and extension; Stephens Junior College, 1912–47: concept of junior college, analysis of women's activities, change in direction, trips, publicity, recruiting, faculty, finances; Women's Foundation; Junior College Association, 1920; women's rights movement; Rockefeller Foundation support; accreditation of junior colleges; Edward Bok and *Ladies Home Journal.* Impressions of many prominent educators.
387 pp. *Open.* 1954. *Contributed by W. H. Cowley of Stanford, California.*

WOOD, John Edmund Fitzgerald (1903–   ) Lawyer.
CARNEGIE CORPORATION

Experiences as the Carnegie Corporation's Counsel; interpretation of the charter.
52 pp. *Permission required.* 1968.

WOOD, Leonard. *Discussed in* Langdon P. Marvin; James T. Williams, Jr.

WOOD, Meredith (1895–1974) *See* Book-of-the-Month Club. *Micro II.*

WOOD, Robert E. (1879–1969) Executive, government official.
Family background, West Point; Philippines, 1901–02; Panama Canal, 1905–15; DuPont, General Asphalt; WWI: shipbuilding program, Army Transport Service, Acting Quartermaster General; Montgomery Ward, 1919–24: establishment of retail stores; Sears, Roebuck, 1924–61: shopping centers, profit sharing, Allstate; New Deal; America First; supply problems in WWII: labor relations.
110 pp. *Permission required to cite or quote.* 1961. *Micro I.*
Discussed in James M. Barker; William Benton; Robert M. Hutchins.

WOODBERRY, George. *Discussed in* Joseph M. Proskauer.

WOODCOCK, Leonard (1911–   ) *See* Social Security. *Micro III.*

WOODS, Henry. *See* Eisenhower Administration. *Micro III.*

WOODS, Louis Ernest (1895–1971) *See* Marine Corps.

WOODS, Mark (1901–   ) Advertising executive.
RADIO PIONEERS
Broadcasting department, NY Telephone Company, 1922; early days at Broadcasting Corporation of America and NBC; administrative view of broadcasting; first commercials; division of NBC into two networks; formation of ABC; President of ABC; future of radio and television. Impressions of various figures in radio.
120 pp. *Open.* 1951.

WOODSON, Carter. *Discussed in* John Warren Davis.

WOODWARD, C. Vann (1908–   ) *See* American Historians.

WOODWARD, Ellen. *Discussed in* Maurine Mulliner.

WOODWARD, Joanne (Mrs. Paul Newman)(1930–   ) *See* Popular Arts.

WOOLLCOTT, Alexander. *Discussed in* Frank Sullivan.

WORLD BANK
Interviews with officers of the International Bank for Reconstruction and Development detail its history and operations from the 1944 Bretton Woods Conference to 1960. Organization, development of policies, management practices, personnel, and the relationship of directors and staff during the presidencies of Eugene Meyer, John McCloy, and Eugene Black are described.
The functions of the World Bank are analyzed, including policy formulation and supervision of end-use of funds, project appraisal, creditworthiness, administration and significance of loans, government banks, equity investment and venture capital, bond issues and corollary legislation, and foreign and domestic bond marketing. The relationship of the Bank to the International Monetary Fund and to other financing institutions is explored. There are descriptions of individual projects in various parts of the world, particularly flood protection, railway rehabilitation, the Indus Basin Settlement Plan, the Mekong River Survey, and the Suez Canal.
Participants and pages: Siem Aldewereld, 31; Gerald Alter, Harold Larsen, and John de Wilde, 32; Eugene R. Black, 62; Robert W. Cavanaugh, 90; Sidney Raymond Cope, 54; Daniel Crena de Iongh, 47; Richard H. Demuth, 91 *(certain pages closed);* William Diamond and Michael Hoffman, 37; Donald Fowler, 44; Robert L. Garner, 100; William F. Howell, 37; Sir William Iliff, 76; Andrew Kamarck, 22; J. Burke Knapp, 76; Harold Larsen, 32; Ansel F. Luxford, 61; Luis Machado, 35; George Martin and Emil Pattberg, 25; Morton Mendels, 76; Lester Nurick, 35 *(closed during lifetime);* Hoyt Peck, 35; Hugh Ripman, 29; Leonard B. Rist, 62; Paul Rosenstein-Rodan, 51 *(closed during lifetime);* Orvis A. Schmidt,

23; Davidson Sommers, 74; Alexander Stevenson, 28; Raymond A. Wheeler, 27.

1,392 pp. *Permission required to cite or quote, except as noted.* 1961. *Underwritten by the International Bank for Reconstruction and Development, Washington, D.C.*

WORLD WAR I *See* Air Force Academy; Will W. Alexander; American Historians; Dana Atchley; Joseph Aub; Aviation Project; Boris Bakhmeteff; Jacques Barzun; Frank B. Berry; Heber Blankenhorn; Henry Breckenridge; Elmer Davis; John W. Davis; Wilbert C. Davison; Goldthwaite Dorr; Caroline K. Duer; Haven Emerson; Bela Fabian; Perrin C. Galpin; Marley F. Hay; Carl H. Henrikson, Jr.; Clarence B. Kelland; William L. Laurence; Walter Lippmann; Marine Corps; Naval History; John L. O'Brian; Jan Papanek; DeWitt C. Poole; George Rublee; Eustace Seligman; Boris Shishkin; James T. Shotwell; John Spargo; Meier Steinbrink; Francis R. Stoddard; Kenneth C. Towe; James W. Wadsworth; James P. Warburg; Sir Robert Watson-Watt; Robert E. Wood; William Yale.

WORLD WAR II *See* Thanassis Aghnides; Air Force Academy; American Historians; Henry H. Arnold Project; Joseph Aub; U H'tin Aung; Aviation Project; John Badeau; George Baehr; Kenneth Bainbridge; Joseph C. Baldwin; James W. Barco; Frank B. Berry; Hugh Borton; William A.M. Burden; Omar Bradley; Emily Chapin; Chinese Oral History Project; Edward D. Churchill; Charles D. Cook; Edward Costikyan; Louis Cowan; Malcolm W. Davis; Lawrence Dennis; Department of Defense; Goldthwaite Dorr; Caroline K. Duer; Ira C. Eaker; Ed Edwin; Edward Elson; Bela Fabian; Flying Tigers; Paul W. Frillman; Muriel Gardiner; Thomas S. Gates; James M. Gavin; Bernard L. Gladieux; Michel Gordey; Richard Hanser; W. Averell Harriman; John Clellon Holmes; Sir Robert G.A. Jackson; Lawrence C. Kolb; James M. Landis; Chester T. Lane; William L. Laurence; Walter Lippmann; Anthony C. McAuliffe; Kenneth D. McCormick; Marine Corps; Robert E. Merriam; Naval History; Vivian Nemhauser; Arthur Nevins; John L. O'-Brian; Occupation of Japan; William

O'Dwyer; Arthur W. Page; Herbert C. Pell; Frances Perkins; William Phillips; Charles Poletti; Norman Ramsey; Isidor S. Ravdin; Nelson A. Rockefeller; Paul L. Ross; Frank W. Rounds, Jr.; Kenneth C. Royall; Sir George Sansom; George Stroganoff-Scherbatoff; Evan Thomas II; Katherine A. Towle; Robert F. Wagner; Henry A. Wallace; Sir Robert Watson-Watt; Warren Weaver; Claude R. Wickard; Jan Wiener; Alexander Wiley; Robert E. Wood.

WORNHAM, Thomas Andrews (1903–) *See* Marine Corps.

WORTON, William Arthur (1897–1973) Marine Corps officer.
Family background; Massachusetts Naval Militia; Quantico; WWI: Verdun, Belleau Wood; Santo Domingo; Chinese language officer, Peking and Tientsin, 1920's; WWII: defense of Iceland, preparation for amphibious assaults; Japanese surrender of North China, occupation of Peking, 1945; Washington during unification discussions, 1947; retirement, 1949; Los Angeles Police Chief. Impressions of Chiang Kai-shek, Madame Chiang, Chou En-lai, and many US military officers.
328 pp. *Permission required to cite or quote.* 1967.

WRATHER, William Embry (1883–1963) *See* Mining Engineers.

WRAY, Lawrence (1899–) *See* McGraw-Hill.

WRIGHT, Basil. *See* Robert J. Flaherty Project.

WRIGHT, Frank Lloyd (1869–1959) Architect.
Opinions on religion, politics, and architecture in two television interviews with Mike Wallace.
45 pp. *Open.* 1957.

ARCHITECTURE PROJECT
Architecture as the basis of culture; profit as the motive of urbanization; necessity of beautifying our housing environment.
15 pp. *Open.* 1959.

WRIGHT, Henry L. *Discussed in* Charles Ascher.

WRIGHT, James. *See* Poets on their Poetry.

WRIGHT, Orville. *Discussed in* Donald W. Douglas; Thomas Milling.

WRIGHT, Richard. *Discussed in* Jean B. Hutson.

WRIGHT, Wilbur. *Discussed in* Ross Browne; Grover Loening.

WRIGHT, Teresa (1918–) *See* Popular Arts.

WRISTON, Henry Merritt (1889–1978) Educator.
CARNEGIE CORPORATION
Relations between the Carnegie Foundation for the Advancement of Teaching and the Carnegie Corporation; trustee of the Foundation, 1933–55; President of Lawrence College, 1925–37, and of Brown University, 1937–50; Frederick Keppel; functions of the Corporation; evaluation of programs and studies; Pennsylvania Study; study in applied mathematics; Alger Hiss case; Harvard Russian Research Center. Impressions of Foundation and Corporation officers and trustees.
219 pp. *Permission required.* 1967.

EISENHOWER ADMINISTRATION
Dwight Eisenhower at Columbia University; Council on Foreign Relations; American Assembly; Goals Commission and other appointments under President Eisenhower.
51 pp. *Permission required to cite or quote.* 1968. *Micro III.*

WU, K.C. *See* Chinese Oral History.

WUNSCH, Alphonse (1902–) *See* Continental Group.

WYATT, Walter (1893–) Lawyer.
General Counsel, Federal Reserve Board; review of emergency banking measures and the Hundred Days of 1933: bank holiday, Federal Reserve banks, Bank Conservation Act, Emergency Banking Act, Glass-Steagall Banking Act, Federal Reserve Act, Federal Deposit Insurance Corporation; devaluation; SEC; impressions of Franklin D. Roosevelt, Carter Glass, Arthur Ballantine, Eugene Black.
98 pp. *Permission required to cite or quote.* 1973. *Micro IV.*

WYATT, Wilson Watkins (1905–) Lawyer.
ADLAI E. STEVENSON PROJECT
First meetings with Adlai Stevenson; nomination of Stevenson at 1952 convention; 1952 campaign: television, Harry Truman's role, Stevenson fund; Elks Club; prison riot; 1956 campaign: choice of a running mate, issues; 1960 convention, Mrs. Eleanor Roosevelt; Stevenson's influence on John F. Kennedy and feelings about UN. Impressions of various aides and politicians.
161 pp. *Permission required.* 1969.

WYNKOOP, Norman Osborne (1893–) *See* McGraw-Hill.

WYZANSKI, Charles Edward, Jr. (1906–) Judge.
Family and early childhood; Harvard College and Law School; private practice with Ropes, Gray; General Counsel at Department of Labor; Solicitor General and Social Security cases; NLRB cases; delegate to ILO; private practice; National Defense Mediation Board.
321 pp. *Closed until 5 years after death.* 1954. Papers: memoranda on Schechter case and on immigration and naturalization problems.

Y

YALE, William (1887–1975) Middle East specialist.
Travel in Middle East for Standard Oil Co., WWI era; special agent, US State Department, Near East, WWI; Versailles Peace Conference; King-Crane Commission; Yale Plan.
   83 pp. *Permission required.* 1969. *Contributed by Garé Le Compte, Old Saybrook, Connecticut.*

YAMAMOTO, Isoroku. *Discussed in* William A. Read.

YANG, Chen Ning (1922–   ) *See* Nobel Laureates.

YARNELL, Harry E. *Discussed in* Thomas C. Hart.

YATES, Charles Richardson (1913–   ) *See* Eisenhower Administration. *Micro III.*

YATES, William R. *See* Radio Pioneers.

YEAGER, Charles (1923–   ) *See* Aviation Project.

YELLEN, Jack (1892–   ) *See* Popular Arts.

YOKEL, Mike (1882–   ) *See* Jackson Hole Preserve.

YOST, Charles W. (1907–   ) *See* International Negotiations.

YOUEL, Harlan E. *See* Occupation of Japan.

YOUNG, Donald Ramsey (1898–1977) *See* Carnegie Corporation.

YOUNG, Howard. *See* Robert A. Taft Project.

YOUNG, Mahonri Mackintosh (1877–1957) Sculptor, painter.
Early life in Salt Lake City; art education; early experiences as an artist; study in Europe; experiences as a professional painter and sculptor; illustrations of his work.
   127 pp. *Permission required to cite or quote.* 1956. *Micro I.*

YOUNG, Margaret Buchner (Mrs. Whitney) Author.
Education; YWCA counseling; teaching at Spelman College; children's books, pamphlets on race relations; Community Action Program counseling; civil rights in Atlanta, 1954–60; Whitney Young's career: Minnesota Urban League, Dean of School of Social Work, Atlanta University, president of National Urban League, 1961–71.
   In process.

YOUNG, Milton R. (1897–   ) Senator.
EISENHOWER ADMINISTRATION
Senate Agricultural Committee; 1952 Republican campaign; President Eisenhower's agricultural policy; Ezra Taft Benson.
   31 pp. *Permission required.* 1967.

YOUNG, Owen D. *Discussed* in Radio Pioneers.

YOUNG, Stanley. *Discussed in* Roger W. Straus.

YOUNG, Whitney. *Discussed in* John Warren Davis; Margaret B. Young.

YOUNGER, Maud. *Discussed in* Alice Paul.

YOUNGSTEIN, Max Emanuel (1913–) *See* Popular Arts.

YOURCENAR, Marguerite. *Discussed in* Roger W. Straus.

Z

ZACHARIASSEN, Aksel. *See* Alexandra Kollontai Project.

ZAFRULLA KHAN, Sir Muhammad (1893–) Jurist.
Education and legal training; government service in India before independence; Round Tables; Muslim League; Indian independence and partition; service in Pakistani Cabinet, High Court; service in UN as delegate and President of the General Assembly, 1947–54, 1961–64; International Court of Justice; discussion of life in India and Pakistan: religion, social customs, economics, education. Impressions of figures such as Mohandas Gandhi, Jawaharlal Nehru, Sir Fazle Husain, Winston Churchill, Lord Willingdon, and Lord Templewood.
488 pp. *Permission required to cite or quote.* 1963. *Micro I.*

ZAGHI, Frederick A. *See* Eisenhower Administration.

ZANGWILL, Israel. *Discussed in* Bernard G. Richards.

ZAZUETA, Armand R. (1928–) *See* Continental Group.

ZECKENDORF, William. *Discussed in* I.M. Pei.

ZEITZ, Abraham. *See* New York Political Studies (C).

ZIEGFELD, Florenz. *Discussed in* Richard Rodgers.

ZILAHY, Mrs. Lajos (1907–) *See* Hungarian Project.

ZIMBALIST, Efrem. *Discussed in* James F. Curtis.

ZIMMERMAN, Harriet. *See* Ethnic Groups and American Foreign Policy.

ZIPPER, Donald H. (1916–) *See* Continental Group.

ZORACH, William (1887–1966) Sculptor, painter.
Early life in Cleveland; study at the National Academy and in Europe; return to NY and first work in stone; commissioned monuments; citizenship difficulties; plate-by-plate discussion of Paul Wingert's *The Sculpture of William Zorach;* work habits; artistic philosophy.

Mrs. Zorach participates in one interview.
  348 pp. *Permission required to cite or quote.* 1957. *Micro IV.*

ZUCOTTI, Salvador. *See* Argentina.

ZUKOR, Adolph (1873–1976) *See* Popular Arts. *Discussed in* William S. Paley.

ZWEIG, Stefan. *Discussed in* Ben W. Huebsch.

COLOPHON

THE TEXT OF THIS EDITION has been set in what was first known as TIMES NEW ROMAN. It was designed exclusively for *The Times* of London by Stanley Morison (1889–1967) in response to a call for type that had color and that would appear larger than conventional design of the time (1932) permitted. Although replaced by *The Times*, Times Roman has won world-wide acceptance. Headings are set in Eric Gill's celebrated Perpetua. The cartouche on the front cover is from the original design by the late Oscar Ogg for the 1964 edition, which won a centennial award from the Metropolitan Printing Trades Council. Ogg's cousin, Warren Chappell, has been the designer of this one, giving it the distinction of carrying the contributions of both. The book was composed, printed and bound by the Haddon Craftsmen. Affixed hereto, at the editors' behest, is the designer's marque.